THE WESTERN EXPERIENCE

THE WESTERN EXPERIENCE

Ninth Edition

MORTIMER CHAMBERS
University of California, Los Angeles

BARBARA HANAWALT
The Ohio State University

THEODORE K. RABB
Princeton University

ISSER WOLOCH
Columbia University

RAYMOND GREW
University of Michigan

LISA TIERSTEN
Barnard College

Boston   Burr Ridge, IL   Dubuque, IA   Madison, WI   New York   San Francisco   St. Louis
Bangkok   Bogotá   Caracas   Kuala Lumpur   Lisbon   London   Madrid   Mexico City
Milan   Montreal   New Delhi   Santiago   Seoul   Singapore   Sydney   Taipei   Toronto

The McGraw-Hill Companies

Higher Education

THE WESTERN EXPERIENCE, VOLUME I: TO THE EIGHTEENTH CENTURY
Published by McGraw-Hill, a business unit of The McGraw-Hill Companies, Inc., 1221 Avenue of the Americas, New York, NY, 10020.
Copyright © 2007, 2003, 1999, 1995, 1991, 1987, 1983, 1979, 1974, by The McGraw-Hill Companies, Inc. All rights reserved. No part of this publication may be reproduced or distributed in any form or by any means, or stored in a database or retrieval system, without the prior written consent of The McGraw-Hill Companies, Inc., including, but not limited to, in any network or other electronic storage or transmission, or broadcast for distance learning.

Some ancillaries, including electronic and print components, may not be available to customers outside the United States.

This book is printed on acid-free paper.

2 3 4 5 6 7 8 9 0 DOW/DOW 0 9 8 7

ISBN-13: 978-0-07-325086-1
ISBN-10: 0-07-325086-4

Vice President and Editor-in-Chief: *Emily Barrosse*
Publisher: *Lyn Uhl*
Senior Sponsoring Editor: *Monica Eckman*
Director of Development: *Lisa Pinto*
Developmental Editor: *Angela W. Kao*
Permissions Coordinator: *The Permissions Group*
Marketing Manager: *Katherine Bates*
Managing Editor: *Jean Dal Porto*
Project Manager: *Emily Hatteberg*
Art Director: *Jeanne Schreiber*
Art Editor: *Ayelet Arbel*
Lead Designer: *Gino Cieslik*
Cover and Interior Designer: *Ellen Pettengell*
Cover credit: Arithmetic, *wool tapestry. Flemish, Tournai, ca. 1500; J. G. Berizzi/Réunion des Musées Nationaux/Art Resource, NY*
Senior Photo Research Coordinator: *Alexandra Ambrose*
Photo Research: *Photosearch, Inc., New York*
Senior Production Supervisor: *Carol A. Bielski*
Lead Media Producer: *Sean Crowley*
Media Project Manager: *Kate Boylan*
Composition: *9.5/12 Trump, by Carlisle Publishing Services*
Printing: *45 # Pub Matte Plus, R.R. Donnelley & Sons*

Credits: The credits section for this book begins on page C-1 and is considered an extension of the copyright page.

Library of Congress Cataloging-in-Publication Data

The Western experience / Mortimer Chambers ... [et al,].—9th ed. [main text]
        6 v. cm.
    Includes bibliographical references and index.
    ISBN-13: 978-0-07-288369-5 (alk. paper)
    ISBN-10: 0-07-288369-3 (alk. paper)
    1. Civilization—History. 2. Civilization, Western—History. I. Chambers, Mortimer.
CB59.W38 2007
909′.09821—dc22

                                                2006041940

The Internet addresses listed in the text were accurate at the time of publication. The inclusion of a Web site does not indicate an endorsement by the authors or McGraw-Hill, and McGraw-Hill does not guarantee the accuracy of the information presented at these sites.

www.mhhe.com

About the Authors

Mortimer Chambers is Professor of History at the University of California at Los Angeles. He was a Rhodes Scholar from 1949 to 1952 and received an M.A. from Wadham College, Oxford, in 1955 after obtaining his doctorate from Harvard University in 1954. He has taught at Harvard University (1954–1955) and the University of Chicago (1955–1958). He was Visiting Professor at the University of British Columbia in 1958, the State University of New York at Buffalo in 1971, the University of Freiburg (Germany) in 1974, and Vassar College in 1988. A specialist in Greek and Roman history, he is coauthor of *Aristotle's History of Athenian Democracy* (1962), editor of a series of essays entitled *The Fall of Rome* (1963), and author of *Georg Busolt: His Career in His Letters* (1990) and of *Staat der Athener*, a German translation and commentary to Aristotle's *Constitution of the Athenians* (1990). He has edited Greek texts of the latter work (1986) and of the *Hellenica Oxyrhynchia* (1993). He has contributed articles to the *American Historical Review* and *Classical Philology* as well as to other journals, both in America and in Europe. He is also an editor of *Historia*, the international journal of ancient history.

Barbara Hanawalt holds the King George III Chair of British History at The Ohio State University and is the author of numerous books and articles on the social and cultural history of the Middle Ages. Her publications include *The Middle Ages: An Illustrated History* (1999), *'Of Good and Ill Repute': Gender and Social Control in Medieval England* (1998), *Growing Up in Medieval London: The Experience of Childhood in History* (1993), *The Ties That Bound: Peasant Life in Medieval England* (1986), and *Crime and Conflict in English Communities, 1300–1348* (1979). She received her M.A. in 1964 and her Ph.D. in 1970, both from the University of Michigan. She has served as president of the Social Science History Association and the Medieval Academy of America and has been on the Council of the American Historical Association and the Medieval Academy of America. She was a fellow of the Netherlands Institute for Advanced Study (2005–2006), a fellow of the Guggenheim Foundation (1998–1999), an ACLS Fellow in 1975–1976, a fellow at the National Humanities Center (1997–1998), a fellow at the Wissenschaftskolleg in Berlin (1990–1991), a member of the School of Historical Research at the Institute for Advanced Study, and a senior research fellow at the Newberry Library in 1979–1980.

Theodore K. Rabb is Professor of History at Princeton University. He received his Ph.D. from Princeton in 1961 and subsequently taught at Stanford, Northwestern, Harvard, and Johns Hopkins universities. He is the author of numerous articles and reviews in journals such as *The New York Times* and the *Times Literary Supplement*, and he has been editor of *The Journal of Interdisciplinary History* since its foundation. Among his books are *The Struggle for Stability in Early Modern Europe* (1975), *Renaissance Lives* (1993), and *Jacobean Gentleman* (1999). He has won awards from the Guggenheim Foundation, the National Endowment for the Humanities, the American Historical Association, and the National Council for History Education. He was the principal historian for the PBS series *Renaissance*, which was nominated for an Emmy.

Isser Woloch is Moore Collegiate Professor of History at Columbia University. He received his Ph.D. (1965) from Princeton University in the field of eighteenth- and nineteenth-century European history. He has taught at Indiana University and at the University of California at Los Angeles, where, in 1967, he received a Distinguished Teaching Citation. He has been a fellow of the ACLS, the National Endowment for the Humanities, the Guggenheim Foundation, and the Institute for Advanced Study at Princeton. His publications include *Jacobin Legacy: The Democratic Movement under the Directory* (1970), *The Peasantry in the Old Regime: Conditions and Protests* (1970), *The French Veteran from the Revolution to the Restoration* (1979), *Eighteenth-Century Europe: Tradition and Progress, 1715–1789* (1982), *The New Regime: Transformations of the French Civic Order, 1789–1820s* (1994), *Revolution and the Meanings of Freedom in the Nineteenth Century* (1996), and *Napoleon and His Collaborators: The Making of a Dictatorship* (2001).

Raymond Grew is Professor of History Emeritus at the University of Michigan. He has also taught at Brandeis University, Princeton University, and at the Écoles des Hautes Études en Sciences Sociales in Paris. He earned both his M.A. and Ph.D. from Harvard University in the field of modern European history. He has been a Fulbright Fellow to Italy and a Fulbright Travelling Fellow to Italy and to France, a Guggenheim Fellow, and a Fellow of the National Endowment for the Humanities. In 1962 he received the Chester Higby Prize from the American Historical Association, and in 1963 the Italian government awarded him the Unità d'Italia Prize; in 1992 he received the David Pinkney Prize of the Society for French Historical Studies and in 2000 a citation for career achievement from the Society for Italian Historical Studies. He has twice served as national chair of the Council for European Studies, was for many years the editor of the international quarterly *Comparative Studies in Society and History,* and is one of the directors of the Global History Group. His recent publications include essays on historical comparison, global history, Catholicism in the nineteenth century, fundamentalism, and Italian culture and politics. His books include *A Sterner Plan for Italian Unity* (1963), *Crises of Development in Europe and the United States* (1978), *School, State, and Society: The Growth of Elementary Schooling in Nineteenth-Century France* (1991), with Patrick J. Harrigan, and two edited volumes: *Food in Global History* (1999) and *The Construction of Minorities* (2001).

Lisa Tiersten is Associate Professor of History at Barnard College, Columbia University. She received her Ph.D. (1991) at Yale University and has taught at Wellesley College and Barnard College. She has been the recipient of a Chateaubriand Fellowship, a French Historical Studies Society Fellowship, and a Getty Fellowship. She also received the Emily Gregory Teaching Award at Barnard College in 1996. Her publications include *Marianne in the Market: Envisioning Consumer Society in Fin-de-Siècle France* (2001). She is currently at work on a history of bankruptcy and the culture of credit in modern France, entitled *Terms of Trade: The Capitalist Imagination in Modern France,* and on an edited volume on the comparative history of children's rights in twentieth-century Europe. Her research interests include modern France, gender, consumer culture, empire, and the comparative culture of capitalism.

This book is dedicated to the memory of David Herlihy, whose erudition and judgment were central to its creation and whose friendship and example continue to inspire his coauthors.

Brief Contents

Contents

Chapter 1

THE FIRST CIVILIZATIONS   3

Chapter 2

THE FORMING OF GREEK CIVILIZATION   33

Chapter 6

THE MAKING OF WESTERN EUROPE 157

Chapter 7

THE EMPIRES OF THE EARLY MIDDLE AGES (800–1000): CREATION AND EROSION 181

Chapter 8

RESTORATION OF AN ORDERED SOCIETY 215

Chapter 9

THE FLOWERING OF MEDIEVAL CIVILIZATION 249

Chapter 10

THE URBAN ECONOMY AND THE CONSOLIDATION OF STATES 279

Chapter 11

BREAKDOWN AND RENEWAL IN AN AGE OF PLAGUE 305

Chapter 15

WAR AND CRISIS 429

Chapter 16

CULTURE AND SOCIETY IN THE AGE OF THE SCIENTIFIC REVOLUTION 459

Chapter 17

THE EMERGENCE OF THE EUROPEAN STATE SYSTEM 491

Maps

Boxes

Primary Source Boxes

Historical Issues Boxes

Chronological Boxes

Global Moment Boxes

Preface

When *The Western Experience* was originally conceived, we sought to write a textbook that would introduce students to the growing field of social history and exciting new ways of thinking about history. We wanted the textbook not merely to set forth information but to serve as an example of historical writing. That means we cared a lot about the quality of the writing itself and also that we wanted the chapters to be examples of a historical essay that set up a historical problem and developed arguments about that problem using historical evidence. We also recognized that for American students the Western Civilization textbook needed to provide an overview of that civilization, giving students an introduction to the major achievements in Western thought, art, and science as well as the social, political, and economic context for understanding them. And lastly, we were determined that our book would treat all these various aspects of history in an integrated way. Too many books, we felt, dealt with cultural or social change entirely separately, even in separate chapters, and we sought to demonstrate and exemplify the connections. To that end, *The Western Experience* is designed to provide an analytical and reasonably comprehensive account of the contexts within which, and the processes by which, European society and civilization evolved.

Now in the ninth edition, this book has evolved with the strength of prior revisions, including Barbara Hanawalt's impressive rewriting and reordering of the six chapters that cover the Middle Ages for the seventh edition. To continue that evolution, we are proud to welcome another distinguished scholar, Lisa Tiersten of Barnard College, to our author team. She has written a new chapter on nineteenth-century empires (chapter 26), one of the first among western civilization textbooks, and she has undertaken the substantial revision and reorganization of chapters 25 and 27. With a fresh voice and lucid approach, Dr. Tiersten has greatly enriched the coverage in these chapters by incorporating recent research on gender, bourgeois and consumer culture, imperialism, technology, and globalization.

EXPERIENCING HISTORY

Everyone uses history. We use it to define who we are and to connect our personal experience to the collective memory of the groups to which we belong, including a particular region, nation, and culture. We invoke the past to explain our hopes and ambitions and to justify our fears and conflicts. The Charter of the United Nations, like the American Declaration of Independence, is based on a view of history. When workers strike or armies march, they cite the lessons of their history. Because history is so important to us psychologically and intellectually, historical understanding is always shifting and often controversial.

Historical knowledge is cumulative. Historians may ask many of the same questions about different periods of history or raise new questions or issues; they integrate the answers, and historical knowledge grows. The study of history cannot be a subjective exercise in which all opinions are equally valid. Regardless of the impetus for a particular historical question, the answer to it stands until overturned by better evidence. We now know more about the past than ever before, and we understand it as the people we study could not. Unlike them, we know the outcome of their history; we can apply methods they did not have, and often we have evidence they never saw.

Humans have always found pleasure in the reciting and reading of history. The poems about the fall of Troy or the histories of Herodotus and Thucydides entertained the ancient Greeks. The biographies of great men and women, dramatic accounts of important events, colorful tales of earlier times can be fascinating in themselves. Through these encounters with history we experience the common concerns of all people; and through the study of European history, we come to appreciate the ideals and conflicts, the failures and accidents, the social needs and human choices that formed the Western world in which we live. Knowing the historical context also enriches our appreciation for the achievements of European culture, enabling us to see its art, science, ideas, and politics in relationship to real people, specific interests, and burning issues.

We think of Europe's history as the history of Western civilization because the Greeks gave the names east and west to the points on the horizon at which the sun rises and sets. Because the Persian Empire and India lay to their east, the Greeks labeled their own continent, which they called Europe, the west. However, we need to be cautious about the view that Western civilization is a united whole, entirely distinct from other civilizations, except perhaps in its cultural development. We will see many occasions when a larger context is appropriate.

The Western Experience thus gives primary attention to a small part of the world and honors a particular cultural tradition. Yet the concentration on Europe does allow us to explore contrasts of worldwide significance; between city and rural life; among empires and monarchies and republics; in life before and after industrialization; among societies that organized labor through markets, serfdom, and slavery; between cultures little concerned with science and those that used changing scientific knowledge; among different ways of creating and experiencing forms of literature and the arts; and among Christian and non-Christian religions and all the major forms of Christianity.

A college course alone cannot create an educated citizen. Moreover, Western history is not the only history a person should know, and an introductory survey is not necessarily the best way to learn it. Yet, as readers consider and then challenge interpretations offered in this text, they will exercise critical and analytical skills. They can begin to overcome the parochialism that attributes importance only to the present. To learn to think critically about historical evidence and know how to formulate an argument on the bases of this evidence is to experience the study of history as one of the vital intellectual activities by which we come to know who and where we are.

A BALANCED, INTERPRETIVE, AND FLEXIBLE APPROACH

At the same time, we recognize that the professional scholar's preference for new perspectives over familiar ones makes a distinction that students may not share. For them, the latest interpretations need to be integrated with established understandings and controversies, with the history of people and events that are part of our cultural lore. We recognize that a textbook

should provide a coherent presentation of the basic information from which students can begin to form their historical understanding. We believe this information must be part of an interpretive history but also that its readers—teachers, students, and general readers—should be free to use it in many different ways and in conjunction with their own areas of special knowledge and their own interests and curiosity.

USE OF THEMES

Throughout this book, from the treatment of the earliest civilizations to the discussion of the present, we pursue certain key themes. These seven themes constitute a set of categories by which societies and historical change can be analyzed.

Social Structure   In early chapters, social structure involves how the land was settled, divided among its inhabitants, and put to use. Later discussions of how property is held must include corporate, communal, and individual ownership, then investment banking and companies that sell shares. Similarly, in each era we treat the division of labor, noting whether workers are slave or free, male or female, and when there are recognized specialists in fighting or crafts or trade. The chapters covering the ancient world, the Middle Ages, and the early modern period explore social hierarchies that include nobles, clergy, commoners, and slaves or serfs; the treatments of the French Revolution, the Industrial Revolution, and twentieth-century societies analyze modern social classes.

The Body Politic   Another theme we analyze throughout this book is what used to be called the body politic. Each era contains discussions of how political power is acquired and used and of the political structures that result. Students learn about the role of law from ancient codes to the present, as well as problems of order, and the formation of governments, including why government functions have increased and political participation of the population has changed.

Technology   From cultivation in the plains of the Tigris and Euphrates to the global economy, we follow changes in the organization of production and in the impact of technology. We note how goods are distributed, and we observe patterns of trade as avenues of cultural exchange in addition to wealth. We look at the changing economic role of governments and the impact of economic theories.

Gender Roles and Family   The evolution of the family and changing gender roles are topics fundamental to every historical period. Families give form to daily life and kinship structures. The history of demography, migration, and work is also a history of the family. The family has always been a central focus of social organization and religion, as well as the principal instrument by which societies assign specific practices, roles, and values to women and men. Gender roles have changed from era to era, differing according to social class and between rural and urban societies. Observing gender roles across time, the student discovers that social, political, economic, and cultural history are always interrelated; that the present is related to the past; and that social change brings gains and losses rather than evolution in a straight line—three lessons all history courses teach.

War   No history of Europe could fail to pay attention to war, which, for most polities, has been their most demanding activity. Warfare has strained whatever resources were available from ancient times to the present, leading governments to invent new ways to extract wealth and mobilize support. War has built and undermined states, stimulated science and consumed technology, made heroes, and restructured nobility, schooling, and social services. Glorified in European culture and often condemned, war in every era has affected the lives of all its peoples. This historical significance, more than specific battles, is one of the themes of *The Western Experience.*

Religion   Religion has been basic to the human experience, and our textbook explores the different religious institutions and experiences that societies developed. Religion affects and is affected by all the themes we address, creating community and causing conflict, shaping intellectual and daily life, providing the experiences that bind individual lives and society within a common system of meaning.

Cultural Expression   For authors of a general history, no decision is more difficult than the space devoted to cultural expression. In this respect, as elsewhere, we have striven for a balance between high and popular culture. We present as clearly and concisely as possible the most important formal ideas, philosophies, and ideologies of each era. We emphasize concepts of recognized importance in the general history of ideas and those concepts that illuminate behavior and discourse in a given period. We pay particular attention to developments in science that we believe are related to important intellectual, economic, and social trends. Popular culture appears both in specific sections and throughout the book. We want to place popular culture within its social and historical con-

text but not make the gulf too wide between popular and high or formal culture. Finally, we write about many of the great works of literature, art, architecture, and music. Because of the difficulties of selection, we have tried to emphasize works that are cultural expressions of their time but that also have been influential over the ages and around the globe.

Attention to these seven themes occasions problems of organization and selection. We could have structured this book around a series of topical essays, perhaps repeating the series of themes for each of the standard chronological divisions of European history. Instead, we chose to preserve a narrative flow that emphasizes interrelationships and historical context. We wanted each chapter to stand as an interpretive historical essay, with a beginning and conclusion. As a result, the themes emerge repeatedly within discussions of a significant event, an influential institution, an individual life, or a whole period of time. Or they may intersect in a single institution or historical trend. Nevertheless, readers can follow any one of these themes across time and use that theme as a measure of change and a way to assess the differences and similarities between societies.

Changes to the Ninth Edition

For us the greatest pleasure in a revision lies in the challenge of absorbing and then incorporating the latest developments in historical understanding. From its first edition, this book included more of the results of quantitative and social history than most general textbooks of European history, an obvious reflection of our own research. Each subsequent edition provided an occasion to incorporate current methods and new knowledge, such as the rise of gender studies: a challenge that required reconsidering paragraphs, sections, and whole chapters in the light of new theories and new research, sometimes literally reconceptualizing part of the past.

Newly Revised Chapter 25: "Progress and Its Discontents"

From the last edition, chapters 25 and 26, "European Power: Wealth, Knowledge, and Imperialism" and "The Age of Progress," have been combined into a new chapter 25, "Progress and Its Discontents." Relevant material on imperial Europe has been moved to chapter 26. This new chapter 25 treats late-nineteenth-century economic transformations that brought the bourgeoisie to power along with the intellectual developments that both reinforced that power and raised doubts about its bases and its legitimacy. It also explores the class identity of the new ruling elite and examines both the pleasures and anxieties evoked by the mass commercial culture it created.

New Chapter 26: "Nineteenth-Century Empires"

In the past fifteen years, European historians increasingly have acknowledged the centrality of imperial experience to European history. Spanning a long nineteenth century from 1780 to 1914, this chapter not only explores the impact of major European economic, cultural, and political developments on imperial practice and attitudes, but also explores the profound impact of imperialism on Europe itself (making use of new scholarship on gender and popular culture, for example, to show how empire increasingly touched upon the lives of everyday Europeans). The chapter thus argues that empire did not happen "out there," but at the center of nineteenth-century European society and culture. This chapter includes fresh new illustrations and photographs, primary source boxes, and a Global Moment box on the Indian Rebellion of 1857.

Newly Revised Chapter 27: "World War I and the World It Created"

The revised chapter 27 brings to bear new scholarship on the war, including research on gender relations and the home front and on the imperial dimension of war. It emphasizes in particular how the military mobilization of the colonies—combined with the postwar rhetoric of national self-determination—raised expectations of colonial reform and gradual self-government. When these hopes were disappointed in the postwar period, the chapter shows, colonial reform movements were transformed into militant movements for colonial independence.

Streamlined Narrative throughout the Book

All of the chapters in the ninth edition have been substantially shortened and streamlined. We have worked to make difficult concepts more understandable and to remove material that interfered with the general flow of the text.

New Global Moment Features

The process whereby worldwide connections have intensified in the past two centuries, usually referred to as globalization, has caused a revision in the way we think about the histories of individual states and regions. Although revolutions in communications and transport have made the interconnections inescapable since the 1800s, it is important to see them in perspective and to pay attention to early signs of cross-cultural activity. Five Global Moment boxed essays highlight significant occasions when Europeans had to come to terms with neighbors in other continents. And we have tried, throughout, to keep students aware of the larger context within which European history has developed.

PEDAGOGICAL FEATURES

Each generation of students brings different experiences, interests, and training into the classroom—changes that are important to the teaching-learning process. The students we teach have taught us what engages or confuses them, what impression of European history they bring to college, and what they can be expected to take from a survey course. Current political, social, and cultural events also shape what we teach and how we teach. Our experience as teachers and the helpful comments of scores of other teachers have led to revisions and new additions throughout the book as we have sought to make it clearer and more accessible without sacrificing our initial goal of writing a reasonably sophisticated, interpretive, and analytic history.

Primary Source Boxes

These excerpts from primary sources are designed to illustrate or supplement points made in the text, to provide some flavor of the issues under discussion, and to allow beginning students some of that independence of judgment that comes from a careful reading of historical sources.

"THEY HAVE A MASTER CALLED LAW"

As King Xerxes leads his army into Greece in 480 B.C., he asks a former king of Sparta, who is accompanying him, whether the Greeks will really fight against the Persians.

"Now, Demaratus, I will ask you what I want to know. You are a Greek and one from no minor or weak city. So now tell me, will the Greeks stand and fight me?" Demaratus replied, "Your Majesty, shall I tell you the truth, or say what you want to hear?" The king ordered him to tell the truth, saying that he would respect him no less for doing so.

"Your Majesty," he said, "I am not speaking about all of them, only about the Spartans. First, I say they will never accept conditions from you that would enslave Greece; second, that they will fight you in battle even if all the other Greeks join your side."

Xerxes said, "Demaratus, let's look at it in all logic: why should a thousand, or ten thousand, or fifty thousand men, if they are all free and not ruled by a single master, stand up against such an army as mine? If they were ruled by one man, like my subjects, I suppose they might, out of fear, show more bravery than usual and, driven into battle by the lash, go up against a bigger force; but if allowed their freedom, they wouldn't do either one."

Demaratus said, "Your Majesty, I knew from the beginning that if I spoke the truth you wouldn't like my message, but, since you ordered me to do so, I told you about the Spartans. They are free men, but not wholly free: They have a master called Law, whom they fear far more than your soldiers fear you. And his orders are always the same—they must not run away from any army no matter how big, but must stand in their formation and either conquer or die. But, your Majesty, may your wishes be fulfilled."

From *Herodotus*, book VII, M. H. Chambers (tr.).

Historical Issues Boxes

These boxes explain major controversies over historical interpretations so that students can see how historical understanding is constructed. They encourage students to participate in these debates and formulate their own positions.

New *Global Moment Boxes*

These boxes focus on particularly vivid occasions when Europeans encountered other world civilizations, in order to suggest the broader context within which Western history unfolded.

HISTORICAL ISSUES: TWO VIEWS OF LOUIS XIV

Implicit in any assessment of the reign of Louis XIV in France is a judgment about the nature of absolutism and the kind of government the continental European monarchies created in the late seventeenth and eighteenth centuries. From the perspective of Frenchman Albert Sorel, a historian of the French Revolution writing at the end of the nineteenth century, the Revolution had been necessary to save France from Louis' heritage. For the American John Rule, a historian who concerned himself primarily with the development of political institutions during the seventeenth century, the marks of Louis XIV's rule were caution, bureaucracy, and order.

Sorel: "The edifice of the state enjoyed incomparable brilliance and splendor, but it resembled a Gothic cathedral in which the height of the nave and the arches had been pushed beyond all reason, weakening the walls as they were raised ever higher. Louis XIV carried the principle of monarchy to its utmost limit, and abused it in all respects to the point of excess. He left the nation crushed by war, mutilated by banishments, and impatient of the yoke which it felt to be ruinous. Men were worn-out, the treasury empty, all relationships strained by the violence of tension, and in the immense framework of the state there remained no institution except the accidental appearance of genius. Things had reached a point where, if a great king did not appear, there would be a great revolution."

From Albert Sorel, *L'Europe et la rèvolution française,* 3rd ed., Vol. 1, Paris, 1893, p. 199, as translated in William F. Church (ed.), *The Greatness of Louis XIV: Myth or Reality?*, Boston: D. C. Heath, 1959, p. 63.

Rule: "As Louis XIV himself said of the tasks of kingship, they were at once great, noble, and delightful. Yet Louis' enjoyment of his craft was tempered by political prudence. At an early age he learned to listen attentively to his advisers, to speak when spoken to, to ponder evidence, to avoid confrontations, to dissemble, to wait. He believed that time and tact would conquer. Despite all the evidence provided him by his ministers and his servants, Louis often hesitated before making a decision; he brooded, and in some instances put off decisions altogether. As he grew older, the king tended to hide his person and his office. Even his officials seldom saw the king for more than a brief interview. And as decision-making became centralized in the hands of the ministers, [so] the municipalities, the judges, the local estates, the guilds and at times the peasantry contested royal encroachments on their rights. Yet to many in the kingdom, Louis represented a modern king, an agent of stability whose struggle was their struggle and whose goal was to contain the crises of the age."

From John C. Rule, "Louis XIV, *Roi-Bureaucrate,*" in Rule (ed.), *Louis XIV and the Craft of Kingship,* Columbus: Ohio State University Press, 1969, pp. 91–92.

Global Moment

THREE EMPIRES AND AN ELEPHANT

Although trade and diplomatic ties between the West and the East diminished in the period of the seventh through the tenth centuries, merchants, pilgrims, envoys, and religious officials still traveled extensively and spread news. If we look at events surrounding the year 800, we find that diplomatic missions among the Franks (a Germanic kingdom), the Byzantines (the Eastern Roman Empire), and the Abbasid caliphate (an Arabic-speaking Muslim empire) continued. The main actors in these negotiations and contacts were Charles the Great or Charlemagne (r. 768–814), king of the Franks and, as of Christmas Day 800, Roman emperor in the West; Irene (r. 796–802), who became empress of Roman Empire in the East after she blinded her son, who subsequently died; and the Caliph Harun al-Rashid (786–809), heir to the Abbasid Dynasty, centered in Baghdad in Persia.

These three rulers dominated the area around the Mediterranean, but their empires were vastly different in terms of economic sophistication, religion, and in-

the scholars were the world's leaders in medicine and science. A great hospital flourished in this period. Harun al-Rashid was said to have sponsored the "golden age" for the Arabic world. It took centuries for Arab learning in geography, astronomy, and medicine to reach the West. Charlemagne's court in Aachen was a long way from this intellectual achievement and cultural splendor.

The three empires had a history of clashes. The Arabic expansions had left the Eastern Roman Empire with far less territory. The Franks and other Germanic tribes had taken over the Western Empire and established independent kingdoms, with the Franks conquering most of them. Charlemagne, as King of the Franks, wanted the title of emperor. But before 800, no other Germanic ruler had had the audacity to take the title of emperor of the Romans, and he had some trepidation over assuming the title without permission or blessings of the real successor to the title in Constantinople. The Franks and the Arabs also had considerable conflicts. After all, Charlemagne's grandfather, Charles Martel, had defeated the Arabs 70 years before (732) and he,

Among the many exotic gifts that Harun al-Rashid gave to Charlemagne was, perhaps, this crystal pitcher. It is certainly a piece of late eighth or early ninth century craftsmanship from Persia. It has long been assumed that this pitcher was among the gifts.
To come

was a rash hope, if he ever had it. He could not, as a Christian, make a real alliance with Arabs. The Church forbade such treaties with non-Christians. What did Charlemagne hope to achieve and what did Harun al-Rashid hope to gain with such a diplomatic overture?

Although the Arabic sources are silent about the exchange, Carolingian sources speak of diplomatic mis-

and the governor of Egypt back with a white elephant named Abu l'-Abbas from India. The elephant and Isaac took four years to travel from Baghdad to Jerusalem and then on to Carthage. From there they went by ship to Italy. It is not clear what ship would have been large enough to hold an elephant in 800. Waiting until spring to cross the Alps, Isaac and the Abu l'-Abbas arrived in

New *Chapter-Opening Timelines*

Each chapter now opens with a new timeline. These timelines are meant to offer students a visual aid with which to track simultaneous developments and important dates to remember. Ultimately, we hope that they will help give readers a grounded sense of chronology.

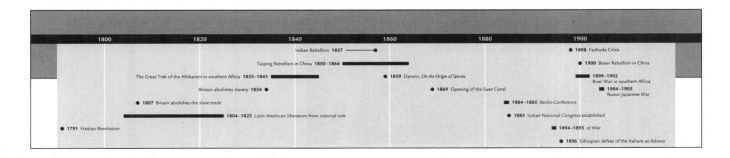

Chapter Twenty

THE FRENCH REVOLUTION

REFORM AND POLITICAL CRISIS • 1789: THE FRENCH REVOLUTION •
THE RECONSTRUCTION OF FRANCE • THE SECOND REVOLUTION

Well into the eighteenth century, the long-standing social structures and political institutions of Europe were securely entrenched. Most monarchs still claimed to hold their authority directly from God. In cooperation with their aristocracies, they presided over realms composed of distinct orders of citizens, or *estates* as they were sometimes known. Each order had its particular rights, privileges, and obligations. But pressures for change were building during the century. In France, the force of public opinion grew increasingly potent by the 1780s. A financial or political crisis that could normally be managed by the monarchy threatened to snowball in this new environment. Such vulnerability was less evident in Austria, Prussia, and Russia, however, where strong monarchs instituted reforms to streamline their governments. Similarly, in Britain the political system proved resilient despite explosions of discontent at home and across the Atlantic.

Unquestionably, then, the French Revolution constituted the pivotal event of European history in the late eighteenth century. From its outbreak in 1789, the Revolution transformed the nature of sovereignty and law in France. Under its impetus, civic and social institutions were renewed, from local government and schooling to family relations and assistance for the poor. Soon its ideals of liberty, equality, and fraternity resonated across the borders of other European states, especially after war broke out in 1792 and French armies took the offensive.

The French Revolution's innovations defined the foundations of a liberal society and polity. Both at home and abroad, however, the new regime faced formidable opposition, and its struggle for survival propelled it in unanticipated directions. Some unforeseen turns, such as democracy and republicanism, became precedents for the future even if they soon aborted. Other developments, such as the Reign of Terror, seemed to nullify the original liberal values of 1789. The bloody struggles of the Revolution thus cast a shadow over this transformative event as they dramatized the brutal dilemma of means versus ends.

New *Chapter-Opening Outlines*

Each chapter now opens with a short outline to give students a sense of what's to come in each chapter.

New *Glossary and Key Terms*

Reviewers of the last edition requested this new feature. Glossary words are bolded in each chapter and compiled in the end-of-book glossary.

Cahiers and Elections   For the moment, however, patriot spokesmen stood far in advance of grass roots. The king had invited all citize their local parishes to elect delegates to toral assemblies and to draft grievan (*cahiers*) setting forth their views. The gre rural cahiers were highly traditional in t plained only of particular local ills or hi pressing confidence that the king would

Anabaptists Individuals who, citing that the Bible nowhere mentions infant baptism, argued that the sacrament was effective only if the believer understood what was happening and that therefore adults ought to be rebaptized. Opponents argued that infant baptism was necessary so that a baby would not be denied salvation if it died young.

anarchists Radical activists who called for the abolition of the state, sometimes by violent means.

The Art

The ninth edition of *The Western Experience* continues the precedent of earlier editions, with more than four hundred full-color reproductions of paintings and photographs and over one hundred clearly focused maps.

The Maps

The maps in *The Western Experience* are already much admired by instructors. Each carries an explanatory caption that enhances the text coverage to help students tackle the content without sacrificing subtlety of interpretation or trying to escape the fact that history is complex. In the ninth edition, each caption has been further improved with a thought question.

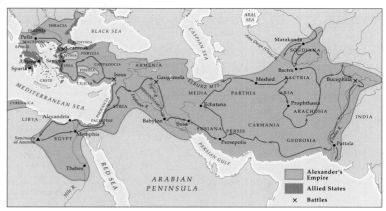

MAP 3.2 THE EMPIRE OF ALEXANDER THE GREAT AND THE ROUTE OF HIS CONQUESTS
Alexander formed the largest empire known down to his own time. He even conquered some territory across the Indus River in India. What were the two major Persian cities near the Persian Gulf?
◆ For an online version, go to www.mhhe.com/chambers9 > chapter 3 > book maps

---

QUESTIONS FOR FURTHER THOUGHT

1. The Greeks invented historical writing. In looking at the past, what are the most important questions a historian should ask?

2. The Greek city-states and their system of alliances gave way to the rising power of Macedonia. How might the Greek states have preserved their strength and political power?

Questions for Further Thought

To encourage students to move beyond rote learning of historical "facts" and to think broadly about history, the authors have added "Questions for Further Thought" at the end of each chapter. These are too broad to be exam questions; instead, they are meant to be questions that stimulate the students to think about history and social, political, and economic forces. Some are comparative, some require students to draw on knowledge of a previous chapter, some ask about the role of great leaders in politics, and some ask about how the less famous people living at the time perceived the events surrounding them.

More Heading Levels

We have given particular attention to adding more descriptive content guides, such as the consistent use of three levels of headings. We believe these will help students identify specific topics for purposes of study and review as well as give a clear outline of a chapter's argument.

Chronological Charts

Nearly every chapter employs charts and chronological tables that outline the unfolding of major events and social processes and serve as a convenient reference for students.

CHRONOLOGY
The Persian Wars
(All dates B.C.)

499, autumn	Greek cities of Ionia in Asia Minor revolt from Persian Empire.
498	Athens and Eretria (on island of Euboea) take part in burning Sardis in Persian Empire.
496	Persians besiege Miletus, the leading city in the revolt.
494	Fall of Miletus.
493	End of Ionian revolt.
492, spring	Persian expedition to northern Greece suffers heavy losses in storms.
490, mid-August	Battle of Marathon near Athens; Persians defeated.
486, November	Death of King Darius of Persia; accession of Xerxes.
484, spring–480, spring	Xerxes prepares for new invasion of Greece.
480, spring	Persian army sets out from Sardis.
480, late August	Battles of Thermopylae and Artemisium.
480, late September	Battle of Salamis.
479, early August	Battle of Plataea.

AVAILABLE FORMATS

To provide an alternative to the full-length hardcover edition, *The Western Experience* Ninth Edition, is available in two-volume and three-volume paperbound editions.

- Volume I includes chapters 1–17 and covers material through the eighteenth century.
- Volume II includes chapters 15–30 and covers material since the sixteenth century.
- Volume A includes chapters 1–12, Antiquity and the Middle Ages.
- Volume B includes chapters 11–21, The Early Modern Era.
- Volume C includes chapters 19–30, The Modern Era.

SUPPLEMENTARY INSTRUCTIONAL MATERIALS

McGraw-Hill offers instructors and students a wide variety of ancillary materials to accompany *The Western Experience*. Please contact your local McGraw-Hill representative for details concerning policies, prices, and availability.

For the Instructor

Instructor's Resource CD-ROM   The Instructor's Resource CD-ROM (IRCD) contains several instructor tools on one easy CD-ROM. For lecture preparation, teachers will find an Instructor's Manual with PowerPoint samples by chapter. For quizzes and tests, the IRCD contains a test bank and *EZ Test*, McGraw-Hill's flexible and easy-to-use electronic testing program. Extras on the IRCD also include map images from the book as well as extra photographs and art images.

Online Learning Center for Instructors   At www.mhhe.com/chambers9. At this home page for the text-specific website, instructors will find a series of online tools to meet a wide range of classroom needs. The Instructor's Manual, PowerPoint presentations, and blank maps can be downloaded by instructors, but are password protected to prevent tampering. Instructors can also create an interactive course syllabus using McGraw-Hill's *PageOut* (www.mhhe.com/pageout).

Overhead Transparency Acetates   This expanded full-color transparency package includes all the maps and chronological charts in the text.

For the Student

McGraw-Hill's Primary Source Investigator (PSI) CD-ROM   This CD-ROM, bound into each copy of *The Western Experience*, provides students with instant access to hundreds of world history documents, images, artifacts, audio recordings, and videos. PSI helps students practice the art of "doing history" on a real archive of historical sources. Students follow the three basic steps of *Ask, Research,* and *Present* to examine sources, take notes on them, and then save or print copies of the sources as evidence for their papers or presentations. After researching a particular theme, individual, or time period, students can use PSI's writing guide to walk them through the steps of developing a thesis, organizing their evidence, and supporting their conclusion.

More than just a history or writing tool, the PSI is also a student study tool that contains interactive maps, quiz questions, and an interactive glossary with audio pronunciation guide.

Student Study Guide/Workbook with Map Exercises, Volumes I and II   Includes the following features for each chapter: chapter outlines, chronological diagrams, four kinds of exercises—map exercises, exercises in document analysis, exercises that reinforce the book's important overarching themes, exercises in matching important terms with significant individuals—and essay topics requiring analysis and speculation.

The Online Learning Center   At www.mhhe.com/chambers9. The Online Learning Center is a fully interactive, book-specific website featuring numerous student study tools such as multiple-choice and true-false practice quizzes; interactive, drag-and-drop games about significant individuals and chronologies; key

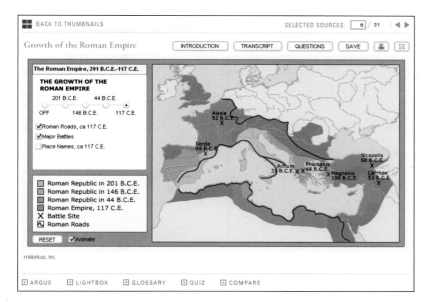

terms with correct identifications; an audio function to help students pronounce difficult terms; and drag-and-drop map exercises. Animated maps from the book are also available through the site. These maps carry a specific URL in their caption.

ACKNOWLEDGMENTS

Manuscript Reviewers, Ninth Edition

Robert Bast, University of Tennessee; Stephen Blumm, Montgomery County Community College; Nathan Brooks, New Mexico State University; Susan Carrafiello, Wright State University; Steven Fanning, University of Illinois at Chicago; Betsy Hertzler, Mesa Community College; Paul Hughes, Sussex County Community College; Mary Kelly, Franklin Pierce College; Paul Lockhart, Wright State University; Eileen Moore, University of Alabama at Birmingham; Penne Prigge, Rockingham Community College; William Roberts, Fairleigh Dickinson University; Steven Ross, Louisiana State University; Charles Sullivan, University of Dallas; Robert Thurston, Miami University.

Manuscript Reviewers, Eighth Edition

Tyler Blethen, West Carolina University; Owen Bradley, University of Tennessee; Dan Brown, Moorpark College; Richard Cole, Luther College; Vickie Cook, Pima Community College; Mary DeCredico, U.S. Naval Academy; Gunar Freibergs, Los Angeles Valley College; Ron Goldberg, Thomas Nelson Community College; Neil Heyman, San Diego State University; Elizabeth McCrank, Boston University; Edrene Stephens McKay, Northwest Arkansas Community College; George Monahan, Suf-

folk Community College; Fred Murphy, Western Kentucky University; Laura Pintar, Loyola University; Anne Quartararo, U.S. Naval Academy; Thomas Rowland, University of Wisconsin–Oshkosh; Charles Steen, University of New Mexico; Sig Sutterlin, Indian Hills Community College; John Tanner, Palomar College; Valentina Tikoff, DePaul University; Guangquin Xu, Northwest Arkansas Community College.

Manuscript Reviewers, Seventh Edition

Frank Baglione, Tallahassee Community College; Paul Goodwin, University of Connecticut; Robert Herzstein, University of South Carolina; Carla M. Joy, Red Rocks Community College; Kathleen Kamerick, University of Iowa; Carol Bresnahan Menning, University of Toledo; Eileen Moore, University of Alabama at Birmingham; Frederick Murphy, Western Kentucky University; Michael Myers, University of Notre Dame; Robert B. Patterson, University of South Carolina at Columbia; Peter Pierson, Santa Clara University; Alan Schaffer, Clemson University; Marc Schwarz, University of New Hampshire; Charles R. Sullivan, University of Dallas; Jack Thacker, Western Kentucky University; Bruce L. Venarde, University of Pittsburgh.

Manuscript Reviewers, Sixth Edition

S. Scott Bartchy, University of California, Los Angeles; Thomas Blomquist, Northern Illinois University; Nancy Ellenberger, U.S. Naval Academy; Steven Epstein, University of Colorado at Boulder; Laura Gellott, University of Wisconsin at Parkside; Drew Harrington, Western Kentucky University; Lisa Lane, Mira Costa College; William Matthews, S.U.N.Y. at Potsdam; Carol Bresnahan Menning, University of Toledo; Sandra Norman, Florida Atlantic University; Peter Pierson, Santa Clara University; Linda Piper, University of Georgia; Philip Racine, Wofford College; Eileen Soldwedel, Edmonds Community College; John Sweets, University of Kansas; Richard Wagner, Des Moines Area Community College.

Focus Group Reviewers from Spring 1992

Michael DeMichele, University of Scranton; Nancy Ellenberger, U.S. Naval Academy; Drew Harrington, Western Kentucky University; William Matthews, S.U.N.Y. at Potsdam.

We would like to thank Lyn Uhl, Monica Eckman, Angela Kao, and Emily Hatteberg of McGraw-Hill for their considerable efforts in bringing this edition to fruition.

THE WESTERN EXPERIENCE

GREAT HALL OF BULLS, LASCAUX CAVES
An example of animals depicted in a prehistoric cave painting.
Musée des Antiquités, St. Germain en Laye/Dagli Orti/The Art Archive

Chapter One

THE FIRST CIVILIZATIONS

THE EARLIEST HUMANS • THE FIRST CIVILIZATIONS IN MESOPOTAMIA
EGYPT • PALESTINE • THE NEAR EASTERN STATES

The subject of this book is the Western experience—that is, the history of European civilization, which is the civilization of modern Europe and America. Yet we do not begin with the mainland of present-day Europe, for our civilization traces its origins to earlier ones in Mesopotamia and around the Mediterranean Sea. Human beings began to abandon a nomadic existence and live in settled agricultural villages about 8000 B.C. This change in human lifestyle points to some of the themes that will run through this book—for example, the rise of technology to contain rivers and to survey and map areas for farming, or the art of cutting and assembling huge stones to build walls and pyramids.

By about 3000 B.C. humans had created settlements of some size along the banks of the Tigris, Euphrates, Nile, and Indus rivers. People's efforts to build a better life transformed the agricultural villages into something we can recognize as cities—having a scale and pattern crucial for the development of civilization. In these valleys, types of behavior and institutions first appeared that have persisted, in varying forms, throughout all periods of Western civilization.

Powerful kingdoms and great empires, centered on sizable cities, gradually arose in Mesopotamia and in Egypt. Their achievement of literacy and their many written records; their long-distance trade; their invention of increasingly ingenious tools, utensils, vehicles, and weapons; their development of monumental architecture and representative art; and their advances in medicine, astronomy, and mathematics marked the change from primitive life and constituted civilization.

Earliest known civilization at Hamoukar, Syria **ca. 3700 B.C.** ●

Invention of writing in Egypt or Sumer **ca. 3200 B.C.** ●

First Dynasty in Egypt **ca. 3100 B.C.** ●

● **ca. 400,000 B.C.** Emergence of Homo Sapiens

Beginning of Bronze Age **ca. 3000 B.C.** ●

● **ca. 11000 B.C.** Beginning of Neolithic Age

THE EARLIEST HUMANS

Our first task as we try to grasp historical chronology is to gain a sense of the overwhelmingly long period that we call "prehistory." The astronomer Carl Sagan reckoned that, if the entire history of the universe were plotted out over the span of one year, everything that we usually think of as European history—the subject of this book—would have taken place in the last two or three minutes of the year.

All human beings are members of the species *Homo sapiens* ("thinking human being"), which evolved, according to present evidence, about 400,000 years ago. The immediate predecessor was **Homo erectus,** which may have emerged as long ago as 1.5 million years. Back in time beyond Homo erectus is an area of doubt and controversy. There is growing support for the theory that humanity originated, in the form of *Homo habilis,* roughly "skillful human being," in east Africa about 2 million years ago. As to humankind's emigration from Africa, recent excavations in the nation of Georgia (part of the former Soviet Union) have discovered two skulls that are considered the most ancient human remains outside Africa. They date to about 1.7 million years ago and suggest that people emigrated when they became carnivorous and had to expand their territory in search of meat; they also show that the emigration must have been under way by this time.

There is no *inevitable* pattern of development in social groups. Hunter-gatherers can remain so forever, and small farming villages may never turn into anything else.[1] But there seem to be certain stages through which many societies have developed on the way to civilization.

Human Beings as Food Gatherers

Human beings have always had to try to come to terms with their environment. For the greatest part of their time on earth, they have struggled simply to hunt and gather food. Only at a later stage did people live in stable settlements—first villages, then cities.

Labor in Early Communities In all observed societies, labor is divided on the basis of sex. In the earliest societies, both hunting and gathering food were the means of survival. Current research suggests that women may have done most of the gathering as well as caring for the young. If hunting animals required longer expeditions, we may guess that men usually performed this duty. Even later, as agriculture became the basis of the economy, modern research suggests that women must have continued their domestic tasks, such as cooking and tending children.

We can surely guess that quarrels of some kind broke out between societies. One hunting band, for example, might have had to turn aside the claims of another band to certain territory. In such clashes, we may guess that men assumed leadership through their strength and thus created a division of roles based on sex that gave them dominance of their communities. One result of this social division has been a comparative lack of information about the role of women in history; the reconstruction of this role, the restoring of women to history, has been a leading theme of historical research in the present generation.

The Old Stone Age The period during which people gathered food is often called the Old Stone Age, or

[1] A point convincingly made by Johnson and Earle, p. 6 (see recommended readings at end of this chapter).

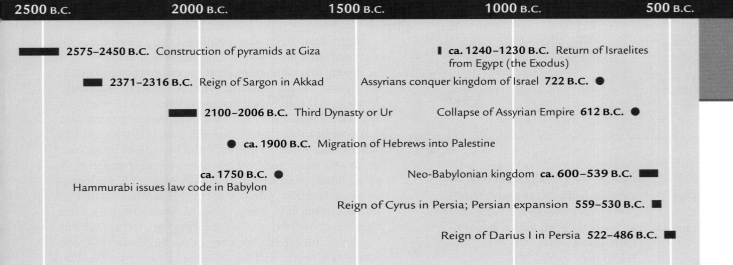

2575–2450 B.C. Construction of pyramids at Giza

ca. 1240–1230 B.C. Return of Israelites from Egypt (the Exodus)

2371–2316 B.C. Reign of Sargon in Akkad

Assyrians conquer kingdom of Israel **722 B.C.**

2100–2006 B.C. Third Dynasty or Ur

Collapse of Assyrian Empire **612 B.C.**

ca. 1900 B.C. Migration of Hebrews into Palestine

ca. 1750 B.C.
Hammurabi issues law code in Babylon

Neo-Babylonian kingdom **ca. 600–539 B.C.**

Reign of Cyrus in Persia; Persian expansion **559–530 B.C.**

Reign of Darius I in Persia **522–486 B.C.**

Paleolithic Age, and ranges from the beginning of human history to about 11,000 B.C. Even in this early period, some human beings developed a remarkably sophisticated kind of painting, the earliest demonstration of the role of artistic creation as another theme in the history of civilization. The most striking creations known from food-gathering societies are a series of cave paintings that survive at their finest in Lascaux in France and Altamira in Spain (28,000–22,000 B.C.). Most of the paintings show wild animals, enemies of human beings and yet part of their essential support. The paintings may have a quasi-religious meaning as symbolic attempts to gain power over the quarry; scars on the walls suggest that people threw spears at the painted animals, as if to imitate killing them. If so, the cave paintings provide our earliest evidence for one of the main themes of history: the attempt to communicate with forces outside human control through symbolic action, art, and thought—that is, through religion and ritual acts.

Human Beings as Food Producers

The Discovery of Agriculture About 11,000 B.C., according to recent research, there occurred the most important event in all human history: People turned from hunting animals and gathering food to producing food from the earth. This event, the rise of agriculture, is called the Neolithic Revolution and introduced the **Neolithic Age,** or New Stone Age.[2] The word *revolution* usually implies dramatic action over a short time, which was in no way true of this one. Yet revolution it was, for it made possible the feeding of larger populations. Agriculture, once mastered, be-

came another enduring theme throughout history and has always been the largest single factor in the economy of the world. Indeed, increasing the food supply was the imperative step to be taken on the path to cities and civilization.

Patterns in Population But *why* did this revolution take place? What caused people to turn from the pattern of roaming the countryside that had lasted hundreds of thousands of years? The driving force was probably an inevitable increase in population. As humans multiplied in the later, or "upper," Paleolithic Age, it became imperative to develop a continuous food supply and to have a secure reserve over the whole year. But traditional foraging might not guarantee such a supply. As people hunted animals, they inevitably made their prey scarcer. Even gathering fruit and grains required ever longer journeys. Therefore farming became a necessity. People grew grain in the summer and stored it in winter, but not all single families could be certain of enough food at all times. Storage of food became a task for the community, and this led to social cooperation, which in turn required social control—an approach to political organization and government.

Moreover, when people invested labor in their settlements and began to depend on land, protecting and even expanding their territory became of immense importance. Therefore one effect of the agricultural revolution was the impetus to gain control over territory—sometimes through negotiation, but sometimes through war. War is another of the constantly recurring themes of Western civilization.

Early Near Eastern Villages

The First Settlements The Neolithic Revolution first occurred probably in the hills of what is now southern

[2] The Mesolithic (Middle Stone) Age, beginning around 8000 B.C., was limited to northwestern Europe.

Turkey and northern Iraq, especially in the Zagros hills east of the Tigris River. But, again, why was *this* region the cradle of agriculture? Historians have concluded that only this location held a sufficient supply of animals for domestication along with the needed vegetables and cereals. The earliest known settlements, dating from about 9000 B.C., were unwalled and unfortified, and their people lived in simple huts. About 8000 B.C. the first somewhat larger villages appeared. The oldest seem to have been Jericho and Jarmo, but even these were still small settlements; by about 8000 B.C. Jericho may have had 2,000–3,000 people. The population of Jarmo, settled about 7000 B.C., is estimated at about 150, crowded into twenty to twenty-five houses of baked clay.

Invention, Travel, Trade   As villages became permanent, they also became more versatile in their inventions; our first evidence of pottery, for example, comes from what is now Syria and dates from about 8000 B.C. This invention allowed the storage of food and sustained the population in periods when hunting and gathering were more difficult. Another invention, the art of weaving, was practiced in Anatolia, now within

modern Turkey, by about 7000 B.C. and provided both new occupations and new resources for a village.

About this time, too, people began to travel in crude rafts and in carts with wheels. Potters gradually learned to fashion their wares on the surface of a turning wheel, and thus could make in minutes what had previously taken hours; and the pot, the raft, and the wheel combined to provide the means to transport grain and other goods. Thus arose another institution of all later societies: the mutually profitable exchange of goods in trade, pursued by people skilled enough to make a living at it. Some archaeologists have suggested that a number of towns were formed not for the sake of local agriculture but to serve as trading centers. Trade needs safe routes and a guarantee of safety for traders, which in turn require some kind of political protection, mutual understanding between communities, and control.

Agricultural Communities   The early farmers were naturally much concerned with fertility. When people feared that their own efforts might not solve life's problems, they turned to divine powers for help. These societies therefore sought to communicate with goddesses in the form of statuettes of unmistakable earthmothers with large buttocks and breasts, whose fertile bodies, it was hoped, would make the soil productive. Such figures also signify the importance of human mothers, for the villages flourished only if women produced and sustained each new generation.

So by stages there arose agrarian communities with communal gods, domesticated animals, simple technologies and economies, and some regulation of social behavior. Yet we must remember how painfully slow was the transition from nomadic hunters to food-producing villagers. And still another 4,000–5,000 years were to separate such agricultural villages from the first civilizations.

THE FIRST CIVILIZATIONS IN MESOPOTAMIA

History has been called an argument without end. It is still not definitely clear where civilization began, but the region of Mesopotamia has at least some claim as the cradle of civilization. The historian can point to the forming of cities, as distinct from farming towns, in this region, and Mesopotamia was also home to one of the two earliest systems of writing. From these beginnings arose two of the earliest civilizations, those of Sumer and of Babylonia. Both have left behind them written documents that are priceless sources for the thoughts and practices of these societies.

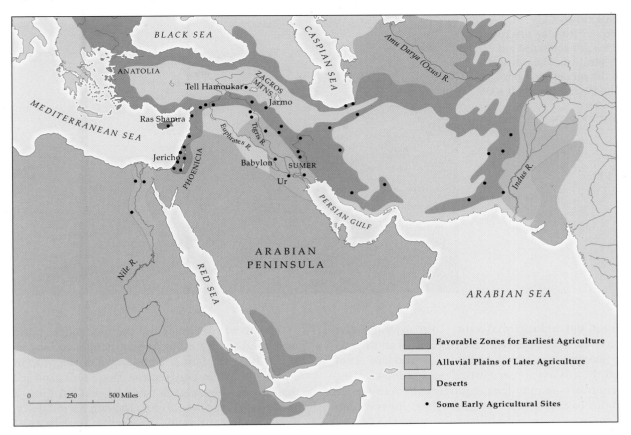

MAP 1.1 THE EARLIEST CIVILIZATIONS
This shows the famous "fertile crescent," which runs north from Jericho and turns southeast to Sumer and beyond. This was the cradle of agriculture from about 11,000 B.C., and here were the first agricultural villages. Which rivers supported agriculture in these regions?
◆ For an online version, go to www.mhhe.com/chambers9 > chapter 1 > book maps

The Emergence of Civilization

We may define civilization as a social organization with more complex rules than those that guided dwellers in caves or the earliest farmers. In a civilization, there are more sophisticated divisions of authority and labor, including duties, powers, and skills that pass down within certain families. A sensational excavation in A.D. 2000 at the site of Tell Hamoukar, in modern Syria, has revealed that people were living there by about 4000 B.C. and that they developed the earliest known civilization at this site about 3700 B.C. (the ancient name of the city has not yet been found). Among the signs of civilization found here are monumental architecture and seals used, perhaps by officials, to stamp valuable goods. Further knowledge of this site must await more excavation.

The Beginnings of Government   The establishment of firm authority requires the acceptance by both gover-

nors and the governed of their status; we shall see this balance throughout history, but we shall also observe its collapse when conflict leads to the replacement of one governing group by another. Rulers, however named, often arise from among the heads of powerful families. But there may be other sources of political strength. Seeking social order, people give authority to a man or woman who seems to have some special quality of leadership or ability.

An equally essential part of the social cement, in all periods of civilization, has been law, formally accepted codes of behavior, as distinct from the simple customs of a village. Law may develop slowly, but eventually it is recorded in detailed law codes, which tell us how societies controlled their people. Such codes can also tell us about ethical values, divisions between citizens, and social structure.

The Power of Cities   Cities are larger and therefore stronger than villages; they have the power to dominate

A Ziggurat from Ur
The stairway leads up to a room in which a god could rest and take his pleasure. The ziggurat formed the core of a temple compound, while around it were storehouses.
Georg Gerster/Comstock

the hinterland and its inhabitants. In many early civilizations, one society even enslaved parts of another society. Slavery, though deplorable in modern eyes, allowed the enslavers more varied occupations by freeing them from the mundane requirements of existence. As people began to use their freedom, however obtained, to pursue special skills, some gained a reputation for religious knowledge and became the state's communicators with divine powers; and such is the strength of religious belief that these priests could form a class of advisers whom even kings could not ignore.

Other citizens used their new freedom to develop new arts and crafts. Along with improved techniques of pottery, weaving, and domestication of animals, a major step forward took place when workers discovered how to blend other metals with copper to fashion bronze, especially for weapons. As the first cities reached significant size, humanity thus entered the Bronze Age, which started about 3000 B.C. and ended between 1200 and 1000 B.C.

Sumer

Cities of Sumer Mesopotamia (the "land between the rivers") is a rich alluvial plain created by deposits from the Tigris and Euphrates rivers. At the southern end of this plain, within modern Iraq, arose a civilization with a more advanced scale of development than that of the people of Tell Hamoukar. This took place in the area known as Sumer. Geography both nourished and threatened the Sumerians. The land was fertile, yet the rivers could roar over their banks, carrying away homes and human lives. Also, the land was open to invasion. Thus survival itself was often uncertain, a fact reflected in a strain of pessimism in Sumerian thought.

The people of Sumer and their language appear to be unrelated to any other known people or language. By about 3000 B.C. Sumer contained a dozen or more city-states—in other words, cities that were each independent of the others, each ruled by its own king (known as the lugal) and worshiping its own patron deity, a god that was thought to offer protection to the city. Sumerian religion held that rule by the king was a divine gift to the people and that the king ruled in the service of the gods. Thus religion and government, two of the large themes of civilization, were combined to comfort the people and, at the same time, to organize and control society.

Sumerian cities were much larger than the early farming villages already mentioned. One of them, Uruk, had a population estimated at 50,000 by around 3000 B.C. and a walled circumference of ten miles. The citizens of each city were divided into three classes: nobles and priests, commoners, and slaves. These classifications are the first example of what we shall often meet in history: a recognized, legal division of people into social orders. The king was not considered divine, but rather a servant of the gods. In practical political terms, he held power only so long as he could command support from the powerful priests and nobles.

The City and Its God At the center of a Sumerian city usually stood a **ziggurat,** a terraced tower built of baked brick and culminating in a temple, probably for the patron god of the city. A ziggurat might be a stupendous structure: The wall surrounding one was some thirty-six feet thick. The Old Testament contains many echoes from Sumer, and it seems likely that the story in the Bible of the Tower of Babel was ultimately based on the memory of a ziggurat.

In Sumerian culture, the patron god theoretically owned the whole city; but in fact, much of the land was private property, held mainly by powerful men and their families but also by private citizens. Most houses were of a single story and were jammed into narrow streets, but some richer houses had two stories and an open court. The people were monogamous, and women held property and took part in business but did not hold political office.

Trade and Mathematics   Geography also forced Sumerians to devise the art of trading. Trade was essential for the growth of Sumerian cities because, despite the region's astonishing fertility, it lacked good timber and stone. Sumerians pioneered the art of building in baked brick, but to obtain other materials they had to export such goods as metalwork, a craft at which they became outstanding.

Perhaps to bolster their expertise in the essential art of trading, the Sumerians developed a precise system of mathematical notation. Their system was the **sexagesimal,** in which the number 60 (*sexaginta* in Latin) is one of the main elements; this system has the advantage of including 3, 10, and 12 as factors. One of the longest-lasting legacies of Mesopotamia to our world is this system: Even today, the foot has 12 inches; the day, twice 12, or 24, hours; the minute and hour, 60 units each; and the circle, 360 degrees.

Sumerian Writing   Historians have long disputed whether the Sumerians or the Egyptians first developed the art of writing; recent research may show a slight lead in favor of Egypt. In any case, the Sumerians were writing by about 3000 B.C. The most important intellectual tool ever discovered, writing enables people to keep records, codify laws, and transmit knowledge. All the record keeping, libraries, and literature of later times are made possible by this invention. Their script was pictographic: Each sign was originally a stylized picture of the article that the scribe had in mind.[3]

Sumerian texts were written on clay tablets by pressing the end of a reed or bone stylus into the wet clay; the resulting wedge-shaped marks are called **cuneiform** (Latin *cuneus,* meaning "wedge"), a name used for all such scripts in whatever language they occur. *Scripts are not languages:* They are symbols that can be used to write several languages, as the Latin script is used to write all the languages of western Europe.

The Epic of Gilgamesh   Sumerian literature has left us a priceless document, a stirring narrative known as *The Epic of Gilgamesh.* There evidently was a king in

[3] The Sumerian system of writing is excellently described by S. N. Kramer, *The Sumerians,* 1963, pp. 302 ff.

A relief showing the Sumerian hero Gilgamesh holding a conquered lion, from the reign of Sargon II of Assyria, eighth century B.C. The relief shows the long continuation of the Sumerian legend.
Giraudon/Art Resource, NY

Sumer with this name (about 2700 B.C.), but in the epic, Gilgamesh is a great hero and ruler, said to be part man and part god. The woodless geography of Sumer dictates part of the story, as Gilgamesh sets out to re-cover cedar from northern lands (probably what is now Syria). He travels with his companion, Enkidu, who is killed by the storm god, Enlil. Gilgamesh, mourning the loss of his friend and confronted with the near certainty of death, plods on through the world in search of eternal life. He finds the plant that restores youth, but a serpent swallows it while Gilgamesh is bathing. In sorrow he returns home, and the epic ends with his death and funeral.

The epic is profoundly pessimistic and gives us a key to the Sumerian view of the universe. The gods, who created the world, established the standards by which people had to live. The storm god, Enlil, lived in heaven. Normally kind and fatherly, Enlil made the rich soil of Mesopotamia fertile and was credited with designing the plow. At times, however, when Enlil had to carry out the harsh decrees of other gods, he became terrifying.

The Fate of Humanity in Sumerian Thought   This fearful alternation between divine favor and divine punishment doubtless reflects the uncertainty bred in the Sumerians by the constant threat of floods. When the rivers overflowed and destroyed the crops, the Sumerians thought the gods had withdrawn their favor, and they rationalized such treatment by assuming that they had somehow offended the gods or failed to observe their requirements.

In Sumerian mythology, humanity was almost completely dependent on the gods. Indeed, Sumerian myth taught that the gods had created people merely to provide slaves for themselves. In another Sumerian epic, *The Creation of Mankind*, Marduk the creator says, "Let him be burdened with the toil of the gods, that they may freely breathe." Other Sumerian myths foreshadow the biblical accounts of eating from the tree of knowledge in paradise and of the flood that covered the earth.

Sargon of Akkad and the Revival of Ur   Wars among the cities of Sumer weakened them and prepared the way for the first great warlord of Western history: Sargon, of the area called Akkad, named for a city just north of Babylon. Sargon ruled from 2371 to 2316 B.C.[4] and conquered all Mesopotamia; his kingdom even reached the Mediterranean Sea. From the name of his city, Akkad, linguists have created the term *Akkadian* to comprise two Semitic languages, Assyrian and Babylonian (there is no separate Akkadian language). Thus, through Sargon, we meet one of the most important of all groups of peoples in Western civilization, the Semites. They spoke a number of related languages including Akkadian, Hebrew, and Canaanite.

Akkadian, also written in cuneiform, now replaced Sumerian as a spoken language, although Sumerian continued as a written language until about the beginning of the Christian era.

Sargon and his successors ruled from Akkad until about 2230 B.C., when invasion, and perhaps internal dissension, dissolved the Akkadian kingdom. The Sumerians then regained control of southern Mesopotamia and established the so-called Third Dynasty of Ur. The chief ruler of this period was Ur-Nammu (2113–2096 B.C.). He created another practice that we will see again and again in history when he issued the first law code and spelled out regulations and penalties for a broad range of offenses. He also established standard weights and measures, a recognition of the importance of trade to the people of his state. Ur-Nammu's law code is preserved in only fragmentary form, but it is clear that he laid down fines in money rather than calling for physical retribution: "If a man has cut off the foot of another man . . . he shall pay ten shekels. . . . If a man has severed with a weapon the bones of another man . . . he shall pay one mina of silver." (Some historians assign this code to his son Shulgi.)

The Babylonian Kingdom

Ur declined, toward the year 2000 B.C., and was destroyed by neighboring peoples in 2006. A Semitic people called Amorites soon established their own capital at Babylon, within the region known as Babylonia. Hammurabi, the sixth king of the dynasty in Babylon itself, finally succeeded in unifying Mesopotamia under his rule.

Hammurabi and His Law Code   Hammurabi (r.[5] 1792–1750 B.C.) is a towering figure whose greatest legacy is the most significant of all the written documents down to his time: a stone column, now in the Louvre Museum in Paris, recording in cuneiform script a long series of legal judgments published under his name. This Code of Hammurabi, like the earlier one of Ur-Nammu, is not a complete constitution or system of law; rather, it is a compilation of those laws and decisions that Hammurabi thought needed restating. Its form is important. The code begins with a preamble, in which the god Marduk is made to declare that he is giving his laws to Hammurabi; this preamble thus validates the laws by assigning them a divine origin.

The code includes 280 sections, much more carefully organized than any earlier one that we know (see "Hammurabi's Law Code," p. 11). Hammurabi has

---

[4] Dates in early Near Eastern history are in constant revision. For dates in this chapter, we normally rely on the *Cambridge Ancient History*, 3rd ed., 1970–2000.

[5] Throughout this book, the letter *r.* before a date or a series of dates stands for "reigned."

HAMMURABI'S LAW CODE

Here are some excerpts from the "judgments" laid down by Hammurabi in his famous law code.

"When Marduk [the patron god of Babylon] sent me to rule the people and to bring help to the country, I established law and justice in the language of the land and promoted the welfare of the people. At that time I decreed:

"1. If a man accuses another man of murder but cannot prove it, the accuser shall be put to death.

"2. If a man bears false witness in a case, or cannot prove his testimony, if that case involves life or death, he shall be put to death.

"22. If a man commits robbery and is captured, he shall be put to death.

"23. If the robber is not captured, the man who has been robbed shall, in the presence of the god, make a list of what he has lost, and the city and the governor of the province where the robbery was committed shall compensate him for his loss.

"138. If a man wants to divorce his wife who has not borne him children, he shall give her money equal to her marriage price and shall repay to her the dowry she brought from her father; and then he may divorce her.

"142. If a woman hates her husband and says, 'You may not possess me,' the city council shall inquire into her case; and if she has been careful and without reproach and her husband has been going about and belittling her, she is not to blame. She may take her dowry and return to her father's house.

"195. If a son strikes his father, they shall cut off his hand.

"196. If a man destroys the eye of another man, they shall destroy his eye.

"197. If he breaks another man's bone, they shall break his bone.

"200. If a man knocks out a tooth of a man of his own rank, they shall knock out his tooth."

From Robert F. Harper (tr.), *The Code of Hammurabi*, Gordon Press, 1904, 1991 (language modified).

---

always been considered the primary example of the lawgiver, the man who grasped the organizing power of royal declarations of law; his example was to be followed by many other potentates, whether or not they consciously looked back to the Babylonian model. The sections of the code, like those of Ur-Nammu's code, are all arranged in the form, "If *A* takes place, *B* shall follow," for example, "If a man strikes his father, they shall cut off his hand."

Hammurabi recognized three classes within his society: We follow the historian H. W. F. Saggs[6] and call them gentleman (one of the landowning families), landless free citizen, and slave. The penalties for various offenses were not uniform; rather, they differed according to the status of the victim. Sometimes the code allowed monetary compensation rather than physical retaliation. For example, "If a man destroys another man's eye, they shall destroy his eye"; but "If a man destroys the eye of another man's slave, he shall pay one half the slave's price." The penalties were severe, to say the least, and the rule of strict retaliation between members of the same class has given us the saying "an eye for an eye, a tooth for a tooth"[7] as a motto for Hammurabi's principles.

[6] *Civilization before Greece and Rome*, 1989, p. 44.

[7] This formulation also reaches us through the Bible (Exod. 21:24).

Women and the Family in the Code   But Hammurabi was not concerned merely with retaliation. Among the most forward-looking provisions in his code were those regarding the family. Hammurabi evidently recognized the vulnerable position of women and children in his society and took care to protect them. If a man's wife became ill, he could marry another woman but had to continue to support the first wife; and she, if she wished, could move out and keep her dowry, that is, the contribution made by her family when she was married. A widower could not spend his dead wife's dowry but had to save it for her sons; and a widow could keep her dowry.

Hammurabi carefully regulated marriage for the sake of future generations. He dealt with breach of promise by decreeing that, if a man had paid a marriage price to his future father-in-law and then decided not to marry the young woman, the woman's father could keep the marriage price. If a man wanted to divorce a wife who had not produced children, he could do so but had to return the dowry she had brought into the marriage.

The Code and Society   The code is not a wholly progressive document. Some decisions in the code show a double standard for the sexes. A wife could divorce her husband for adultery and reclaim her dowry, but only if she had been chaste; if not, she was thrown into the

CHRONOLOGY
Dates in Egyptian History
3100–332 B.C.

The basic source for Egyptian chronology is a list of the rulers compiled about 280 B.C. by Manetho, an Egyptian priest, who wrote in Greek. He grouped the kings into thirty dynasties (later chronicles added a thirty-first). Modern scholars accept Manetho's divisions. The following approximate dates rely on *Cultural Atlas of Ancient Egypt*, rev. ed., 2000, by J. Baines and J. Malek. All dates are B.C.

Late Predynastic Period	ca. 3100
Early Dynastic Period (Dynasties 1–3)	2950–2575
Old Kingdom (Dynasties 4–8)	2575–2125
First Intermediate Period (Dynasties 9–11)	2125–1975
Middle Kingdom (Dynasties 11–14)	1975–1630
Second Intermediate Period (Dynasties 15–17; Hyksos era)	1630–1539
New Kingdom, or Empire (Dynasties 18–20)	1539–1075
Third Intermediate Period (Dynasties 21–25)	1075–715
Late Period (Dynasties 25–31)	715–332
Conquest of Egypt by Persia	525
Conquest of Egypt by Alexander the Great	332

Top: The ceremonial palette of King Narmer is a symbolic representation of the unification of Upper and Lower Egypt. This side of the palette shows the king, wearing the white crown of Upper Egypt, smashing the head of an enemy. The god Horus, in the form of a falcon, holds a rope attached to a captive of Lower Egypt, a region symbolized by six papyrus plants.

Bottom: On this side of the palette King Narmer has completed his conquest of Lower Egypt and wears the red crown of that kingdom. He is reviewing the bodies of decapitated victims. The exotic beasts with necks intertwined may symbolize the unity of the two Egypts.
Hirmer Fotoarchiv

Euphrates River (and, presumably, drowned) along with her lover. Nowhere does the code state that a husband will suffer the same punishment if he has been unfaithful.

At the end of his long document, Hammurabi added a proud epilogue, reading in part, "The great gods called me, and I am the guardian shepherd whose beneficent shadow is cast over my city. In my bosom I carried the people of the land of Sumer and Akkad; I governed them in peace; in my wisdom I sheltered them." He thus combined the power of both law and religious belief to create a civic order for his society.

Mesopotamian Culture

Hammurabi's subjects used all manner of commercial records (bills, letters of credit, and the like), and their knowledge of mathematics was amazing. They built on foundations laid by the Sumerians, using the sexagesimal system, with the number 60 as the base. They had multiplication tables, exponents, tables for computing interest, and textbooks with problems for solution.

The Mesopotamians also developed complex systems of astrology (the art of predicting the future from the stars) and astronomy. It is not certain which science inspired the other, but we have both astrological predictions and astronomic observations from the second millennium. The Babylonian calendar had twelve lunar months and thus had only 354 days, but astronomers learned how to regularize the year by adding a month at certain intervals. When the Hebrews and Greeks wanted to order time through a calendar, they learned the method from the Babylonians. In fact, the calendars of both Jerusalem and Athens were also lunar, with 354 days and a month added from time to time.

EGYPT

The early cities of Mesopotamia had turbulent histories, falling now to one warlord, now to another. The kingdom of Egypt, by contrast, achieved a nearly incredible permanence. The basic element in the long history of Egyptian civilization is the Nile River. The Nile flows down to the Mediterranean Sea over a series of granite thresholds known as cataracts. Each summer it overflows its banks, reviving the land with fresh water and depositing a thick layer of soil for cultivation. Only this yearly flood protected the early Egyptians from starvation.

The geography of Egypt must also have played a part in the social organization of the state. In effect, Egyptians could live only along the Nile and could not withdraw into any kind of interior. Moreover, the need to live close to the river isolated Egypt from other peoples and allowed a long, generally unbroken development. The climate is usually equable, and the river was a friend, not the potential enemy that it was in Sumer.

These conditions allowed the kings to control their subjects through governors and, if need be, with troops up and down the river. The narrow bed of the Nile as it flows down to the Mediterranean Sea is almost a metaphor for the highly "vertical" structure of Egyptian society. Egyptians must have thought that the regularity of their agricultural life was a gift from the gods. The kings and their servants saw to the maintenance of religion, and the faith of Egypt was a large factor in the strength and longevity of their society.

The Old and Middle Kingdoms

Unification of Egypt and Its Kings   Historians divide Egyptian history into nine periods, which include the Old, Middle, and New Kingdoms (see "Dates in Egyptian History," p. 12). These periods in turn are divided into thirty-one groups of kings, or dynasties. Before the First Dynasty, Egypt was divided into two regions, Upper Egypt (the Nile Valley) and Lower Egypt (the delta, to the north, where the water spreads into a shape like an upside down Greek letter delta). It seems likely that the two Egypts went through a gradual unification near the beginning of the First Dynasty, but decisive impetus to this movement may have come from Narmer, who lived about 3100 B.C. A famous plaque shows him as king of both Upper and Lower Egypt. The first king of the First Dynasty is recorded as Menes (some historians have identified him with Narmer), who established a capital of the whole land at Memphis, at the southern point of the delta, the site of modern Cairo.

Egyptian rulers enjoyed a supremacy that we can hardly imagine today. The king (he was not called **pharaoh** until the New Kingdom, about 1540 B.C.) was the owner of all Egypt and was considered a god as well. The entire economy was a royal monopoly; serving the king was a hierarchy of officials, ranging from governors of provinces down through local mayors and tax collectors. Artisans, peasants, and servants, all working for the king, nourished the whole system.

The supreme monuments of the Old Kingdom are the three immense pyramids, tombs for kings, built at Giza (now within the city of Cairo) in the Fourth Dynasty between 2575 and 2450 B.C. These staggering feats of engineering dwarf any other monuments from any age. The Egyptians were the unchallenged masters in cutting and manipulating stone. They fitted the tremendous blocks of the pyramids together with nearly perfect tightness, and the sides of these pyramids are exactly aligned toward the four cardinal points of the compass. Building such a pyramid may well have been the chief activity of a king during his reign. The ability to move and arrange such huge weights was a sign of an omnipotent ruler.

Religion   The king was seen as a god—specifically, the incarnation of the god Horus, who is represented in art as a falcon. Here Egypt differs from the Mesopotamian kingdoms, in which the ruler was not considered divine. Thus Egypt offers another example of the political power of religion in organizing early societies. Other gods, who occupied lesser positions in Egyptian religion, appeared in a variety of forms, often as animals, and in origin were probably deities of the villages up and down the Nile. The Egyptians believed in a pleasant life after death, in which people would perform their usual tasks but with more success. The king, already a god, would become a greater god; soothsayers, priests, and administrators would hold even higher positions. For everyone who had lived a good life, there would be delights such as boating and duck hunting.

In Egyptian mythology, the god who ruled over the dead was **Osiris**, a god of vegetation and fertility. At

THE PYRAMIDS OF GIZA
Left to right, the pyramid of Menkaure, Khefre, and Khufu (the "Great" pyramid).
Henning Bock/AKG London

times he was identified with the Nile, which gives fertility to Egypt. Myths said that he had given Egypt its laws and had shown the people how to prosper. Legend also told that he was murdered by his treacherous brother and his body cut into fragments. His loving wife and sister, Isis, resurrected him by reassembling these parts. Osiris' son, Horus, was identified with the king, who was, as we have said, seen as the incarnation of Horus on earth.

In harmony with their expectation of survival beyond death, the Egyptians made careful preparations for the physical needs of the afterlife, especially by placing favored possessions, such as jewelry and wine cups, into a tomb; above all, by embalming and making mummies of the dead. Statues sat in the tombs of kings and those high officials who could afford them, as receptacles for their spirits in case their bodies should be destroyed.

Maat   The Egyptians recognized an abstract ethical quality called ***maat***, which Egyptologists translate roughly as "right order." Maat existed if everything was in the order that the gods had ordained. All ancient societies valued order—most of them had a monarchic system that naturally prized discipline—but the notion of maat seems to show a new way of advocating moral behavior. When a society can give a name to the abstract idea of right order, a subtler kind of thinking is taking place. Right order would, indeed, help to hold Egyptian society together. The king maintained maat

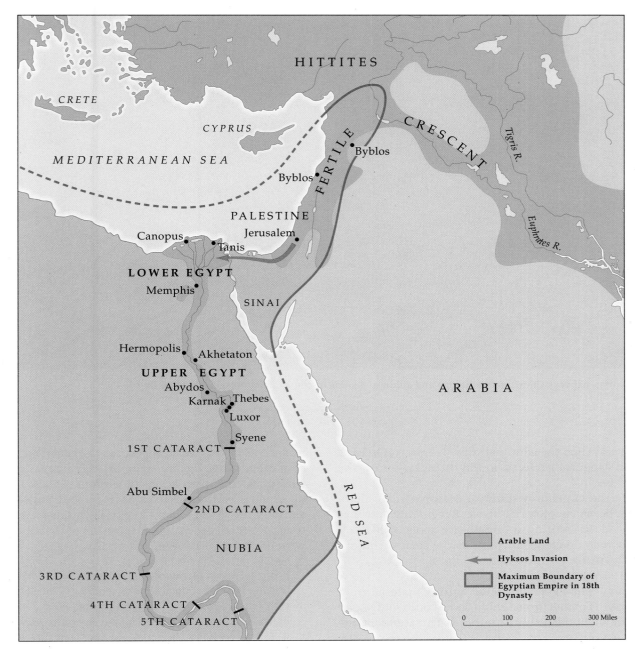

MAP 1.2 ANCIENT EGYPT
The kingdom of Egypt was centered on the Nile River, which provided the fertile soil for agriculture. Notice that the river flows over a series of cataracts into the Mediterranean Sea. At the northern mouth, in Lower Egypt, the river fans out into a larger area called the delta. Which are some of the main towns along the river?

◆ For an online version, go to www.mhhe.com/chambers9 > chapter 1 > book maps

and acted in accordance with it; he could not, therefore, be evil or act wrongly. Thus maat illustrates another frequent use of religion throughout history: as a carefully crafted tool to promote and maintain social order and political control. Egyptian religion also taught that Osiris, ruler of the underworld, judged human beings and decided whether the dead truly deserved admission to the hereafter.

Writing Egyptians developed a form of writing known as **hieroglyphs** ("sacred carvings"). The indispensable key to the Egyptian past is the Rosetta Stone, found when Napoleon occupied parts of Egypt in A.D. 1798. This stone, now in the British Museum, contains a partly preserved hieroglyphic text from 196 B.C., along with a translation in Demotic, at that time the "modern" form of Egyptian, and another in Greek,

An Egyptian papyrus showing an antelope and a lion in a game of chess; a playful scene from daily life.
© British Museum

which was then the administrative language. Greek, a known language, offered a way of deciphering the other two.

Like the cuneiform script of Mesopotamia, hieroglyphs began as pictorial signs. Recent research has suggested that writing in Egypt began about 3200 B.C. If so, Egypt could claim the prize as the society that invented writing, a little ahead of Sumer.

Papyrus   The Egyptians made writing material from the papyrus plants (from which comes our word *paper*) that grew abundantly in the Nile. The stems of the plant were placed crosswise in layers, then soaked, pressed, and dried to produce sheets and rolls. The dry climate has preserved thousands of papyri in legible condition. In later times many Greek texts were also preserved on papyri.

Literature and Instructions   Egyptians developed a rich, lively literature. Their works, like their art, are full of mythology and the afterlife, and their hymns to various deities, poems celebrating the king's victory over death, and stories about the gods all reflect the serene Egyptian confidence in the beneficence of divine powers. Various texts, collectively known as the *Book of the Dead*, provide charms and other methods of ensuring a successful transition to the other world.

Success in this world appears as the central concern of another literary genre, appropriately known as "instructions" or "instructions in wisdom." These books, in which a wise man gives advice about how to get ahead in the world, offer a key to Egyptian social attitudes, especially the supreme position of the king. The writers counsel discretion and loyalty:

> If you are a man of note sitting in the council of your lord, fix your heart upon what is good. Be silent—this is better than flowers. Speak only if you can unravel the difficulty . . . to speak is harder than any other work. . . . Bend your back to him that is over you, your superior in the king's administration. So will your house endure with its substance, and your pay be duly awarded. To resist him that is set in authority is evil.[8]

We also have Egyptian love poetry: "I love to go to the pond to bathe in your presence, so I may let you see my beauty in my tunic of finest royal linen, when it is wet." And there are meditations, songs, ghost stories, and fables of all kinds. In fact, not until the Greeks did the ancient world have another literature with variety and beauty equal to that of Egypt.

[8] Adolf Erman, *The Ancient Egyptians: A Sourcebook of Their Writings*, 1966, pp. 61–62 (language modified).

Mathematics The Egyptians were pioneers in applied science. The need for careful planting in the silt deposits of the Nile forced them to master arithmetic, geometry, and the art of surveying; an unusually rich overflow might wipe out the boundaries between plots of land, and when this happened the land had to be remeasured.

Medicine Medicine in Egypt depended largely on driving out demons from the body. The Egyptians believed that a separate god ruled over each organ and limb, and treatment consisted largely in finding the right chant to appease the appropriate deity and then delivering it in the right tone of voice. Sometimes a sorcerer simply threatened a demon by promising to invoke the aid of the gods if it did not depart at once.

But medicine was not based entirely on magic. We have recipes for toothache, for depression, for constipation, and much more. The Edwin Smith Papyrus, a treatise on surgery, discusses some forty-eight medical problems, classified according to the various parts of the body. Whenever possible, the author gives a diagnosis and suggests a treatment through surgery. A verdict is often given in one of three forms—"An ailment that I will treat," "An ailment with which I will contend," or "An ailment not to be treated"—probably according to whether the prognosis was favorable, uncertain, or unfavorable. This text is a witness to the birth of a kind of inquiry that transcends haphazard folk medicine. Such maturing and broadening of knowledge independent of magic characterize the civilizing process throughout history.

The New Kingdom

The Period of the Hyksos Beginning about 1630 B.C. the delta region, in Lower Egypt, was largely under the control of the people known as the Hyksos. The name means, roughly, "rulers of foreign lands," and the Egyptians farther south called them the Aamu, "Asiatics" (that is, from western Asia). They appear to have immigrated from the southern Levant or Palestine. By about 1520 B.C. Egyptian warriors from Thebes had come north and driven the Hyksos back into their homeland. The period following their departure is called the New Kingdom, sometimes also the Egyptian Empire.

The Eighteenth Dynasty During the Eighteenth Dynasty the kings from Thebes, now called pharaohs, strengthened the power of the central government and organized the country into a military state. They enlarged their domain by invading Asia Minor, fighting in what is roughly modern Syria, where they clashed above all with a kingdom known as Mitanni.

Queen Hatshepsut of Egypt (1473–1458 B.C.), history's first female ruler, pictured as a sphinx, which was a divine animal. She is depicted as a sphinx with a ceremonial false beard, as if to emphasize her right to rule.
Metropolitan Museum of Art, Rogers Fund, 1931 (31.3.166).
Photograph © 2002 The Metropolitan Museum of Art, New York

Hatshepsut (1473–1458 B.C.) Within the Eighteenth Dynasty there reigned the most powerful female ruler of ancient times, Hatshepsut. This dynamic woman seized power and had herself crowned king of Egypt. It was an act of breathtaking audacity in a social system in which men had always held the absolute power of monarch. Perhaps to emphasize her right to rule as king, she had herself portrayed as a sphinx with a beard.

Hatshepsut wanted to be remembered above all as a builder, the restorer of Egypt. "I have repaired," she proclaimed on inscribed walls, "what was destroyed by the Hyksos; I have raised up what was in pieces ever since

Akhnaton and Nefertiti in a familial scene hold three of their children while the sun-disk blesses and cherishes them. The style of art (round bellies, slender bodies, elongated jaws) is typical of the Amarna period.
M. Büsing/BPK Berlin/Art Resource, NY

the Asiatics had been in the Delta, overthrowing what had been made." Her great temple tomb in the Nile valley is among the most majestic of temples in Egypt.

Thutmose III (1479–1425 B.C.)   Thutmose III, Hatshepsut's successor, became Egypt's greatest military leader. He made seventeen expeditions into Asia and expanded the empire as far as the Euphrates River. He proudly recorded his victory over Mitanni (about 1440 B.C.). His successors, exploiting these conquests, grew rich on the tribute paid by subject peoples. With this economic power the Egyptians expanded their trade, honored their gods with more temples, and continued working the rich copper mines in the Sinai peninsula.

Akhnaton's Religious Reform   After the conquests of Thutmose III, a dramatic conflict of religions took place in the New Kingdom. This struggle arose from a contest between the pharaoh and certain priests and nobles, as each party strove to make its own god the supreme one. Thus the apparent religious battle—not for the last time in history—was, in reality, a political one. Although this battle was but one event during the centuries of the New Kingdom, the reforming aims of one side in this conflict have fascinated modern observers.

Early in his reign, King Amenhotep IV (1353–1336 B.C.) began to oppose the worship of **Amon-Re**, for centuries the traditional god of Thebes, and sponsored the worship of the **aton**, the physical disk, or circle, of the

sun. Supported by his wife, Nefertiti, Amenhotep appears to have been trying to overcome the influence of priests and bureaucrats in Thebes. To advertise the new faith among his people, he changed his own name to Akhnaton, meaning "he who serves Aton." He moved his capital from Thebes to a completely new city called Akhetaton, "the horizon of Aton" (a village called El Amarna today), where he built a temple to Aton. He composed a soaring hymn in praise of Aton, hailing him as the creator of the world—an account of creation comparable to those of the Sumerians and the Israelites.[9] Art of the Amarna period showed a different style from that of the earlier periods. The king was portrayed with a pot belly and elongated head and jaw, and this style was reflected in portraits of common people as well.

Akhnaton evidently fought the worship of other gods, even hacking the name of Amon-Re from monuments. His devoted worship of Aton has even led some historians to call him the first monotheist. But such a view is anachronistic and overlooks how Aton was worshiped: The royal family alone worshiped this god, while the Egyptian people were expected to continue to worship the pharaoh himself. Scenes in art show priests and nobles in attitudes of reverence, but they are addressing their prayers to the pharaoh, not directly to Aton.

[9] Strong resemblances have been seen between this hymn and Psalm 104. See J. A. Wilson, *The Culture of Ancient Egypt*, 1951, p. 227.

Syrian subjects presenting tribute to the pharaoh of Egypt on a wall painting at Thebes in the period of the empire.
C. M. Dixon/© British Museum

The Reaction against Akhnaton   The more conservative priests, and probably most Egyptians, continued to worship Amon-Re, and Akhnaton's religious reform ended with his death. The second following ruler (1332–1322 B.C.) changed his name from Tutankhaton to Tutankhamen, thus indicating that Amon-Re, the older chief deity, was again in favor. The royal court moved back north to Memphis, and the city named for Aton, Akhetaton, was abandoned and destroyed. Akhnaton's name was savagely hacked off monuments and king lists, and he was now known as "the criminal of Akhetaton." The young king Tutankhamen reigned for only nine years and was buried with dazzling splendor. His tomb, discovered in 1922 intact with all its treasures, is one of the most stunning finds in the history of Egyptology.

Ramses II (1279–1213 B.C.)   In the Nineteenth Dynasty, the New Kingdom emerged from the period of religious conflict with renewed strength and was led by ambitious pharaohs, the most famous of whom was Ramses II. After warfare between Egypt and the Hittite kingdom of Asia Minor, the two kingdoms signed a peace treaty in 1259 B.C.;[10] this may have been the

world's first nonagression pact and brings forth another of the themes that run through history, namely, diplomacy and negotiation between states.

Ramses II devoted much of Egypt's wealth to amazing building projects. At Karnak, for example, he completed an enormous hall of columns sacred to Amon-Re, who had now fully regained his old position. Ramses' supreme achievement as a builder is the colossal temple that he had carved out of the rocky cliffs along the Nile at Abu Simbel. In front of the temple sit four 65-foot-high statues of the king. The building of the Aswan Dam by the modern Egyptians would have drowned the temple and its statues beneath the water of an artificial lake, but an international group of engineers preserved Ramses' desire to be remembered for all time by cutting the outer monuments free and raising them above the level of the water.

A View of Egyptian Society

Administration and Slavery   In antiquity, communication by ship was greatly superior to overland transportation because of the greater speed and economy of sailing. The Nile therefore imposed a natural administrative unity on Egypt. The kings secured their power through the help of ministers and advisers, especially the class of priests, while a complex bureaucracy carried out the routine work of government and saw to the

[10] Both the Hittite and Egyptian texts of this document are translated in J. B. Pritchard (ed.), *Ancient Near Eastern Texts Relating to the Old Testament*, 1969, pp. 199–203.

economy, which was a royal monopoly with the exception of marketing the simplest household products.

Slaves existed, but the economic difference between free citizens and slaves was not always vast. Both classes worked the fields, labored on the pyramids, and were indeed the ultimate economic basis for the regime, although their own lives changed little from one generation to another.

Education   For all its controls, the Egyptian hierarchy did allow youths to enter and rise through education. The kings and their gods needed all manner of scribes, treasurers, and functionaries, and Egyptian children might learn the art of writing in a school run by a temple or a palace or even from a private teacher in a village. They normally studied from age four to age sixteen and could then enter the army or the royal service. Scribes were also needed for the arts of medicine and architecture and for priesthoods; most priests were men, but some were women.

Women and the Family   Egypt had no formal marriage. Men and women simply started to live together, often as teenagers. The desire for children was universal as insurance against the future. One wise man of the Eighteenth Dynasty advised, "Take a wife when you are young, so that she might give you a son. Happy is the man with a large family, for he is respected on account of his children." A woman held the title "mistress of the house," and the house and its management were her responsibilities. Agricultural work was by far the main occupation of Egyptians, and women participated in the task; they also went shopping, a fact noted with surprise by the Greek historian Herodotus on his visit to Egypt.

Most women were peasants with little education, but they had certain powers not granted, for example, to women of Israelite or Greco-Roman societies. Most remarkably, in view of the critical importance of ownership of land in Egypt, land passed down from mother to daughter; probably, it has been said, because it is always clear who one's mother is, while paternity can be uncertain. Likewise, men commonly identified themselves by citing the name of their mother, not of their father.

Women and Occupations   This method of passing on property meant that women could own and manage both land and other property. Thus a woman did not have to turn her property over to her husband at the time of marriage. Women could also initiate legal action, buy and sell property, and execute wills. But women were legally equal to men only within their own class. Most women were peasants and shared the daily work of planting crops, picking fruit, and carrying baskets; above all, they had to produce children.

Men normally held the important positions in the state and the bureaucracy (again the amazing position of the queen Hatshepsut should be remembered). Below this level of political influence, women performed tasks like overseeing weavers, singers, and cooks; some were treasurers in private businesses. A respected occupation was that of midwife, and midwives delivered most Egyptian babies. A great many women were singers, dancers, and professional mourners at funerals. Among higher positions open to women were priesthoods, often including priestesses who chanted or played instruments in temples.

Women were buried along with their men, sharing in the elegance of the tomb according to the rank of their husbands. Privileged women could be given in death a profusion of jewels, necklaces, and other ornaments.

The Permanence of Egypt   We must not overlook the turmoil within Egyptian history: the invasion of the Hyksos, wars in Asia, the collapse of the New Kingdom, and its conquest by Assyria and then by Persia (see "Dates in Egyptian History," p. 12). Yet there remains the awesome *permanence* of Egypt: No other state, in the history of the nations we call Western, ever survived so long. On the whole, over the span of some thirty centuries, life flowed predictably, like the Nile, making severe demands but bringing the material for a well-earned reward.

PALESTINE

We have already discussed the Semitic society of Babylonia and turn now to Semites in the area of Palestine. They include the Phoenicians, who were famous as sailors and explorers; they also developed an alphabet that became the mother of all the scripts of Europe. Even more important to the Western experience was the society of Israel, which gave the Western world its greatest book—the Bible.

Canaanites and Phoenicians

The region of Palestine was originally inhabited by a group of Semitic tribes known as the Canaanites, among whose cities were Jericho and Jerusalem. By about 1200 B.C. the Canaanites had settled mainly in Phoenicia, a narrow region along the Mediterranean Sea (roughly modern Lebanon). The Phoenicians drew part of their culture from the Mesopotamian and Egyptian states nearby, but they were also brilliant innovators.

The Phoenician Alphabet   Their outstanding contribution was a simplified alphabet with 22 characters that was later adopted by the Greeks and became the

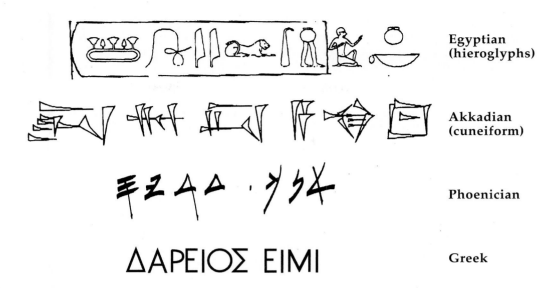

Egyptian (hieroglyphs)

Akkadian (cuneiform)

Phoenician

Greek

ΔΑΡΕΙΟΣ ΕΙΜΙ

Several translations of "I am Darius," in hieroglyphic, Akkadian, Phoenician, and Greek.

ancestor of Western alphabets. The political and social importance of this invention is impossible to overstate. It ended the long period during which people had to learn thousands of pictorial symbols to be reasonably literate and writing was a mysterious art known to only a few. Especially in the hands of the Greeks, writing brought a knowledge of law codes and historical records within the intellectual reach of ordinary citizens and led to reevaluation of the past and a critical spirit about received tradition.

Phoenician Exploration   The Phoenicians lacked the military power to create an empire, but they influenced other cultures, especially through trade on both land and sea. They established trading posts or colonies far from Palestine, the most famous of which was Carthage, a powerful city on the north coast of Africa that controlled parts of North Africa and Spain. The Greek historian Herodotus records that some Phoenicians for the first time sailed completely around Africa.

Among the Phoenician articles of trade was a reddish dye that the ancients called *purple;* cloth dyed in this color became a luxury and has remained a mark of royalty or eminence. The Phoenicians' wide explorations made them masters of the sea, and because of their sailing ability they provided the navy for the Persian Empire. They and other Canaanite peoples had thus developed a high urban civilization by the time the Israelites began their invasion of the Palestinian coast.

Hebrew Society and the Bible

South of Phoenicia is the region of Palestine that today is known as Israel, also settled in antiquity by speakers of the Semitic Hebrew language. The Hebrew Bible, or Old Testament, provides a continuous record of how this people viewed its past, but before historians can use the narratives and chronicles of the sacred books as a source, they must take a stand on the credibility of the documents. Scholars in the nineteenth century questioned whether the Old Testament contained unchallengeable, divinely revealed truth. Archaeology in recent years has often confirmed the Bible, at least in questions of geography and topography, but literal accuracy is not, after all, the central issue to the historian. Religious traditions of any society, whether or not they are strictly verifiable, can instruct us about a society, just as do law codes and lists of kings.

The Israelite chroniclers concentrated on a single god and on humanity's relationship to him. This great theme, varied in countless ways, fuses the Old Testament into a story about one god and the history of his chosen people. Unlike Mesopotamian epics, the Bible deals with real people and real times; it combines ethics, poetry, and history into the most influential book in the Western tradition.

The Early Hebrews and Moses   Hebrew tradition tells that a nomadic tribe led by Abraham migrated into Palestine from the east. A probable date for this movement is about 1900 B.C. His grandson, Jacob, is said to have organized the settlers into twelve tribes under the leadership of his twelve sons. Jacob himself also took the name Israel (meaning "God strove" or "God ruled"), and this name is also used for the people. Israel was therefore a tribal society, unlike the urban society of Sumer or the unified monarchy of Egypt.

THE SALVATION OF ISRAEL

The Old Testament book of Exodus narrates the return of the Israelites from Egypt and preserves the hymn of praise sung by Moses and his people after they reached the holy land. The poem celebrates the strength of God and his generosity in saving Israel. It also shows that Israel saw itself as having a special compact with God.

"I will sing to the Lord, for he has triumphed gloriously; the horse and his rider he has thrown into the sea. The Lord is my strength and my song, and he has become my salvation; this is my God, and I will praise him, my father's God, and I will exalt him. The Lord is a man of war; the Lord is his name. Pharaoh's chariots and his host he cast into the sea; and his picked officers are sunk in the Red Sea. The floods cover them; they went down into the depths like a stone. Thy right hand, O Lord, glorious in power, thy right hand, O Lord, shatters the enemy. . . .

Thou hast led in thy steadfast love the people whom thou has redeemed, thou hast guided them by thy strength to thy holy abode . . . the sanctuary, O Lord, which thou hast made for thy abode, the sanctuary, O Lord, which thy hands have established. The Lord will reign for ever and ever."

From Exodus 15, Revised Standard Version of the Bible, National Council of Churches of Christ, 1946, 1952, 1971.

Egypt and the Exodus   Some Israelite tribes settled in Canaan. Others migrated to Egypt, according to the Bible to escape a severe famine, although immigration into Egypt had long been allowed. They remained there, but evidently suffered such harsh conditions that they determined to return to their homeland. Their return took place probably about 1240–1230 B.C., in the "exodus" (see "The Salvation of Israel," above). At their head was Moses, who led them across the Sinai peninsula during a period of general unrest in the Near East. Their return was the critical formative event in their history. Moses organized the tribes of Israel and some neighboring Canaanites into a confederation bound by a covenant to the god he named YHWH (by convention, we write this word Yahweh; in English it later became Jehovah) and placed all the people in Yahweh's service. Moses proclaimed the new covenant between God and his people on Mount Sinai, in the wastes of the desert. According to the Old Testament Book of Exodus, he received his instructions directly from Yahweh. These instructions, a document of the greatest historical interest, include the Ten Commandments, in which Yahweh issues the terse order, "Thou shalt have no other gods before me." Most scholars interpret this command as a declaration that Yahweh was the one and only God: No others existed at all. So far as we can tell, this was the first time that any people in Western civilization embraced genuine monotheism.

But *why* did Israel accept a single god, in contrast to the rest of the ancient world, in which families of deities were the rule? Was Moses, who had lived in Egypt, perhaps influenced by Akhnaton's worship of Aton as the only true god? We do not know, but we may guess that Moses saw the need to unify his people so that they would be strong enough to regain their home in Palestine; and what could forge a stronger bond than having the whole people swear allegiance to one god above all?

Moses also laid down a code of laws, which, unlike earlier codes, is a series of laws prescribing ethically right conduct. Far more than other ancient codes, this one respects people over property, lays down protection for the oppressed, and insists on respect for parents. This code appears to be the first intervention of religion into the private behavior of human beings. The historical reality of Moses, the fact that his laws are connected with the experience of a people, and the power of the ethical concerns of that people have given the faith of Israel an immediacy to which Sumerian or Egyptian religion could hardly pretend.

Israel and Its Society   Early Israelite society was clearly father-dominated through the patriarchs and God, whom they considered their supreme father. This structure led to a patriarchal family and shaped the legal status of women. Marriage occurs through purchase throughout the Old Testament, and a daughter might be bestowed on a man as a kind of salary, as in the moving story of Jacob and Rachel. Jacob loved Rachel dearly, and this is the point of the story, but he worked seven years to gain her in lieu of the purchase price (Gen. 29). Sometimes women were awarded as prizes for military success.

Some women did indeed rise above such a level of dependence on the family, and their heroism is all the greater. For example, the book of Ruth tells the story of Naomi, a woman of Bethlehem who moves to Moab (east of the river Jordan and the Dead Sea). When she

JEREMIAH REPROACHES ISRAEL

The people of Israel discovered monotheism, but to maintain it was not easy. The prophet Jeremiah warned his people that they were backsliding into worshiping false gods such as Baal, rather than retaining allegiance to the one true God.

"The Lord said to me, 'There is revolt among the men of Judah and the inhabitants of Jerusalem. They have turned back to the iniquities of their forefathers, who refused to hear my words; they have gone after other gods to serve them; the house of Israel and the house of Judah have broken my covenant which I made with their fathers. Therefore, thus says the Lord, Behold, I am bringing evil upon them which they cannot escape; though they cry to me, I will not listen to them. . . . The Lord once called you, "A green olive tree, fair with goodly fruit"; but with the roar of a great tempest he will set fire to it, and its branches will be consumed. The Lord of hosts, who planted you, has pronounced evil against you, because of the evil which the house of Israel and the house of Judah have done, provoking me to anger by burning incense to Baal.'"

From Jeremiah 11, Revised Standard Version of the Bible, National Council of Churches of Christ, 1946, 1952, 1971.

decides to return to Bethlehem, her loving Moabite daughter-in-law Ruth refuses her orders to remain behind. Ruth toils faithfully in the field and meets Naomi's relative Boaz, whom she marries. Her grandson is Jesse and her great-grandson is David, who became King of Israel and whom Christians consider an ancestor of Jesus (Matthew 1). Again, there is the strong figure of Deborah. The book of Judges (5) preserves her hymn of praise to God, which many scholars consider the oldest passage in the Bible. She was also one of the judges, leaders of the villages of Israel before there was a united kingdom, and is said to have served forty years.

The Israelite Monarchy   By a series of attacks on Canaanite cities and by covenants made with other tribes, the Israelites established themselves in Palestine. About 1230 B.C. they invaded Canaanite territory in a campaign aimed at expansion. Biblical stories say that Joshua, the successor of Moses, led the tribes of Israel across the Jordan River and followed God's instructions to take the Canaanite city of Jericho by siege. Many modern scholars would modify the biblical account and assume a more gradual process of occupation.

During the years of the conquest of Canaan, Israel still lacked a central government. The judges managed to reunite the people in periods of crisis, but the tribes then habitually drifted apart. They were also under pressure from the Philistines, a warlike people living along the coast of Palestine. According to the Bible, the people finally demanded a king, evidently wanting to imitate the practice of the Canaanites and also as protection against the Philistines: "We will have a king over us; then we shall be like other nations, with a king to govern us, to lead us out to war and fight our bat-

tles" (1 Sam. 8:20). The first king was Saul (ca. 1020–1000 B.C.). His successor, David (ca. 1000–961 B.C.), captured Jerusalem and made it Israel's capital. The entire nation now took the name Israel, and David extended the kingdom to its farthest boundaries. In modern terms, his domain comprised modern Israel, Lebanon, much of Jordan, and part of Syria even north of Damascus.

Solomon   Solomon, David's son and successor (ca. 961–922 B.C.), was famed for his wisdom. Like all great kings of the period, Solomon was a builder. He left behind him the physical memorial that symbolized the faith of Israel through the centuries—the Temple in Jerusalem. But the temple could not compare in size with his magnificent palace and citadel, whose stables, according to tradition, housed twelve thousand horses.

Solomon's autocratic rule and extravagance may have caused resentment among his people, who were heavily taxed to pay for his palace and army. After his death the kingdom split into two parts. The northern half, centered on the ancient town of Shechem, retained the name of Israel; the southern half, ruled from Jerusalem, was now called Judah, and only it remained from Solomon's kingdom. Weakened by internal quarrels, the northern kingdom of Israel was conquered in 722 B.C. by the Assyrians to the northeast, who deported much of the population into Babylonia.

The Dissolution of Israel   Judah was now the only Israelite kingdom. The Greeks called this people *Ioudaioi*, from which comes the name Jews. Judah also fell in 586 B.C. to the Neo-Babylonian Kingdom ruled by Nebuchadnezzar. The captives were deported to Babylon, in the so-called Babylonian captivity, but

An extreme rarity, the only example of frescoes in a Jewish synagogue showing scenes from the Bible. From Dura Europus, ca. A.D. 239; now in a museum at Damascus.
Princeton University Press/Art Resource, NY

later in the same century they were allowed by King Cyrus of Persia to trickle back into Palestine. In general the Jews became pawns of the various forces that ruled Palestine until A.D. 1948, when a revived Jewish state—the republic of Israel—took its place among sovereign nations.

The Faith and the Prophets Judaism was also shaped by a few resolute critics, known as the prophets: men of the people, tradesmen, and preachers, such as Amos, Micah, Hosea, Jeremiah, and Isaiah. These prophets were not kings and had no military power that could make the people listen to their message. The most authoritative prophet had been Moses, and all successors looked back to him for guidance. The later prophets spoke one general message: Israel was becoming corrupt and only a rigid moral reform could save it. Worship of Yahweh had sometimes been blended with that of the gods, or Baalim, of the Canaanites. Luxury, promiscuity, and extravagance were weakening the discipline of Israelite society (see "Jeremiah Reproaches Israel," p. 23). Perhaps most important, they warned

that worship of Yahweh had become, for many, only a matter of form and ritual. They insisted that their people should put their faith in God and live in a just and righteous manner.

But even as they denounced the prevalent wickedness, the prophets promised that God would forgive Israel if the people repented and that he would further prove his love to Israel by sending a Messiah. The word **Messiah** (*mashiah* in Hebrew) means a person or even a thing possessing a divine power or purpose; referring to people, it came to mean one "anointed" by God to perform a special mission. From about 200 B.C. onward, Jewish thought held that a king would someday appear, a descendant of David, who would restore the power and glory of Israel on earth. The famous Dead Sea Scrolls (discussed in chapter 5), ranging in date from the second century B.C. through the first century A.D., often speak of the awaited Messiah. Christians, too, developed their theory of a Messiah, who would return to rule on earth over all humanity: To them, the "anointed one" (*ho christós* in Greek) is Jesus, but to Jews, the hero is still unborn or unknown.

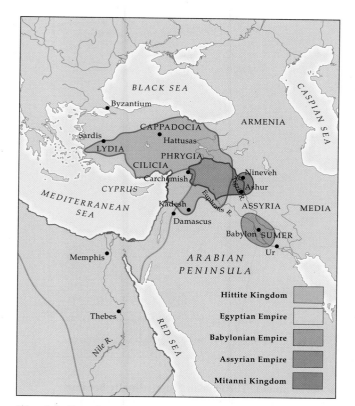

MAP 1.3 FIVE ANCIENT STATES
Over the years, these five states developed in the same general region. Assyria would later dominate the other states including Egypt. What was the greatest extent of the Egyptian Empire?
◆ For an online version, go to www.mhhe.com/chambers9 > chapter 1 > book maps

The Jewish Legacy

The Jews are the only society originating in the ancient Near East whose social and religious traditions have continued to influence modern European civilization. For reasons that no one can fully explain, adversity has never broken the Jewish spirit, and over many centuries the Jews have persisted as a society even without an independent state. Their faith provided the most persuasive answer to the problem that also troubled their neighbors—the nature of the relationship between humanity and God.

To Israel, there was only one god; unlike the gods of the pagans, he tolerated the existence of no others. He judged severely, but he was also prepared to forgive those who sincerely regretted wrong behavior. He had created the world but stood outside the world; he never appeared as an animal or in any other form. Above all, he was a god for everyone, not just for nobles, priests, and kings. Christianity, the religion of medieval and modern Europe, and Islam, the chief religion of the

Near East, are both children of Judaism and preserve the morality and ethics of the older faith.

THE NEAR EASTERN STATES

A series of general disruptions about 1250 to 1150 B.C. left no state dominant for the next few centuries until the Assyrians began their conquests. They became the first people to accomplish a political unification of large parts of the Near East (see map 1.3). The Persians, the next great imperialists of this region, built on foundations laid by the Assyrians and ruled with an administrative skill that only the Roman Empire would equal in ancient times. The Persians also developed a widely accepted religion, Zoroastrianism, some of whose doctrines persisted long after the Persian Empire had disappeared.

The Assyrian State

The Assyrians   The Assyrians were descended from Semitic nomads who had entered northern Mesopotamia about 2500 B.C. and founded the city of Ashur, named after their chief god. From this name comes the designation *Assyrian* for the people. Their language was a Semitic dialect closely resembling that of the Babylonians, and they wrote in the cuneiform script that had originated in Sumer and had remained in general use.

Assyrian Conquests   About 900 B.C. the Assyrians began their most important period of conquest and expansion. Their territory included Babylonia to the south, the cities of Palestine to the west, and northern Egypt. By the middle of the seventh century B.C. their dominion embraced most of the Near East.

If any one concept could characterize Assyrian society, it would be militarism. The army was especially dominant and efficient. The Assyrians faced a greater challenge than any earlier state in absorbing large kingdoms such as Egypt and Babylonia. They ruled with a degree of control unknown in any of the earlier conglomerates.

Assyrian Rule   The Assyrian kings exacted heavy payments of tribute as the price of leaving the conquered territories in peace. Some peoples, such as the inhabitants of Judah, escaped further burdens, but other less independent peoples had to accept a vizier, or governor, serving the king. In some cases the imperial government deported subject peoples who might prove troublesome—for example, inhabitants of Israel who were dispersed within the Assyrian domain. Assyrian armies stationed in the provinces were a further guarantee of stability. We must also record that Assyrian kings took

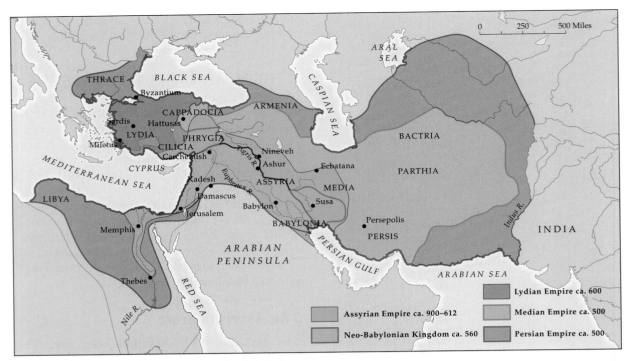

MAP 1.4 FIVE KINGDOMS OF THE NEAR EAST, TO 500 B.C.
This map shows five kingdoms and records their chronological development. The Persian Empire finally became the greatest of all and dominated the entire Near East. Notice that it even reached into Europe in the region of Thrace. Which bodies of water were the outer limits of the Persian Empire?
◆ For an online version, go to www.mhhe.com/chambers9 > chapter 1 > book maps

pride in their brutal treatment of enemies and victims. Certainly, brutality has always existed in war, but the boast of one king is repellent:

> 3000 of their combat troops I felled with weapons. . . .
> Many of the captives taken from them I burned in a fire.
> Many I took alive; from some (of these) I cut off their hands to the wrist, from others I cut off their noses, ears, and fingers; I put out the eyes of many of the soldiers. . . .
> I burnt their young men and women to death.[11]

Language became another means of unifying the Assyrian domain; the Semitic language known as Aramaic (originally spoken by the Aramaeans, who controlled parts of Mesopotamia from about 1100 to about 900 B.C.) was ultimately spoken everywhere in lands dominated by Assyria. It later became the common tongue of the Near East and was the official language of the Persian Empire. In Palestine, Aramaic was spoken by the Jews, including Jesus.

Assyrian Art and Writings   For all their harsh militarism and their brutal rule over their conquered subjects, the Assyrians created magnificent works of art.

Much of the wealth extracted from the empire was spent on glorifications of the king and his conquests. Most notable are the reliefs cut on the palace walls at Nineveh, the capital, and elsewhere. The last powerful Assyrian king, Ashurbanipal (668–627 B.C.), also created a library of cuneiform texts. The largest single group of these texts covers omens, divination, or observations of the stars, because Assyrian kings relied heavily on omens and their interpretation by priests to guide royal policy.

It is hardly surprising that the subjects of the Assyrians watched for any chance to rebel. Finally, in 612 B.C., a combination of forces led by Babylonians captured Nineveh, and the Assyrian Empire collapsed. Within a few years Assyria was reduced to a primitive state of nonurbanized living. Greek explorers 200 years later found it only sparsely populated.

The Neo-Babylonian Kingdom and the Medes

The Assyrian Empire gave way to two states: the Neo-Babylonian Kingdom and the Kingdom of the Medes. Babylon, the ancient city of Hammurabi, was the capital of the Neo-Babylonian Kingdom. It was notorious as a center of luxury and wealth. The dominant tribe in

[11] From H. W. F. Saggs, *The Might That Was Assyria*, 1984, p. 261.

An Assyrian relief showing Ashurbanipal's soldiers attacking a city. Some soldiers swim to the attack; others scale the walls with ladders while defenders fall from the ramparts.
Hirmer Fotoarchiv

the kingdom was the Chaldeans, south of Babylon. They were the most learned astronomers of antiquity. They kept minute records of eclipses, charted a plan of the heavens, and calculated the length of the year. Their discoveries were passed on to the Greeks and Romans and influenced all medieval and modern astronomy.

Nebuchadnezzar (604–562 B.C.), the most famous Neo-Babylonian king, built lavish temples and is said to have constructed a terraced roof garden known as the Hanging Gardens, which was considered one of the Seven Wonders of the ancient world. It was he who captured Jerusalem in 586 B.C., destroyed the city and its holy temple, and scattered thousands of Jews within Babylonia, a tragedy recorded by the prophet Jeremiah.

The Iranians Down to this point we have met the Sumerians, the Egyptians, and some Semite peoples. We come now to a people who spoke an Indo-European language, the Iranians. No documents have been found in the original Indo-European language, but from this language almost all the modern languages of Europe descend. Germanic languages (including English), Greek, Latin, Romance languages, Slavic languages including Russian, and the languages of India, Pakistan, and Iran all belong to this family. Perhaps about 6000–5000 B.C. the Indo-European peoples began a slow dispersion across Europe and parts of Asia. Some of them finally settled on the Indian subcontinent, while others moved westward into Greece, Italy, central Europe, and Asia Minor.

A new people, the Iranians, appeared, another branch of the family that spoke Indo-European languages. Two noteworthy Iranian societies were the

Medes and the Persians. The Medes, living in the area of Media to the east of Mesopotamia, formed a coherent kingdom about 625 B.C., and they took part in the capture of Nineveh in 612 B.C. We know little of their society because no written documents from Media have yet been found.

Their neighbors, the Persians, lived in the same general area and eventually subdued the Medes. Yet the Medes had enough prestige to be named first in official documents in which both Medes and Persians are mentioned. The Greeks, too, used *Medes (Medoi)* as the term embracing both Medes and Persians, and they called their two wars with the Persian Empire the *Medic* wars.

The Persian Empire

Cyrus (559–530 B.C.) The Persians proceeded to form the largest, most efficient state down to their time. The founder of the Persian Empire was King Cyrus. His actions show him as a determined imperialist, and his first conquest was his victory over Media, to the north, in 550 B.C. A few years later Cyrus led his forces into western Asia Minor and conquered the kingdom of Lydia. This advance brought the Persian Empire westward as far as the Aegean Sea, which separates Asia Minor from Greece, and set the stage for a direct clash between the vast empire of the Near East and the new culture of the Greeks; but this clash was not to come for another two generations.

To secure the southern flank of his growing empire, Cyrus led his forces against the Neo-Babylonian Kingdom and captured Babylon. The inhabitants evidently

and the rich valley of the Nile remained under Persian rule until Alexander the Great captured it in 332 B.C.

Part of the Bisitun inscription in Iran, showing King Darius of Persia (522–486 B.C.) receiving the submission of rebels. Carved in three languages, this inscription provided the key to deciphering cuneiform writing.
Dr. G. G. Cameron, The University Museum, University of Pennsylvania (Neg #ANEP Plate 462)

Darius (522–486 B.C.) The most skillful administrator of the Persian Empire was Darius. He left behind a superb monument—a proud summary of his reign written in three languages (Old Persian, Akkadian, Elamite). Carved under a relief showing Darius and some of his captives, this text survives high on the face of a rock at Bisitun in Iran. In a series of paragraphs, each beginning "Saith Darius the king," he records his conquests, including that of Babylon, and the defeat and mutilation of his enemies. He also clarifies that he is the only source of law: "As was said by me, thus it was done." The tone and physical setting of this grandiose monument confirm the lofty position of the king in the Persian state. A later inscription on his tomb also proclaimed his devotion to justice: "I am a friend to right, not to wrong. Whoever does harm, I punish him according to the damage he has done." This statement reminds us of the insistence on restitution built into Hammurabi's code and shows how some Near Eastern kings, for all their unchallengeable power, tried to earn a reputation for fairness.

The Administration of the Empire Darius divided his empire into some twenty satrapies, or provinces, each ruled by a satrap ("protector of the realm"). The king, naturally, was the supreme head of the state, but the satraps had a high degree of independence; they dispensed justice, designed foreign policy, and were in charge of finance. Each satrap, for example, was responsible for collecting an assigned amount of revenue from his province. This system of delegating authority became the model for the Roman Empire when it expanded Rome's domain outside Italy.

The Greek historian Herodotus, writing in the fifth century B.C., mentions with admiration the Persian system of roads begun by Cyrus and perfected by Darius. A great highway ran across the empire from the capital at Susa westward to Sardis in Lydia, a distance of more than one thousand miles. The first long highway built anywhere, this road served trade and commerce and also bound the far-flung empire together.

Zoroaster The Persian king was never considered divine, but he often served as a priest and claimed to have received his authority from the god of the Persians, Ahura Mazda. The prophet who formed the Persian faith was Zoroaster (also known as Zarathustra). We are not sure of the date of his life and work, but a number of historians think he lived about 600 B.C. or soon after.

Zoroaster was not considered divine; rather, he taught that the supreme god, Ahura Mazda, a god of

welcomed him, for they offered little resistance. Their judgment was sound; Cyrus treated the city with moderation, not sacking it, as an Assyrian conqueror might have done. In fact, his administration was marked by a notable toleration of the customs and religions of the people he brought under his control. We have seen that he allowed as many as 40,000 refugees from Judah to return to their homeland.

Cambyses and Egypt Cyrus' successor, Cambyses (530–522 B.C.), made the third conquest that completed the Persian Empire: He conquered Egypt in 525 B.C.,

Two panels on a staircase of the great reception hall at the Persian capital, Persepolis. In each panel an official leads a messenger whose followers bear tribute for the king of Persia. George Holton/Photo Researchers, Inc.

light, had created the world and directed the heavens and seasons. The Persian conception of God as creator of the world, and of light and darkness, seems to have influenced Judaism to some degree. Within the book of the prophet Isaiah, God says, "I form light and create darkness. . . . I made the earth, and created humankind upon it; it was my hands that stretched out the heavens" (ch. 45).

The Dualist Religion of Persia   Around Ahura Mazda gathered good deities such as "Truth," "Righteous Thought," "Devotion," and so on, whose ideals humanity should follow. But the Persian faith taught that Ahura was opposed by Ahriman, a wholly evil spirit—a devil, in fact. Thus Zoroaster taught a dualist religion, that is, one with two divine forces, although only Ahura is the true god whose message we are to hear. A concern with the devil was to expand greatly in the New Testament. Another similarity to Christian thought is found in Zoroaster's proclamation that, after thousands of years, a day of judgment will see the final triumph of good, and those people who have followed Ahura in morally good lives will gain paradise, while the rest will suffer in the realm of endless night. Zoroaster also rejected such ancient practices as the sacrifice of animals. The faith he taught demanded recognition of the one good spirit and a life of devotion to Ahura's ideals. His noble thought far outlasted the Persian Empire and still has followers today in Iran and in India.

In this chapter we have observed several historical themes. The rise of agriculture, which enabled humanity to live in permanent villages, led to the expansion of such villages into cities. In the cities, civilization arose with more ingenious tools that led to monumental architecture. Trade and its companion, writing, emerged. Monarchy became and remained the form of government, and rulers issued law codes to control their societies.

Summary

The mighty legacy of the ancient Near Eastern societies—including the art of writing, monumental architecture, and the development of pottery and weaponry—also influenced the development of their neighbors, the Greeks. The Greeks further learned from the older societies the use of coinage, the measurement of time, and forms of diplomacy. They added to this heritage a radical individualism and a passion for logical argument; their policies and institutions have influenced our own, even more directly and profoundly than those of the Near East, as will be apparent when we turn to the Mediterranean and the peoples of Greece.

QUESTIONS FOR FURTHER THOUGHT

1. This chapter has looked at religious practices in several societies. How does the religion of Israel resemble some other religions? How does it differ from them?

2. In the forming of societies, which contributes more, intellectual skills or the dominance and administration of a strong government?

RECOMMENDED READING

Sources

Lichtheim, Miriam. *Ancient Egyptian Literature: A Book of Readings.* 3 vols. 1973–1980. Excellent gathering of original sources in modern translation.

Metzger, B. M., and M. D. Coogan (eds.). *The Oxford Companion to the Bible.* 1993. Best general introduction to the Bible.

The New Oxford Annotated Bible. 1991. The New Revised Standard Version, with helpful annotation throughout.

Pritchard, James B. (ed.). *Ancient Near Eastern Texts Relating to the Old Testament.* 1969. More than the title implies; a wide-ranging collection of cuneiform and hieroglyphic texts on many subjects, with brief commentaries by eminent scholars.

*Sandars, N. K. (tr.). *The Epic of Gilgamesh.* 1972. The great Sumerian epic, in a highly readable translation with informative introduction.

Studies

Albright, William Foxwell. *The Biblical Period from Abraham to Ezra.* 1963. A brief history of Israel from a giant in the field.

The Cambridge Ancient History. 3d ed. 14 vols. 1970–2000. The standard history of the ancient world; chapters by numerous scholars, with large bibliographies.

Crawford, H. *Sumer and the Sumerians.* 1991. A new history of the earliest civilization.

Dandamaev, Muhammad A. *A Political History of the Achaemenid Empire.* 1990. The Persian Empire and its organization.

Ehrenberg, Margaret. *Women in Prehistory.* 1989. On women's roles in the rise of agriculture and in the early cities.

Frye, Richard N. *History of Ancient Iran.* 1984. All-inclusive history of Persia.

*Gardiner, Sir Alan. *Egypt of the Pharaohs.* 1969. A detailed political narrative.

Gimbutas, Marija. *The Goddesses and Gods of Old Europe, 6500–3500 B.C.: Myths and Cult Images.* 1984. Challenging work that argues for a matriarchal structure in earliest Europe that gave way to male domination.

*Grimal, Nicolas. *A History of Ancient Egypt.* 1992. A recent complete history in one volume.

*Hallo, William W., and William K. Simpson. *The Ancient Near East: A History.* 2d ed. 1998. American textbook survey of Mesopotamian/Egyptian history.

*Johnson, Allen W., and Timothy Earle. *The Evolution of Human Societies: From Foraging Group to Agrarian State.* 2d ed. 2000. Anthropological study that allows deductions about developments in earliest times.

Kemp, Barry J. *Ancient Egypt: Anatomy of a Civilization.* 1989. Social and intellectual history.

Kramer, Samuel Noah. *The Sumerians: Their History, Culture, and Character.* 1963. Full portrait of Sumerian society by a leading authority.

Læssøe, Jørgen. *People of Ancient Assyria, Their Inscriptions and Correspondence.* 1963. Good collection of original Assyrian texts.

Lerner, Gerda. *The Creation of Patriarchy.* 1986. Studies, from a feminist perspective, the rise of the social system in which men assume roles of command and leadership.

Meyers, Carol L. *Rediscovering Eve: Ancient Israelite Women in Context.* 1988. Women in Israelite society and in the Bible, with attention to folk customs.

Oates, Joan. *Babylon.* 1979. A survey for the nonspecialist.

Redford, Donald B. *Akhenaten: The Heretic King.* 1984. Highly readable study of this king in historical setting.

Reeves, Nicholas, and Richard H. Wilkinson. *The Complete Valley of the Kings: Tombs and Treasures of Egypt's Greatest Pharaohs.* 1996. A stunning photographic record of Egyptian architecture.

Robins, G. *Women in Ancient Egypt.* 1993. Well-illustrated treatment.

Roux, Georges. *Ancient Iraq.* 3d ed. 1992. Detailed, readable survey of ancient Mesopotamia.

Saggs, H. W. F. *Civilization before Greece and Rome.* 1989. Chapters on law, trade, religion, and so on; not a continuous narrative.

———. *The Greatness That Was Babylon.* 1988. General history of Mesopotamia; good survey of everyday life.

———. *The Might That Was Assyria.* 1984. Sympathetic portrait of this militaristic society.

Shanks, Hershel (ed.). *Ancient Israel: From Abraham to the Roman Destruction of the Temple.* Rev. ed. 1999. Eight chapters by experts, forming a concise modern history.

Wilson, John A. *The Culture of Ancient Egypt.* 1951. A timeless classic, superb for the history of ideas.

*Available in paperback.

A magnificent mask of gold foil, found pressed on the face of a ruler of Mycenae, ca. 1500 B.C. This is one of the first Europeans on whose faces we can look.
Nimatallah/Art Resource, NY

Chapter Two

THE FORMING OF GREEK CIVILIZATION

CRETE AND EARLY GREECE (CA. 3000–1100 B.C.)
THE GREEK RENAISSANCE (CA. 800–600 B.C.) • THE POLIS • THE CHALLENGE OF PERSIA
THE WARS OF THE FIFTH CENTURY (479–404 B.C.)

Greek civilization has been praised by our own more than any other for its creativity, its artistic genius, its intellectual daring. It created forms of thought and expression that have been imitated ever since, including philosophy, drama, and historical writing. Its immortal epic poetry, above all that of Homer, has traveled worldwide, even into India. Greek civilization also assigned a leading role to reason, debate, and logical argument. This civilization honored personal heroism and independence, and its literature is the oldest one with many individually known writers.

In Greece, for the first time, we see another theme that runs through Western civilization: a body politic, a political system with laws fashioned by the people and with guaranteed participation for citizens. The Greeks developed a civic culture that broke with the Near Eastern traditions of monarchy. They lived in independent communities, or city-states. These cities were normally dominated by an upper class of some kind, but even this structure extended power beyond the all-powerful ruler of older civilizations.

Citizens of Greek city-states took pride in their temples, their civic traditions, the qualities of their own state, their participation in its life. In Athens the government was a democracy in which the male citizens themselves, not their representatives, made political decisions directly. This democracy allowed no role for women, foreigners, or slaves. Sparta, Athens' leading rival, chose by contrast a severe, authoritarian form of rule and was the only Greek state to retain monarchy after it had vanished in all others.

These two states led Greece into its most brilliant victories in war, the defeat of forces twice sent from the vast Persian Empire. They also became the nuclei of alliances that followed this triumph with tragedy, as their rivalry escalated into the long, destructive Peloponnesian War.

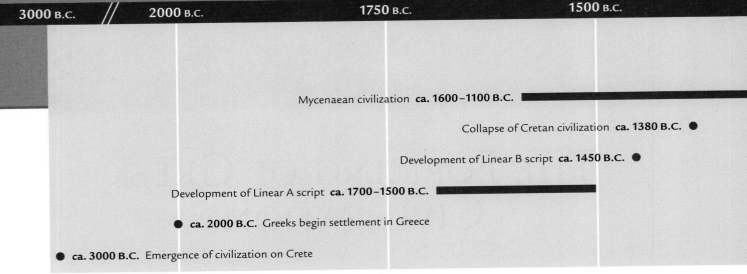

Mycenaean civilization **ca. 1600–1100 B.C.**

Collapse of Cretan civilization **ca. 1380 B.C.** ●

Development of Linear B script **ca. 1450 B.C.** ●

Development of Linear A script **ca. 1700–1500 B.C.**

● **ca. 2000 B.C.** Greeks begin settlement in Greece

● **ca. 3000 B.C.** Emergence of civilization on Crete

CRETE AND EARLY GREECE (CA. 3000–1100 B.C.)

The first important society in the Greek world developed on the island of Crete, just south of the Aegean Sea. The people of Crete were not Greek and probably came from western Asia Minor well before 3000 B.C. They traded with the nearby Greeks and left their influence in art, in religion, and in a system of writing. They were followed in history by a number of cities in Greece governed by monarchs. The most imposing such city was Mycenae, where tombs have disclosed stunning works of art. Greek legend also tells of a war against Troy in which Mycenae was the leading Greek power.

Cretan Civilization

We have no reliable historical narratives about early Cretan civilization. Therefore we must rely on archaeological evidence, found especially in a magnificent villa at Knossos. The historian must recognize that archaeological evidence often calls for much conjecture in its interpretation. The villa is known as the Palace of Minos; the civilization of Crete is thus often called Minoan.

King Minos and His Palace   Greek legend told of the Minotaur ("Minos-bull"), a monster that lived in a labyrinth (surely a memory of the complex palace) and devoured girls and boys sent to it as tribute. The story suggests that Greeks had at least a dim recollection of a ruler, perhaps only a mythical one, called Minos, and the historian Thucydides tells of Minos, the powerful king who "cleared the seas of piracy, captured islands, and placed his sons in control over them."

Other palaces on Crete exist, but none is so elegant as that at Knossos. For our knowledge of the palace, and much of Cretan culture generally, we must thank (Sir) Arthur Evans, a wealthy Englishman who began to excavate at Knossos in 1900 and spent some forty years at his task: he named the palace the Palace of Minos and restored much of it, including its colorful wall paintings.

The Palace of Minos was built over a period of about 700 years from ca. 2200 to ca. 1500 B.C. It was an extensive structure, with a vast eastern courtyard, an impressive grand staircase leading to upper rooms, and many wings and storage chambers. The palace even had a plumbing system with water running through fitted clay pipes.

The walls of the palace at Knossos were decorated with frescoes showing the Cretans' delight in nature. Gardens, birds, and animals are vividly portrayed, and one spectacular painting shows young men vaulting over the horns of a bull. The absence of walls around the palace suggests that **Minoan** civilization was essentially peaceful.

Cretan Society and the Roles of Women   Knossos was clearly the wealthiest of the Cretan cities, and the king was served by an efficient bureaucracy. The rulers were probably men; one wall painting shows a man, often identified as a priest or king, leading an animal to some kind of ceremony. Women were respected in this society, and jeweled ladies in elegant gowns appear in Minoan wall paintings.

Some historians have argued that women on Crete had actual political power in a system of matriarchy, or rule by women. This theory descends from a book published in 1861 by a Swiss scholar, Johann Bachofen, who theorized that early societies worshiped a goddess

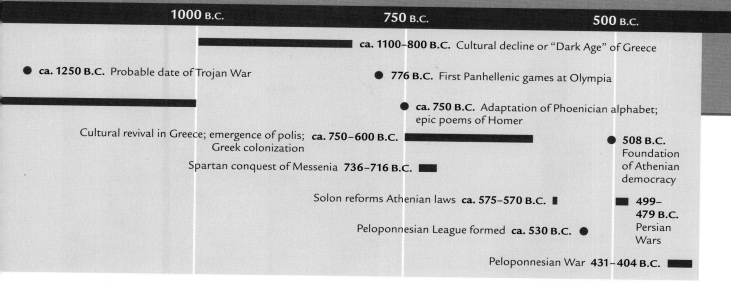

| 1000 B.C. | 750 B.C. | 500 B.C. |

ca. 1100–800 B.C. Cultural decline or "Dark Age" of Greece

ca. 1250 B.C. Probable date of Trojan War

776 B.C. First Panhellenic games at Olympia

ca. 750 B.C. Adaptation of Phoenician alphabet; epic poems of Homer

Cultural revival in Greece; emergence of polis; **ca. 750–600 B.C.** Greek colonization

508 B.C. Foundation of Athenian democracy

Spartan conquest of Messenia **736–716 B.C.**

Solon reforms Athenian laws **ca. 575–570 B.C.**

499– 479 B.C. Persian Wars

Peloponnesian League formed **ca. 530 B.C.**

Peloponnesian War **431–404 B.C.**

MAP 2.1 EARLY GREECE DURING THE BRONZE AGE
This map shows the areas in which Greek speakers settled between about 2000–1100 B.C. There was never a king or supreme ruler of the whole region, but rather rulers in the various cities. Which islands lay at the extreme boundaries of Greece, and where was Mycenae, where the Mycenaean culture originated?
◆ For an online version, go to www.mhhe.com/chambers9 > chapter 2 > book maps

This marble statuette of a goddess is a product of the Cycladic culture (named for its home in the Cyclades Islands of Greece), which preceded the coming of the Greeks. Carved ca. 2800 to 2300 B.C., the statuette represents the early emphasis on female rather than male gods. Neolithic art preferred abstraction to Paleolithic realism and points the way toward later abstract thought. In the twentieth century, artists like Brancusi and Mondrian returned to this type of noble, elegant simplicity.
© British Museum

Roman wall painting, showing Theseus having killed the Minotaur; he is surrounded by grateful Athenian children, whom he has saved from possibly being devoured by the half-man, half-beast monster.
Scala/Art Resource, NY

women are known from Crete, holding snakes or grain in their hands and thus dominating nature. This much need not surprise us, since *earth* is a noun of the feminine gender in many languages and is clearly the mother of all crops. But these facts fall short of proving the existence of a true matriarchy on Crete; it is better simply to accept that these figurines probably represent goddesses of nature.

On the other hand, paintings found at Knossos show women in elegant coiffures, dressed in splendid robes and wearing dramatic makeup. Their faces show no hint of hard labor; these women, at least, enjoyed an upper-class lifestyle, whether or not they had political influence.

A Cretan Empire?   Much of the wealth of Crete came from trade, and Cretan pottery has been found far and wide throughout the Mediterranean world. About a dozen sites in the Greek world, probably trading posts, are called *Minoa*, obviously named after Minos. But we cannot speak of a true Cretan empire with political control of wide areas like the dominions of Assyria or Persia, for Crete lacked the population to conquer and permanently subdue overseas possessions.

called the Great Mother, Mother Goddess, or Earth Goddess. Only over time, the theory holds, did men wrest political power away from women. Statuettes of

A wall painting from Knossos, showing athletes vaulting over the horns of a bull. The figure at the right will catch the leaper in the center. The location of this painting in the palace suggests that the sport was a kind of ceremony. The bull may represent raw nature being tamed in this agricultural society.
Erich Lessing/Art Resource, NY

THRONE ROOM AT PALACE OF KNOSSOS
Bridgeman Art Library

Crete and the Greeks

Minoan civilization reached its height between 1550 and 1400 B.C. Greek art of this period shows Minoan influence, and at least two Greek goddesses, Athena and Artemis, were probably adopted from Crete.

Cretan Writing   The Minoans also had interchange with the Greeks through writing. Clay tablets have been found at Knossos in two similar scripts, called Linear A and **Linear B.** Both scripts are syllabic: Each symbol represents a sound, such as *ko,* rather than a letter of an alphabet. The language written in Linear A, the older script (used ca. 1700–1500 B.C.), has not yet been deciphered; but Linear B, the younger of the two scripts (used ca. 1450–1400 B.C.), has been deciphered as an early form of Greek. The decipherment was the work of a brilliant English architect, Michael Ventris, not a professional classical scholar. He achieved this feat in 1952 and tragically died in a motoring accident in 1956. The tablets contain inventories, rosters, and records of all kinds, listing footstools, helmets, vessels, seeds, and the like. They thus show that the rulers on Crete governed through fairly elaborate bureaucracies.

That these Linear B tablets were written in a form of Greek is a startling discovery, for it shows that the Greeks, who at this time had not developed writing of their own, learned to write their language in a Cretan script. Their presence on Crete during this period suggests that Greeks had come to dominate Knossos, perhaps through outright military seizure. Probably the only Greek community that could have done this was that of Mycenae.

The Collapse of Cretan Civilization   About 1380 B.C., a catastrophe, whose causes are uncertain, engulfed Knossos and other Cretan cities; several of the stately palaces were burned or destroyed. A massive earthquake shook the island at this time, but the disaster may also have been connected with a quarrel or rebellion against Greek rule.

A "marine style" vase by a Greek artist, ca. 1500 B.C., clearly imitating Cretan models. Sea creatures were often used in Minoan pottery in a free, naturalistic style.
C. M. Dixon

A large vase from Crete in the Late Minoan II style, ca. 1450 to 1400 B.C., when Cretan art came under Greek influence and became more disciplined and geometric. Note the double ax motif; found in the palace at Knossos.
C. M. Dixon

Some historians have tried to link the collapse of Knossos with a tremendous earthquake on the island of Thera (or Santorini) about seventy-five miles north of Crete. This earthquake is now dated to about 1625 B.C. It must have done damage on Crete, but the exact relationship, if any, between this natural disaster and the destruction of Knossos remains unclear.

Mycenaean Civilization (ca. 1600–1100 B.C.)

The Greeks, the people who spoke and imported the Greek language, began to settle in Greece about 2000 B.C., arriving from the Balkan areas to the north; they were members of the general family of Indo-Europeans who had started to migrate into Europe at an uncertain time, perhaps around 5000 B.C. (see chapter 1, p. 27). They called themselves Hellenes and their country Hellas; the Greeks still use these names, and only in West European languages are they called *Greeks*, a name given them by the Romans.

The City of Mycenae   Geography divides Greece into many small valleys and forced the Greeks to develop independent communities with kings, but without the direction—or oppression—of a central ruler like a pharaoh. By about 1600 B.C., the Greeks had created wealthy, fortified cities, among which the most prominent was Mycenae, a huge citadel built on a hill in the Peloponnese. The years from 1600 to 1100 B.C. are therefore often called the Mycenaean Age.

The Work of Heinrich Schliemann   Another pioneer of archaeology, the German Heinrich Schliemann, is mainly responsible for the rediscovery of Mycenae. Arriving here in 1876, he discovered six graves, probably those of a ruling dynasty, containing gold masks and ornaments of stunning workmanship. The graves at Mycenae have given us a glimpse of the wealth and artistic accomplishments of this city. They contained such luxuries as masks of gold foil that were pressed on the faces of the dead and a complete burial suit of gold foil wrapped around a child, as well as swords, knives, and hundreds of gold ornaments. Tablets written in Linear B, attesting a palace bureaucracy, have been found at Mycenae and other sites of the Mycenaean Age.

A tablet in Greek, written in the Linear B script, from Pylos, about 1200 B.C. Note that each line contains a brief listing, probably items from an inventory, followed by a number. Such tablets reveal a complex bureaucracy within the monarchy at Pylos during the Mycenaean Age.
C. M. Dixon

The Zenith of Mycenaean Power and the Trojan War

Between 1400 and 1200 B.C., Mycenae reached the height of its prosperity and created the most imposing monuments in Bronze Age Greece. A mighty decorated gateway with a relief of lions carved over it, known as the Lion Gate, formed the entrance to the walled citadel. Some rulers were buried in immense vaulted beehive-shaped tombs, of which the grandest and best preserved is the so-called Treasury of Atreus, named by archaeologists for the legendary father of King Agamemnon; but we do not really know which ruler or rulers were buried here.

Each city of the Mycenaean Age was probably independent under its own king. The only time these cities appear to have united was during the war against Troy, a rich city of obscure ethnic origin in Asia Minor near the Dardanelles. The evident wealth of the city must have offered a tempting prey to pirates and looters. Such was probably the real cause of the war against Troy, but Greek legend explained the war by the romantic story in Homer's *Iliad* about the seduction by a Trojan prince of Helen, the wife of a king of Sparta.

The Troy of Homer
Because Homer is the only source recording the Greek attack on Troy, we must proceed with caution if we are to believe that there really was such a war, for Homer was a poet, not a historian. Still, excavations at Troy have revealed several layers of building, among which one layer, called Troy VII A, was destroyed by some invaders about 1250 B.C., and this layer may well be the Troy that Homer says the Greeks attacked; some historians, however, would favor Troy VI, the preceding city.

The Decline of Mycenae
The war against Troy was the last great feat of the Mycenaean Age. Between about 1300 and 1200 B.C., marauders, called sea-peoples, made trade by sea so dangerous that the export of Mycenaean pottery virtually ended. The identity of these warriors is still uncertain, but their homes were probably somewhere in Asia Minor. Even

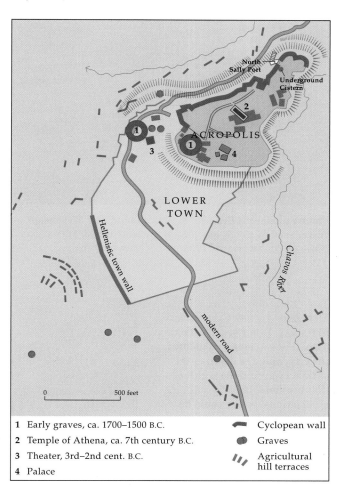

1 Early graves, ca. 1700–1500 B.C.
2 Temple of Athena, ca. 7th century B.C.
3 Theater, 3rd–2nd cent. B.C.
4 Palace

Cyclopean wall
Graves
Agricultural hill terraces

MAP 2.2 MYCENAE
The most important city in Bronze Age Greece, Mycenae, was first settled on its citadel or Acropolis. As the population expanded, a lower town developed, also surrounded by a wall. Outside the town were terraced agricultural plots. Where was the palace of the king?
◆ For an online version, go to www.mhhe.com/chambers9 > chapter 2 > book maps

more significant to the collapse of the Mycenaean Age was a series of attacks by land, lasting roughly from 1200 to 1100 B.C.; around 1100 B.C., Mycenae itself was overrun, though not obliterated. This invasion by land was probably the work of a later wave of Greeks who spoke the Doric dialect of the Greek language. Between about 1200 and 1100 B.C., these Greeks made their way southward from central Greece and settled mainly in the Peloponnese, especially in Corinth and Sparta, which became the most important cities in which Doric Greek was spoken.

The Dark Age   The period 1100–800 B.C. is called the Dark Age of Greece, because throughout the area there

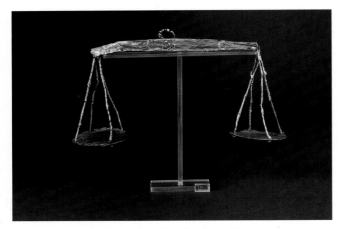

Picture of elegant little set of scales found in a Mycenean grave, used to weigh out gold in the next world, 16th c. B.C.
National Archaeological Museum, Athens, Greece

was sharp cultural decline: less elegant pottery, simple burials, no massive buildings. Even the art of writing in Linear B vanished, perhaps because the more learned class was killed off, or perhaps because the economy was so weakened that the keeping of records became pointless. Nor do we have written sources about the period. But the decline was not a total collapse. Farming, weaving, making pottery, the Greek language in spoken form, and other skills survived.

The invasions of the twelfth century B.C., in which the **Dorian** Greeks played at least a part, ended forever the domination of the palace-centered kings. The shattering of the monarchic pattern of the Mycenaean Age may even have been liberating. If these monarchies had survived, Greece might have developed as Egypt and Asia Minor did, with centralized rule and priests who interpreted religion in ways that justified kingship. Self-government in Greece might have been delayed for centuries, if it appeared at all.

THE GREEK RENAISSANCE (CA. 800–600 B.C.)

It is really the historian who is in the dark during the Greek Dark Age. At least near the end of this period, there must have been a revival of confidence and a nourishing of civic life.

With the passing of time, Greek culture revived after the Dark Age and entered a period of extraordinary artistic and intellectual vitality. Poetry and art broke new frontiers; the economy expanded, partly through overseas colonization; and the **polis,** or independent city-

THE "LION GATE," THE ENTRANCE TO THE CITADEL AT MYCENAE, BUILT CA. 1350 B.C. Two lionesses stand guard over the city; note the depth of the entranceway and the width of the threshold. In early civilizations, power could be demonstrated by moving enormous stones.
Michael Holford Photographs

The most spectacular tomb at Mycenae, the "Treasury of Atreus," built in beehive style ca. 1300 B.C. The long entrance alley and the tomb itself are almost perfectly preserved.
Michael Holford Photographs

state, emerged. Historians borrow a term from a later period and call this movement the Greek Renaissance.

Greek Religion

The Greeks brought with them, during their earliest immigration around 2000 B.C., the worship of some of their gods, above all **Zeus,** the sky god, whose name is Indo-European; his counterparts are Dyaus in early India, Jupiter in Rome, and Tiu in Norse myths. Other gods were adapted from other regions: Apollo, the sun god, from western Asia Minor; Aphrodite, goddess of love, from Cyprus; Athena, goddess of wisdom, and Artemis, the hunter goddess, from Crete. At a much later stage, Greeks adopted some Egyptian gods (Isis, for example), but there is no solid evidence for the belief, recently put forth, that they received all or even many of their gods from Egypt (see "The Debate over Black Athena," p. 43).[1]

The Relationship of Greeks to Their Gods   Greek gods are not the remote, transcendent deities of Mesopotamian peoples. They intervene in human affairs, they assist their favorites, and they are anthropomorphic: That is, they are humanlike superbeings, differing from people only in their physical perfection and im-

[1] Herodotus, the first historian, writing around 440 B.C., does say this, but he was perhaps so impressed with the antiquity of Egypt and with the resemblance of some gods in the two cultures that he drew this false conclusion.

The "warrior vase" from Mycenae, currently housed in the National Archeological Museum in Athens, Greece, showing armed warriors departing for battle; at the left, a woman waves her farewell.
C. M. Dixon

mortality. Even Mount Olympus, their legendary home, is an actual mountain in northern Greece.

The Greeks never developed a code of behavior prescribed by religion, as Israel did. Some acts, such as killing a parent or leaving a relative unburied, were obviously wrong, as were offenses against generally accepted conduct, such as betraying a friend. If people became too arrogant, Nemesis, an avenging force,

MAP 2.3 ARCHAIC AND CLASSICAL GREECE, CA. 800–400 B.C.
Four main dialects of the Greek language were spoken in the Greek world. Similarity of dialect could lead to political sympathy within the dialect group. Notice that Greeks never penetrated far into the Persian Empire. What was the most extreme reach of the Greek language to the north?
◆ For an online version, go to www.mhhe.com/chambers9 > chapter 2 > book maps

would sweep down on them and destroy them. But on the whole, Greek religion had no spirit of evil and scarcely any demanding spirits of good.

The gods were viewed as generally benevolent, but they had to be appeased through offerings and suitable ceremonies. The most remarkable feature of Greek religion—especially in contrast to monarchies of Egypt and Mesopotamia—was that the Greeks had priests and priestesses for their temples and smaller shrines but no priestly class that intervened in politics. To put it simply, the Greeks had no church. The societies all around Greece seem to have needed priestly hierarchies to interpret religion and sacred lore. Only thus could they be sure that they were not offending divine powers.

Forms of Worship   Why the Greeks felt they could worship without such a hierarchy we do not know, but the reason must be connected to the independence of the more than one thousand individual Greek city-states. There was no king, pharaoh, or emperor who had the power to install such a system. Religion and civic life were intertwined, and the beautiful temples all over Greece were built by decision of the governing power, but not at the orders of priests or viziers.

Most gods were common to all Greeks, and their worship is a sign of a Panhellenic culture that arose during the Greek Renaissance. Each locality, while recognizing the several gods generally, could have its own patron. For example, various gods had temples in

HISTORICAL ISSUES: THE DEBATE OVER BLACK ATHENA

Martin Bernal, in Black Athena, *has set forth the challenging thesis that Greek civilization and even much of the Greek language rest on cultural borrowings from Egypt and the Levant from about 2100 to about 1100 B.C. Bernal also holds that anti-Semitic nineteenth-century scholars deliberately concealed the contribution of Egypt and the Phoenicians. This excerpt, in Bernal's words, summarizes his thesis.*

"The scheme I propose is that while there seems to have been more or less continuous Near Eastern influence on the Aegean over this millennium, its intensity varied considerably at different periods. The first 'peak' of which we have any trace was the 21st century. It was then that Egypt recovered from the breakdown of the First Intermediate Period, and the so-called Middle Kingdom was established by the new 11th Dynasty. This not only reunited Egypt but attacked the Levant and is known from archaeological evidence to have had wide-ranging contacts further afield, certainly including Crete and possibly the mainland. . . . It is generally agreed that the Greek language was formed during the 17th and 16th centuries B.C. Its Indo-European structure and basic lexicon are combined with a non-Indo-European vocabulary of sophistication. I am convinced that much of the latter can be plausibly derived from Egyptian and West Semitic. This would fit very well with a long period of domination by Egypto-Semitic conquerors. . . . [I] discuss some of the equations made between specific Greek and Egyptian divinities and rituals, and the general belief that the Egyptian were the earlier forms and that Egyptian religion was the original one."

From Martin Bernal, *Black Athena,* Vol. 1, Rutgers University Press, 1987, pp. 17–23, abridged.

Mary R. Lefkowitz and Guy MacLean Rogers, professors of classics at Wellesley College, have edited a 500-page volume, Black Athena Revisited, *in which 24 scholars give their reactions to Bernal's theories. The following is one excerpt from the discussion.*

"No expert in the field doubts that there was a Greek cultural debt to the ancient Near East. The real questions are: How large was the debt? Was it massive, as Bernal claims? Was it limited to the Egyptians and the Phoenicians? . . .

"All of the contributors agree that the early Greeks got their alphabet from the Phoenicians; but little else. Indeed, in terms of language, the evidence that Bernal has presented thus far for the influence of Egyptian or Phoenician on ancient Greek has failed to meet any of the standard tests which are required for the proof of extensive influence. . . .

"Similarly, in the area of religion, Egyptian and Canaanite deities were never worshiped on Greek soil in their indigenous forms. . . .

"Archaeologists, linguists, historians, and literary critics have the gravest reservations about the scholarly methods used in *Black Athena.* Archaeologists cite a constant misconstruing of facts and conclusions and misinterpretation of such archaeological evidence as there is. . . . Linguists see Bernal's methods as little more than a series of assertive guesses, often bordering on the fantastic."

From Mary R. Lefkowitz and Guy MacLean Rogers, *Black Athena Revisited,* University of North Carolina Press, 1996, pp. 449–452, abridged.

Athens, but Athena was accepted as the protecting goddess of the city. Zeus, though worshiped everywhere as the chief god, was the main local deity at Olympia. Apollo was the chief god at Delphi and supposedly inspired the oracle, a woman who gave guidance to inquirers after payment of a fee. New research supports the ancient tradition that she inhaled vapors from a chasm.

This woman, or the priests who interpreted her answers, was careful to express these answers in ambiguous language, so that the oracle could be justified no matter what happened. The historian Herodotus reports that, when King Croesus of Lydia asked whether he should invade Persia, he was told that "if Croesus crosses the Halys River [the frontier of Persia], he will destroy a mighty kingdom." He took this to be encouraging, attacked Persia—and destroyed his own kingdom.

The Greek faith in this oracle is another sign of growing common identity among the Greeks. Though never more than a small village, Delphi was adorned with treasure houses built by the various cities to house the gifts they dedicated to Apollo when seeking his guidance.

Public Games

Another sign of a growing community among Greeks is the founding of Panhellenic athletic games in 776 B.C. This date is commonly agreed to mark

Α Β Γ Δ Ε Ζ Η Θ

Ι Κ Λ Μ Ν Ξ Ο Π

Ρ Σ Τ Υ Φ Χ Ψ Ω

A Comparison of Greek and Phoenician Alphabets

the beginning of the "historic" period of Greek civilization: broadly speaking, the period when writing began and we begin to have fairly solid dates for events.

The first games were held at Olympia, in the Peloponnese, and were dedicated to Zeus; thus, from the beginning the games were connected with religion and demonstrate that religion can have wide uses in a community. But they were also a way of celebrating human perfection and heroism, aspirations typical of Greek civilization. Originally, the Olympics featured only foot races and wrestling, but gradually they came to include horse and chariot races, boxing, javelin throwing, and other events. Only the winner gained a prize, an olive wreath, but victory also brought rich awards from one's city and lifelong glory; the modern myth of the "amateur athlete" was unknown to the Greeks. In imitation of the Olympics, other cities founded games, and there was eventually one set of Panhellenic games (that is, open to all Greeks) each year, as well as games in many individual cities. The games also give us some of our dates in the archaic period, for the Greeks themselves used the Olympic games especially as chronological reference points.

Colonization (ca. 750–ca. 550 B.C.)

The growth in population during the Dark Age probably strained the natural resources in Greece, especially the limited farming land, and finally drove the Greeks into foreign colonization. In effect, the mainland Greeks, starting around 750 B.C., tried to relieve social tension by exporting their surplus population. They colonized vigorously from ca. 750 to ca. 550 B.C., and by the end of this period Greeks were spread throughout the Mediterranean. Wherever they went, they settled on the edge of the sea, never far inland. Colonies, when founded, were wholly independent cities, and among them are some of the great ports of modern Europe: Byzantium (today Istanbul in Turkey), Naples, Marseilles, and Syracuse.

This expansion overseas led to a revival of trade after the stagnation of the Dark Age. The Greeks now had access to a greater food supply, above all grain from southern Italy and the Black Sea. Trade brought prosperity to many Greek cities and, even more important, spread Greek civilization throughout the Mediterranean.

The Alphabet

Origin of the Alphabet The Greeks apparently lapsed into illiteracy when the Linear B script vanished, soon after 1200 B.C.; but by about 750 B.C. their trade had brought them to Palestine and into contact with the Phoenicians, who used a Semitic script called the alphabet. This alphabet had only twenty-two characters, but their precision and versatility made this script far easier to master than pictorial cuneiform scripts (see above). Fortunately for the future of European literacy, the Greeks adopted the alphabet and gave even greater precision to their script by changing some of the characters, which were all consonants, to vowels.

Two versions of the Greek alphabet developed. A Western version made its way to Cumae, a Greek town in Italy, and then to the Etruscans, the people in Italy who then controlled Rome. They passed it on to the Romans, who turned it into the alphabet used throughout the Western world. The Eastern version became the standard alphabet in Greece itself. Much later, many letters of the Greek alphabet were used in the Cyrillic script of Russian and other Slavic languages. Thus large parts of the world today use one or another derivative of the Phoenician alphabet in the form in which it was received from the Greeks.

The Alphabet and Greek Life The Greeks first used the alphabet in public for the proclamation of laws, which ordinary people could read and grasp; information could circulate more rapidly, with dynamic consequences for political life. Later, from about 500 B.C.,

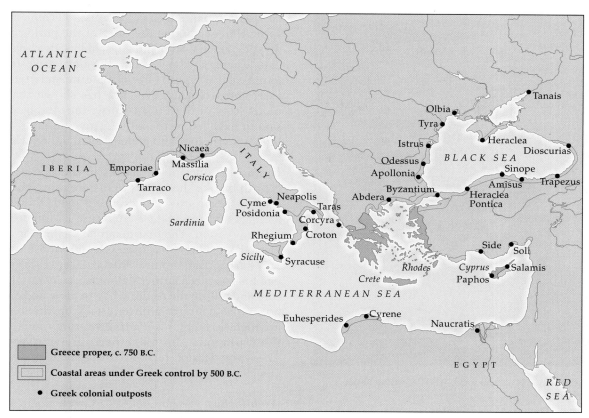

MAP 2.4 GREEK COLONIZATION, CA. 750–CA. 550 B.C.
Partly to seek trading partners, partly to solve the problem of excessive population, Greek cities sent out many colonies in the Mediterranean and Black seas. Notice that all the colonial cities remained on the coastlines. Which were the farthest Greek cities in east and west directions?
◆ For an online version, go to www.mhhe.com/chambers9 > chapter 2 > book maps

especially in Athens, people began to publish all kinds of public decisions and records on prominently displayed stone inscriptions; these were not simply boastful monuments to a king's victories but were documents enabling citizens to understand, criticize, and control the activities of the state.

Archaic Literature

The Homeric Epics The greatest literary creations of the Greek Renaissance are the epic poems about the glorious heroes who had supposedly led the war against Troy. The supreme achievements of this poetic tradition are two epics ascribed to Homer, the *Iliad* and the *Odyssey*.

The *Iliad* is a portrait—in rolling, majestic verse—of a warrior aristocracy in which greatness in combat is the highest virtue. The chief hero is the proud warrior Achilles, who withdraws from the siege of Troy when his concubine is taken from him; he then allows his friend Patroclus to wear his armor in combat and, after

Patroclus is killed by the Trojan hero Hector, avenges his friend's death by killing Hector in a scene of savage power. The gods take sides with their favorites, but the *Iliad* is essentially a poem about men and women.

The *Odyssey*, by contrast, celebrates cleverness rather than sheer military prowess. Its hero, Odysseus, makes his way home after the Trojan War through dozens of adventures that test his skill and tenacity and that enable Homer to explore human character and behavior in widely different situations. Eventually Odysseus reaches his home, the island of Ithaca, and drives off a band of suitors who are wooing his faithful wife Penelope.

The Homeric Question These epics were probably first recited at feasts by traveling bards, but over the years they became known to all through presentation at festivals and finally through study in schools. We have no idea who wrote these great epics. This is the famous "Homeric question." Neither ancient Greeks nor modern scholars have been able to prove whether a

AN ETRUSCAN VASE (CA. 520 B.C.), WITH A SCENE FROM GREEK LITERATURE
Odysseus and his men escape from the Cyclops, Polyphemus, by putting out his only eye (Homer's *Odyssey*, book 9). This scene is found on several other vases from Greece.
Michael Holford Photographs

person named Homer really lived, whether the epics are the work of one writer or several, and whether they were originally composed orally or in writing.

It is clear, however, that the texts we have date from long after the Trojan War of ca. 1250 B.C. Most scholars date the poems to around 750 B.C., and this disparity raises the question of how any knowledge of the war could have been preserved. The traditions were evidently passed down through the centuries. The poems themselves were probably composed orally, recited for generations, and written down later, after the Greeks had become fluent in the art of writing. In any case, Homer remained the chief inspiration for Greek literature in all periods.

Homeric Legends Far from Greece Over the centuries Greek legends were known far and wide, reaching even the land of India. Greek gods, including Zeus, Athena, and others, were portrayed on Indian coins in later times. Sometimes Greek gods were transformed into, or identified with, Indian ones. Zeus became the Indian god Vajrapani, while Nike, a minor Greek god-

dess whose name means "victory," became an Indian spirit who celebrated the birth of the philosopher and mystic, Buddha. Some Indian scholars also hold that Indian legends and fables made the journey westward and found their way into Greek literature and myth. In any case, archaeological evidence has shown that the famous story of the Trojan Horse, the stratagem that is said to have led to the fall of Troy, found its way into Indian mythology and perhaps even Indian warfare.

Hesiod Homer never speaks in the first person (except to invoke the Muses to inspire him), but his successors began to express their own thoughts and feelings and to create a literature of intensely frank self-expression. The first major post-Homeric poet was Hesiod of Boeotia (in central Greece), whose *Works and Days* dates from around 700 B.C. Hesiod was a farmer, and his poem is a farmer's almanac, celebrating agriculture and telling the reader when to plow and plant. The poem also contains a bitter attack on the injustice of aristocratic landlords ("gift-devouring rulers") toward their peasants. In his other surviving poem, the *Theogony*, Hesiod recounts the genealogy of the various gods.

Archilochus About 650 B.C. Greek poets began to work with more personal themes. Archilochus of Paros has left us brief poems of brilliant vigor and audacity, written as bursts of self-revelation, a typically Greek kind of literature that has no predecessors in the ancient Eastern cultures. He was a traveler, a man of action, and a mercenary soldier who fell in battle. He criticizes traditional forms of chivalry and can be cynical about supposed aristocratic conduct. He boasts, for example, that he once threw away his shield to save his life and laughs off this unmilitary act: "Never mind, I'll buy another one just as good." His love poetry can be astonishingly frank. In one poem he tenderly yet passionately describes his seduction of a girl, including his own sexual fulfillment.

Sappho The most intense and subtle poet of the age was Sappho of the island of Lesbos (about 600 B.C.). We have only one complete poem from her pen and many short quotations (see "Sappho's Love Poetry," p. 48). In her poetry she writes about an association of young women, but it is not certain precisely what kind of group this was. They worshiped Aphrodite and the Muses, minor goddesses who inspired poetry and other arts.

The most tantalizing question, to which the surviving fragments of her work supply no exact answer, is what kind of experiences the group shared. Sappho was a widow and apparently taught the girls poetry, dance, music, and elegant dress as preparation for marriage.

A superb red-figure vase (the figures are left in the natural red of the clay), illustrating a scene from Homer's *Odyssey*, book 12. Odysseus, bound to the mast of his ship, listens to the song of the Siren, who guides him into troubled waters; by the Siren Painter, ca. 490 to 480 B.C. Michael Holford/© British Museum

Sometimes she sings of the beauty of the girls, sometimes of her pain when one leaves the circle (probably to marry) or is unresponsive to her affection. At other times she speaks frankly of the pleasures of love, and there is little question that she shared physical love with some of the girls. But, unlike Archilochus, she does not boast of her sexuality or of her conquests; rather, she writes of shared experience and love felt mutually.

THE POLIS

"The human being," said the Greek philosopher Aristotle, "is a political creature." By this he probably meant that humans normally want to live within a community of people sharing cultural traditions and common citizenship. The Greek city, at its largest, had about 40,000 adult male citizens. Originally, monarchs ruled, as they did at Mycenae, but over the years most cities reached at least an approach to government by a body of citizens. In their cities, the Greeks created architecture, dramas, and philosophic writings that are still worshiped and imitated.

Organization and Government

For the social and political history of Western civilization, the most important event in the Greek Renais-sance was the emergence, soon after 800 B.C., of the independent city-state, the polis (plural, *poleis*). Physically, the polis had a central inhabited area (the *astu*), often surrounding a citadel called the acropolis ("high city"). Over time, the acropolis came to be reserved for temples, shrines, treasuries, and other official buildings. Within the astu, the nucleus of the city, the people dwelt in closely packed houses, each normally built on more than one level, without internal staircases but with the rooms opening to a courtyard. A wall usually surrounded the astu; outside it, but still part of the polis, were suburbs and fields. Those who owned land might live in the urban center and walk or ride a donkey to their land. Or they might live in smaller villages, which were still legally part of the polis.

General Structure of the Polis   Greek cities usually had a large open space, the **agora,** that served as a main public square and civic center. Although used as a public market, the agora was always a sacred place and, like the acropolis, it housed temples and official buildings. In Athens, the agora was also the site of trials, of buildings containing laws and other documents, and of many free-standing inscriptions on marble recording further public business.

In a Greek polis, only male citizens could vote, pass on their property through wills, and generally participate in civic life. Females did not vote but, like men, were protected against seizure and violence. Outside

SAPPHO'S LOVE POETRY

The poetry of Sappho of Lesbos is amazingly sensitive and original. This short excerpt from a poem frankly acknowledges her need for love.

"You have come, and done,
And I was waiting for you
To temper the red desire
That burned my heart."

The following is addressed to a young woman.

"He seems to be a god, that man
Facing you, who leans to be close,
Smiles, and, alert and glad, listens
To your mellow voice.

"And quickens in love at your laughter
That stings my breasts, jolts my heart
If I dare the shock of a glance.
I cannot speak,

"My tongue sticks to my dry mouth,
Thin fire spreads beneath my skin,

My eyes cannot see and my aching ears
Roar in their labyrinths.

"Chill sweat slides down my body,
I shake, I turn greener than grass,
I am neither living nor dead and cry
From the narrow between.

"But endure, even this grief of love."

From Guy Davenport (tr.), *7 Greeks*, New Directions, 1995.

---

this group, and without civic rights, were slaves and resident aliens. No citizen of a polis had rights in any other polis; thus poleis were both cities and small states.

Population of the Poleis   When Greeks referred to the size of the citizen body, they reckoned only adult males, and by this measure the poleis ranged from a few hundred citizens to tens of thousands. Athens, the largest, had between thirty-five and forty-five thousand citizens; if to this we add the estimated number of women, children, resident foreigners, and slaves, the total population of Athens and the outlying villages, which were also part of the polis, was between two and three hundred thousand (the whole region is known as Attica). Sparta, by contrast, probably had an adult male population of no more than twelve thousand.

Origins of Self-Government   Despite considerable diversity within the six to seven hundred poleis, one development seems to have been common to all those poleis that we know anything about, namely, the growth of some kind of self-government by the male citizens. The major social problem that Greek poleis solved was how to harness the energies of all the citizens in support of a city rather than allow the rivalries inherent in such crowded quarters to erupt into civil war. In many poleis (Corinth, for example), oligarchy (a

system in which a small number of citizens governed) held sway, while other cities, especially Athens, developed control of affairs by the masses.

Evolution toward self-government is rare in history, and the various forms of self-government that arose in Greece may, like the Greeks' lack of a priestly class, be the result of topography and the scale of their towns. In a small state, locked within a ring of hills, no monarch could long remain a remote, transcendent figure like the rulers of Eastern kingdoms. Homer attests that the Greeks of the Mycenaean era had kings, but by about 700 B.C. they had vanished—though we can seldom say precisely how—in nearly all poleis. Sparta, the most authoritarian Greek state, was an exception and retained a system with two kings, each descended from a royal family, ruling together. The Spartans apparently felt safer in a system in which one king could act as a control over the other.

Hoplites and Society   The wealthier classes—using the term loosely, we may call them aristocrats, but there was no hereditary nobility—must have governed, if Homer is to be believed, through assemblies that originated as the armed forces of the poleis. But as populations increased and armies came to include citizens outside the circle of the elite, the upper classes could no longer ignore the wishes of others. In particular, Greek infantry soldiers, called hoplites (Greek *hopla,* arms), may have been an impetus toward self-government, because numbers of armed citizens could more effectively demand a say in political decisions. It is significant that the first Greek legal codes defining citizens' rights were published soon after the disappearance of kings, within the seventh century B.C.—evidence that the populace was no longer willing to accept direction from the wealthy.

Tyrants and Tyranny   Also in the seventh century we hear of the first popular leaders who united the masses and overturned the rule of the old aristocracy. These men installed themselves as "tyrants" (the Greek word *tyrannos* meant an autocrat who ruled without strict legal foundation, not necessarily a cruel oppressor). The tyrants, though certainly no sponsors of democracy, did help to undermine rule by the traditional aristocracy and in a way opened the path to self-government. They sometimes built grandiose temples and other public works to beautify their cities and ensure the support of the people. Some sponsored industry and trade of their city's products overseas. Most saw to the buildup of armies, doubtless for their own security. On the whole, tyrants forced progress within their cities and helped lead the cities away from the rule of the older aristocratic class.

Greek Armies   In the period of the Greek Renaissance, we also see the formation of the armies that were to make the Greeks supreme in battle against their neighbors. Infantry soldiers, or hoplites, were grouped into the formation called the phalanx. This was a close-packed formation of men, usually eight deep. A soldier carried a shield on his left arm and protected his right side by standing close to his neighbor's shield. The weapons were either swords or, especially in the fourth century B.C., long spears. The phalanx became a formidable instrument in battle, especially when moving forward to attack.

As the ranks pushed forward, one adversary or the other would give way. Once the front ranks of either side were broken, the Greeks normally broke off the battle, for they lacked the manpower to sustain huge casualties. Infantry soldiers had to provide their own equipment. This meant that they were men of the middle class, and many historians have concluded that solidarity among the hoplites contributed to the growth of political consciousness and pointed the way to a greater degree of self-government.

The Economy of the Poleis (ca. 700–400 B.C.)

A Modest Lifestyle   The poleis were sufficiently similar to allow a general picture of their economy. The basic activity was agriculture, but in many areas of Greece the soil is thin and rocky, not suited to raising grain or pasturing animals. A shortage of food was therefore a constant threat to economic stability. Some states, as we have seen, drained away part of their excess population through colonization and imported grain from areas on the fringe of the Greek world.

All Greek dwellings were modest, and sanitation was primitive, although the Athenians had a main drain under their central market. Grain, and occasionally fish, were staples of the diet; meat was usually reserved for festival days. Breakfast, if taken at all, was a lump of bread dipped in olive oil, which also served as fuel for lamps and even as a kind of soap. Sugar was unknown; the only sweetening agent was honey. With few luxuries available, Greeks could subsist on small incomes. Fishing and farming were suspended in winter, so Greeks had considerable leisure time, which they spent mainly in public places, as is still true today.

Coinage and Public Expenses   The development of an economy based on coinage was slow. Coinage itself began in the kingdom of Lydia, in western Asia Minor, about 600 B.C. or a little later. Soon the Greeks began to use coins, but at first they played little part in daily trade: The smallest coin was usually a drachma, said to have been at that time the price of a sheep. In the fifth century the use of coinage expanded rapidly, as fractions of the drachma came into use. Taxation in poleis paid for the upkeep of walls, drains, roads, harbors, and the like, though Greeks had little grasp of the mechanics of public finance. There were no permanent military treasuries until the 300s B.C., a surprising fact since the cities were so often at war. Infantry soldiers had to arm themselves, but they were paid at the expense of the state. When large projects such as public buildings and maintenance of ships were planned, the expenses were assigned to citizens who were judged capable of bearing the cost.

Use of Slave Labor   A great social-economic historian, M. I. Finley, once asked the challenging question: Was Greek civilization based on slave labor? Undeniably, slave owners had freedom to pursue civic affairs. Many Greeks looked down on manual labor as beneath their dignity, and it was usually the task of poor citizens or slaves. The troubling institution of slavery was accepted by all ancient societies and was justified by philosophers like Aristotle, who asserted that nature had divided humanity into natural masters and natural slaves—the latter including all "barbarians," that is, non-Greeks. Nor did anyone in antiquity ever recommend abolishing slavery on the ground that it was morally wrong: The only criticism of it was the occasional warning to manage it efficiently.

Greeks commonly obtained slaves through conquest of other territory, though kidnapping and even the sale of children added to recruitment. An ordinary slave might cost about 150 drachmas, roughly four months' pay for a laborer, but a highly skilled one could cost much more.

Industry   Greece, unlike Rome, did not use gangs of slaves in agriculture, and industry was rarely more than household craft. The only industries in which slaves worked together in large numbers were mining and stone quarrying, where conditions were atrocious. These industries and domestic service were the only tasks always assigned to slaves. In a unique exception to this rule, Athens had a police force composed of three hundred slaves from Scythia. The Athenian writer Xenophon said, "A man buys a slave to have a companion at work." Potters, shoemakers, and stone-cutters might have a slave or two, though a few larger workshops are known: One shield maker, for example, had 120 slaves.

The availability of slaves and the prejudice against manual labor may explain why some slaves worked, along with citizens, on the building of the Parthenon in Athens and were paid the same as free men—one drachma a day, about the same wage paid to soldiers and sailors—and they partly explain the lack of inventions among the Greeks that could have made industry more productive.

Sparta and Athens (ca. 700–500 B.C.)

We know little about the internal workings of most poleis, and the two we know best, Sparta and Athens, were not typical; but their importance requires detailed discussion.

Early Sparta   Sparta, the most influential of all the Dorian states, chose to solve its problem of overpopulation by conquering Messenia, the territory to its west, in a war usually dated 736 to 716 B.C. Many, probably most, of the Messenians were then enslaved. Only males of demonstrably pure Spartan descent could be full citizens, and they were each given an allotment of land to be worked for them by the enslaved Messenians, who were known as **helots.** They were public slaves, with no rights whatever, but they differed from other slaves in Greece in that they could not be bought and sold. Spartan landowners spent their lives in constant military training in order to maintain control over the helots, who outnumbered them by about seven to one.

Around 650 B.C. the Messenians tried to rebel, but the uprising failed, and the Spartans responded by making their army more invincible and their state even more rigid. The new arrangements, attributed to a law-giver named Lycurgus, date from about 600 B.C. The identity of Lycurgus was obscure even in antiquity, though such a man apparently lived around 800 B.C., and many historians believe that Spartan reformers of around 600 B.C. ascribed their system to him in order to give it the appearance of ancient authority.

Sparta's Government   In the Spartan regime, **oligarchy,** or rule by a small number, was tempered with some measure of democracy. The public assembly included all males over the age of thirty, who elected a council of twenty-eight elders over age sixty to serve for life and to plan business for the assembly. The assembly also chose five ephors ("overseers") each year; they received foreign delegates, summoned the assembly to meet, and in general acted as a check on the power of the kings. When proposals came before the assembly, voting was limited to yes or no, without debate. As a further safeguard against too much popular control, the ephors and council could simply dismiss the assembly if, in their opinion, it made the wrong choice. Thus, the limited democracy of Sparta yielded to its ultimate faith in oligarchy. To Greek political philosophers, Sparta was a superb example of a "mixed" constitution, in which the kings represented the element of monarchy, the council, oligarchy, and the assembly, a kind of democracy.

For a time Sparta tried to dominate some other Peloponnesian states by outright conquest. But by around 560 B.C. this policy had failed, and about 530 B.C. the Spartans sought strength through negotiation rather than warfare by forming an alliance, known as the Peloponnesian League, with their neighbors. The league is one of the earliest examples of alliance in the Greek world and is a rare instance of the Greeks' transcending the normal exclusiveness of city-state politics. The Spartans led the league but did not wholly control it, and action required approval of the member states.

Men and Women in Spartan Society   The Spartan male dedicated most of his life, from age seven through age sixty, to soldiering. The warriors lived and trained together, and their discipline could be sadistic. As tests of their courage and resourcefulness, young men were taught to steal if necessary, to go without food and shelter, even at times to kill a helot.

Spartan women also had a lifestyle that other Greeks found extraordinary. Again the military commitments of the state played a role in shaping social practices, for the girls trained in games in order to become physically strong mothers. Spartan men, living with one another, seldom visited their wives, and if a marriage was childless, a woman could bear a child by a man other than her husband. These customs were meant to ensure enough manpower for the army and to focus loyalty on the state, not on the individual family.

An Attic Kouros, or Young Man, in the "Severe" Style, ca. 510 b.c.
The figure is one of ideal physical perfection, typical of the humanity-centered aesthetics of Greece.
Nimatallah/Art Resource, NY

Spartan Isolationism   Spartans were cut off from the other Greeks by two mountain ranges, and they traded little with other people, even adopting an intrinsically worthless iron currency to maintain their isolation.

Their lifestyle was one of extreme austerity. They rarely traveled, did not welcome visits by foreigners, and deliberately shielded themselves from new ideas that might have inspired intellectual pursuits such as philosophy or historical writing. Their short, abrupt speech is usually called "laconic" from the name of the plain where they lived, Laconia.

Though they did make fine pottery, at least until about 525 b.c., when the art declined, their military regime left little time for or interest in the arts. Thus the isolation of Sparta from other Greeks was both geographic and psychological, but it reflected the deliberate choice of the people.

Early Athens   The city of Athens also had expansionist beginnings, extending its domain by about 700 b.c. to include the whole plain of Attica. It was a large polis with widespread trading interests, and its political currents were strong and turbulent. As the people experimented again and again with their constitution, their political history became the most varied of all the city-states of Greece.

Athens, like other states, once had kings; but the monarchy ended in 683 b.c. (we do not know exactly how), and the city was managed by three (later nine) archons, or administrators, elected annually by an assembly in which all adult male citizens could vote. After their year in office, the nine archons moved permanently into a council called the **Areopagus,** which eventually numbered about three hundred men. Because it comprised senior men with permanent membership, the Areopagus was probably more influential than the board of archons in setting public policy.

Draco and Homicide Law   Our first information about a reform in Athens after the monarchy is dated around 621 b.c. when Draco, an otherwise unknown statesman, codified the law on homicide, apparently distinguishing between voluntary and involuntary homicide. This reform was a large step forward, for early societies often looked on any kind of homicide as defiling the community in the eyes of the gods. This reform was also another in the series of law codes that established a recognized basis for justice and did away with forcing citizens to rely on the dictates of tribal elders.

Crisis in the Athenian Economy   An economic crisis in the 500s b.c. forced Athens into far-reaching social changes, the likes of which no Greek state had ever seen. As often happens in history, economic conditions demanded a social response. Down to about 600 b.c. the

Athenian economy was trying to do the impossible, namely, feed the growing population of Attica from its own limited area; this strategy caused a nearly desperate social and economic crisis. Some farmers had evidently borrowed food from others who were better off and had gone so deeply into debt in the form of grain that they had lost their own land and had even fallen into slavery by pledging their bodies as security for more food.

Their frustration might have exploded into violent revolution had the Athenians not found a rational solution by giving (probably in the 570s) powers of arbitration to Solon, who had been archon in 594 B.C.[2] He was a poet and statesman whose courageous, compassionate work has made him a towering figure in Greek history, indeed in the history of civilization.

Solon and Economic Reform Aware that the poor farmers could probably never repay their debts, Solon took the daring step of canceling all agricultural debts and forbade further borrowing against the body. At one stroke the enslaved men were free, but the land they had lost probably remained in the hands of its new owners, who were thus compensated for the cancellation of debt. This legislation left many families without land and made them seek work elsewhere, but the crucial fact was that Solon had prevented civil war. Such arbitration by a private citizen without an army to fight with is heretofore unknown in history.

Because an economic crisis had threatened the community and brought him to power, Solon determined to transform the economy of Athens. He decreed that no product from the soil could be exported except olive oil; by this means he forced the Athenians to cultivate olive trees, which they could grow more successfully than grain. He also changed the commercial weights used by the Athenians, making them the same as those more widely used in Greece, a reform that brought Athens into a wider circle of trade.

Solon's Political Reforms Solon now seized the opportunity to reform the Athenian state with the aim of breaking the grip of the wealthy and those with eminent family backgrounds on public office. He therefore divided all Athenian citizens into four classes based on their income from farmland and allowed members of the two highest classes to hold office. The significance of this reform is that men could improve their status economically and thus achieve positions of leadership regardless of their ancestry.

[2] That Solon was archon in 594 B.C. is fairly certain, and most historians follow ancient sources in dating his reforms to this year as well. But the assumed linkage between his archonship and his reforms was probably only an inference drawn in antiquity, and there is good reason to think that the reforms took place in the 570s; see C. Hignett, *A History of the Athenian Constitution*, 1952, p. 316.

Solon also created a court of appeal, the Heliaea, somehow drawn from the people, but our sources tell us little of how it worked. His chief contribution was to see the common people as a group with grievances and to take bold steps to help them. He thus pointed the state toward eventual democracy, but he did not want to go too far and by no means gave the masses supreme power; in his own poetry he declared, "I gave the people just enough privilege and no more." Nor did his legislation, humane though it was, wholly end the agricultural problem; freeing farmers from servitude was not the same as guaranteeing them enough to eat, and the agony of those peasants who had lost their land continued.

The Tyrant Pisistratus Pisistratus, a popular Athenian military leader supported by poorer farmers from the hill country in eastern Attica, saw his chance in this turmoil. In 561 B.C. he and his followers seized power; though twice driven out, he returned in 546 with a mercenary army to gain permanent control and ruled from that year until his death in 528.

Pisistratus fits well the pattern of the Greek tyrants sketched earlier. He rewarded his supporters with grants of land, surely taken from the estates of landowning aristocrats who had opposed him, thus completing the work of Solon, who lacked the power and probably the will to redistribute land. And like many another "big city boss," he saw to a splendid program of public works. He built temples to Athena and Zeus and established a yearly festival to the god Dionysus. By encouraging dramatic contests at this festival, he opened the way for the development of Athenian tragedy in the next century.

He ruled by cloaking his despotic power in legal form. The assembly still chose archons, but from trusted men picked by the tyrant himself. The legal facade was actually one of his chief contributions, for the Athenians now became familiar with democratic procedures, which gave them experience with the working of real democracy when it came into existence at the end of the sixth century.

Cleisthenes and Demokratia Pisistratus' son, Hippias, ruled securely until 514 B.C., when a conspiracy frightened him into using terror as a means to maintain his control. He forced many Athenians into exile, including Cleisthenes, the leader of the Alcmaeonids, a powerful family. While in exile in Delphi, Cleisthenes and his supporters enlisted the help of the Spartans to overthrow Hippias. According to Herodotus, Cleisthenes and his family had spent lavishly to rebuild the temple at Delphi, and the Delphic priests had the oracle urge the Spartans to "liberate the Athenians." Moreover, Hippias had given his daughter in marriage to the son of a Persian vassal ruler, and this move may have looked to the Spartans like a dangerous act that could bring about Persian influence over Greece. In any case, a Spartan force led by

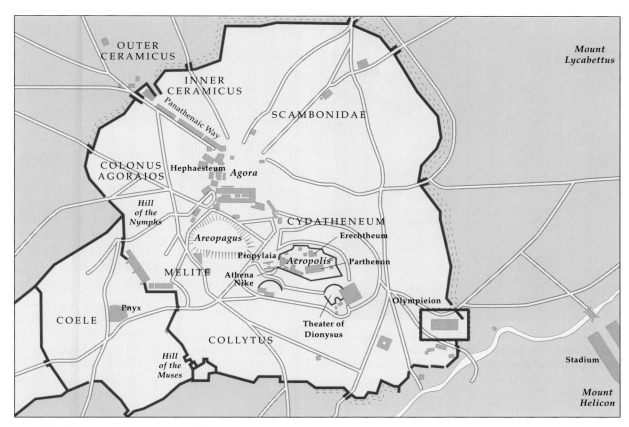

MAP 2.5 CLASSICAL ATHENS, CA. 400 B.C.
Athens became the largest Greek city in population and political importance. It also had the most impressive collection of public buildings and temples, especially on the Acropolis or "high city." The urban area was surrounded by a wall. Where was the temple of Athena or Parthenon?
◆ For an online version, go to www.mhhe.com/chambers9 > chapter 2 > book maps

the king Cleomenes drove out the Pisistratid family in 510 B.C. and ended the Athenian tyranny.

Cleisthenes returned to his native city and in 508—perhaps to secure his own political supremacy—carried the social revolution further by proposing a scheme whereby the masses would actually direct the state. The Greek word *demos* means "the people," but in Greek political language it also means "the masses," and the domination of the Athenian state by the whole mass of voters came to be called *demokratia*. Participation extended only to the adult male citizens of Athens, for women, aliens, and slaves did not vote; but this system was by far the closest to a democracy that had ever existed.

Cleisthenes anchored his system in popular support by a stroke of genius: He created a council of five hundred members (called the boulé) to prepare business for the assembly; all male citizens above age thirty were eligible to serve in it for a year. In later times (and perhaps from the beginning, though our sources do not say so) councillors were chosen by drawing lots, and no man could serve more than twice. There was a fair

chance that every eligible Athenian would be chosen to serve during his lifetime, and this widespread participation in the council ensured that the people would want to maintain the new regime. Within about fifty years, this new council came to surpass in political power the old Areopagus council, which continued to exist.

The End of Regional Factions in Athens   Our sources tell us that the Athenians were loosely divided into three groups in Attica: those who lived in the central plain, or along the coast, or "beyond the hills" in eastern Attica. Cleisthenes set out to break up these regional factions through a complex system of building blocks. Every man was now enrolled as a citizen within the single village, or *deme,* in which he lived, and which kept registers of its citizens. These villages throughout Attica were then grouped into ten tribes, so composed that each tribe contained citizens from all parts of Attica. The council's five hundred men included fifty men from each tribe and were, like the tribes, automatically a cross section of Athenian citizens. Thus within the council, too, no local faction could dominate.

Athenians used sherds of pottery, called *ostraka*, to vote men out of town for ten years. The sherd at the lower left bears the name Hippokrates; the others are directed against Themistocles, son of Neocles.
Scala/Art Resource, NY

As a result, when the council met to prepare business for the assembly, no single region could dominate the discussion. Each of the ten tribes fought as a unit in the army, and here, too, men from all over Attica, not from a single region, stood together in each tribal regiment.

The sovereign body was, as before, the assembly, including all adult male citizens, whether landowners or not. The assembly passed laws and resolutions brought before it by the council, elected magistrates, voted for or against war, and accepted alliances with other states. Unfortunately, as a democratic assembly, it was vulnerable to being misled or corrupted by unscrupulous politicians. Sometimes it gave way to disastrous or vindictive decisions.

The Use of the Lot in Elections   After passing his reforms in 508 B.C., Cleisthenes vanishes from our sources, but the Athenians continued to refine his system, especially through the use of the lot. In 487 B.C. they began to choose their nine annual archons, the executive committee, by drawing lots from a slate of candidates. Later, in the fifth and fourth centuries B.C., all manner of officials, such as public auditors and managers of public land and mines, were so chosen. The theory behind this practice held that many men were equally honest and capable of serving in a democracy and choosing officials by lot reduced corruption and angry competition in the process of selection.

Choosing civic officials by lot greatly diminished the prestige of such positions and caused the most ambitious men not to bother to seek them. As a result, political power shifted to the ten generals, who were elected annually and could be reelected. From this point onward, the great Athenian politicians competed for the position of general.

Ostracism   Also in 487 B.C., for the first time, a man was expelled from Athens for ten years by the process of **ostracism.** In this colorful procedure, the whole people could vote once a year to expel any man whom they considered potentially dangerous. They voted by scratching a name on *ostraka,* or potsherds. If the total number of votes was six thousand or more, the "win-

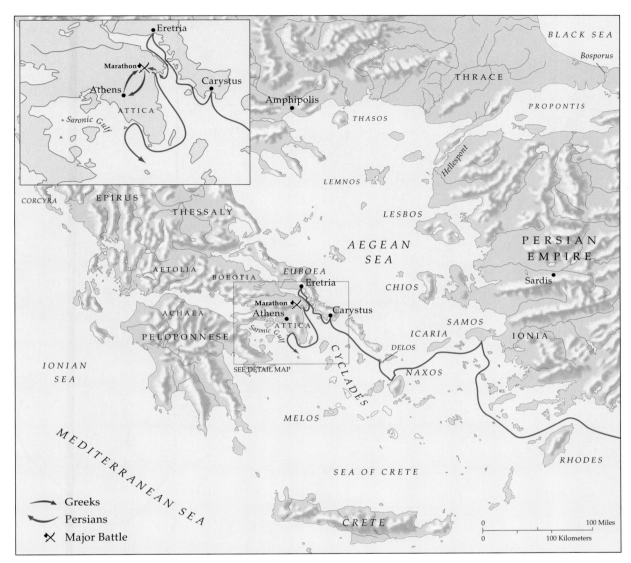

MAP 2.6 THE FIRST PERSIAN WAR, 490 B.C.
The king of Persia sent an expedition against Eretria and Athens to punish them for their part in an attack on Sardis. The battle of Marathon turned the Persian invasion back. On the way to Marathon, at which islands did the Persian fleet stop?
◆ For an online version, go to www.mhhe.com/chambers9 > chapter 2 > book maps

ner" had to depart Attica for ten years; but neither his property nor his family suffered any penalty. Aristotle attributed the practice to Cleisthenes himself, but this statement remains controversial.

THE CHALLENGE OF PERSIA

By the beginning of the "classical" period of Greek history, lasting from about 500 to 323 B.C., the Greek states had reached the political form they would retain for more than two centuries. But almost at once they faced their supreme challenge, a clash with the great Persian Empire. In two brief but intensely dangerous

wars, they turned the Persian armies back. Their morale was heightened because they were fighting for their own land, and the poet Aeschylus, in his play *The Persians*, records their battle cry: "Now the struggle is about everything." Daring and even trickery played their parts in the remarkable victory.

The Invasion under Darius and Marathon (490 B.C.)

King Darius of Persia (r. 522–486 B.C.) had expanded his empire throughout Asia Minor, including the Greek cities in the region called Ionia, on the west coast. Some of these Greeks sought their liberty from Persian

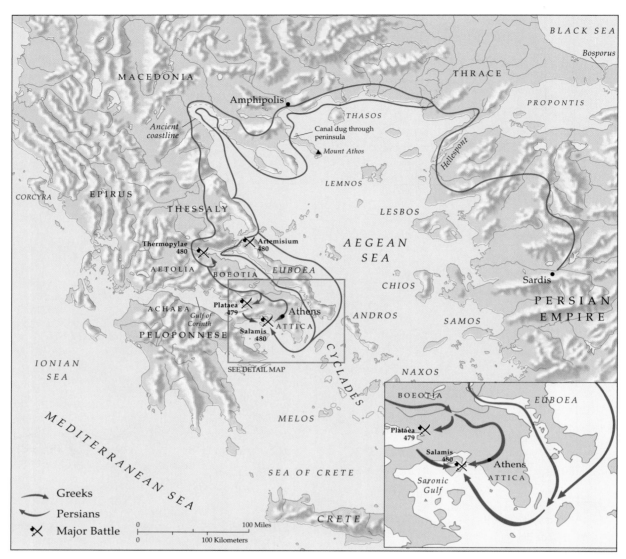

MAP 2.7 THE SECOND PERSIAN WAR, 480–479 B.C.
Ten years after the first war, the Persians attacked Greece again. The Persian navy and army invaded in parallel routes. The critical battles were at the island of Salamis and at Plataea in Boeotia. Where is the island of Salamis? Note the canal cut through Mt. Athos in 492 B.C.
◆ For an online version, go to www.mhhe.com/chambers9 > chapter 2 > book maps

control in 499 B.C. in the "Ionian revolt." The rebels obtained a promise of help from the Athenians, who sent them twenty warships. The historian Herodotus declares that "these ships turned out to be the beginning of trouble for both Greeks and non-Greeks," since they led directly to the two Persian wars. The revolt collapsed in 493 B.C., and Darius now proposed to invade Greece itself, largely for the sake of revenge against Athens, which had helped the rebels in the burning of Sardis, one of his cities.

After a brief campaign in 492, he sent a fleet across the Aegean in 490. The Persians first attacked Eretria, on the island of Euboea, and then landed in Attica on the beach at Marathon, a village north of Athens. The Athenian in-

fantry routed them in a brilliant victory and even marched back to Athens in time to ward off a Persian naval attack. A later legend told of an Athenian, Eucles, who ran back to Athens in his armor with the good news; he cried out, "Hail, we rejoice," and dropped dead (the origin of the marathon race).[3] The Athenians never forgot

[3] The name Eucles is preserved by Plutarch in his *On the Glory of the Athenians.* The usual popular version calls this man Phidippides or Philippides, but Herodotus, our oldest source, says that Phidippides ran from *Athens to Sparta* in one day to ask for Spartan help *before* the battle of Marathon (book 6, chapter 105). A much later writer, Lucian, improves on Herodotus by having him run with the good news from Marathon back to Athens, but there is no trace of this run in Herodotus.

this immortal feat of arms; they lost only 192 men, according to Herodotus, and the Persians lost about 6,400.

The Second Persian War (480–479 B.C.)

Preparations for War   To avenge this defeat, Darius' son, Xerxes (r. 486–465 B.C.), readied a huge force and swore that this time there would be no mistake. Fortunately for Greece and Europe, the Athenians were guided by a shrewd strategist, Themistocles. In 483 B.C., seeing the Persian menace on the horizon, he had persuaded the Athenians to use some newly found veins of silver in their mines to increase greatly the size of their fleet.

With this money they raised the number of their ships to two hundred. These ships were the famous **triremes,** on which nearly two hundred men rowed, seated in three banks. So powerful were these ships that they became, in effect, missiles, capable of smashing and disabling the enemy's ships. By thus greatly multiplying the striking power of one man, the trireme became the naval equivalent of the phalanx, in which hundreds of men could strike together on land.

The Invasion of 480 and Thermopylae   Early in 480 some thirty Greek states, also fearing annihilation, formed a military alliance and entrusted to the Spartans command on both land and sea. A few months later Xerxes began his march toward Greece with a force of perhaps sixty thousand men and six hundred ships, in a grandiose amphibious invasion of Europe. The first Greek force sent out in 480 against the Persians was defeated at the pass of Thermopylae in central Greece. The Spartan king in command, Leonidas, dismissed many of his allies, with the result that the Spartans defended the pass almost alone in a stand always remembered for its heroism. A poet, in two simple, grave lines on a stone, immortalized the heroism of the three hundred Spartans and their king who fell there: "Stranger, tell the Spartans that we lie here, faithful to their orders." At the same time, a sea battle at nearby Artemisium was inconclusive.

Themistocles and the Victory at Salamis   As the Persian army marched southward, the Athenians abandoned Athens and the Persians burned down the city. In this nearly desperate situation, Themistocles assembled the Greek fleet off the island of Salamis, near the Athenian coast. The Persians attacked with their ships into the narrows between Salamis and the shore, where the Greek fleet, with heavier ships, utterly defeated them. His navy shattered, Xerxes, who had watched the battle from a height, abandoned Greece and marched back to Persia (see "They Have a Master Called Law," p. 58).

Themistocles, the great Athenian strategist, was ostracized about 472 B.C. This ostrakon, cast against him, says, "Themistocles, son of Neocles, let him depart" (*ITO*).
American School of Classical Studies at Athens: Agora Excavations

The Battle of Plataea (479 B.C.)   Yet the Persians could still have won the war, for a large Persian army remained in central Greece. The reckoning with this force came in a battle in 479 B.C., at the village of Plataea. Once more a Greek army, under the Spartan general Pausanias, crushed the Persians; out of perhaps fifty thousand Persians, only a few thousand survived.

The Greeks won a further battle at Mycale on the shore of Asia Minor in 479. The Ionian Greeks now proclaimed their freedom and thus completed the work of throwing off Persian control that they had begun twenty years earlier in the Ionian revolt. Thus the Greeks crowned the most brilliant victory in the history of their civilization.

THE WARS OF THE FIFTH CENTURY (479–404 B.C.)

After a brief period of cooperation, the two leading Greek cities, Athens and Sparta, led their allies into the long, tragic war that fatally weakened the Greek poleis.

The Athenian Empire

The victorious Greeks continued the war against Persia in 479 and 478 B.C., liberating, for example, the Greek city of Byzantium on the Bosporus from Persian control. But in 478 Sparta returned to its perennial isolationism and withdrew from the alliance that had been formed to oppose Persia. In response, many of the

"THEY HAVE A MASTER CALLED LAW"

As King Xerxes leads his army into Greece in 480 B.C., he asks a former king of Sparta, who is accompanying him, whether the Greeks will really fight against the Persians.

"Now, Demaratus, I will ask you what I want to know. You are a Greek and one from no minor or weak city. So now tell me, will the Greeks stand and fight me?" Demaratus replied, "Your Majesty, shall I tell you the truth, or say what you want to hear?" The king ordered him to tell the truth, saying that he would respect him no less for doing so.

"Your Majesty," he said, "I am not speaking about all of them, only about the Spartans. First, I say they will never accept conditions from you that would enslave Greece; second, that they will fight you in battle even if all the other Greeks join your side."

Xerxes said, "Demaratus, let's look at it in all logic: why should a thousand, or ten thousand, or fifty thousand men, if they are all free and not ruled by a single master, stand up against such an army as mine? If they were ruled

by one man, like my subjects, I suppose they might, out of fear, show more bravery than usual and, driven into battle by the lash, go up against a bigger force; but if allowed their freedom, they wouldn't do either one."

Demaratus said, "Your Majesty, I knew from the beginning that if I spoke the truth you wouldn't like my message, but, since you ordered me to do so, I told you about the Spartans. They are free men, but not wholly free: They have a master called Law, whom they fear far more than your soldiers fear you. And his orders are always the same—they must not run away from any army no matter how big, but must stand in their formation and either conquer or die. But, your Majesty, may your wishes be fulfilled."

From *Herodotus*, book VII, M. H. Chambers (tr.).

newly liberated Greek states met on the island of Delos in 478 and formed an alliance, known as the **Delian League,** to continue the war and take further vengeance on Persia. Athens was recognized as head of the league and determined which members should supply ships to the common navy and which members should contribute money.

The military campaigns, often fought under the command of the Athenian general Cimon, were successful until the warfare between Greeks and Persians ended about 450. Meanwhile, Athenian control of the league had become stricter through the years. Sometimes Athens forcibly prevented members from withdrawing from the league; sometimes it stationed garrisons or governors in the supposedly independent member states. Athenian domination became unmistakable in or near 454, when the league transferred its treasury from Delos to Athens. The cash contributions were now nothing but tribute to Athens, and the alliance of equals had become an Athenian Empire.

The Age of Pericles

The Golden Age of Athens The leading statesman in the period of the Athenian Empire was Pericles (ca. 490?–429 B.C.), an aristocrat who had the support of the common people. Now that the archonship was no longer a position for an ambitious man, Pericles held only the post of general, to which he was reelected

from 443 to 429. He was a powerful orator and a highly competent general and was renowned for his personal honesty; moreover, his policies generally favored the common people.

He won them over by establishing pay for Athenian jurors and for those who served in the council. These measures not only supported the people but worked to ensure the fullest possible participation in government by all citizens. In 447 B.C. he proposed that the Athenians restore the damage done by the Persian invasion of 480 and rebuild the temples on the Acropolis.

Between 447 and 432 B.C. they built for their goddess Athena the most nearly perfect of all Greek temples, the Parthenon. Inside it was a statue of Athena bearing more than a ton of gold. It was the work of the sculptor Phidias, who probably directed the reliefs on the temple as well. They also built a magnificent gateway to the Acropolis. These public works both beautified the city and served the political aim of providing work for the people.

Moreover, Pericles' lifetime coincided with the zenith of Athenian literature, when Athenian drama, especially, reached its highest development in the plays of Sophocles (a friend of Pericles) and Euripides. (On drama see further chapter 3, p. 71.) So brilliant was this era, and so strongly marked by his leadership, that historians often call the era from 450 to 429 the Age of Pericles. His political dominance drew praise from the historian Thucydides because "he controlled the

A portion of the frieze within the Athenian Parthenon, showing officials carrying the robe that will be presented to Athena. On the right, gods sit in conversation, awaiting the procession; note that they are portrayed as larger than the human beings.
Hirmer Fotoarchiv

masses, rather than let them control him. . . . Though the state was a democracy in name, in fact it was ruled by the most prominent man."[4]

The Athenian Judicial System   The expansion of the empire must have been one of the causes of the development of the Athenian judicial system. Juries were chosen by lot and comprised two to five hundred or even more citizens drawn from all classes. There was no detailed body of civil or criminal law, and in trials there was no judge, merely a magistrate to keep order. Juries had wide powers of interpretation without the possibility of appeal from their decision. Nor were there professional attorneys, although a man facing trial could pay a clever rhetorician to write a courtroom speech for him. Juries heard all manner of cases with the exception of homicides, which were tried by the Areopagus council (see p. 51). Critics of this system saw it as too democratic, but it expressed the spirit of the Greek state: that the average citizen could and should play a part in governing the city.

The Peloponnesian War (431–404 B.C.)

The Athenians became more and more imperialistic and menacing to other states. The tension that followed led to the war that sealed the doom of the Greek city-states. By far the longest and most dramatic of all collisions in Greek history, the Peloponnesian War received an immortal analysis from the greatest of ancient historians, Thucydides of Athens (ca. 455–395 B.C.).

The Outbreak of War   In the 430s aggressive action by Athens convinced the Spartans and their allies that they must declare a preventive war on Athens. The war opposed two kinds of states. Sparta, the head of the Peloponnesian League, controlled no empire but had the strongest army in Greece and maintained itself through its own resources. Athens, which had the strongest navy, relied on its empire to provide grain for its people and tribute to pay for its fleet.

The Archidamian War (431–421 B.C.)   The first ten years of the war are called the Archidamian War, so named for Archidamus, one of the kings of Sparta when the war began. The battles were inconclusive and neither side devised a winning strategy. Far more damaging to Athens than the annual Spartan invasions was a devastating plague, not yet identified with any known disease. It attacked the Athenians, who were packed inside their walls, in 430 B.C. The plague took thousands of lives in the crowded, unsanitary city; Thucydides survived it and has left us a horrifying description of its effects on the body.

Unfortunately for Athens' effectiveness in the war, Pericles died in 429 B.C., perhaps from the plague. None of his successors maintained his stable leadership, and

[4] Thucydides 2.65.

A Roman copy of an idealized portrait of Pericles, the leading Athenian statesman of his time. The helmet symbolizes his position as commander.
Scala/Art Resource, NY

some were unscrupulous demagogues playing only for their own power. Casualties finally made both sides ready to end, or at least suspend, the war. A peace treaty, supposed to make Athens and Sparta allies for fifty years, was signed in 421 B.C. It is called the Peace of Nicias for the Athenian general who led the negotiations.

The "Suspicious Truce" (421–415 B.C.) and the Affair of Melos

At this point the Greeks could have turned their backs on war, for both Athens and Sparta had shown courage and neither had gained a decisive advantage. Thucydides called the next few years a time of suspicious truce, but during this period one event demands attention, the brutal subjugation of the small island of Melos by the Athenians in 416.

The Athenians sailed up to this neutral island and commanded the Melians to join the Athenian Empire.

Thucydides describes the negotiations in a brilliant passage, called the Melian Dialogue, in which envoys on each side argue their cases. It is by no means clear how he could have known what was said by either side, and this dialogue is probably based on his own conjectures. In any case, the Melians protest that they are so few in number that they cannot in any way threaten the Athenians, to which the Athenians reply that it is precisely their weakness that makes them dangerous: If the Athenians allow so small a state to remain neutral, this will show weakness in the Athenians themselves and may tempt their subjects to rebel.

In the Dialogue the Athenians brush aside all arguments based on morality and justice and finally seize the island, kill most of the adult men (probably two to three thousand), and sell the women and children as slaves. Without explicitly stating any moral conclusion, Thucydides shows the Athenians giving way to the corrupting influence of war; as he says in another passage, "War teaches men to be violent."[5]

The Syracusan Expedition

In 415 B.C. another occasion for war arose. The people of Segesta, a city in Sicily, appealed to Athens for help in a war they were fighting against Syracuse, the leading power on that island. In commenting on the death of Pericles, Thucydides noted that his successors were often lesser men of poor judgment. It was so now, as Alcibiades, a talented young political leader of enormous ambition and—as it later turned out—few scruples, persuaded the Athenian assembly, against the advice of the Athenian general Nicias, to raise a large fleet and attack Syracuse, with him as one of the generals. This campaign in effect reopened the Peloponnesian War despite the peace treaty of 421 B.C.

Thucydides makes it clear that a quick, resolute attack might well have succeeded, but the Athenians failed to strike when they had a clear advantage. One event that blunted the Athenian attack was the loss of Alcibiades. He was recalled to Athens to stand trial on two scandalous charges: that he had been part of a gang of rowdies that had mutilated small statues of the god Hermes and that he and his friends had mocked some religious ceremonies known as mysteries. Fearing that his political enemies would be able to secure his conviction, he defected to Sparta and advised them how to fight the Athenians. His defection left Nicias, who had opposed the campaign from the start, in command.

In Syracuse, the Athenians finally decided to break off the campaign, but they lost a critical battle in the harbor and could not sail away. Trying to retreat toward the interior of the island, they were cut off and decimated. Those who survived this calamity were imprisoned in

[5] Thucydides 3.82.

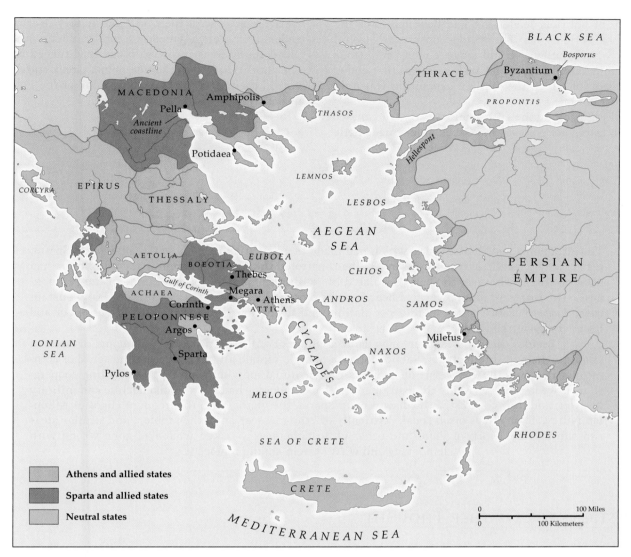

MAP 2.8 GREECE IN 431 B.C. AT THE OUTBREAK OF THE PELOPONNESIAN WAR
The two main cities, Athens and Sparta, had allies throughout Greece. Most of the allies of Athens were members of the Delian League, which became the Athenian Empire. Which states or regions were neutral at the opening of the war?
◆ For an online version, go to www.mhhe.com/chambers9 > chapter 2 > book maps

terrible conditions in a quarry at Syracuse; as Thucydides grimly says, "Few out of many returned home."[6]

Athens Defeated The disaster in Sicily led to many defections among Athens' subjects, but Sparta still could not strike the final blow. The war dragged on for another eight years until, in 405 B.C., the Spartan admiral Lysander captured the Athenian fleet at a spot called Aegospotami, in the Dardanelles (the ancient Hellespont). Athens, now unable to bring grain through the straits, had to surrender in desperate hunger in 404.

[6]Thucydides 7.87.

It abandoned its empire and, as a guarantee for the future and a symbol of humiliation, had to pull down the "long walls" that had protected the population during the war. Sparta proclaimed this event, in language often used by victors in war, as the "liberation of Greece" and imposed on the Athenians a cruel regime (known as the Thirty Tyrants). Pro-Spartan and anti-Spartan factions assailed one another during the rule of this hated clique, with atrocities and murders committed on both sides. After eight months the Spartan king Pausanias restored the democracy in 403 B.C.

Athens never regained its former power, although democracy survived for long years after the war. The quality of political leadership had declined after the death of Pericles, as Thucydides observed. Several times when the war could have ended, ambitious politicians raised support for rash ventures that ended in disaster, of which the Sicilian expedition was only the most notable.

Looking back at the fifth century B.C., we can see that, in interstate politics, the Greek poleis made little constructive use of their brilliant victory over the invaders from Persia. Freed of a foreign enemy, they divided themselves into two blocs that turned against one another and, like characters in a Greek tragedy, involved themselves in the catastrophe of the Peloponnesian War.

Summary

The Athenians lost their empire, which had made them the richest polis in Greek history. Sparta, persuaded by its allies to go to war in 431, had shattered the Athenian Empire, but this empire had been no threat whatever to Sparta's isolated life within the protecting mountains of the Peloponnese. The losses in manpower had been heavy on both sides, but Sparta could less easily sustain these losses because of its smaller population, and in the fourth century it could put fewer and fewer troops in the field.

Besides these losses, there now came a failure of will, a spirit of pessimism and disillusion among Athenian intellectuals. Such a collapse of civic morale all but destroyed the sense of community that was the very heart of the polis. Self-centered individualism replaced willing cooperation between citizens. Many thought uncontrolled democracy had led to social decline and military disaster, and they contrasted the discipline of Sparta, the victor, with the frequent chaos of Athenian policy. Thucydides often speaks critically of "the masses" and "the rabble," and similar ideas run through the work of Plato and other philosophers, who asked what had gone wrong with democracy and what system should replace it.

QUESTIONS FOR FURTHER THOUGHT

1. There was no single ruler of ancient Greece, as there was in Egypt. If there had been such a ruler, how might Greek history and society have been different?

2. In what ways would you have liked to live in ancient Greece? What features of Greek life would you have found undesirable?

RECOMMENDED READING

Sources

*Herodotus. *The Histories.* Robin Waterfield (tr.). 1998. A new translation with precise notes by Carolyn Dewald.

*Homer. *The Iliad.* Robert Fagles (tr.). 1990. A stirring translation in verse.

———. *The Odyssey.* Robert Fagles (tr.). 1996. A worthy companion to Fagles' *Iliad.*

*Thucydides. *The Peloponnesian War.* Rex Warner (tr.). 1972. The masterpiece of Greek historical writing.

*———. *The Landmark Thucydides.* Robert B. Strassler (ed.). 1996. The Crawley translation, older but still a classic, with many helpful maps, notes, and appendixes.

Studies

*Boardman, John. *Greek Art.* 1973. One of many books by this great authority.

*Boardman, John, et al. (eds.). *The Oxford History of Greece and the Hellenistic World.* 1991. Sixteen chapters by leading authorities on topics like art, literature, religion, and history.

Burkert, Walter. *Greek Religion.* 1987. By the most original and profound expert of our times.

*———. *The Orientalizing Revolution.* 1992. Brief but close-packed study of Eastern influence on Greek art, religion, and culture.

*Chadwick, John. *The Decipherment of Linear B.* 2d ed. 1970. Study of the Cretan scripts, with notes on the method of decipherment.

Drews, Robert. *The Coming of the Greeks.* 1988. Important on the arrival of the Greeks and movement of Indo-European peoples.

*Ehrenberg, Victor. *From Solon to Socrates.* 1968. Standard textbook on the central period of Greek history, with good references to sources.

Fantham, Elaine, et al. *Women in the Classical World.* 1994. Chapters on women in both Greece and Rome. Many good illustrations.

*Finley, M. I. *The World of Odysseus.* 2d ed. 1977. Brilliant discussion of the historical material in Homer, both *Iliad* and *Odyssey.*

Flacelière, Robert. *Daily Life in Greece at the Time of Pericles.* 1965. Social and economic history of Greek life.

Forrest, W. G. *A History of Sparta, 950–192 B.C.* 1980. Brief history of Sparta, taking the story down through the state's collapse.

Garlan, Yvon. *Slavery in Ancient Greece.* Rev. ed. 1988. Thorough treatment of this institution.

Green, Peter. *The Greco-Persian Wars.* 1996. Modern, accurate narrative of the two Persian Wars.

Hansen, Mogens Herman. *The Athenian Democracy in the Age of Demosthenes: Structure, Principles, and Ideology.* 1991. History of the democracy with careful attention to how it functioned.

Lawrence, A. W. *Greek Architecture.* 1987. Introductory survey of temples and private buildings.

Lazenby, J. F. *The Spartan Army.* 1985. History and operation of the Spartan army.

Lenardon, Robert J. *The Saga of Themistocles.* 1978. Readable, sound study of the great strategist.

MacDowell, Douglas M. *The Law in Classical Athens.* 1978. Good discussion of all aspects.

*Morrison, J. S., and J. F. Coates. *The Athenian Trireme: The History and Reconstruction of an Ancient Greek Warship.* 1986. Essential treatment, solving at last the problem of how the Greek trireme was built.

Page, Denys L. *History and the Homeric Iliad.* 2d ed. 1966. Especially good on Near Eastern connections with the epic.

Patterson, Cynthia B. *The Family in Greek History.* 1998. A good, modern study.

*Pomeroy, Sarah B. *Goddesses, Whores, Wives, and Slaves.* 1975. The pioneering work that opened the modern study of women in the ancient world; includes chapters on Rome.

*Renault, Mary. *The King Must Die.* 1958. An evocative historical novel set in the mythical time of Theseus.

Sealey, Raphael. *Women and Law in Classical Greece.* 1990. Carries the discussion beyond Athens into other Greek societies.

West, M. L. *The East Face of Helicon: West Asiatic Elements in Greek Poetry and Myth.* 1997. Superb treatment of the contribution of the non-Greek world to Greek culture.

Wycherley, R. E. *How the Greeks Built Cities.* 1976. Greek town planning with description of major urban public buildings.

*Available in paperback.

A superb statue of the god Apollo from the west pediment of the Temple of Zeus at Olympia. In a commanding gesture, the god controls a centaur and symbolically brings Hellenic rationality to bear over an undisciplined universe. The statue combines the power and dignity of a god with the ideal perfection of a human being.
Erich Lessing/Art Resource, NY

Chapter Three

CLASSICAL AND HELLENISTIC GREECE

CLASSICAL GREEK CULTURE (CA. 500–323 B.C.) • THE RISE OF MACEDONIA
• THE HELLENISTIC AGE (323–30 B.C.)

The Peloponnesian War left the two main Greek political alliances, those built around Athens and Sparta, weak and demoralized. The war thus prepared the way for the conquest of Greece in the next century by the Macedonian king Philip II. His son, Alexander the Great, went on to conquer Egypt, Persia, and vast stretches of Asia Minor.

Despite the tumultuous conditions of Greek politics—and perhaps because of the uncertainties and upheavals—the fifth and fourth centuries B.C. gave the world an extraordinary flowering of intellectual and artistic achievement. This burst of creative energy was concentrated in time and space to a degree that had never been seen in history and, some would argue, has never been duplicated. The theme that runs through Greek civilization was now the inquiry into philosophy and analytical thought. At about the same time,

Confucius, a philosopher in China, which the Greeks never visited, formulated his own rules for living by correct ethical standards.

In these centuries the Greeks wrote their greatest tragic dramas; they invented historical writing and developed firm dating systems for historical events. Within society, the classical structure of the family and the several roles of women now become visible.

During the last decades of the fourth century, the Greeks, having lost the world of the independent polis, entered the world of Alexander's empire, which brought them into contact with peoples outside Greece. There followed a series of intellectual experiments, especially in science and technology, art and literature, philosophy and religion. The Greek language sank deep roots in the Near East and ultimately became the language for the Christian Bible, or New Testament.

Life of Pericles, Athenian statesman **ca. 495–429 B.C.**

Flowering of Greek drama **ca. 470–385 B.C.**

ca. 600 B.C.
Beginnings of philosophic speculation

Life of Socrates of Athens **469–399 B.C.**

The *Oresteia* of Aeschylus **458 B.C.**

Sophistic influence in Athens **ca. 450–400 B.C.**

Herodotus writes history of the Persian Wars **ca. 440–430 B.C.**

Life of Plato **428–347 B.C.**

CLASSICAL GREEK CULTURE (CA. 500–323 B.C.)

In less than two centuries, Greek society went through a profound intellectual transformation, apparent above all in literature, philosophy, drama, and historical writing. In all these spheres, reasoned argument became supreme. This cultural trait was hardly to be found among their older eastern neighbors. This era was one of Athenian preeminence, and the study of this "golden age" inevitably focuses on Athens.

Greek Philosophy

The Inspiration for Philosophic Thought The supreme intellectual invention of the Greeks is the special search for knowledge called philosophy—the attempt to use reason to discover why things are as they are. Philosophy is born when people are no longer satisfied with supernatural and mythical explanations of the world or of human behavior. It is hard to say just why Greeks gradually became skeptical about the accounts that they inherited in their own mythology, but around 600 B.C. they began to suspect that there was an order in the universe beyond manipulation by the gods—and that human beings could discover it.

Life in Greek poleis was conducive to argument and debate, and such conditions encouraged rational inquiry and even dispute. Philosophy, like drama and history, became a means to analyze and understand change and upheaval. Yet philosophy never turned its back on religion. The earliest philosophers were seeking nothing less than a cosmic plan, a divine world order.

The Beginnings of Philosophy in Miletus The first Greek philosophers lived in the city of Miletus, a

prominent trading center on the western shore of Asia Minor in the region of Ionia. Its citizens had direct contact with the ideas and achievements of the Near East, and these intellectual currents must have helped form the city as a center of thought. Soon after 600 B.C., certain Milesians were discovering a world of speculation in an apparently simple yet profoundly radical question: What exists? They sought their answer in some single primal element. One philosopher, Thales, for example, taught that everything in the whole universe was made of water, a notion that echoes Babylonian myths of a primeval flood. He may have reasoned that water is found in several states—as ice, as mist, and as water itself. Moreover, all the first civilizations—Sumer, Egypt, Babylonia—were nourished by great rivers.

The hypothesis of Thales inspired various replies. For example, one of his pupils, Anaximander of Miletus, held (probably about 560 B.C.) that the origin of everything was an infinite body of matter, which he called "the boundless." A whirling motion within the boundless divided its substance into the hot, which rose to form the heavens, and the cold, which sank and assumed form in the earth and the air surrounding it. A further separation into wet and dry created the oceans and the land. Human beings, he thought, had emerged from the sea; in this way he expressed a primitive theory of evolution. This theory points toward a common later classification of all matter into four elements: earth, air, fire, and water. Moreover, he said, all things will pass away into that from which they came: Thus—a dark but clearly religious statement—"will they pay one another the penalty and the fine for their wrongdoing according to the ordinance of time."

Pythagoras and Numbers Among the theories proposed to explain the order or substance of all things were those of Pythagoras of Samos (around 530 B.C.),

ca. 287–212 B.C.
Life of Archimedes

● **306 B.C.** Epicurus establishes school in Athens

● **ca. 312 B.C.** Zeno founds Stoicism in Athens

Hellenistic Age **323–30 B.C.**

336–323 B.C. Reign of Alexander the Great in Macedonia; invasion of Persia and Egypt

359–336 B.C. Reign of Philip II in Macedonia

384–322 B.C. Life of Aristotle

AN ATTIC RED-FIGURE VASE (CA. 470 B.C.), SHOWING SCENES FROM A SCHOOL
At left, a master teaches a boy to play the lyre; at right, a boy learns to recite poetry from a scroll held by a master while another master supervises the class.
Johannes Laurentius, 1992/BPK Berlin/Art Resource, NY

who developed a strikingly different theory to explain the structure of the world. He saw the key to all existence in mathematics and approached the universe through the study of numbers. He discovered the harmonic intervals within the musical scale and stated the Pythagorean theorem in geometry about the area based on the sides of a right triangle. Pythagoras went on to say that all objects are similar to numbers, by which he probably meant that objects always contain a numerically balanced arrangement of parts. He lacked, of course, the experimental methods of modern physicists; yet his theory is remarkably similar to the modern discoveries of mathematical relationships within all things, including even the genetic code in our bodies.

The Atomic Theory Yet another way of looking at the universe came from Leucippus (home uncertain) and his contemporary, Democritus of Abdera, about 450 B.C. They saw the world as made up of invisibly small particles, or atoms (*a-toma* in Greek, meaning "things that cannot be divided"), which come together and cohere at random. Death, according to this theory, leads simply to the redistribution of the atoms that make up our body and soul and thus need hold no terror for humanity. The validity of the atomic theory was eventually to be recognized in the modern era. It is another example of the astonishing ability of Greek theorists to hit part of the scientific truth, even though they could not prove it in laboratories.

The Sophists Around 450 B.C. philosophers turned away from speculations about the structure of the universe and toward the study of human beings and the ways they led their lives. The first Greeks to undertake this study were those commonly known as **Sophists** (*sophistés* in Greek means "expert" or "learned man"). They came to Athens from various places and challenged nearly all accepted beliefs. One of the early Sophists, Protagoras, declared that "man is the measure" of everything; that is, human beings and their perceptions are the only measure of whether a thing exists at all. The very existence of the gods, whom people cannot really perceive, is only an undemonstrable assumption. From such a statement it is only a short step to the belief that it is almost impossible to know anything; in the absence of objective knowledge, the only recourse is to make your way through the world by coolly exploiting to your own advantage any situation you encounter.

The Sophists also drew an important distinction between human customs on the one hand and the law of nature on the other. Thus they argued that what was made or designed by people was arbitrary and inferior; what existed naturally was immutable and proper. This argument called into question all accepted rules of good behavior. Freed of moral constraints, the Sophists suggested that intellectual activity was valuable only in helping one succeed in life. They accepted pupils and said they could train these pupils for success in any calling, since in every line of work there are problems to be solved through reasoning. They taught the art of rhetoric, persuasive speech making that could be used to sway an assembly or to defend oneself in court. Their pupils, they implied, could gain power by analyz-

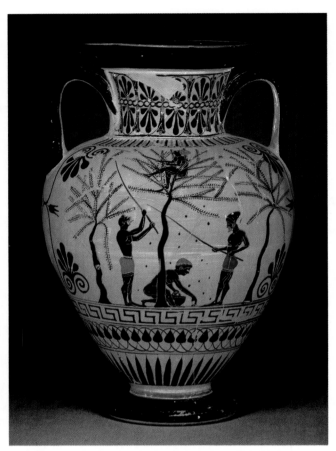

The olive was one of the basic crops in Greek agriculture. In this black-figure vase (the figures are painted black, while the background is the natural red of the clay), two men knock olives off a tree at harvest time, while another climbs the branches and a boy gathers the fruit.
© British Museum (PS227411)

ing the mechanics of politics and by using the skills the Sophists taught them.

Socrates of Athens The main critic of the Sophists was Socrates (469–399 B.C.). He was active during the intellectually dynamic period before and during the Peloponnesian War. Socrates faulted the Sophists for taking pay for teaching, yet failing to recognize moral absolutes and teach ethically right behavior. In the course of his critique, Socrates transformed philosophy into an inquiry about the moral responsibility of people. His basic questions were not, What is the world made of and how does it operate? but rather, What is right action and how can I know it is right? His mission was to persuade the young men of Athens to examine their lives in the pursuit of moral truth, for "the unexamined life is not worth living."

His technique was to engage his pupils in a dialogue of questions and answers and to refute, correct, and guide them by this "Socratic" method to the right answers. He held that no one is wise who cannot give a logical account of his or her actions and that knowledge will point to the morally right choices; this belief led to his statement that "knowledge is virtue," one of several Socratic theses that seem paradoxical, for even ignorant men may be virtuous. Another such paradox is his statement that he was the wisest of men because he knew that he knew nothing. It was through ironic statements like these that he made people think critically and thus discover moral truths. The Roman orator and essayist Cicero said that Socrates had brought philosophy down from the heavens and placed it in the cities of the world.

Socrates' Trial and Death   Socrates had political critics, for he was the tutor of several Athenians who had opposed democracy during the last years of the Peloponnesian War. One, Critias, was a member of the pro-Spartan oligarchy known as the Thirty Tyrants, who ruled Athens after the war. Alcibiades, who joined the Spartan side during the war, was another of his followers. As a result, Socrates was suspected of sympathy with the enemies of Athenian democracy, and in 399 B.C. he was brought to trial on charges of "worshiping strange gods and corrupting the youth"—a way of implying that Socrates had connections with enemies of the democratic state.

One can understand why Athenian jurors, who had just regained their democratic constitution from a short-lived oligarchy that fell in 403, would have wanted to punish anyone who had collaborated with the oligarchs. But there is little reason to think that Socrates was disloyal to the state. Nevertheless, persuaded by Socrates' enemies and acting in misguided patriotism, the jury convicted him. He proposed as his penalty a fine of 100 drachmas, which was about two months' pay, thus not a trifling sum; but when he also ironically requested the honor of dining rights at the town hall, the jury reacted in anger by voting for the death penalty (see "Socrates Is Sentenced to Death," p. 70).

Socrates accepted his fate and declined to seek exile. Perhaps he thought that life outside his polis, at age seventy, offered little pleasure. He may also have wanted to show his young followers that the duty of a good citizen was to obey the laws of the state. He drank a cup of poison with simple courage.

Plato: What Is Reality?   Our knowledge of Socrates' thought comes mainly from the writings of his most famous pupil, Plato (428–347 B.C.), for Socrates wrote nothing. Plato continued Socrates' investigation of moral conduct by writing a series of complex and pro-found philosophical books, mainly in the form of dialogues in which Socrates is the main speaker. In these works, Plato went far beyond the ironic paradoxes proposed by Socrates and sought truth through a subtle process of reasoning and inquiry that modern readers still endlessly discuss and probe.

Plato made his greatest impact on the future of philosophy with his theory of knowledge. Socrates' answer to the question, How can I know what is right? was simply that one must listen to one's conscience. Such reliance on the inner voice within each human being did not satisfy Plato, who believed that we must go beyond the evidence of our senses to find ultimate reality and truth. Moreover, Socrates thought that everyone could recognize and practice right behavior; but Plato believed that moral goodness was restricted to the elite who could master it through philosophic study. He developed and taught his theories in his school in Athens called the **Academy.**

The Republic   According to Plato, we see objects as real, but in fact they are only poor reflections of ideal models, or "forms," which are eternal, perfect originals of any given object or notion.[1] In his *Republic*, Plato illustrates our lack of true perception with a famous metaphor. Imagine men sitting in a cave, facing a wall, with a fire behind them. As others carry objects through the cave, in front of the fire, the men see only vague shadows of the objects and therefore cannot make out the reality. Everything that we see is like these imprecise shadows; so what we see as justice, for example, is nothing but an approximation of the true "form" of justice. Only through long training in philosophy can we learn how to perceive and understand the true ideal forms, which exist outside our world.

Plato presents this thesis in several dialogues, of which the most widely read is *The Republic*. Like other Athenian intellectuals, Plato opposed democracy as a political system dominated by emotion rather than logic. His repudiation of democracy intensified when a jury was persuaded to condemn Socrates to death, even though he had served the state as a soldier and had committed no crime. Socrates is the main speaker in the *Republic*, and in the work's long debate over the right form of state he expresses severe criticisms of democracy as a volatile, unpredictable, and ineffective system. Yet it is by no means certain that these opinions were really those of the historical Socrates. It is probable that Plato was the real antidemocrat and that he put these opinions into the mouth of Socrates for dramatic purposes. Whatever its source, Plato's denunciation of

---

[1] Plato used the Greek word *idéa*, which means an image that one can see. Thus "form" is a better translation than the English "idea," even though the latter is widely used.

SOCRATES IS SENTENCED TO DEATH

Plato's version of Socrates' words to the jury that sentenced him to death:

"You too, gentlemen of the jury, must look forward to death with confidence, and fix your minds on this one belief, which is certain: that nothing can harm a good man either in life or after death, and his fortunes are not a matter of indifference to the gods. This present experience of mine has not come about mechanically; I am quite clear that the time had come when it was better for me to die and to be released from my distractions. . . . For my own part I bear no grudge at all against those who condemned me and accused me, although it was not with this kind intention that they did so, but because they thought they were hurting me. . . . However, I ask them to grant me one favor. When my sons grow up, gentlemen, if you think that they are putting money or any-

thing else before goodness, take your revenge by plaguing them as I plagued you; and if they fancy themselves for no reason, you must scold them just as I scolded you, for neglecting the important things and thinking that they are good for something when they are good for nothing. If you do this, I shall have had justice at your hands, both I myself and my children.

Now it is time that we were going, I to die and you to live; but which of us has the happier prospect is unknown to anyone but God."

From Plato, *The Last Days of Socrates*, Hugh Tredennick (tr.), Penguin Classics, 1954, 1972, 1980, p. 76.

---

broad participation by the people in governing has remained a challenge to political theorists ever since.

Aristotle: Form and Matter   Plato had a pupil of equal genius, Aristotle (384–322 B.C.), who was for a time the teacher of Alexander the Great of Macedonia. Aristotle founded a school within a grove in Athens called the **Lyceum.** His investigations, in which he was assisted by his pupils in Athens between 336 and 322 B.C., embraced all fields of learning known to the ancients, including logic, metaphysics, astronomy, biology, physics, politics, and poetry.

Aristotle departed from Plato's theory of an ideal reality that cannot be perceived by the senses. Rather, he saw reality as consisting of both form and matter. In this way, he turned his pupils to empirical sciences, the study of what can be seen to exist. He also had an overall theory of the world of nature. For Aristotle each object has a purpose as part of a grand design of the universe. "Nature does nothing by accident," he said. The task of the philosopher is to study these individual objects to discover their purpose; then he may ultimately be able to determine a general pattern.

Aristotle and the State   Like Plato, Aristotle wanted to design the best state. In one of his works, the *Politics,* he classified the types of political constitutions in the Greek world and distinguished three basic forms: monarchy, aristocracy, and moderate democracy. He warned that monarchy can turn into tyranny; aristocracy, into oligarchy; and moderate democracy, into radical democracy, or anarchy.

Of the three uncorrupted forms, Aristotle expressed a preference for moderate democracy—one in which the masses do not exercise too much power. The chief end of government, in his view, is a good life for both the individual and the community as a whole. This idea is an extension of the view expressed in his *Ethics,* that happiness is the greatest good of the individual. To achieve this end, people must seek moderation, often called the Golden Mean: a compromise between extremes of excessive pleasure and ascetic denial—a goal that reflected the Greek principle of harmony and balance in all things.

Aristotle's Physical Theories   Aristotle's conception of the universe remained influential in scientific speculation for two thousand years. By 350 B.C. philosophers generally recognized four elements: earth, air, fire, and water. Aristotle gave the elements purpose and movement. Air and fire, he said, naturally move upward; and earth and water, downward. He explained movement by saying that elements seek their natural place. Thus, a stone falls because it seeks to return to the earth. It also seeks to be at rest; all motion is therefore involuntary and unnatural and must be accounted for by an outside force.

To the four elements Aristotle added a fifth, ether, the material of which the stars are made. He explained that the stars move in a natural circular motion, and outside the whole universe there exists an eternal "prime mover," which imparts movement to all the other parts. This prime mover, or God as Aristotle finally designates him, does not move or change; God is

An Attic relief, showing the goddess Athena leaning on her spear and gazing at a tablet, perhaps a list of men fallen in battle. If so, this would justify the name often given to this relief, the "Mourning Athena."
Pentelic marble, ca. 460 B.C. Acropolis Museum, Athens

THE SO-CALLED TEMPLE OF CONCORD FROM AGRIGENTO, SICILY
Superb example of a fifth-century Doric temple. The stone was of inferior quality and was originally covered with stucco, still visible on some columns.
John Snyder/Corbis Stock Market

a kind of divine thought or mind that sets the whole universe in motion.

Greek Tragedy

One of the most lasting achievements of the fifth century B.C. was the creation and perfection of a new literary and theatrical form, tragedy. Greek dramas were written in the most sublime poetry since Homer, and they first appeared in Athens, at religious festivals honoring the god Dionysus. At these celebrations, also marked by dancing and revelry, dramatic performances addressed increasingly profound moral issues.

Themes in Greek Tragedy Writers of tragedies drew most of their plots from tales of gods and heroes in Greek mythology. They used these characters to ask some of the basic questions of human life: What is our relationship to the gods? What is justice? If the gods are just, why do they allow people to suffer? How can worldly success lead to destruction? Greek tragedies are still performed and filmed, and they continue to inspire operas, plays, and ballets more than two thousand years after their creation.

Aeschylus: Fate and Revenge Playwrights presented dramas in sets of three, accompanied by a comic playlet known as a **satyr play** (probably meant to relieve the heavy emotion of the main drama). Only one such "trilogy" has survived: the *Oresteia*, the tragedy of Orestes, the son of Agamemnon, by Aeschylus, which was produced in 458 B.C. Its central theme is the nature of justice, which Aeschylus explores in a tale of multiple murders and vengeance. Agamemnon, the leader of the war against Troy, found his fleet becalmed and had to sacrifice his daughter to revive the winds so that he could fulfill his oath to make war on Troy. On his return, his wife, Clytemnestra, kills him and is in turn killed by her son, Orestes, who is finally tried and acquitted in an Athenian court presided over by the goddess Athena. The cycle of retribution runs its course as the themes of fate and revenge focus on the family, all developed through majestic poetry and intense emotion.

Sophocles: When Is Civil Disobedience Justified?
Sophocles wrote mainly during the Peloponnesian War of 431–404 B.C. He changed the form of drama by

OEDIPUS' SELF-MUTILATION

In Sophocles' tragedy King Oedipus, *Jocasta, the mother of Oedipus, hangs herself after learning that she has married her own son. An attendant then narrates what follows. (Those he "should never have seen" are the daughters Oedipus fathered by his mother-wife.)*

"We saw a knotted pendulum, a noose,
A strangled woman swinging before our eyes.
The King saw too, and with heart-rending groans
Untied the rope, and laid her on the ground.
But worse was yet to see. Her dress was pinned
With golden brooches, which the King snatched out
And thrust, from full arm's length, into his eyes—
Eyes that should see no longer his shame, his guilt,
No longer see those they should never have seen,
Nor see, unseeing, those he had longed to see,
Henceforth seeing nothing but night. . . . To this wild tune
He pierced his eyeballs time and time again,

Till bloody tears ran down his beard—not drops
But in full spate a whole cascade descending
In drenching cataracts of scarlet rain.
Thus two have sinned; and on two heads, not one—
On man and wife—falls mingled punishment.
Their old long happiness of former times
Was happiness earned with justice; but to-day
Calamity, death, ruin, tears, and shame,
All ills that there are names for—all are here."

From *Sophocles,* The Three Theban Plays, *E. F. Watling (tr.),* Penguin Classics, 1971, pp. 60–61.

adding a third actor (Aeschylus never had more than two actors on the stage at any time) in order to concentrate more on the interplay of characters and the larger issues of society that they explore. He also shows a greater interest in personality than does Aeschylus.

His *Oedipus the King* is perhaps the most nearly perfect specimen of surviving Greek tragedy; its central concern is the relationship of the individual and the polis. The play is about Oedipus, the revered king of Thebes, who has unknowingly committed the terrible crimes of killing his father and marrying his mother. As the play opens, some unknown offense has brought a plague on his people. Oedipus orders a search to discover the person who has caused this pollution. As the search narrows with terrifying logic to Oedipus himself, he discovers that his crimes of patricide and incest, though unintentional, have disturbed the order of the universe and his polis in particular. The only remedy is for him to serve justice and atone for his offenses. When the truth emerges, Oedipus' wife-mother hangs herself and Oedipus, in a frenzy of remorse and humiliation, plunges the brooches from her robe into his eyes and begins a life of wandering as a blind outcast; the once powerful monarch is now a broken, homeless fugitive (see "Oedipus' Self-Mutilation," above).

Sophocles' *Antigone* continues the saga of Oedipus' family as his daughter Antigone grapples with another dilemma about justice. One of her brothers has been killed while attacking his own city, Thebes. Antigone wants to give him a traditional burial despite his traitorous actions, but the ruler of Thebes forbids such honor for an outlaw. Antigone must therefore decide which laws to obey—those of the gods or those laid down by a man.

Antigone defies the ruler by burying her brother and thus willingly goes to prison, where she hangs herself in heroic loyalty to her beliefs. The play, like most Greek tragedies, raises moral questions that still resonate: When is civil disobedience justified, and is it our duty to resist laws that we consider wrong?

Euripides: Psychology and Human Destiny   The Athenian poet Euripides, a contemporary of Sophocles, emphasized above all the psychology of his characters. Reacting to the violence of his times, he throws his characters back on their own searing passions. They forge their own fates, alienated from their societies. As a result, we see in Euripides how the workings of the mind and emotions shape a person's destiny. His intense, even fanatical, characters determine the course of events by their own often savage deeds. Compared with Aeschylus and Sophocles, Euripides seems less confident in a divine moral order. In this uncertainty, he reflects the wavering spirit of his age.

In Euripides' *Medea*, for example, Jason, Medea's husband, has deserted her for a princess of Corinth. Driven by overwhelming emotion to take revenge, Medea kills the Corinthian girl and then turns on her own children. As love and hatred battle within her, she weeps over her children but, despite a momentary weakening of will, completes her vengeance and kills

Roman wall paintings often show scenes from Greek drama and mythology; this painting shows Medea, in Euripides' play, about to kill her children. "My friends, I am resolved to act, to slay my children quickly and depart from this land." Naples, Archeological Museum. Photo © Luciano Pedicini/Index

them. The powerful woman has found her own way of dealing with the terrors of the world. We should note that she is not punished for her horrible crime, as probably would have happened in a tragedy of Aeschylus or Sophocles.

Greek Comedy: Aristophanes

Comedy abandoned these serious themes and satirized contemporary situations and people in the real world. Almost the only comedies that have come down to us are those written by the Athenian Aristophanes, a younger contemporary of Sophocles and Euripides. Again and again he emphasized the ridiculous in individual lives as well as in society at large. Aristophanes used fantasy and burlesque to satirize the Peloponnesian War, political leaders, intellectuals—including Socrates—and the failings of democracy. Whatever his political motives in writing his satires, they sometimes exposed the folly of human behavior more devastatingly than the tragedies did. And they were particularly cutting in their depiction of the absurdities of arrogant persons in Athenian society.

The earliest of Aristophanes' eleven surviving plays is *The Acharnians* (425 B.C.), an antiwar comedy from the early years of the Peloponnesian War (Acharnae was an Athenian village). Aristophanes continued his antiwar theme in other plays, notably *Lysistrata*, which he wrote after the disastrous Athenian expedition to Syracuse. In this comedy the women of Athens, despairing of any other means of ending the long war, go on a sex strike that humiliates their blustering menfolk, and they succeed in enlisting the other women of Greece in their cause.

Aristophanes reserved some of his sharpest attacks for the democratic leaders who succeeded Pericles. In *The Knights* (424 B.C.) a general tries to persuade an ignorant sausage-seller to unseat Cleon, one of those leaders:

Sausage-Seller: Tell me this, how can I, a sausage-seller, be a big man like that?

General: The easiest thing in the world. You've got all the qualifications: low birth, marketplace training, insolence.

Sausage-Seller: I don't think I deserve it.

General: Not deserve it? It looks to me as if you've got too good a conscience. Was your father a gentleman?

Sausage-Seller: By the gods, no! My folks were scoundrels.

General: Lucky man! What a good start you've got for public life!

Sausage-Seller: But I can hardly read.

General: The only trouble is that you know anything. To be a leader of the people isn't for learned men, or honest men, but for the ignorant and vile. Don't miss the golden opportunity.[2]

Historical Writing

Drama is one way of examining the human condition; writing history is another. The constant wars in the fifth century B.C. prompted some men to seek to explain why war was their perpetual companion. They looked to the past to understand what causes war and how people behave during conflict. In so doing, they invented a new literary form: history.

Herodotus: Father of History Herodotus, a Greek from Asia Minor, is rightly called the "Father of History." In his history of the Persian Wars, he laid down forever the historian's main question: Why do events happen? The most impressive dimension of his work is his recognition that all the cultures of the ancient world were connected. Much as a modern anthropologist does,

[2] From L. S. Stavrianos, *Epic of Man to 1500*, 1970.

THUCYDIDES: THE MELIAN DIALOGUE

In 416 B.C., the Athenians mercilessly inform the people of the small island of Melos that they must join the Athenian Empire. Thucydides presents the cold logic of their demand.

Athenians: We will use no fine phrases saying, for example, that we have a right to our empire because we defeated the Persians, or that we have come against you now because of the injuries you have done us. And we ask you not to imagine that you will influence us by saying that you have never done us any harm. You know as well as we do that the strong do what they have the power to do and the weak accept what they have to accept.

Melians: So you would not agree to our being neutral, friends instead of enemies, but allies of neither side?

Athenians: No, because it is not so much your hostility that injures us; rather, if we were on friendly terms with you, our subjects would regard that as a sign of weakness in us, whereas your hatred is evidence of our power.

Melians: We trust that the gods will give us fortune as good as yours, because we are standing for what is right against what is wrong.

Athenians: Our opinion of the gods and our knowledge of men lead us to conclude that it is a general and necessary law of nature to rule wherever one can. This is not a law that we made ourselves, nor were we the first to act upon it when it was made. We found it already in existence, and we shall leave it to exist forever. We are merely acting in accordance with it, and we know that you or anybody else with the same power as ours would be acting in precisely the same way.

From *Thucydides, The Peloponnesian War*, Rex Warner (tr.), Penguin Classics, 1954, 1980, pp. 403–404 abridged.

Herodotus described the character of the several peoples of the Near East, without the help of any earlier narrative. He explained the Persian Empire as the work of powerful monarchs, constantly striving for a larger realm. He showed his Greek heritage with his verdict that the Greek triumph was the inevitable triumph of a free society over a despotic one. He also brought the supernatural into his work through dreams, omens, and oracles, and he declared that the Athenians—"next to the gods"—were mainly responsible for the victory.

Thucydides: Analyst of War   The Athenian Thucydides is said to have heard Herodotus read from his work, and this experience may have inspired him to write the history of the Peloponnesian War, in which he served as an officer. He did not live to finish his work, which breaks off in 411 B.C., seven years before the end of the war. He has a narrower theme than Herodotus, but he is the more profound inquirer into causation and evidence.

He brought to bear on events the kind of logical analysis that philosophers developed in the late fifth century. He presented a series of speeches and debates about various issues and decisions, in which the speakers sweep aside all arguments based on justice and mercy. It is by no means clear that Thucydides himself rejected compassion, but he presented the whole war as a cold pursuit of power.

In his view, the Athenian state was in good order under Pericles because he could control the Athenian democracy. His successors, by contrast, played to the masses with disastrous results, including above all sending a force to Sicily in 415 B.C. Thucydides combined accuracy and concentration on detail with descriptive powers that rival those of the dramatists and were perhaps drawn from them. No reader can avoid feeling a chill when reading his clinical description of the plague that attacked Athens in 430 B.C. or the shattering defeat of the proud armada that sailed against Syracuse. He is the undisputed master among ancient historians, and for gripping narrative power and philosophical breadth he remains unequaled (see "Thucydides: The Melian Dialogue," above).

The Family in Classical Greece

Recovering Greek Attitudes   Greek society assigned certain roles to people according to their sex. Men were the rulers and leaders, and in no Greek state did women vote or hold offices, with the exception of certain priesthoods. They were, however, citizens and so could not be violated or sold into slavery.

Thus, roughly half the citizens of Greek poleis must have been women, but to reconstruct their place in Greek society is not easy, mainly because nearly all our sources were written by men. Probably there was no

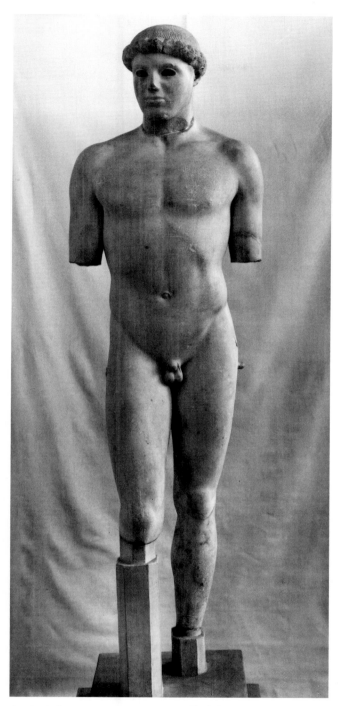

An Attic kouros, or young man, called the Kritios boy, leaning on one foot; it shows a movement away from the severe toward a more natural style.
Hirmer Fotoarchiv

slave, while the Trojan hero Hector honors and cherishes his wife, Andromache; equally, in Homer's *Odyssey* Penelope, the wife of the absent Odysseus, is an admired model of wisdom and fidelity.

As we look from the idealized figures of Homer to the women of the polis, we see a much less benign attitude toward women. Certainly there was no equality between the sexes. A woman was always under the control of her **kyrios,** or master—at first her father, then her husband, then her father again if she became divorced or widowed. Her father gave her in marriage with a dowry, normally at about age fifteen, to a man perhaps ten to fifteen years her senior. Xenophon describes the education of a young wife in obedience and household skills, and the picture is like the training of a young animal (see "The Training of a Wife," p. 76).

Women and Property A wife's main duty, apart from managing the household, was to provide a male heir in order to maintain the family's hold over its property. In Athens, if the family had no male heir, the property came to a daughter, but she held it only temporarily. The heiress must then be married to the nearest available male relative, thus preventing the property from passing from the family. In this respect Athenian women were far less privileged than, for example, Egyptian women. Yet the duty of women to provide heirs did not cause Greeks to think of a woman as a mere breeding machine. On the contrary, the power, possessed only by women, to bear children seems to have made them objects not only to be cherished but also to be feared.

Restrictions in Women's Lives Widows and heiresses had to be given new husbands in order to maintain control of property within the family. Since women could thus be transferred from one husband to another, Greeks were not sure about their fidelity; adultery by women was a grave threat because it could bring outsiders into the family and threaten the preservation of property within the correct line. It is always clear who a child's mother is, but doubts can exist about the identity of a father. Such suspicions may partly account for some passages by Greek poets and philosophers in which women are viewed as undisciplined, emotionally unstable, and sexually inexhaustible. By contrast, infidelity in men was looked on as permissible.

To preserve a woman's fidelity, the door of the home was considered her proper frontier, but such restrictions were not possible for families without servants; yet even when women did go out, they were normally accompanied by a handmaiden, a slave, or a relative. The statesman Pericles, in a speech given him by Thucydides, says that the most honored woman is she who is least talked about in society.

single view of women in Greek society, as we can see from our oldest source, the Homeric poems. In the *Iliad,* the story opens as Achilles and Agamemnon quarrel over a concubine who is nothing but a sexual

THE TRAINING OF A WIFE

The Athenian writer-soldier Xenophon wrote a work (The Deconomicus) in which one Ischomachus explains how he trained his wife in her duties. He instructs her as follows.

"Your duty will be to remain indoors and send out those servants whose work is outside, and superintend those who are to work indoors, and to receive the incomings, and distribute so much of them as must be spent, and watch over so much as is to be kept in store, and take care that the sum laid by for a year be not spent in a month. And when wool is brought to you, you must see that cloaks are made for those that want them. You must see too that the dry corn [i.e., grain] is in good condition for making food. You will have to see that any servant who is ill is cared for.

"There are other duties peculiar to you that are pleasant to perform. It is delightful to teach spinning to a maid who had no knowledge of it when you received her; to take in hand a girl who is ignorant of housekeeping and service; to have the power of rewarding the discreet and useful members of your household, and of punishing anyone who turns out to be a rogue. The better partner you prove to me and the better housewife to our children, the greater will be the honour paid to you in our home."

From *Xenophon*, E. C. Marchant (tr.), Vol. 4, Harvard University Press, 1979, 7. 35–42 abridged.

Some Greek thinkers were able to rise above such a limiting view of a woman's place. Plato, in his *Republic*, recommended that women share in education with men, although he stopped short of what we would call a truly liberal attitude regarding sexual equality.

The Power of Women in Myth In several ways, then, men could feel uncertain about their control over women. If we have rightly understood some of this uncertainty, we may be near to understanding why women of Greek drama such as Clytemnestra, Antigone, and Medea are such powerful characters, far stronger and more dangerous than the men in Greek plays. Again, in mythology the Furies, who could drive people mad, were female; Greeks tried to appease them by calling them the "kindly ones." Female too were the powers called Nemesis and Ate, which brought punishing destruction on those who became too arrogant and self-confident; so were the three Fates, who spun out the thread of life and cut it off at the end.

Men, Women, and Sex Men, unlike women, were allowed to find sex where they liked. Elegant single women were paid companions at men's social affairs; the most famous courtesan of all, Aspasia, had a long affair with the statesman Pericles and bore him a son. Only these women could participate in the refined intellectual life of the city. Poorer women worked, for example, as seamstresses, nurses, or sellers in the market. Prostitutes, who were normally slaves or foreigners, were not difficult to find; a man might have sex with a slave whom he owned. Homosexuality between men

was tolerated and is often illustrated in ribald scenes on Greek pottery.

Yet we must not expect perfect consistency where such emotions are at play. By modern Western standards, and even some ancient ones, Greek women suffered severe restrictions. On the other hand, women whose households had slaves may have had to work less than many women in modern emancipated societies. Our museums contain copious statues of beautiful Greek maidens. And many of the most revered deities are women: Athena, who was respected for her warlike nature and never had lovers in myth, was also the protecting goddess to the Athenians, who held her in affection and built for her one of the world's architectural masterpieces, the Parthenon. Aphrodite, who could involve human beings in ruin through sexual passion, was treasured as the model of ideal beauty and was so portrayed in hundreds of statues.

It is impossible to estimate in scientific terms the emotional love between Greek men and women. The recommendation of Plutarch, that a man should sleep with his wife three times a month, suggests that love played only a modest part in marriage. On the other hand, gravestones from many poleis show the affection in which some women were held; typically, a woman is seated, members of her family stand nearby, and a son or her husband takes her hand in a quiet farewell.

THE RISE OF MACEDONIA

The Peloponnesian War had caused terrible losses in manpower for the Greek city-states. Instead of the

Unknown, perhaps a pupil of Lysippos
STATUE OF A VICTORIOUS YOUTH, LAST QUARTER OF FOURTH CENTURY B.C.
Surviving bronze statues from Greece are rare.
Bronze, H: 151.5 cm. Collection of the J. Paul Getty Museum, Malibu, California (77.AB.30)

needed healing period, there followed decades of interstate warfare—the perennial tragedy of Greece—that further weakened the poleis. These battles opened the way for an old kingdom from the north of Greece, Macedonia, to become the leading power in the Greek world. Moreover, the Macedonian king Alexander the Great drove the Greek language and many features of Greek culture deeply into Asia Minor and Egypt.

The Decline of the Independent Poleis

Athens had lost the Peloponnesian War and Sparta had imposed on the Athenians a puppet regime, known as

the Thirty Tyrants, in 404 B.C.; but within a few months popular opposition swept this group away. As the Athenians sought to regain power, they revived their naval league in 394 B.C., though with many fewer members than it had had in the fifth century. But their arrogance had not subsided. Despite their promises to respect the independence of the league's members, the Athenians began to demand tribute from them as they had done under the Delian League. Rebellions followed, and this second league collapsed about 355 B.C.

By now there were no longer only two dominant cities in Greece. The polis of Thebes was becoming an important power, siding now with Athens, now with Sparta, in a series of never-ending quarrels. There was no clear trend in these struggles except that the constant intrigue and war, spanning several decades, drained the energies of all the antagonists. In 371 B.C. the brilliant Theban general Epaminondas won a victory over Sparta and thus finally exploded the long-held belief in Greece that the Spartan infantry was invincible. The Thebans liberated Sparta's slaves, the helots, and helped them to found their own city, called Messene, in the Peloponnese.

The Spartans thus lost much of their territory and many of the slaves who had worked their land. A shortage of manpower accelerated the decline in Sparta's strength. Aristotle informs us about 335 B.C. that Spartan armies in the field had fewer than one thousand men, rather than the four or five thousand who had gone into battle during the wars of the fifth century. Epaminondas himself died in another battle near Sparta in 362 B.C., and no comparable leader in any polis took his place. The era of independent city-states was all but over, doomed by the constant wars of the fourth century.

Philip II of Macedonia

The Rise of Philip   Macedonia, a kingdom in northern Greece, emerged as a leading power under an ambitious, resourceful king, Philip II, who reigned between 359 and 336 B.C. With shrewd and ruthless political skill Philip developed his kingdom, built up a powerful army, and planned a program of conquest.

Using both aggression and diplomacy, Philip added poleis and large territories to his kingdom and extended his influence into central Greece. The great Athenian orator Demosthenes (384–322 B.C.), in a series of fiery speeches called **Philippics,** beginning in 351, called on his countrymen to recognize the danger from Macedonia and prepare to make war against it. But by the time the Athenians responded, it was too late to halt the Macedonian advance.

Philip's Victory and Death   Philip won a decisive battle against Athens and several other poleis at Chaeronea

MAP 3.1 MACEDONIA UNDER PHILIP II, 359–336 B.C.
King Philip II greatly increased the territory controlled by the once isolated kingdom of Macedonia. He brought his power southward into central Greece and greatly extended his domain to the north. What was the eastern limit of his kingdom?
◆ For an online version, go to www.mhhe.com/chambers9 > chapter 3 > book maps

in 338 B.C. All the city-states of southern Greece, except isolated Sparta, now lay at his mercy. He could have devastated many of them, including Athens, but his sense of tactics warned him not to do so. Instead, he gathered the more important poleis into an obedient alliance called the League of Corinth, which recognized Philip as its leader and agreed to follow him in his next project, an invasion of Persia.

But before Philip could open his Persian war, he was murdered in 336 B.C. by one of his officers who apparently had a personal quarrel with the king. Some historians have wondered whether Philip's wife or his son,

Alexander, may have been involved in a plot to kill Philip and put Alexander on the throne; but tempting as such speculations may be, the sources do not give them clear support.

Alexander the Great

The empire built by Philip now passed to his son, Alexander III (r. 336–323 B.C.), known as Alexander the Great, and never has a young warrior prince made more effective use of his opportunities. During his brief reign Alexander created the largest empire the an-

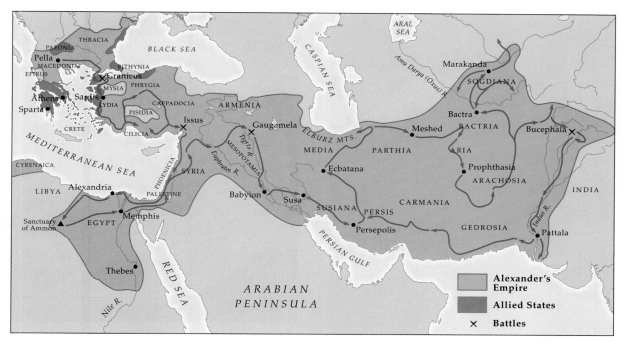

MAP 3.2 THE EMPIRE OF ALEXANDER THE GREAT AND THE ROUTE OF HIS CONQUESTS
Alexander formed the largest empire known down to his own time. He even conquered some territory across the Indus River in India. What were the two major Persian cities near the Persian Gulf?
◆ For an online version, go to www.mhhe.com/chambers9 > chapter 3 > book maps

cient world had known and, more than any other man, became responsible for the eastward expansion of the Greek world.

Alexander's Invasion of Persia   In the next year, 335, a rumor of Alexander's death caused a democratic revolution in the city of Thebes. Alexander marched on Thebes and sacked it with the utmost brutality, destroying every building except temples and the house of the poet Pindar. Having thus warned the Greek cities against any further rebellions, Alexander began the invasion of the Persian Empire. The Persia that he attacked was a much weaker state than the one that had conquered Babylon or the one that Xerxes had led against the Greeks in 480 B.C. Intrigue and disloyalty had weakened the administration of the empire. Moreover, the king, Darius III, had to rely on Greek mercenary soldiers as the one disciplined element in his infantry, for native troops were mainly untrained. The weakness of Persia helps explain Alexander's success, but in no way does it diminish his reputation as one of the supreme generals in history. His campaigns were astonishing combinations of physical courage, strategic insight, and superb leadership.

Alexander in Egypt   Alexander swept the Persians away from the coast of Asia Minor and in 332 B.C.

drove them out of Egypt, a land they had held for two centuries. The Egyptians welcomed him as a liberator and recognized him as their pharaoh. He appointed two Egyptians to administer the country, along with a Greek to manage the finances; he was to follow this pattern of dividing power throughout his reign.

While he was in Egypt (also in 332), Alexander founded the city of Alexandria. He intended this city to serve as a link between Macedonia and the valley of the Nile, and he had it laid out in the grid pattern typical of Greek city planning. Although he did not live to see it, Alexandria remained one of the conqueror's most enduring legacies: a great metropolis throughout history.

Victories and Death of Alexander   In the next season, 331 B.C., Alexander fought Darius III at Gaugamela, winning a complete victory that guaranteed he would face little further opposition in Persia. Darius III was murdered by disloyal officers in 330 B.C., and Alexander assumed the title of king of Persia. Again he followed his policy of placing some areas in the control of natives: Babylonia, for example, was given to a Persian named Mazaeus.

The expedition had now achieved its professed aim; yet Alexander, for whom conquest was self-expression, continued to make war. During the next few years he campaigned as far east as India, where he crossed the

THE VENUS OF CYRENE IN ROME (EARLY THIRD CENTURY B.C.)
A most elegant, graceful depiction of ideal female beauty.
Scala/Art Resource, NY

THE HEAD OF ALEXANDER THE GREAT IN HEROIC PROFILE
The obverse of a silver coin issued by Lysimachus, one of Alexander's bodyguards, who after his master's death became king of Thrace.
Museum of Fine Arts, Boston. Gift of Mrs. George M. Brett. Reproduced with permission. © 2001 Museum of Fine Arts, Boston. All Rights Reserved.

The Reputation of Alexander   Alexander is a figure of such stature and power that he defies easy interpretation, and even today radically different biographies are written about this most famous man in Greek history. Part of our difficulty is that our best narrative source for his life, the Greek historian Arrian, lived four centuries after Alexander's death, and Arrian, for all his merits, was not the kind of probing historian who might have given us a rounded psychological portrait of the king. Yet it is clear that along with Alexander's courage and drive, perhaps as their necessary accompaniment, came a personality sometimes barely containing a raging animal. He ordered the execution of a number of his friends for supposedly being aware of conspiracies against him; another friend he murdered himself in a sudden fury. On the other hand, Arrian tells the moving story of Alexander's pouring a cup of water, offered him by his parched troops, into the desert because he refused to drink if his men could not.

Alexander's Rule   Alexander established democratic regimes in the Greek states in Asia Minor that he had freed from Persian rule. But he also established some policies that brought Persians and their ways into his

Indus River (see map 3.2), and finally, in 326 B.C., he began his march back. But at Babylon in 323 B.C., he caught a fever after a bout of heavy drinking, and within a few days he died, not yet thirty-three.

A scene from the magnificent "Alexander Sarcophagus" found at Sidon, now in the Archaeological Museum, Istanbul; fourth century B.C. Alexander, left, is shown hunting, accompanied by a Persian. Although we have no reason to think Alexander was ever buried in this sarcophagus, the scene symbolizes Alexander's heroism and virility and calls attention to his conquest of the Persian Empire.
C. M. Dixon

regime. We have seen that he used Persians as administrators. He also had young Persians trained in Macedonian style and even enrolled them within Macedonian regiments. These measures were intended to strengthen his empire by enlisting support from natives. Some historians have gone further and have declared that Alexander had a vision of the unity of the human race and was trying to establish an empire in which different peoples would live in harmony as within one family, but this view is widely, and rightly, rejected as sentimental and too idealistic.

Other historians focus on his acts of cruelty and vindictiveness and see him as a paranoiac tyrant. In any case, no portrait of him should overlook his patronage of scholarship, which extended even to his bringing scientists and geographers with him as he invaded Persia. His foundation, Alexandria, became the intellectual center of the next age. However we interpret Alexander, he has remained the prototype of a world conqueror. Some of his successors sought to maintain his memory by putting his portrait on their own coins, and even Roman emperors issued medallions portraying him, as if to borrow his glory and power for their often threatened reigns.

THE HELLENISTIC AGE (323–30 B.C.)

The Classical Age of Greek civilization began about 500 B.C. and ended in 323 B.C., with the death of Alexander the Great. The next period, the **Hellenistic Age,** began with that event and extended to the death of Cleopatra VII of Egypt in 30 B.C. During this period the Greeks carried their culture throughout the Near East in the movement known as Hellenization. Broadly speaking, Hellenization refers to the increasing use of the Greek language and customs among non-Greeks. This movement had begun well before the death of Alexander, but his invasion of the Persian Empire gave a decided stimulus to such a widespread acceptance of Greek culture. The Greeks in turn received legacies, especially in religion, from the peoples whom they met in this age.

The Dissolution of Alexander's Empire

New Kingdoms   Alexander's empire was shattered almost at once after his death, as his generals seized various parts for themselves. By about 275 B.C., after years of warfare and diplomatic intrigue, three large kingdoms emerged. These were the kingdom of Macedonia and its territories in Greece; Syria, formed by the Macedonian Seleucus; and Egypt, governed by the Macedonian Ptolemy and his successors. A fourth kingdom was formed about 260 B.C. around the city of Pergamum in western Asia Minor (see map 3.3).

In the Hellenistic kingdoms the richer classes gained more and more influence, but they sometimes used their wealth to endow spectacular temples and other buildings and to sponsor games and festivals. We may guess that they were acting partly to indulge in prideful display, partly to gain favorable public opinion. In Athens, for instance, Attalus II of Pergamum (r. 158–138 B.C.) donated a magnificent stoa, or colonnaded building, that was rebuilt in A.D. 1956.

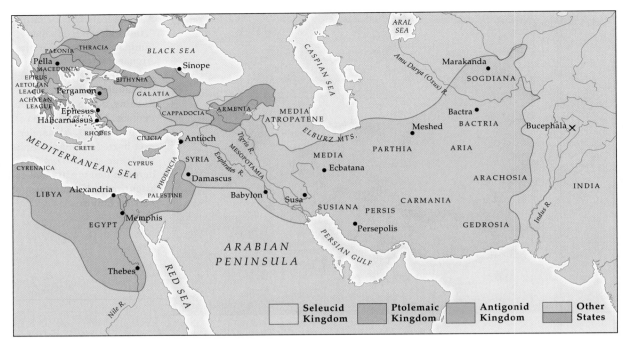

MAP 3.3 HELLENISTIC KINGDOMS AFTER ALEXANDER, CA. 240 B.C.
After the death of Alexander, three of his generals (Antigonus, Seleucus, and Ptolemy) became rulers of large portions of his empire and formed kingdoms of their own. A fourth kingdom, Pergamon or Pergamum, appeared about 260 B.C. Which kingdom controlled the area of Palestine about 240 B.C.?
◆ For an online version, go to www.mhhe.com/chambers9 > chapter 3 > book maps

Kingdoms and Leagues   The subsequent history of these kingdoms is one of continual warfare until they were all eventually absorbed by the Roman Republic. The king of Macedonia controlled northern Greece. The poleis in the south retained their autonomy, and some of them formed defensive leagues to protect their independence from the monarchy. The most influential were the Aetolian League in western Greece and the Achaean League on the northern coast of the Peloponnese.

These leagues tried to strengthen themselves by awarding citizenship in the league to all citizens of their member cities; but this principle of confederation for mutual security arrived too late in Greek history to take firm root before Greece fell to the expanding Roman Republic. As to the Egyptians and inhabitants of the Near East, they had long seen their rulers as divine or semidivine beings, and the Hellenistic kings in these areas exploited this tendency and established themselves as absolute monarchs who owned the kingdom.

Hellenistic Rulers   Remarkably, considering the military roots of these kingdoms, the Hellenistic Age witnessed the reemergence of women as rulers. Their power first became evident in Macedonia, where Olympias, the mother of Alexander, was a more important political figure than any other woman in classical Greece. The most famous and skillful of all Hellenistic queens was Cleopatra of Egypt, who manipulated such Roman military leaders as Julius Caesar and Mark Antony to the advantage of her kingdom.

Hellenistic monarchs ruled through strong armies and large bureaucracies, and their systems of taxation were extremely efficient. Certain products, such as oil in Egypt, were royal monopolies and could be traded only at official prices. Greeks usually held the chief public offices in the army and bureaucracy, and rulers did allow some democratic institutions, such as a town council, to function in Near Eastern cities, but the autonomy of these cities was limited to local affairs. The king collected tribute from the cities and controlled all foreign policy, and he alone granted and could cancel such rights of self-government as the cities enjoyed.

Economic Life

Agriculture and Industry   One of the sharpest contrasts between the classical and Hellenistic worlds was the scale of economic activity. In classical Greece,

Panels from the altar to Zeus at Pergamum, in the Pergamon-Museum, Berlin, showing gods in combat with giants. Greek art preferred abstraction to reality, and such scenes probably represent the triumph of Greek civilization over non-Greek peoples. The violence and dramatizing are in the "baroque" tradition of Hellenistic art of the second century B.C.
C. M. Dixon

farmers worked small plots of land, and industry and commerce were ventures of small entrepreneurs. In the Hellenistic states of Egypt and the Seleucid Kingdom, vast estates predominated. Industry and trade operated throughout the Near East on a larger scale than ever before in the ancient world, requiring the services of bankers and other financial agents.

The Hellenistic world prospered as ambitious Greeks, emigrating from their homeland to make their fortunes, brought new vigor to the economies of Egypt and the Near East. They introduced new crops and new techniques in agriculture to make production more efficient. For example, Greeks had long cultivated vines, and they now enhanced the wines of Egypt. At the same time, they improved and extended the irrigation system and could thus devote more acreage to pasturing animals, which provided leather and cloth for the people and horses for the cavalry.

Hellenistic Cities   Agriculture remained the major industry in the vast lands of the new kingdoms, but it was in the numerous Greek cities founded by Alexander and his successors that the civilization that we call Hellenistic took form. Most of these new cities were in western Asia, in the Seleucid Kingdom. Alexander had founded the brilliant city of Alexandria, in Egypt, but the Ptolemies who ruled Egypt did not follow his example by founding many cities. They considered a docile, rustic civilization far easier to control than citizens of a politically active urban society.

Some Hellenistic cities were magnificently ornate and spectacular. Besides their political institutions, the Greeks brought from their homeland many of the amenities of polis life—temples, theaters, gymnasiums, and other public buildings. Pergamum, an outstanding example of city planning, contained a stupendous altar to Zeus, a renowned library, and a theater high above the main city with a superb view. The city may have had as many as one hundred thousand inhabitants (under the Roman Empire its population was about two hundred thousand), while Alexandria, the largest of all, had at least a half million people.

Local families in the upper classes copied Greek ways and sent their children to Greek schools. Moreover, a version of Greek, koiné ("common") Greek, became an international tongue. Now, for the first time, people could travel to virtually any city in the Mediterranean world and make themselves understood.

Literature, Art, and Science

Libraries and Scholars   The most significant literary achievements in the Hellenistic Age were in the field of scholarship. The kings of Egypt took pride in constructing a huge library in Alexandria that probably contained, by 200 B.C., a half-million papyrus rolls. Along with the library, they built the Museum, a kind of research institute, where literary, historical, and scientific studies flourished, each employing its own experts. One of the main interests of literary scholars in Alexandria was the literature of the classical period, and among their achievements was the standardization of the Greek text of Homer. By comparing the many versions that had been handed down in manuscripts over the centuries, scholars were able to establish the text on which modern editions of Homer are based.

The specialization of scholars was characteristic of the growing professionalism of the age. The citizen of fifth-century Athens could be a farmer, a politician, and a soldier at the same time, but now each of these roles was filled by a professional. The army consisted of professional soldiers, while professional bureaucrats ran the government.

A New Spirit in Art   Hellenistic rulers also wanted to glorify their cities and provided generous subsidies for art and architecture. The architecture of the age sometimes emphasized size and grandeur, as compared with the simplicity and human scale of classical architecture. Thus, the Altar of Zeus from Pergamum, now in Berlin, included a great stairway, flanked by a frieze four hundred feet long. The figures on the frieze, typical of Hellenistic sculpture, are carved in high relief, with an almost extravagant drama and emotionalism

BRONZE STATUE OF A BOXER FROM ROME, SECOND CENTURY B.C.
Greek sculptors had abandoned statues of ideal beauty and were now experimenting with scenes of frank realism. Note the boxer's battered face and bandaged hands.
Scala/Art Resource, NY

that make them seem to burst out of the background. Hellenistic sculpture also differed from that of the classical period through its devotion to realism. Instead of creating figures of ideal perfection, artists now showed individuality in faces and bodies (see picture of bronze statue of boxer), even depicting physical imperfection or frank ugliness.

Hellenistic Science   Advances in the field of science drew strength from the cross-fertilization of cultures in the Hellenistic Age. The Greeks had long speculated about the nature of the universe, and the Near East had an even longer scientific tradition, particularly in the fields of astronomy and mathematics. After Alexander's conquests joined the two cultures, other conditions favored scientific advance: the increased professionalism of the age, the use of Greek as an international language, and the facilities of the Museum in Alexandria. The result was a golden age of science that was not surpassed until the seventeenth century.

Euclid's Geometric Theorems

Unlike their eastern neighbors, Greeks had a strong desire for theoretical understanding, even beyond the solving of immediate mathematical and engineering problems. Their work in the realm of theory descends from their skill in philosophic debate.

In mathematics, Euclid (home unknown, about 300 B.C.) compiled a textbook that is still the basis for the study of plane geometry. Some of his theorems were already known, and others (for example, his demonstration that nonparallel lines must meet somewhere) may seem obvious. His accomplishment was to construct a succession of elegant proofs for these theorems, each based on earlier proofs, starting with the simple proposition that the shortest distance between two points is a straight line. The analytical method of his proofs is a characteristic of Greek thought, for Greek philosophers believed that knowing something entailed being able to prove it. The restatement of Euclid's theorems through the study of geometry in schools around the world has made him perhaps the most widely read Greek author.

Archimedes: Advanced Mathematics and Engineering

The greatest mathematician of antiquity—indeed, one of the greatest ever, in the class of Newton and Einstein—was Archimedes of Syracuse, who also lived during the Hellenistic era (ca. 287–212 B.C.). He calculated the value of *pi* (the ratio between the circumference and diameter of a circle); he developed a system for expressing immensely large numbers, by using 100 million as the base (as we use 10); and he discovered the ratio between the volumes of a cylinder and a sphere within it, namely, 3:2. In a testament to his love of theoretical knowledge, he wanted this proportion engraved on his tombstone.

Archimedes was also a pioneer in physics; he demonstrated that a floating body will sink in a liquid only to the point at which it displaces its own weight. He understood the principle of using the lever for lifting massive weights and is said to have proclaimed, "Give me a place where I can stand and I will lift the earth" (that is, standing outside the earth entirely and with a long enough lever). He also invented the water screw, still used for irrigation in Egypt. As the Romans besieged Syracuse in 212 B.C., he devised engines to fight them off; but, tragically, he was murdered by a Roman soldier as the city fell—while he sat drawing a mathematical figure in the sand.

Aristarchus and the Orbit of the Earth

About 280 B.C., Aristarchus of Samos, an astronomer and mathematician, advanced a heliocentric theory of the movement of the planets. The view that the earth revolves around the sun was not new, but Aristarchus refined it by stating that the earth revolves on its own axis while it, together with the other planets, circles the sun. Not until the sixteenth century did astronomers prove the soundness of Aristarchus' system; meanwhile, the Greek astronomic tradition continued to follow an older geocentric theory, which held that the earth was the center of the solar system and that the sun revolved around it. The false geocentric theory was, however, the basis for the most important Hellenistic text on astronomy, the *Almagest* of Ptolemy of Alexandria (about A.D. 140). This book systematized the Greek study of astronomy and remained the accepted text on the subject for more than one thousand years.

Other Mathematical Discoveries

Hellenistic scientists also made important advances in the realm of measurements. Hipparchus calculated the length of the average lunar month to within one second of today's accepted figure. Eratosthenes of Cyrene about 225 B.C. computed the circumference of the earth to be about twenty-eight thousand miles, only three thousand miles more than the actual figure. Other scientists worked out the division of time into hours, minutes, and seconds and of circles into degrees, minutes, and seconds.

Philosophy and Religion

Philosophies of Comfort

The change in lifestyle from the relative security of the polis to the increasing uncertainties of a larger world shifted the direction of Greek philosophy. Plato and Aristotle had been philosophers of the polis in the sense that they were concerned with the individual's role in the intimate world of the city-state; the ideal state in their theories would have only a few thousand citizens. But when the city-state came to be governed by a large kingdom headed by a remote ruler, individual men and women could hardly influence its policies even though they were caught up in its wars and its many changes of fortune.

Moreover, the large Hellenistic cities lacked the cohesiveness, the sense of belonging among citizens, that had made the classical poleis internally united. In such conditions, philosophers sought means of accommodation with the larger Hellenistic world that was shaping their lives. They tried to provide people with guidance in their personal lives and were less concerned about the nature of the political framework. Thus, the two most important schools of Hellenistic philosophy, Epicureanism and Stoicism, were philosophies designed to provide comfort and reassurance for the individual human being.

Epicurus and Atomism

Epicurus of Samos (341–270 B.C.), who taught in Athens, believed that people should strive above all for tranquillity, which he sought to provide through the atomic theory of Democritus. Our bodies and souls, Epicurus taught, are made up of atoms that cohere only for our lifetimes. When we die, the atoms will be redistributed into the universe again, and nothing of us will remain behind to suffer any desire for the life we have lost. Because death therefore holds no terrors, we should concern ourselves only with leading pleasurable lives, above all avoiding physical and mental pain. Sensuality, gluttony, and passionate love, in Epicurus' view, are equally unrewarding, since they may lead to disappointment and pain. Thus, the wise person withdraws from the world to study philosophy and enjoy the companionship of a few friends. Some later Epicureans came close to advocating an almost heedless pursuit of pleasure, but such was not the message of Epicurus, whose philosophy was intended as a powerful antidote to anxiety and suffering.

Zeno and the Universe of Stoicism

Zeno of Cyprus, who was a contemporary of Epicurus, taught a different approach to life's problems. He founded a philosophical school known as Stoicism, so named because he taught his pupils in a building in Athens called the Stoa. Zeno was a man of Semitic ancestry, and the fact that he taught at Athens is a notable example of the mixing of cultures that took place in the Hellenistic Age. A later Stoic, Chrysippus of Soli, stated Stoicism in its best-known form: One must act in accordance with nature, choosing one's actions with attention to reason. Such a program will lead one to virtue. A successful life includes pleasure; good health is desirable, provided one uses it in the pursuit of virtue. If one acts in accordance with nature, one cannot be other than happy.

To **Stoics,** the universe was wholly created and held together by a force sometimes called fire, sometimes *pneuma* or "breath." At certain intervals, the universe is destroyed by fire, but it is born again, and we are reborn with it. Because a single divine plan governs the universe, to find happiness one must act in harmony with this plan. One should be patient in adversity, for adversity is a necessary part of the divine plan and one can do nothing to change it. By cultivating a sense of duty and self-discipline, people can learn to accept their fate; they will then become immune to earthly anxieties and will achieve inner freedom and tranquillity.

Ethical Duties of the Stoics

The Stoics did not advocate withdrawal from the world, for they believed that all people, as rational beings, belong to one family. Moreover, to ensure justice for all, the rational person should discover his or her place in the world and consider it a duty to participate in public affairs.

The Stoics advanced ideas that were to have a profound influence on later Western history, especially as they were interpreted in the Roman and Christian visions of civilization: the concept that all humanity is part of a universal family; the virtues of tolerance; and the need for self-discipline, public service, and compassion for the less fortunate members of the human race. Stoicism is thus part of a great intellectual revolution that led some thinkers to consider similarities among humans more important than differences.

Again, while most earlier Greeks had accepted without question the institution of slavery, the Stoics believed that the practice of exploiting others corrupted the owner (the slave could endure bondage by achieving inner freedom). Stoicism became the most influential philosophy among the educated of the Hellenistic Age and achieved great influence among the Romans, who adopted with conviction the ideals of discipline and fulfillment of public and private duty.

New Religions

The search for meaning in life preoccupied all levels of Hellenistic society, but none so painfully as the great masses of the poor. The answers of philosophy were addressed to an intellectual elite: wealthy scholars, as it were, meditating in the study. But the poor—lacking the education, leisure, and detachment for such a pursuit—looked elsewhere for spiritual and emotional sustenance in their daily encounters with the problems of life. For many, religion answered their need for escape and consolation.

Among the new religious practices were the Near Eastern mystery cults that had some features in common as a result of the frequent intermingling of cultures in the cosmopolitan Near East. They are called mystery cults because they centered on the worship of a savior whose death and resurrection would redeem the sins of humanity; their rituals were secret, known only to the participants, and were elaborate, often wildly emotional; and they nourished hope by promising an afterlife that would compensate for the rigors of life on earth. One of the most popular mystery cults was the worship of the Egyptian deities Isis and Osiris. In Egyptian mythology, Osiris had been murdered and dismembered but was reassembled and saved by Isis, his devoted wife; he then became the god of the underworld. Thus, the myth suggested that its followers might also attain salvation and life after death.

Summary

All these political, scientific, and intellectual explorations were parts of the legacy of Alexander, the Macedonian who brought Greek civilization and the Greek language into the world beyond the Mediterranean Sea. Greek was to be the language in which the New Testament was written, and therefore some historians have also seen his campaigns as preparing the way for Christianity and have even called Christianity his most important legacy. Be this as it may, the Greeks and Macedonians could not maintain permanent control over the remains of Alexander's empire. Not Greece but Rome became the uniting force that passed the legacy of classical civilization to medieval and then to modern Europe.

QUESTIONS FOR FURTHER THOUGHT

1. The Greeks invented historical writing. In looking at the past, what are the most important questions a historian should ask?

2. The Greek city-states and their system of alliances gave way to the rising power of Macedonia. How might the Greek states have preserved their strength and political power?

RECOMMENDED READING

Sources

*Aristotle. *The Athenian Constitution.* P. J. Rhodes (tr.). 1984. The great philosopher's brief history and description of the Athenian state, with helpful commentary.

*Arrian. *The Campaigns of Alexander the Great.* Aubrey de Slincourt (tr.). 1958. Our main source for the life of the great conqueror.

*Grene, David, and Richmond Lattimore (eds.). *The Complete Greek Tragedies.* 9 vols. 1953–1991. The best collection of modern translations.

Lefkowitz, Mary, and Maureen B. Fant. *Women's Life in Greece and Rome: A Source Book in Translation.* 1982. Translated documents and literary excerpts on all features of women's lives.

*Phillips, David D. *Athenian Political Oratory.* 2004. Sixteen speeches on political affairs including eight by Demosthenes, with historical commentary.

*Plato. *The Republic.* Desmond Lee (tr.). 1974. The central work of Greek philosophy.

*Plutarch. *Nine Greek Lives.* Robin Waterfield (tr.). 1998. Biographies of prominent statesmen and commanders, including Pericles and Alexander the Great.

*Xenophon. *A History of My Times.* Rex Warner (tr.). 1979. A narrative, often less than profound, of Greek history down to 362 B.C.

Studies

Bosworth, A. B. *Conquest and Empire: The Reign of Alexander the Great.* 1988. Now the standard treatment of Alexander's life and reign.

Cawkwell, George. *Philip of Macedon.* 1978. Macedonia before Philip II, father of Alexander, and the expansion of the kingdom.

*Dodds, E. R. *The Greeks and the Irrational.* 1951. Brilliant investigation of the Greek mind, showing its irrational and psychological complexity.

Dover, K. J. *Greek Homosexuality.* 1989. Scientific, nonsensational study of this social phenomenon. By today's leading Hellenist.

*———. *Greek Popular Morality in the Time of Plato and Aristotle.* 1994. Goes beyond the ethical doctrines of philosophers to discover the values of ordinary Greeks.

Errington, R. Malcolm. *A History of Macedonia.* Catherine Errington (tr.). 1990. Compact one-volume treatment, carrying the story down through Alexander's successors.

Garland, Robert. *The Greek Way of Life: From Conception to Old Age.* 1990. Reconstruction of normal life cycle of Greeks in classical and Hellenistic Age.

Green, Peter. *Alexander to Actium: The Historical Evolution of the Hellenistic Age.* 1990. The most comprehensive historical and cultural survey; a colossal study.

Guthrie, W. K. C. *A History of Greek Philosophy.* 6 vols. 1962–1981. Encyclopedic history, brilliant and sensitive.

Just, Roger. *Women in Athenian Law and Life.* 1989. Brief, admirably up-to-date treatment of marriage, inheritance, freedom and seclusion, and more.

*Kitto, H. D. F. *Greek Tragedy: A Literary Study.* 1969. Probably still the best general book on one of the supreme achievements of the Greeks, written without literary jargon.

Lacey, W. K. *The Family in Classical Greece.* 1984. Survey of the family in the Greek world, especially in Athens and Sparta.

Lloyd, G. E. R. *Aristotle: The Growth and Structure of His Thought.* 1968. Good survey of all areas of Aristotle's philosophy.

Long, A. A. *Hellenistic Philosophy: Stoics, Epicureans, Sceptics.* 2d ed. 1986. Readable survey of the postclassical Greek philosophers.

Miller, Stephen G. *Ancient Greek Athletics.* 2004. History and details of competition among Greeks; excellent illustrations.

Osborne, Robin. *Greece in the Making, 1200–479 B.C.* 1996. Now the most recent survey of archaic and classical Greek history. Reliable and thorough.

Pickard-Cambridge, A. W. *The Dramatic Festivals of Athens.* 2d ed. by John Gould and David M. Lewis. 1968. Detailed description of dramatic festivals, costumes, and much more.

Pomeroy, Sarah B. *Women in Hellenistic Egypt.* 1989. Especially good on the status of women in this society.

Rowe, C. J. *Plato.* 1984. Modern introduction with ample bibliography.

Sansone, David. *Greek Athletics and the Genesis of Sport.* 1988. On the place and history of games in Greek society.

Sinclair, R. K. *Democracy and Participation in Athens.* 1988. On the opportunities for average citizens to share in running the Athenian state.

*Stockton, David L. *The Classical Athenian Democracy.* 1990. Comprehensive description of the working of the state, not excessively technical.

Travlos, John. *Pictorial Dictionary of Ancient Athens.* 1980. Precise locations of and essays on all major buildings and sites in Athens.

Vlastos, Gregory. *Socrates: Ironist and Moral Philosopher.* 1991. Most important recent study of style and significance of Socrates' thought.

*Walbank, F. W. *The Hellenistic World.* 1982. The best brief survey of the period.

White, K. D. *Greek and Roman Technology.* 1984. Describes entire range of classical technology.

*Available in paperback.

"Noble" Romans, those whose ancestors had been consuls, had the right to have masks representing them carried in funeral processions. This republican noble of about 30 B.C. shows the masks of two of his ancestors.
Scala/Art Resource, NY

Chapter Four

THE ROMAN REPUBLIC

THE UNIFICATION OF ITALY (TO 264 B.C.) •
THE AGE OF MEDITERRANEAN CONQUEST (264–133 B.C.) •
THE ROMAN REVOLUTION (133–27 B.C.) • THE END OF THE ROMAN REPUBLIC •
THE FOUNDING OF THE ROMAN EMPIRE

The Greeks flourished in small, intensely competitive communities, but the Romans formed a huge, long-lived empire. The Greek historian Polybius, who lived many years in Rome, has left us his analysis of Rome's successful policy. Drawing on theories of Aristotle, he praised Rome for its mixed constitution. He saw the element of monarchy in the two Roman consuls. The Roman Senate represented oligarchy, or the rule of a few. And the Roman common people supplied the element of democracy. The state, he thought, so long as it was balanced on these three supports, could not fail to prosper and expand.

The history of Rome brings to the fore another of the themes that run through the Western experience: the use of warfare as a deliberately chosen instrument of policy. Sometimes Rome got its way through diplomacy, but when this failed, the military machine did not. An army is not a democracy but a body governed by a few experienced men—in fact, an oligarchy.

The Romans exploited the family as a force, a weapon, in society. Political power was based on the strength of a man's family and on the alliances he formed with other families. The state united first the Italian peninsula, then the whole Mediterranean basin. Finally, the Romans came to know a culture that they recognized as superior to their own: that of Greece. The poet Horace said that "Greece, once captured, conquered its captor," as Greek literature and art inspired those of Rome.

In the process of domination, a series of warlords became so powerful that, through their rivalry, they destroyed the republic and the political freedom that Rome had achieved. The response was the formation of an even more powerful autocracy, from which Europe was to descend: the Roman Empire.

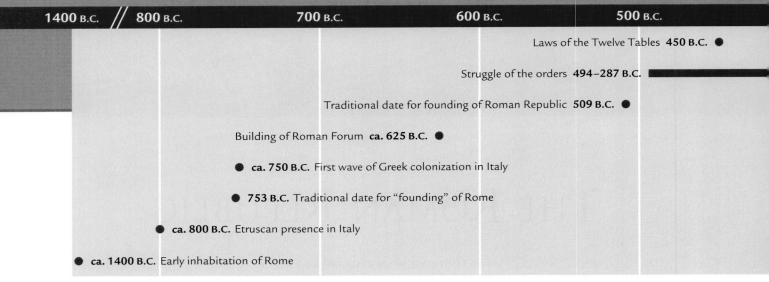

Laws of the Twelve Tables **450 B.C.** ●

Struggle of the orders **494–287 B.C.** ▬

Traditional date for founding of Roman Republic **509 B.C.** ●

Building of Roman Forum **ca. 625 B.C.** ●

● **ca. 750 B.C.** First wave of Greek colonization in Italy

● **753 B.C.** Traditional date for "founding" of Rome

● **ca. 800 B.C.** Etruscan presence in Italy

● **ca. 1400 B.C.** Early inhabitation of Rome

THE UNIFICATION OF ITALY (TO 264 B.C.)

The inhabitants of Italy greatly outnumbered those of Greece in antiquity. Unlike the Greeks, they became unified under the leadership of a single city, Rome. This movement required centuries, and during this period Rome itself was transformed from a monarchy into a republic with a solid constitution. Families were not only the binding force of the household but became the building blocks of political power. Guided by the Roman Senate, the city expanded its territory until the whole peninsula of Italy was under Roman control.

The Geography of Italy

Italy is not, like Greece, divided into many small valleys or islands. The main geographic feature is the Apennine range, which runs diagonally across Italy in the north and then turns southward to bisect the peninsula. North of the Apennines, the Po River flows through a large, fertile valley that was for centuries the home of Celtic peoples known as Gauls. The hills of Italy, unlike those of Greece, are gentle enough for pasturing. The landscape is of unsurpassed beauty; some of the best Roman poetry—by Virgil, Horace, and Catullus—hymns the delights of the land and the pleasure of farming. But the geography of Italy could also be a challenge. The mountains divide the land into sections and made the task of unifying Italy a long and arduous one.

Early Rome

The legends about the founding of Rome by Aeneas, a Trojan hero who reached Italy after the Trojan War, or by Romulus and Remus (two mythical sons of the war god Mars) are myths, so we must depend on archaeology to recover early Roman history. Pottery finds suggest that the site of Rome, along the Tiber River in the plain of Latium, was inhabited as early as 1400 B.C. Ancient scholars relied on myths to date the "founding" of Rome in 753 B.C. We need not take this date seriously as the moment at which Rome came into existence, but there must have been considerable habitation in the area by that time, especially on the seven hills that surround the city. About 625 B.C. the settlers drained the marshes below the hills and built a central marketplace, the Forum. This area was to be forever the center of Roman history.

Etruscan Origins Besides the Romans themselves, two other peoples laid the basis for Roman history. The first were the Etruscans, who actually dominated early Rome from about 625 to 509 B.C. The name *Roma* is Etruscan, and at least some of the kings of Rome, as their names show, were Etruscans. The origin of the Etruscans themselves is obscure and has provoked a famous controversy. Some ancient sources say that they were a native European people, but the Greek historian Herodotus asserts that they arrived from Asia Minor. In any case, the Etruscans appeared in Italy soon after 800 B.C., in the region north of the Tiber River known as Etruria (their name is preserved in modern Tuscany). Their language is still mostly undeciphered even though thousands of short Etruscan inscriptions exist.

The Etruscans had a technologically advanced culture and traded with Greeks and Phoenicians; Greek vases, especially, have been found in Etruscan tombs, and Etruscan art largely imitates that of the Greeks. They also bequeathed to the Romans the technique of building temples, and they introduced the worship of a triad of gods (Juno, Minerva, Jupiter) and the custom of examining the innards of animals to foretell the future.

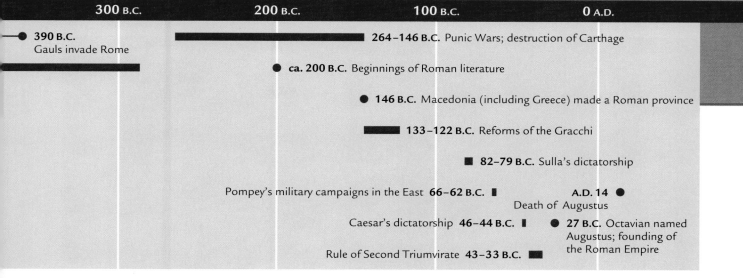

390 B.C.
Gauls invade Rome

264–146 B.C. Punic Wars; destruction of Carthage

ca. 200 B.C. Beginnings of Roman literature

146 B.C. Macedonia (including Greece) made a Roman province

133–122 B.C. Reforms of the Gracchi

82–79 B.C. Sulla's dictatorship

Pompey's military campaigns in the East **66–62 B.C.**

A.D. 14
Death of Augustus

Caesar's dictatorship **46–44 B.C.**

27 B.C. Octavian named Augustus; founding of the Roman Empire

Rule of Second Triumvirate **43–33 B.C.**

SARCOPHAGUS FROM A LATE-SIXTH-CENTURY ETRUSCAN TOMB
The reclining couple on the lid reflects the influence of Greek art on the style of the Etruscans.
Alinari/Art Resource, NY

Greek Influence　The second non-Roman people who helped shape Roman culture were the Greeks. Beginning about 750 B.C., they established some 50 poleis in southern Italy and on the island of Sicily. So numerous were the Greek cities in southern Italy that the Romans called this region *Magna Graecia* ("Great Greece") and thus gave us the name *Greeks* for the people who have always called themselves Hellenes.[1]

Greek culture from these colonies influenced the Etruscans and, in turn, the Romans. For example, from the village of Cumae, the oldest Greek colony in Italy,

[1] The name *Graikoi* (*Graeci,* or Greeks) was sometimes used, according to Aristotle (*Meteorology* 352) and other sources, for the people generally called Hellenes. The name probably comes from one or more villages in central Greece called Graia; one such place is mentioned in Homer (*Iliad* 2.498).

the Etruscans learned the Western version of the Greek alphabet and passed it on to Rome; it became the basis for the alphabet used throughout the Western world. And virtually all Roman literature is inspired by Greek models.

The Early Roman Republic

About 500 B.C. (the Romans reckoned the date as 509) Rome freed itself of its last Etruscan king and established a republic. Much of the history of the Roman Republic concerns the growth of its constitution; this was never a written document but a set of carefully observed procedures. The Roman system, like that of Sparta, had three major supports, which offset and balanced one another. First, the supreme civil and military officers were two men called **consuls.** From time to time the Romans appointed a man as **dictator,** whose authority surpassed that of the consuls, but he could not hold office longer than six months. Second, there was an advisory body of elder statesmen, the Senate. Third, there were assemblies that included all adult male citizens.

The Consuls and the Assemblies　The consuls were elected annually by the Assembly of the Centuries (or Comitia Centuriata), which was made up of the entire army divided, in theory, into 193 groups of 100 men each (that is, "centuries"); in this assembly the wealthier citizens voted first and could determine the result if most of them voted the same way. This arrangement illustrates the hierarchical and conservative instincts of the Roman mind; so does the law providing that, in cases in which the two consuls disagreed, one could block the action of the other, and the consul advocating no action prevailed. Consuls possessed a right known as **imperium,** which gave them the power to command

The art of Etruscan tombs often showed dancing and banqueting in the afterlife. This fifth-century painting, from the Tomb of the Lionesses at Tarquinia, shows two dancers with jugs of wine.
Scala/Art Resource, NY

troops and to execute any other assignments they might receive from the Senate.

There were two other assemblies, the more important being the Assembly of Tribes (Comitia Tributa), which was divided into thirty-five large voting blocs called tribes. Membership in a specific tribe was determined by a man's residence. This tribal assembly elected officers who did not command troops and therefore did not have imperium; and these magistrates, known as quaestors and aediles, looked after various financial matters and public works. The other assembly, actually the oldest of the three, was the Assembly of Curiae (Comitia Curiata), or wards of the city; this assembly met only to validate decisions taken elsewhere and gradually lost importance. In time, the Assembly of Tribes became the most active of the three assemblies and passed most of Rome's major laws.

The Senate   The Senate, which existed in the period of the kings, was the nerve center of the whole state. It

did not, in the Republic, pass laws, but it did appoint commanders, assign funds, and generally set public policy. The letters *SPQR* (standing for "The Senate and the Roman People") were carried on the army's standards and showed the preeminent status of this body. The Roman Senate house, which still stands (rebuilt about A.D. 290) in the Forum, was thus the shrine of Roman power. The senators in the Republic (usually about 300) were men who had held elected offices, and membership was for life. Their solid conservatism acted to restrain hot-headed politicians, and more than once they provided the moral leadership that saw the state through a military crisis. Indeed, the word *patres* (fathers) was often used to refer to the Senate.

The Struggle of the Orders (494–287 B.C.)

Patricians and Plebeians   Within the citizen body, the Romans established a distinction that had no parallel in any Greek state. The **patricians,** a small number of clans

This temple in central Rome, from the second century B.C., perhaps dedicated to Portunus, the god of harbors, is a typical Roman temple with a closed room for an image of the god. An altar stood in front. The columns are in the Greek Ionic order, and the temple has a deep basement, common in Etruscan building. Thus the temple unites the three cultures that went into the making of Rome.
Trëe

Many names, written by professional painters in favor of this or that candidate in elections, have been found on the walls of Pompeii, the city buried in the eruption of A.D. 79.
Alinari/Art Resource, NY

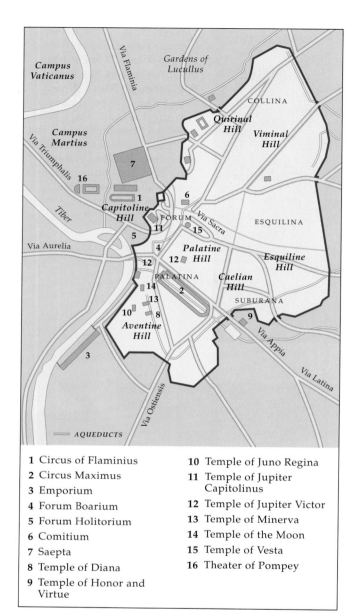

1 Circus of Flaminius
2 Circus Maximus
3 Emporium
4 Forum Boarium
5 Forum Holitorium
6 Comitium
7 Saepta
8 Temple of Diana
9 Temple of Honor and Virtue
10 Temple of Juno Regina
11 Temple of Jupiter Capitolinus
12 Temple of Jupiter Victor
13 Temple of Minerva
14 Temple of the Moon
15 Temple of Vesta
16 Theater of Pompey

Map 4.1 The City of Rome in Republican Times
The original city of Rome was built along the left bank of the Tiber River, which flows down to the Adriatic Sea. There are many hills within the city, but seven of them became famous as the seven hills on which the city stood. Which are these hills? Where is the main Forum, called simply by that name?

◆ For an online version, go to www.mhhe.com/chambers9 > chapter 4 > book maps

(about five to seven percent of the whole people), were recognized as being socially and legally superior to the vast majority, who were called **plebeians.** Ancient sources do not explain how the distinction arose; it was probably based on wealth gained from owning land and on the less easily defined criterion of social eminence.

Membership in the patrician class was based on birth (or, occasionally, adoption), and originally only patricians could belong to the Senate (the *patres*) and hold office.

The plebeians did win a number of privileges in a long process called the struggle of the orders (or classes). When the struggle ended, the plebeians could point to significant gains, but the great families were still secure in their domination. Indeed, one effect of the struggle of the orders was to make the state an even more efficient machine for conquest: The plebeians could now feel that they had a more favorable position within the system and were thus more willing to fight for their country.

Concessions to the Plebeians   The plebeians' first victory in the struggle came in 494 B.C., when they evidently threatened to secede from the state.[2] They now obtained the right to elect annually two men, called **tribunes,** to represent them; the number eventually rose to ten. The powers of the tribunes reveal the Roman genius for political compromise in the interests of a united state. The patricians evidently recognized that spokesmen for the people were a necessary evil, and oaths were exchanged that made it a religious crime to violate or injure the body of a tribune. The "sacrosanctity" of the tribunes allowed them to interfere in any action, since no one could lay hands on them. Out of this protected status arose the famous veto power of the tribunes (sometimes called *intercession*); they could forbid any magistrate from acting and could even arrest consuls. Such power might have threatened to cause anarchy, but in fact, because it reassured the plebeians, it proved to be a stabilizing influence.

Other concessions to the plebeians included the publication of a code of laws, in 450 B.C., on the so-called twelve wooden tablets, and the right, in 445, to intermarry with patricians. Intermarriage created a patrician-plebeian aristocracy that replaced the original one restricted to patricians alone.

The Licinian-Sextian Laws   The plebeians won their greatest victory in 367 B.C. Two tribunes, Licinius and Sextius, carried a bill that reserved one consulship every year to a plebeian (there were occasional exceptions, but the principle remained). Their bill also created another office—that of praetor, a kind of assistant consul who also held imperium. His main duty, probably taken away from the consuls, was to be the chief officer for cases at civil law. Eventually in the Republic eight praetors were elected every year, but there were never more than two consuls at a time.

[2] The sources give contradictory dates for, and accounts of, many events in Roman history down to about 280 B.C.; the order adopted here cannot always be proved right in every detail.

CHRONOLOGY
The Struggle of the Orders

The main stages by which the Roman plebeians attained a measure of equality with the patricians are as follows:

494 B.C. First "secession" of plebeians; appointment of two tribunes (later rising to ten).

450 The Laws of the Twelve Tables, Rome's first written law code, is published.

445 The Lex Canuleia permits marriage between patricians and plebeians.

367 Licinian-Sextian laws limiting amount of public land anyone could hold.

366 First plebeian consul.

287 Laws passed by plebeians are binding on the whole state; final victory of plebeians.

Therefore, as the road to the highest office narrowed, a praetor who wanted to become consul was well advised to observe the generally traditional ways of Roman politics.

The laws of Licinius and Sextius also restricted the amount of public land that any citizen could occupy (the precise acreage allowed is disputed). This measure was supposed to prevent the upper classes from occupying more than a fair share of public land for themselves; but over the years they did precisely this, and the lower orders were often denied their proper amount of farming territory.

The End of the Struggle of the Orders

The plebeians of Rome had for a long time met in an assembly called the "council of the plebeians" (*concilium plebis*), which patricians could not attend. Resolutions formed in that assembly were called plebiscites (*plebiscita*). In 287 B.C. a law (the Lex Hortensia)[3] established that such decisions should be binding on the whole state. Thus the common people now had the absolute legal right to pass laws, and this assembly became the most important one of all in legislation; but in practice most proposals had the sponsorship of the Senate before they came to the assembly of the plebeians for passage. Another assembly, which all citizens could attend—patricians along with plebeians—developed out of the

[3]All Roman laws were named for their proposers, in this case a dictator, Hortensius. Because *lex* (law) is a feminine noun in Latin, the adjective naming it must end in -*a*.

concilium plebis and was called the Assembly of Tribes (or Comitia Tributa). But in fact patricians seldom attended this assembly because their votes would have been swamped by the far larger numbers of plebeians, and ancient authors usually ignored the distinction between these two assemblies.

The struggle of the orders was a bitter conflict, and only the need for Rome to remain united against outside enemies kept it from degenerating into civil war. It led to greater power for the plebeians; but the patrician-plebeian upper class managed to control the changes in the constitution before they could lead to actual direction of affairs by the masses. A brake against radical democracy was the fact that the assemblies could not initiate political action. They could meet only when summoned to do so by an elected officer and even then could vote only on motions placed before them.

Roman Society in the Republic

The Structure of the Roman Family

The forceful part played by the family in Roman politics was reflected in the organization of the family itself. The Romans accepted direction from the top in most areas of their society, and this kind of structure was built into the family of patricians and plebeians alike. The father of the family, the *paterfamilias*, was the absolute owner of the whole family, which included children, land, other property, animals, and slaves. So long as he lived, his sons, even if married with their own households, remained in his power. On the death of the father, each of his sons became a paterfamilias in his own family. Such a severe system differs from anything known in Greece but has parallels in Israelite society.

Women in the Early Republic

The nature of the Roman state, an organization aimed at military defense and expansion, required a constant supply of soldiers. Therefore society designed a role for women that would guarantee the fulfillment of motherhood. Roman legend told that Romulus, the city's mythical founder, led a raid against the Sabines, a neighboring tribe, in which the Romans seized thirty virtuous women to become their wives. This "rape of the Sabines," as it became called, supposedly gave the infant city of Rome a class of strong, loyal women.

Other legends reaffirm the heroic role of women in the early Republic. For example, about 490 a Roman commander, Coriolanus, took sides with a neighboring people in attacking Rome itself. Only the pleas of his wife and his mother persuaded him to halt his troops and lead them away. The legend further says that the women asked the Senate only one reward for their service to the state, namely, to recognize Female Fortune (Fortuna Muliebris) as a goddess and dedicate a temple to her.

A Late Republican Gravestone Showing One Lucius Vibius and His Wife and Child **Roman realism is evident in the portraiture. The face of the man suggests the determined conservatism that shaped the Roman character during the Republican period.** Scala/Art Resource, NY

Customs in Marriage   Despite these tributes to the virtues of Roman women in legend, the early Republic generally kept women in the position of second-class citizens. A young woman normally married at about age fifteen, as in Greece, and was transferred to her new family and lost her right to her native family's property. Her husband was sometimes considerably older and might have been married before, perhaps having lost a wife in childbirth. Wives were legally within the power of their fathers or husbands (again as in ancient Israel), and their chief virtues were considered to be silence and obedience. The sources tell stories about women legally executed by their families for adultery or other offenses.

Women in the Later Republic   But this system could not last forever. As Rome became wealthier, the narrow framework of women's lives was loosened, and they began to own significant property. Marriage less often involved the placing of a woman under the absolute power of her husband. The reason for this change was not necessarily a wish to respect women's rights; rather, it was that wealthy families with well-off daughters did not wish to lose control over their property by transferring their wealth out of the family.

Marriages now became less stable, and we find women of prominent families, especially in Rome itself, moving in society and even from husband to husband, with a freedom impossible in Greece. In apparent alarm at the emancipation of women, Marcus Cato, a prominent conservative, spoke in favor of an existing law that forbade women to possess jewelry and wear colored dresses; but his opposition to this luxury tells us that women were doing so in the second century B.C. Despite Cato's dislike of such women's liberation, we do not find in Rome that undercurrent of fear of the mysterious powers of women that can be seen in Greek myth and literature.

Women and Family Politics   As in Greece, Roman women could not hold office or vote, but they greatly surpassed Greek women as influences behind the scenes. One especially eminent woman was Cornelia, the daughter of Scipio Africanus, the victorious general in the second Punic War. On the death of her husband she refused all offers of marriage, including one from a king of Egypt, and devoted herself to the education of her twelve children, among whom were the tribunes Tiberius and Gaius Gracchus. She was a woman of high education who maintained a salon and whose letters were praised for their elegant style; indeed, she had a position and prominence unparalleled by that of any woman in classical Greece.

Other women in the Republic also became important as links between powerful families in marriage alliances, which were arranged by fathers, often for the political advantages they could bring with them. One notable such marriage made Julius Caesar the father-in-law of Pompey and cemented the alliance of the two men during Caesar's rise to supreme power. Julia, the daughter of the first emperor, Augustus, was also married to men favored by this emperor in order to continue his family line. The influence of women in politics continued to grow enormously during the Roman Empire, when the long periods of an emperor's reign allowed wives and mothers of rulers to learn and control the levers of power in the imperial court. Yet we must not exaggerate the degree to which Roman women were liberated. In all periods, as in Greece, sarcophagi and tomb reliefs portray men with their wives in conventional poses, and one gravestone for a woman praises her for her domestic virtues: "She was chaste, she was thrifty, she remained at home, she spun wool."

Religion and Roman Values   Roman religion consisted largely of forms of worship that upheld Roman tradition. Within the household, the father acted as the priest and led the family in its worship of household gods—for example, Janus, the god protecting the doorway; Vesta, the spirit of the hearth; and household spirits known as Lares and Penates.

Public religion, on the other hand, was closely connected with the interest of the state. Priesthoods were mainly political offices, held only by men. Women were, however, responsible for one of the most important religious duties: It fell to six virgins to maintain the sacred fire of Vesta that guarded the hearth of the state. These Vestal Virgins were held in high honor and lived in a spacious, elegant villa in the Forum; by a remarkable exception, these women were freed of the power of their father.

Roman religion, unlike Greek, often served to maintain conservative old Roman values, such as *pietas* (proper devotion), *dignitas* (the respect that was owed to a good citizen), and *gravitas* (the wish to take things seriously). As to Roman rites, they seem to have been designed mainly to placate the gods, almost to keep them at arm's length, through sacrifices. The Romans believed that their gods would protect them if the gods were shown proper devotion, or *pietas*. The Romans also went to elaborate lengths before declaring war, seeking reasons to believe that the war was just and holy. Eventually some rites hardened into patterns whose original meaning had been forgotten; but so long as the priests did not deviate from routine, the Romans assumed that the gods were satisfied and would not frustrate their enterprises.

Roman Mythology   Nearly all of Roman mythology was an adaptation of Greek legend, and Roman gods were often Greek deities with Roman names. The Greek father-god, Zeus, became Iuppiter, or Jupiter; his wife, Hera, became Juno; Athena became Minerva; Hermes became Mercury; and so on. Romans worshiped these gods officially in public and also in the home along with the household deities, these latter being minor gods with no connection to the Greek pantheon. Perhaps because Greek myths often show gods behaving spitefully or immorally, the Romans also created certain uplifting ideals—such as Virtus (manly conduct), Pax (peace), Fides (loyalty), and Pudor (modesty)—and transformed them into gods.

Early Roman Literature

It may seem surprising that it took the Romans centuries to develop a literature. Homeric epic is older than the Greek city-states themselves, but Rome had been independent of the Etruscans for the better part of three centuries before a significant literature emerged. Evidently the Romans needed contact with Greek civilization, which came about during the age of conquest, to stimulate their own literary efforts. After the first Punic War, one Naevius wrote an epic poem about Rome's victory (thus imitating Homer), but it has not survived.

Comedy   The earliest preserved Latin literature is the comedies, influenced by the Greeks, of Plautus (ca. 250–ca. 184 B.C.) and Terence (ca. 190–ca. 159 B.C.). These playwrights imitated Greek New Comedy, as it is called, in which the plays were entirely fiction. The Romans did not approve of Old Comedy, such as the plays of Aristophanes, which savagely lampooned active politicians.

Plautus filled his comedies with stock situations and characters, such as mistaken identities, lecherous old men, and frustrated romances. One of his plays about mistaken identities, the *Menaechmi*, gave Shakespeare the model for his *Comedy of Errors*. Terence wrote comedy in a more refined and delicate style than Plautus. His characters are less earthy, and the humor emerges from more subtle situations or such human foibles as greed.

Roman Historians: Polybius   Historical writing, too, began rather late in Rome, around 200 B.C., and the writings of the earliest Roman historians are all lost, surviving only through quotations in other writers. The earliest preserved historical narrative on Rome is from the Greek writer Polybius (ca. 200–ca. 118 B.C.). He was deported from Greece as a hostage to Rome in the 160s, where he met many Roman statesmen and became an expert in Roman history. He wrote a general history of the Greco-Roman world from the first Punic War down to his own times, largely to demonstrate the inevitable domination of the Mediterranean by the Romans.

Polybius believed that much of Rome's success in government was due to its well-designed constitution—a commendable mixed form of state that would long maintain Rome's power. He traveled widely and insisted on the need to visit sites in order to grasp the importance of geography to history. His work is analytic and methodical and attempts to revive the high standards of historical writing that Herodotus and Thucydides had established. He is both the most important historian of the Hellenistic Age and the most reliable guide to earlier Roman history.

Early Expansion of Rome

Rome's First Conquests   While the Romans were developing their form of government, they were also expanding their holdings on the Italian peninsula. Sometimes they could use peaceful diplomacy, for example, by making a treaty with neighboring peoples in the plain of Latium. More often they turned to outright military conquest in wars that were clearly long and strenuous. They gained one important victory over the last remaining Etruscan stronghold, the town of Veii, just across the Tiber River, which they took and destroyed in 396 B.C.

The Invasion by the Gauls   The period of conquest was not uniformly successful and in fact included one major disaster. In 390 B.C. a marauding tribe of Gauls left their stronghold in the Po valley and captured the city of Rome. The event led to an action that Roman tradition remembered as a heroic deed performed by wealthy Roman women. Rome negotiated a ransom with the Gauls to secure their withdrawal, but only a contribution from women brought the funds up to the full amount demanded. The state honored the women by proclaiming that laudatory orations could be spoken at their funerals. Rome then renewed its policy of expansion, showing the resilience that made it, in the words of the historian Edward Gibbon, "sometimes vanquished in battle, always victorious in war."[4] By the 290s Rome dominated the Italian peninsula as far south as the Greek city-states of Magna Graecia.

The Roman Army   No small element in Rome's military victories was the new formation of its army. The Greek phalanx gave way to the system of maniples, or groups of either 60 or 120 men, each commanded by a centurion (roughly a lieutenant in a modern army). The advantage of this system was that the army had both power and versatility, because the maniples could maneuver independently and could hold together even if the main unit, the **legion** (6,000 men), lost its formation. About 100 B.C. the maniple was replaced by the cohort (*cohors*), usually a group of 600, but this change was not one of principle, and the cohorts maintained the flexibility of the maniples.

[4] *Decline and Fall of the Roman Empire*, chap. 38.

Pyrrhus Invades Italy   In the 280s some of the Greek cities of southern Italy, threatened by the growing imperialism of Rome, enlisted Pyrrhus, the king of Epirus (near modern Albania), to save their independence with a campaign against Rome. He brought a large force that included 20 war elephants, a weapon that the Romans had never before confronted. Pyrrhus fought two successful battles in 280 B.C., but at a heavy cost in casualties to his own men (hence the phrase "a Pyrrhic victory"). The Romans again rebounded from defeat, and Pyrrhus abandoned his allies in 275 B.C., leaving the Romans free to pursue their conquests. By 265 B.C. Rome controlled the entire Italian peninsula but had not yet mastered the Po valley.

The Roman Federation   Rome showed great administrative skill in organizing the conquered communities by establishing different degrees of privilege and responsibility among them. Residents of a few favored communities received the most highly prized status, full Roman citizenship. This status meant that they were on the same legal footing as the Romans; they had the protection of Roman law, they could make legal wills to pass on their property, and they could even hold office in Rome. Members of some other communities became citizens who could not vote but had the right of intermarriage with Romans. At a lower level of privilege were the allied states (*socii*). They enjoyed Rome's protection from other peoples and were also liable to provide troops.

This carefully designed system of confederation enabled the Romans to solve an administrative problem that had frustrated the Greek poleis: how to control a large territory without having to demolish or transform the conqueror's own institutions. Even more important, the creation of this chain of alliances greatly expanded the manpower available to Rome in its progressive domination of the Mediterranean. And as the various communities under Rome's control came more and more to resemble Rome in social structure, they could climb the rungs up to full Roman citizenship: a powerful stimulus to loyalty that served Rome well in all its conquests.

THE AGE OF MEDITERRANEAN CONQUEST (264–133 B.C.)

Rome had now established its control over the whole Italian peninsula. There followed a period of imperialistic expansion that many historians consider partly involuntary, as Rome became embroiled with other Mediterranean powers. One result, important for the future history of Europe, was the inevitable forming of a system of administering Rome's new territories.

MAP 4.2 ITALY IN 265 B.C., ON THE EVE OF THE PUNIC WARS By 265 B.C., Rome had united the entire peninsula of Italy, but not everyone living under Rome's domain was a Roman citizen. The last territory to be conquered was Apulia, in southeastern Italy (312 B.C.). Where was the area irrigated by the Po River, not yet under Rome's control?

◆ For an online version, go to www.mhhe.com/chambers9 > chapter 4 > book maps

The Punic Wars

Rome—by which we now mean not only the ancient city but also the group of peoples in Italy allied with the city—at last had the strength in population to become a world power. The Romans achieved that goal in three wars with Carthage, a city that had been founded by Phoenicians about 700 B.C. and over the next century had established its own Mediterranean empire. By the time Rome had unified the Italian peninsula, Carthage controlled cities in northern Africa, parts of Spain, the islands of Corsica and Sardinia, and much of Sicily. It was beyond comparison the leading naval power in the western Mediterranean and could live off the tribute paid by its possessions. With good reason a German historian called Carthage "the London of antiquity."

The First Punic War The wars between Rome and Carthage are called Punic Wars (from *Poeni*, the Latin name for the Phoenicians who had founded Carthage). The first opened in 264 B.C. when the Romans sent a force to assist the town of Messana (modern Messina) in Sicily, which was under siege from Carthage. The quarrel soon escalated into a battle for control of the whole island of Sicily. In the war, the Romans showed the virtues of which they were most proud—above all the refusal to accept defeat no matter how heavy the casualties. Rome won the war in 241. Carthage abandoned Sicily entirely, large parts of the island passed to Rome, and it became the first Roman "province" (a territory outside Italy under Roman control).

In 238 B.C. the Carthaginian garrison on the island of Sardinia rebelled, and the Romans unscrupulously took the opportunity to seize the island and also its neighbor, the island of Corsica. The two islands, administered together, formed the second Roman province. Carthage was furious over this humiliation, which made a second war with Rome all but inevitable.

The Second Punic War and Hannibal The second of the three wars (219–202 B.C.) was the most critical of all. Carthage, still angry over Rome's seizure of Sardinia and Corsica, sought to build up an empire in southern Spain as some compensation for its losses. In 219 B.C. a quarrel arose over Saguntum, a town in Spain to which Rome had promised protection. The great figure on the Carthaginian side was Hannibal. In 219 he seized Saguntum, thus in effect opening war with

Rome. A brilliant and daring strategist, second to almost none in history, he determined to carry the war to the enemy. In autumn 218 he led his army from Spain through the snow across the Alps and down into Italy. He brought with him 37 elephants, the irresistible weapon in ancient war (all but one of them soon died).

Once in Italy Hannibal hoped to arouse the tribes of Gauls in the Po valley and end the alliances of the various peoples with Rome, following which he would conquer Rome itself. Despite his energy, his twofold strategy failed. In 216 B.C. he won a stupendous victory over the Romans at Cannae, in southeastern Italy, which has remained a classic study for strategists ever since; but not even then could he bring about a revolt of the allies. At least half of them remained faithful to Rome, and without their help Hannibal's manpower was no match for that of Rome.

Publius Cornelius Scipio   While Hannibal was in Italy, the Roman commander Publius Cornelius Scipio, only 26 years old, carried the war into Spain. Scipio was the first man given such a command without having held higher office. He apparently had absolute faith in the favor of the gods and could inspire his men with this conviction. In 209 B.C. he captured the important Spanish city of New Carthage and by 206 he controlled most of Spain. In 204 B.C. he landed in Africa, near Carthage itself, where his victories brought about the recall of Hannibal from Italy and set the stage for a final clash between these two great generals and their forces. Scipio won the decisive battle in 202 B.C., at Zama in North Africa. In honor of the victory, Scipio received the name *Africanus* and proudly added it to his traditional Roman name. Besides paying Rome a huge indemnity, Carthage had to give up all its territory except its immediate surroundings in Africa and was forbidden to raise an army without Roman permission.

Thus the second war ended in a hard-earned victory for Roman perseverance and skill; but a large bill would later have to be paid. Hannibal had laid waste large tracts of farming land in southern Italy and had driven many farmers off their soil. In casualties, too, the cost to Rome had been severe: It is estimated that Roman military manpower fell from about 285,000 in 218 to about 235,000 in 203.

The Third Punic War   After the second war, Rome made an alliance with Masinissa, the king of Numidia, just west of Carthage. Over the years Masinissa began to plunder Carthaginian territory and drove Carthage to the point of armed resistance against him. In Rome a bitterly anti-Carthaginian group was led by Marcus Cato, whose name has become symbolic of narrow intolerance. He and his group argued that Carthage was still dangerous; he constantly urged that it be de-

stroyed. Finally he succeeded in persuading Rome to declare war against Carthage and in making it a campaign of punishment (149–146 B.C.).

Another Scipio, known as Scipio Aemilianus, captured Carthage in 146. The Romans utterly destroyed the city and formally cursed the site (the tale that they poured salt into the soil is only a modern fiction), and the territory became the Roman province called simply Africa. The conquest of the territory formerly held by Carthage in Europe was made complete when Rome conquered almost all of Spain by 133 B.C.

Expansion in the Eastern Mediterranean

Wars with Macedonia and Syria   In the following decades the Romans continued their conquests until they had mastered the whole Mediterranean basin. Historians have long debated whether this policy represented deliberate imperialism or was at least partly accidental. Certainly the first stage was forced on Rome by the king of Macedonia, Philip V (r. 221–179 B.C.). He drew Rome into war by forming an alliance with Hannibal in 215 B.C. and thus opened the gate through which, over centuries, Roman troops and administrators poured as far east as Armenia and changed the course of European history.

During this era Rome also became involved in war with Antiochus III, the Macedonian ruler of Syria, the kingdom founded by Seleucus after the death of Alexander. Roman forces defeated his army at Magnesia in Asia Minor in 190 B.C.—another significant moment in Rome's expansion, as Roman legions left Europe and fought in Asia Minor for the first time.

Annexation of Greece   For a time, the Romans tried to stay out of Greek affairs and proclaimed that they were allowing the Greeks freedom. To the Greeks, freedom meant the liberty to do as they liked, but for the Romans it meant behaving as obedient Roman clients. After further quarrels and battles, the Roman Senate realized that outright annexation of the Greek mainland was the only way to secure Rome's interests.

Therefore, in 146 B.C., Macedonia and Greece were combined into a province. This decision brought the Romans into permanent contact with Greek culture, which they passed on over the centuries to Europe. They had already destroyed Carthage, and as they took over Greece their dominance in the Mediterranean could not be denied or reversed. But this domination came at a price. Without the need for unity against outside enemies, Roman society began to lose its cohesiveness; this in turn led to the decline of the Republic.

The Province of Asia   Some experienced rulers in the region were shrewd enough to perceive what had

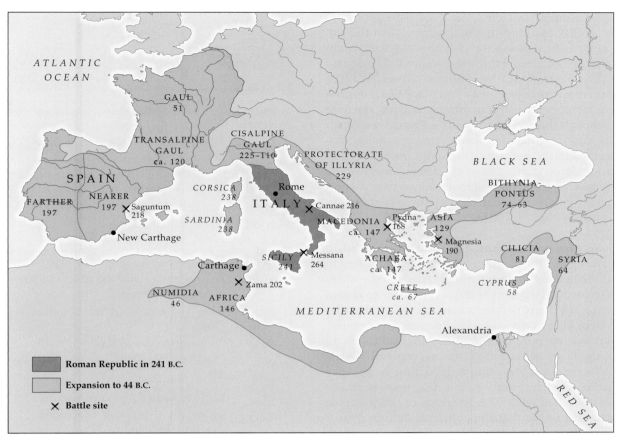

MAP 4.3 THE EXPANSION OF THE ROMAN REPUBLIC, 241–44 B.C.
After the first Punic War (264–241 B.C.), Rome ruled over Italy itself and the island of Sicily. Rome then extended its rule through the conquest of other areas in the Mediterranean which were called provinces. This map shows the growth of the Roman dominion to 44 B.C. When was the province of northern Gaul added?
◆ For an online version, go to www.mhhe.com/chambers9 > chapter 4 > book maps

happened and began a process of accommodation to Rome. For example, in 133 B.C., the last king of Pergamum died without leaving a successor and the Romans found that he had willed his kingdom to Rome—surely because he had seen that the kingdom of Pergamum could not long survive without Roman protection. Four years later Rome created the province of Asia, based on the territory of Pergamum (see map 4.3). This province possessed great wealth and offered tempting opportunities for a governor of Asia to enrich himself through corruption; the post became highly desirable for ambitious politicians and also brought with it a posting to the pleasant climate of the beautifully built Greek cities.

The Nature of Roman Expansion

Organization and Force   Rome's success in its domination of the Mediterranean rested on certain unique historical conditions. Early in its history, events had

forced the city to seek defensive alliances. After the expulsion of the Etruscan monarchs, for example, Rome had to unite militarily with its neighbors in the plain of Latium against a possible Etruscan counterattack. Constant wars in the fourth and third centuries, such as the invasion by the Gauls in 390 B.C., further emphasized the need for common security.

The result was a commitment to, and mastery of, military force that proved to be unsurpassed, and this military force soon developed into a highly effective and (when necessary) utterly ruthless policy of conquest. Scipio Aemilianus, for example, forced the people of Numantia, in Spain, to surrender in 133 B.C., by reducing them to cannibalism and even cut off the hands of four hundred young men in a neighboring city who had advocated aiding their Spanish brethren. The Senate at home considered Aemilianus' achievements worthy of a triumphal parade, the highest military honor that Romans could bestow on a successful commander.

Provincial Administration   The Latin word *provincia* means "a duty assigned to a magistrate," and the Romans extended the meaning to denote the various regions that they acquired through conquest. The Senate chose the governors for the various provinces, often giving them the title *proconsul* ("in place of a consul"). These governors ruled their provinces with absolute power, though they could not violate Roman law or act illegally against Roman citizens. Some provincial governors ruled fairly, but others were notorious for their corruption. From the Roman view, the advantage of the system was its efficiency: Rebellions were not common, and troops stationed in the provinces could maintain control without resorting to massacres.

Tax Collectors, or Publicani   The provinces furnished financial support for the Roman Republic. Some had to pay tribute in various forms, usually food, while others were assigned a fixed sum of money. In order to obtain these taxes, the state devised a convenient but corruptible system of tax collection. Companies of tax collectors, known as *publicani*, bid for the contracts to collect the taxes of certain provinces, especially Asia. The collectors paid the state a fixed sum in advance and then made their profit by collecting taxes in excess of what they had paid. The governor of the province was supposed to see that the publicani did not collect more than a specified sum. Unfortunately, however, the collectors could use their funds as bribes to persuade the governor to overlook their rapacity.[5]

The Equestrians   The tax collectors came from a class known as **equestrians**. The *equites* originally formed the cavalry in Rome's military forces, but over the years the equestrians stopped fighting on horseback and became a social class, roughly the businessmen of Rome. Equestrians did not serve in the Senate. They had to be of high financial standing, and some of them could far outstrip senators in wealth. They held no political offices but formed companies to build roads and aqueducts and to conduct businesses of all kinds.

THE ROMAN REVOLUTION (133–27 B.C.)

The year 133 B.C. saw the final conquest of most of Spain, in the west, and the acquisition of the province of Asia, in the east. This was also the beginning of the Roman revolution, a long political transformation that ended the Roman Republic. Imperialism demanded

[5] Cicero, a firm supporter of the *publicani*, called them "the flower of the Roman equestrians, the ornament of the state, and the foundation of the Republic."

CHRONOLOGY
The Roman Revolution

The main landmarks in the Roman revolution were as follows:

133 B.C.	Tiberius Gracchus elected tribune; is killed in riot.
123–121	Gaius Gracchus tribune; equestrians gain control of extortion court; Gaius killed.
107	First consulship of Marius.
91–88	War with Italian allies.
81–79	Sulla's dictatorship.
70	First consulship of Pompey and Crassus.
66	Pompey given command against Mithridates in Asia.
59	Julius Caesar consul, receives command in Gaul.
58–50	Caesar's conquest of Gaul.
49	Caesar invades Italy, opening of civil war.
44	Caesar murdered.
31	Battle of Actium, defeat of Mark Antony.
27	Supremacy of Octavian, later called Augustus; beginning of Roman Empire.

---

powerful military commanders, and the selfish rivalry among them burst the bounds of the constitution.

Social Change and the Gracchi

The Changing World of Italy   The breakdown of the Roman Republic has been called Hannibal's legacy, for the ravages of years of fighting up and down Italy had brought many farmers to the point of ruin. On the other hand, wealthy citizens had enriched themselves with booty and the spoils of war. The less fortunate had often lost their land or were willing to sell it to these newly wealthy men. There had also been a great increase in the slave population on Italian soil from prisoners of war, and these slaves depressed the wages paid to private workers.

Often the displaced farmers had little choice but to join the ranks of the permanently unemployed. Their poverty threatened to impede the recruitment of soldiers into the Roman army, for Rome had nothing like a modern war treasury, and only men who had enough money to buy their own armor could be drafted into the legions. Without sufficient recruits, the gains from the conquests might be lost. Moreover, those who could no longer find work lost the spirit of cohesion and loyalty to their society. They became prey to demagogues and many became supporters of this or that warlord. The Senate, which might have provided moral leadership to the state, also showed itself unable to stand firm as the long revolution rolled on.

Tiberius Gracchus Two ambitious young Roman statesmen, Tiberius and Gaius Gracchus, moved to solve the problems of those who had lost their land. Their mother, Cornelia, was a well-known daughter of a great family; her father was Publius Cornelius Scipio Africanus, who had won the war against Hannibal. She had married a prominent plebeian politician, Tiberius Gracchus. Because patrician or plebeian status came down through the male line, her sons were plebeian, though descended from the loftiest aristocracy.

Tiberius, the older brother (162–133 B.C.), became tribune in 133 and proposed a bill to the Assembly of Tribes that would assign parcels of publicly owned land to dispossessed farmers. The state would obtain and redistribute such land by enforcing a long-ignored law that limited the amount of public land that anyone could occupy. To serve in the Roman army, a man had to have at least a modest amount of wealth, and Tiberius' aim, a moderate one, was to create prosperous farmers and thus increase the supply of potential recruits for the army. He made the mistake of not submitting his bill for the approval of the Senate before proposing it. Angered at this slight, some senators found another tribune willing to oppose the bill with his veto. Tiberius then persuaded the people to remove that tribune from office. This action was both illegal and dangerous. Once such a step had been taken, what tribune would be safe in the future from an identical threat? But the people followed Tiberius and passed the bill.

Tiberius Murdered The distribution of land was in progress when Tiberius decided to run for reelection. This move was a breach of custom, for tribunes held office for only one year. Some of his opponents feared that he might seize permanent leadership of the propertyless and lead them into social revolution. A group of senators, late in 133, took the law into their own hands and provoked a riot in which Tiberius was clubbed to death—an event that gave grim warning of a new intensity in Rome's political struggles. Above all, this action violated the taboo against assassination of a tribune, and this first step, once taken, became easier to repeat. Despite Tiberius' death, the distribution of land continued, and his enemies even took credit for the success of the project.

Gaius Gracchus Tiberius' younger brother, Gaius, became tribune ten years later, in 123 B.C. He was the harsher and less compromising of the two plebeians. He remembered that some senators had inspired the murder of his brother, and he wanted to reply with several measures that sought to limit the powers of senators. He proposed, and the people accepted, that the Senate's freedom in assigning governors to provinces should be restricted. One of the most important powers of the Senate was membership in the extortion court, which investigated cases of alleged extortion by provincial governors and tax collectors. The jurors, all senators, were usually not severe in judging governors, who were fellow members of the Senate. Gaius had a bill passed that assigned the seats on this jury to members of the equestrian class. Thus the courts became the prize of political victory.

All tax collectors were equestrians, and it was now they who had the potential to favor members of their group who might be accused and brought to trial for extortion. Gaius' arrangements were later revised, but he was the first to make the extortion court the subject of a bitter political quarrel.

The Fall and Death of Gaius Gracchus Gaius had also followed his brother Tiberius in authoring a bill that continued the distribution of public land. It included provisions for the founding of colonies where more citizens could be settled. But he committed a major blunder in proposing to found a colony of Roman citizens on the site of Carthage, the hated enemy in the three Punic wars. This ill-judged action aroused widespread criticism.

Like his brother, Gaius Gracchus came to a violent end. He failed to be elected to a third year as tribune, and his enemies asserted that he and his followers were planning a revolution. The Senate then ordered one of the consuls for the year 121 B.C. to "see to it that the state suffered no harm," thus inviting the consul to use force to suppress the younger Gracchus. This resolution, which was later passed against others whom the Senate wanted to eliminate, was known in Roman politics as the **"last decree"** (*Senatus consultum ultimum*). It was in effect the declaration of martial law. When the consul raised up a mob to hunt Gaius down, he had one of his own slaves kill him.

The Gracchi and History The Gracchi had unleashed a whirlwind when they invited the Assembly of Tribes to take a more activist role. It is true that the people had long possessed the right to legislate in this assembly, but they had not always had the will; nor had ambitious tribunes always dared to use such a weapon. But now demagogues began to turn more and more to this assembly to pass bills in favor of their military patrons. From this moment began the slow but sure Roman revolution.

The Years of the Warlords

The Gracchi could not protect themselves from the violence of the Senate because they had no army. But as Roman conquests brought the state into further wars, powerful generals appeared who did have the support of their armies and used it to seize power. Their struggles against one another undermined the republican constitution and the state finally collapsed into dictatorship.

Marius and a Changed Roman Army

The first general to play this game was Gaius Marius (ca. 157–86 B.C.), from the countryside near Rome. In Roman terminology, he was a "new man," or **novus homo,** that is, a man none of whose ancestors had been consul. He was a roughneck, of little education, but stalwart and fearless. He is a crucial figure because he changed, radically and forever, the membership of the Roman army and the direction of its loyalty. He gained high prestige by winning a war (111–106 B.C.) against Jugurtha, the king of Numidia in North Africa. Marius had obtained this command after the generals who had been sent out by the Senate had proved incompetent; and Marius showed his hatred for the feeble aristocrats who had thoroughly bungled the campaign.

Marius' reputation grew even more after he drove back an attempted invasion (105–101 B.C.) by some Germanic tribes moving toward northern Italy. Such was his stature in this period that he was consul for five consecutive years and dominated politics from 107 to 100 B.C.

In order to raise large numbers of men for his army, Marius abolished the old requirement that a soldier had to own at least a modest amount of property, and he also accepted volunteers instead of just drafting men for service (the men so enrolled were known as *capite censi,* "enrolled by head count"). As a result, the army came to be composed largely of poor men who served their commander, received booty from him, relied on him as their main patron, and expected him to obtain for them a grant of land that they could farm after they were discharged. Thus Marius converted the army into an instrument for ambitious commanders during the remaining years of the Republic and even throughout the Roman Empire.

The War with the Italians

The Italian peoples who were Rome's allies had never been granted Roman citizenship, and in 91 B.C. another reform-minded tribune, Marcus Livius Drusus, tried to carry a bill that would have made them citizens. The Senate declared his law null and void, and Drusus, like the Gracchi, was murdered. At this outrage some of the allies proclaimed themselves independent and opened a war that continued until 88. In the end the Romans negotiated with the Italians and allowed them to acquire citizenship. But the fact that it required a war to obtain this concession shows that both the Roman upper classes—the senators and equestrians—and the Roman masses were still ready to fight for their privileges.

Sulla the Dictator

The Italian War made the reputation of another powerful general, Lucius Cornelius Sulla (ca. 138–78 B.C.). He was a man without any scruples, a glutton and sensualist who helped himself to whatever women he liked. In the 80s civil war broke out in Rome over who should obtain the command in a war against Mithridates, the king of Pontus in Asia Minor (r. 120–63 B.C.). One group rallied behind Sulla and his legions, seeing in him the best vehicle for their own ambitions. In 88 B.C. he invaded the city of Rome with his supporters—the first but not the last time that Romans themselves marched on and seized the ancient city.

Mithridates had extended his kingdom until it included the Roman province of Asia and even large parts of the Greek mainland. In 88 B.C. he gave orders for the massacre of at least 80,000 Romans and Italians residing in Asia Minor—a testimony to the unpopularity of Roman rule in this province. This massacre could not go unanswered, and Sulla received the command against Mithridates.

Sulla departed for his campaign in 87 B.C., and during his absence Marius and his supporters seized Rome in turn. They conducted a reign of terror, publishing lists ("proscriptions") of those to be killed either with or without "trials" and exhibiting their maimed bodies and even their heads in the streets. But as soon as Sulla was free of his Eastern war, he returned to Italy and once more occupied Rome (November 82). Our sources tell us that he had thousands of his opponents executed and had himself named dictator without limit of time, thus breaking the customary six-month limit for holding that office.

Sulla's Reforms

For all Sulla's brutality and self-indulgence, he did have a political program: to reshape the state on strictly authoritarian and conservative lines. Two forces, he thought, had menaced the rigid control over Rome that the Senate should enjoy: the tribunes of the people, who had made the Assembly of Tribes more conscious of its power, and the generals who had used the loyalty of their armies to gain political leverage. To deal with the first of these threats, Sulla forced through a law that blocked tribunes from holding any other office; they also had to wait ten years to be reelected. These measures were meant to discourage any ambitious politicians from seeking this office.

Sulla handled the army commanders through a law that forbade them to leave their provinces or make war

This idealized statue of the first century B.C. shows the ruthless tyrant Cornelius Sulla in the dignified pose of a classical orator.
Giraudon/Art Resource, NY

outside their borders without instructions from the Senate; thus, no ambitious commander could blunder into a war or make himself into a conqueror. Sulla further established minimum ages at which a man might hold the various offices in a political career (a consul, for example, had to be 42 or older). He also canceled the work of Gaius Gracchus on the jury system; as one might expect from this strict traditionalist, he gave all the seats on the juries back to senators.

Sulla resigned the dictatorship in 79 B.C., a rare act in any supreme ruler, but he evidently thought he had put the Senate so firmly in control that he was no longer needed; he died in 78. To his enemies he was pitiless, and his executions of Roman citizens were horrifying, but he was also a political strategist. He had done his part for the conservative cause by putting the Senate in charge, but this body proved unable to manage the next generation of warlords.

The Rise of Pompey   Sulla had used the tool forged by Marius—an army loyal to a commander—and another warlord soon followed his example, namely Gnaeus Pompeius (106–48 B.C.), usually called Pompey. He first gained a reputation in 77 B.C., when he was sent to Spain to end a revolt there. After completing this task, and while his army was still intact, he helped suppress a rebellion of slaves in Italy led by a Thracian slave named Spartacus. This campaign was already under the command of another ambitious Roman, Marcus Licinius Crassus, the richest man of his time. Pompey and Crassus were rivals, but they worked together in suppressing the revolt. No sooner did the slave revolt collapse in 71 B.C. than the joint commanders, Pompey and Crassus, marched their armies to the gates of Rome and demanded both consulships for the year 70. Pompey was legally unqualified for this office, for he was only 36 and had held no previous magistracy. If Crassus, Pompey's rival, had refused to join in this bargain, he might have preserved the Sullan system. But, like him, the Senate also lacked the will to enforce the constitution and resist the two men, and they won election as consuls. This was little short of a coup d'état.

During their consulship Pompey and Crassus canceled several of Sulla's arrangements. They restored to the tribunes their right to propose legislation, and they mixed senators and equestrians in the always controversial juries. At the end of their year in office, both consuls retired without demanding any further appointment—an action that, though at first surprising, was really consistent with Pompey's ambitions. He wanted to be the first man in the state, but he disliked committing himself to open revolution. A modern historian has compared him to Shakespeare's Macbeth: He would not play false and yet would wrongly win.

Pompey's Military Commands   In 67 B.C. Pompey obtained the command to deal with pirates operating in the Mediterranean who were interfering with the grain supply for Rome—a critical matter since the city had to live on grain shipped to its harbor. Pompey fulfilled his orders and cleared the seas in a swift campaign. He also recognized the economic roots of piracy and settled many of the captured pirates on land that they could cultivate in Asia Minor and Greece. Then in 66 B.C. he received through the Tribal Assembly an even more important command in Asia Minor, where Rome was involved in war with Mithridates, Sulla's old enemy, who was still on his throne.

Another Roman general, Lucullus, had practically wiped out Mithridates' forces, so Pompey's campaign was essentially a mopping-up operation. But Pompey took action that had permanent results; he set up a system of client kings, rulers of smaller states whose loyalty to Rome was ensured by the device of "friendship" (*amicitia*). Through this bargain Rome would protect local rulers, who paid no taxes to Rome but were expected to assist with manpower and resources when needed. He also captured Syria in 64 B.C.; it became a Roman province in 62 B.C. In 63 B.C. he captured Judaea and Jerusalem.

Cicero: Nonmilitary Statesman   During Pompey's absence overseas, Marcus Tullius Cicero (106–43 B.C.) became the chief nonmilitary statesman in Rome. Like Marius, he was a "new man" from the countryside, but unlike Marius, Cicero chose a career in law and administration rather than in the military. His administrative skill won for him each successive political office at the earliest possible legal age. His polished prose style became the model for clarity and elegance. He was genuinely dedicated to compromise and political negotiation and thought that such procedures would establish the combined rule of the two upper classes, the senatorial and equestrian.

Cicero was elected consul for 63 B.C. One of his defeated rivals for the office, Catiline (Lucius Sergius Catilina), formed a conspiracy to take over the city by force. Cicero learned details of this plan and denounced Catiline in four famous speeches (the "Catilinarian" orations). He obtained the Senate's support to execute some of the captured conspirators without trial (a wholly illegal act); Catiline himself died in battle against an army of the state.

Pompey Returns to Rome   Pompey returned to Rome in 62 B.C. from his Eastern victories with two political aims. He wanted the Senate to ratify the arrangements he had made in Asia Minor, and he requested a grant of land for his men. This latter request, as we have seen, was nothing unusual. It reflected the relationship between a general and his troops, which was that of pa-

MAP 4.4 GAUL IN THE TIME OF CAESAR
In a famous sentence, Julius Caesar said, "Gaul as a whole is divided into three parts." This map shows these parts (Gallia Aquitania, Lugdunensis, and Belgica) with the dates when they were subdued. Gallia Narbonensis, named from the town of Narbo (modern Narbonne) was already a Roman province. Germania was controlled later. Which part of Gaul was closest to Britain, which Caesar also attacked?
◆ For an online version, go to www.mhhe.com/chambers9 > chapter 4 > book maps

tron and client—one of the oldest traditions in Rome. But some senators, either jealous or fearful of his prestige, combined to frustrate his wishes. This short-term victory practically doomed the Senate and the Republic, for it drove Pompey into a political alliance with Julius Caesar, who proved to have the revolutionary will that Pompey lacked.

The First Triumvirate

The Partners and Their Desires   Gaius Julius Caesar (100–44 B.C.), a descendant of an old patrician family, returned to Rome in 60 B.C. from his post as governor of Spain. Intellectually, he was a brilliant man who wrote elegant, lean Latin. Politically, he is an example of the aristocrat who bases his power on the common people. In this respect he resembles Pericles in Athenian history. Caesar had enemies within the Senate, where many looked on him as a brash upstart or a potential tyrant. They refused his request to be allowed to run for the consulship of 59 in absence and then lead a triumphal parade through the city. Faced with this direct affront to his dignity, Caesar made a political bargain with Pompey. Crassus joined them because he was at odds with some powerful senators over a financial matter. The three

Perhaps the most spectacular classical monument in Europe, the Pont du Gard was built in the first century A.D. to carry water to Nîmes (ancient Nemausus) in France. The water ran through a trough above the top layer of arches. The aqueduct is an example of the Romans' mastery of hydraulic technology and construction in arches.
Michael Holford Photographs

formed a coalition known to historians as the First **Triumvirate** ("body of three men"; it had no official mandate or status). Their united influence at the polls over their clients elected Caesar as one of the consuls for 59. To confirm the bargain in a manner customary in Roman politics, Pompey married Caesar's daughter, Julia.

Caesar's Consulship and the Gallic War   Caesar's influence secured allotments of land for Pompey's army and the approval of his arrangements in the East. Crassus' financial quarrel was also settled to his satisfaction. Caesar then secured for himself the command over Cisalpine Gaul (the Po valley) and the coast of Illyria for a guaranteed period of five years beginning on March 1,

59 B.C. About this time the governor of Transalpine Gaul (Provence, in the south of France) died, and the Senate added this province as well to Caesar's command.

Caesar intervened in the politics of the Gallic tribes and opened a series of campaigns that finally brought the whole area of modern France and Belgium under Roman rule. The Romans implanted in Gaul the Latin language (the origin of modern French), Roman architecture and technology, and Roman ways in general. Caesar narrated and defended his actions in his *Commentaries on the Gallic War,* which to this day remains a superb textbook in political-military decision making.

The Gallic War lasted from 58 to 50 B.C. Caesar's two partners in the triumvirate, Pompey and Crassus, were always suspicious of each other, but they maintained fairly good relations and even held a second consulship together in 55. They also had Caesar's command in Gaul renewed for another five years, so that it would not expire until March 1, 49 B.C., and they obtained commands for themselves. Crassus went out to Syria, from which he launched a disastrous campaign against the kingdom of Parthia, across the Euphrates River. Here he lost his life in 53 B.C. Pompey was given command over the two provinces of Spain, which he governed through assistants, preferring to remain at the center of power near Rome.

The Supremacy of Julius Caesar

The Break between Caesar and the Senate   Caesar's conquest of Gaul greatly enriched the state, but to his enemies it was a cause of dismay. They feared that he might use his victories and his popularity among the people to become another, and perhaps a permanent, Sulla. As protection against Caesar, his enemies in the Senate began to draw Pompey into their camp. Some of them had quarreled with him in the past, but they were willing to gamble that they could eliminate him when they no longer needed him.

As 49 B.C. opened, the Senate met in a state near hysteria. A small band of implacable senators forced through a motion ordering Caesar to lay down his command, even though he was then taking no action beyond remaining in his province of Cisalpine Gaul. The Senate passed a decree establishing martial law (that is, the "last decree," which had been invented for use against Gaius Gracchus) and ordered Pompey to command the armies of Rome against Caesar. The ill-advised Pompey accepted the command; but in doing so he signed his own death warrant and condemned the Republic to extinction in yet another civil war.

The Attack on the Tribunes of the People   Finally, the Senate defied the oldest of Roman traditions by threatening the lives of any tribunes who opposed these extreme measures. They thus handed Caesar a superb theme for his own propaganda: He could proclaim that he was defending the rights of the tribunes, of the common people of Rome who had elected them, and of the men in his army who had loyally served in the Gallic wars.

Caesar's Invasion of Italy   Caesar saw that his enemies were in effect challenging him to war and decided that he had no course but to fight for his dignity and, as he could now assert, for the people and their sacred tribunes. On about January 11, 49 B.C., he spoke the words "Let the die be cast" in Greek, and crossed the boundary of his province, the small Rubicon River north of

MARBLE BUST OF JULIUS CAESAR
Archaeological Museum Naples/Dagli Orti/The Art Archive

Ravenna, thus invading his own country at the head of Roman legions. Yet perhaps his conscience was not wholly clear: The biographer Plutarch records the tale that, on the night before the crossing, he dreamt that he was having sexual relations with his own mother.

Caesar advanced swiftly, and Pompey and his followers had to retreat to Greece; Caesar pursued them and won a decisive battle in 48 B.C. at the town of Pharsalus, in Thessaly. Pompey sought refuge in Egypt, but advisers to the pharaoh realized that Caesar had won the victory and that it was not safe for them to give Pompey protection. As Pompey approached the shore, he was stabbed to death by a former Roman officer of his. His head was cut off and his body thrown into the sea. Caesar followed to Egypt in October 48 B.C. and found that Pompey was dead. He now intervened in a civil war between the young king, Ptolemy XIII, and his sister, the famous Macedonian ruler Cleopatra VII. Caesar arranged that Ptolemy and Cleopatra should share the rule and proceeded to have a long affair with the queen. A boy, called Caesarion

ARENA IN EL-DJEM, TUNISIA, IMITATING THE COLOSSEUM IN ROME
Built in the second/third century A.D., this arena could seat 50,000 spectators. Wild animals were housed in the long rectangular pit in the center. Roman buildings were widely copied throughout the Empire as other cities sought to identify themselves with the great capital.
Photo Researchers, Inc.

(the Little Caesar), was born.[6] Politics played as much a role as love, because Cleopatra's affection guaranteed Roman control over the rich resources of Egypt; Caesar did not follow the usual practice of making Egypt a province but left it as a kingdom to be ruled by Cleopatra and Ptolemy. After other victories Caesar returned to Rome in 46 B.C.

Caesar's Rule to 44 B.C. Caesar now decided to make his rule impregnable and assumed the positions of both dictator and consul. On the model of Sulla, he extended

his dictatorship beyond the legal six-month limit; then, in 44, he had himself named dictator for life. He swept aside all restraints on his power that Roman tradition might have imposed and took complete authority to pass laws, declare war, and appoint men to office.

As dictator, Caesar saw to a series of rapid reforms in many areas of Roman life. He raised the membership of the Senate to about nine hundred, packing it with many of his veteran officers. From this time onward the Senate lost its former authority as the bulwark of the state. He scaled down his large army by settling many of his soldiers in newly founded colonies and extended Roman citizenship into some of the provinces. His most lasting reform was one by

---

[6] Scholars have always been uncertain whether Caesar was really the father of this boy.

THE MURDER OF JULIUS CAESAR

The biographer Plutarch, who wrote about A.D. 120, looked back to describe the scene when Caesar was killed, 44 B.C.

"The place chosen for this murder, where the Senate met on that day, contained a statue of Pompey, one of the adornments for the theater he had built; this made it clear to all that some divine power had guided the deed and summoned it to just that spot. As Caesar entered, the Senate rose as a sign of respect, while those in Brutus' faction came down and stood around his chair. Tillius Cimber seized Caesar's toga with both hands and pulled it down from his neck, which was the signal for the assassination. Casca was the first to strike him in the neck with his sword, but the wound was neither deep nor fatal, and Caesar turned around, grasping and holding the weapon. Those who knew nothing of the plot were terrified and did not dare run away or help Caesar or even utter a sound. But those who came prepared for the murder whipped out their daggers, and Caesar was encircled, so that wherever he turned he met with blows and was surrounded by daggers leveled at his face and eyes and he was grappling with all their hands at once. Everyone was supposed to strike him and have a taste of the murder; even Brutus stabbed him once in the groin. Some say that, as he fought off all the rest, turning his body this way and that and shouting for help, he saw Brutus draw his dagger and pulled his toga down over his head and let himself fall at the base of Pompey's statue, whether by chance or because he was pushed by the assassins. There was blood all around the statue, so that it seemed that Pompey was presiding over the vengeance taken against his enemy, who now lay at his feet and breathed out his life through his wounds. They say he was struck 23 times, and many of the assassins were wounded by one another as they all directed their blows at his body."

Plutarch, *The Life of Caesar,* chap. 66, M. H. Chambers (tr.).

which we still regulate our lives—the establishment of a calendar year based on the old Egyptian reckoning of 365 days, with one day added every fourth year.[7] This "Julian" calendar lasted until 1582, when it was revised by Pope Gregory XIII to our present Gregorian calendar.

The Death of Caesar   The full effect of Caesar's plans was not to be realized, for on March 15, 44 B.C. (the date known as the Ides of March), after four years of supremacy, he fell to the daggers of conspirators led by two of his lieutenants, Marcus Brutus and Gaius Cassius. His autocracy had been a grave affront to the upper class; because he had undermined their dignity as members of the governing class, they united against him and carried out the most famous political murder in all history. It is said that Caesar was warned that morning of an imminent conspiracy and that he brushed the warning aside. As the Senate met near a theater built by Pompey, the killers plunged on him; when he recognized his protégé Marcus Brutus in the group, he said in Greek, "You, too, my boy?" and covered his head with his toga as he fell. His body was carried to the Forum and burned on a rock that still stands in a small temple built to his memory (see "The Murder of Julius Caesar," above).

Caesar's character is baffling and controversial, even as it was to his contemporaries. He was pitiless toward Gauls and Germans, and he enriched himself by selling prisoners of war as slaves; but indifference toward captured foreigners was common in the ancient world. In Rome he showed too little respect for the Senate and republican forms once he became dictator, and for this mistake he paid with his life. On the other hand, in the civil war he was generous enough to dismiss opposing generals whom he had captured, and they lived to fight him another day. Such actions may have rested on cool calculation of their value as propaganda, but they may also show genuine gallantry. No one can question Caesar's fiery leadership. He was wiry and tough, he ignored heat and rain, he swam unfordable rivers, and his troops followed him into Italy with enthusiasm and fought with amazing discipline.

Caesar clearly thought that the old institutions of the Senate and the assemblies were obsolete. "The Republic," he is said to have remarked, "is only a name without body or face, and Sulla did not know the ABCs of politics in resigning his dictatorship."[8] The political weakness of the late Republic largely confirms this harsh evaluation. But in the end Caesar's arrogance was too much for the experienced politicians whom he needed for his administration. His career thus blends triumph and tragedy. He rose to the absolute summit of Roman politics, but in doing so he destroyed both the Roman Republic and himself.

---

[7] The added day was inserted between Feb. 23 and 24 in leap year. The date "Feb. 29" is a modern error.

[8] Suetonius, *Life of Caesar,* chap. 77.

THE END OF THE ROMAN REPUBLIC

Julius Caesar's dictatorship had all but killed the Roman Republic, but after his death the question still remained whether the republican constitution could be revived. Some politicians tried to restore the republic, and the issue hung in the balance for thirteen years, until Caesar's adopted son, Octavian, eliminated his rival, Mark Antony, and gained supreme control.

The Second Triumvirate

Antony and Octavian   Brutus, Cassius, and the other assassins imagined that republican government could be restored with Caesar out of the way. Yet partisans of Caesar commanded armies throughout the Roman world, and they were not men who would meekly surrender their powers to the Senate. One survivor was Marcus Antonius, or Mark Antony, a follower of Caesar and consul for the year 44 B.C. Antony tried to seize for himself the provincial command in Cisalpine Gaul, even though the Senate had already assigned it to another governor for the year 43. The Senate turned on him, with Cicero, now a senior statesman, leading the attack. The state sent an army out to bring Antony to justice, and it must have seemed to many that the old institutions of the Republic had indeed come back to life.

Among the commanders whom the Senate put in action against Antony was a young man of 19—Caesar's grandnephew, whom Caesar adopted in his will. His name, originally Gaius Octavius, became Gaius Julius Caesar Octavianus upon his adoption; modern historians call him Octavian, but he called himself Caesar. He used his name skillfully to win a following among Caesar's former soldiers, but he also played the part of a discreet young supporter of the Senate in its battle against Antony. Cicero, the chief supporter of the old constitution, naively wrote of Octavian after their first meeting, "The young man is completely devoted to me."[9]

Formation of the Second Triumvirate   Octavian had been assigned the duty of capturing Antony, but they both recognized that the Senate was really seeking the destruction of the Caesarian faction from which they both derived their political support. If either man were overthrown, the Senate would soon discard the other. Octavian thus calculated his own advantage and turned his back on the duty of attacking Antony. The two Caesarians formed an alliance near Bologna in 43 B.C. They brought into their partnership a lesser commander, Marcus Lepidus; then, following the example of Sulla

and others, they invaded Rome and made themselves the military rulers of the ancient capital.

Faced with their armies, the Senate had to acknowledge their leadership, and a tribune proposed a law that turned the state over to their control for a period of five years; their official title was Triumviri (body of three men) "to provide order for the state"—a charge broad enough to supply a legal basis for nearly any action they might wish to take. Thus was formed the Second Triumvirate. In due course they had their collective power renewed for another five years.

Brutus and Cassius, seeing that they did not have popular support, left for the East and in 43 B.C. were given control over all the eastern provinces. But in 42 B.C. the triumvirs eliminated these enemies at the Battle of Philippi in northern Greece. To reward their troops with land, the rulers had already marked out the territory of no fewer than eighteen prosperous towns in Italy. The rule of the Second Triumvirate (43–33 B.C.) was thus made secure by the seizure and redistribution of property. A series of "trials" mounted against those who had had the bad luck to be on the losing side provided further security. As in the time of Marius and Sulla, the autocrats brushed aside the traditional guarantees of Roman law as they coldly purged their enemies. The number of the slain was said to be the largest ever. Cicero had placed himself in special danger through a series of orations denouncing Antony (the "Philippics," a term recalling Demosthenes' attacks on Philip II of Macedonia; see p. 77). He paid the price and was murdered on Antony's orders in 43 B.C.

Octavian Triumphant

Antony and Cleopatra   Suspicion now began to grow between the two major partners, Antony and Octavian (Lepidus had been forced into retirement when he tried to take control of Sicily away from Octavian). They now both lusted for supreme power, and Antony did his own cause grave harm by remaining in the East for long periods. On the one hand, he fought a disastrous war against the Parthian Kingdom, which had taken certain Roman territories after the death of Crassus in 53. On the other, he carried on a long affair with Cleopatra VII of Egypt. Octavian stayed in Rome and skillfully exploited the rumors that surrounded this romance with Cleopatra. In particular, Octavian falsely asserted that Antony was planning to place this Eastern queen in command of the state.

Octavian's Victory over Antony   The final break between the two men came in 32 B.C. Octavian raised a large force from Italy and the western provinces; led by his skillful general Marcus Agrippa, this force defeated Antony in 31 B.C. at Actium, a promontory on the western coast of Greece. Antony shamefully abandoned his

---

[9] Letters to Atticus, 14.11 (April 25, 44 B.C.).

The Ara Pacis (Altar of Peace) was built in Rome in 13 B.C. to celebrate the establishment of peace by Augustus. Relatives of the imperial family are portrayed in idealizations of their stations in life rather than in strict Roman realism.
C. M. Dixon

men and sailed back to Egypt with Cleopatra, and his army surrendered to Octavian.

The next year Octavian unhurriedly advanced on Alexandria for the reckoning with Antony and Cleopatra. Antony took his own life, and Cleopatra soon did the same—according to the version immortalized in Shakespeare, by letting a poisonous snake bite her. With Cleopatra's death ended the last Macedonian kingdom and, therefore, the Hellenistic Age, which had begun with the death of Alexander the Great in 323 B.C.

THE FOUNDING OF THE ROMAN EMPIRE

Those Romans, like Cicero, who had hoped for the restoration of the Republic lost their hopes or their lives. Only one warlord from the Republic, Octavian, had survived the confused years after Julius Caesar. By a supreme political charade, he combined his own autocracy with the restoration of the forms of the Republic. This skillful compromise in effect created the Roman Empire, which he ruled until his death in A.D. 14.

Augustus and the Principate

Octavian Becomes Augustus   On January 1, 27 B.C., Octavian appeared in the Roman Senate and announced

that the state had returned to peace and that he needed no more extraordinary authority. He resigned his commands and took credit for restoring the Republic. But he arranged that the Senate, full of his loyal creatures, should "voluntarily" give him an enormous provincial command, consisting of Spain, Gaul, and Syria. Most of the legions were concentrated in these provinces; thus Octavian was the legal commander of most of the Roman army. Egypt was handled in a special manner. It was treated as a private possession of Octavian's and managed by his own appointee; therefore it was strictly not one of the Roman provinces.

The older, more pacified provinces (Asia, Africa, Greece, and others) were ruled by governors appointed by the Senate; thus historians speak of "imperial" (governed by the emperor) and "senatorial" provinces. Through this arrangement, Octavian showed respect to the Senate, which Caesar had largely ignored. This is another element in the statesmanship that Octavian was careful to display.

A few days later the Senate met again and conferred on Octavian the name **Augustus,** meaning "most honored" or "revered." This title brought with it no powers, but its semidivine overtones were useful to Augustus (as we shall now call him) in establishing his supremacy. To this date we may fix the beginning of the Roman Empire. In 23 B.C. he resigned the consulship but received two additional powers from the Senate. His imperium

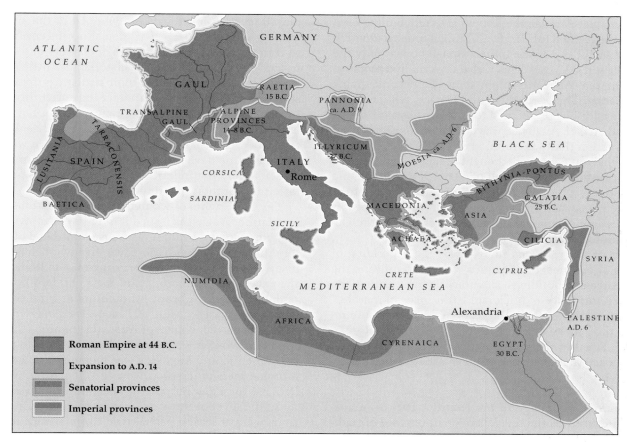

MAP 4.5 THE ROMAN PROVINCES, 44 B.C.–A.D. 14
This map shows the Roman provinces at the death of the emperor Augustus. The more pacified provinces, governed by the Senate, are outlined in green; those governed by the emperor through his legates are outlined in yellow. Which was the last province added before A.D. 14?

◆ For an online version, go to www.mhhe.com/chambers9 > chapter 4 > book maps

was extended to cover not only his provinces but the whole Roman world. He also obtained the authority of a tribune (*tribunicia potestas*). As a patrician (by his adoption into Caesar's family), Augustus could not actually be a tribune. Yet his having the "power" of a tribune suggested that he was the patron and defender of the common people of Rome. This power also gave him the legal right to veto any actions and to offer legislation. He was usually called the *princeps*, an old republican word meaning roughly "first citizen," but not an official title. This was another of his skillful pretensions to have restored the Republic. Modern writers often refer to the system that Augustus established as the **Principate.**

Augustus, the First Roman Emperor

The Administration   The long reign of Augustus from 27 B.C. to A.D. 14 laid down many abiding features of the Roman Empire. He provided a cash payment from the public treasury to soldiers who had served for twenty years, thus securing the loyalty of the legions to

the state, not to their generals. To collect the money, he had to establish a reliable civil service and reform the taxation system, enrolling in effect the whole Roman world. He made the Empire more secure by extending and solidifying the northern frontier (see map 4.5) to reach the Rhine and Danube rivers. His control was all but absolute, but most people were relieved at the ending of the long period of civil war.

He created a permanent fire department and a postal service. He formed a body of soldiers in Rome, the Praetorian Guard. This force of some nine thousand men served as the city's police force and as Augustus' personal bodyguard, but after a few decades it came to play a decisive and violent role in the designation of new emperors.

The Manipulation of Religion   Augustus also assumed the office of Pontifex Maximus, or high priest, and made attempts to revive the old Roman religion, probably as a device to promote political stability. He also grasped the possibilities of a ruler-cult. First, he assigned Julius

Caesar a place among the Roman gods and built a Temple to the Deified Julius. He also called himself *Divi Filius*, or son of the divine Julius, though he was only the adopted son of Caesar. This verbal trick invited people to imagine that Augustus might some day become divine like Caesar. The poets Virgil and Horace, who wrote at his court, discreetly referred to Augustus as a future deity; and, in fact, Augustus was deified on his death, a political action that was imitated on the deaths of several later emperors who were thought to have ruled well. He also sponsored the building of temples to "Rome and Augustus"—a further suggestion, though not an offensive demand, that the emperor should be worshiped. It also became customary to make an offering to the Genius (protecting spirit) of the emperor.

Part of the religious revival was the rebuilding of scores of temples, but temples were by no means the only Augustan buildings; a famous saying was that "he found Rome made of brick and left it made of marble." The prosperity of the later years of Augustus' rule reflects the general peace that he brought to the Roman world. Freed of the expense of wars, Rome enjoyed a confidence that expressed itself in artistic and literary creativity.

Legislation, Women, and the Family　Part of Augustus' program was the revival and maintenance of traditional Roman values. In this effort religion naturally played its part, but he also intervened in the areas of marriage and the family. His proclaimed intention was to restore the old Roman values of chastity and stability within the family, and the historian has little reason to doubt his sincerity. But a more realistic purpose was surely to rebuild the population of Italy after the losses in the civil wars. He therefore awarded special privileges to fathers of three or more children. The Augustan laws even penalized both men and women who did not marry or have children: for example, unmarried persons could not inherit a trust, and childless persons forfeited half their inheritances.

The legal rights of women also advanced under his legislation. Augustus issued strong laws against adultery, and women could now accuse a husband of adultery through a witness. Moreover, freedwomen (that is, former slaves) could now marry any man in Rome with the exception of senators, and their children held the rank of citizens. A beautiful monument from the Augustan period, the Altar of Peace (*Ara Pacis*), prominently displayed women of Augustus' family—the first time that women were shown alongside men in public monumental art. Augustus was probably not working for what we would see as women's liberation, nor did he have the fixed purpose of bringing women's rights up to the level of those enjoyed by men; but these actions were at least a partial result of his work toward the repopulation of Italy.

Summary

The Roman Republic never gave so much power to the people as the Athenian democracy did. The dominant forces were the great political families, allied through strategic marriages. As success in war created powerful commanders, their rivalry shattered the republican constitution. Augustus was Caesar's adopted son and also his final successor, the last warlord of the Republic. He rose to power in shameless disloyalty and bloodshed. Through his careful control of the army and magistrates, he then gave Rome three decades of healing after the civil wars, and the success of his work is shown by the fact that the state did not relapse into civil war after his death. His personality seems to lack the panache of Caesar, who was invincible in the field and a talented man of letters, but his greatness before history is that he formed the structure from which modern Europe has descended—the Roman Empire.

QUESTIONS FOR FURTHER THOUGHT

1. What features and conditions of life in Rome were especially conducive to the constant expansion of Rome's territorial holdings?
2. The Roman Republic had a constitution that resembled that of a Greek city-state in many ways, but it collapsed and gave way to one-man rule. How might Roman statesmen and the Senate have preserved the republican constitution?

RECOMMENDED READING

Sources

*Caesar, Julius. *The Gallic War*. Carolyn Hammond (tr.). 1996. An unsurpassed textbook in political-military decision making.

*Cicero. *Selected Political Speeches*. Michael Grant (tr.). 1977.

Gardner, Jane F., and Thomas Wiedemann (eds.). *The Roman Household: A Sourcebook*. 1991. Translated sources of all kinds on marriage, inheritance, and relations within the family.

*Livy. All surviving portions of his history of Rome are in four volumes published by Penguin (various translators). 1965–1982.

Mellor, Ronald (ed.). *The Historians of Ancient Rome: An Anthology of the Major Writings*. 1998. Collection in one volume of long excerpts from the Roman historians.

*Plutarch. *Fall of the Roman Republic*. Rex Warner (tr.). 1972. Biographies of Caesar, Pompey, Cicero, and other leading politicians of the Republic.

*Polybius. *The Rise of the Roman Empire*. Ian Scott-Kilvert (tr.). 1979. A generous selection from the surviving portions of the historian of Roman imperialism.

*Sallust. *Jugurthine War and War with Catiline*. S. A. Handford (tr.). 1963.

*Shelton, Jo-Ann (ed.). *As the Romans Did: A Sourcebook in Roman Social History*. 2d ed. 1998. Compilation of many interesting sources, arranged by categories (families, housing, education, and so on).

Studies

*Boatwright, Mary T., Daniel J. Gargola, and R. J. A. Talbert. *The Romans*. 2004. Most recent textbook treatment covering Roman history down to the death of the emperor Constantine, A.D. 337. Not excessive in length.

Bradley, Keith R. *Slavery and Rebellion in the Roman World*. 1989. A good study of the economic and political role of slavery.

———. *Discovering the Roman Family*. 1991. Chapters on child labor, the role of the nurse, divorce, and so on.

*Cornell, T. J. *The Beginnings of Rome*. 1995. Extensive narrative of all aspects of the Republic down to the Punic Wars. Now the best source.

Cornell, T. J., and J. Matthews. *Atlas of the Roman World*. 1982. Historical narrative, well illustrated by excellent maps.

Dixon, Suzanne. *The Roman Family*. 1992. On the development and practices of the family, following her *The Roman Mother*, 1988.

Dupont, Florence. *Daily Life in Ancient Rome*. 1992. On housing, amusements, the economy, the family.

Earl, Douglas. *The Age of Augustus*. 1980. The best survey of political and social life in the Augustan age.

Galinsky, Karl. *Augustan Culture*. 1966. Art, architecture, and culture of the age.

Gardner, Jane F. *Women in Roman Law and Society*. 1986. On the legal position of women and its changes in Roman life.

Habicht, Christian. *Cicero the Politician*. 1990. Admirably concise treatment, placing Cicero within the circle of Roman politicians.

Keaveney, Arthur. *Sulla: The Last Republican*. 1983. Study of Sulla, stressing his program of reform.

Keppie, Lawrence. *The Making of the Roman Army: From Republic to Empire*. 1984. Good history and analysis of the working of the army.

Kleiner, Diana E. E. *Roman Sculpture*. 1992. Complete history and survey of sculpture down to A.D. 330, superbly illustrated.

Meier, Christian. *Caesar*. 1995. The most modern, comprehensive biography of Rome's greatest warrior.

Nicolet, Claude. *The World of the Citizen in Republican Rome*. 1980. On the relation between citizen and state: taxation, military service, membership in assemblies, and so on.

Pallottino, Massimo. *A History of Earliest Italy*. 1991. Culture, economics, and history of the peoples of Italy by a great Etruscologist.

Richardson, Lawrence, Jr. *A New Topographical Dictionary of Ancient Rome*. 1992. Lists all known buildings and topographic features; first work to consult on any such question.

*Scullard, H. H. *From the Gracchi to Nero*. 5th ed. 1982. The best textbook narrative of the central period of the Republic and the early Empire.

Seager, Robin. *Pompey: A Political Biography*. Rev. ed. 2002. Brief, readable study of the man involved in many central political crises.

Southern, Pat. *Augustus, Emperor of Rome, 63 B.C.–14 A.D.* 1998. Most recent comprehensive biography of the first emperor.

Stockton, David. *The Gracchi*. 1979. The best modern study of the two politicians who discovered and used popular support.

*Syme, Ronald. *The Roman Revolution*. Originally 1939. The greatest study of the classical world in the last century. Brilliant analysis of the collapse of the Republic. For advanced students.

*Available in paperback.

GAIUS OCTAVIUS
Given the title "Augustus" by the Roman Senate, he is portrayed as ruler and military commander in this idealized statue.
Scala/Art Resource, NY

Chapter Five

THE EMPIRE AND CHRISTIANITY

THE EMPIRE AT ITS HEIGHT • THE PERIOD OF CRISIS (192–284) •
THE LATE ROMAN EMPIRE • CHRISTIANITY AND ITS EARLY RIVALS

The history of the Roman Empire is one of amazing continuity. The system of government devised by Augustus and maintained by his successors gave the Empire two centuries of solid prosperity. Historians call this the period of the *Pax Romana,* "the Roman Peace," and the Empire as a system of government remained an ideal in Europe for centuries. In the history of the Empire, the first main theme is the working of a cohesive political organization. The carefully crafted administration managed the greatest of all ancient empires, and its remains—stadiums, public baths, marketplaces, temples, official buildings—have inspired imitations down into our own times.

At the height of the Empire, the Roman world enjoyed a period of enviable prosperity. Remarkably, trade reached as far as China, where Rome obtained the luxury of silk, brought back along the famous Silk Road. But at the beginning of the third century, the Empire entered a period of crisis. Control of the army became the key to power, and emperors and would-be emperors followed one another in confusing succession. When order finally returned during the late third and fourth centuries, the old Roman Empire was no more. In the East, the Byzantine Empire was formed; in the West, the Empire steadily declined, finally ceasing to be governed by Rome in A.D. 476.

But even as antiquity was passing, its peoples were laying the basis for a new form of civilization. A change of religion became the second large historical theme in the Empire, as a new set of beliefs emerged— Christianity, which was destined to transform the life and culture of the Western heirs of the Roman Empire.

The "five good emperors" **96–180**

Flavian Dynasty **69–96**

Period of Crisis **192–284**

"Year of the four emperors" **69** ●

Rebellion of Jews in Judea **66–70**

131–135 Second Jewish Rebellion; Jews expelled from Jerusalem

ca. 33–62 Mission of St. Paul

14–68 Julio-Claudian Dynasty

ca. 4 B.C.–A.D. 30 Life of Jesus

27 B.C.–A.D. 14 Reign of Augustus

THE EMPIRE AT ITS HEIGHT

Three unifying elements preserved the Roman Empire that Augustus founded. First was the figure of the emperor, whom all subjects identified as the head of the regime. With some exceptions, the emperors were competent, stable rulers until about A.D. 200. Second were the civil servants and city councils, who collected taxes and maintained urban life. Third was the army, both the ultimate security of the emperor himself and the protector of the frontiers. The three elements supported one another, and the failure of any one of them threatened the other two and thus the fabric of the state (see "Tacitus on the Powers of Augustus," p. 121).

The Successors of Augustus

The Julio-Claudian Dynasty   The first emperor, Augustus, had no male heir. His last wife, Livia, was from the old patrician clan of the Claudians and evidently persuaded him to adopt her son, Tiberius, and to designate Tiberius as his successor. She thus played a leading role in shaping the imperial dynasty.

After the death of Augustus in A.D. 14, the Senate recognized Tiberius as ruler and thus confirmed the principle of dynastic succession, establishing the fact that an empire, not a republic, now existed. The dynasty founded by Augustus is known as the Julio-Claudian, because of a complex series of marriages between the Julian and Claudian clans. This dynasty reigned until A.D. 68. Much can be said against the rule of the **Julio-Claudians.** Tiberius was morbid, suspicious, and vengeful. His successor, Gaius (nicknamed Caligula), suffered from insanity and was murdered by the emperor's bodyguard, known as the Praetorian Guard. Claudius was gullible and was manipulated by his assistants and wives, the last of whom probably poisoned him to secure the throne for her son Nero. Nero ruled with some efficiency for his first five years but then became one of the worst emperors, whose tyranny led to a rebellion in Gaul. When the revolt spread to Rome, he saw that he was doomed and killed himself.

Yet these emperors did maintain, and even expand, the heritage left by Augustus. Claudius, for example, saw to the conquest of southern Britain, which became a Roman province in A.D. 47. He established new provinces and founded the city of Cologne in what is now Germany. Moreover, the Empire remained at peace internally, and the provincial administration that Augustus had established continued to function effectively.

Imperial Administration   The process of centralization of power in the person of the emperor and away from the Senate continued. Tiberius transferred election of magistrates from the people to the Senate; in effect, those whom he "recommended" were automatically elected. Claudius turned many affairs of state over to his trusted assistants, usually Greeks freed from slavery (thus called *freedmen*), who helped to found the bureaucracy that more and more ran the Empire.

Interventions by the Army   Another factor that weakened senatorial power was the frequent interference in affairs of state by the Praetorian Guard. The Guard first intervened in politics in 41, when it forced the Senate to recognize Claudius as emperor. It did the same for Nero in 54. This repeated invasion of civil authority by the Praetorian Guard was a step on the road toward militarization; within little more than a century, the emperors were to become totally dependent for power on their ability to buy the good will of the soldiery. The army, which had kept the emperors secure, sometimes became a force beyond control.

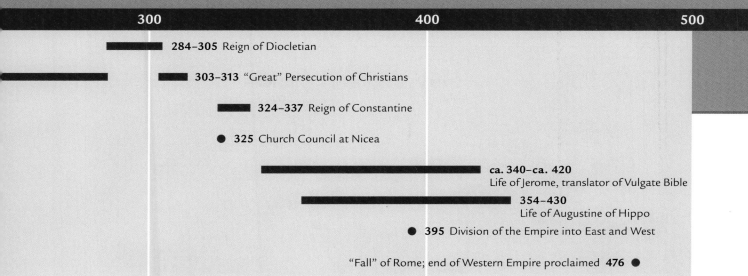

	300		400		500

284–305 Reign of Diocletian

303–313 "Great" Persecution of Christians

324–337 Reign of Constantine

● **325** Church Council at Nicea

ca. 340–ca. 420
Life of Jerome, translator of Vulgate Bible

354–430
Life of Augustine of Hippo

● **395** Division of the Empire into East and West

"Fall" of Rome; end of Western Empire proclaimed **476** ●

TACITUS ON THE POWERS OF AUGUSTUS

The first emperor of Rome, Augustus, maintained that he had restored the Republic after years of civil war. The historian Tacitus, writing about A.D. 120, gave a different evaluation of his work.

"After Brutus and Cassius were killed, the state had no military force. . . . Even the party of Julius Caesar had no leader left but Augustus, who laid aside the title of Triumvir and called himself a consul. For controlling the people, he contented himself with the rights of a tribune. When he had seduced the army with gifts, the people with distributions of food, and everyone with the pleasure of general calm, he began little by little to increase his authority and to gather to himself the powers of the Senate, the magistrates, and the laws. No one opposed him, since the strongest men had fallen either in battle or through legalized executions, and the rest of the nobles, according to who was more ready to accept servitude, were awarded gifts and public offices; since they profited from the new arrangements, they preferred their present security to the previous uncertainties. The provinces, too, accepted this state of affairs, since the former government by the Senate and people was suspect, owing to the struggles among the powerful and the greed of local governors; the protection of the laws had been worthless, because the laws were constantly overturned by violence, intrigue, and finally outright bribery."

From Tacitus, *Annals*, Book 1, ch. 2, M. H. Chambers (tr.).

The military played a significant role in the struggle over the succession after Nero's death in 68, as troops in various quarters of the Empire backed their own candidates for emperor. The year 69 is often called "the year of the four emperors" because in the course of the year four men claimed to be emperor. Vespasian finally stabilized the situation and emerged as sole ruler late in 69. He founded the Flavian Dynasty (so called from his second name, Flavius), which lasted through his reign and those of his two sons, Titus and Domitian.

The Five Good Emperors

The Flavian Dynasty ended in violence in 96, when a group of senators instigated the murder of the emperor Domitian, Vespasian's despotic son. The Senate then picked a quiet older senator, Nerva (r. 96–98), to be the new emperor. Nerva, who was childless, adopted an experienced military officer, Trajan, and designated him as his successor. The next two emperors, also childless, did the same. This system remained in use for nearly a century: An emperor would choose a qualified successor and adopt him as his son, thus ensuring a peaceful transfer of power. The men thus chosen were so capable that historians have called Nerva and the next four rulers the "five good emperors."

Trajan and Hadrian On the whole, in the period of the five good emperors, the Empire remained stable and even expanded. Trajan was an active military emperor

121

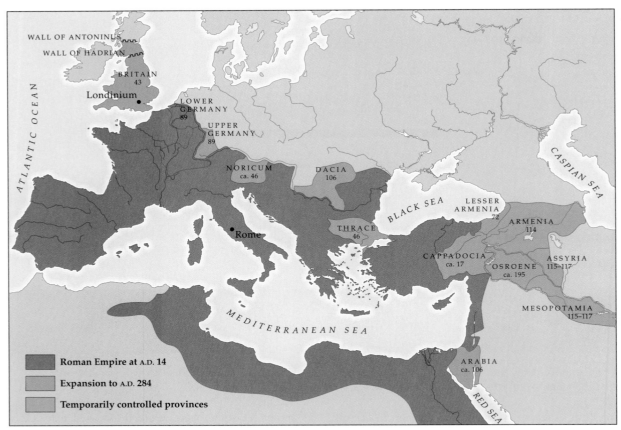

MAP 5.1 THE ROMAN EMPIRE, A.D. 14–284
This map shows the state of the Empire—the world's largest down to this time—from the death of Augustus to the accession of Diocletian. The largest permanent conquest was that of Britain. Note that the expansion in the extreme East was only temporary. Which was the last permanent acquisition in this period?
◆ For an online version, go to www.mhhe.com/chambers9 > chapter 5 > book maps

and conquered the region of Dacia, north of the Danube River. This was Rome's only permanent conquest north of the Danube and established a home for speakers of Latin; their descendants occupy modern Romania. In 116 Trajan drove the Empire to its farthest extension to the east as he established control over the Tigris-Euphrates valley as far as the head of the Persian Gulf, but he died while trying to return to Rome. Hadrian, his successor, decided to withdraw from this extreme eastern position; he thus changed from a policy of aggressive to defensive imperialism.

Trajan and Hadrian also undertook vast building programs. Trajan erected many structures throughout the Empire. Especially, he built a huge new forum (the Forum of Trajan) in central Rome and placed there an impressive column, which preserves a series of scenes recording episodes in his wars north of the Danube. This new Forum had a large group of buildings—shops, offices, a library—to the east of his column. Hadrian's

most famous building project is Hadrian's wall (much of it still stands), built across Britain to protect the frontier between the Roman province of Britain and the areas controlled by Celtic tribes to the north. In Italy, among other projects, he had built an immense luxurious "villa," actually a small town, south of Rome near Tivoli.

Hadrian continued the development of a frank autocracy. Laws now came down straight from the emperor and were known as "decisions" (*constitutiones*). Often the Senate was not even formally invited to approve such laws. He sought advice from an informal council known as the "friends" (*amici*) of the emperor, which included the leading experts in Roman law. One of these, Salvius Julianus, collected the edicts that Roman praetors had issued over the centuries, in an attempt to standardize the procedures of civil law; this action pointed the way toward the great codification of law in the sixth century under the emperor Justinian (see chapter 6). Hadrian's laws, though issued without any pretense of democratic process, were generally fair and humane. They tried to improve the condition of soldiers and slaves and gave women the same rights in court as men.

Antoninus Pius, Marcus Aurelius   Hadrian arranged the succession of the next two emperors, Antoninus Pius (r. 138–161) and Marcus Aurelius (r. 161–180), who are the last of the "five good emperors." The rule of Antoninus was peaceful, and under the reign of Marcus Aurelius the Empire enjoyed its last years of prosperity. Meanwhile, hostile new peoples were massing to the north and east of the imperial frontiers. In the final years of Marcus' reign, the gathering storm broke in all its fury, and he had to spend years fighting invasions by peoples on the Danube River and in the East.

One campaign was especially disastrous, because the army returning from Asia Minor in the 160s brought with it a devastating plague that spread through much of Europe. This plague must have been one cause of the later weakening of Rome, but the nearly total lack of records prevents our knowing how many died.

Unfortunately, Marcus abandoned the principle of adoption and passed the throne to his worthless son, Commodus (r. 180–192), whose extravagance and cruelty were reminiscent of Nero and Domitian. His murder on the last day of 192 opened a period of terrible instability, to which we shall return (pp. 133–134).

In A.D. 113 the emperor Trajan erected a monumental column to celebrate his war against peoples living across the Danube River. These panels show preparations for the war. Note the figure of the river god at the bottom, under a bridge built for the army.
Trëe

HADRIAN'S WALL
The emperor Hadrian had this famous wall built across Britain to mark off the Roman Empire and keep foreign peoples out.
C. M. Dixon

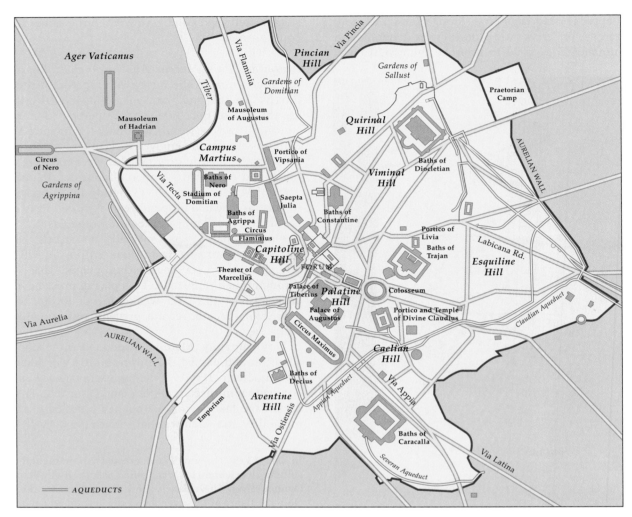

MAP 5.2 THE CITY OF ROME IN THE EMPIRE
On this map, note the buildings—above all, large public baths—built by several emperors. Please compare this map to map 4.1 (p. 96) to observe the growth of the city. The westward expansion across the Tiber River is known today as Trastevere ("trans-Tiber"). On which hill was the Palace of Augustus?
◆ For an online version, go to www.mhhe.com/chambers9 > chapter 5 > book maps

Roman Imperial Civilization

The Economy of the Cities   The first two centuries of the Empire are often called the "higher" Empire. In this period Italy and the provinces reached a level of prosperity and of flourishing population that Europe would not see again for a thousand years. The results of Roman censuses, which have partially survived, indicate that Italy at the death of Augustus contained about 7.5 million inhabitants. (In about 1500, the earliest date at which we can make a comparable estimate, the same area contained about 10 million people.)

Cities in the Empire   In the Western provinces, cities were, for the most part, small; to judge from the area enclosed by Roman walls, most towns contained only a few thousand residents. Yet they usually imitated Rome with temples, markets, arenas, courthouses, and other public buildings and thus displayed an authentic urban character. In the East, cities were often much larger. Alexandria in Egypt is estimated to have had about 400,000 inhabitants; Ephesus in Asia Minor, 200,000; Antioch in Syria, 150,000. The size of the cities in the East is surely one reason why the economy in the Eastern part of the Empire was stronger than that in the Western part.

Largest of all the imperial cities, and a true wonder of the ancient world, was Rome. Estimates of its size generally suggest about 1 million inhabitants. Not until the eighteenth century would European cities again contain such a concentration of people; in the 1780s, for example, Paris held about 600,000 people. Roman

An arch built by the emperor Trajan at Beneventum. Some panels show sacrifices to the gods, and the whole was intended to commemorate Trajan's generosity to his people. Triumphal and commemorative arches were among the proudest monuments in Rome and have been imitated in many modern cities.
Nimatallah/Art Resource, NY

civil engineering maintained, even under crowded conditions, acceptable standards of public hygiene and supplied enormous quantities of pure water and food.

Agriculture   Agriculture still remained the basic support of the economy, supplying, according to rough estimates, more than 75 percent of the total product of the Empire. One important change in Italian agriculture in the last century of the Republic had been shrinkage in the number of small peasant farms. They gave way to great slave-run estates, called **latifundia,** which generally produced cash crops. The owners of the big latifundia were wealthy senators and equestrians, even entrepreneurs from outside the traditional governing classes. Trimalchio, a freed slave who appears as a character in Petronius' novel, the *Satyricon,* boasted that he could ride from Rome to the area near Naples without leaving his own land.

The managers of these vast plantations favored varied forms of agriculture—cultivating vines, olives, and fruit and raising large numbers of cattle, sheep, and goats. Only enough grain was cultivated to feed the resident staff of workers, most of them slaves. The great estates also supplied the cities with building stone, lumber, and firewood; huge quantities of wood were required, for example, to keep the Roman baths at comfortable temperatures. In the view of many historians, extensive deforestation and overgrazing led inevitably to erosion of the land and the loss of fertile topsoil—principal reasons for the economic decline of Roman Italy. Even ancient peoples had the power to injure their environments.

Economies in the Provinces   In the provinces, the "Roman peace" favored the development of what had once been backward areas to the point that they threatened

A well-preserved apartment house (second to third century A.D.) in the city of Ostia, which served Rome as a port. The dwelling space is located over shops on the ground floor. The tradition of snack bars everywhere in Rome and Italy is an old one.
C. M. Dixon

Italy's economic leadership. The wine market, for example, passed into the hands of Spanish cultivators in the second century, for Spanish wine rivaled Italian in quality and was cheaper to produce, thanks to lower labor costs. In some areas of industry, too, the provinces began to outrun Italian production.

One of the main Italian industries was pottery, but by about A.D. 50 pottery made in Gaul had replaced Italian pottery even in Italy and had also taken over the market in the provinces and military camps. Thus Rome's success in establishing a commercial network created markets for products from the provinces and eventually contributed to Italy's own economic decline.

City Life in Italy   The upper class in Rome lived on a far higher scale, and was more widely separated from the common people, than the rich of Greece. The wealthy had running water tapped into their homes, slaves to tend them hand and foot, and elegant country villas for recreation. Hadrian's villa, or country retreat, near Rome was the size of a small city. These villas approached economic self-sufficiency, because slaves manufactured articles of light industry (clothing, leather goods, domestic utensils) on the farms.

A modern feature of Roman cities was the existence of suburbs and resorts. Pompeii was a commercial town, but its neighbor Herculaneum was a residential suburb. Both towns, buried and thus preserved by the volcanic eruption of Mt. Vesuvius in 79, contain examples of the airy Roman house, built around a central open court, or atrium, and decorated with graceful wall paintings.

The Working Classes   The workers of Rome had no such elegant housing, living rather in flimsy and inflammable apartments in high-rise buildings. They often had to plod up a hundred steps or more to their crowded rooms. A bed was the only place for sitting or eating, and the window opened to a noisy street. Rooms lacked running water, but a complex system of aqueducts gave easy access to water outside the home, and Rome always took pride in its enormous, cheap public baths.

There were associations in Rome for every kind of worker: fishermen, engineers, cobblers, silk workers, and so on. Despite their small, crowded apartments, city laborers had working conditions that were beyond the dreams of a Near Eastern peasant. They worked only about six or seven hours a day, and the Roman year contained about 160 holidays, to which the state added from time to time special days of celebration. The modern American actually works longer hours than the ancient Roman, despite our labor-saving devices.

Social Conditions   The major amusements for the people during days of leisure were public games, especially chariot races, which brought honor and wealth to the skilled charioteers, in arenas such as the huge Circus Maximus. Besides races, the Romans gave themselves over to brutal contests, which sometimes went on to death, between professional gladiators or between men and animals. The main arena for these spectacles was the grandiose Colosseum, begun by the emperor Vespasian in the 70s. It held about 50,000 spectators, and much of it still stands in central Rome, probably the one monument that most vividly recalls the classical city.

Rome was wealthy enough to support roughly half its population at public expense through free allotments of food, especially grain, which was the most common item in the diet. In the less prosperous years after 200, the cost of these subsidies placed a heavy strain on the Empire's economy.

Expansion of Trade   In the late Republic, and even more during the general prosperity of the Empire, industry and trade broke new frontiers. In 25–24 B.C. the emperor Augustus directed an expedition into Arabia for the sake of expanded trade; at about the same time he received envoys from India, surely for the same purpose, and he made treaties with the Parthians of Asia Minor to seek trading facilities in that region. Such commercial explorations were dramatically enhanced by long-distance trade, in both directions, with China, along the famous Silk Road (see "Rome and China: The Silk Road," pp. 128–130).

The Mixture in Society   Social mobility became easier under the Empire. For example, some Greeks who had been freed from slavery enjoyed enviable careers as secretaries to emperors or as businessmen. The need for more troops opened new opportunities for provincials, who entered the Roman legions, especially during the second century and later; and even the Senate began to include men born in the provinces. In time the Empire became less "Roman," for in both manpower and economic strength the primacy of Italy was of the past.

Women and the Family   The gains in the status of women continued in the Empire, above all within the families of the ruling elite, who lived in remarkable luxury. But more than this, women in the court of the emperor could even achieve political power comparable to that of such queens in the Hellenistic Age as Cleopatra. Livia, the last wife of Augustus, is said to have met with ambassadors of foreign states in the absence of Augustus and to have seen to the advancement of her political favorites. As we have seen, Augustus adopted her son, Tiberius, who became the second emperor of Rome; when Augustus died and was officially proclaimed a god, Livia became the priestess of his cult and received the title Augusta, a parallel to his own name Augustus.

Later in the history of the Julio-Claudian dynasty, Agrippina the Younger, a descendant of Augustus, showed equal political skill in getting her son chosen as the emperor Nero. She married the emperor Claudius, who already had a son from another marriage, and then persuaded Claudius to adopt her son; she probably poisoned Claudius and then obtained the support of the Praetorian Guard for Nero, whom the Senate recognized as emperor. Her influence over Nero in his early years made her almost a co-emperor, and her face appeared on official coins along with his.

The faces of other mothers and wives of emperors were struck on coins, and there were statues to women of the imperial court at many places in the Empire. Of course, not many women could attain such eminence, and the traditional values remained for most women: chastity and deference to the husband, loving care toward the children. In a famous epitaph, a Roman butcher said of his wife,

> She preceded me in death, my one and only, chaste in body, loving in spirit, faithful to her faithful husband, always cheerful, never neglecting her duty through greed.

Roman Law   A complex system of law and procedure was one of the chief cultural contributions of Roman civilization. Roman law had already developed under the Republic, but its further development under the Empire made it even more all-embracing. The Stoic philosophy influenced Roman legal thought, through the idea that the universe is inherently rational and that life should be guided by reason. Moreover, Roman legal thought recognized a kind of *natural law,* valid for all people, which could be discovered through rational inquiry. At times, especially in periods of crisis, weaker members of society could not always obtain justice; but the overriding social purpose of Roman law was to provide justice rather than simply maintain the stability of the state. As an example, natural law denied the legality of slavery.

The Growth of the Roman Legal System   The assemblies of the Republic, both that of the Centuries and that of the Tribes (see chapter 4), issued laws mainly on large public issues, such as distributions of land or assignments of military commands overseas. Another influence on the law came from magistrates, especially praetors, who issued edicts that explained the principles by which they would interpret the law during their year in office; these edicts acquired the authority of tradition and ultimately passed into permanent law.

Normally, cases came before a judge, who was a private citizen relying on the advice of other private citizens who were reputed to understand the law but did not actually practice law. These advisers were called jurists (**iurisprudentes** or **iurisconsulti**), and their opinions constantly influenced the growth of the law, especially in the first two centuries of the Empire. They could also rise to high political office. Among the most important jurists were Ulpian, Paulus, and Gaius. They delivered written responses, with authority delegated to them by the emperors, to questions raised by presiding judges and relied mainly on "natural law" for their opinions. Their responses thus shaped Roman laws, even when the laws themselves were issued by emperors as constitutiones. They also wrote voluminous commentaries on the law, and their opinions are widely preserved in the final great codification of the law by Justinian in the sixth century.

Global Moment

ROME AND CHINA: THE SILK ROAD

The Silk Road captivates the popular imagination today as one of the oldest and most productive links between East and West in ancient history. The road was a key trade route by which commodities and ideas were exchanged from as far east as China and as far west as the Roman world. It got its popular name in the nineteenth century from the German geographer F. von Richthofen, who named it the "Seidenstrasse" (Silk Road) after one of the chief products to come out of China. Those who used this road traveled across harsh deserts and hostile territories to profit from the trade in merchandise such as fine silks, spices, and jewels. This trade flourished during the Han Dynasty of China (206 B.C.–A.D. 220) and during the height of expansion in the Roman Republic and early Roman Empire.

The Silk Road was not one single road as the name suggests, but actually comprised several different routes; in general, it ran for more than 4,000 miles between eastern China and the seaports of the Mediterranean. We do not have precise dates for when the different sections were developed, but we can describe the route at its most nearly complete stage. Its easternmost point is usually identified with modern-day Xi'an (or Sian). Proceeding from there, south of the Great Wall of China, it ran west to Dunhuang. From there, it split and reunited many times, across desert and over mountains before reaching its westernmost point, just south of modern Baghdad, on the Euphrates River (see map). Ships could then sail up the Euphrates to a Roman camp named Zeugma. Goods could travel a short distance westward by land and reach the great port of Antioch, near the mouth of the Orontes River. From here ships could sail through the Mediterranean Sea until they reached the west coast of Italy and Rome.

Silk was not the only product transported on the road, but it was probably considered the most remarkable one in the West, desired chiefly for its luxurious quality (the Chinese guarded the source and process

with the utmost secrecy). In fact, the Latin name for the Chinese was *Seres,* which means silk, and China thus became known as the "land of silk," *Serica* or *Terra Serica.* From the West, China received clothing, glass, rugs, and precious metals—including prized gold from the Roman world.

Roman writers were well aware of the trade among the Empire, India, and China. One Roman source states that one pound of silk was considered equal in value to the same weight in gold (*Scriptores Historiae Augustae,* Life of Aurelianus, chap. 45). This may be an exaggeration, like our saying that something is "worth its weight in gold," but in the first century A.D. the encyclopedist Pliny the Elder (*Natural History,* 12.84) looked with disfavor on the trade in such luxuries, recording that the Roman trade with India, China, and Arabia cost the Romans 100 million sesterces (small silver coins, perhaps about five million dollars) in trading deficits. That is, the balance of trade was in favor of the eastern nations.

As the different cultures came into contact through trade, they also learned something about each other's appearances, customs, and practices. Chinese impressions of the Romans are documented in sources that refer to the Roman Empire as Ta Ch'in; this was actually the general region of Syria, where the Silk Road ended in the West. Chinese sources report as follows:

> The country of Ta Ch'in is situated on the western part of the sea. The defenses of the cities are made of stone. The inhabitants of that country are tall and well-proportioned, somewhat like the Chinese, whence they are called Ta Ch'ins. The country contains much gold, silver, and rare precious stones, especially the "jewel that shines at night" [the diamond?], "the moonshine pearl," corals, amber, glass, green jadestone, gold-embroidered rugs, and thin silk-cloth of various colors. They make gold-colored cloth and asbestos cloth. All the rare gems of other foreign countries come from there. They make coins of gold and silver. Ten units of silver are worth one of gold. They traffic by sea with Ahn-si (Parthia) and T'ien-chu (India), the profit of which trade is ten-fold. They are honest in their transactions, and there are no double prices. Their kings always desired to send embassies to China, but the

An-his (Parthians) wished to carry on trade with them in Chinese silks, and it is for this reason that they were cut off from communication.

These records are interesting not only because they reveal some of the earliest known Chinese impressions of the Romans, but because they tell of the many products that exchanged hands, and of the role of the Parthians, whose kingdom included the territory of Persia located directly between Rome and China. While it is likely that merchandise changed hands many times over such a long route, the Parthians were especially well placed to profit as middlemen along the Silk Road. In an effort to cut off the Parthians' profit, both Rome and China sent emissaries in search of each other. For instance, in A.D. 97 Gang Ying, a Chinese ambassador, traveled as far west as Mesopotamia but was prevented (or persuaded) from going directly west into Syria. Instead, he was conveyed south to the head of the Persian Gulf and was told, "The sea is vast and great; with favorable winds it is possible to cross within three months; but if you meet slow winds, it may also take you two years." At this point, he returned home.

Romans also traveled toward China. Coins of the emperor Marcus Aurelius and his predecessor, Antoninus Pius, have been found in the Far East, and Chinese sources from A.D. 166 report the arrival of Romans claiming to represent Marcus Aurelius. Very little information on this encounter is preserved, but sources do reveal that the Romans presented modest gifts or ivory, rhinoceros horns, and tortoise shells, which suggest that it was an expedition of private traders rather than one sent by the emperor of Rome, who likely would have produced more lavish gifts.

Over the next few centuries, the Western demand for silk, especially for church and royal garments, continued to grow to such a degree that in A.D. 552 the Byzantine emperor Justinian in Constantinople intervened in the trade. The historian Procopius (*History of the Wars*, 1.20.9–12) reports that Justinian proposed to the king of the Ethiopians that he should cooperate with Justinian in securing a supply of silk for the two nations. At this time, the once weakened Persian Empire had revived under the Sassanid Dynasty and was finding ways to use its new influence by blocking trade in silk from India and China by land routes, including the Silk Road. Moreover, Persian merchants often placed themselves in harbors where the ships from India, carrying silk, used to dock. They often bought up the whole cargo of silk and thus frustrated the Byzantine Empire's access to it.

Apparently Justinian was not successful in his attempt to work with the Ethiopians to acquire more silk, and the Chinese were not eager to let the source, the valuable silkworms, escape their control. According to Procopius, who continues the story (*Wars*, 8.17.1–8), two monks, who had traveled in India and China and learned the secrets of silkworm cultivation and weaving, assured Justinian that they could free him from having to buy silk from the Persians. The precious silkworms could not be brought to Constantinople alive, but it would be possible to convey their offspring as unhatched eggs. The monks faithfully transported some of the eggs back to Constantinople—according to another source, in hollow canes. The eggs were then buried in dung and, when sufficiently heated, they produced the worms. The worms then fed on the leaves of the mulberry tree, which grew widely in Syria. This stratagem laid the foundation for the manufacture of silk in Europe. In the Byzantine Empire, silk production was a carefully guarded secret, and its manufacture and distribution became a royal monopoly.

The Silk Road continued in use by merchants and travelers, but by about 1100 the trade with the West was seriously weakened through attacks on the Byzantine Empire. For example, the Seljuk Turks began an onslaught against the Empire from the east. At the battle of Manzikert (modern Malazgirt in eastern Turkey), north of Lake Van, in 1071, the Seljuks annihilated a

continued

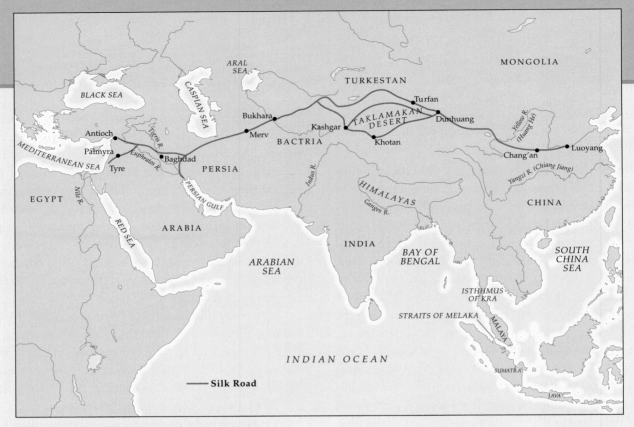

THE SILK ROAD BETWEEN CHINA AND THE WEST
Merchants and traders carried silk and other products on this road for centuries. It also became an important artery for all kinds of cultural exchange. What was the farthest point that the road reached toward the West?
◆ For an online version, go to www.mhhe.com/chambers9 > chapter 5 > book maps

Byzantine army and took the emperor Romanus IV Diogenes prisoner. He died in the next year, and soon afterward Byzantine power in Asia Minor collapsed. However, by this time the manufacture of silk had spread to Sicily and Spain in the hands of the Arabs, and later it also spread through the cities of Italy northward into Europe. As the West was able to produce more of its own silk, its demand for silk from China lessened. In addition, the development of sea routes offered alternatives to the challenging land routes. The Silk Road traffic declined.

To the historian, the importance of the Silk Road is not limited to its commercial aspects. Valuable commodities had been exchanged overland for millennia by way of the Road, but as merchants and traders met one another along the Road a significant series of intellectual exchanges also took place. The great trade route may have reached its supreme importance in the world of faith. The major religions of modern times—first Buddhism, then Christianity (of the "Nestorian" kind), and finally Islam—followed the ancient traders on this long highway and planted their beliefs among the peoples. Seen in this light, the Silk Road must also be called one of the most important arteries of intellectual and spiritual life in the history of the world.

The Chinese sources quoted here, known as Dynastic Histories, are taken from F. Hirth, *China and the Roman Orient*, Shanghai 1885, reprinted Chicago 1975 (language modified).

Citizens and Noncitizens in Roman Law   The Romans distinguished their own citizens from the other peoples under their control. Roman citizens were subject to the "civil law" (***ius civile***), or law applying to citizens. The number of people subject to this law grew constantly as citizenship was extended to more and more inhabitants. Finally, the emperor Caracalla decreed that all free men and women in the Empire should be citizens, thus subject to the ius civile.

Down to the time of this mass grant of Roman citizenship, inhabitants of the Empire who were not citizens had the right to maintain many of their own customs, which came to form the ***ius gentium,*** or law applying to other nations. These two kinds of law fell, logically enough, to two magistrates for administration, the "urban praetor" (*praetor urbanus*) and the "traveling praetor" (*praetor peregrinus*). But when all free men and women became citizens, the ius gentium in this sense was no longer needed.[1]

The Romans' respect for their law is consistent with the remarkable cohesiveness that one sees throughout their society. In war they were often brutal, but then so were many others in all periods of history. Rome's achievement in designing and preserving a system of laws governing the behavior of citizens toward one another has served as a model for much of the law of Western Europe. Codes of law, as we have also observed, are a feature of several other ancient societies, but in richness and complexity the codifications of the late Roman Empire easily surpass all the rest.

Engineering and Architecture   The Romans showed brilliance in the fields of engineering and construction. The most enduring monument to Roman civilization is the impressive network of roads found everywhere from Britain to Africa. Originally designed as highways for the rapid movement of legions, these roads became trade routes in more peaceful times and eliminated all barriers to travel.

From the earliest times the Romans also built aqueducts that converged toward the cities, sloping down and carrying fresh water from the mountains; Rome's imposing system of sewers was constantly flushed by water from the aqueducts. The Romans placed more emphasis on personal cleanliness than did any other civilization until modern times. Several emperors commissioned the building of immense public baths, of which the grandest of all were the Baths of Caracalla at Rome, built in the third century. The English city of Bath is named for the facilities that the Romans built there.

[1] In Roman legal theory, *ius gentium* came to mean a kind of universal law observed by all nations, in effect, a system of law that could be discovered by reason.

The Sacred Way leads into the Roman Forum through the Arch of Titus, which was erected to celebrate the end of the great Jewish rebellion in A.D. 70. A triumphal procession would enter the Forum through this elegantly placed arch and parade up to the Temple of Jupiter on the Capitoline Hill. Trëe

Roman temples, imitating those of the Greeks, were supported by columns, usually in the Corinthian style, crowned with a bell-like acanthus flower. Their temples had large interiors and were often completely walled at the rear, because Romans performed their ceremonies indoors. They were the first to grasp the possibilities of using arches and vaults on a large scale, thus giving their buildings a vastness that the Greeks could not achieve.

Large Buildings in Concrete   The Romans also invented concrete, which is inexpensive and can be laid by relatively unskilled labor. It can be shaped into forms impossible in marble, and it is lighter in weight and can easily be supported in vaulted buildings. One of its most successful applications is the spacious Pantheon—built in the time of Augustus and then rebuilt under Hadrian—covered by a dome with a striking opening in the center. Sculpture and architecture coincided in triumphal arches, which often bear reliefs depicting the historical event that the arch commemorates.

Literature in the Empire: Virgil   In Rome, literature was generally the entertainment of the upper classes.

Augustus, the first emperor, favored several of the most famous Latin poets at his court. Perhaps the leading Latin poet was Virgil (70–19 B.C.). He borrowed from Greek models, as Roman poets often did. His early poems, the *Bucolics* (also called *Eclogues*) and *Georgics,* are polished hymns of praise to the Italian landscape that reflect the style of Theocritus and Hesiod; but the gentle, human spirit of Virgil himself is always present. The best qualities of Virgil appear when he treats civilized emotions—mercy, compassion, and sadness; then his work echoes with a graceful melancholy.

These qualities appear in his patriotic epic, the *Aeneid,* which adopts and transforms materials from Homer. In this work Virgil narrates the wanderings of Aeneas, the Trojan whose descendants were the legendary founders of Rome. Leaving his native city after the fall of Troy, Aeneas reached Carthage and had a romance with its queen, Dido; but his sense of duty compelled him to abandon her in order to reach Italy and fulfill his destiny. Virgil's aim was to sing the glory of Rome and its salvation by Augustus after the civil wars of the late Republic. Virgil knew Augustus, was a favorite at Augustus' court, and at times wrote what could be considered official propaganda.

Satire: Horace, Juvenal

A contemporary of Virgil's was Horace, whose *Odes, Epodes,* and *Satires* examine love, amusement, annoyance, contentment—in short, the feelings of everyday life. He too was well connected with the court of Augustus. Now and then Horace makes an attempt at serious patriotic verse, but these poems are self-conscious and moralizing and do not speak with the real Horatian voice of gentle, amusing irony.

Juvenal, a more pungent satirist than Horace, wrote shortly after A.D. 100. He took as his motto "Indignation inspires my poetry" (*facit indignatio versum*). His poems denounce the excess of pride and elegance in Roman society. His language is colorful, often bitter and obscene. One of his richest and wisest satires concerns the vanity of human wishes. After reviewing the foolishness of human beings, Juvenal gives his advice in a famous epigram: One should pray for "a sound mind in a sound body" (*mens sana in corpore sano*).

Poetry of Love

There was also a rich literature of sexuality. The poet Ovid (43 B.C.–A.D. 17) wrote a handbook for seduction, *The Art of Love,* and a treatise on love affairs. Perhaps because of his frankly sexual subject matter, Augustus exiled him to a distant town in the Black Sea region: a reminder that the peace and order under the Empire did not always guarantee personal freedom. The poet Propertius (ca. 47 B.C.–ca. 2 B.C.) and others also wrote of their mistresses; and the Greek satirist Lucian (ca. A.D. 120–ca. 185) has left a racy *Dialogue of the Courtesans.*

Historians: Livy

The histories of Rome written during the Republic were usually the work of men directly involved in politics. Under the Empire this situation changed because political contest had almost vanished. It therefore seemed appropriate to look back on the Republic and write a final history of its politics and imperialism. Titus Livius, or Livy (59 B.C.–A.D. 17), undertook this task during the reign of Augustus, when the decisive political transformation occurred. Livy narrated Roman history from its legendary beginnings until 9 B.C. Because he usually drew on the work of earlier historians, he was sometimes unable to escape the influence of the myths that had clouded the history of the early Republic; thus he is at his best when he uses a good source such as the Greek historian Polybius.

Livy's *Roman History* is a kind of prose epic, filled with patriotism and admiration for the great men who had led Rome when the Republic was conquering the Mediterranean. He also suggests that Rome had declined in moral standards. Livy was the last writer in Latin to attempt a full history of Rome. His work inspired many later writers who looked back at the Republic as the Golden Age of Rome; it was accepted as authoritative until soon after 1800, when historians began to be more skeptical about Roman tradition.

Tacitus

The leading Roman historian in intellectual stature was Publius Cornelius Tacitus (ca. 55–ca. 120). His first major work is *The Histories,* in which he treats Roman history from 69, the year of the four emperors, through the death of Domitian in 96, emphasizing the analysis of character. Deeply influenced by satire, the dominant literary form of his age, Tacitus loved to fashion stinging epigrams aimed at members of the governing class, and he treated nearly all his main characters as selfish or corrupt. His disillusioned attitude was partly the result of his being an outsider, probably from southern Gaul; he saw Roman society through the cool eyes of a man from a province who became a senator and even rose to the office of consul.

His most important work is the *Annals,* which covers the reign of the Julio-Claudian emperors from Tiberius through Nero. Tacitus looked back at the early Empire from the vantage point of a later period. Though he said he wrote "without anger or partisanship" (*sine ira et studio*),[2] he found little good to say about the first emperors, and few modern critics would call him impartial. At his best, Tacitus sets a high standard of accuracy, but his wish for accuracy was sometimes at war with his desire to send a moral message about the failings of this or that regime.

[2] *Annals,* 1.1.

The ancient Greek city Ephesus, on the coast of Turkey, remained prosperous in the Empire. Tiberius Julius Celsus, consul in A.D. 92, endowed this magnificent library, which his son completed about 135.
Comstock

THE PERIOD OF CRISIS (192–284)

The Roman Empire, at its height, was in modern language the superpower of the Western world. There was no other state or system that could be called an empire, and certainly none that could challenge or threaten it. But in the third century of our era the Empire faltered and stumbled. The three unifying elements all appeared to be at the end of their strength. Emperors proved to be either weak or corrupt; the civil service was demoralized; and the army was broken up into factions that supported now one emperor, now another. The collapse of these three bulwarks of the state brought the economy crashing to ruin.

The Crisis of Leadership

The centuries of the "Roman peace" ended with the death of the emperor Commodus in 192, and in the following years the political balance shifted to the military. The next generation faced an all but fatal military and political crisis. Wars broke out on the European frontiers, and most emperors could survive only a few years. During the third century, dozens of emperors claimed the throne, but many of these men were really no more than political gamblers or warlords who for a short time purchased the loyalty of their soldiers. Thus two of the stabilizing elements of the Empire—the strong, effective emperor and the disciplined army—began to fall apart.

The Roman Senate, which had once been the inspiration and bulwark of the state, now had neither interest nor ability to intervene in affairs of state, while the emperors assumed more and more dictatorial powers and governed through court favorites. The economy of

the Empire, too, nearly collapsed during this period, largely because defense costs had risen as raiders plundered the wealth of the Empire on several frontiers. Moreover, the emperors had been supplying the inhabitants of Rome with free food and public games, or "bread and circuses," in the phrase of Juvenal the satirist—a fairly effective means of political domination, but a heavy drain on the economy. Adding to these financial problems was a shortage of silver, on which the imperial currency was based. The emperors resorted to debasing the currency, but this action forced people to hoard what silver they had and actually drove more of the metal out of circulation.

A further problem was the increasing reluctance of people of independent means to hold civic offices, which paid no salary. Moreover, office holders were forced to pay from their own pockets any deficiency in the collection of taxes. Finally, the government had to compel people to take office, a step that pointed to the practice of binding people to their occupations. This in turn led to the collapse of the third crucial element of stability in the state, the efficient administrators and civil servants. Many of the emperors during the century of crisis were men of little leadership; but some of them must have been among the ablest rulers in the history of Rome, for otherwise the Empire would have totally disintegrated.

Weaknesses in Roman Slavery

The Numbers of Slaves Like most other ancient states, Rome used slaves widely. The historian's duty is not simply to denounce this repugnant practice but to understand its place in Roman society. Ancient slavery, unlike slavery in America, never comprised members of only one ethnic group. Anyone might have the bad luck to be rounded up, especially in war, and forced into slavery. During the late Republic, the number of Roman slaves increased dramatically, as Rome overran Greece, Asia Minor, Spain, and Gaul. Of the 7.5 million inhabitants of Italy at the death of Augustus, an estimated 3 million were slaves.

Slavery allowed an expansion of the great plantations of the last century of the Roman Republic. In most places they were more or less adequately fed. They had a better life in the cities, where they served as artisans and personal servants. Greeks in particular acted as tutors. Others supplied entertainment, especially girls and boys who could sing and dance. There was also traffic in beautiful young slaves of both sexes, often for sexual purposes. Gladiators were slaves and probably fought harder because of it. Victory over opponents might lead to freedom; if they lost, they forfeited little more than a miserable existence.

Slavery and the Economy   Judged solely as an economic system, slavery allowed a calculated use of labor in relation to land and capital. But slavery had serious weaknesses, which we must include in the causes for the decline of the Empire in the West. Rome declined in part because the economy could no longer support the army against invaders. One principal reason for this weakness was that slavery could not solve two basic economic problems. First, there must be incentives to ensure an effective labor force. The possibility of being freed provided some incentive, but on the whole the plight of the slave was not to be envied. Especially on the land, the principal incentive for slaves was the dread of punishment. Their work required little skill and was almost entirely physical labor. This drained their work of dignity and dampened interest in technological innovation.

Second, demoralized slaves were poor producers of children, even when they were allowed to marry. Why pass misery down the generations? And conquests ceased from the time of Hadrian (117–138), a fact that threatened the continued supply of slaves.

The Plight of the Poor

The spread of great estates in the late Republic had driven many small farmers off the land. Many displaced workers drifted into Rome, where free bread and circuses purchased their docility. In provinces, too, rural depopulation and the abandonment of cultivated fields became a major problem for the economy. Faced with shrinking numbers of cultivators and taxpayers, the government sought desperately to resettle the abandoned fields. For example, Marcus Aurelius started a policy of settling foreigners on deserted lands within the Empire. The state also sought to attract free Roman farmers back to the countryside. The free cultivator who settled on another's land was called a **colonus,** and this institution was called the *colonate.*

The Poor and the Land   Roman policy toward the *coloni* and other free cultivators was ambivalent and shifting. In many cases the colonus did well, with a light and fixed rent that he paid to the landlord, or *dominus.* He could sell the land he improved or pass it on to his heirs, and he could depart from it at will. But by the fourth century the picture was much worse: The colonus was bound to the soil, as were his children after him, and he was subject to the personal jurisdiction of his lord. The long-term interests of society dictated that resettlement within family-owned farms should be encouraged. On the other hand, the hard-pressed government could not overlook any source of revenue, and it often resorted to outrageous fiscal practices. It ruthlessly requisitioned food; it forced settlers to pay the taxes of their absent neighbors; and it subjugated settlers to the authority of their landlords, who could be held responsible for collecting from them services and taxes. By the fourth and fifth centuries, under conditions of devastating fiscal oppression, some peasants preferred to flee the Empire rather than face ruin at home.

THE LATE ROMAN EMPIRE

The crisis of the third century came close to a disaster that might have carried the Empire straight to its death. But some of the many emperors, both desperate and determined, managed to hold off invasions on the frontiers. The system designed by Augustus and maintained by his successors proved to have enough resources to weather the storm. As the Empire regained stability, it could not return to the old system in which the Senate provided a measure of guidance and contributed efficient governors. The only promise for the future lay in a strict vertical system. Meanwhile, in the world of faith the old Roman deities commanded less and less devotion, and a change of gods could not be halted or reversed.

Restoration under Diocletian

The Rule of Diocletian (r. 284–305)   The political crisis of the third century finally ended in 284 when Diocletian, a high army officer, seized the imperial throne. He was from the peasantry of Illyria and was a strong, ruthless man who ruled through an authoritarian bureaucracy. Recognizing that the Empire was too large and too unstable to be directed by one man, Diocletian

The Tetrarchs (Diocletian and his corulers), shown supporting each other, on a corner of St. Mark's cathedral in Venice: Diocletian and Maximian are on the right; Galerius and Constantius on the left. The heads on the swords are Germanic.
Michael Holford Photographs

natural economic forces led to further inflation, and he had to let the edict lapse after a few years.

Diocletian's severe rule stabilized the Empire, though it is hard to find in it much to praise. Many of his practices continued throughout the fourth century, especially his establishment of a despotism that resembled the ancient kingdoms of the Near East in its absolute monarchic rule. All laws came directly from the emperor, and the jurists, who had shaped the growth of law in the first two centuries of the Empire, played no further role. Thus Rome had moved from a "principate," the system of Augustus, to a "dominate" (*dominus*, "master").

The Accession of Constantine   Diocletian retired in 305, and soon afterward his system of shared rule broke down. Years of complex intrigue and civil war followed, as several leaders fought for the throne. One of the ruling circle was Constantius, the father of Constantine. When Constantius died in 306, Constantine began to fight for supreme power; in 324 he defeated his last rival and became sole emperor of Rome. Thus, forty years after the accession of Diocletian, the Empire once again had a single ruler. In 330 Constantine renamed the old Greek city of Byzantium as New Rome and established it as his capital; popular usage gave it the name Constantinople.

Constantine and the Bureaucracy

By the end of his reign in 337, Constantine had set the pattern that remained throughout the fourth and later centuries. The whole state was now one rigid structure, almost one massive corporation that brutally discouraged individual initiative. A totally impassable gulf existed between the monarch's court and the common people. Even within the court, the emperor stood apart from the rest, surrounded by ceremony. Fourth-century rulers wore expensive cloaks dyed in purple, and courtiers had to kiss a corner of the emperor's robe when approaching the throne. Diadems, the custom of kneeling before the emperor, and other marks of royalty became traditional and have remained so in European monarchies.

The Decline of the Western Empire

After Constantine's death in 337, the chief administrative question for more than a century was whether one man could be strong enough to rule as sole monarch. For most of the time, this solution proved impossible, and some kind of shared rule became common. On the death of Theodosius in 395, the Empire split into an Eastern half and a Western half, with the dividing line just east of Italy.

enlisted three associates to assist him in ruling. The two senior men (Diocletian and Maximian) bore the title Augustus; the two younger (Galerius and Constantius) were known as Caesar. Modern historians call this arrangement the **Tetrarchy** (rule of four). Each of the four rulers was placed wherever he was needed.

In order to solve the financial crisis, Diocletian had every plot of land taxed at a certain amount, to be paid to the emperor's agents. Trades and professions were also taxed so that the burden would not fall solely on landowners. The cities in the Empire had long had a local council or **curia;** the officials, called **curiales,** were personally responsible for the required tax and had to pay it themselves if they could not collect it from others. Diocletian tried to hold back inflation with a famous Edict on Prices, which fixed maximum prices for nearly all goods and also fixed maximum wages. But

The emperor Constantine tried to increase his glory by commissioning colossal portraits of himself, such as the one in Rome shown here. The original full-length statue was some forty feet tall.
Hirmer Fotoarchiv

In the last centuries of the Empire, society became more and more rigid; it did not, and perhaps could not, allow people to move freely from one class to another. As the central government weakened, local estates, usually called *villas*, became self-sufficient units with hunting lands and workshops that supplied the goods that the local population needed; they therefore became the main economic and political units of the Western Empire. At the same time, trade was declining because of a shortage of new markets and the constant threat of invasions along the frontiers. Moreover, a shortage of labor caused fertile lands to lie fallow and mines to remain unexploited.

The "Fall" of Rome?   Such was the background for the dramatic turning point in history that is the end of the Western Empire. The formal end of the Western Empire is traditionally dated to 476, when a Germanic warlord, Odoacer (sometimes called Odovacar), deposed the youth whom we call the last Western emperor, Romulus Augustulus, and the Senate resolved not to try to name any further Western emperors. To symbolize the end of the Western emperors, an embassy was sent to Constantinople to surrender the imperial insignia. Modern readers inevitably think of this event in the terminology imposed by the historical masterpiece of Edward Gibbon—that is, as the "decline and fall" of the Empire. But no political structure as large as the Roman Empire really falls like a tree in a forest without further influence or legacy. Moreover, some emperors in Constantinople, notably Justinian in the sixth century, saw themselves as the head of the whole traditional Empire, West and East, and tried to reunite the two geographic parts.

The Survival of the Eastern Empire   Even though historians take care to speak of the transformation of the Empire rather than of its disappearance, there is no doubt that the Empire in the West did pass away, while the Eastern part, based on Constantinople and called by historians the Byzantine Empire, survived for nearly another thousand years. The problem is to explain why the Western regions could not maintain themselves under a continuous government while no similar dissolution threatened the Eastern portion of the Empire.

Theories about the Fall   Some historians have been enticed into trying to state the one great cause for the fall of Rome—and this quest may be impossible. Gibbon, for example, blamed the destructive work of barbarism and religion. But to say that Rome declined because of invasions by Germans, Franks, and Goths only pushes the inquiry back one step: Why were these peoples able to defeat an Empire that had ruled the civilized world for centuries? And why did the Eastern part of the Empire not decline along with the Western?

Some historians suggest that the emperors unintentionally paved the way for the fall of Rome by exterminating possible political rivals in the upper class, thus weakening the group that could have supplied leader-

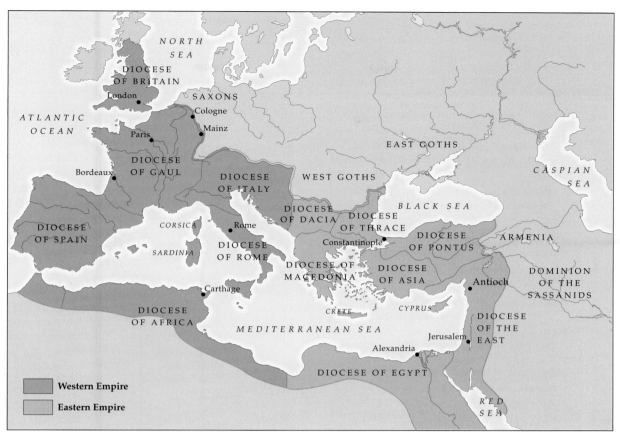

MAP 5.3 THE EASTERN AND WESTERN EMPIRES IN 395
By the time of the division of the Empire in 395, it was divided into several "Dioceses," corresponding roughly to the former provinces. Dacia, north of the Danube River, had been lost, but the name was retained in a Diocese south of the river. Where were the two major locations of Goths?

◆ For an online version, go to www.mhhe.com/chambers9 > chapter 5 > book maps

ship for the state. Others have advanced an economic argument, saying that the Empire was bound to decline because it never really emerged from a domestic economy. But this economic theory is hardly convincing, for some societies—admittedly much less complex than the Empire—have existed for many centuries with no more than a domestic economy. If there had been no convulsions and strains in the Empire, the production of goods and food could have continued more or less unchanged. Other historians have proposed exhaustion of the soil and fluctuating cycles of rainfall and drought in order to explain Rome's economic depression, but there is little exact knowledge about the cycles of crops and weather conditions that would indubitably account for the fall of the Empire.

A Crisis in Manpower   Still other historians have suggested that the weakness of the Western Empire was due to a shortage of manpower. This explanation does have some merit, because the Eastern cities appear to have been more populous than the Western ones, and

thus they had more strength and resilience. The numerical inferiority of the West became even more serious when the villas became self-sufficient units and there was no longer a centralized military system. It was much easier for outsiders to invade the Empire when they met haphazard resistance from local forces. As early as the third century, many Germanic captives and volunteers entered the army, which was scarcely "Roman" in any true sense. The Germanic troops felt little loyalty to Roman tradition and were unwilling to submit to severe discipline. Thus the army—the power base of the Augustan age—sank and pulled the Empire down with it. Also, the relocation of the capital to Constantinople moved the administrative center even farther from the Western provinces and probably accelerated the dissolution of the regions of Italy and Gaul.

The Routes of Invasion   But the shortage of manpower was not the only factor in the weakening of the Western Empire. Possibly an even stronger threat was simply the physical geography of Europe. The Western

CHRONOLOGY
The "Fall" of Rome

476 is known to all readers of history as the year of the fall of Rome, but the true chronology is more complex.

393	Theodosius I, ruling in Constantinople, installs his son Honorius as emperor in the West.
395	Death of Theodosius; the division of the Empire into Eastern and Western parts is maintained.
423	Death of Honorius in West; other Western emperors continue to be appointed.
474, June 24	Leo I, emperor in East, appoints Julius Nepos as emperor in West.
475	Nepos appoints Orestes, a former lieutenant of Attila the Hun, as Master of the Soldiers. Orestes insists that his young son, Romulus Augustus (or Augustulus), be recognized as Western emperor. Nepos flees to Salona in Dalmatia. Romulus is proclaimed emperor in Ravenna on October 31, but the act is without legal force, and Nepos continues to be recognized as official Western emperor.
476	The German warlord Odoacer leads a rebellion against Orestes and kills him, August 28. He deposes Romulus in Ravenna (September 4) and exiles him with a pension to Campania. The Roman Senate sends an embassy to Zeno, the Eastern emperor (r. 474–491), proclaiming no further need for a Western emperor; but Zeno continues to recognize Nepos.
480, April or May	Nepos is murdered in his villa at Salona.
ca. 520	Marcellinus, in his Latin *Chronicle* written in Constantinople, states that the Western Empire (*Hesperium imperium*) "perished" with the deposition of Romulus Augustulus in 476, thus establishing this date for the "fall" of Rome.

Empire seems to have been far more vulnerable to invasion than the Eastern Empire. Warlike peoples streamed along the Danube valley and through the terrain of Central Europe into the Western provinces, which offered a less hazardous route than the journey south through the difficult mountains of the Balkans, Greece, and Asia Minor into the Eastern Empire.

Social Conditions and Decline Other conditions, too, made the Western Empire less able to resist invasion. In the late second and third centuries the emperors had deliberately increased the prestige of the army and depressed the Senate and the civil service. The creature that they fashioned soon began to rule them, for the armies and their leaders made and unmade emperors at will. The only way to preserve civilian control over the military machine would have been to entrust more responsibility to the Senate and to maintain strong civil servants. But the emperors simply continued along the path of absolute coercion, stifling initiative and making the lower classes apathetic and resentful. These conditions gave citizens only slight motivation to defend their oppressive government; domination by invaders may have seemed not much worse than being in the grip of the Roman state.

We must also consider the large number of holidays and many forms of amusement within the city of Rome: To what degree did such luxuries contribute to the transformation of the Western Empire? There is evidence here and there that the masses in the city gradually lost their feelings of responsibility. For example, in 69, as Tacitus reports, the crowd cheered with pleasure as rival troops fought in the streets for the throne.[3] When the masses no longer had to exert more than minimal effort to survive, they abandoned the discipline and civic cooperation that had created the Empire. The people shunned public office, non-Italians supplied the troops, and appeals for traditional Roman firmness in danger found little response.

The Role of Christianity Finally, historians must take into account the great upheaval in ideas and faith. We cannot express this view in the language of science or statistics, but the new religion, Christianity, may also have weakened the defenses of the Empire. This thesis was first supported by Edward Gibbon, who had rejected the Catholic faith in his own life and scorned Christianity. But even as we recognize Gibbon's prejudices, we must allow that he may have hit a part of the truth. In the Roman scheme, the emperors, governors, and administrators stood far above the people, and Roman religion pro-

---

[3] *Histories*, 3.83.

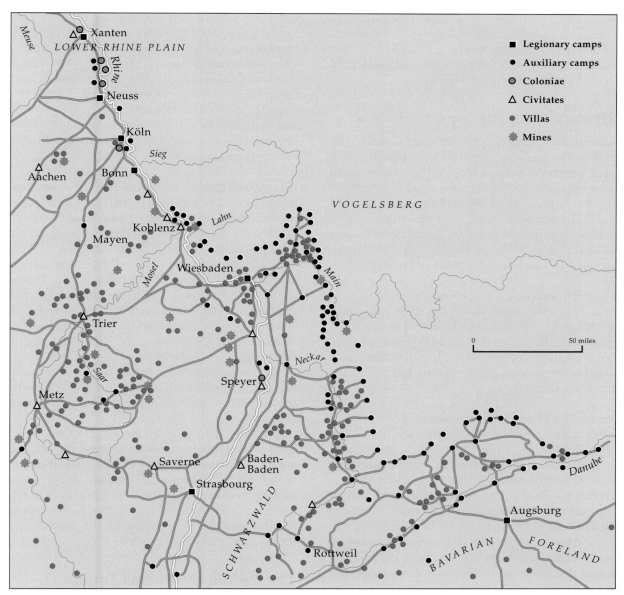

MAP 5.4 THE RHINE FRONTIER OF THE ROMAN EMPIRE
This map shows the fortifications that ran largely east of the Rhine and north of the Danube rivers. Their purpose was defense against Germanic tribes. Legions of Roman soldiers were stationed at larger centers (Bonn, Köln or Cologne, Strasbourg or Strassburg), and at a lower level there were many camps of auxiliary troops, all connected by a system of roads. Which legionary camp was located south of the Danube River?
◆ For an online version, go to www.mhhe.com/chambers9 > chapter 5 > book maps

vided little spiritual compensation for a low rank in the world. The Christian faith offered something better: the message that all persons are potentially equal in the eyes of God and may hope for a better afterlife through salvation. As the Western Empire came under constant attack, the increasing number of Christians may have been less than eager to fight to preserve the old system. This spiritual rejection, as we might call it, worked along with the mighty pressures of invasion to cause the "fall" of Rome.

CHRISTIANITY AND ITS EARLY RIVALS

The triumph of Christianity within the Roman Empire was one of the most remarkable cultural revolutions in history—all the more extraordinary because its values were opposed to those of classical thought, which sought the good life in the present world. *Carpe diem,* "Seize the day," said Horace; there is no certainty about tomorrow. But classical values were failing to reach the disadvantaged, the subjugated, the losers. Small wonder that people sought a new meaning for their existence. More than this, Christianity was born into a world alive with religious fervor.

The Mystery Religions

One element of a spreading religious ferment under the Empire was the growing popularity of the so-called mysteries, which promised a blessed life after death to those who were initiated into secret (therefore "mysterious") rites. Through these rites, the believer attained a mystical identification with the renewing cycles of nature. The mysteries are generally described in various sources as thrilling, bringing one into another world, carrying one to a summit of emotion and perception.

The Mysteries of Eleusis   The oldest and most famous rites were held each fall at Eleusis, a day's walk from Athens. A drama-filled night culminated in the initiate's conviction that he or she would be given a lovely life after death by Demeter, the goddess of grain, just as she caused beautiful new grain to come forth from the apparently dead seed.

Mithraism   This hope for survival after death did not bring with it any expectation of a changed moral life, nor did initiation lead to membership in any kind of community of believers or "church," with one notable exception: the religion known as Mithraism. Mithras was originally a Persian god of light and truth and an ally of the good god, Ahura Mazda; he symbolized the daily triumph of life over death by bringing back the sun to the dark heavens. Initiation was open only to men, and Mithraism—with its emphasis on courage, loyalty, self-discipline, and victory—became especially popular in the Roman army.

Christianity and Mysteries   When Christians began, around A.D. 30, to proclaim the good news (or "gospel") of the recent death and resurrection of their leader, Jesus of Nazareth,[4] throughout the Empire, many who responded thought they were hearing about the best "mystery" of all: A historical person had conquered death and promised a blessed afterlife to all who believed in him. Yet much early Christian literature was written to teach believers that Christianity was far more than a "mystery." In fact, the historian should

---

[4] "Jesus" was his name. After his death he was called *ho Christós*, "the anointed one," or the Messiah, by his followers. Thus the names "Christ" and "Jesus Christ," though universally used, are not historically accurate, and "Jesus, called the Christ" is cumbersome.

not class Christianity among the mystery religions. First, rites in mystery religions were secret, and participation required a period of instruction or purification. The experience, however thrilling, was temporary. Above all, the rituals usually did not lead to forming a community of believers or a church. Christianity, by contrast, demanded that every believer practice love and justice in new communities made up of Jew and Greek, slave and free, male and female, rich and poor, educated and ignorant.

Characteristics of Christianity   This new religion hardly looked "religious." Christians had no temples or other holy places, no priests, no ordinary sacrifices, no oracles, no visible gods, no initiations; they made no pilgrimages, did not practice divination, would not venerate the emperor, and challenged the final authority of the father (or oldest male) in family life. No wonder some pagans accused Christians of being atheists who undermined traditional society. The roots of these radical beliefs and practices go back to the long Judaic tradition and its sacred writings. Christians maintained that prophecies in the Hebrew Bible, which in the light of new revelation they began to call the *Old* Testament, had foretold the coming of Jesus as the Messiah, the deliverer of the Jewish people, and the future lord of the world.

Like the Jews, Christians emphasized their god's wish to create a community of men and women who practiced justice and mercy. All the first Christians had been Jews, but they parted company with Jewish tradition by insisting that Jesus' life, his sacrificial death, and his resurrection all meant that God's community had become open to everyone, on absolutely equal terms, from every background.

The Jews in the Roman Empire

The Jews and Other Powers   The Jews had been favored subjects of the Persian Empire until Alexander's invasion of the East (334–323 B.C.) swept away Persian rule. In the Hellenistic Age they were governed during the third century B.C. by the Ptolemies of Egypt and then by the Seleucid kings of Syria, who began to force Greek culture on them and finally outlawed the Jewish religion altogether. One Seleucid king, Antiochus IV (r. 175–164 B.C.), defiled the holy Temple in Jerusalem by erecting within it an altar to Zeus and an image of himself. Pious Jewish nationalists responded under the leadership of Judas Maccabaeus with guerrilla warfare. This successful Maccabean Revolt (167–164 B.C.) is remembered today with Hanukkah, the eight-day Festival of Lights, which celebrates the reported miracle of a one-day supply of oil that burned for eight days. After a century of virtual independence, the Jews in Judea

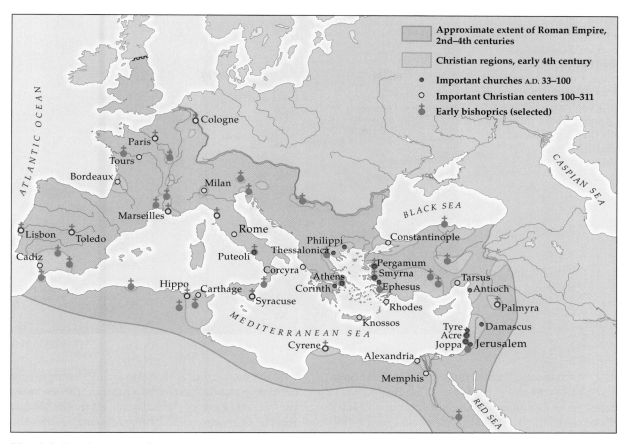

MAP 5.5 THE SPREAD OF CHRISTIANITY
This map shows the successive stages of the spread of Christianity. Note that there were some important churches within the first century A.D. in the eastern Mediterranean. Later, churches appeared on the very edges of the Roman Empire. What were the northernmost and southernmost bishoprics in the period of the Empire?
◆ For an online version, go to www.mhhe.com/chambers9 > chapter 5 > book maps

(the province created out of the Jewish kingdom of Judah) fell under Rome's control after the arrival in Jerusalem of the Roman general Pompey in 63 B.C.

When Julius Caesar was at war with Pompey in 47 B.C., he had the help of a Jewish force, and he rewarded the Jews with reduced taxes and exemption from military service. The Romans also agreed that Jews could not be called to court on the Sabbath and that they could continue to worship in their synagogues, even in Rome itself. Thus, despite the loss of their century-long freedom, the Jews enjoyed at least some measure of toleration.

Roman Control over the Jews   Rome permitted client kings, local rulers who pledged loyalty to Rome, to rule Judea. The most notorious was Herod the Great (r. 40–4 B.C.), hated by most Jews, whom he sought to win over by remodeling the Temple in Jerusalem into one of the wonders of the ancient world. But Herod's son was a weak ruler, and the Romans assumed direct control over Judea through civil servants from Rome; they

were usually called procurators, the most famous of whom was Pontius Pilate.

Constant quarrels between the Roman officers and the Jews reached a climax in A.D. 66, when Jerusalem burst into rebellion. This great Jewish War, as the Romans called it, lasted until 70, when the Romans under the emperor Titus demolished the Temple, except a remnant of the Western Wall, at which Jews were allowed to pray once a year. This portion of wall still stands and is a holy shrine to Jews today. Hoping to retain the favor of the Jews by respecting their god, the Romans did not at first try to eliminate the Jewish faith itself; but they finally did attempt its suppression after another Jewish rebellion (131–135). Nonetheless, Judaism retained its coherence and strength, assuring its people that God would one day send them their redeemer.

Jewish Factions   The attractiveness of Hellenistic culture, combined with the insult of Roman occupation, led to a continuing crisis of identity among the Jews.

MITHRAEUM, OR SHRINE TO THE
SAVIOR GOD MITHRAS, WITH
BENCHES FOR WORSHIPERS.
It was built in the second or
third century within a large first-
century apartment. On the altar,
Mithras is shown sacrificing a
bull to Apollo. Above this level
was built the church of San
Clemente in Rome.
C. M. Dixon

After the Maccabean Revolt, three principal factions arose, each stressing the part of Jewish tradition that it considered most essential for the survival of the Jews as God's people.

First, the landed aristocracy and high priests formed the **Sadducees,** religious conservatives who rejected belief in an afterlife and in angels because they did not find such teaching in the five Books of Moses (the Pentateuch, called the *Torah* by Jews).

A second faction, the **Pharisees,** were pious middle-class laypersons who taught the resurrection of the dead, believed in angels, and accepted gentile converts.[5] During the century following the Roman expulsion of the Jews from Jerusalem in 135, the spiritual heirs of the Pharisees, the great rabbis, organized their oral legal traditions, which updated the practice of the Torah, into a book called the Mishnah. This compendium became fundamental for all subsequent Jewish thought and was augmented in the East by an authoritative commentary (the Gemara) to form the Babylonian **Talmud,** or general body of Jewish tradition. A similar process in the West created the less elaborate Persian Talmud.

The Essenes The third faction was the Essenes, who have drawn the most attention in recent years because of the astonishing discovery of the Dead Sea Scrolls, documents found from 1947 onward in eleven caves near the Dead Sea. Although scholarly debate contin-

[5] The Latin word *gentiles* means "foreigners," those born to non-Jewish mothers.

ues, the consensus is that the writers were Essenes, ascetic priests who settled at Qumran, fifteen miles into the desert east of Jerusalem, after the Maccabean Revolt; they were evidently protesting against the leadership of the Temple by high priests whom they considered corrupt and unworthy.

These rolls and many fragments of leather have given historians an extraordinary view of the apocalyptic beliefs and strict practices of this protesting faction, which was active from ca. 150 B.C. to A.D. 70. The Essenes were convinced that evil in the world had become so powerful—even prevailing in the Temple—that only a cataclysmic intervention by God, which would soon arrive, could cleanse the world and open the way for righteousness to prevail.

Doctrines of the Essenes A certain "Teacher of Righteousness," the priestly champion of the forces of light, is thought to be the anonymous author of many of the scrolls; his opponent in Jerusalem, who he says serves the powers of darkness, is called the Wicked Priest. The scrolls foresee at least two God-anointed leaders: the Messiah of David (a military commander) and the Messiah of Aaron (a high priest). The writers also predict the return of the "Teacher."

The relations of the Essenes at Qumran to Jesus and the first Christians remain much debated. The Essenes never appear in the Christian Bible, or New Testament. To be sure, in the spectrum of Jewish factions, these two groups could hardly have differed more widely. The Essenes were exclusive, hierarchic, priestly, and withdrawn from society. Jesus and his followers wel-

The church of Santa Costanza in Rome, built in the early fourth century as a mausoleum for Constantia and Helena, daughters of the emperor Constantine, contains some of the oldest Christian mosaics. This scene from daily life shows workers bringing in the grape harvest.
Erich Lessing/Art Resource, NY

comed everyone; they were egalitarian, uninterested in sacrifices in the Temple, and wholly "in the world."

Origins of Christianity

The Person of Jesus   The modern historical investigation of Jesus of Nazareth has challenged scholars for two centuries. He seems to have been a charismatic Jewish teacher, yet he wrote nothing that we know of.

His existence and his execution by the Romans are confirmed by such first- and second-century historians as Josephus, Tacitus, and Suetonius.

For details we must sift the writings of early converts, such as Saul of Tarsus (who did not know Jesus) or the authors of the Gospels (the first four books of the New Testament), which focus on Jesus' power over evil forces, his message of hope and moral demands, his healing miracles, and his radical inclusiveness (even lepers were welcomed into the faith). But ancient writers had little interest in presenting his biography in chronological order or in probing his inner life. We know almost nothing about his career as a youth and young adult apart from his being raised a Jew in Galilee; thus, despite the efforts of many, it is impossible to write a biography of Jesus.

Jesus as Teacher

As his followers recalled his career, Jesus was born of a virgin named Mary, who was betrothed but not yet married to a man named Joseph, in the last years of Herod the Great, at a date that modern scholarship sets about 4 B.C. At around age thirty, Jesus went to John the Baptist, an outspoken prophet, to be baptized—that is, to become purified through a ritual washing—and join his apocalyptic movement, which foresaw the coming end of the world. Soon afterward John was imprisoned, and Jesus began a program of itinerant teaching and healing, apparently rejecting John's apocalyptic message by proclaiming instead the "good news" that God's rule had already begun *before* the final judgment. Jesus affirmed the Pharisees' belief in resurrection, yet he urged his disciples to pray that God's will be done here on earth as it is in heaven, that God's kingdom should come to people here. Jesus was, therefore, a man in the tradition of the Hebrew prophets, who brought their message to the people directly.

In the Sermon on the Mount, the summary of Jesus' basic principles recorded in the Gospel of Matthew, Jesus declared that when God rules, the poor, the meek, the pure in heart, the peacemakers, and the justice seekers will be honored. He said too that prayer and piety were matters of personal commitment, not public gestures to win society's acclaim.

Doctrines of Jesus

With all other Jews, Jesus believed that God was a gracious, welcoming God. The related questions were: To *whom* is God gracious? and, therefore, Whom must I treat as my neighbor? As Jesus demonstrated by his fellowship at open meals, every person was potentially such a neighbor, especially a person in need.

Jesus' fellowship at meals reached its climax at his last supper at the time of Passover, a Jewish religious holiday. At this meal he urged his disciples to continue a ritual practice in memory of him, using bread and wine to symbolize the gift of his body and the sacrifice of his blood. The early Christians regularly did so, calling this meal the eucharist, or thanksgiving. Jesus' doctrines included the assurance that belief in his message would bring redemption from sin and salvation with eternal life in the presence of God; above all, he called himself the Son of Man—but also the Son of God, who would sit at God's right hand.

Jesus' Death

For the passing of Jesus, only Christian sources give us a narrative, which we cannot compare with others. Christian writers state that the high priests in Jerusalem accused Jesus of blasphemy (he had challenged their authority in the Temple), of pretending to be God's Messiah and a king, and of opposing paying taxes to the Roman emperor. The Roman governor, Pontius Pilate, apparently feared that a riot, led by Jesus' enemies, was about to break out at the Passover. It is said that he washed his hands to make himself innocent of Jesus' blood and handed him over to the crowd, which then brought about his crucifixion, a horribly painful form of execution (about A.D. 30).

Jesus' followers became convinced that God raised him from the dead after three days and that this resurrection confirmed the truth of his deeds and words despite his rejection and persecution. The Christians further believed that he ascended bodily into heaven but would return to save his followers and establish his kingdom. Armed with this conviction, they followed the example of Stephen, the first Christian martyr, and began to convert other Jews to their faith.

Paul and His Mission

A Pharisee, Saul of Tarsus (in today's southern Turkey), known to us as Paul, became a leader in persecuting Jews who had become Christians. Luke, the author of one of the four Gospels, narrates Paul's life in the *Acts of the Apostles*. About A.D. 33, on his way to Damascus to organize further persecutions, Paul saw on the road an apparition of the risen Jesus, who asked, "Saul, Saul, why do you persecute me?" Paul realized that he had been given a special mission to the gentiles and became Christianity's chief advocate. He traversed the Roman world, organizing Christian communities of both Jews and gentiles and advising their members through his letters. He was executed in Rome about A.D. 62 while planning a mission to Spain (see map 5.6).

Paul became the best known of all the early Christian teachers. His letters, or epistles, written to guide the congregations he had founded, were widely circulated and then collected as part of the Christians' inspired Scriptures. Luke devotes nearly half of the Acts to Paul's career as a courageous witness who fought with burning missionary fever for his new lord.

Paul and the Conversion of the Gentiles

Above all, Paul rejected the policy of some early Jewish Christians who wanted to restrict membership in the new faith to Jews or to gentiles who had become Jews through circumcision. In one of his tautly argued letters in the Bible's Book of Romans he asked: "Is God the God of the Jews only? Is he not also the God of the Gentiles? Yes, of the Gentiles also." By rejecting circumcision as a condition of membership, Paul helped firmly establish the Christian church on the basis of personal faith,

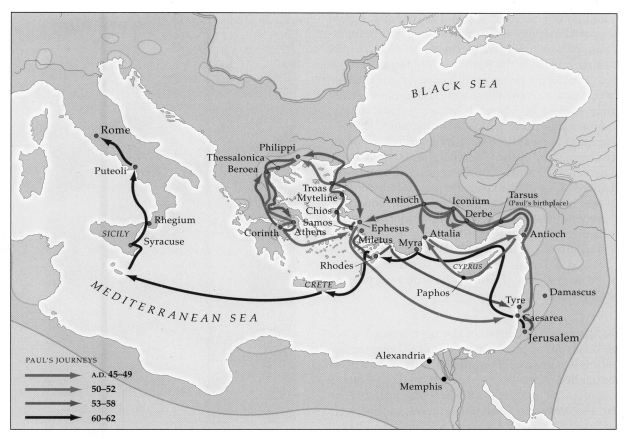

MAP 5.6 THE JOURNEYS OF ST. PAUL
**The journeys of St. Paul over 17 years, as he visited and wrote to Christians everywhere, were tireless and complex.
In his last two years he reached Rome, where he died. Where did he first concentrate his efforts?**
◆ For an online version, go to www.mhhe.com/chambers9 > chapter 5 > book maps

not limited by ethnic identity, bloodlines, or observation of the Mosaic law.

Paul and Christian Communities   Paul taught Christians to regard themselves as citizens of heaven and to begin living with one another in humility and love, in joyous expectation of their final destiny. Christians were sure that God would soon consign their world's system of honor and shame based on violence, pride, and class discrimination to the trash heap of history. Paul also redefined the notion of the Messiah. For Jews, this leader would someday arrive and create another kingdom on earth. For Paul, the messianic age had begun with Jesus, interrupting the age of violence and death as the sign and promise of what the future would bring.

Paul's vision of human freedom and a renewed human community characterized by mutual service is one of the most compelling social images in Western culture. Taking this message throughout the lands of the eastern Mediterranean, Paul and his successors brought converts by the thousands into the new church.

Persecutions   The Roman government adopted a general policy of toleration toward the many religious sects of the Empire, seeking the blessings of all divine powers on the Empire. The Romans even paid for sacrifices to be performed on behalf of the Empire in the temple in Jerusalem. They asked only that veneration be shown on official occasions to the traditional gods and to the deceased and deified emperors—little more than public patriotism. But the Christians, like the Jews before them, refused even this apparently small compromise with polytheism.

Rome's attitude toward Christians wavered between lack of interest and cruel persecution. The first serious persecution took place under Nero in A.D. 64. A vast fire had ravaged the crowded areas in central Rome, and Nero had many Christians brutally killed as scapegoats. The historian Tacitus, in reporting the affair, declares that Christians were thought guilty of a wicked style of life, but he makes it clear that the persecution was based on a false charge.[6] From time to time other anti-Christ-

[6] *Annals*, 15.44.

ian actions took place, but it is unlikely that the mild doctrines of Christians were the reason. Their main offense was, rather, their stubbornness, or *contumacia*, which caused many in the Roman world to see them as enemies of society. The emperor Trajan, giving instructions to his civil servant Pliny, agreed that laws against Christians should be followed, but he warned against anonymous accusations, which he would not tolerate.

Occasional persecutions and long periods of peace marked the history of the Church—that is, the Christian community—into the fourth century. Then, in the period 303–313, came the Great Persecution under Diocletian and his successors, when the rulers sought to eliminate what they saw as a potential menace to the state. Their unsuccessful efforts testify to the widespread strength of Christianity. Moreover, the persecutions created a list of venerated Christian martyrs, which led to the cult of saints, thereafter an integral part of Christian piety.

Female Martyrs   In Christian thought, women could receive God's favor just as men could. Therefore Roman officials persecuted women as well as men. Our sources (called Acts of the several martyrs) record many stories of horrific punishments inflicted on women. According to Christian sources, virgins were thrown into brothels and women were fastened naked to trees by one foot and left to perish as they hung downward. One woman of Alexandria boldly refused to abandon her faith and is said to have been tortured to death by having boiling pitch poured over her body.

A famous martyr was St. Perpetua, who was put to death in Carthage in 203. A narrative in Latin records her fate. The emperor Septimius Severus had forbidden any subjects to become Christians, but Perpetua and five others fearlessly confessed their Christianity. Her mother was a Christian, but her father was a pagan. In vain he begged her to renounce her faith in order to spare his family the disgrace of having a Christian daughter. She was tried before a procurator, who also urged her to recant, but she refused the customary sacrifice for the emperor. Perpetua and her slave, who became St. Felicitas, welcomed their martyrdom; they and their fellow Christians were mauled by wild animals before being killed by the sword.

St. Agnes and St. Cecilia   The narratives of the martyrs are meant to show the steadfast courage of early Christians and the solace they found in their faith. Christian sources preserve, for example, the story of St. Agnes, in the time of Diocletian. She was exposed in the stadium of Domitian in Rome (now the Piazza Navona, where a church stands bearing her name), but her nakedness was covered by the miraculous growth

The fourth-century emperor Valentinian I shown as Christian ruler in a colossal statue from Barletta in southeast Italy. In one hand, he holds an orb (restored) to signify his imperial power; in the other, the cross to show his devotion to the Church. The portrait thus unites the two forces that sustained the later Empire.
Scala/Art Resource, NY

of her hair. She was then tied to a stake to be burned, but the flames would not touch her and the emperor had her beheaded.

Again, St. Cecilia, the purported inventor of the organ and the patron saint of music, was according to tradition imprisoned in her own bath to be scalded. She emerged unscathed and was then beheaded (the date of her death is uncertain). A church to her memory stands on the spot of her house in Rome, where she lived with her husband, whom she converted.

An Emperor Becomes the Church's Patron   One of the most amazing changes of face in Roman history is the radical shift in the policy of the government toward the Christians initiated in 313 by the emperor Constantine. In the traditional story, first appearing around the period 318–320, Constantine had a dream on the evening before he was to fight a rival for supremacy over Italy in 312, at the Milvian Bridge near Rome. In the dream he was told to decorate the shields of his soldiers with the Greek letters *chi* and *rho*, the monogram of Christ: "In this sign you shall conquer." Constantine won the battle and thereafter recognized divine power in the name of Christ.

At what point Constantine himself converted to Christianity is debated. In any case, in 313, at a conference held at Milan, he ended the age of persecutions by extending complete freedom of worship to the Christians and ordering the return of their confiscated goods. As to Constantine himself, his conversion had certain political reasons, for there were now so many Christians that he naturally wanted to include them within the state. But his own letters and actions show a serious personal commitment to Christianity.

The Victory of Christianity   Just before his death in 337, Constantine received baptism from the bishop Eusebius of Nicomedia, but Christianity was not yet the official religion of the Empire. The emperor Julian, known as the Apostate, turned his back on the church and tried in the period 361–363 to restore the position of the traditional gods, but by then the wave of Christianity could not be stopped. In 391 and 392 Theodosius the Great forbade the practice of all religions except the form of Christianity recognized by the government, thus transforming in one move the character of both the Empire and Christianity. He reversed Rome's long-standing policy of religious toleration and changed the Church from a brave alternative society sharply critical of "this world" into a friend of worldly power; it thus began attracting some "converts" who sought personal gain rather than spiritual renewal.

Christianity and Roman Law   The law had been moving for many years toward more humane regulations, partly under the influence of philosophic conceptions of natural law that could apply to all persons. For example, the old supreme power of the father had long since fallen away. Christianity moved this spirit forward. Constantine and his successors gave more and more privileges to the church. Christians became exempt from the much-resented burdens of civil service in local curiae. Churches could own property and enjoyed exemptions from certain taxes, and bishops were allowed to judge the legal disputes of the members of their congregations. The clergy had the power to preside over the freeing of slaves by their owners, and freed slaves became citizens at once. Thus the Church acquired a privileged juridical status that it would re-

tain, in many Western lands, until the eighteenth and nineteenth centuries.

Constantine repealed the old laws of Augustus that regulated marriage and punished celibacy—a lifestyle now tolerated more easily because celibacy in priests was seen as a virtue. Emperors tried, though without great success, to discourage the ease with which people could be divorced (St. Jerome writes of a man living with his twenty-first wife, a woman who had already had twenty-two husbands), and cases in divorce could be heard by priests. Women were given greater protection with regard to dowries; husbands had less power over a dowry during marriage, and it became easier for a wife to recover it after divorce (Hammurabi of Babylon had long ago seen to similar rights for women).

Battles within Christianity

Usually the Christian community did not bother to define matters of dogma or discipline until disputes threatened its internal unity. The losers in these disputes, if they did not amend their beliefs, were regarded as heretics (from the Greek word *hairesis*, meaning "choice"—that is, a wrong choice). This word was used from the earliest days of Christianity.

The Heresies of Marcion and Montanus   A **heresy** that threatened the character of the Christian revelation was that of Marcion of Sinope in Asia Minor (ca. 150). He sought to reform Christianity by restricting it to the message of St. Paul alone. He therefore edited his version of the New Testament, which included and recognized as divine only the Gospel of Luke and the Epistles of Paul.

Another heresy was that of a bishop from Asia Minor, Montanus (ca. 170–200), who maintained that certain living believers were prophets who were continuously receiving direct inspiration from the Holy Spirit. Women were prominent among these prophets, and Montanus' ideas eventually won the allegiance of the great North African writer Tertullian. The movement forced Christians to ask: Who should rule the Christian congregations—teachers, who could only interpret texts from the past, or living prophets, who might expect continuing new revelations?

Christian Responses to Heresy   Christians who accepted the standard doctrines of the Church branded the ideas of Marcion and Montanus as heresy. Because such heresies have vanished over the centuries, one might well ask: What is their historical importance? The answer is that they stimulated the early Church to redefine its positions. Out of the turmoil and disagreement, the Church emerged stronger, even though the price was sometimes the blunt suppression of sincerely held opinions.

Orthodox theologians of the second century answered Marcion by defining the canon of sacred writings to include, in effect, the modern Bible—the entire Old and New Testaments. And the Church answered Montanus by declaring that the age of divine inspiration had come to an end. All the truths needed for salvation, the Church now said, were complete with the work of St. John, the last inspired author (ca. 100), and no new revelations were admitted. In the fourth century, too, the Church refused to accept as inspired certain other writings, calling them the Apocrypha (obscure or unclear writings).

The Government of the Church   Evidence from the first century indicates that James, a relative (perhaps a brother) of Jesus, was the recognized head of the Christians in Jerusalem. During this period, too, we meet the terms deacon (*diakonos*), bishop (*episkopos*, or "overseer"), and elder (*presbuteros*), which at first were nearly synonymous. Then, in the second century, the bishop became the elected leader of a group of elders (later called priests) and of deacons (both men and women), who became responsible for collecting donations, distributing charities, and managing the Church's material affairs.

Bishops gained the right to appoint priests, define doctrine, maintain discipline, and oversee morals. This political structure gave Christianity a stable administration and a hierarchy that no ancient mystery religion enjoyed. In the West, the number of bishops remained small; they thus obtained power over fairly large areas. Bishops in cities with the largest Christian communities—Rome, Alexandria, Antioch—became the most influential. Finally, the bishop of Rome became the head of the Church in the West. The general name for a bishop was *papa*, or father, but eventually the bishop of Rome was the only one who could so call himself (in English, *pope*).

Women in the Church   The role of women in early Christianity presents some contradictions to the historian. The figure of Mary, mother of Jesus, was of course universally revered, and Gospel accounts associate other women with Jesus: Mary Magdalene and another Mary are said to have been the first to see Jesus risen from his tomb. Paul names one Junia in the Book of Romans as "outstanding among the apostles." Other gifted women served as teachers and coworkers with Paul.

On the other hand, the Christian writer Tertullian says of women, "You give birth to suffering and anguish. You are Eve. The Devil is in you. You were the first to abandon God's law. You were the one who de-

Mosaic of the Three Magi, kings or wise men, Balthasar, Melchior, and Gaspar in Sant' Apollinare Nuovo, sixth century A.D. Ravenna.
Sant' Apollinare Nuovo, Ravenna/Dagli Orti (A)/The Art Archive

ceived man." Such a stern condemnation of women reminds us of the much milder words of Paul commanding women to be silent in church: "Let the woman learn in silence with all subjection. But I suffer not a woman to teach, nor to usurp authority over the man, but to be in silence" (1 Tim. 2).

Widows and Virgins in the Church   But as the Church developed, it made more and more use of the devotion and abilities of women. Widows, for example, had always inspired compassion as people in need of help, and special honor was paid to widows who had led a chaste life and could show that they had done good works. Their duty was to pray at home but also to visit the sick and pray at their bedsides. But, in accordance with Paul's words, they were not to teach the Gospel.

Later, in the third and fourth centuries, widows and virgins could become deaconesses and thus rise higher in status within the Church. Though they were members of the clergy, they still could not teach or interpret the Scriptures. Their main duty was to maintain order and assist the male clergy in performing duties such as baptism, especially for women. They continued to visit the sick and to pray at their bedsides; in doing so they confirmed the Church's role as the loving protector of humankind.

Powerful Christian Women   If women could not perform the duties reserved for priests, they could still be powerful behind the scenes. St. John Chrysostom (ca. 345–407), a priest at Antioch and later archbishop at Constantinople, complained that influential women could get their favorites chosen as priests. Among the women whom he accused of greed and immorality was the empress Eudoxia, wife of the emperor Arcadius (r. 383–408). In the end she got Chrysostom exiled to a remote place in Armenia.

Women, especially those in the court, could also contribute stupendous fortunes to the founding of churches. St. Helena, the mother of the emperor Constantine, founded churches in Palestine, and others are known to have endowed hospitals and monasteries. Above all, historians have pointed to the ability of women in the field of conversion as their most important contribution to the early church. Paul refers to the power of women to maintain and pass on the faith in a letter to his lieutenant Timothy: "Recalling your tears, I long to see you so that I may be filled with joy. I am reminded of your sincere faith, a faith that lived first in your grandmother Lois and your mother Eunice" (2 Tim. 1). Again, St. Helena was a Christian before her son Constantine became one and probably influenced his conversion. St. Monica, the mother of St. Augustine, was a Christian and lovingly worked for the conversion of her husband and for the salvation of her son.

Donatists   In 303, Diocletian issued an edict ordering that churches and sacred books should be destroyed throughout the Empire. Some Christians sought to escape punishment by surrendering their copies of the Scriptures. Those who did so were called *traditores* ("those who handed over" the Scriptures—thus our word *traitor*), and the more steadfast Christians hated them. When the persecutions ended in 313, a party of North African Christians led by a bishop named Donatus declared that the "traitors," even if repentant, had forever lost membership in the Church; all the sacraments they had ever administered—all baptisms, marriages, ordinations, and the like—were declared worthless. Because the traitors were many, acceptance of the Donatist program would have brought chaos to the North African Church.

The result was violent schism, which mounted on occasion to civil war. Refusing to accept the rule of traitors, the Donatists established their own bishops and hierarchy. In response, the more forgiving orthodox Church declared that the sacraments conferred grace on the recipients *ex opere operato*, simply "from the work having been performed," and that the spiritual state of the priests at the time did not matter. This attitude remained the official Christian doctrine until challenged during the Protestant Reformation of the Middle Ages.

Arius and Arianism   The heresy of Donatus, which insisted on proper order in the Church, partakes of the Roman heritage of law and discipline within the Western Church. Another heresy reflects the Greek interest in theosophical and philosophical issues. This was the movement beginning about 311 when Arius, an Alexandrian priest, began to teach that Jesus was not coequal with God the Father but had been created by him at a moment in time. Arius stated, "There was a time when he [Jesus] was not." The teachings of Arius raised a furor in Egypt and soon throughout the Empire. To restore peace, Constantine summoned the first "ecumenical" council (that is, one representing the entire inhabited world) of the Church, which met at Nicaea in Asia Minor in May 325. The council condemned Arius in the **Nicene Creed,** which declared that Jesus was coeternal with the Father and of one substance with God.

Arius was exiled but was later allowed to return to Alexandria. **Arianism** persisted in many places, and even Constantine gradually moved to a more tolerant policy toward it. A later council, meeting at Constantinople in 381 under the emperor Theodosius, restated the Nicene Creed. These declarations had behind them the full power of the state and could be enforced as a matter of law, although belief might waver with political currents. Finally, at the Council of Chalcedon of 451, Jesus was clearly defined as one person with two natures. As a human being, he was the son of Mary; as God, he was coequal with the Father and had reigned and would reign with him eternally. This definition has since remained the belief of Christians in general.

The Church and Classical Culture   Christian writers, although they proclaimed themselves enemies of pagan culture, had no choice but to accept classical traditions. The basic grammars and texts, the authoritative models of argument and style, were all pagan. To defend the faith, Christian apologists had to master the art of rhetoric and use the arsenal of pagan learning. This Christian accommodation with pagan learning had decisive repercussions. Nearly all the texts of the great classical authors have reached us in copies made by Christians, who believed they were useful in education. Paradoxically, these outspoken enemies of pagan values actually preserved a rich cultural heritage that they sought to undermine.

The Fathers of the Church

Christianity became the chief religion of Europe partly because it reached the people through the languages and thought of Greco-Roman civilization. Even before the birth of Jesus, Greek-speaking Jews in Alexandria had translated the Old Testament into Greek; this version, said to have been made by seventy-two scholars, is called the Septuagint (from the Latin *septuaginta*, meaning "70"), and the authors of the New Testament

An early mosaic (ca. 400) showing Christ holding a book and surrounded by apostles in Roman dress. Two women, perhaps saints, crown St. Peter and St. Paul, with the holy city of Jerusalem in the background. The commanding figure of Jesus resembles that of Jupiter in Roman art. From the church of Santa Pudenziana, Rome.
Scala/Art Resource, NY

referred to it and wrote their own works in the common Greek of the day. On the basis of these sacred texts, there grew an ocean of commentary and persuasion by the so-called Fathers of the Church, the leading theologians of the second to fifth centuries.

Origen and Eusebius   The most learned Church father writing in Greek was Origen (ca. 185–ca. 253), a priest in Alexandria. Both the volume and the profound scholarship of his writings were a wonder of late antiquity. He worked especially on the text of the Scriptures by comparing the original Hebrew and the Septuagint; he also wrote extensive commentaries on books of the Bible and a tract, *Against Celsus,* in which he answers the arguments of an elitist critic of the Christians.

Another highly influential Greek father was Eusebius of Caesarea (ca. 260–ca. 340). His most original work was a history of the Church, which became the model for later such histories. The most learned man of his time, he also wrote a *Chronicle* of universal history, which is one of our most important sources for ancient history in general.

The Latin Fathers: Ambrose and Jerome   Among the fathers who wrote in Latin was Ambrose, bishop of Milan from 374 to 397. His most important doctrine was that the Church must be independent of the emperor and that bishops should have the right to chastise rulers. In 390 Ambrose excommunicated the emperor Theodosius after he had massacred the rebellious citizens of Thessalonica, forbidding him to receive the eucharist and thus placing him outside the body of the Church. Theodosius admitted his guilt and repented, and the popes of later centuries who struggled with secular officials owed much of their power to the resolute example of Ambrose.

AUGUSTINE IS BROUGHT TO HIS FAITH

St. Augustine describes how, after many struggles to overcome his lustful nature, he was inspired at age thirty-one to pick up and read in the New Testament; this was the critical moment in his conversion.

"And, not indeed in these words, but to this effect I spoke often to you: 'But you, O Lord, how long? Will you be angry forever? Do not remember against us the guilt of past generations.' I sent up these sorrowful cries—'How long, how long? Tomorrow, and tomorrow? Why not now? Why is there now no end to my uncleanness?'

"I was saying these things and weeping in the most bitter contrition of my heart, when I heard the voice of a boy or girl, I do not know which, coming from a neighboring house, chanting, and often repeating, 'Take up and read; take up and read.' Immediately my face changed, and I began to consider whether it was usual for children in any kind of game to sing such words; nor could I remember ever hearing anything like this. So, restraining the torrent of my tears, I rose up, interpreting it as nothing but a command from heaven to open the Bible, and to read the first chapter I saw. So I returned to where I had put down the apostles. I grasped it, opened it, and in silence read the first paragraph I saw—'Not in rioting and drunkenness, not in debauchery and lust, not in strife and envy; but let Jesus Christ be your armor, and give no more thought to satisfying bodily appetites' [Romans 13–14]. I read no further, I did not need to; for instantly, as the sentence ended—by a light of security that poured into my heart—all the gloom of doubt vanished."

From *Confessions*, 8.12, J. G. Pilkington (tr.), in Whitney Oates (ed.), *The Basic Writings of Saint Augustine*, Vol. 1, Random House, 1948, p. 126 (language modified).

Jerome (ca. 340–420) succeeded Eusebius as the most learned Church father of his time. His translation of both the Old and the New Testaments into Latin, usually called the Vulgate version of the Bible, is probably the most influential book ever written in the Latin language. It became the medium through which the Judeo-Christian writings permeated the Latin-speaking nations of Europe and was the biblical text most often used during the Middle Ages. It also ensured that Latin would survive deeply into the Middle Ages as the medium of debate and would thus provide a necessary link to the classical past.

Augustine   Augustine (354–430), the best known of the fathers, was born in North Africa of a pagan father and a Christian mother and accepted Christianity under the influence of Ambrose in 387 (see "Augustine Is Brought to His Faith," above). He became bishop of Hippo in North Africa in 395 and spent the remaining years of his long life writing, preaching, and administering his see.

In his voluminous writings Augustine had something to say about almost every question of Christian theology. He profoundly influenced, for example, Christian teachings on sexual morality and marriage. Like some of his pagan contemporaries, he believed that the world was already filled with people. "The coming of Christ," he wrote, "is not served by the begetting of children." He therefore urged all Christians to a life of celibacy, even though this would cause their number to decline: "Marriage is not expedient, except for those who do not have self-control." He banned all sexual activity for the unmarried. Within marriage, husband and wife should unite sexually only for procreation, and even the pleasure they took in this act, representing a triumph of libido over reason, was a small, though pardonable, sin.

The Working of Grace   Augustine was passionately interested in the operations of grace. He sought the work of grace in his own life, and the result was his *Confessions*, an intensely personal autobiography; it is both a record of his early life, when he gave way to material and sexual temptations, and a celebration of the providence that had guided him in his struggle toward God. This masterpiece of introspective analysis is a type of literature virtually unknown in the classical tradition.

In theological matters, Augustine distinguished between God the creator (the author of nature) and God the redeemer (the source of grace), and insisted that these two figures not be confused. God as creator had given humanity certain powers, such as intelligence superior to that of beasts, but those powers, injured by the original fall of Adam and Eve, are insufficient to earn salvation. Only through grace, which Jesus' sacrifice had earned, could humanity hope to be saved. Moreover, God had already decided on whom he would bestow grace; hence, even before we are born, we are all predestined either to heaven or to hell.

THE CATHEDRAL IN SYRACUSE, SICILY
The interior, in powerful historical symbolism, shows a Doric temple to Athena (fifth century B.C.) with its original columns,
now supporting the walls and roof of a Christian church built in the seventh century A.D.
Art Resource, NY

Augustine on Salvation   Augustine deeply pondered the problem of sin—the breaking of God's law—and quarreled with Pelagius, a British monk who argued that sin was only the result of a wrong choice and that people could achieve perfection, do good works, and thus attain salvation. For Augustine, sin descended from Adam into every human being, and doing good works, no matter how many, could not guarantee salvation, which was the gift of God alone through his grace. Humanity's salvation must await a glorious transformation at the end of time.

Augustine further believed that the power of grace might redeem the whole course of human history. In his greatest work, *The City of God,* he set out to show that there was order in history: Behind the manifold events of the past the hand of God was evident, directing people through his grace to their destiny. Into this immense panorama, Augustine brought the sacred history of the Jewish Testament, the history of his own times, and the Christian expectation of resurrection. He held that the grace of God united the chosen in a form of community or city that stood against the community of those joined by the love of earthly things. The city of God, in which live those chosen for salvation, was as yet invisible, and the elect who were its members should recognize that this present earth was not their true home. Augustine saw history as moving in a straight line toward humankind's salvation, as compared with cyclical views among some Greeks. Therefore, to Christians of his own troubled age and to those of later ages, Augustine held out the beckoning vision of a heavenly city, a celestial Jerusalem, where at last they would be at home with God.

Summary

In the history of the Roman Empire, several great themes are seen. The body politic soon lost direct elections by the people, and the structure of society became constantly more monarchic. As success in war led to an established empire, a long period of peace nourished the economy and saw the development of urban centers throughout Europe. The Empire managed to avoid a near-collapse, and within its survival the Christian religion won the victory of faith. Christians felt able to ignore or transcend the "fall" of Rome—an event that the modern world sees as a possible model of its own fate. The transformation of the Empire, as it is better called, is a challenge and a warning to all who read history; it is also the recognized end of the ancient world and the beginning of a long period in which new nations would use the legacy of antiquity in their own development.

QUESTION FOR FURTHER THOUGHT

It may well surprise the historian that the Roman Empire, which controlled almost all of Europe in its time, suffered a catastrophic decline. By what means, if any, might this decline have been mitigated or even prevented?

RECOMMENDED READING

Sources

Early Christian Writings: The Apostolic Fathers. M. Staniforth (tr.). 1968.

*Suetonius. *Lives of the Caesars.* Robert Graves (tr.). 1972.

*Tacitus. *Annals of Imperial Rome.* Michael Grant (tr.). 1978.

*———. *The Histories.* Kenneth Wellesley (tr.). 1976. The two works give the history of the Empire in the first century A.D. by the leading Roman historian.

Studies

Ando, Clifford. *Imperial Ideology and Provincial Loyalty in the Roman Empire.* 2000. Excellent modern study of the relationship between the governing power in the Empire and the subjects in the several provinces.

Birley, Anthony. *Marcus Aurelius: A Biography.* 1987. Study of the only philosopher-king in the Roman world.

Bradley, Keith R. *Slaves and Masters in the Roman Empire: A Study in Social Control.* 1987. Slave families, freeing of slaves, rewards, and punishments.

Brown, Peter. *Augustine of Hippo: A Biography.* 1986. Masterly study of the greatest of the church fathers.

*———. *The World of Late Antiquity, A.D. 150–750.* 1971. One of many illuminating books by this great scholar. Brief, well illustrated.

Cameron, Averil. *The Mediterranean World in Late Antiquity, A.D. 395–600.* 1993. A brief, accessible modern survey.

Chadwick, Henry. *The Early Church.* Rev. ed. 1993. The development of the religious institution that was to conquer Europe.

Crook, J. A. *Law and Life of Rome.* 1967. Survey, arranged by topics, of the relationship between law and daily life in the Empire.

Cross, Frank M. *The Ancient Library of Qumran and Modern Biblical Studies.* 1976. Excellent introduction to the study of the Dead Sea Scrolls.

Gruen, Erich S. *Diaspora: Jews amidst Greeks and Romans.* 2002. Wide-ranging examination of how Jews lived outside the Holy Land among peoples who did not share their faith.

Luttwak, Edward. *The Grand Strategy of the Roman Empire from the First Century A.D. to the Third.* 1979. Realistic appraisal of how the Empire maintained itself, by an internationally known strategic thinker and writer.

MacMullen, Ramsay. *Christianizing the Roman Empire.* 1986. The spread of Christianity, with attention to the conversion of Constantine and its results.

———. *Constantine.* 1988. Biography of the emperor who pointed the Empire toward Christianity.

———. *Paganism in the Roman Empire.* 1981. Study of pagan beliefs, worshipers, and cults in the Empire.

Musurillo, Herbert (ed.). *The Acts of the Christian Martyrs.* 1979. Translations of accounts of torture and martyrdom in early Christianity.

Potter, David S. *The Roman Empire at Bay, A.D. 180–395.* 2004. Detailed history of the critical period for the Empire, arguing that centralization of control was the major factor in the decline.

Stambaugh, John E. *The Ancient Roman City.* 1988. The development of the city and comparisons with other ancient cities.

Wells, Colin. *The Roman Empire.* 2nd ed. 1995. The best one-volume modern narrative.

Whittaker, C. R. *The Frontiers of the Roman Empire: A Social and Economic Study.* 1994. On the Germans and other neighbors of the Empire.

*Available in paperback.

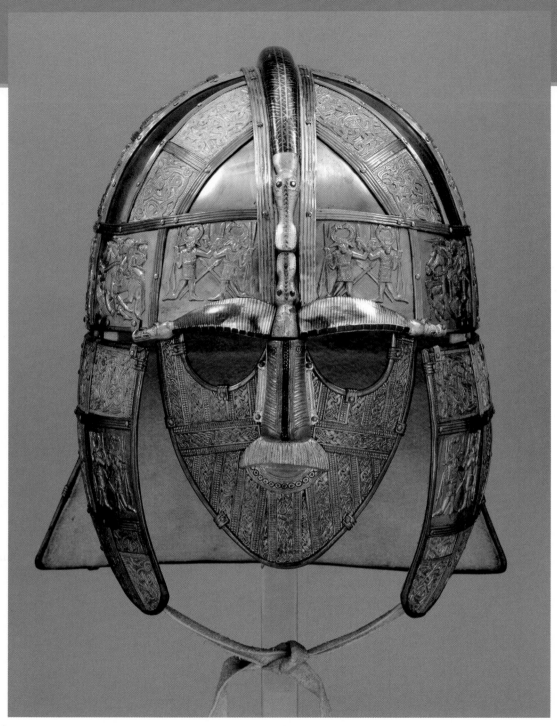

ANGLO-SAXON HELMET FROM THE SHIP-BURIAL AT SUTTON HOO
The Anglo-Saxons traveled and traded widely in Europe. Still pagan, they buried their leaders in ships equipped for the journey to the afterlife. The Sutton Hoo burial mound in England was discovered in 1939. In addition to this helmet (a reconstruction of the one now housed in the British Museum), the ship contained coins; silver bowls, cups, and spoons; and gold objects. A brass bowl came from the Near East and a large silver bowl came from Byzantium. Coins put the date of the burial in the first quarter of the seventh century.

Courtesy of the Trustees of the British Museum

THE MAKING OF WESTERN EUROPE

The "Dark Ages" is the popular conception of the period after the decline of the Roman Empire in Western Europe, but the period was one that saw continuities as well as radical changes. The civilization that took root in the west and north of Europe after the decline of the Roman Empire was the direct ancestor of the modern Western world. Historians call the millennium between the fall of the Roman Empire and approximately 1500 the Middle Ages, or the medieval period of European history. As various Germanic and Hunnish peoples moved into Europe, the former Celtic and Roman populations gradually intermarried with the invaders; classical Latin ceased to be the ordinary language of people and instead evolved into Spanish, Portuguese, French, and Italian. Roman law blended with the law of the invaders. Settlement patterns also changed. Roman cities fell into a decline, and aqueducts, roads, walls, baths, and the general infrastructure that made the cities comfortable were no longer maintained.

Christianity continued to gain widespread acceptance among the Roman population and among the invading tribes. Monasteries, religious communities for men and women, provided a refuge for those who wished to lead a life of prayer and scholarly pursuits. Monasteries also preserved Latin and the classics of Roman literature.

For the ordinary people, both Roman and tribal, these centuries were ones of violence, danger, and movement. Waves of invasions made agriculture and even survival unpredictable. Even during these political disruptions, innovations were improving agriculture, including a better plow, a new system of crop rotation, the horse collar, and the stirrup.

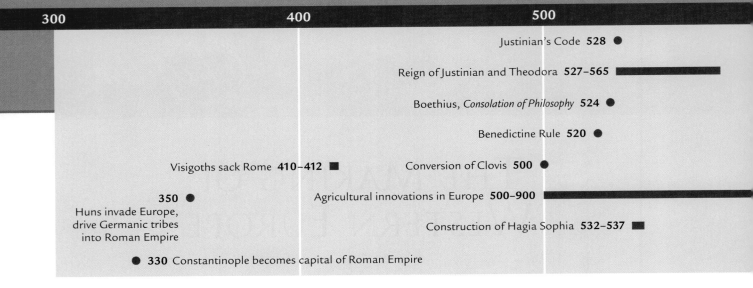

| 300 | 400 | 500 |

Justinian's Code **528** ●

Reign of Justinian and Theodora **527–565** ▬

Boethius, *Consolation of Philosophy* **524** ●

Benedictine Rule **520** ●

Visigoths sack Rome **410–412** ■   Conversion of Clovis **500** ●

350 ●   Agricultural innovations in Europe **500–900** ▬
Huns invade Europe,
drive Germanic tribes
into Roman Empire

Construction of Hagia Sophia **532–537** ■

● **330** Constantinople becomes capital of Roman Empire

THE NEW COMMUNITY OF PEOPLES

The Early Middle Ages, roughly the fifth through the eighth century, witnessed the emergence of new types of social and cultural organization based partly on Roman tradition but incorporating Christianity and the customs of new peoples who moved into the Empire. The Greeks and Romans called all these peoples *barbarians* because of their unintelligible languages and strange customs.[1] There was no single barbarian nation: These peoples were many and differed considerably in language and culture.

The Great Migrations

Among the earliest barbarian peoples were the Celtic tribes. While those in Scotland, Ireland, and Wales are best known today, Celts had settled in France and Spain as well. Although Roman occupation imposed its government and civilization on the Celts, it did not destroy their conquest and culture.

More numerous and more formidable than the Celts were the Germans, who were settled in a great arc that stretched from Scandinavia to the Black Sea. Historians have given these peoples the generic names of Germans or Goths, based loosely on their membership in the Germanic linguistic group to which their various dialects belonged. The term does not imply unity of culture, a self-designation by the people, or a relationship to modern Germans. Many of the Germanic tribes had long been exposed to Mediterranean influences and had some understanding of the Roman economy, warfare, and culture. From about 350, Christianity spread among the Germans north of the Danube, but in its Arian form. Beyond this Germanic cordon lived the still pagan Slavic tribes, also identifiable by their linguistic group.

Huns and Germanic Peoples Fear and hunger set the tribes in motion in the fourth century. Germanic tribes had for centuries challenged the Roman frontiers. Their primitive agriculture forced them to search constantly for new lands to plunder or settle. The wealth and splendor of the Roman world attracted the Germans. The Romans brought them into the Empire initially as slaves or prisoners of war, then as free peasants to settle on deserted lands, and finally as mercenary soldiers and officers. By the fourth century, however, the barbarian penetration of the Empire became more violent.

Sweeping out of their central Asiatic homeland, the Huns, a nomadic people of Mongolian or Tartar origins, terrified the Germanic tribes, who sought refuge in the Roman Empire. Because climatic changes desiccated their grazing lands, the Huns moved north and west with their horses and families. They formed a hoard under the leadership of their great chief Attila (r.ca. 433–453). Christian writers called him the "scourge of God." He established his hoard on the Danube, where their raiding parties struck at both Gaul and Italy. With Attila's death in 453, the Hunnic Empire disintegrated, but the Huns had already given impetus to the great movement of peoples that marks the beginning of the Middle Ages.

Visigoths The Visigoths (or West Goths) were the first of the Germanic tribes to experience the Hunnish raids. Fleeing before them, the Visigoths asked the Byzantine emperor to settle them in a depopulated area south of the Danube. In 376 the emperor Valens admitted them into the Empire. Although the Visigoths were willing to settle peacefully, the Byzantine officials

---

[1] The Greeks invented the word *barbaros* to imitate the strange sounds of unintelligible languages.

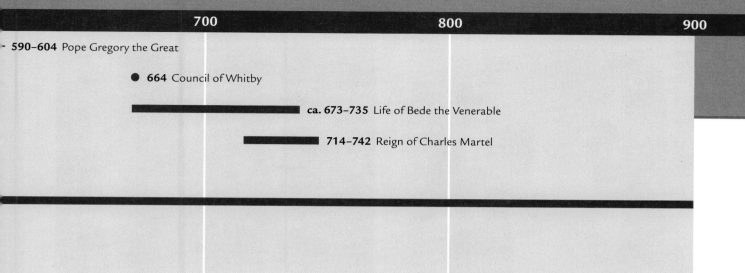

700	800	900

590–604 Pope Gregory the Great

● **664** Council of Whitby

ca. 673–735 Life of Bede the Venerable

714–742 Reign of Charles Martel

CHRONOLOGY
The Germanic Invasions

ca. 310	Goths and other Germans on the Danube.	r. 485–511	Clovis: Conversion of Franks to Roman Christianity.
ca. 350	Huns invade Europe, destroy Ostrogoths, and drive Visigoths to seek settlement south of the Danube in Byzantine territory.	r. 493–526	Theodoric and the Ostrogothic Kingdom of Italy: Boethius and Cassiodorus.
378	Battle of Adrianople: Visigothic defeat of Byzantine army.	r. 527–565	Justinian: Conquest of Vandal Kingdom of North Africa and part of Spain and Italy.
ca. 400	Franks, Alamans, Burgundians, Vandals, and others cross the Rhine into Gaul.	r. 590–604	Pope Gregory the Great: Mission of Augustine (597) to England.
410–412	Visigoths sack Rome and move on into Gaul.	664	Council of Whitby: United English Christians under the papacy.
429	Visigoths in Spain and South Gaul.	r. 714–741	Charles Martel: Defeats the Arabs at Tours (Poitiers) in 732.
ca. 430–500	Anglo-Saxons in England, Vandals in Africa, Franks in Gaul, Alamans in Alsace and upper Danube, Burgundians in Rhone Valley.	751	Pepin III: Becomes King of Franks with papal support, anointed by pope in 754.
d. 461	St. Patrick: Conversion of Ireland.		

treated them miserably, raping their women and forcing them to sell children into slavery in return for food. The starving Goths rebelled and Valens led an expedition against them. The triumph of the Visigothic cavalry over the Byzantine army at the battle of Adrianople in 378 showed the superiority of the Gothic mounted warrior (the prototype of the medieval knight) over the Roman foot soldier.

Continuing their westward movement, the Visigoths sacked Rome in 410, the first time in 800 years that a foreign army had occupied Rome. The Visigoths took gold and silver treasure, slaves, and movable property.

The devastated Romans asked the Visigoth leader what he would leave for them, and he is reputed to have replied, "Your lives." Crossing the Alps into Gaul, the Visigoths established in 418 the first autonomous kingdom on Roman soil. At its height in the mid-fifth century, the kingdom of the Visigoths extended from Gibraltar to the Loire River. Another Germanic people, the Franks, conquered the Visigothic Kingdom in Gaul in the sixth century and confined the Visigoths to Spain.

Vandals and Burgundians The Vandals were another Germanic people that the Huns forced out of their

159

VISIGOTHIC FIBULAE
Fibulae were decorative pins used to fasten clothes. These sixth-century Spanish examples are typical of the sophisticated metalwork practiced by medieval artisans. Gems set in gold and bronze reveal the outline of an eagle form, as well as a delight in pattern that was characteristic of the age.
Walters Art Gallery, Baltimore

The gilded copper relief of the Lombard king Agilulf, flanked by his warriors, shows Germanic adaptation of kingship in imitation of the Roman emperors. The Lombards conquered much of the Italian peninsula in 568. Agilulf became king shortly afterward.
Scala/Art Resource, NY

territory. Coming from eastern Germany, the Vandals crossed the Rhine River into Gaul in 406. Perhaps eighty thousand in number, they continued south through the Iberian Peninsula (Spain) and crossed to North Africa, where they established a permanent kingdom in 429. Like the Visigoths, the Vandals were Arians, and they persecuted orthodox Christians. They became so powerful on the Mediterranean Sea that in 455 they were able to plunder Rome. This act, their religious persecutions, and their piracy in the Mediterranean earned the Vandals a reputation for senseless violence, which the modern word *vandal* still reflects. The Vandal Kingdom survived until the Byzantine emperor Justinian destroyed it in the sixth century.

The Burgundians, another Germanic tribe from eastern Europe, followed the Vandals into Gaul, probably in 411. The Burgundians established an independent kingdom in the valleys of the upper Rhône and Saône rivers in 443, which gave the region its permanent name, Burgundy (see map 6.1).

Ostrogoths The ease with which all these Germanic peoples invaded the Roman frontiers shows that the Empire had lost virtually all authority in the West by the middle of the fifth century. The emperor Valentinian III was the last Roman to exercise any real power in the West. A series of feeble emperors were raised to the throne and then deposed or murdered. One of the rebels, Odoacer, deposed the last emperor in 476. Although no more than a palace mutiny, this coup marks

the final passage of power from Roman to German hands in the West.

The Ostrogoths (eastern Goths) moved into the territory vacated by the Visigoths at the invitation of the Byzantine emperor. Young Theodoric, son of one of their kings, was sent as a hostage to Constantinople. There he learned at least something of Greek and Roman culture, although he continued to adhere to Arian Christianity. The emperor so favored him that he was even made a Roman citizen. When Theodoric united all of the Ostrogoths under his command, they became too dangerous to keep in the East and the emperor dispatched Theodoric and the Ostrogoths to deal with Odoacer. Theodoric led his troops into Italy in 489 and conquered it, overthrowing Odoacer in 493.

Germanic Tribes in Gaul In the third and fourth centuries the Germanic tribes living just beyond the Roman frontier in the Rhine valley coalesced into two large federations, the Alemanni in the upper valley and the Franks in the lower valley. The Alemanni pushed beyond the Rhine into the middle of Gaul and founded a kingdom in 420. They give to both modern French and Spanish their names for Germany (*Allemagne, Alemania*). The Franks slowly penetrated into northern

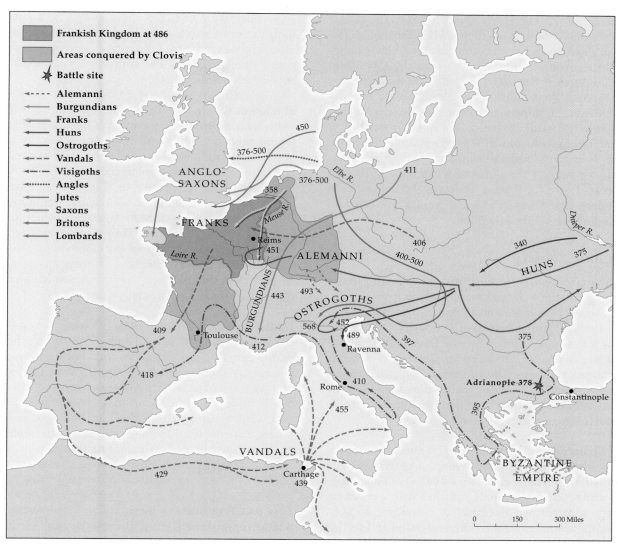

MAP 6.1 INVASIONS, FOURTH THROUGH SIXTH CENTURIES
This map indicates the enormous movement of peoples throughout Europe in the fourth through the sixth centuries.
While most of these people were Germanic in origin, it is interesting to note the range of all the migrations. What
conditions do you suppose prompted this movement of the peoples of the fifth and sixth centuries?
◆ For an online version, go to www.mhhe.com/chambers9 > chapter 6 > book maps

Gaul, moving across the valley of the Seine up to the Loire River. Francia, as it was called, gives us the modern name France. The first-mentioned king of the Franks, a figure who stands on the dark margin between legend and history, was called Merovech, and he gave his name to the first dynasty of Frankish kings, the Merovingians.

Anglo-Saxons in Britain   The Romans had withdrawn their legions from Britain in 407 to defend Rome against the Visigoths, leaving the island open to invasion. The Germanic settlement of Britain differed from the conquests on the continent. Rather than traveling as family groups, the Angles, Saxons, Jutes, and even

some Franks came in small bands under the authority of chiefs. These Germanic peoples did not settle and assimilate with the native peoples (the Britons) as they did in most other Roman provinces; they either exterminated the Britons or pushed them westward into Cornwall and Wales.

For a few decades in the early sixth century, the Britons unsuccessfully rallied against the Germanic invaders under a king whom later sources call Arthur, but after 550 the invaders triumphed and imposed their language on the region. So sharp was the linguistic change thus enforced that modern English, apart from place names, shows little trace of the speech of the original Britons.

The Early Slavs   The Slavic tribes living to the east of the Germans embarked on their own extensive migrations. In the fifth and sixth centuries some Slavic tribes pushed their settlements as far west as the Elbe River and as far north as the Baltic Sea; they are the ancestors of the modern West Slavs—the Poles, Czechs, and Slovaks. During the same years, other Slavic tribes penetrated into the Balkan peninsula and Greece; their descendants are the modern South Slavs—the Serbs, Croats, Bulgarians, and Macedonians. Still other tribes moved east beyond the Dnieper River and north into the forest regions of Russia; they are the ancestors of the modern East Slavs—the Russians, Ukrainians, and Belarussians (or White Russians).

Germanic Society

The tribal groups who moved into the Roman Empire had a very different economy and society from the Romans. Much of what we know about Germanic society comes from a Roman historian and writer, Cornelius Tacitus (ca. A.D. 56–120). While he lived before the period of the invasions, he knew of Germanic customs from talking to Germanic soldiers and slaves. Studies of Germanic law codes written after they settled in the Empire and archaeology have done much to increase our knowledge of these peoples.

Social Structure   Germanic society was based on the households, each headed by a man, a patriarch, who controlled his women, children, and slaves. The households coalesced into kindreds, families with a common ancestry, that formed the basis of Germanic society. The families fought for each other, migrated and settled together, and held some property (forests and wastelands) in common. But each individual held his own property as well, so that some individuals and families were richer than others. The kindred groups formed together into clans under chiefs who distinguished themselves by success in battle and were able to draw free warriors and their families to their leadership.

In times of migration, these loosely organized kindred groups and clans came together as a tribe, which gives us such names as Ostrogoths, Franks, and so on. Before the Germanic invasions of the Roman Empire, the tribes or peoples did not usually have kings; only the invasions, which required a continuing military command, made the king (who also served as chief priest) usual within Germanic society.

Economy   The agricultural economy of the Germanic peoples was rudimentary. They cleared forest land for small fields of grain, grazed herds, hunted, and relied on plundering other clans or the Romans. Women, slaves, and children produced the agricultural products, while men hunted.

Because they changed their homes so frequently, their finest art was jewelry made from precious metals, often embodying forms of animals (see photos of Visigothic fibulae, p. 160). The animal forms strongly influenced early medieval art.

Women made essential contributions to the Germanic household at every social level. A free German male who aspired to be a warrior needed a wife who would tend his fields and watch over his flocks and herds during his absences on campaigns. The social importance of Germanic women was not, however, an unmixed benefit. According to Tacitus, they worked harder than the men did. In addition to doing much of the agriculture, women brewed, spun cloth, and made clothing for their families. They were often the prized booty for raiding expeditions and constant targets of abduction. Their life expectancy seems to have been shorter than that of males, and their resulting smaller number added to their social value.

Comitatus, or Warrior Bands   Warfare was a way of life and an integral part of the economy for the Germanic peoples. The Germans raided other peoples and eventually the Roman territory to get metals, slaves, and precious objects. The warriors were organized into bands under the leadership of a chief. Tacitus called this warrior band a **comitatus** ("following"), in which young warriors would join the retinue of an established chief, follow him to battle, and fight under his leadership in return for his protection and a share of his booty.

Law and Procedures   Germanic laws were not written down until the sixth century, so dispute settlement relied on oral traditions. When the laws were recorded, they indicate much about these traditions. Kinsmen were to avenge a death or injury to a member of their family group. Because such feuds could cause social unrest, a system of compensations developed. The amount of compensation, called **Wergeld** (literally, "man money"), depended on the social rank of the individual. Offenders could also pay the family compensation for the loss of an arm, an eye, teeth, or a nose. The high wergeld for women indicates their value in the society.

One of the most distinctive features of tribal government was its reliance on large councils or assemblies. The chief or king had only limited power and never made decisions alone; he always acted in an assembly or council of free warriors who aided him in making his judgments (see "Tacitus on the Early Germans," p. 163).

The Literary Legacy of Germanic Poetry   Literature, like law, passed through oral transmission. The earliest surviving examples of Germanic poetry were not written down until the ninth century, but they still provide

TACITUS ON THE EARLY GERMANS

The short book by Cornelius Tacitus, Germania, *published in 98, is virtually the only surviving portrait of early Germanic society. In this passage Tacitus describes the customs of the Germans in government.*

"On matters of minor importance only the chiefs deliberate, on major affairs the whole community; but, even where the people have the power to decide, the case is carefully considered in advance by the chiefs. Except in case of accident or emergency they assemble on fixed days. . . . When the mass so decide, they take their seats fully armed. Silence is then demanded by the priests, who on that occasion have also power to enforce obedience. . . . If a proposal displeases them, the people roar out their dissent; if they approve, they clash their spears.

"One can launch an accusation before the Council or bring a capital charge. The punishment varies to suit the crime. The traitor and deserter are hanged on trees, the coward, the shirker and the unnaturally vicious are drowned in miry swamps under a cover of wattled hurdles. The distinction in the punishment implies that deeds of violence should be paid for in the full glare of publicity, but that deeds of shame should be suppressed. Even for lighter offences the punishment varies. The man who is found guilty is fined so and so many horses or cattle. Part of the fine is paid to the King or State, part to the injured man or his relatives."

From H. Mattingly (tr.), *The Germania,* Penguin Classics, 1970, pp. 11–12.

---

an authentic reflection of Germanic culture, testifying to a violent age.

In the Anglo-Saxon epic *Beowulf,* the king of the Danes, Hrothgar, is powerless against the terrible monster Grendel; his plight illustrates the weakness of tribal kingship. Hrothgar must appeal for help to the hero Beowulf, a great warrior who comes from a tribe in southern Sweden. Beowulf succeeds in defeating Grendel by tearing off his arm. Grendel flees and dies. When Grendel's mother, a sea-witch, comes seeking revenge, Beowulf chases her to her underwater cave, where he finds a giant's ancient sword and slays Grendel's mother. Beowulf becomes king and dies years later while battling a dragon. The poem is rich in descriptions of drinking halls, court intrigues, kingship, and personal loyalties of a follower to his leader.

Religion and Superstition Germanic religion displayed an abiding sense of pessimism. The Germans saw nature as a hostile force. Minor deities, both good and bad, dwelt in groves, streams, fields, and seas and directly affected human beings. Through incantations, spells, or charms, people tried to influence the actions of these spirits. Such practices added a large element of superstition, which lasted through the Middle Ages and long beyond.

The higher gods lived in the sky and took a remote interest in human affairs. Some of our modern words derive from those of the German gods: Tuesday comes from Ti or Tyr, god of war; Wednesday comes from Woden or Odin, god of victory; Thursday comes from Thor, the thunderer; and Friday from Woden's wife, Friia or Frig.

Germans and Romans

Historians have estimated, although on flimsy evidence, that the Germans who settled within the Roman Empire constituted no more than 5 percent of the total population. The Germans did not exterminate the Romans; rather, through gradual settlement and intermarriage with Romans, the Germans adopted lives that made them almost indistinguishable from their Roman counterparts.

Historians no longer speak, as they once did, of the Germans being responsible for the destruction of the Western Roman Empire. Even before entering the Empire, many Germans, particularly those settled near the frontiers, had achieved a cultural level that resembled that of Romans living in those areas. In the northern part of Gaul, Celtic influences had already reemerged, and Roman influence proved to be a rather thin veneer on the region and its peoples. Assimilation, however, was slow and had a definite impact on Roman society. In the course of time, the Germanic chiefs and armies obtained perhaps a third of the territory of the former Western Empire. The letters of Sidonius Apollinaris (431–480) are eloquent about the experiences of a Roman patrician living in Gaul (see "Sidonius Apollinaris on Living with Germans," p. 164).

Changes Following Settlement The settling tribes changed the landscape and language of the areas they invaded. Before the invasions, the tribes had lived in nucleated villages (houses in a central area and fields surrounding the housing area). When they moved into the Roman Empire, the Germanic tribes showed a

SIDONIUS APOLLINARIS ON LIVING WITH GERMANS

A Roman of patrician birth and training living in Gaul, Sidonius (ca. 431–ca. 480) wrote a series of letters to friends commenting on the loss of the Latin language, the wreck of the Roman Empire, and the crudity of the Germanic tribes.

"Though you descend in the male line from an ancestor who was not only consul—that is immaterial—but also (and here is the real point) a poet . . . yet here we find you picking up a knowledge of the German tongue with the greatest ease; the feat fills me with indescribable amazement. . . . You can hardly conceive how amused we all are to hear that, when you are by, not a barbarian but fears to perpetrate a barbarism in his own language. Old Germans bowed with age are said to stand astounded when they see you interpreting their German letters; they actually choose you for arbiter and mediator in their disputes. You are a new Solon in the elucidation of Burgundian law. . . . You are popular on all sides; you are sought after; your society gives universal pleasure. You are chosen as adviser and judge; as soon as you utter a decision it is received with respect. In body and mind alike these people are as stiff as stocks and very hard to form; yet they delight to find in you, and equally delight to learn a Burgundian eloquence and a Roman spirit.

"Let me end with a single caution to the cleverest of men. Do not allow these talents of yours to prevent you from devoting whatever time you can spare to reading. Let your critical taste determine you to preserve a balance between the two languages [Latin and German], holding fast to the one to prevent us making fun of you, and practicing the other that you may have the laugh of us."

From O. M. Dalton, *The Letters of Sidonius,* 2 vols., 5.5: To his friend Syagriius, Clarendon Press, 1915.

preference for continuing this settlement pattern. Since those Romans who had villas also preferred to live in the countryside, urban populations shrank and the infrastructure of the cities, such as aqueducts, disappeared. With education abandoned except in the Church and among some Romans, the Latin language was no longer commonly written or spoken, and vernacular languages (the romance languages, or languages derived from the Roman one) began to develop.

As the invaders settled and their kings established governments modeled as much as possible on their understanding of the Roman one, they needed written law rather than oral tradition. The Germanic law codes were modeled on Roman law codes but codified Germanic law.

Intermarriage in the population was inevitable. If there were anxieties among Roman or Germanic parents about intermarriage or among free warriors about becoming peasants, these anxieties were not expressed in written accounts.

Christianity and the Tribes   By the time many of the tribes entered Europe, they had already converted to Christianity. The conversion began with Ulfila (ca. 310–ca. 381), the son of Christian parents who lived in the land of the Goths. His parents had been captured by the Goths, so he grew up a Gothic-speaking Christian. He received a Christian education and was consecrated in 341 by the bishop of Constantinople, who was an Arian. Ulfila brought the Arian version of Christianity to the Goths and translated the Bible into their language. From these early missionary activities Arian Christianity spread to the Visigoths, Vandals, and Ostrogoths.

The difference between the Arian Goths and the Roman Christians was one of the most serious barriers to peaceful settlement of the tribes. Most of the Arian kings persecuted the native Christian population. Only the Franks, under Clovis, converted to Roman Christianity. Because of this early conversion, the Frankish rulers developed a close relation with the Roman Church.

THE NEW POLITICAL STRUCTURES

By the beginning of the sixth century, the initial wave of tribal migrations into the West had eased and the tribes began to settle, forming monarchies. While the Western Empire was undergoing a major reconfiguration of its political landscape, the Eastern Empire continued to flourish.

The Early Byzantine Empire

The name Byzantine is, strictly speaking, a historical misnomer. The inhabitants of the Eastern Empire recognized no break between their civilization and that of classical Rome. Throughout their history they called themselves *Romans,* even after Rome had slipped from their power and they had adopted Greek as their official language. Indeed, modern Western historians

This Byzantine gold cup, dating from the sixth or seventh century, was found at Durazzo in modern Albania. Four female figures in gold repoussé symbolize the cities of Rome, Cyprus, Alexandria, and Constantinople. The detail shows the figure of Constantinople. The representation of cities in allegorical form indicates the prominence of urban centers in Byzantine thought and society.
Metropolitan Museum of Art, Gift of J. Pierpont Morgan, 1917 (17.190.1710). Photograph © 2001 The Metropolitan Museum of Art, New York

from the Balkans to Asia Minor and the maritime route between the Black and Mediterranean seas. Moreover, the city at once acquired the aura of a Christian city, the capital of the Christian Empire.

Abandonment of the West   The successors of Constantine had no intention of abandoning the powers of the old Roman Empire in either the West or the East. However, the Eastern emperors lacked the resources to defend the West. They could only try to preserve the boundaries in the East by a combination of warfare against the barbarians and paying tribute to them to remain in peace within the borders. When the Visigoths and Ostrogoths became rebellious, the emperors paid them to go west. The idea of restoring the Empire to its former size, power, and glory was never lost.

Justinian the Great (r. 527–565) of Byzantium

Justinian pursued three principal goals in his reign: the restoration of the Western provinces to the Empire, the reformation of laws and institutions, and an ambitious program of splendid public works.

Justinian and Theodora   Historians have much information, or at least many allegations, about Justinian from his court historian, Procopius. While the emperor lived, Procopius praised him in two official histories: *On the Wars* recounts Justinian's victorious campaigns, and *On Buildings* describes his architectural achievements. But after Justinian's death, Procopius also wrote one of the most vicious character assassinations in history. *The Secret History* paints Justinian, empress Theodora, and several high officials of the court as monsters of public and private vice. Historians still have not satisfactorily reconciled the contradictory portraits that the two-tongued Procopius has left to us.

Justinian's name is linked to that of his empress, Theodora, with whom he shared power. Born in about 500, Theodora became a famous actress and a celebrated courtesan before she was twenty. She traveled through the cities of the Empire, earning her way, according to Procopius, by skilled prostitution. In her early twenties she returned to Constantinople, where she mended her morals but lost none of her charm, and married Justinian.

Theodora's influence on her husband was decisive from the start. In 532 the popular factions of Constantinople rose in a rebellion known as the Nike Revolt (Nike means "win"). The two parties at the chariot races at the hippodrome in Constantinople were known as the Blues and the Greens. In addition to supporting their own horses and drivers, they had taken different sides on religious and political divisions in the Empire. Uniting against Justinian and Theodora, they

sometimes forget that the Roman Empire did not fall in the East until 1453.

Capital at Constantinople   Byzantine history began when the emperor Constantine transferred the capital of the Roman Empire from the West to the East in 330. The emperor probably had many motives for moving the capital further east, including the larger Christian population in the east. It was also the wealthiest and most populous part of the Empire. Constantine chose as his new capital the site of the ancient Greek colony of Byzantium.

The site of this capital on a narrow peninsula that appears as a hand trying to connect Europe and Asia, influenced the character of Byzantium and the course of its history. The city stood at the intersection of two heavily traveled trade routes: the overland highway

EMPEROR JUSTINIAN, RAVENNA
The mosaics—patterns made from small chips of tinted glass backed with gold leaf—that cover the wall of the church of San Vitale in Ravenna are one of the greatest achievements of the Byzantine era. Here, the emperor Justinian is surrounded by both priests and warriors, emphasizing his power over the religious as well as the secular domain.
Scala/Art Resource, NY

rebelled. Justinian panicked and planned to flee. But in a moving speech, as recorded by Procopius, Theodora urged her husband to choose death rather than exile. Justinian remained and crushed the uprising.

Reconquest of the West   To restore imperial rule over the lost Western provinces, Justinian sent armies to attack the kingdoms of the Vandals, Ostrogoths, and Visigoths and sought a precarious peace with the Persians beyond his eastern frontier. By 554 his troops had destroyed the Vandal Kingdom in North Africa and established Byzantine rule there; had forced the Visigoths in Spain to cede the southern tip of the Iberian peninsula; and had triumphed, at least for a while, over the Ostrogothic Kingdom in Italy (see map 6.2). The Byzantines could not defend this territory, so it soon fell to other invaders. Only Sicily and southern Italy retained a strong Greek presence.

Justinian sought to reconcile the Eastern and Western branches of the Church, which were bitterly divided over a theological question concerning the nature of

Christi.[2] He had the pope abducted from Rome and taken to Constantinople, where he bullied him into accepting an unwelcome compromise. Justinian's coercive tactics did not bring union and peace to the Church, and all the conflicting parties bitterly resented them.

Codex Justinianus   In 528 Justinian appointed a commission to prepare a systematic codification of Roman law. The result was the *Corpus Iuris Civilis* ("Body of Civil Law"), often called **Justinian's Code.** It consisted of four compilations: the *Codex*, an easily consulted arrangement of all imperial edicts according to topic; the *Digest*, or *Pandects*, a summary of legal opinions; the *Institutes*, a textbook to introduce students to the reformed legal system; and the *Novellae*, a collection of

[2] The Monophysite theory holds that Jesus has one nature, partly divine and partly human; he was not, in other words, simply true man. Condemned as heretical at the Council of Chalcedon (451), the belief remained strong in the East. The orthodox view is that Jesus has two natures, one human and one divine, and is both true God and true man.

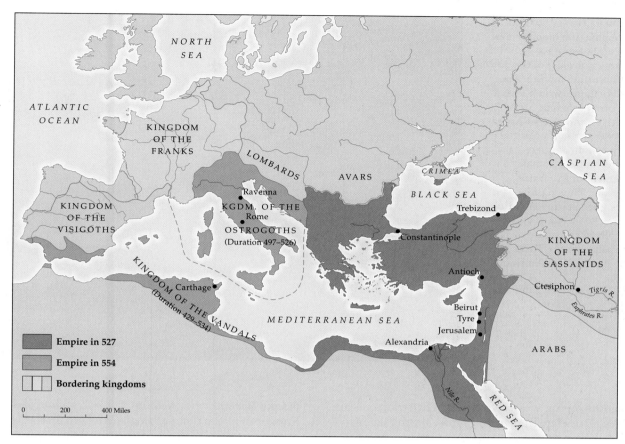

MAP 6.2 EUROPE IN THE AGE OF JUSTINIAN
The map shows Western and Eastern Europe, or the Greek and Latin halves of the Roman Empire. Notice the location of Constantinople, Rome, and Ravenna. What is the significance of the location of these cities? Where did the various Germanic tribes establish kingdoms? Where was the Persian Kingdom?
◆ For an online version, go to www.mhhe.com/chambers9 > chapter 6 > book maps

new imperial edicts issued after 534. These works are the last major ones written in Latin in the East; the language of the Empire was now Greek.

It would be hard to exaggerate the importance of the *Corpus Iuris Civilis*. It has remained for all subsequent generations the largest and richest source of information concerning the legal institutions and thought of Roman antiquity. In the Middle Ages international and commercial law were based on it, as was much of Church law. The modern legal systems of most Western countries incorporate the principles of Roman law as preserved in the *Corpus*.[3]

Hagia Sophia   The destruction resulting from the Nike revolt in Constantinople gave Justinian an opportunity to

start a rebuilding program. The most spectacular of his many new churches, palaces, and public works was the great church of Hagia Sophia, or Holy Wisdom. Begun in 532 and completed in 537, it became the model for churches all over the Empire. As Procopius described it, its great dome seems to float in the air, as if suspended by a chain from heaven. Hagia Sophia is one of the acknowledged architectural masterpieces of the world. Like other Byzantine churches, it was decorated with brilliant mosaics, but most of these were destroyed by the iconoclasts (people who regarded the use of icons for worship as a form of idolatry) in the eighth and ninth centuries.

Historical Assessment of the Reign   Justinian was remarkably successful in all his ambitious policies until the last years of his reign. Beginning in 542, terrible plagues (the same type of plague as the Black Death in the fourteenth century) repeatedly struck the imperial lands. Justinian was waging a two-front war against the Persians (Sassanids) to the east and the resurgent

---

[3] The British Commonwealth and the United States (except Louisiana) follow common law, based on cases decided in medieval England; but common law too was strongly influenced by Roman legal concepts.

INTERIOR OF HAGIA SOPHIA
Hagia Sophia, the monumental project of the emperor Justinian, is a lasting reminder of the power of the Byzantine Empire. The saucerlike dome, which rises 180 feet, is carried on four pendentives (the wedge-shaped supports that allow a circular dome to rest on a square structure) and is a notable achievement of Byzantine engineering. The original mosaics were destroyed during the iconoclastic controversy, redone afterward, and whitewashed by the Turks after the conquest of Constantinople in 1453.
© 1993 Tibor Bognár/Corbis Stock Market

Ostrogoths on the western frontier. The strains on human resources left the entire Empire on the defensive at his death.

Historians have viewed Justinian's policies as unrealistic, excessively ambitious, and ultimately disastrous. Memories of ancient Roman greatness blinded him to the inadequacy of his own resources. Yet Hagia Sophia and the *Corpus Iuris Civilis* ensure him a permanent reputation in both the East and the West.

The Frankish Kingdom

Unification under Clovis   The founder of the kingdom of the Franks was Clovis (r. 485–511), putative grandson of Merovech, king of the Franks. Clovis' great accomplishment was the political unification of nearly the whole of Gaul, corresponding roughly to most of modern France. According to the bishop and historian Gregory of Tours (538–594), one of the reasons Clovis succeeded in becoming the sole ruler was that he killed all his relatives who might challenge him.

No less important than military force for unification was Clovis' conversion (c. 500) to Roman, rather than Arian, Christianity. Gregory of Tours tells us that Clovis' wife, Clotilda, urged him to convert and that he had promised to be baptized if he won a battle that he was losing. Winning it, he and all his troops were baptized. This step facilitated his conquests and made possible the peaceful assimilation of the diverse peoples he ruled. As the first barbarians to accept Roman Christianity, the Franks became the Western Church's chief defender from both internal dissension and external attacks.

The Later Merovingians   Clovis had established a strong Frankish kingdom in Gaul, but his Merovingian successors, known traditionally as the "do-nothing kings," showed the weaknesses of tribal monarchy. Unable to conceive of the kingdom as anything but a private estate, they divided and redivided their lands among their heirs. Frankish custom dictated partible inheritance, that is, all surviving sons inherited the property equally. To resolve territorial disputes, the Merovingians relied primarily on violence to define their powers. The history of their reigns is largely a dismal story of intrigue and destructive feuds.

Because of the Merovingian kings' negligence, their chief household official, known as the mayor of the palace, gradually took over the real powers of government. The mayor's functions were to manage the palaces and supervise the royal lands; he was also able to distribute the lands largely as he saw fit. One mayor, Pepin of Heristal (d. 714), who already administered the eastern lands of the kingdom, gained control over the western lands in 687, thus unifying nearly the whole kingdom of Gaul under his administration.

Charles Martel   Pepin's son and successor, Charles Martel, or "The Hammer" (r. 714–741), succeeded in defeating the Arab advance into Europe at the battle of Tours in 732 (see p. 185). This great victory saved the

BAD AND GOOD REGIMENT, CA. 1125
This manuscript illustration shows a typical medieval plow team of oxen. The heavy plow used on the plains of Northern Europe included three indispensable parts: a colter, or knife, to cut the soil; a share, or wedge, to widen the breech and break up the clods; and a moldboard to lift the earth and turn the furrow.
Photo, D. Pineider, Biblioteca Medicea Laurenziana, Florence

As a consequence, horses were not universally used in agriculture in the Middle Ages.

The Three-Field System   Northern Europeans also developed a new method of crop rotation: the **three-field system.** An estate's arable land was divided into three large fields of several hundred acres each, with two-thirds of the land cultivated each year on a rotating basis. The system was first documented in 763. A field was planted in winter wheat, then in a spring crop— oats, barley, peas, or beans—then permitted to lie fallow for a year. (See map 8.1 for an illustration of the three-field system.) The older two-field system, based on the yearly alternation of winter wheat and fallow, continued to be used in Mediterranean lands, where spring crops were difficult to raise because rain was scarce in the spring and summer. The north, however, had abundant year-round rainfall.

The three-field system kept a larger portion (two-thirds) of the soil in crops each year. The fallow became pasture for village animals, and their manure returned the soil to fertility. With only one-third rather than one-half of the land lying fallow, the other two-thirds produced grain and other crops. Yields from the new crop rotation show the increased productivity: In the Mediterranean system, one bushel of planted grain yielded only two or three bushels at harvest, while in the new system the yields might be as high as seven bushels harvested.

A spring crop of legumes restored fertility to the soil, provided a more varied diet for the people, and lessened the risk of total failure, because two crops were planted in one year. A spring crop of oats was used for fodder and thus helped support a larger number of animals, which in turn provided manure for more abundant crops. Barley was turned into beer.

Peasant Life   A glimpse of the life of peasants comes from the estate books of the great abbey of Saint-Germain-des-Prés near Paris. The list of peasants shows that remnants of the old Roman *latifundia* system were still present, since some of the inhabitants were called slaves and others were free. Both the status listings and the names show that there had been considerable intermarriage among the original population of the estate and the newly settled Franks. Thus, Maurisius (a Roman name), a half-free man, was married to Ermegardis (a Germanic name). The peasants paid rent for their farms and had to provide labor for their lords, such as carting, plowing, harvesting, and hay making on the estate. True manorialism did not develop until the eleventh century (see chapter 8).

The settlement of the Germanic peoples as peasants brought its own revolution in the roles of men and women. Women, children, and slaves had done all the agriculture during the period before migration, but once settled, men became the farmers, as had been true in the ancient world. Handling the heavy plow and the large oxen teams was considered men's work. Women, in addition to caring for children, tended to domestic animals, produced cheese, brewed beer and mead (a fermented honey drink), and did spinning and weaving.

Trade and Manufacture

The movement of peoples and the wars of Justinian had a negative impact on towns and trade.

Trade and Commerce   The Mediterranean had been a great commercial artery for the exchange of Western goods, for the spices and fine cloths of the Levant, and for papyrus and grain from Egypt. Trade in Eastern luxury items never disappeared, because the Church and

FRENCH ILLUMINATIONS OF PEASANTS
The division of labor by sex was a prominent part of the peasant economy. Men did the heavy fieldwork, including beating the grain of the stalk with a flail. Women did spinning and weaving. The symbol for the peasant man was the flail and for the woman the spindle.
Giraudon/Art Resource, NY

wealthy individuals demanded such items as silk, dyes, perfumes, olive oil, wine, and papyrus. Jews and Syrians carried on the trade with the East. Slaves (the word *slave* derives from *Slav,* which were the people most often sold) were traded to the East to pay for the luxury goods. Archaeological evidence shows some trade with Africa, mostly gold in exchange for amber and salt. The trade that had characterized the western Mediterranean in Roman times had decreased significantly in the fifth century. The eastern Mediterranean continued to provide vital trade in luxury items until well into the seventh century.

A northern trade was gaining in importance. The Frisians were the most active traders, relying on the Rhine River to export cloth and luxury items into the hinterland of Europe. Through ports on the North Sea, the Frisians also traded with England, the coast of France, Denmark, and other Baltic countries. The cloth they traded, which was valued for its thick, waterproof quality, probably was the surplus production of estates and monasteries in northern Europe.

Towns and Production   Like trade, towns suffered from the political disruptions. Archaeology shows that the inhabited area of those Roman towns that continued to exist had shrunk to little more than ecclesiastical buildings, inns, and some residences. Towns ceased to serve as administrative centers except for Church business. Craft production was done at the village and estate level.

THE EXPANSION OF THE CHURCH

The Church in the early Middle Ages was both a dynamic leader, guiding the West in the period of the collapse of Roman authority, and the preserver of the classical educational traditions of literacy, rhetoric, and logic. The development of **monasticism** provided a new opportunity for pious men and women to live a life of prayer and service in a world in which much was changing. Within the walls of monasteries and nunneries as well as in bishops' residences, classical learning was preserved, copied, and taught. Missionaries went to frontier areas and converted to Christianity people who had never been exposed to the Roman civilization. By the beginning of the seventh century, all of Christian Western Europe had abandoned Arianism and adopted Roman Christianity. The papacy developed as the religious and often the political leader in the West.

Origins of the Papacy

The papacy—*pope* derives from *pappas,* a Greek word for *father*—had its origins in the bishopric of Rome. The pope's authority gradually grew in importance and power so that he became the head of the Roman Catholic Church.

Doctrine of Petrine Succession   According to the traditional Catholic (and medieval) view, Jesus himself endowed the apostle Peter with supreme responsibility for his church: "And I say unto thee, thou art Peter and upon this rock I will build my church. . . . I will entrust to you the keys of the kingdom of heaven. Whatever you bind on earth shall be bound in heaven. Whatever you loose on earth shall be loosed in Heaven" (Matt. 16:18–19). In the Aramaic language that Jesus spoke, as well as in Greek and Latin, *Peter* and *rock* are the same word. This play on words has been called the most momentous pun in history. Medieval tradition further held that Peter became the first bishop of Rome and was martyred there about the year 60. Historical evidence does not conclusively establish Peter's presence in Rome.

Growth of Papal Primacy   Several factors led to the predominance of the Bishop of Rome and the subsequent growth of papal power. Rome was the original imperial capital and the center of Latin culture. As the authority of the emperors waned and disappeared in the West, people still looked to Rome for leadership, and increasingly its bishop provided it. The emperors, eager to use the Church as an adjunct to their own imperial administration, favored the concentration of religious authority in the West in the Bishop of Rome's hands. During the invasions, the papacy represented the orthodox Christian practice as opposed to the Arian heresy of the Germanic invaders and so became the focal point of orthodox Christians in the West.

Great popes in the fourth and fifth centuries contributed to papal primacy. Pope Leo I (r. 440–461) sent a delegation to Attila the Hun to persuade him not to attack Rome. In numerous letters and sermons, Leo identified the living pope as the successor of Peter and enjoyed the same powers that Peter had as the chosen disciple. Not all bishops recognized the papal claims to authority, but the popes' prestige in the Western world was unrivaled. The patriarch of Constantinople, primate of the Eastern Christians, did not recognize the superior authority of the papacy.

Gregory the Great   The popes increasingly assumed responsibility for the security of Italy and the defense of the Church. The pope who best exemplifies the problems and accomplishments of the early medieval papacy is Gregory I (r. 590–604).

When Gregory became pope, the Lombards were plundering the Roman countryside and threatening Rome with destruction and starvation. Under these difficult conditions, Gregory kept food coming to Rome, ransomed captives, aided widows and orphans, and organized the defense of the city. Gregory finally negotiated a truce with the Lombards in 598, although they continued to pose a threat to the security of Rome for more than a century.

Gregory was no less solicitous for the welfare of the entire Church. During his pontificate, Gregory gave

Pope Gregory the Great was one of the key figures in the transition from the ancient world to the Middle Ages. He is regarded—along with Jerome, Ambrose, and Augustine—as one (and the last) of the four fathers of the Latin Church. His efforts to defend Rome against the Lombards and to advance missionary work gave added prestige to the papal see.
Art Resource, NY

new momentum to missionary efforts. The Spanish Visigoths were converted from Arian to Roman Christianity. By establishing a tradition of active involvement in the affairs of the world, to which most of his medieval successors would faithfully adhere, Gregory widened enormously the influence of the Roman see.

Like many of the early church leaders, Gregory came from a Roman patrician background and had been educated to be an imperial administrator. Using the experience of his career in the civil administration, he organized the estates belonging to the papacy around Rome to provide a more solid financial base for the papacy.

Monasticism

Monks (from the Greek *monos*, "single" or solitary") were even more effective than the papacy in shaping medieval civilization. Men and women who wanted to devote themselves to prayer, retain their virginity, and live abstemiously withdrew from daily life to live in isolated communities. The ascetic ideal of fleeing the world in order to devote oneself to worship is common to many religions.

People who lived alone were called hermits. The most renowned of these was St. Anthony, who lived a life of rigid asceticism in the desert of Egypt for more than twenty years (from ca. 285). Some of the early Syrian hermits, such as Simon Stylites, lived on a pillar for years, eating only millet seeds. The Church father Jerome criticized hermitic excesses, commenting that if beards made a man holy, all goats were holy.

The more common practice for people who wished to follow an ascetic life was to live and work together in cenobitic ("living in common") monasticism. Even Anthony found that the numbers of people who flocked to his isolated retreat had to be organized and given rules for guidance. Egypt was the home of the first true monasteries and nunneries, with the days divided by work and prayer. St. Basil, the father of Greek monasticism, spent a year in Egypt before establishing a monastery (ca. 360) in Greece. The Basilian order, which is still in existence today, favored living in small clusters of residences, closer to a hermit's life. It became the predominant order in the Eastern Empire.

Benedict and the Benedictine Rule

The man who designed the most common Western form of monasticism—St. Benedict, a Roman patrician—founded a community at Monte Cassino in ca. 520 and drew up a rule, or manual of conduct, for its members. Benedictines lived in contained communities, sharing meals, sleeping quarters, and common prayers. The Benedictine rule dealt with all the main problems of monastic life, including food (the rule provided for an allotment of wine each day) and clothing, discipline, prayer, the work of monks, and sleeping arrangements. The rule was a flexible one, applicable to many individual communities. The abbot was to be elected for life, with full authority over the community, but he was to consult the elder and even the younger monks. One of the most famous regulations required some manual labor, lending to it a dignity that both the Greeks and Romans had denied. "Idleness," said the regulation, "is the enemy of the soul." The core vows for joining the Benedictine order were poverty, chastity, and obedience (see "The Rule of St. Benedict on the Clothing of Monks," p. 175).

Early Nunneries

From the earliest days of monasticism, women joined communities of nuns. St. Jerome

ST. BENEDICT PRESENTING HIS RULE
This fourteenth-century image depicts St. Benedict presenting his rule to a group of nuns. His connection with female spirituality went back to his own lifetime, because his sister, Scholastica, was also devout and lived at a convent near Benedict's at Monte Cassino.
Biblioteca Seminario Vescovile, Florence. © P. Tosi/Index

designed a rule for the women in his family and their friends. St. Basil's mother and sister were already living in a nunnery when he founded his monastic order. St. Scholastica, Benedict's sister, lived in a nunnery near Monte Cassino. In Anglo-Saxon England abbesses, such as Hilda of Whitby (657–680), headed double monasteries that included houses for both monks and nuns. Abbess Hilda encouraged learning at Whitby; five of its monks went on to become bishops.

Relationship of Monasteries to Lay Society

Monks were the most successful agriculturists of the age, first as farmers in their own right and then, gradually, as managers of ever larger estates. They set an example of good farming practices and estate management from which laypeople could benefit.

Monasteries and nunneries came to play a major role in early medieval society and government. Powerful families established religious communities on their lands. The abbots and abbesses were often closely related to these prominent laypersons, administering the monastery's lands and resources in the interest of their lay relatives.

Kings, too, relied heavily on monastic farms to supply food for their administrations and armies and often appropriated part of the monks' income to finance their own needs. Able abbots served as advisors and administrators for the kings.

Education and Preservation of Learning

Culturally, monks and nuns were almost the only people who

THE RULE OF ST. BENEDICT ON THE CLOTHING OF MONKS

The rule of St. Benedict (ca. 480–ca. 550) tried to anticipate all the needs of monks and all the problems that might arise in monastic communities in terms of regulation of work, prayers, relations among the monks, visitors to the monastery, travel, and monastic vows. This humane rule became the basis of monastic rules in Western Europe.

"The clothing distributed to the brothers should vary according to local conditions and climate, because more is needed in the cold regions and less in warmer. This is left to the abbot's discretion. We believe that for each monk a cowl and tunic will suffice in temperate regions; in winter a woolen cowl is necessary, in summer a thinner or worn one; also a scapular for work, and footwear—both sandals and shoes.

"Monks must not complain about the color or coarseness of all these articles, but use what is available in the vicinity at a reasonable cost. However, the abbot ought to be concerned about the measurements of these garments that they not be too short but fitted to the wearers.

"Whenever new clothing is received, the old should be returned at once and stored in a wardrobe for the poor. To provide for laundering and night wear, every monk will need two cowls and two tunics, but anything more must be taken away as superfluous. When new articles are received, the worn ones—sandals or anything old—must be returned.

"Brothers going on a journey should get underclothing from the wardrobe. On their return they are to wash it and give it back. Their cowls and tunics, too, ought to be somewhat better than those they ordinarily wear. Let them get these from the wardrobe before departing, and on returning put them back.

"For bedding the monks will need a mat, a woolen blanket and a light covering as well as a pillow.

"The beds are to be inspected frequently by the abbot, lest private possessions are found there. A monk discovered with anything not given him by the abbot must be subjected to very severe punishment. In order that this vice of private ownership may be completely uprooted, the abbot is to provide all things necessary: that is, cowl, tunic, sandals, shoes, belt, knife, stylus, needle, handkerchief and writing tablets. In this way every excuse of lacking some necessity will be taken away."

From Timothy Fry (ed.), *The Rule of St. Benedict in Latin and English with Notes*, Liturgical Press, 1980, pp. 261–265.

---

were literate and learned. The Benedictine rule assumed that the monk could read. Although not expressly obliged to do so, monasteries maintained both libraries and schools for the training of young monks and nuns and, sometimes, lay children.

Monasteries organized *scriptoria*, or writing rooms, in which manuscripts that were needed for liturgy or education were copied. The great bulk of the surviving Latin literary works of both pagan and Christian antiquity were preserved in copies made in monasteries and nunneries. Sometimes monks decorated, or illuminated, the manuscript pages; manuscript illuminations are among the loveliest art forms that have come from the age. Monastic scribes wrote nearly all the administrative records, lay and ecclesiastical, that have survived from the early Middle Ages.

The Appeal of the Ascetic Life Part of the monks' importance to society came from their communal organization, which enabled them to cope effectively with the problems of a turbulent age. Monasteries and nunneries provided a haven for people like Gregory the Great, St. Benedict, and St. Scholastica, to compensate for the disappearance of Roman intellectual life. At the same time, they extended charity to the poor and to pilgrims who stopped at their doors. The community provided a valued sense of continuity over generations.

Missionaries and Popular Religion

One of the major achievements of the Church was to spread Christianity, including Roman culture, to parts of Europe that had never experienced extensive contacts with Rome. The missionary initiative was often made individually. St. Patrick was a Briton who was captured and became a slave in Ireland. Escaping from his captors, he went to Gaul, where he was ordained a bishop. He returned to Ireland in 430 and converted the Irish, establishing monasteries there.

The Irish monks converted northern Anglo-Saxon England, establishing monasteries in northern England, including Lindisfarne and Whitby. These monasteries and nunneries became great centers of learning and religious crafts. They preserved many texts that were destroyed on the continent during the invasions. The illuminated manuscripts of these Celtic/Anglo-Saxon monasteries combined elements of Christianity with the indigenous designs of dragons, snakes, animals, and

This Spanish manuscript illumination of daily life in the monastery shows that the writing of manuscripts was one of the monks' principal occupations. In addition, one of the monks is ringing the bells that marked the different services of the day and that also served to remind the surrounding countryside of the activities of the monastery.
The Pierpont Morgan Library/Art Resource, NY

PHILOSOPHY CONSOLING BOETHIUS, EARLY ELEVENTH CENTURY
In his *Consolation of Philosophy*, Boethius described the embodiment of philosophy as a mature woman who had grown as tall as the heavens and carried a scepter and books. This image, from an eleventh-century manuscript, depicts philosophy as equal in height to the building whose solid façade and row of small windows may be the prison in which Boethius wrote his famous work.
Bibliothèque Nationale de France, Paris

plants, as can be seen in the *Book of Kells* and the *Lindisfarne Gospel*.

Benedictines as Missionaries

Gregory the Great understood the potential of the Benedictines as missionaries. According to legend, he saw some fair-haired Anglo-Saxon children in the slave market and asked about their origins. Being told that they were Angles, he commented that they looked like angels. Further questions revealed that the Angles still worshiped trees and stones. Gregory sent a bishop, Augustine, with other priests to England in 597. Augustine found that the Kentish king's wife, Bertha, the great-granddaughter of Clovis and Clotilde, had been prevailing on the king to convert, and he eventually did convert to Roman Christianity.

The conversion of the Frisians and other groups to the east of the Rhine was more challenging. Anglo-Saxon Benedictines moved into this rough land with the blessings of the pope. They established churches where the pagans had formerly worshiped trees, sometimes even cutting down the sacred trees to build the church.

Elements of the former religion remained a part of Christianity, so that many of the days that had been pagan holidays were coordinated with saints' feasts. Conversion was gradual, and the new converts only partially understood the religion.

Council of Whitby

As the Roman variety of Christianity, brought by Augustine of Canterbury, spread in England, it came into conflict with the Irish and Anglo-Saxon versions. The two versions had differences in the date for the celebration of Easter and in some points about monasticism. Finally, at the Council of Whitby in 664, the king of Northumbria questioned both sides about their belief in St. Peter. When both agreed on Peter's primacy, he concluded that his people should observe Roman practices.

The Role of Miracles   One of the convincing tools of conversion was miracles and stories of miracles. Stories of how saints cured sick people who worshiped at their tombs or how saints punished the ungodly when they stole sacred objects from churches conveyed a persuasive message about the power of the Christian God and his faithful followers. The miracle stories are historians' best source of popular culture during the Early Middle Ages, because they record instances in daily life that were changed as a result of divine intervention.

The Church and Classical Learning

Christian writers had an ambiguous attitude toward classical texts: Many prominent Christian writers condemned classical literature as foolishness and an incitement to sin, and yet the classical authors provided both the language for study and philosophical texts that demanded reconciliation with Christian teachings. Because the Church had not yet established its own schools, its scholars studied in secular schools, learning the techniques of philosophical argument and rhetorical expression that were traditional among pagan scholars.

Preservation of Classical Texts   An important part of Christian scholarship was devoted to the preparation of textbooks that would preserve a modicum of ancient learning and the ability to read the ancient authors. One of the most influential of these textbooks was *Introductions to Divine and Human Readings* by Cassiodorus, a sixth-century monk and official in Theodoric's government. In it he listed the religious and secular books that he thought a monk should copy and read. This book is about as appealing to modern readers as a library catalog, but at the time it was carefully studied and used to determine the holdings of medieval libraries.

Another sixth-century Christian scholar in Theodoric's service, Boethius, translated portions of Aristotle's treatises on logic from Greek into Latin. His translations were the main source of early medieval writers' limited but significant familiarity with Aristotelian logic until the thirteenth century. Boethius wrote on many other subjects as well and is most famed now for his *Consolation of Philosophy*, a meditation on death that does not mention the Christian religion. Boethius wrote the *Consolation* while imprisoned by Theodoric at the end of his reign. The book helped preserve the dignity of learning by showing the role that reason and philosophy play in solving human problems.

CHI-RHO, *BOOK OF KELLS*
The Greek letters *chi* and *rho*, the first two letters of Christ's name, were frequently used as symbols of Christianity by early believers. This page, from the late eighth-century Irish manuscript *The Book of Kells*, is an example of the complex interlacing that was characteristic of Anglo-Saxon manuscript illumination in this period.
The Board of Trinity College Dublin

In Spain classical learning was preserved by Isidore, bishop of Seville, in his *Etymologies*, which were a vast encyclopedia of ancient learning, covering in twenty books subjects from theology to furniture and providing a rich source of classical lore and learning for medieval writers.

Christian Writings   Scholars also helped through original works to shape the character and interest of the age, especially by writing *exegeses*, or comments and interpretation, on the Bible. In this field the most important writer after St. Augustine was Pope Gregory. His commentary on the Book of Job used allegory to explain the biblical text and set the style for biblical exegesis in the medieval world. Pope Gregory also taught readers, notably through his *Dialogues*, about the lives of the saints and the miracles that God wrought through them. Gregory had an ability to simplify works of theology and wrote the *Pastoral Care* as instruction for bishops.

The study of history also evoked great interest among scholars. One of the most influential accounts was the *History of the Franks* by Gregory, bishop of Tours. Like many of the early medieval historians, Gregory began with creation; he then recounted the history of the human race up to 591.

Scholarship on the continent sank to its lowest level in the seventh and early eighth centuries, but it flourished in Ireland in the seventh and in England in the early eighth century. Scholars there enjoyed the relative shelter of an insular home. They had the zeal of new converts and a strong monastic system that supported the schools. Since they did not speak a language derived from Latin, they could learn a correct Latin in schools without being confused by related vernacular forms. Thus, their Latin was closer to classical Latin than that used on the continent.

The finest English scholar was Bede the Venerable (ca. 673–735), whose *Ecclesiastical History of the English People*, an account of the conversion of the English and the growth of their Church, established his fame even until today. His high sense of scholarship is evident in his excellent Latin and in the careful way he cites his sources: oral interviews with knowledgeable eyewitnesses, documents from local archives, and accounts written at his request. His book is the product of a medieval writer, not a modern one; Bede recounted miracles, and the principal theme of his history is the story of salvation. But his belief that history was the unfolding of God's plan did not lead him to distort the material in his sources. He is a man who in any age would be recognized as a scholar.

Summary

By the close of the seventh century, Europe was much changed from the days of the Roman Empire. The new Visigothic kingdom controlled the territory that would become modern Spain; the Merovingians ruled over the former Roman province of Gaul, which had roughly the borders of modern France. Anglo-Saxon England under the Northumbrian hegemony included all of modern England. In Italy the pope had proved a powerful force not only in religion but also in politics. The people who moved into the old Roman Empire came as settlers. While their customs of governing were different from those of the Roman population, they soon blended their own practices with those of the Romans. Christianity proved one of the most powerful tools of assimilation because it taught both the Christian and Roman culture. Missionaries, drawn from the Benedictine monastic order, went beyond the borders of the old Empire and converted those who had no exposure to the Roman world. The monastic orders provided a refuge for those who wanted to live a life of prayer and those who wanted to read classical philosophy and Christian theological texts. The preservation of texts was largely the work of monasteries. The medieval economy was based on agriculture, and the period of the sixth and seventh centuries saw the development of new technologies: stirrups for the better use of horses for fighting, the horse collar that allowed horses to replace oxen, the heavy-wheeled plow for cultivating the fields of northern Europe, and a crop rotation system that permitted two-thirds of the land to be cultivated each year. With increased agricultural production, Europe was on the verge of greater wealth, which would be concentrated in the north rather than on the Mediterranean. In Europe and the eastern Mediterranean major political changes were again on the horizon as the Franks continued to consolidate their power, the Byzantine Empire faced renewed invasions, and Islam inspired the Arabs to conquer the old Persian Empire and much of the Byzantine Empire.

QUESTIONS FOR FURTHER THOUGHT

1. What were the problems that the Germanic folk encountered in trying to assimilate with the Romans? What problems did the Romans have in living side by side with the tribesmen?

2. Historians have long argued that three elements went into the making of what we call "medieval civilization"—Roman government and culture, Germanic government and social customs, and

Christianity. What elements did each of these contribute to the emerging medieval culture in the West?

3. What was the influence of the technological developments in the sixth and seventh centuries on warfare and on agriculture?

RECOMMENDED READING

Sources

Colgrave, B. (ed.). *The Life of Bishop Wilfrid . . . , Two Lives of Saint Cuthbert . . . , Felix's Life of Saint Guthlac, and The Earliest Life of Gregory the Great.* 1985. The hagiographies of the missionary saints.

Gregory of Tours. *History of the Franks.* Ernest Brehaut, (tr.). 1916.

*Mattingly, H. (tr.). *Tacitus on Britain and Germany: A Translation of the "Agricola" and the "Germania."* 1967. A description of the life and culture of Germanic tribes, including his experience living in Roman Britain.

*Procopius. *Secret History.* Richard Atwater (tr.). 1964. A scandal-filled history of Justinian's reign.

Studies

*Brown, Peter. *The Cult of the Saints: Its Rise and Function in Latin Christianity.* 1980. Locates the cult of the saints not in popular religion but in the power structures of late ancient society.

*Burns, Thomas S. *A History of the Ostrogoths.* 1984. Based on archaeological as well as literary evidence.

Carver, Marvin. *Sutton Hoo: Burial Grounds of Kings.* 1998.

*Geary, Patrick. *Before France and Germany: The Creation and Transformation of the Merovingian World.* 1988. A comprehensive summary of recent research, stressing the importance of the Roman heritage for the growth of Frankish institutions.

*————. *The Myth of Nations: The Medieval Origins of Europe.* 2001.

Heather, Peter. *The Goths and Romans.* 1996.

*Herwig, Wolfram. *History of the Goths.* Thomas J. Dunlap (tr.). 1988. Stresses the instability of Gothic tribal formations.

Hodges, Richard, and David Whitehouse. *Mohammad and Charlemagne: The Origins of Europe.* 1983. A reevaluation of the Pirenne thesis using archaeological evidence. The authors explore the shift of trade from the Mediterranean to northern Europe.

*Lawrence, C. H. *Medieval Monasticism: Forms of Religious Life in Western Europe in the Middle Ages.* 2d ed. 1989. On the rule of Benedict, the rise of Cluny, and other topics.

*Lynch, Joseph. *The Medieval Church: A Brief History.* 1992. A very readable introduction to the history of the Church.

*Moorhead, John. *Justinian.* 1994. A lively discussion of the reign of Justinian in the context of his times.

*Wallace-Hadrill, J. M. *The Barbarian West.* 1962. Brief and readable essays.

Wemple, Suzanne Fonay. *Women in Frankish Society: Marriage and the Cloister, 500 to 800.* 1981. An important study of a neglected topic.

*Available in paperback.

DOME OF THE ROCK, JERUSALEM
This mosque is sometimes called the Mosque of Omar. It was built between 685 and 691 and is the oldest extant Islamic monument. The rock over which it is built is sacred to both Muslims and Jews. Muslims believe that Muhammad ascended to heaven on this spot. To Jews it is the side of Solomon's temple. Medieval Christians believed that it was actually Solomon's temple.
© Richard T. Nowitz/Corbis

Chapter Seven

THE EMPIRES OF THE EARLY MIDDLE AGES (800–1000): CREATION AND EROSION

ISLAM • THE BYZANTINE EMPIRE (610–1071) •
THE CAROLINGIAN, OR FRANKISH, EMPIRE • THE VIKINGS, KIEV, AND ENGLAND

Europe's fate was inextricably bound with that of the old Roman world in the period of the seventh through the eleventh century. New conquests, the spread of Christianity to previously non-Christian peoples, and the rise of a new religion, Islam (*Islam* means "submission"), had major impacts on the West. Frankish kings, like the Byzantine emperors, spread their power through missionary activity to tribes living in northern Europe and Slavic areas. While Muhammad, the founding prophet of Islam, enjoined his followers, the Muslims (believers in Islam) to do battle for their faith, he did not preach a missionary zeal. His successors conquered in rapid succession the Persian Empire and much of the Byzantine Empire to Constantinople. The Arabs became intellectual intermediaries, combining Classical Greek science and mathematics with that of India and spreading it to the West.

The old Roman world was now divided into three vast empires: Charlemagne's Frankish Empire was largely located in northwest Europe and the northern Mediterranean. The Byzantine Empire included parts of Turkey and the areas to the north and west of Constantinople. The Arabic Caliphate extended from Persia all along the southern Mediterranean and included the Iberian Peninsula. In addition, there were the smaller political units of Anglo-Saxon England and the Kievan state. The empires and kingdoms provide rich opportunities for contrasting military organization, government and religious structures, the position of women, and the inherent weakness of these states.

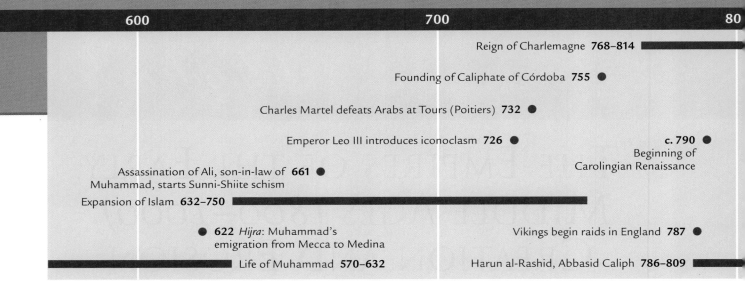

Reign of Charlemagne **768–814**

Founding of Caliphate of Córdoba **755** ●

Charles Martel defeats Arabs at Tours (Poitiers) **732** ●

Emperor Leo III introduces iconoclasm **726** ●

c. 790 ●
Beginning of
Carolingian Renaissance

Assassination of Ali, son-in-law of **661** ●
Muhammad, starts Sunni-Shiite schism

Expansion of Islam **632–750**

622 *Hijra*: Muhammad's
emigration from Mecca to Medina

Vikings begin raids in England **787** ●

Life of Muhammad **570–632**

Harun al-Rashid, Abbasid Caliph **786–809**

ISLAM

Sometime about 610 in the Arabian town of Mecca, a merchant's son named Muhammad began to preach to the people, summoning them to repentance and reform. Gradually, he brought his teachings together to form a new system of religious belief that he called **Islam.** The explosive impact of his preaching was one of the most extraordinary events of world history. Within a century after Muhammad's death his followers had conquered and partially converted territories larger than the old Roman Empire. Today Islam remains the faith of perhaps 800 million people, more than an eighth of the world's population.

The Arabs

The Arabian peninsula, the homeland of the Arabs, profoundly influenced their culture and history. Its vast interior and northern regions have steppes, wastelands, and some of the hottest and driest deserts of the world. The Arabs, however, adapted to this harsh environment. They supported themselves by raising sheep and camels that provided nearly all their necessities: meat, milk, wool, skins for clothes and tents, and fuel from dried camel dung. The Arabs were extremely proud of their family, race, language, skill, and way of life. The harsh environment and their fierce pride made them spirited, tenacious, and formidable warriors.

The Arabian peninsula was in a state of intense political and social ferment on the eve of Muhammad's appearance. The stronger political powers—the Persians, Byzantines, and Abyssinians across the Red Sea—tried repeatedly to subdue the Arabs but could not dominate them in their desert home. Religious ferment was no less explosive. Muhammad was the religious leader who fused all these contending pagan,

Christian, and Jewish ideas into a single, commanding, and authentically Arabian religion.

Muhammad

Historians have little certain information about the founder of Islam. Muhammad was born in Mecca about 570 or 571. His father died before his birth, and his mother died when he was 6. Raised by his uncle, Muhammad worked as a camel driver in caravans. He may have been illiterate and may have had no direct knowledge of the Jewish and Christian scriptures, but he acquired a wide, if sometimes inaccurate, knowledge of the history and teaching of those two religions. At about the age of twenty-five Muhammad married the widow of a rich merchant and they had four daughters. Freed from economic concerns, he gave himself to religious meditations in the desert outside Mecca.

Preaching   In 610 and throughout his life, Muhammad heard the voice of the angel Gabriel telling him to recite the words that God, or Allah, revealed to him. Muhammad began to preach publicly, but only his wife and a small group of relatives initially accepted his teachings. The people of Mecca feared him because his strictures against paganism seemed to threaten the position of Mecca as a center of pilgrimages. Rejected in his native city, Muhammad accepted an invitation to expound his ideas in Medina, about 270 miles to the north.

Hijra   Muhammad's emigration from Mecca to Medina is called the **hijra** and occurred in 622, which later became year 1 of the Islamic calendar. The hijra was a turning point in Muhammad's career for two reasons: He became the political leader and governor of an important town, which gave him a base for the military expansion of the Islamic community; and his responsi-

- **843** Treaty of Verdun divides Carolingian Empire
- **862** Cyril and Methodius become missionaries to Slavs

Conversion to Christianity of Vladimir **988** ●

Schism between Eastern and Western Churches **1054** ●

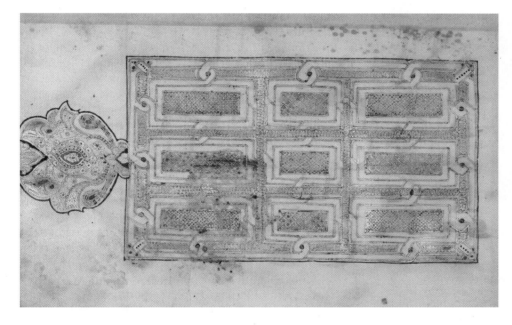

LEAF FROM A QUR'AN. EGYPT, NINTH OR TENTH CENTURY
The Koran, the sacred book of Islam, in a ninth- or tenth-century edition. From the ninth century the design of sacred books followed specific forms that remained standard in Islamic art. Color and gilding are added not only as ornament but also to separate verses; the leafy projection to the left signals the beginning of a new chapter.
Courtesy of the Freer Gallery of Art, Smithsonian Institution, Washington, D.C.

bilities as head of an independent town affected the character of his religious message. More and more, his message was concerned with public law, administration, and the practical problems of government.

Muhammad was more successful in making converts at Medina than he was at Mecca. He told his followers that God ordered them to convert or conquer their neighbors. With the support of his followers, Muhammad marched against the Meccans, defeating them in battle in 624 and taking Mecca in 630. He destroyed all the pagan shrines, keeping only the Kaaba (Arabic for "square building"), which Muslim tradition says that the prophet Abraham built as a temple. By his death in 632, Muhammad had given his religion a firm foundation.

The Religion of Islam

Muhammad passed on to his followers the words or prophecies of **Allah** (from *al ilah*, meaning "the God").

The Koran   The collection of prophecies is known as the **Koran** (or Qur'an). In Islamic theology, Allah is its true author. The Koran was written down in its present version in 651 and 652. It imparts to the sympathetic reader a powerful mood, one of uncompromising monotheism, of repeated and impassioned emphasis upon the unity, power, and presence of Allah. The mood is sustained by constant reiterations of set formulas praising Allah, his power, knowledge, mercy, justice, and concern for his people.

PILGRIMAGE GUIDE
This sixteenth-century illustration of a pilgrimage guide written around 900 shows the Kaaba at Mecca. The Kaaba, said to have been built by the Prophet Abraham, is the black rectangular building surrounded by domed arcades.
Courtesy of The Arthur M. Sackler Museum, Harvard University Art Museums, The Edwin Binney, 3rd Collection of Turkish Art at the Harvard University Art Museums. © President and Fellows of Harvard College, Harvard University

The chief obligation that Muhammad imposed on his followers was submission (the literal meaning of *Islam*) to the will of Allah. Those who submit are **Muslims.** (*Muhammadan,* which suggests that Muhammad claimed divinity, is an inappropriate usage.) Muhammad was little concerned with the subtleties of theology; he was interested in defining for Muslims the ethical and legal requirements for an upright life. Unlike Christianity, Islam retained this practical emphasis; jurisprudence, even more than speculative theology, remained the great intellectual interest of Muslim scholarship. Also in contrast to Christianity, Islam did not recognize a separate clergy, for there was no need for specialized intermediaries between Allah and his people. Allah was the direct ruler of the faithful on earth; he legislated for them in the Koran, which was administered through Muhammad, the Prophet, and his successors, the **caliphs.** Religion and state were not separate entities, at least in theory. There was only the single, sacred community of Allah.

Law and Government Because Islam recognized no distinction between religion and government, the caliph was the supreme religious and civil head of the Muslim world. He was not free, however, to change the laws at will, since Allah had already provided all the laws his people needed. The caliph's role was primarily to be a military chief and a judge. Administration at the local level was done by a judge, whose task was to see that the faithful lived according to the law of the Koran.

Relationship to Other Religions The message of Islam exerted a powerful appeal to the Arabs. Compared with Christianity and Judaism, Islam was a starkly simple belief, easily explained and easily grasped. It was an effective fusion of religious ideas from Arabic paganism, Christianity, Judaism, and perhaps Zoroastrianism. Judaism influenced the legal code regulating diet and behavior. Judaism and Christianity provided the notion of prophecy, for Muhammad considered himself the last of a line of prophets that began with Abraham and included Jesus. More than that, the Bible tells that Abraham fathered Ishmael by Hagar, an Egyptian slave girl (Gen. 16–17), and Muslims believe that Ishmael was their ancestor and lies buried with Hagar in the Kaaba at Mecca. Christianity contributed the concepts of Last Judgment, personal salvation, heaven and hell, charity to the poor and weak, and a universal religion. Christianity, or perhaps Zoroastrianism, suggested the figures of Satan and evil demons. Paganism contributed the veneration of the Kaaba and the requirement of pilgrimage to the sacred city. The Arabs saw themselves as replacing the Jews as God's chosen people, with a sacred right to his holy places, including Jerusalem (see "The Koran on Christians and Jews," p. 185).

Expansion of Islam

Conquests Several factors aided the extraordinary expansion of Islam in the first century of its existence. Islam fused the once contending Arab clans and tribes into a unified and dedicated force. The Arabs, long familiar with camels, were masters of desert warfare. Their enemies, relying on horses, could not challenge them on desert terrain. The Arabs moved armies and

THE KORAN ON CHRISTIANS AND JEWS

In the Koran, Muhammad proclaims that the faith of Islam also welcomes "the people of the Book"—that is, Christians and Jews who have the Bible as their sacred book—and that Islam is the fulfillment of these earlier faiths.

"Believers, Jews, Christians, and Sabaeans [of the kingdom of Saba in southwest Arabia]—whoever believes in Allah and the Last Day and does what is right—shall be rewarded by their Lord; they have nothing to fear or regret. To Moses We [that is, Allah] gave the Scriptures and after him We sent other apostles. We gave Jesus the son of Mary veritable signs and strengthened him with the Holy Spirit. And now that a Book [the Koran] confirming their Scriptures has been revealed to them by Allah, they deny it, although they know it to be the truth and have long prayed for help against the unbelievers.

"May Allah's curse be upon the infidels! Evil is that for which they have bartered away their souls. To deny Allah's own revelation, grudging that He should reveal His bounty to whom He chooses from His servants! They have incurred Allah's most inexorable wrath. An ignominious punishment awaits the unbelievers. The unbelievers among the People of the Book, and the pagans, resent that any blessings should have been sent down to you from your Lord. But Allah chooses whom He will for His mercy. His grace is infinite.

"Abraham enjoined the faith on his children, and so did Jacob, saying: 'My children, Allah has chosen for you the true faith. Do not depart this life except as men who have submitted to Him.' Say: 'We believe in Allah and that which is revealed to us; we believe in what was revealed to Abraham, Ishmael, Isaac, Jacob, and the tribes; to Moses and Jesus and the other prophets. We make no distinction between any of them, and to Allah we have surrendered ourselves. Your God is one God. There is no God but Him.'"

From N. J. Dawood (tr.), *The Koran*, Penguin Books, 1968, condensed.

supplies with facility across vast arid stretches, struck the enemy at places and times of their own choosing, and retreated to the safety of the desert when the odds turned against them. Moreover, the Arabs' immediate neighbors, the Byzantines and Persians, were mutually exhausted by their recurrent wars. Both the Byzantine and Persian empires included large Semitic populations that were linguistically and culturally related to the Arabs and could, therefore, comprehend the message of Islam.

The Arabs were able to make and hold their conquests through a unique combination of fanaticism and toleration. Warriors were inspired by the Prophet's promise of vast rewards to those who died in the Holy War against the nonbelievers and by the prospect of considerable booty if victorious. The Prophet, however, also enjoined a policy of partial toleration toward Christians and Jews, who were both known as the "people of the Book" (the Bible). Thus, Christians and Jews continued to live under their own laws, but they paid a special tax for the privilege. Many Persian, Greek, and Semitic people converted voluntarily because they found the religion close to their own beliefs. Finally, because the Arabs did not have the numbers and the skills to govern all the territories they conquered, they opened the ranks of government to men from the newly conquered peoples. This move added stability to Arabic rule.

Islam expanded rapidly in the period following Muhammad's death in 632 and coinciding with the rule of the first four caliphs, as Muhammad's successors were called. Arabian forces seized the Byzantine provinces of Palestine and Syria, overran Persia, and conquered Egypt by the 640s. By 661 the Arabian Empire was firmly established as a world power.

Umayyads Islamic conquests continued under the caliphs of the Umayyad family, who were the first line of hereditary rulers of the Arab Empire. The Umayyads moved the capital from Mecca to Damascus. Under their rule the Muslims conquered North Africa and overran the kingdom of the Visigoths in Spain. After crossing the Pyrenees into the kingdom of the Franks, Muslim raiders were finally defeated by Charles Martel at Tours in 732. This battle, 100 years after Muhammad's death, marked the extent of the Arabs' western advance and stabilized the frontier of Islam for the next several centuries (see map 7.1).

Sunni-Shiite Schism As the territory under Islamic control grew to enormous size, internal dissensions shattered Islamic unity. Relations among the various peoples who had accepted Islam became fractious, and religious divisions appeared. Islam had been an open and fluid religion at the death of Muhammad, but scholars and teachers gradually elaborated a theology

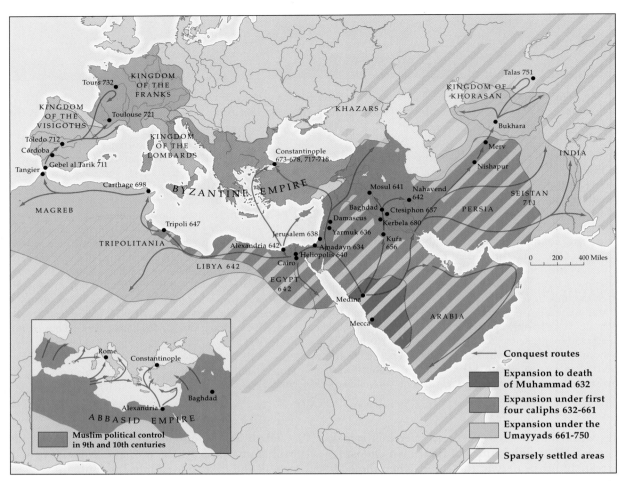

MAP 7.1 EXPANSION OF ISLAM
Consider the vast extent of the Arab expansion from the Arabian peninsula. The Muslims conquered Persian, Byzantine, and Germanic kingdoms. The whole area became Arabic speaking. What cities mark the defeat and turning back of Muslims? How rapidly did the Muslims expand?
◆ For an online version, go to www.mhhe.com/chambers9 > chapter 7 > book maps

that a majority of the believers accepted as orthodox. The scholars based the new orthodoxy not only on the Koran but also on the *Sunnas,* or traditions, which were writings that purported to describe how the first companions of Muhammad or how Muhammad himself dealt with various problems. Some Muslims, however, rejected the new orthodoxy of the *Sunnites,* as they came to be called. Those who opposed the Sunnites were called the *Shiites* ("party" or "faction" of Ali).

This earliest schism was more a political than a religious one. The Shiites maintained that only the descendants of Muhammad's son-in-law, Ali (r. 655–661), who was the fourth caliph, could lawfully rule the Islamic community; they rejected the Umayyads (and later the Abbasids) as usurpers. Shiism soon became a cloak for all sorts of antagonisms, protests, and revolts. It struck deep roots among the mixed populations, reflecting the dissatisfactions of non-Arabs with the Arab

preponderance and channeling the antagonism between the poorer classes and their masters.

The growing social and religious dissensions finally destroyed the Umayyad caliphate. A descendant of Abbas, the uncle of Muhammad, revolted against the Umayyads, captured Damascus, and ruthlessly massacred the caliph's family in 750. This victor founded the Abbasid Dynasty. Only one member of the Umayyads, Abdurrahman, escaped. He fled to Spain, where he set up an independent caliphate at Córdoba in 755. Other independent regimes soon arose: Morocco in 788, Tunisia in 800, eastern Persia in 820, and Egypt in 868. All became virtually independent under their local dynasties. The new Abbasid caliph moved the capital from Damascus to a new city, Baghdad. The Abbasid Dynasty, which endured until 1258, marked a high point in Islamic culture, but the political community of Islam was never again to be united.

Islamic Economy and Society

Despite disunity, medieval Islamic civilization reached its peak of prosperity, refinement, and learning in the ninth and tenth centuries. Arabic, the language of the Koran, served to unify literature, learning, and commerce across the Islamic lands.

Diverse Economic Systems As Islam expanded, it embraced numerous economic systems. The Bedouins in the Arabian peninsula, the Berbers in North Africa, and the Turkish people of Eurasia continued to have a pastoral economy. The majority of those living in Egypt, Persia, Sicily, and Spain lived from settled agriculture. The inhabitants of cities, especially those along the caravan routes that tied the Middle East to India and central Asia, relied on commerce.

Arabic was universal and made commercial communications easy. Muhammad had been a merchant, and Islamic law favored commerce. Maritime commerce in the Mediterranean provided, until the sixteenth century, the chief commercial link among India, Egypt, and the West. A large collection of letters from Jewish merchants living in Cairo in the eleventh and twelfth centuries has survived and marvelously illuminates trade and many other aspects of social life in the medieval East.[1]

Trade stimulated urban artisans to improve the quality of their products. The steel of Damascus and Toledo, the leather of Córdoba, and the fine cotton, linen, and silk of many Eastern towns (damask, for instance, was named for the weaving of Damascus) were desired and imitated in the West. Merchants shipped these products to India and Indonesia, where they were traded for spices and other products. Borrowing technology from China, India, and Byzantium, the Arabs improved on what they found. They improved on siege weapons and fortress building that they learned from the Byzantines. Serving as a conduit to the West of inventions from China, they introduced the windmill and the spinning wheel as well as paper making, block printing, and specialized textile weaving.

Cosmopolitan Cities A vigorous urban life, concentrated in the cities of Damascus, Baghdad, Cairo, and Córdoba, distinguished medieval Islamic society. According to travelers' reports, Damascus had 113,000 homes and 70 libraries. Baghdad surpassed all other cities in the number of palaces, libraries, and public baths. Products from almost all parts of the known world could be purchased at the markets, or bazaars, in all the major cities. The streets teemed with slaves, servants, artisans, merchants, administrators, and beggars. The aura of the Islamic cities was preeminently cosmopolitan.

Mixed Role for Women In the early days of Islam, women played a major role in conversion. Muhammad's wife, Khadija, was his first convert. His second wife, daughter of a wealthy Meccan, was an early convert who shared the exile in Medina before Muhammad married her. The wives of two of the first caliphs were also early converts.

The Koran placed a high value on preserving and enhancing the family. It encouraged people to marry and enjoined men to support their wives. It allowed male Muslims to have as many as four legal wives, but only if they could support them and treat them all fairly. Divorce was difficult because the husband had to allow his divorced wife to keep gifts he had given her and support her and her children. Women could inherit from their male kin, but their portion was less than a male heir would receive: "A male child shall have the equivalent of two female children."

The position of women depended on their social class and on the period in which they lived. Islamic society became more restrictive of women in later centuries. Muhammad had urged his wives to live in seclusion, but eventually the harem (rooms reserved for women) was recommended for all women after puberty. But the strict seclusion of the harem was something that only the very wealthy could afford for their wives, daughters, and concubines. Peasant and artisan women would have to be in public. Women who left the seclusion of home did so with a veil covering the head and face.

Arabic Contributions to Global Culture

The Islamic conquests brought the Arabs into contact with older and more accomplished civilizations than their own, particularly with the intellectual achievements of the Greeks, which they were eager to preserve. During the eighth and ninth centuries, scholars translated into Arabic many Greek authors: Aristotle, Euclid, Archimedes, Hippocrates, and Galen. Islamic scholars were especially interested in astronomy, astrology, mathematics, medicine, and optics, and in these areas their writings exerted a great influence on the Western world.

Medical Education Al-Razi (known as Rhazes in the West) of Baghdad was director of the state hospital in Baghdad, and he had practical experience with medicine

---

[1] These letters are called the *Geniza documents.* The *geniza* was a storeroom attached to a synagogue; records mentioning God's name (including merchants' letters) could not be destroyed and were stored in the geniza. The geniza of the Cairo synagogue was sealed up and not rediscovered until the nineteenth century. Its contents were then sold to collectors of Jewish documents and to libraries and thus dispersed throughout the world. For examples of these extraordinary records, see S. D. Goitein, *Letters of Medieval Jewish Traders,* 1973.

HISTORICAL ISSUES: WRITING MEDIEVAL WOMEN'S HISTORY

One of the most important new directions for historical writing has been the history of women. Books and articles on women from all time periods and all countries are now abundant, and courses on women's history are readily available. Writing the history of women in the Middle Ages, however, presents major interpretive problems.

Very few writings by women survive from the Middle Ages. Few women in the West were literate, and those who were knew vernacular languages rather than Latin, the language of learning. Still, learned nuns left devotional literature, plays, and histories. Arabic was the language of both literature and speech, and some women's poems in Arabic survive. Greek women wrote histories. Another source of women's own thoughts were accounts of their visions or of their lives that their priests recorded.

Most information about women, therefore, is filtered through sources written by men. Men wrote about women from a number of motives, and these biases must be taken into consideration when interpreting the sources. Religious sources, for instance, seek to organize society and instruct believers. To understand and interpret these sources, a historian needs to know a great deal about the context in which they were written. The strictures from the Koran, for example, could be read as being very repres-

sive of women. When seen in the context of Muhammad's desire to preserve and strengthen the family, however, they take on a different meaning. Add the pre-Islamic context, and the Koran can be viewed as improving the position of women by protecting them against abuses they had previously experienced.

Other sources, such as laws, provide sparse information about the women they seek to regulate and protect. The researcher does not know whether the laws were actually applied. A variety of other sources help to elucidate this information. Court cases, of course, provide ready information when they are available. Historians have also creatively used archaeological evidence and even place names. For example, the Anglo-Saxons had the custom that the husband presented the wife with a gift, the *morgangifu*, the day after the marriage. Present-day names such as Mayfield or Morgay Farm indicate that these were bridal gifts to women.

The historian's craft is partly one of solving mysteries; the study of women's history provides rich opportunities for the historically minded sleuth. Both the subject itself and the problems of researching it contribute to the dynamics of the field.

---

and medical education. He wrote some 140 medical treatises, including a description of smallpox. Among the accomplishments of the Abbasid caliphate were courses in pharmacy and licensing of all people practicing medicine.

Mathematics and Astronomy   Arabic mathematicians adopted their impressive numbering system from the Hindus but made the critical addition of the zero, which is itself an Arabic word. The use of the zero allows figures to be arranged in columns and permits the use of a decimal system. Italian merchants became familiar with the Arabic numbers shortly before the year 1200 and carried them back to the West. Arabic mathematicians also developed algebra. Astronomers and astrologers invented an improved astrolabe (which measures the angular declination of heavenly bodies above the horizon) and were able to improve the astronomical tables of antiquity.

Philosophy and Theology   Scholars also wrote philosophical and theological treatises. The most important Islamic philosopher was the Spaniard ibn-Rushd, or Averroës (ca. 1126–1198), who wrote commentaries on Aristotle and exerted a profound influence on Christian

as well as Islamic philosophy in the Middle Ages. Islamic philosophical speculations nourished intellectual life in the West in two ways: Western philosophers gained a much broader familiarity with the scientific and philosophical heritage of classical Greece through translations made from Arabic, chiefly in Spain; and Islamic philosophers explored issues central to religious philosophy much earlier than did Christian thinkers. What is the relation between faith and reason, between an all-powerful God and the freedom, dignity, and individuality of the human person? In posing these problems and in suggesting answers, the Muslims stimulated and enriched thought in the West.

Centers of Culture   Baghdad under the Abbasid Dynasty was a great cultural center. Caliph Harun al-Rashid's reign (r. 786–809) (see "Three Empires and an Elephant," pp. 200–202) was the high point of Islamic culture. The *Arabian Nights* was first written in this period and put into its present form in the fourteenth century. The stories convey a glamorous and idealized, but not a false, picture of the luxurious life at Baghdad. Harun's son Al-Mamun (r. 813–833) reigned even more splendidly than his father did. He was also a patron of learning. Al-Mamun founded an observatory for the

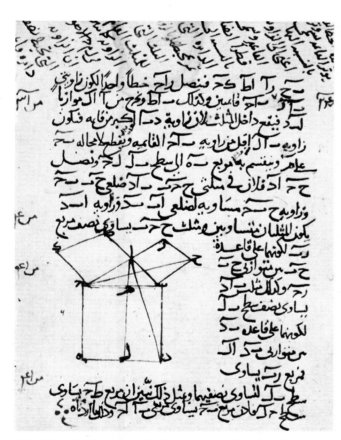

This thirteenth-century Arab commentary on the *Geometry of Euclid* illustrates the proof of the Pythagorean theorem. Mathematics was one science in which the Arabs surpassed the classical achievements.
© British Museum

study of the heavens and established a "House of Wisdom" (sometimes referred to as the first Islamic institution of higher education), where translations were made and a library collected for the use of scholars.

Spain was a notable center of medieval Islamic civilization. The brilliance of Islamic-Spanish civilization is best reflected in three great architectural monuments: the mosque (now a cathedral) at Córdoba, the Alhambra Palace in Granada, and the Alcazar at Seville. Jewish communities in Spain, the most creative of Jewish communities in the West, contributed to the high quality of intellectual life. It was also in Spain that Western Christians came into intimate contact with Islamic learning and drew from it the greatest benefits.

Decline of Medieval Islamic Civilization

The earliest indication of decline was the growing military weakness of the various Islamic states in the face of new invasions in the middle of the eleventh century. In the West, Christian armies embarked on the recon-

quest of the Iberian Peninsula, and Christian fleets broke the Islamic domination of the western Mediterranean islands. The Byzantine offensive gave rise to the First Crusade, which wrested Jerusalem from Islamic control in 1099. In the East, Turkish nomads infiltrated the Abbasid caliphate in considerable numbers, and the Seljuks (converts to Islam) seized Baghdad in 1055. Turkish rulers gained supremacy in all the eastern Islamic states over the next few centuries.

The Arabic economic base was changing. By the thirteenth century, maritime and commercial supremacy on the Mediterranean Sea passed to Italians and other Westerners. Arabian coins largely disappeared from circulation in the West, documenting a headlong retreat from commerce. Simultaneously, the Islamic states no longer supported their warriors with salaries but with grants of land, which weakened central authority. The growing importance of an aristocracy of rural warriors seems to have brought a new militarism and rigidity into society.

FORMS OF THE FIXED STARS, CA. 1009–1010
One of the earliest examples of Islamic book illustration, this manuscript, written around 1009–1010, contains seventy-five drawings noting the forms of the fixed stars. Sagittarius, shown as an armed rider, is traced from the pattern of the constellation and indicates the sophistication of Muslim astronomy.
The Bodleian Library, University of Oxford. MS. Marsh 144, page 273

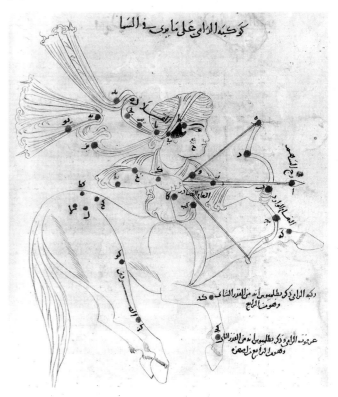

ALHAMBRA PALACE
The remarkable series of rooms and courtyards that make up the Alhambra Palace in Granada are one of the supreme achievements of Islamic art. The delicate tracery, the elegant details, and the constant presence of running water create a mood of luxury and refinement that can still be experienced by the visitor today.
J. Messerschmidt/eStock Photo

MOSQUE AT CÓRDOBA, 784–990
Begun around 784, the Mosque at Córdoba was enlarged throughout the ninth and tenth centuries. The flexible plan of parallel aisles creates a complex visual forest of double-tiered arches that originally supported a wooden roof. This immense structure, with 850 columns and 19 aisles, was one of the largest buildings in the Islamic world.
Fridmar Damm/eStock Photo

THE BYZANTINE EMPIRE (610–1071)

The Byzantine Empire developed a decisively Eastern orientation, a characteristic already observable in Justinian's reign. Although Justinian's great codification of Roman law was in Latin, he issued his own edicts in Greek, now the common language of the Empire. Court ceremonials resembled those of an Eastern ruler, in which the subjects were distanced from the ruler by space, dress, and submissive behavior. Byzantium remained wealthy, aggressive in defending its borders, and expansive in its missionary activity, but it was under constant attack and its physical territory shrank to an area in Europe and Asia surrounding Constantinople.

Strains on the Empire

Heraclius and the Persian Wars   Heraclius (r. 610–641) came to power amid repeated military disasters. The Avars, a nomadic tribe from Central Asia, and Slavs invaded the Balkans right up to the walls of Constantinople. While the Avars withdrew again to above the Danube River, the Slavs remained in the Balkans. The aggressive Persians took Antioch, Jerusalem, and Alexandria. They Persians even removed from the Church of the Holy Sepulcher in Jerusalem the cross on which Jesus was crucified. Raising money through treasures donated by the churches, Heraclius strengthened the army and then boldly opened a successful war against the Persians in 622. The Persians agreed to a humiliating peace and returned the Holy Cross.

The Persian wars left Byzantium financially depleted and its army exhausted. The Empire was not in a position to defend itself immediately against a new menace on its borders. After the death of Muhammad in 632, his Muslim followers from the Arabic world embarked on a tidal wave of conquests, overrunning much of the Empire in scarcely more than ten years.

Territorial Losses to Muslims   A century elapsed before the Byzantines were able to take the offensive against the Muslims. The Empire had lost Egypt and Syria, but the loss had positive as well as negative effects. Those regions had never become entirely Greco-Roman and had resisted Byzantine administration, taxation, and religion. These regions embraced the Arian (see chapter 5) and monophysite (see chapter 6) heresies. Their religious beliefs were closer to Islam, thus making the Arab conquest easier. (See maps 6.2 and 7.1.)

Military Revival   The emperor Leo III (r. 717–741) beat back a Muslim attack on Constantinople in 717 and 718 and then began to reconquer Asia Minor. The military revival reached its height under the great warrior emperors of the ninth through eleventh centuries. Byzantine armies pushed the Muslims back into Syria

ICONOCLAST WHITEWASHING AN IMAGE OF CHRIST, CA. 900 Byzantine iconoclasts, protesting the worship of images and the leadership of a Latin pope, destroyed the decorations of numerous churches. This page from a Psalter illuminated around 900 depicts the obliteration through whitewashing of an icon of Christ.
Moscow, Historical Museum; photo, Ecole des Hautes Etudes, Paris

and waged successful wars in southern Italy, the Balkan Peninsula, and the Caucasus. Their principal military accomplishment was in the Balkan Peninsula, where they defeated the nomadic people known as the Bulgars. The modern Bulgarians are entirely Slavic in language and culture and retain only the name of the original nomads. During the late ninth and tenth centuries, Byzantium experienced once again a period of stability, wealth, and artistic glory.

Leo III and Iconoclasm While Leo III's military campaigns marked the turn of the tide against the Arab expansion, his religious policies plunged the Empire into turmoil. Leo had grown up in Asia Minor, where he had contact with both Islam and heretical Christians, and he absorbed some of their suspicions that the use of holy images, or icons (from the Greek *eikon,* "image"), in worship was akin to idolatry. He introduced *iconoclasm* ("image-breaking") in the Empire in 726. Not only did he forbid the veneration of images within churches, he pursued a policy of actively destroying them. Iconoclasm was a drastic policy, because many of the worshipers had come to regard particular icons, images of Jesus, Mary, and the saints, as being efficacious as intercessors for divine help. Leo and the iconoclasts argued that people were worshiping pieces of wood and stone rather than God, Jesus, or Mary.

Leo's iconoclastic policy had a disastrous effect on relations with the West. It contributed to the pope's decision to recognize Pepin the Short as king of the Franks and defender of the papacy (see chapter 6). After 843 the Byzantine Empire restored the worship of images, but the iconoclastic policy helped to widen the cleavage between the Western and Eastern churches.

Byzantine Government

Position of the Emperor The relationship between religion and the state was close in Byzantium. The Byzantines believed that if the Empire performed the sacred duty of aiding the salvation of the human race, God would never permit its destruction, an idea that inspired Byzantines with the courage to resist for centuries a nearly continuous onslaught of invaders. The emperor was a holy figure as the head of the state. A Christian emperor could not claim divinity (as pagan Roman emperors had), but the emperor lived surrounded by ceremony that imparted an aura of sanctity to his person. The term *sacred* was liberally applied to his person, palace, and office.

Although the Byzantine emperor had a prominent role in both Church and state, his theological role was limited. He was not a priest and he could not say Mass or administer the sacraments. Yet the emperor exercised a wide authority over ecclesiastical matters. He supervised the qualifications for ordination of priests, created bishoprics and changed their boundaries, investigated the monasteries and reformed them when necessary, and appointed patriarchs. The emperor summoned councils, supervised their proceedings, and enforced their decisions.

Elaborate Bureaucracy The emperor, like his predecessors in the old Roman Empire, enjoyed absolute authority and governed with the aid of a civil service. Literate and trained laymen staffed the bureaucracy.

At a time when Western governments operated almost without a budget, the Byzantine government collected large revenues from the 10 percent tariff on trade and from the profit from the state monopolies. The government also employed skilled diplomats, whom contemporary observers celebrated for their ability to keep enemies divided and for their liberal use of bribes, tributes, and subsidies. The modern phrase, "Byzantine diplomacy," indicates our respect for their complex skill.

The Eastern Church and the Western Church

The contrasting experiences in the early Middle Ages deeply affected the character and spirit of the two major branches of Christianity. The differences between the two churches clarify other contrasts in the history of the Eastern and Western peoples. The Eastern Church developed and functioned under the supervision of the emperor. In the West, on the other hand, the collapse of central authority in the Roman Empire gave the clergy a position of leadership in secular affairs.

Theological Differences   Both the Eastern Church and the Western Church considered themselves catholic (that is, universal) and orthodox (that is, holding true beliefs); the terms **Roman Catholic** and **Greek Orthodox** used to identify the churches today are exclusively modern usages. The two churches maintained nearly identical beliefs. Perhaps the principal, or at least the most famous, disagreement was and still is the *filioque* dispute (meaning "and from the son"), which concerns the relationship between members of the Trinity: the Father, Son, and Holy Spirit. The Eastern Church held, and still holds, that the Holy Spirit proceeds only from the Father, while the Western Church maintained that the Holy Spirit proceeds from the Father "and from the Son."

The Eastern Church permitted, as the Western Church did not, divorce for reasons of adultery and the ordination of married men to the priesthood, although bishops had to be celibate.

Languages in Liturgy   The most significant liturgical difference between the two churches was that the Eastern Church allowed the use of vernacular languages—Greek, Coptic, Ethiopian, Syriac, Armenian, Georgian, Slavonic, and others—in the liturgy. Liturgical usage added great dignity to these Eastern languages and stimulated their development. The East Slavs, for example, possessed a rich literature in Slavonic within a century after their conversion to Christianity. Western vernacular literature was much slower in developing. On the other hand, the toleration of many vernacular languages weakened the unity of the Eastern Church. An Eastern cleric using his own vernacular language could not easily communicate with clerics from other regions, whereas a Western cleric who used Latin could make himself understood anywhere in the West. Because of linguistic differences from their neighbors, Eastern churches tended to develop in isolation from one another.

The Eastern Church developed into a loose confederation of independent national churches. In contrast, with the unity of Latin as its liturgical and literary language, the Western Church began to develop a centralized control over Christianity under the papacy.

Missionary Activities   The two churches came into direct conflict in the Balkans over the conversion of the Slavs. Two Christian brothers of Slavic descent, Cyril and Methodius, set out in about 862 as missionaries from the Byzantine Empire to preach to the Slavs. Cyril developed a Slavonic script based on Greek letters called the **Cyrillic alphabet.** The brothers used the Yugo-Slav or South Slav dialect, translating the Bible and the liturgy into Slavonic. With modifications, the Cyrillic alphabet remains in use in parts of Eastern Europe and Russia today.

In the West the sword opened the way for missionaries. The papacy relied on the Frankish rulers to expand the boundaries of the Western Church through conquest. The struggles between Rome and Constantinople for conversion of the Slavic peoples brought about the area's religious configuration that still exists today. Croatia, Albania, and Moravia (the Czechs and Slovacs) came under the Roman Church, but the Serbs and the rest of the Balkan area adhered to the Greek Church. Russia was converted to the Eastern Church in the tenth century.

East-West Schism   The final schism between the Eastern Church and the Western Church occurred in 1054, destroying hope for a united Christian Church. Even today, more than nine hundred years later, the Western and Eastern traditions are still trying to overcome the rift.

Byzantine Economy and Society

Urban and Rural Population   The outstanding feature of Byzantine civilization, compared with that of Western Europe, was the continuing vitality of its cities. At one time the Byzantine Empire included such great urban centers as Alexandria, Antioch, Beirut, Constantinople, Trebizond, and Tyre. At its peak under Justinian, Constantinople probably contained more than three hundred thousand inhabitants. The city had paved and illuminated streets and splendid churches and palaces. Urban society was, however, marked by a wide division between rich and poor. The rich lived among magnificent surroundings in huge palaces; the

AGRICULTURE
Cultivating their own plots was the principal work of Byzantine peasants. This manuscript illustration shows the various labors of digging, harvesting, and watering taking place in a fanciful landscape.
Bibliothèque Nationale de France, Paris

poor, in sprawling slums. Crimes committed in broad daylight were commonplace.

Rural society was organized on a theme system. The themes were administered by generals, who became the elite of the Empire. Soldiers and sailors were paid by granting them their own farms. They fought in their own theme army or navy to defend their land. The village organization was similar to the one that developed in the West.

Trade and Manufacture

The Byzantine Empire was wealthy compared with other states of the age. One great source of wealth came from the commerce that passed through the ports and gates of Constantinople. The Slavs from the north carried amber, fur, honey, slaves, wax, and wheat; Armenians and Syrians from the east brought clothing, fruit, glass, steel, and spices; merchants from the west contributed arms, iron, slaves, and wood. The vigorous commerce attracted large colonies of foreign merchants. The commercial importance of Byzantium is revealed in the prestige of its gold coin, the *bezant*. Its weight and purity were kept constant from the reign of Constantine to the late eleventh century.

Constantinople was also the producer of luxury items. When the Persian Empire blocked the trade in silk from China and India across the land routes (the Great Silk Road) (see "Rome and China: The Silk Road," pp. 128–130), Justinian tried to find other ways to import silk from China. He experimented with send-

ing missionaries to Ethiopia and the Arabian peninsula to create a route through the Red Sea. Finally, two monks who had returned from northern India revealed to him the secret of silkworm cultivation and weaving, which the Chinese had known for at least two millennia. Justinian established silk production as a state monopoly; it enriched the state and meant that the emperor controlled the distribution of prestigious quality silk fabrics and dyes among aspiring tribal kings who wished to imitate the emperor. The best silk, rich purple-dyed cloth, was reserved for the imperial family. So significant was the symbolic value of purple silk that it became a particular distinction of legitimacy to "be born in the purple," indicating that the emperor's mother gave birth in a chamber hung with purple cloth. One emperor, Constantine Prophyrogenitus ("born in the purple," r. 913–957), took it as a name.

Byzantine artisans producing luxury goods such as silk, goldwork, icons, and glass objects were organized into *guilds* (organizations of craftsmen who trained skilled workers and organized artisans to ensure quality products).

Limited Role of Women

Women in the Byzantine Empire continued as they had in the ancient world. Their lives centered around the home, and their contact with men outside the family was strictly limited. They wore veils over their heads, but not their faces. Whereas in Western monasticism nuns performed charity work and ran schools, Byzantine nuns were strictly cloistered and performed none of these functions, which were reserved for monks. Only at the imperial and aristocratic level could women play an active role, including acting as regent and even becoming sole ruler, as did Empress Irene (r. 797–802) and Theodora (r. 1042, 1055–1056) (see "Three Empires and an Elephant," pp. 200–202). It was another Theodora, a regent, who initiated the return to icon veneration in 843. Aristocratic women played a role in administering family lands.

The streets and fields were not devoid of women. Poor women had no recourse but to aid in family agriculture, to become street vendors of food and drink, or even enter into the theater and prostitution.

The law placed women and children under the protection of male relatives, so they could not act legally on their own. Nonetheless, the law afforded women the protection of their dowries—the goods, money, and land that the wife brought to the marriage. The dowry was an important economic asset to the family, and the husband could administer but not sell it during the marriage. On his death the wife regained it for her widowhood. Widowhood did not leave women legally free, as it did in the West, because the Eastern Church intervened and discouraged women from remarrying.

WOMEN WEAVING AND SPINNING
Textile production was an important industry in Byzantine culture. This manuscript illustration depicts one woman weaving on a simple rectangular frame and another woman spinning.
Bibliothèque Nationale de France, Paris

Byzantine Culture

Education   Byzantine wealth supported a tradition of learning that benefited not only the clergy but also many laymen. There were three types of institutions of higher learning: a palace school, primarily for laymen, trained civil servants in language, law, and rhetoric; a patriarchal school instructed priests in rhetoric and theology; and monastic schools taught young monks the mystical writings of the past. With the demise of public grammar schools in the sixth and seventh centuries, the poor depended on their guild for what education they received.

Scholarship   Scholars used the Greek rather than the Latin language almost exclusively after the sixth century. They composed school manuals, histories, saints' lives, biblical commentaries, and encyclopedias of ancient science and lore. On the whole, Byzantine scholars did not show the fascination with Aristotle and science that the Arabs and the Western scholars did, but concentrated instead on Plato and religious writers. Their greatest accomplishment was the preservation of classical Greek literature. With the exception of some few works preserved on papyri, virtually all that the Western world possesses of classical Greek authors has come down through Byzantine copies, most of which date from the tenth to the twelfth centuries.

Art and Architecture   With the final rejection of iconoclasm in the middle of the ninth century, art and architecture flourished once again. Byzantine artisans designed and decorated many churches throughout the Empire. Their work is found in such places as Messina and Palermo in Sicily and Venice in Italy. Artists were summoned to such distant places as Kiev to aid in the design, construction, and decoration of churches.

The mosaics make vividly concrete the Byzantine concepts of empire, emperor, and church. The emperor is always presented as the august figure. Christ is never shown as suffering; he is, in other words, always God and never man. The mosaics have no sense of movement, admission of human frailty, or recognition of the reality of change. Operating within this picture of the world, the artists nevertheless portrayed their solemn figures with a rich variety of forms, garments, and colors. Byzantine mosaics may be static, but they are neither drab nor monotonous.

Popular Culture   The Hippodrome in Constantinople and similar sports centers in other cities continued some of the entertainments of the Roman coliseums. Chariot racing was the most popular sport, but animal shows, theater, and other spectacles also enjoyed considerable vogue. The spectators divided into rival fan groups called the "Blues" and the "Greens," whose members adopted strange haircuts and clothing, carried weapons, and generally acted as rowdy sports fans. These "clubs" could form more serious factions if they involved themselves in religious or political issues and were responsible for some of the more serious riots.

Decline of the Byzantine Empire

Social Transformations   The theme system of free peasant-warriors began to collapse. From the early tenth century, these free peasant-warriors, apparently to escape mounting fiscal and military burdens, began to abandon their farms to more powerful neighbors. In the eleventh century many of them became serfs; they gave up their freedom of movement and paid landlords a rent for their property.

A powerful rural aristocracy made up of the estate owners weakened the strength of the central government. The emperors tried to limit the size and number of great estates, but by the late eleventh century, their weaker successors preferred to purchase the loyalty of the rural aristocracy by distributing imperial estates to them. Byzantium was being transformed from a disciplined society of peasant-warriors under a strong central government to a society with a dependent peasantry, strong local landlords, and a weak central government.

Defense of the Empire Without a pool of free peasants to recruit for the army and navy, the emperors had to rely on mercenary soldiers to defend the territory. The mercenaries often became involved in imperial politics and overthrew emperors. Among the mercenaries were Varangians from Scandinavia (see p. 205). Constantinople did have the benefit of Greek Fire, a compound based on naphtha, which could burn on water or be put in clay pots with a fuse and hurled across a wall, causing fires where they landed.

The Seljuk Turks A new people emerged from the east and overwhelmed the Byzantine territory. The Byzantines gave the name *Turk* to a number of nomadic tribes that lived in the region east and north of the Caspian Sea (modern Turkestan). In the eleventh century, members of one tribe, the Seljuks, penetrated beyond the eastern borders of the Empire into Asia Minor. They shattered the largely mercenary army of the Byzantines and took the emperor captive at Manzikert in 1071.

As the Byzantine defenses broke down, Asia Minor lay open to the Seljuk forces. One Turkish chieftain, Suleiman, established himself and his warriors at Nicaea, only a few miles from Constantinople. The virtual loss of Asia Minor forced the Byzantine emperor to appeal to the West for help, a request that led to the First Crusade. This appeal signaled the end of the Byzantine Empire as a great power in the East.

THE CAROLINGIAN, OR FRANKISH, EMPIRE

The Frankish Empire was already strong when Charles the Great (r. 768–814) became its king. Charles Martel, Charlemagne's grandfather, had defeated the Arabs in a battle at Tours in 732, thus sparing Frankish lands the same fate that befell the Visigothic kingdom in Spain. Charles Martel's son, Pepin the Short, had elevated the family role in government from that of mayor of the palace to that of king of the Franks. Forming an alliance with the Frankish aristocracy and the pope, he had deposed the last of the Merovingians and was crowned king (see p. 169). Through careful alliances with the aristocracy, continued warfare with neighbors, and good management, the Frankish kings established a large empire in the former Roman province of Gaul and ex-

CHARLEMAGNE
This twelfth-century silver reliquary from Aachen represents Charlemagne as emperor, saint, and protector of the Church. After his death, through all the subsequent medieval centuries, Charlemagne was remembered and viewed as the ideal Christian emperor.
Scala/Art Resource, NY

tended their control beyond the Rhine River. Charles the Great was a worthy successor to his able ancestors.

Charlemagne

Pepin's son Charles the Great, or Charlemagne, pursued the policies of his predecessors with unprecedented energy. His biographer, the court scholar Einhard, says that he was a large man, and that he delighted in physical exercise (see "Einhard on Charlemagne," p. 197). His taste for food and women seems to have been no less exuberant. Perhaps more remarkable in this man were his intellectual curiosity and alertness. He was probably illiterate, but he inspired a revival of learning modern scholars call the "Carolingian Renaissance." The vast empire that Charlemagne built (called the "Carolingian" Empire from "Carolus," his Latin name) was in large measure a personal accomplishment, a tribute to his abounding physical energy and intelligence.

Victorious Wars Charlemagne's success as king depended on his success in waging long wars on every

EINHARD ON CHARLEMAGNE

The most important Western ruler of the Early Middle Ages was Charles the Great, or Charlemagne. A member of his court, Einhard, wrote of his life and described him as follows.

"Charles was large and strong, and of lofty stature; his height was seven times the length of his foot. In accordance with the national custom, he took frequent exercise on horseback and in hunting. He often practiced swimming, in which he was so skilled that none could surpass him. He was temperate in eating, and particularly so in drinking, for he hated drunkenness in anybody, much more in himself and in members of his household. While dining, he listened to reading or music. The subjects of the readings were the stories and deeds of older times; he was fond, too, of St. Augustine's books, and especially of 'The City of God.'

"Charles had the gift of ready and fluent speech, and could express himself with the utmost clearness. He was not satisfied with a command of only his native language, but studied foreign ones, and was such a master of Latin that he could speak it as well as his native tongue; but he could understand Greek better than he could speak it. He zealously cultivated the liberal arts, held those who taught them in great esteem, and conferred high honors on them. He also tried to write, and used to keep tablets under his pillow, so that in leisure hours he might train his hand to form the letters; but as he began his efforts late in life, he had poor success."

From Einhard, *Life of Charlemagne*, S. E. Turner (tr.), University of Michigan Press, 1960.

frontier. He perceived that spreading Christianity along with conquest led to submission to Frankish authority among pagan peoples. Where permanent conquest and conversion were not possible, the expeditions would still weaken neighboring enemies and prevent them from striking into the Frankish domains. At the pope's request Charlemagne campaigned four times in Italy against the Lombards and against factions in Rome opposed to the pope. He suppressed the independent Bavarians and overcame the Saxons after thirty-three years of fighting, thus bringing them fully and finally into the community of Western peoples. His conversions could be brutal. When the Saxons resisted Christianity, he threatened to kill them if they did not convert. These victorious wars added new territories to his empire (see map 7.2).

Imperial Title   On Charlemagne's fourth visit to Italy in 800, when he was praying before St. Peter's altar on Christmas night, Pope Leo III crowned him emperor of the Romans. The coronation added nothing to his possessions but was of great symbolic importance. It confirmed the alliance of the papacy and the Frankish monarchy. The coronation proclaimed the complete political and cultural autonomy of the Western community of peoples from Byzantine (Roman) control.

Carolingian Government

Imperial Ideology   The coronation added much to Charlemagne's dignity, and a grandiose imperial ideology developed around his person. But the elevation at

the hands of the pope also led to later conflicts between future emperors and popes over who had the right to grant imperial power. A cult developed around the emperor that played a vital role in preserving the unity of the Empire. In imperial propaganda Charlemagne became the new David (the ideal king of the Old Testament), the new Augustus (the greatest of the pagan emperors), and the new Constantine (the champion of the Church).

Administering the Empire   The emperor was the head of the government. He ruled with the aid of a small group of officials. The chaplain, head of the palace clergy, advised the emperor and the entire court in matters of conscience. The chaplain also supervised the chancery, or secretariat, where the official documents were written. The chief lay official, the count of the palace, supervised the administration, judged cases that the emperor did not personally handle, and acted as regent during the emperor's frequent absences. Other officials included the chamberlain, who looked after the royal bedroom and treasury; the seneschal, who kept the palace in food and servants; and the constable, who cared for the horses.

At the local level the fundamental administrative unit was the county, which resembled in its extent the Roman provinces. The count was the administrator, judge, and military leader of the county.

Charlemagne's chief administrative problem was to maintain an effective supervision and control over the local officials. He used three devices to resolve this problem. First, Charlemagne himself traveled widely to

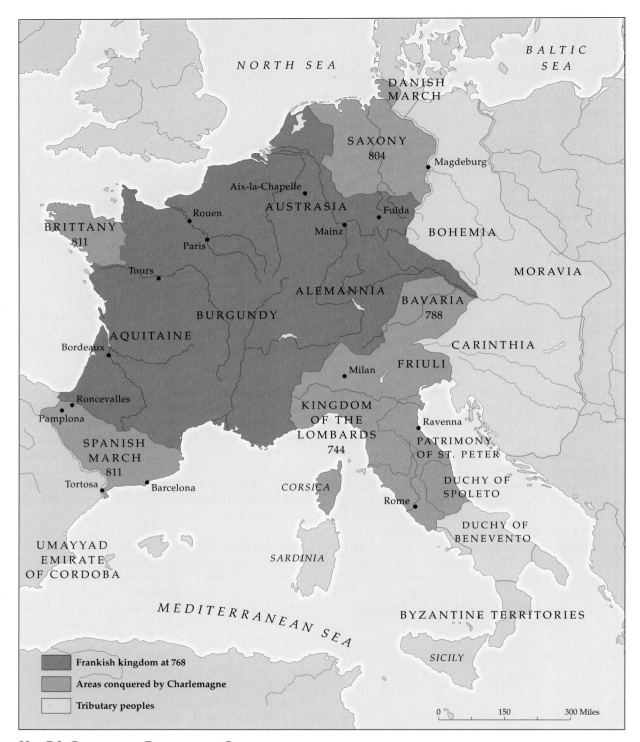

MAP 7.2 CAROLINGIAN EMPIRE UNDER CHARLEMAGNE
This map shows the additions that Charlemagne made to the Frankish Empire. Marches were the frontier provinces organized for the military defense of the Empire. Aix-la-Chapelle, also called Aachen, was the capital of the Empire. Where were the tributary people? Compare this map to map 5.1, showing the extent of the Roman Empire. What did the Carolingian Empire include that the Roman Empire did not? What parts of Europe did the Romans control that the Carolingians did not?
◆ For an online version, go to www.mhhe.com/chambers9 > chapter 7 > book maps

This ninth-century manuscript illumination is the Beatus page from Psalm 1 and displays the Carolingian minuscule, which is the model for the letters used today in what printers call Roman type.
The British Library, London. 12714.tif, Harley 2793, f. 33

ascertain how the land was being administered and to hear appeals from the decisions of the counts. Second, he appointed special traveling inspectors, called *missi dominici* (or "emperor's emissaries"), to inspect a particular county every year. These men scrutinized the behavior of both the lay and the ecclesiastical officials, heard complaints, published imperial directives, and reported their findings to the emperor. Third, Charlemagne required that the important men of his realm, both laymen and ecclesiastics, attend a general assembly almost every year. There they reported on conditions in their local areas, advised the emperor on important matters, and heard his directives. Many of the imperial directives have survived. Divided into chapters (*capitula*), these informative records are known as *capitularies.*

Currency   To promote unity, Charlemagne standardized weights, measures, and money throughout his Empire. The monetary system came to be based on a single minted coin, the silver *denarius,* or penny. Twelve of these made a *solidus,* or shilling (although such a coin was not actually minted), and twenty shillings made a pound.

The Carolingian Renaissance

Charlemagne and his successors promoted learning within their domains in what is now called the Carolingian Renaissance. These rulers were interested in education for several reasons. In the sixth and seventh centuries, when the continent was divided among many small kingdoms, different styles of writing, known as *national hands* (Visigothic, Merovingian,

Lombard, and so on), had developed. The Latin grammar used by scholars had also absorbed many regional peculiarities.

Literate persons in one part of Europe had great difficulty recognizing or reading a text written in another. The widespread decline in education had left few persons who could read at all. Poorly educated priests could not properly perform the liturgy, and variations in religious rituals were also growing. Both situations weakened the unity of the Church as well as the state.

Carolingian Minuscule   Pepin and Charlemagne sought to remedy the lack of literacy. One great achievement of this educational revival was a reform in handwriting. About the year 800, monks at the monasteries of Corbie and Tours devised a new type of formal literary writing, a "book-hand," using lowercase letters and known as the **Carolingian minuscule.** Previously, the book-hands had been based on various styles of capital letters only and were difficult to read rapidly. The Carolingian minuscule used capital letters for the beginning of sentences and smaller (or lowercase) letters for the text. Our modern printing is based on this Carolingian innovation. It was easier to read a page written in this way; also, more letters could be written on a page, and thus more books were produced at less expense. Use of this graceful new script eventually spread across Europe.

Latin Language   Another achievement of this educational revival was the development of a common scholarly language. Carolingian scholars perfected a distinctive language now known as medieval Latin, which largely retained the grammatical rules of classical Latin but was more flexible and open in its vocabulary, freely coining new words to express the new realities of the age. Medieval Latin was also clearly different from the vulgar, or Romance, Latin spoken by the people. The establishment of medieval Latin as a distinct language of learning thus freed the Romance vernaculars to develop on their own. One of these vernacular languages is Old French, whose oldest surviving text dates from 842.[2]

The Latin created by the Carolingian scholars enabled travelers, administrators, and scholars to make themselves understood in all parts of Europe; and it continued to serve this function until the modern era. Even when it disappeared as an international language, it helped promote European unity. All the modern vernacular tongues of Europe developed under the strong influence of these scholars' Latin. One of the

[2] At Strasbourg in 842, Charles the Bald and Louis the German, two of the sons of Louis the Pious, took an oath that was recorded in Latin, Old French, and German. The oath at Strasbourg not only preserves the oldest surviving text in Old French but also marks the first use of German in a formal legal document.

Global Moment

THREE EMPIRES AND AN ELEPHANT

Although trade and diplomatic ties between the West and the East diminished in the period of the seventh through the tenth centuries, merchants, pilgrims, envoys, and religious officials still traveled extensively and spread news. If we look at events surrounding the year 800, we find that diplomatic missions among the Franks (a Germanic kingdom), the Byzantines (the Eastern Roman Empire), and the Abbasid caliphate (an Arabic-speaking Muslim empire) continued. The main actors in these negotiations and contacts were Charles the Great or Charlemagne (r. 768–814), king of the Franks and, as of Christmas Day 800, Roman emperor in the West; Irene (r. 796–802), who became empress of Roman Empire in the East after she blinded her son, who subsequently died; and the Caliph Harun al-Rashid (786–809), heir to the Abbasid Dynasty, centered in Baghdad in Persia.

These three rulers dominated the area around the Mediterranean, but their empires were vastly different in terms of economic sophistication, religion, and intellectual and cultural achievements. Charlemagne established his capital in the far north of his territory, in Aachen, an old Roman town located between his Frankish lands and newly conquered areas in Germany. He built what was, by western European standards, a grand palace and a church. He began to reform the Latin language and revive learning in his empire in what has come to be known as the Carolingian Renaissance (a name derived from Charles). His church and palace were small, however, compared to the grandeur of Hagia Sophia in Constantinople or the palaces that Empress Irene controlled. Greek, not Latin, was the language of Irene's empire. Although both the former western and eastern parts of the Roman Empire were Christian, differences, including those of language and church policy were already dividing them.

Farther to the east, in Baghdad, where Harun al-Rashid ruled, the language was Arabic, the religion was Islam, the opulence of the palaces was remarkable, and the scholars were the world's leaders in medicine and science. A great hospital flourished in this period. Harun al-Rashid was said to have sponsored the "golden age" for the Arabic world. It took centuries for Arab learning in geography, astronomy, and medicine to reach the West. Charlemagne's court in Aachen was a long way from this intellectual achievement and cultural splendor.

The three empires had a history of clashes. The Arabic expansions had left the Eastern Roman Empire with far less territory. The Franks and other Germanic tribes had taken over the Western Empire and established independent kingdoms, with the Franks conquering most of them. Charlemagne, as King of the Franks, wanted the title of emperor. But before 800, no other Germanic ruler had had the audacity to take the title of emperor of the Romans, and he had some trepidation over assuming the title without permission or blessings of the real successor to the title in Constantinople. The Franks and the Arabs also had considerable conflicts. After all, Charlemagne's grandfather, Charles Martel, had defeated the Arabs 70 years before (732) and he, himself, made campaigns against them in Spain.

Charlemagne, who had never seen the magnificence of Constantinople or Baghdad, was not deterred from diplomatic missions to the east. At the end of the eighth century, he tried to reach an agreement with Empress Irene and her Eastern Empire, perhaps with the hope of legitimizing his power in the West. Neither part of the old Roman Empire had the military strength to attack each other, and thus Irene entertained the negotiation. Diplomats on both sides even tried to arrange a marriage between Irene and Charlemagne to smooth over relations. Meanwhile, Harun al-Rashid's armies were threatening Constantinople and Irene desperately resorted to paying a tribute to Harun to keep his army from attacking.

Charlemagne must have heard of the shift in the diplomatic winds and perhaps thought that by establishing ties with Harun al-Rashid, he could pressure Irene into accepting his assumption of the imperial title. It

Among the many exotic gifts that Harun al-Rashid gave to Charlemagne was, perhaps, this crystal pitcher. It is certainly a piece of late eighth- or early-ninth-century craftsmanship from Persia. It has long been assumed that this pitcher was among the gifts.
Treasury of the Abbey of Saint-Maurice, Valais, Switzerland. Lauros/Giraudon/Bridgeman Art Library

was a rash hope, if he ever had it. He could not, as a Christian, make a real alliance with Arabs. The Church forbade such treaties with non-Christians. What did Charlemagne hope to achieve and what did Harun al-Rashid hope to gain with such a diplomatic overture?

Although the Arabic sources are silent about the exchange, Carolingian sources speak of diplomatic missions to Baghdad in 797 and later. One of Charlemagne's contemporary biographers wrote, with obvious bias:

> With Harun al-Rashid, King of the Persians, who held almost the whole of the East in fee, always excepting India, Charlemagne was on such friendly terms that Harun valued his good will more than the approval of all other kings and princes in the entire world, and considered him alone as worthy of being honored and propitiated with gifts.

The same biographer spoke of Charlemagne's mission to Harun and said that "a few years earlier Harun had sent Charlemagne the only elephant he possessed, simply because the Frankish king asked for it."

Legend has woven fabulous stories around the elephant. One legend is that two Frankish envoys and a Jewish merchant Isaac, probably acting as a translator, went to Baghdad to meet with Harun. The two diplomats did not return to Europe, but the caliph sent Isaac

and the governor of Egypt back with a white elephant named Abu l'-Abbas from India. The elephant and Isaac took four years to travel from Baghdad to Jerusalem and then on to Carthage. From there they went by ship to Italy. It is not clear what ship would have been large enough to hold an elephant in 800. Waiting until spring to cross the Alps, Isaac and the Abu l'-Abbas arrived in Aachen in July of 802. The elephant must have caused a great stir in Aachen and Charlemagne was known to have traveled with it throughout his kingdom. He later used the elephant in a war against the Danes to frighten them from a northern port they were besieging. The elephant succumbed to disease in this northern climate and died in 810.

The elephant was not the only precious gift from Harun al-Rashid. Charlemagne also received a carved horn of ivory, a gold tray and pitcher, and a chess set. There was also a water clock, common in the Abbasid Empire, which had a twelve-hour mechanism that dropped little balls on a cymbal to mark the hour. Twelve horsemen also stepped out of twelve windows on the hour.

We are told by another of Charlemagne's biographers that Charlemagne sent diplomatic gifts to Harun
continued

al-Rashid as well. Spanish horses and mules, "cloaks from Frisia, white, grey, crimson and sapphire-blue, for these, so he discovered, were in short supply in those parts and extremely expensive." One can imagine that the Abbasid caliph, who had access to the best woven cloth from China and his own realms, would not be impressed by the roughly woven cloaks made in Frisia near the North Sea. The author confessed that the only thing that Harun showed much interest in were hunting dogs, which he immediately set on hunting a lion. According to the account, the Frankish ambassadors and their dogs were successful in bringing down the lion.

The diplomatic missions among empires in the year 800 show that an emperor, an empress, and a caliph did not live in complete isolation from each other. The traveling diplomats, traders in luxury goods, and the transfer of mechanical marvels, let alone an elephant, indicated a capacity for trade and communication among these different linguist and religious groups, despite their tensions. Communications were inadequate and distances were so great that any real alliances were impossible. At most, the communication between Charlemagne and Harun al-Rashid were expressions of respect for the perceived power of each other's empires. Although the diplomatic exchanges of Charlemagne with the Byzantine Empire were of a more serious nature, the divisions between the Eastern and Western halves of the Old Roman Empire were too deep to form an alliance. All three empires went into a decline in the ninth century. One remnant of the exchange between Charlemagne and Harun al-Rashid lived on, however. When the Franks initiated the First Crusade, the legend still persisted that among the gifts the Abbasid caliph had given to Charlemagne were the keys to Jerusalem. The Franks used this myth to legitimize their capture of that city.

Quotes are from Lewis Thorpe (tr.), *Einard and Notker the Stammer: Two Lives of Charlemagne,* Hammondsworth, Middlesex, UK: Penguin Books, 1969, pp. 70, 143–149.

reasons why it is possible to translate quickly from one European language to another is that their learned vocabularies are in large measure based on common Latin models.

Standardization of Texts A further achievement of the educational revival was the standardization of important texts. Pepin sought to standardize the liturgy on the basis of Roman practice, and Charlemagne continued his policy. Charlemagne had Alcuin of York, an Anglo-Saxon scholar who served as a sort of minister of cultural affairs from about 783 until 794, prepare a new edition of Jerome's Vulgate translation of the Bible. This edition became the common biblical text for the entire Western Church. Charlemagne procured from Monte Cassino a copy of the Benedictine rule and had it copied and distributed, so that monks everywhere would follow a standard code.

Schools and Curriculum Expanding educational opportunities were essential for the success of Charlemagne's program. To increase the supply of locally trained scholars, he ordered all bishops and monasteries to establish schools to educate boys. Charlemagne himself set the example by founding a palace school for the sons of his own courtiers. Alcuin helped devise the standards for the school curriculum, based on the seven liberal arts. He divided the curriculum into the **trivium,** or verbal arts (grammar, rhetoric, and logic), and the **quadrivium,** or mathematical arts (arithmetic, astronomy, geometry, and music). In the twelfth century this curriculum would become the standard program of study for a bachelor of arts at universities.

Court Scholars Charlemagne brought scholars from all around Europe to his court, including Anglo-Saxons and Italians. They formed an academy to discuss major intellectual issues in imitation of the classical world and used names drawn from the Bible or classics when they met together. Charlemagne was known as David and Alcuin as Horace.

Most of the scholars were grammarians and educators, engaged in producing teachers' manuals, textbooks, and school exercises. Their work was neither original nor possessed of rhetorical grace, but it was of the greatest importance for the intellectual growth of

EZRA RESTORING THE BIBLE
The image of Ezra restoring the
Bible, in this eighth-century
English manuscript, gives the
work of the medieval monk an
exalted self-justification. Here
we see a biblical figure doing
exactly what monks did—
namely, writing and copying. In
this case, Ezra was purifying the
text of the Bible, and the
implication was that monks
were engaged in the same task.
The vivid depiction of the
bookshelves, with their open
doors, and the table and stool is
clearly an attempt to bring to life
a scene from a monastery of the
time.
Scala/Art Resource, NY

Europe. The revived mastery of correct Latin equipped
scholars of later generations to return to the classical
heritage and to recover from it philosophic and aesthetic values.

Carolingian Society and Culture

Aristocratic Culture   While Charlemagne was trying
to raise the educational level of his people and the
clergy, popular culture remained chiefly oral. The upper classes, including Charlemagne himself, enjoyed
heroic poems of warfare, but only a fragment of this
poetry remains. Fighting and hunting were the chief
occupations of the aristocrats, and with the many
wars and the large forests, they had much to occupy
themselves. The aristocrats surrounded themselves
with as much luxury as they could make on their
estates or could purchase from traveling merchants.
They bought goods whose origins were in Byzantium,
and they had gold and silver objects made for them by
local craftsmen. (See "Three Empires and an Elephant," pp. 200–202.)

This small (8 5/8 inches) ivory depiction of the Virgin was probably executed at Aachen, one of the capitals of Charlemagne, in the ninth century. Note that the Virgin holds spindles in her left hand; spinning was typically woman's work. But surprisingly, she also wears armor—gauntlets on her wrists and what look to be shoulder pieces. Though a woman doing woman's work, she is a militant, imperious figure, strikingly different from the motherly madonnas of later medieval art.
Metropolitan Museum of Art, Gift of J. Pierpont Morgan, 1917 (17.190.49). Photograph © 2001 The Metropolitan Museum of Art, New York

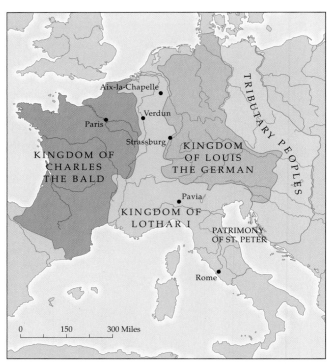

MAP 7.3 PARTITION OF THE FRANKISH EMPIRE
This map indicates the division of the Frankish Empire among the three surviving sons of Louis the Pious. In making the division, the language that the inhabitants spoke was not a consideration. Did the tripartite division of the Empire under Charlemagne's grandsons follow natural boundaries such as rivers or mountains? What tensions might have arisen from the division of the Empire?
◆ For an online version, go to www.mhhe.com/chambers9 > chapter 7 > book maps

Economy and Society As described in chapter 6, the agricultural economy was gradually improving as new tools and farming techniques permitted cultivation of the fertile river-valley soils. Large landed estates, farmed by serfs, provided most of the food. Ordinary woolen and linen cloth was made on these estates, which also produced wine, cheeses, and other food. Aside from Venice and some Mediterranean port cities, the towns were small. Many of the artisans worked directly on estates rather than in towns, and long-distance trade was conducted by traveling merchants.

Art and Architecture The increased prosperity is visible today in the number of fine churches and monasteries that date from this period. As Charlemagne conquered new territories, monks, nuns, and clergy moved into them and established new religious foundations. The period was one of major building. Byzantine architecture became the model for most of the churches, including the magnificent one that

Charlemagne built at Aix-la-Chapelle (modern Aachen) and that still stands today.

Mosaics in imitation of Byzantine models graced many church walls, and if mosaics were too expensive, wall painting took their place. The clergy commissioned artisans to make ecclesiastical objects, especially reliquaries for the bones of saints, out of precious metals and precious gems and stones.

Decline of the Carolingian Empire

Division of the Empire Charlemagne at his death left a united and apparently strong empire to his single surviving son, Louis the Pious. Louis, a weak and indecisive man, soon lost control over his own family, and his sons rebelled against him. After Louis' death, the three surviving sons partitioned the Empire at the Treaty of Verdun in 843 and established their own kingdoms (see map 7.3; see also footnote on p. 199).

As the family of Carolingian rulers divided amid civil wars and partitions of territory, the loyalty of the mili-

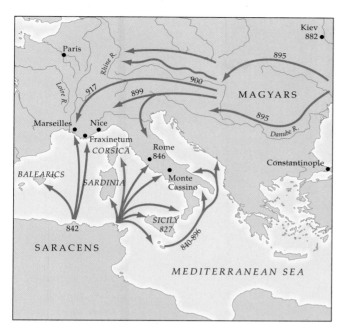

MAP 7.4 INVASIONS OF SOUTHERN EUROPE, NINTH THROUGH TENTH CENTURIES
This map shows that the Muslims (Saracens as the Western Europeans called them) and Magyars made incursions, if not permanent settlements, into Europe in the ninth through tenth centuries. Were there natural boundaries to stop the Magyars, who traveled by horseback? What probable conveyance did the Saracens use to raid?
◆ For an online version, go to www.mhhe.com/chambers9 > chapter 7 > book maps

PICTURE-STONE
This carving shows a Viking horseman at the top with his round shield and helmet. In the center section is a Viking boat. The prow was raised and cut into the shape of a dragon's head or some other ferocious beast. A rudder was used to guide the boat. The two occupants are shown wearing chain mail, the typical armor of the time.
Werner Forman/Art Resource, NY

tary aristocracy also waned. The new rulers conquered no new lands; so they had no new offices or properties with which to buy the loyalties of the aristocracy. The office of count, appointive under Charlemagne, became hereditary under his successors. The Carolingian rulers no longer summoned the great men of the realm to the yearly assemblies and no longer dispatched the *missi dominici* on their circuits. The institutional and moral bonds tying their central governments to the peripheral territories were thus broken or abandoned.

New Invasions   Under Charlemagne's weak successors, invasions of the Frankish Empire resumed, and centrifugal forces tore at the empire as well. To the south, Muslims from North Africa invaded Sicily and southern Italy in 827, attacked the valley of the Rhône in 842, and raided Rome in 846. Concurrently, from the east a new nomadic people, the Magyars, established themselves by about 895 in the valley of the Danube; from this base for the next fifty years, they struck repeatedly into the areas that are now France, Germany, and Italy (see map 7.4). Eventually they settled in modern-day Hungary. But none of these raids were as devastating to the Carolingian lands as those of the Scandinavians.

THE VIKINGS, KIEV, AND ENGLAND

For both Western and Eastern Europe, the migration and raids of the Vikings (Danes, Norwegians, and Swedes) altered the political map during a long period from the mid-eighth to the early tenth century. The Scandinavian migrations had a profound effect throughout the northern part of Europe, including the founding of the Kievan Rus principality and the invasion of Anglo-Saxon England and Carolingian France.

The Vikings

Scandinavia's sparse farmland could not support the populations that developed there. Parts of the population had migrated out in the fourth century and joined the Germanic invasions of Europe. The ninth and tenth centuries saw a resurgence of out-migration. Contemporary sources called them Northmen or Vikings (a name applied to all Scandinavians in the eighth century); the East Slavs called them Verangians.

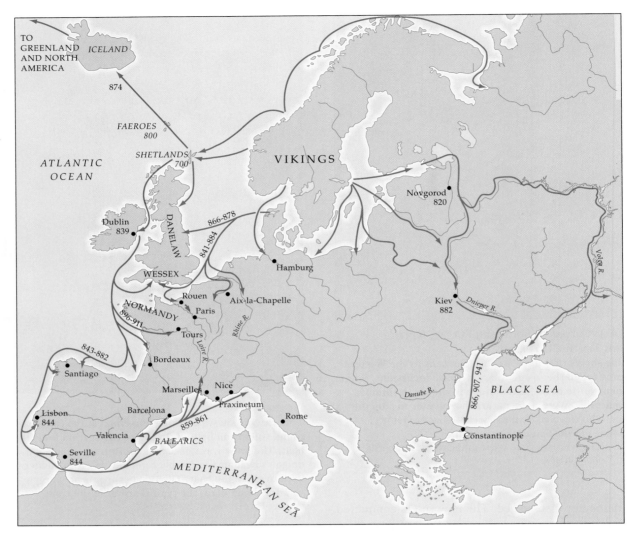

MAP 7.5 INVASIONS OF NORTHERN EUROPE, EIGHTH THROUGH NINTH CENTURIES
The Viking or Scandinavian invasions of the eighth through the ninth centuries were extensive and resulted in permanent settlements. The Vikings relied on their shallow draft boats for both trading and raiding permitting them to travel on both oceans and rivers. What areas did they explore and raid? What cities did they found (see dates on map)?
◆ For an online version, go to www.mhhe.com/chambers9 > chapter 7 > book maps

Viking Ships and Exploration One major factor in the migration of Northmen was their ships. These were shallow draft craft equally capable of traveling up rivers and on the high seas. A large square sail propelled the ship in winds and oarsmen propelled it in the calm. The ships were large enough to carry horses and provisions as well as men.

The ships permitted both exploration and trade. As skilled and versatile seamen, the Vikings' explorations took them as far as a western territory they called Vinland, undoubtedly part of the North American continent. Iceland, settled as a result of these explorations, became a major center of medieval Scandinavian culture. The Vikings were constantly at war with one another because there was no stable kingdom; a defeated chief, rather than becoming subservient his conqueror, often preferred to seek out new land overseas.

Eastern Expansion To the east the Vikings engaged in both trade and raiding. In about 830, Vikings from Scandinavia, known as the Rus, were invited to intervene in wars among the East Slavs. They staked out their own claims in Novgorod and Kiev, eventually establishing a principality composed largely of East Slavs (see more later in this chapter). The internal river systems of central Europe provided a conduit to Constantinople and the Black Sea. Some Vikings came to trade with Byzantium and Persia, but others made their wealth by hiring themselves out as mercenaries to the Byzantine emperor (see map 7.5).

JEWELRY OF VIKING HANDICRAFT AND PLUNDERED COINS
The Viking artisans were skilled at stone and wood carving as well as making fine jewelry. They used their own designs, which included serpents, animals, and plants intertwined. They also incorporated plundered objects, such as coins, directly into their designs.
© Universitetets Oldsaksamling, Oslo. Photo: Ove Holst/University Museum of National Antiquities, Oslo, Norway

Western Expansion   In England and on the continent, the Vikings appeared first as merchants and pirates, then as conquerors and colonists. Vikings, chiefly Danes, began raiding England in 787. One story tells of the attack on London: Unable to move up the Thames River because of London Bridge, the Vikings attached ropes to the pilings holding up the bridge and rowed downstream as the tide was going out; the pilings easily pulled out and the Vikings raided upstream. By 866 a Danish army landed in eastern England and established a permanent settlement. In Ireland and Scotland, Norwegians were the invaders and settlers. Dublin was a Norwegian settlement.

On the continent Danes began their attack along the western coast of France as early as 800, eventually penetrating far inland. Viking raiding parties even ventured around the Iberian Peninsula into the Mediterranean Sea and up the Rhône valley. In 911 the Viking Rollo secured from Charles the Simple, the king of France, the territory near the mouth of the Seine River, which became known as Normandy (from the name *Northmen*).

Conversion to Christianity   Christianity only gradually made inroads in Scandinavia. Some Vikings converted in order to carry on trade in Western Europe. In the middle of the ninth century, Anskar, a Dane trained in a Saxon monastery, made conversions in Denmark and southern Sweden, establishing churches and winning adherents among the nobility. The conversions, however, were often incomplete. Gravestones in the shape of a cross display carvings of the old gods as well. Burials continued to have grave goods (objects from daily life for use of the dead in afterlife), often with some Christian objects as well. Christianity did not have a strong enough hold to dissuade the Vikings from attacking and looting monasteries in England and France.

Treatment of Women   The violent nature of Scandinavian society suggests that women were treated roughly. Polygamy was normal and concubines common. Other evidence, however, indicates that women were esteemed and played the role of advisers in politics. Archaeology has also indicated the value placed on women. For instance, one ship burial at Oseberg in Sweden is that of a noblewoman who was fifty years old. Her grave contained another woman, perhaps a servant (thirty years old), several beds with quilts and cushions, a chair, two lamps, tapestries, and spinning and weaving implements.

Poetry and Sagas   The Edda are the legends of the Norse gods, telling their exploits and fights. They were recorded in the thirteenth century in both poetry and prose. According to the "Lay of Volund," warriors who died in battle joined the following of Odin in a great banquet hall, Valhalla. But the entire company of gods and heroes would be doomed to destruction by fire during a cosmic twilight when the ravaged earth would sink entirely into the sea. The myth became the basis for Richard Wagner's opera *Götterdammerung*.

The **sagas,** although written down in Iceland during the thirteenth century, are prose stories that actually cover the Viking period to about 1000, when Iceland converted to Christianity. The sagas are adventure stories recounting a fierce sense of bravery and violence on the part of both men and women. In the Eddic poems, Gudrun does not slay her brothers after they kill her husband, Sigurd, whereas in the *Gisla Saga* the widow has her brother killed after he kills her husband. *King Harald's Saga* recounts Harald's adventures traveling down the Eastern rivers to Constantinople and his exploits as a Verangian Guard (mercenary) in Constantinople. The saga describes his invasion of England in 1066 and his defeat.

The Kievan Rus Principality

The East Slavs invited the Vikings to aid them in their internal wars in the first half of the ninth century. The Vikings then became instrumental in establishing the

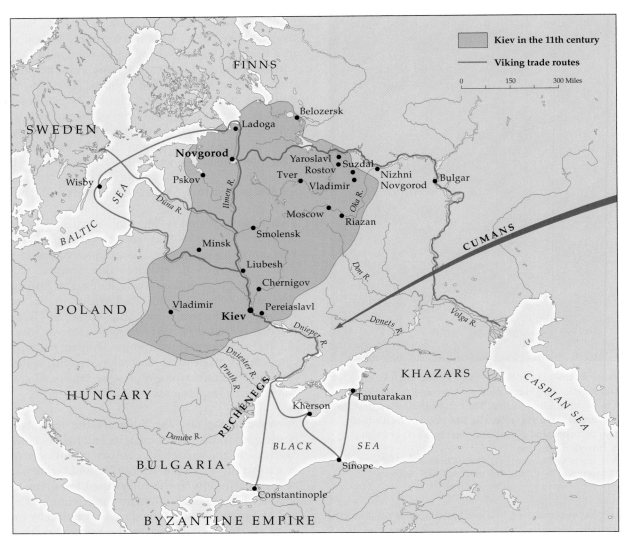

MAP 7.6 PRINCIPALITY OF KIEV
The East Slavs invited the Scandinavians, the Rus, to settle and unify them. The Scandinavians had traded extensively in the Black Sea. What were the trading routes that the Rus used? What were the capitals of the Kievan state?
◆ For an online version, go to www.mhhe.com/chambers9 > chapter 7 > book maps

first East Slavic state centered around Kiev on the Dnieper River and Novgorod on Lake Ilmen.

Origins   The *Primary Chronicle*, the most detailed and important source for the origin of the Rus state, recounts that the Rus (Vikings or Verangians) ruled Novgorod. Prince Oleg (r.ca. 873–913) united the two cities of Novgorod and Kiev under his rule. In 907 he led a fleet on a raid against Constantinople. The Byzantine emperor granted both tribute and trading concessions in order to purchase peace with the Rus.

In 988 the Kievan ruler, Vladimir, converted to the Eastern form of Christianity and imposed baptism on his subjects. As was so often the case, the influence of a woman was important in the conversion. In exchange

for military help in the defense of Byzantine territory, Vladimir demanded a Byzantine princess in marriage. The woman in question, Anna, sister of the emperor, would not marry Vladimir unless he converted to Christianity. He agreed, and she arrived with a group of missionaries. The missionaries translated the Bible and the liturgy by adapting the Cyrillic alphabet to East Slavic—the forerunner of modern Russian.

Reign of Yaroslav the Wise   The Principality of Kiev (see map 7.6) reached its height of power under Vladimir's son Yaroslav (r. 1015–1054). Yaroslav won self-government for the Rus Church from the patriarch of Constantinople in 1037, creating an independent bishop in Kiev.

YAROSLAV PRESENTING MODEL OF CHURCH
Although now destroyed, a group of eleventh-century frescoes in St. Sophia Cathedral in Kiev once depicted the family of Prince Yaroslav. This re-creation of the frescoes in a drawing by the seventeenth-century Dutch artist A. V. Westvelt shows Yaroslav presenting a model of a church to Prince Vladimir.
New York Public Library. Astor, Lenox, Tilden Foundations

During his reign Yaroslav issued the first written codification of East Slavic law, the *Russkaia Pravda.* He patronized church building, bringing in skilled Byzantine artisans to decorate them. The cathedral at Kiev was the masterpiece. Yaroslav, a writer himself, promoted learning in his principality and assembled many scribes to translate religious books from Greek into Slavic. Kiev kept close ties with Western Europe. Yaroslav's own daughter Anna married King Henry I of France. Charters with her signature survive, carefully inscribed with Cyrillic letters; she seems to have been the only layperson in the French court who could write.

Agriculture and Trade   Kiev was a leader in the agricultural revival of early medieval Europe, having been one of the designers of the heavier plow and among the first to use horse collars. Every year a great fleet of boats, led by the princes themselves, assembled at Kiev and floated down the Dnieper River to the Black Sea and across to Constantinople. There they exchanged amber, fur, honey, slaves, and wheat for silks, spices, and other luxuries of the East.

Kievan Cities   Trade supported the development of urban centers. Within the many towns, a wealthy aristocracy of princes, warriors, and great merchants rubbed shoulders with artisans, workers, and large numbers of destitute persons. Kiev in the eleventh century was one of the great cities of the age. A German chronicler, Thietmar of Merseburg, said it had 400 churches, 8 marketplaces, and unnumbered inhabitants. Kiev must have included 20,000 to 30,000 people—more people than any contemporary Western city.

Learning and Literature   The clergy established a formal educational system primarily to train the clergy; but their schools were open to the sons of ruling families. A number of women, too, were educated in convents. Birch bark letters discovered by archaeologists show that women could read and perhaps write. Their letters are about business and love.

The *Primary Chronicle,* the literary masterpiece of the age, recounts the conversion of the Rus to Christianity and their battles against the pagan peoples who surrounded them. The *Song of Igor's Campaign* represents poetry in a short heroic epic. It records an unsuccessful campaign that the Rus princes conducted in 1185 against the pagan Polovtsi people.

Art and Architecture   Christianity had an immense influence on architectural and artistic development. The East Slavs built many churches based on Byzantine models. The familiar "onion" domes of Russian churches, for example, were a late effort to imitate in wood the domes on ecclesiastical structures at Constantinople. The Kievan principality appreciated magnificence and splendor in its churches and liturgical services. It hired Byzantines to train its artisans and to decorate its churches with icons.

Decline of the Principality of Kiev   As was true of the Byzantines, Arabs, and Carolingians, both internal and external troubles destroyed the peace of the land

CHRONOLOGY
Chronological Chart

Byzantium	Islam	Frankish Empire	Vikings/England/Rus
Heraclius (r. 610–641)	Muhammad (d. 632)	Merovingians	
Defeat of Persia (622–629)	Hijra (622)		
Loss of Egypt, Syria to Arabs	First four caliphs (632–666)		Council of Whitby (664)
	Expansion into N. Africa		
Leo III (r. 717–741) Iconoclasm	Conquest of Visigoths Defeat at Tours (732)	Charles Martel (714–741)	Bede (d. 735)
Siege of Constantinople (718)			
Bulgarian wars	Umayyads in Córdoba	Pepin becomes king (741)	Viking invasions
	Harun al-Rashid (r. 786–809)	Charlemagne (r. 768–814)	
		Imperial coronation (800)	
		Louis the Pious (r. 814–840)	
Cyrillic alphabet	Disintegration of Arab Empire	Division of Empire (843)	Alfred of Wessex (r. 871–899)
			Yaroslav the Wise (r. 1015–1054)

after Yaroslav's death. Like the Carolingians, Yaroslav divided his territory among all male heirs. The result was frequent bickering and civil wars. These internal struggles left the people unable to resist the renewed menace of the steppe nomads. In 1061 the Cumans, a nomadic Turkish people, began harassing the frontier, and they eventually cut off Kiev from contact with the Black Sea. This sundering of the trade route to Constantinople was a disaster for commerce and culture because it deprived Kiev of contact with the Byzantine Empire and the Western world.

Anglo-Saxon England

The Viking attacks on England had begun in the late eighth century, and by 793 the famous centers of Anglo-Saxon learning, Lindisfarne and Jarrow, were looted and destroyed. The Vikings successfully established themselves in the north of England and were pushing south when they encountered King Alfred of Wessex (r. 871–899).

Alfred the Great   King Alfred, after experiencing military defeats by the Danes in the early years of his reign, reorganized the defense of the kingdom. He reformed the militia to keep a larger and more mobile army in the field and built fortresses to defend the land and ships to defend the coast. His reforms proved successful. Before 880 several Danish chiefs received baptism as part of a treaty with Alfred, and in 886 the Danes agreed to confine themselves to a region in the north and east of England. This region, which the Danes continued to dominate for several generations, was later known as the *Danelaw*, in recognition of the fact that the Danish laws in force there differed from the English laws of other parts of the country.

Intellectual Life   Anglo-Saxon England was perhaps the most literate country of Europe at the time. Schools and tutors educated upper-class boys and girls in Old English. There was an audience for poetry and prose.

Alfred renewed intellectual life in England. He gathered a group of scholars and began a program of translating into Anglo-Saxon the works of such writers as Bede, Gregory the Great, and Boethius. During his reign, an unknown author compiled a history of England known as the *Anglo-Saxon Chronicle.* Continued thereafter by various authors and now extant in several versions, the *Chronicle* is an indispensable source for the later Anglo-Saxon period in English history.

Summary

The period from the seventh to the beginning of the eleventh century included the rise of a new religion, Islam, and an Arab conquest of the southern Mediterranean and the Persian Empire; a revival of the Byzantine Empire; the rise of Kiev; prosperity in Anglo-Saxon England; and the Carolingian Empire. But all these empires and kingdoms had internal weaknesses that left them too disorganized to resist fresh invasions. The Arabs, Byzantines, and Kievans lost territory to Turkish tribes. In the West Vikings, Magyars, and Muslim pirates disrupted peace. The Vikings plundered and eventually settled in large parts of Ireland, England, and France. The Carolingian Empire split into French-speaking and German-speaking halves.

Islamic civilization became a conduit from east to west in terms of trade items, intellectual ideas, and technological innovation. Global exchange, not simply fragile empires, was part of the seventh through the eleventh centuries.

QUESTIONS FOR FURTHER THOUGHT

1. In both chapter 6 and chapter 7, one of the dominating themes was the migration of various peoples from northern and eastern Europe (Germanic tribes, Vikings, and Slavs), from Central Asia (Huns, Avars, Bulgarians), and from the Arabian peninsula. Why were these people on the move? Speculate on both the conditions that might stimulate movement and those that attracted them to the West.

2. We have seen in chapter 6 that, aside from some outstanding figures such as Boethius and Bede, intellectual life suffered in the West during the invasions. What brought about the flourishing of Arabic, Carolingian, Anglo-Saxon, and Russian learning during the subsequent centuries? What political conditions give rise to intellectual advances?

3. The decline and fall of empires continues to challenge historians to look for causes. In this chapter we have seen the Byzantine, Arabic, Carolingian, and Kievan Empires go into decline after a period of expansion, consolidation, and brilliance. What influence does the personality of the emperor or ruler have, and what influence do internal and external events have on the fate of empires? Compare these empires to the Roman one.

RECOMMENDED READING

Sources

*Dmytryshyn, Basil. *Medieval Russia: A Source Book, 850–1700.* 3rd ed. 1991. Primary sources for the period covered.

*Einhard. *The Life of Charlemagne.* 1962. Personal account by someone who lived in Charlemagne's court.

*Ibn, Khaldun. *The Muqaddimah: An Introduction to World History.* Franz Rosenthal (tr.). 1969. Reflections on societies and empires by a North African Muslim; written in the fourteenth century.

Zenkovsky, Serge A. (ed.). *Medieval Russia's Epics, Chronicles, and Tales.* 1974. Includes sermons and saints' lives.

Studies

Bulliet, Richard W. *The Case for Islamo-Christian Civilization.* 2004. Examines the common roots and history of Islam and Christianity.

Fine, John V. A. *The Early Medieval Balkans: A Critical Survey from the Sixth to the Late Twelfth Century.* 1983. The only work of its kind in English.

*Geanakoplos, Deno J. *Byzantine East and Latin West: Two Worlds of Christendom in the Middle Ages and Renaissance.* 1966. The Western debt to Byzantium.

Gregory, Timothy. *A History of Byzantium.* 2005.

Hussey J. M. *The Orthodox Church in the Byzantine Empire.* 1986. History of Orthodox Church in Byzantium.

Keddie, Nikki, and Beth Baron (eds.). *Women in Middle Eastern History: Shifting Boundaries in Sex and Gender.* 1991. Essays explaining the position of women in Islam.

Laiou, Angeliki E. *Gender, Society, and Economic Life in Byzantium.* 1992. A study of the lives of women, peasants, and more ordinary people in thirteenth- and fourteenth-century Byzantium.

*Lewis, Bernard (ed.). *Islam from the Prophet Muhammad to the Capture of Constantinople.* Vol. 1: *Politics and War.* Vol. 2: *Religion and Society.* 1987. Collected essays.

*Martin, Janet. *Medieval Russia, 980–1584.* 1995. Short history of medieval Russia that also covers recent interpretations.

*Riché, Pierre. *Daily Life in the World of Charlemagne.* Jo Ann McNamara (tr.). 1975. A very good read on the social and cultural history of the period.

Sawyer, P. H. *Kings and Vikings: Scandinavia and Europe A.D. 700–1100.* 1984. Excellent summary of recent research on the Vikings.

Stenton, Frank. *Anglo-Saxon England.* 1971. Basic introductory text.

Walther, Wiebke. *Women in Islam.* 1993.

*Available in paperback.

URBAN GROWTH IN THE TWELFTH CENTURY: MEDIEVAL BRUGES
The economic prosperity and population growth of the twelfth century permitted the development of urban centers of trade and commerce. Urban centers continued to prosper throughout the Middle Ages. They all had walls and defensive gates as well as town squares and houses reaching three stories. Some European cities, such as Bruges, preserve their medieval center to modern times. See map 8.4 for a plan of medieval Bruges.

© Charles & Josette Lenars/Corbis

Chapter Eight

RESTORATION OF AN ORDERED SOCIETY

ECONOMIC AND SOCIAL CHANGES • GOVERNMENTS OF EUROPE 1000–1150
THE REFORM OF THE WESTERN CHURCH • THE CRUSADES

The year 1000 was greeted at the time with anxiety. It was the first millennium since the birth of Jesus of Nazareth, and people thought that the end of the world was at hand. To historians looking back at the period from 1050 to 1200, however, the outlines of medieval society, government, culture, and the economy have become clear. Rudimentary castles, the origins of feudalism (a type of patron-client relationship between lords and vassals), and the economic and social arrangement of manors and serfs for agriculture began to organize the people and the countryside of Europe. The society that evolved in the Middle Ages was very hierarchical, with a small elite group of nobles and a large peasant population that supported it through agriculture. Rulers used feudal ties with the elite as a basis for establishing their governments and extending their power. The geographical and political boundaries of Europe formed during this period, and the rulers' governmental innovations laid the groundwork for late medieval states. With a restoration of order and an increase in agricultural productivity, trade once again prospered. Surpluses of grain supported an urban population, and towns once again grew in Europe. Reformed monasticism kindled the spark of popular piety that had begun in the tenth century. Taking advantage of the enthusiasm for religion and reform, the papacy underwent a period of major change and consolidation of power. Europeans began to look from the local scenes of their own estates and towns to the larger world. Through both warfare and long-distance trade, they expanded to the east into Slavic lands and into the eastern Mediterranean in a series of campaigns called the crusades. The period was one of global expansion for Europe.

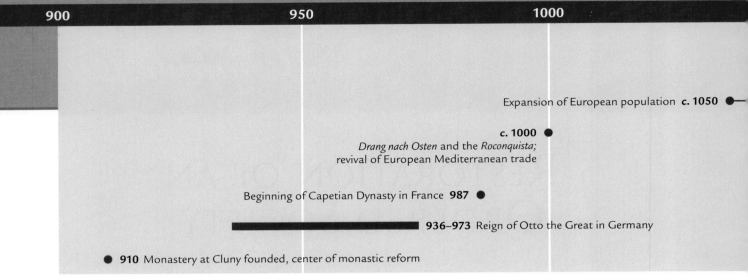

Expansion of European population **c. 1050** ●——

c. 1000 ●
Drang nach Osten and the *Roconquista;*
revival of European Mediterranean trade

Beginning of Capetian Dynasty in France **987** ●

936–973 Reign of Otto the Great in Germany

● **910** Monastery at Cluny founded, center of monastic reform

ECONOMIC AND SOCIAL CHANGES

Historians use shorthand terms to refer to the period's major changes. **Manorialism** refers both to the economic organization of agricultural production and to the organization of the lives and labor of peasants who did the actual cultivating. Approximately 90 percent of the population were peasants. **Feudalism** refers to approximately the top 5 percent of the population. Feudalism governed relationships of the lay and some clerical elite of society and consisted of a patron (lord) and clients (vassals). Some historians favor the historical interpretation of Karl Marx and use *feudalism* to refer to both the social and economic organization of the manor and the personal, military, and governmental role of feudalism. The other roughly 5 percent of the population was made up of clergy and urban dwellers.

Europe experienced a period of growth and prosperity that began in about 1050. A shift in weather to a warmer and dryer period, the release from the threat of external invasion, and the development of new agricultural practices discussed in chapter 6 all added to increased productivity. The new political order that feudalism began to offer brought at least a measure of peace and an expansion of trade. Economic and demographic growth led to a revival of cities and to internal and external colonization.

Feudalism

The new stability in Europe altered the power structures and lives of the warrior class. Material comforts, housing, gender relations, and even the nature of warfare changed. But perhaps the most important factor for understanding the European Middle Ages was that the power relationships of the nobility to each other and to the monarch became more personal and private rather than being based on citizenship as in the Roman Empire.

Definition Although historians debate the accuracy of using the term *feudalism* as shorthand for the personal bonds among the elite in the Middle Ages and the date of its origins, the term is still a useful one. In its restricted meaning, *feudalism* refers to a patron-client relationship between two freemen (men who are not serfs), a lord and his vassal. **Vassal** derived from a Celtic word for servant, but in feudal terms *vassal* meant a free person who put himself under the protection of a lord and for whom he rendered loyal military aid. In practice, both lord and vassal came from the upper echelons of society, lay and clerical. Feudal arrangements did not include the serfs and the poorer freemen.

Historians have traced the development of feudalism to both the patron-client arrangements in the Roman Empire and to the chief-warrior relationship (*comitatus*) among the Germanic tribes. During the Carolingian period, changes in warfare made equipping and training warriors more expensive. Few warriors could afford the horse and new body armor, so the Carolingians began granting land or other support to their warriors. Charlemagne imagined a pyramidal plan for recruiting an army, with the king at the top, followed by counts and dukes, and under them the warriors. This simple plan proved unfeasible, and it took until about 1300 to work out the nuances of feudal relations.

The Feudal Milieu To understand the growth of feudalism, we must first recall the chaotic conditions that marked the Viking invasion and the decline of the Carolingian Empire. In a milieu in which the kings could

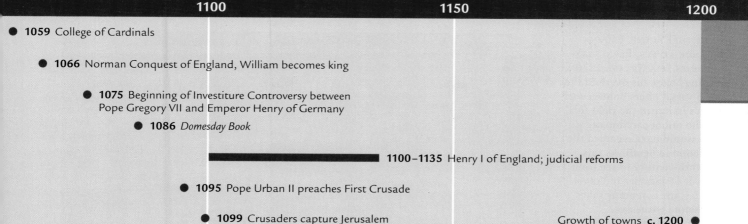

not protect their realm from raids and could not rein in local counts and freebooters, an individual sought the protection of a neighbor stronger than himself. If the neighbor accepted, the two men entered into a close, quasi-familial relationship. Like the bonds between father and son, the relationship between the strong "lord" and the weak freeman was initially more ethical and emotional than legally binding.

The true homeland of Western feudalism was the region between the Loire and Rhine rivers. The institutions that developed there were subsequently exported to England in the Norman Conquest and to southern Italy. Gradually, the organization of government and society in southern France, Spain, and the Kingdom of Jerusalem copied the feudal model. Many parts of Germany did not develop full feudalism because of the continued importance of free land tenure. The Celtic areas (Ireland, Scotland, Wales, Brittany) did not develop classical feudalism, because powerful clans traditionally extended such protection. Perhaps because of the early importance of towns in Northern Italy, the use of feudal ties was stunted but not suppressed.

Vassalage   Vassalage was an honorable personal bond between a lord and his man. An act of **homage** established the relationship. In this simple ceremony the prospective vassal placed his hands within those of his lord (sometimes they exchanged a kiss of peace) and swore to become his man. He might also swear **fealty** (swearing to be faithful to his oath of homage) on the Gospels or a saint's relic. The "joining of hands" was the central act in the ceremony of homage.

In its fully developed form, vassalage imposed obligations on both the vassal and his lord. The vassal owed his lord material and military aid and counsel (advice). He had to perform military service in the lord's army and usually had to bring additional men in numbers proportionate to the wealth he derived from his land (fief). As military aid became more precisely defined in the twelfth century, it was more a matter of contract than of emotional bonds. The contract could stipulate that the vassal serve, for example, forty days a year in a local war, less time if the lord intended to fight in foreign lands. The vassal could not refuse service, but if the lord asked for more than the customary time, the vassal could demand compensation or simply return home. The lord could demand other financial aids, such as paying the ransom if the lord was captured and paying for the ceremonies surrounding the knighting of his eldest son or the marriage of his eldest daughter.

The obligation of counsel required the vassal to give advice and to help the lord reach true judgments in legal cases that came before his court. Cases usually involved adjudication of disputes among the vassals and complaints brought by the lord against his men. By custom, only a jury of his peers, that is, his fellow vassals, could judge a vassal.

The lord, in turn, owed his vassal protection and maintenance (military and material support). He had to come to his vassal's aid when requested, repel invaders from his vassal's land, and help a vassal being sued in another's court.

Disloyalty on the part of the vassal, such as refusing military service, gave the lord the right to terminate the bonds of homage and take back any property that he had given to the vassal.

The Fief   The lord's concession of land and the serfs who cultivated it to his vassal was called a **fief** (rhymes with *leaf*). The granting of a fief superimposed on the personal relationship of vassalage a second relationship, one involving property.

217

INVESTITURE SCENE, FRESCO, FERRANDE TOWER, PERNES-LES-FONTAINES, FRANCE, CA. 1270 **Kneeling before his overlord the king, a vassal offers homage and receives in return the right to a fief—the roll of parchment, which would have recorded the transaction in detail. As this thirteenth-century fresco from Pernes-les-Fontaines in France indicates, the ceremony takes place before witnesses.** Giraudon/Art Resource, NY

The lord granted the fief to his vassal (usually immediately following the act of homage). As a symbol of the land the vassal was receiving, the lord gave to his vassal a clod of earth or sprig of leaves. In a strict juridical sense the fief was a conditional, temporary, and non-hereditary grant of land or other income-producing property, such as an office, toll, or rent. At the vassal's death, disability, or refusal to serve his lord, the fief at once returned to the lord who granted it.

Although technically not inheritable, the fief gradually became hereditary. From the start, lords had found it convenient to grant a fief to the adult son of a deceased vassal, because the son could at once serve in his father's stead. The son had to make a special payment to the lord (the relief) to acquire the fief.

Women and Minors

Because women and young sons of vassals could not perform military service, their right to inherit initially was not guaranteed. But the advantages of orderly succession to valuable property led lords to recognize the right of a minor son to inherit. The lord retained the right of wardship, taking the heir and his property back into his hands or granting them to another noble until the heir reached the age of twenty-one.

Only reluctantly did feudal practice permit daughters to inherit a fief. Nevertheless, in most areas of Europe women could inherit. Their lord had the right to select their husbands for them, because their spouses assumed the obligations of service connected to the fief.

Subinfeudation

Initially, vassals were forbidden to sell the fief, grant it to the Church, or otherwise transfer it in whole or in part. Vassals, however, commonly sold or granted portions of their fiefs, but only with the lord's permission and usually accompanied by a money payment.

When lords regranted portions of their fiefs to other vassals, the process was called subinfeudation. Subinfeudation complicated the hierarchy that Charlemagne had initially envisioned. Subinfeudation permitted vassals to have their own vassals. A vassal could acquire fiefs from several different lords, swearing homage and fealty to each. In case of conflict among his different lords, whom should he serve? To escape this dilemma, feudal custom required that the vassal select one of his lords as his liege lord, that is, the one whom he would serve against all others.

Castles

With the later invasions and breakdown of Carolingian government, those lords who could afford it invested in defensive fortress-homes, or castles. Initially these castles were a motte, a wooden tower built on a hill with an external courtyard, the bailey, surrounded by a wooden palisade. A castle-holder could offer weaker neighbors a place to shelter their animals and families in the event of attack. By the eleventh and twelfth centuries, castles became more elaborate, with thick stone walls for the tower and larger stone-walled courtyards that contained outbuildings such as stables, kitchens, and gardens. The moat, the ditch surrounding

THE TERMINOLOGY OF FEUDALISM AND MANORIALISM

FEUDALISM

An economic, political, and social organization of medieval Europe. Land was held by vassals from more powerful overlords in exchange for military and other services.

Vassal   A free warrior who places himself under a lord, accepting the terms of loyal service, fighting in time of war, and counsel in time of peace. As the system developed, women and minor sons also could become vassals, as could members of the clergy.

Aid   Aid was the military service that the vassal owed the lord.

Fief (sometimes called benefice)   Land given to a vassal from his lord in exchange for specified terms of service. A ceremonial presentation of a sheaf of grain often accompanied the grant of land.

Homage   An oath sworn by the vassal to the lord, acknowledging allegiance to the lord. The vassal took his oath by placing his hands within the hands of the lord.

Fealty   An oath, often accompanying the oath of homage, in which the vassal swears to uphold his homage. This oath was sworn on the Gospels or on a saint's relics.

Relief   An inheritance tax on the vassal at his death when the fief passed to his heir.

Subinfeudation   The grant of a fief by a vassal to a subordinate who becomes his vassal.

Liege Lord   That lord whom the vassal must serve even if he has conflicting oaths with subinfeudation.

MANORIALISM

An agricultural, legal, and social organization of land, including a nucleated village, large fields for agriculture, and serfs to work the land. The land and its inhabitants were called a manor and both belonged to the lord.

Manor   An estate held by the lord that included land, the people on the land, and a village, usually with a mill. A fief might contain a number of manors or sometimes just a part of one.

Open Fields   The agricultural area was divided up into three large fields (500 acres or more). The lord held land for his direct profit in these, and the serfs rented strips of land in all three fields for their profit and to pay their rent.

Manorial Court   The lord had the right to administer justice on his manor in order to regulate services and rents owed to him. Peasants also used manorial court for their own business and to keep peace within their village.

Serf or Villein   Peasant who was personally free, but bound to the lord of the manor and the land of the manor. Serfs rented land from the lord to cultivate to produce their own crops. In addition, they owed work for the lord and various gifts of produce.

Week Work   Work that the peasant owed to the lord every week.

Boon Work   Work that the peasant owed to the lord for special tasks such as plowing or harvesting.

Demesne Land   Land that the lord held for his own crops and profit. Serfs worked this land.

Glebe Land   Land held by the parish priest.

---

castles and sometimes filled with water, added to the defense. Castles were built throughout Europe and can still be seen today. The pace of castle building was rapid. In Florence and its surrounding countryside in Italy, for example, only two castles are mentioned in the sources before 900, 11 before 1000, 52 before 1050, 130 before 1100, and 205 before 1200.

Life of the Nobility

Feudalism brought many changes to the elite's family arrangements, housing, fighting, and leisure activities. To proclaim their identity and distinctiveness from the rest of society, the nobles adopted family names, which usually recalled the name of the revered founder or of the ancestral castle. Other symbols also denoted elite

status—coats of arms, mottoes, fanciful genealogies, and castles.

Noble Families   The appearance of a hereditary nobility in the eleventh and twelfth centuries reflected a fundamental change in the structure of the elite families. Abandoning the older system of partible inheritance among all sons, the custom came to be that the firstborn son would inherit the fief (primogeniture). If there were no sons, daughters inherited and the fief was divided equally among them.

Primogeniture had the advantage of keeping the estates intact, but it had implications for the younger sons and for the daughters. The great families provided their daughters with dowries but otherwise excluded them from a full share in the inheritance. Anxious to

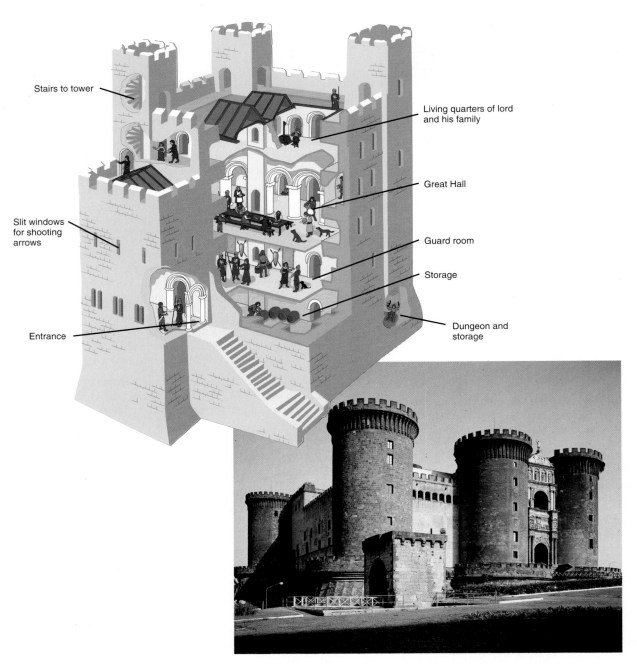

Stairs to tower

Living quarters of lord
and his family

Great Hall

Slit windows
for shooting
arrows

Guard room

Storage

Entrance

Dungeon and
storage

CASTEL NUOVO (NEW CASTLE), THIRTEENTH CENTURY, WITH TRIUMPHAL ARCH, NAPLES, CAMPANIA, ITALY
Castles developed from mounds of earth with a stockade on top. A major development in the twelfth century was the elaborate square keep shown in the diagram above. The keep included areas for storage of large quantities of food in the event of siege, a guard room, the great hall where meals were served and the guard slept, and finally, on the top, quarters for the family. Square keeps were vulnerable to attack so round towers were developed to protect the corners of the castle as seen in the photograph.
Dagli Orti/The Art Archive

attract a suitable husband for a daughter and settle her future early, noble fathers offered a large dowry. Unmarried daughters usually became nuns. Younger sons had no lands unless they could win them in war or marry an affluent heiress. Unattached young warriors abounded. Some entered the Church and rose to high offices. Others drifted from court to court as warriors for hire. Some found new opportunities in the aggressive expansion of Europe in Spain, eastern Europe, and the Holy Land.

A MEDIEVAL KNIGHT IN ARMOR The knight is fully armed with chain mail on his arms and steel plates on his shoulders and legs. He is equipped with spurs and a sword, and he is wearing a leather cap. His wife holds up his helmet and lance, and a daughter or court lady holds his shield. The surcoat he wears, the horse cover, and the shield represent his coat of arms. The illustration is from the fourteenth-century English *Lutteral Psalter.*
The British Library, London. Add. 42130. folio 202v

Tancred de Hauteville's Sons Among such aggressive young nobles were the sons of Tancred de Hauteville, a minor Norman vassal. Three of the brothers—William Iron-Arm, Humphrey, and Drogo—sought their fortunes as warriors, sometimes acting as mercenaries and sometimes as brigands. On their way to pilgrimage in Jerusalem, they found that Sicily and southern Italy were fine places to practice their skills of warfare. The Arab and Greek factions, who were fighting each other, were both willing to hire mercenaries. Soon the Hauteville brothers were carving out their own estates rather than working for the local rulers. William's half-brother, Robert Guiscard ("the Sly" or "the Fox") managed to conquer southern Italy and receive papal recognition for the territory. Robert's brother, Roger, captured Sicily and held it with papal approval in 1072. The brothers established a Norman Kingdom in these two areas.

Knights and Armor Improvements in fighting equipment meant that a long period of training was necessary to become a skilled warrior.

A warrior cult that grew up surrounding the training was transformed into knighthood. Young sons of the elite started at an early age to learn to ride and use the weapons of war. Vassals might send their sons to the lord's household at age seven or eight to act as pages,

becoming squires in their teenage years. Twenty-one was the age of majority and was usually accompanied by knighthood, which gave the person the honorific title of "sir." Knights had to be skilled in arms, brave, loyal to a leader, and conventionally pious.

Song of Roland The heroic poems, or *chansons de geste,* of the eleventh and twelfth centuries underscore the values fostered by knighthood and the lord-vassal relationship. The best known of these poems is *The Song of Roland,* which was probably composed in the last quarter of the eleventh century. The subject of the poem is the ambush of the rear guard of Charlemagne's army under the command of Roland by the Basques at Roncesvalles in 778, but poetic imagination (or perhaps older legend) transformed this minor Frankish setback into a major event in the war against Islam.

With fine psychological discernment, the poem examines the character of Roland. The qualities that make him a heroic knight—his dauntless courage and uncompromising pride—are at war with the qualities required of a good vassal—obedience, loyalty, cooperation, and common sense. Although most of his army is dead, Roland is too proud to summon Charlemagne to his aid. His pride leads to his downfall and the loss of an army.

MAKING COATS OF CHAIN MAIL
This depiction of a craftsman making chain mail suggests the high skills and hard labor that were needed to bend the metal into elaborate shapes. Armor made of chain mail allowed the knight far greater freedom of movement, but it could be penetrated by the sharp thrust of a sword or arrow.
Stadtbibliothek Nürnberg (Ms.) Amb. 317.2°, f. 10r

Noblewomen While the young sons in a noble family were being trained for the battlefield, their sisters were taught to live in or travel between castles. The fathers, if still alive—and if not then the lord—arranged the marriages of these young women to men they might never have seen and who might have been much older or younger than themselves. Even as widows, these women's lord could arrange for their remarriage. Noblewomen's marriages cemented alliances, transferred property, and produced heirs.

During periods of internal warfare in Europe and the Crusades, husband and wife often were separated for long periods of time. Noblewomen were called upon to administer the fief in their husbands' absence or to defend castles against siege.

Noblewomen were often knowledgeable in herbal cures, and they could care for the sick and wounded in their households. They spun wool and flax. The elaborate embroideries for church vestments, wall and bed hangings, and personal adornment were often the work of noblewomen and their servants. Leisure activities included music, games, feasts, and stories.

Not all women who were married wanted to be; some would have preferred to become nuns. Christina of Markyate, daughter of a well-to-do family in England (d. after 1155), was forced into marriage by her parents but refused to consummate it. Her mother beat her and pulled her hair, and her father stripped her and threatened to force her out of the house. She fled and finally became a nun. Some young women whose families forced them into nunneries were as miserable as those women forced into marriage. For a pious woman with a calling for monastic life, a nunnery offered an environment with educational opportunities, training in skilled crafts, and even the opportunity to administer nunnery property.

Manorialism

Medieval Europe had a mix of cultivation strategies. Some areas were farmed by free peasants (those who owned their own land) who mixed cultivation with fishing or herding. Most of the grain, however, came from large manors with **serfs** (*villeins* was a term used in England and France) or unfree peasants working the land. As described in chapter 6, the major tool of agriculture was the heavy-wheeled plow with oxen or horses to draw it.

The **manor,** a community of serfs living under the authority of a lord, was a fundamental unit of economic, judicial, and social organization during the Middle Ages. The lord or his appointed officials regulated cultivation of the land as well as the rents, labor services, and fines that the peasants owed to the lord in return for the land they cultivated for themselves. Manors were characteristic of much of England, northern France, western Germany, and certain areas of the south, such as the Rhône and Po valleys. These areas were regions of fertile soil in which grains were cultivated intensively.

Division of Land The lands of most manors were divided into two or three **open fields** (see map 8.1). Within these fields, the land was further divided into strips for cultivation. The lord owned all the land, but he rented strips of land in all three fields to the peasants, who also had a house and garden area. A peasant's strips were not contiguous, but were scattered in each of the three fields. The strips and housing plots were protected by custom, and the right to rent them was passed on through inheritance. Peasants did not have equal holdings; some might have as many as thirty acres and others as little as two acres. These pieces of land formed the peasants' own farms to support their families and pay their rent.

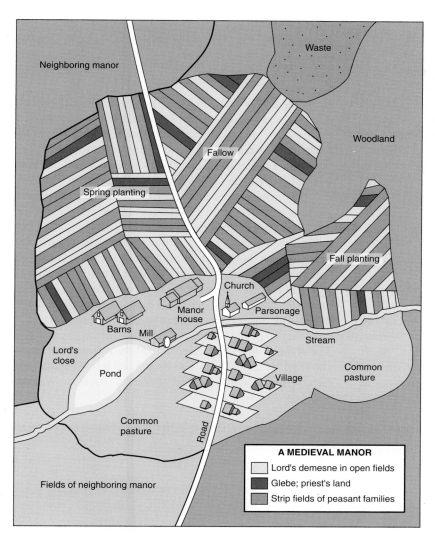

MAP 8.1 IDEALIZED DIAGRAM OF MEDIEVAL MANOR
This is an idealized diagram of a medieval manor showing the location of the village and the open fields surrounding it. Look up the three-field system discussed in chapter 6. Describe how it worked. Identify the peasants' strips and those belonging to the priest and lord.
◆ For an online version, go to www.mhhe.com/chambers9 > chapter 8 > book maps

Interspersed with the peasants' land was the **demesne** (rhymes with reign) **land,** or land that the lord reserved for his own use and that the peasants cultivated for him. In addition, a manor might have land reserved for the parish priest, called **glebe land,** which the priest either worked himself or hired laborers to work for him.

Many manors had extensive meadows, forests, and wastelands, where the lord hunted and the peasants grazed their animals, collected firewood, and procured timber for their houses. Peasants paid fees to use the forests and wastelands that were part of the lord's demesne. Peasants often had their own common, a collectively owned meadow in which each resident had the right to graze a fixed number of animals. Peasants who had too little land to support themselves worked as agricultural laborers or had an additional occupation on the manor such as blacksmith, carpenter, or baker.

The Lord's Control   The lord's control over his serfs was considerable. Serfs and their children were not chattel property, as were slaves, but they could not leave the manor without the lord's permission. The lord or his steward ran the manorial court, which was a way of regulating the serfs and an important source of profit from the manor. Peasants who did not pay their rent, who trespassed on the lord's property, or who otherwise broke the manorial rules paid fines in the court. The lord charged peasants for the use of his mill and winepress and required them to buy salt or iron from him. For many peasants, the manorial lord was the only government they ever directly confronted. Peasants paid to use the manorial court to settle their own disputes and to have a record kept of these transactions. The court also regulated and punished disturbances of the peace among villagers, including assaults, petty thefts, and trespass.

Serfdom   Most of the peasants inhabiting the manor were serfs. They had to work for the lord a set number of days a week and at intense periods of harvest and planting. Men were usually obliged to work three days a week on the lord's land, a service called week work. The additional service at planting and harvest was called boon work. The serfs also paid a yearly monetary rent on their land. Lords received mandatory gifts at holidays, such as eggs at Easter or a chicken at Christmas—the origins of our holiday eating traditions. When a serf died and his farm passed to his son, or to a daughter if there were no sons, the family paid the lord an inheritance tax, either the best animal or money.

Manors had free peasants as well. Freedom did not bring a substantially better standard of living, but it meant that the free peasant could leave the manor.

Peasant Life

While the life of the serf was one filled with heavy labor, the position had some security and advantages. Because serfs had a customary right to their land, they and their children could profit from the improvements they made on it. Moreover, the serfs' obligations and rents were traditional and fixed and could not be raised from year to year. Thus, in periods of economic prosperity, their rents remained fixed so that their profits increased.

Housing and Food   Peasant housing varied from region to region. Where stone was plentiful, peasants built stone houses. Other places had more rudimentary housing that resembled an A-frame of beams with the wall areas filled in with woven branches and covered with clay. Whatever the living arrangements, housing for the animals was connected to human housing, in part for warmth and in part because animals were the peasants' most valuable possessions.

Peasants largely ate a grain diet, with the addition of eggs, cheese, beans, and some meat for protein. Bread was made of a rough whole wheat or rye or a mixture of grains. Oats, peas, and beans were made into a gruel. For their ordinary drink, peasants made wine or beer, depending on the part of Europe in which they lived.

Sex Roles   Sex roles were strongly differentiated on the manors. Men did the plowing and heavy fieldwork, cutting of firewood, carting, and construction. Women

The peasant house contained one or two rooms with a fire in the center of the room in the early Middle Ages, or in a fireplace at the side of the room by the late Middle Ages, as this illustration indicates. Stables were attached to the houses to protect the livestock, which were the peasants' most valuable possessions. Pegs and poles held clothing. Furniture was sparse. The beehives lining the fence in the garden area provided honey, the only sweetener available to peasants. Grain was valuable; in this picture a stone tower protects the grain.
Giraudon/Art Resource, NY

tended the domestic animals, milking them, making butter and cheese, and collecting eggs. Women raised the children, did the brewing, cooked the simple meals, and made thread from wool and flax. They also spun rough cloth.

It would be a mistake to assume that peasant households were like American pioneer households, in which most things were made at home. In the eleventh century even peasants had access to a market economy, selling their surplus grain and animals and buying ready-made goods in market towns. Clothing, metal pots, fine ceramics, animals, and luxury items were all bought at markets. Markets stimulated the growth of cottage industries, especially in the vicinity of towns.

Popular Culture Popular entertainment included singing and dancing, wrestling and archery contests, and various ball games. The peasant year, although filled with labor, was punctuated by festivals. Christmas celebrations lasted for twelve days, Mayday was a time for singing contests and maypoles, and Midsummer Eve was celebrated with bonfires.

Expansion of Europe

Europe's population in the Early Middle Ages, to about the year 1050, was small and was not distributed evenly across the countryside. The end of invasions, the relative stability that feudalism was bringing to government, the increased agricultural productivity, and new economic opportunities encouraged growth in family size. For the first time since the fall of the west-ern Roman Empire, Europe experienced a sustained and substantial population growth. Europe became too densely populated for its existing cultivated land and began to expand both internally and externally.

Internal Colonization In England, France, and Germany, the peasants cleared forests and drained marshes to expand agricultural space; in the Low Countries, they began building dikes and draining marshes by the sea. Lords were willing to offer freedom from labor services and/or rents to encourage peasants who would take up new land. This internal colonization can be seen in place names that indicate the home village, such as Great Horewood and the new settlement of Little Horewood. Other new settlements carry names such as Newcastle or Villenova (new town).

Conquest of Frontiers German nobles pushed east-ward beyond the former borders of the Frankish Empire (see map 8.2) into territories that were thinly inhabited by Slavs, Prussians, Letts, and Lithuanians. Some Germans settled just beyond the Elbe River and established the Principality of Brandenburg. Other Germans advanced along the shores of the Baltic Sea at the same time that Swedes began to move across Finland. The Russian prince of Novgorod, Alexander Nevsky, defeated the Swedes on the Neva River close to the Baltic Sea in 1240 and repulsed the Germans in another victory in 1242. Although these defeats halted further advances in northeastern Europe, the Germans and Swedes retained control of the shores of the Baltic Sea. The Germans had by then pushed through the middle

PEASANT WOMEN'S WORK
Women's work included a number of cottage crafts in addition to rearing children and helping out in the fields during harvest. Women did shearing, washing, and spinning of wool thread. They also wove rough cloth of both wool and linen.
Trinity College Library, Cambridge

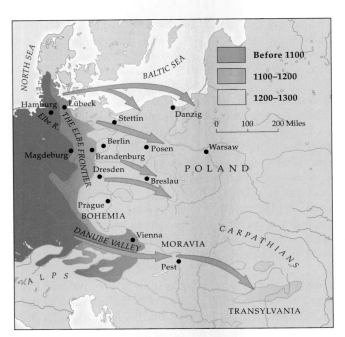

MAP 8.2 GERMAN MIGRATION EASTWARD
The *drang nach Osten* or German migration to the east settled western Europeans in the sparsely settled Slavic lands in the East. What was the period of migration and where did the emigrants come from? What states and cities did they establish that still exist?
◆ For an online version, go to www.mhhe.com/chambers9 > chapter 8 > book maps

Danube valley and founded another principality: Austria. Offering land and low rents, the nobles advertised in the West for peasants to migrate and settle the newly opened territories. By the early fifteenth century the *drang nach Osten* ("drive to the east") had clearly spent its strength, but it had tripled the area of German settlement over what it had been in Carolingian times (see map 8.2).

Settlers also moved into the Iberian Peninsula (present-day Spain and Portugal). In the mid-eleventh century the Christian kings, whose kingdoms were confined to the extreme north of the peninsula, began an offensive against the Muslims, who ruled most of Iberia. The Christians pushed south over two centuries until they held most of the peninsula. By 1275 only the emirate of Granada remained under Muslim rule. The Christian kings actively recruited Christian settlers for the territories they reconquered and gave them land under favorable terms. The reconquest and resettlement of the peninsula, known as the *Reconquista,* proved lasting achievements; the Iberian frontier remained almost unchanged for the next 280 years, during which time Castile, Aragon, Portugal, and other states developed and flourished.

In Italy the Hauteville brothers, as we have seen, succeeded in defeating the Muslims and Byzantines in southern Italy and Sicily and united the two regions into the Kingdom of Naples and Sicily. This victory opened new areas for European settlement.

European power swept over the sea as well as the land. The leaders were the maritime cities of Venice, Pisa, and Genoa. In 1015 and 1016 fleets from Pisa and Genoa freed Sardinia from Islamic rule.

Commercial Expansion

The European economy remained predominantly agricultural, although trade and manufacture revived. Most of the trade was local, between rural areas or between city and countryside, but a dramatic rebirth of long-distance trade also took place. Three trading zones developed, based on the Mediterranean Sea in the south, the Baltic Sea in the north, and the overland routes that linked the two seas (see map 8.3).

Mediterranean Trade   Venice, Pisa, and Genoa led this commercial expansion. In 998 and again in 1082 the Venetians received from the Byzantine emperors charters that gave them complete freedom of Byzantine waters. In the twelfth century Pisans and Genoese negotiated formal treaties with Islamic rulers that allowed them to establish commercial colonies in the Middle East and North Africa. Marseilles and Barcelona soon began to participate in the profitable Eastern trade.

In this Mediterranean exchange, the East shipped condiments, medicines, perfumes, dyes, paper, ivories, porcelain, pearls, precious stones, and rare metals such as mercury—all of which were known in the West under the generic name of *spices.* Eastern traders also sent a variety of fine linens and cottons (damask, muslin, organdy) as well as brocades and silks. Western North Africa supplied animal skins, leather, cheese, ivory, and gold. Europe shipped wood and iron and products made from them (including entire ships), as well as grain, wine, and other agricultural commodities. By the year 1200 manufactured goods, especially woolen cloth woven in Flanders and finished in Italy, began to play an increasingly important role in the Mediterranean exchange. This cloth gave European merchants a product valued in the Eastern markets; with it they were able not only to pay for Eastern imports but also to generate a flow of precious metals into Europe.

Baltic and Northern Trade   Trade in northern Europe among the lands bordering the Baltic Sea linked the great ports of London, Bruges, Bergen, Cologne, Lübeck, and Novgorod with the many smaller maritime towns. The eastern Baltic regions sold grain, lumber and forest products, amber, and furs. Scandinavia supplied wood and fish. England provided raw wool and grains. Flanders, the great industrial area of the north, imported food stuffs and wool to support its cloth industry.

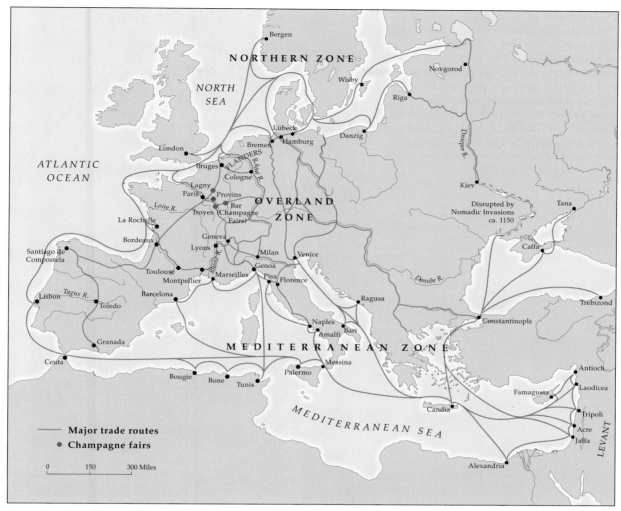

MAP 8.3 MEDIEVAL TRADE ROUTES
European merchants greatly expanded their trade within Europe and to the south and the east in the twelfth and thirteenth centuries. This map shows the numerous trade routes that they used to exchange goods. Where were the major trade fairs held? Who were the major trading partners of London, Paris, Milan, Venice, Naples, and Constantinople?

◆ For an online version, go to www.mhhe.com/chambers9 > chapter 8 > book maps

Overland Trade   The northern and Mediterranean trading zones were joined by numerous overland routes. After 1100 the most active exchange between north and south was concentrated at six great fairs, held at various times of the year in the province of Champagne in France. Trade included local products, but the fairs' chief importance was as redistribution points for luxury goods. The fairs guaranteed the merchants personal security, low tariffs, fair monetary exchange, and quick and impartial justice.

Milan became a center for overland trade that funneled the luxury goods from the Mediterranean trade to the north into Germany and products from that region back to Venice, Genoa, and Pisa.

Rebirth of Urban Life

Although the towns in Western Europe were increasing in size and social complexity, their growth was slow even in this age of economic expansion. Before 1200 probably no town in Western Europe included more than 30,000 inhabitants. These small towns, however, were assuming new functions.

In theEarly Middle Ages the towns had been chiefly administrative centers, serving as the residence of bishops—or, much more rarely, of counts—and as fortified enclosures to which the surrounding rural population fled when under attack. (The original sense of the English word *borough* and of the German word

MAP 8.4 THE GROWTH OF MEDIEVAL BRUGES
Bruges (in modern Belgium) presents a fine example of the topographical dualism of many commercial towns of northern Europe. This map shows that the town grew from two centers: the central fortress (A) and the merchants' settlement (B), gradually absorbing surrounding parishes and villages. Identify the various stages of urban development. Note that the town walls indicate the expansion of the city. What classes of people lived in cities?
◆ For an online version, go to www.mhhe.com/ chambers9 > chapter 8 > book maps

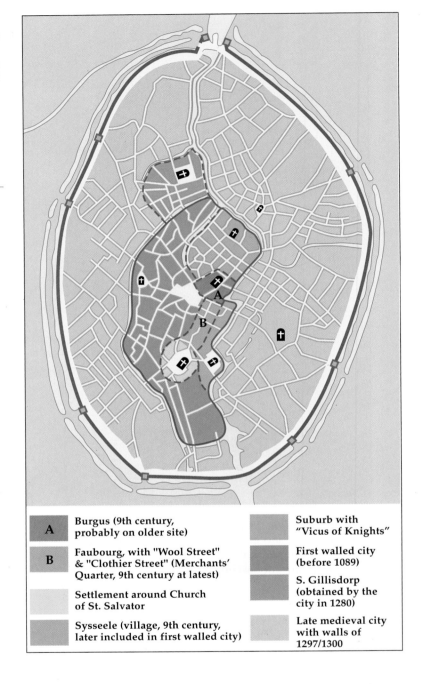

A	Burgus (9th century, probably on older site)		Suburb with "Vicus of Knights"
B	Faubourg, with "Wool Street" & "Clothier Street" (Merchants' Quarter, 9th century at latest)		First walled city (before 1089)
	Settlement around Church of St. Salvator		S. Gillisdorp (obtained by the city in 1280)
	Sysseele (village, 9th century, later included in first walled city)		Late medieval city with walls of 1297/1300

Burg is "fortress.") As the revival of trade made many of these towns centers of local or international exchange, permanent colonies of merchants grew up around the older fortresses. These merchant quarters were sometimes called a *faubourg* ("outside the fortress") or suburb (*sub urbis*) (see map 8.4).

Urban Society Urban social organization was hierarchical, as was the rest of medieval society. At the top was a small elite group, usually referred to as *patricians*.

In Italy the elite included nobles, merchants engaged in long-distance trade, and great landlords from the countryside, who lived for part or all of the year in the towns. In contrast, in northern Europe the nobles and great landlords tended to keep to their rural estates. The powerful urban families in the north came chiefly from common origins, and most of them had founded their fortunes on commerce or the management of urban property. The most distinctive feature of urban society was the opportunity for vertical social mobility.

A TWELFTH-CENTURY DESCRIPTION OF LONDON

William Fitz Stephen introduced his biography of Thomas Beckett (written in 1183) with a description of his beloved city of London. He describes a busy commercial town with vendors of food catering to those on limited budgets as well as to nobles. Prepared food is available to take home or eat at a tavern. Peasants participate in the market economy by bringing livestock and other wares.

". . . there is in London upon the river's bank, amid the wine that is sold from ships and wine-cellars, a public cook shop. There daily, according to the season, you may find viands, dishes roast, fried and boiled, fish great and small, coarser flesh for the poor, the more delicate for the rich, such as venison and birds both big and little. If friends, weary with travel, should of a sudden come to any of the citizens, and it is not their pleasure to wait fasting till fresh food is bought and cooked and 'till servants bring water for hands and bread,' they hasten to the river bank, and there all things desirable are ready to their hand. However great the infinitude of knights or foreigners that enter the city or are about to leave it, at whatever hour of night or day, that the former may not fast too long nor the latter depart without their dinner, they turn aside thither . . . and refresh themselves. . . .

"In another place apart stand the wares of the country-folk, instruments of agriculture, long-flanked swine, cows with swollen udders and [sheep] 'woolly flocks.' Mares stand there, meet for plows, sledges and two-horsed carts."

From William Fitz Stephen, *Norman London*, Italica Press, pp. 52, 54.

Below the patricians were shopkeepers and artisans. While the patricians had a single guild (from *gegyld*, "association") in most towns before 1200, after that date guilds multiplied, showing an ever greater diversification in the commercial enterprises of the mercantile classes. Goldsmiths (also bankers), spice merchants, and those importing such items as salt fish and cloth, formed guilds. Artisans and less prominent merchants organized trade guilds to regulate their crafts, such as those of the shoemakers, bakers, saddlers, fishmongers, and so on. As urban economies developed in the thirteenth century, some industries, such as cloth making, became prominent and supported a number of skilled laborers.

Urban Life   The urban milieu provided entirely different living conditions than did that of the castle or the manor. The houses were close together and faced streets that could be narrow and smelly, because they served for general rubbish disposal. The houses were two to three or four stories high. The area behind the house might contain a garden, a courtyard, and work space. In some towns the house completely surrounded the courtyard. Patricians had full houses to themselves, but many people rented portions of houses for business and suites of rooms for residences. The poorer people rented one room on the upper floors or even shared the rent for such spaces.

Rather than growing their own food, urban dwellers relied on the surrounding countryside to provide their sustenance. The diet of urban residents varied very much by the wealth of the inhabitant, but an idea of the variety of foods available can be seen in William Fitz Stephen's description of London (see "A Twelfth-Century Description of London," above).

Medieval cities were not the anonymous places that cities are now. Rich and poor lived side by side, often in the same house. The parish church served a very local population. London, for instance, had 104 churches for a city that included only a square mile of space within its walls.

Urban centers provided a rich variety of entertainment. Church feast days, civic celebrations, and visits of lords were all events calling for parades. Traveling entertainers—such as tumblers, animal trainers with their performing animals, players, and jugglers—offered diversion.

GOVERNMENTS OF EUROPE 1000–1150

The expansion of Europe, growth of towns, increased prosperity, and framework of feudalism permitted larger governmental units, including monarchies, principalities, and a strengthened papacy (see map 9.3 for political developments and boundaries).

Norman England

We could use the history of any one of several principalities to illustrate the political reorganization characteristic of the new monarchies, but England offers the best example of feudal concepts in the service of princes. The growth of feudalism in England was intimately connected with the Norman Conquest of 1066, so we can look at feudalism as a system of government imposed on England by William the Conqueror.

The Norman Conquest   Duke William of Normandy (1026–1087), the architect of the Conquest, is the epitome of the ambitious, energetic, and resourceful prince of the central Middle Ages. A bastard who had to fight 12 years to make good his claim over the Norman duchy, William early set his ambitions on the English crown. His claims were respectable, but not compelling. He was the first cousin of the last Saxon king, the childless Edward the Confessor, who allegedly had promised to make William heir to the throne. But the Witan, the English royal council, supported the claim of the Saxon Harold Godwinson.

Edward died in 1066. William immediately recruited an army of vassals and adventurers to support his claim to the throne, but unfavorable winds kept his fleet bottled up in the Norman ports for six weeks. Meanwhile, Harold Hardrada, king of Norway, who also disputed Harold Godwinson's claim, invaded England with a Viking army. The Saxons defeated his force near York on September 28, 1066. That same day, the channel winds shifted and William landed in England. Harold Godwinson foolishly rushed south to confront him. Although the Saxon army was not, as was once thought, technically inferior to the Norman army, it was tired and badly in need of rest and reinforcements after the victory over the Vikings. At the Battle of Hastings on October 14, fatigue seems eventually to have tipped the scales of an otherwise even struggle. The Normans carried the day and left Harold Godwinson dead upon the field. Duke William of Normandy had won his claim to be king of England.

Impact of the Conquest   The Norman Conquest provided areas of both continuity and change for the Anglo-Saxon population. Although local and central government remained similar, the society and economy underwent major reorientation.

The basic unit of local administration remained the shire, or county, under the supervision of the sheriff, who had primary responsibility for looking after the king's interests. The sheriff, chief official in the shire, administered the royal estates, collected the taxes, summoned and led contingents to the national militia, and presided over the shire court to enforce royal justice. William left all these institutions of local government intact.

THE BAYEUX TAPESTRY
More of an embroidery than a true tapestry, the Bayeux Tapestry is a strip of linen 231 feet long and 20 inches wide depicting the Norman Conquest of England in 1066. The story is laid out as a running narrative, like a cartoon strip. The tapestry was commissioned by Odo, Bishop of Bayeux and half brother of William, and was embroidered by women. In the portion shown here, William arrives at Pevensey (top); King Harold fights in the Battle of Hastings and is shot in the eye by an arrow, killing him (bottom). The tapestry was completed toward the end of the eleventh century and is now housed in a museum connected with the Cathedral of Bayeux in Normandy in France.
Erich Lessing/Art Resource, NY

The Conquest also brought major changes to Anglo-Saxon society. The Saxon *earls*, as the great nobles were called, and most of the lesser nobles, or *thanes*, lost their estates and fled. William redistributed the lands among his followers from the continent—his barons (a title of uncertain origin, now used to connote the immediate vassals of the king). He allotted land liberally to his followers as he conquered England. Thus, unlike France where lords held huge blocks of land, English nobles had theirs scattered through the kingdom. William insisted that all English land be considered fiefs held directly or indirectly (subinfeudated) from the king. In other words, he imposed a feudal hierarchy with the king as the recognized owner of all land and his vassals as recipients of fiefs from the king.

The peasant population, which had consisted of free peasants and slaves, was organized into manors on which most peasants became serfs.

Domesday Book   In 1086 William conducted a comprehensive survey of the lands of England, the report of which became known as the *Domesday Book*. In line with William's policy of maintaining control over his land and assets, he sent out royal officers to every shire. The taxes, tolls, markets, mints, and services owed the king were all recorded. The survey shows a population of about 1.1 million people. The *Domesday Book* also shows that the Normans had brutally killed or evicted the resisters and adopted a scorched earth policy.

Curia Regis, or King's Council   To maintain close contact with his barons and vassals, William adapted the Anglo-Saxon Witan to resemble a continental king's great council, or **curia regis.** Essentially, the great council was an assembly of bishops, abbots, and barons—in fact, anyone whom the king summoned. The council fulfilled the feudal functions of giving the king advice and serving as his principal court in reaching judgments. Because the great council could not be kept permanently in session, a small council, consisting of those persons in permanent attendance at the court whom the king wished to invite, carried on the functions of the great council between its sessions. The great council was the direct ancestor of Parliament, whereas the small council was the source of the administrative bureaus of the royal government.

Henry I   William the Conqueror had three sons. The eldest became Duke of Normandy, the second, William Rufus, became king of England, and the youngest, Henry, was given a cash settlement. When William Rufus died of an arrow wound while hunting, Henry (r. 1100–1135) seized the royal treasure and became king. It was rumored at the time that Henry had a hand in his brother's death; the man who shot the arrow later received land grants from him. Henry I surrounded himself with able bishops who helped him organize the government. He also managed to take over the Duchy

of Normandy when his eldest brother died, and once again united it with the kingdom of England. Both England and Normandy needed reorganization.

Using the curia regis for settling feudal disputes, Henry began to make inroads in the autonomy of feudal lords by making his court one of appeal. He also began to reestablish the royal prerogative to try felonies, including homicide, robbery, arson, burglary, and larceny, which were offenses against the king's peace and punishable by death. The court business was profitable because the crown confiscated the goods from those convicted of crimes, but business was soon so brisk that the court was overwhelmed. The solution was to send itinerant justices around to the counties to try cases in the shire courts and to investigate infringements of royal rights in the countryside.

Exchequer   To make the curia regis more efficient, Henry created separate departments. The financial department became known as the Exchequer—a name derived from a tablecloth marked out in squares like a checkerboard on which accounts were audited. The tablecloth was really a large abacus on which pennies were in one column, shillings in the next, and pounds and their multiples in the other columns (12 pennies = 1 shilling and 20 shillings = 1 pound sterling). The Chancellor who headed the Exchequer audited the sheriffs' accounts and kept track of other revenues. The Chancellor of the Exchequer is still the financial officer in the British cabinet today. Because wealth was the basis of power for any medieval king, Henry had established an efficient way to collect revenue owed him and to control his barons. With able administrators in charge of his government, he was free to spend more time in Normandy, staving off rebellions.

Capetian France

In France the pattern of feudal development was much different from that of England. Central government all but disappeared in the turmoil following the age of Charlemagne. What governmental functions could still be performed were carried out by counts and other lords of small territorial units. These factors alone would have made rebuilding an effective national monarchy considerably more difficult in France than in England; but, in addition, France was a much larger country, and its regions preserved considerable cultural diversity.

Larger units of feudal government, however, emerged in the Duchy of Normandy, the counties of Flanders and Champagne, the royal lands of the Ile-de-France, and others. French kings sought with some success to establish a lord-vassal relation with the great

The Exchequer, or treasury, took its name from the checkered tablecloth, a type of abacus on which they tallied the fines they had collected for the king. Officials presented their accounts and the money that was due. The Chancellor of the Exchequer and his clerks kept a record of the accounts and imprisoned those who did not pay the full amount.
'Facsimiles of National Manuscripts of Ireland,' Classmark Tab.b.253 vol. 3. Cambridge University Library

dukes and counts who governed these principalities. The kings did not envision, and could not have achieved, the unification of the entire realm under their own direct authority.

The Capetians In 987 the great nobles of France elected as their king Hugh Capet, whose descendants held the throne until 1792. Hugh was chosen primarily because his small possessions in the Ile-de-France, which included Paris, as the recognized capital, and the surrounding region, made him no threat to the independence of the nobles. He and his successors for the next century made no dramatic efforts to enlarge their royal authority. They carefully nursed what advantages they had: the central location of their lands; the title of king, which commanded a vague prestige; and a close association with the Church, which gave them an avenue of influence extending beyond their own territory. They also pursued a remarkably prudent policy of consolidating control over their own lands, and they had the good fortune to produce sons for generations. The Capetians built the tradition that the crown was theirs not by election but by hereditary right.

The Capetian policy first bore fruit under Louis VI, the Fat (r. 1108–1137). He achieved his goal of being master of his own possessions by successfully reducing to obedience the petty nobles who had been disturbing his lands and harassing travelers seeking to cross them (see "Louis VI Subdues a Violent Baron," p. 233). By the end of his reign, he had established effective control over the lands between the cities of Paris and Orléans. This move gave him a compact block of territory in the geographic heart of France. Louis VI encouraged economic growth of towns, which added to his own fiscal resources as he collected revenues from trade.

The German Empire

In the tenth and eleventh centuries the German lands east of the Rhine showed a pattern of political development very different from that of France or England. Whereas William forced central control over his territory in England by conquest and the Capetians established hereditary right to the French throne, Germany kept a strong tradition of elective kingship and a concentration of wealth and power in large territorial

LOUIS VI SUBDUES A VIOLENT BARON

This selection describes the attempt of Louis VI (1108–1137), a strong monarch, to keep the peace in his realm. It comes from The Life of Louis VI, *a chronicle by Suger, the head of a French monastery and a great admirer of the king. It is a good example of the chronicles that form one of the historian's basic sources for studying medieval history.*

"A king is obliged by virtue of his office to crush with his strong right hand the impudence of tyrants. For such men freely provoke wars, take pleasure in plunder, oppress the poor, destroy the churches, and give themselves free reign to do whatsoever they wish. . . .

"One such wicked man was Thomas of Marle. For while King Louis was busy fighting in the wars which we mentioned earlier, Thomas ravaged the regions around Laon, Reims, and Amiens. . . .Thomas devastated the region with the fury of a wolf. No fear of ecclesiastical penalty persuaded him to spare the clergy; no feeling of humility convinced him to spare the people. Everyone was slaughtered, everything destroyed. He snatched two prize estates from the nuns of Saint-John of Laon. And treating the two castles of Crècy-sur-Serre and Nouvion-Catillon as his own, he transformed them into a dragon's lair and a den of thieves, exposing the nearby inhabitants to the miseries of fire and plunder.

"Fed up with the intolerable afflictions of this man, the churchmen of France met together (on December 6, 1114) at a great council at Beauvais. . . . The venerable papal legate Cuno, bishop of Praeneste, was particularly moved by the numerous pleas of the church and the cries of the orphans and the poor. He drew the sword of Saint Peter against Thomas of Marle, and with the unanimous assent of the council, declared him excommunicated, ripped from him in absentia the titles and honors of knighthood, branded him a criminal, and declared him unworthy of being called a Christian.

"Heeding the wishes of so great a council, King Louis moved quickly against Thomas. Accompanied by his army and the clergy, he turned at once against the heavily defended castle of Crècy. There, thanks to his men at arms, or should we say on account of divine aid, Louis achieved swift victory. He seized the new towers as if they were no more than the huts of peasants; he drove out the criminals; he piously slaughtered the impious; and as for those who had showed no pity, he in turn showed no pity towards them. . . . Flushed by the success of his decisive victory, the king moved quickly against the other illegally held castle, Nouvion."

From C. W. Hollister et al., *Medieval Europe: A Short Source Book,* New York: McGraw-Hill, 1992, pp. 207–208.

---

blocks—Saxony, Franconia, Swabia, and Bavaria. Originally districts of the Carolingian Empire, these territories became independent political entities under powerful dukes. Paradoxically, the German populace also retained Charlemagne's Empire as the political ideal. The result of strong territorial allegiances and a desire for a larger political unit brought clashes between the nobles and their rulers throughout the Middle Ages.

Otto I, the Great The last direct descendant of Charlemagne in Germany, a feeble ruler known as Louis the Child, died in 911. Recognizing the need for a common leader, the German dukes in 919 elected as king one of their number, Henry of Saxony. His descendants held the German monarchy until 1024. The most powerful of this line of Saxon kings, and the true restorer of the German Empire, was Otto I, the Great (r. 936–973). Otto was primarily a warrior, and conquest was a principal foundation of his power. He routed the Magyars near Augsburg in 955 and ended their menace to Europe; he organized military provinces, or marches, along the Eastern frontier and actively promoted the work of German missionaries and settlers beyond the Elbe River. In 951 he marched into Italy.

Restoration of the Empire The immediate rationale for Otto's entrance into Italy was the appeal of Adelaid, widow of one of the Italian kings, who was about to be forced into an undesirable marriage. He rescued the queen and married her himself. Historians have debated the real reasons Otto wished to secure power in Italy. Apparently, Otto conceived of himself not just as a German king, but as the successor to Charlemagne and as the leader of all Western Christians. He could not allow Italy, especially Rome and the papacy, to remain in chaos or permit another prince to achieve a strong position there. In 962, during Otto's second campaign in Italy, the pope crowned him "Roman Emperor," a title with more prestige than power.

CROWN OF THE GERMAN EMPIRE, TENTH AND ELEVENTH CENTURIES
The crown of the German Empire may originally have been given to Otto I by Pope John, but throughout the tenth and eleventh centuries various pieces were added by different emperors. It eventually consisted of eight panels, decorated with cloisonné enamels, which are hinged together with gold filigree and surrounded with jewels and pearls.
Art Resource, NY

CHRONOLOGY
Political Events

Germany:	Otto I, the Great (**r. 936–973**)
	Otto II (**r. 973–983**)
	Henry III (**r. 1039–1056**)
	Henry IV (**r. 1056–1106**)
France:	Hugh Capet (**r. 987–996**)
	Louis VI, the Fat (**r. 1108–1137**)
	Council of Clermont and preaching of First Crusade (**1095**)
England:	Edward the Confessor (**r. 1042–1066**)
	Norman Conquest (**1066**)
	William I (**r. 1066–1087**)
	Domesday Book (**1086**)
	Henry I (**r. 1100–1135**)
Italy:	Pope Sylvester II (**999–1003**)
	College of Cardinals (**1059**)
	Pope Gregory VII (**1073–1085**)
	Canossa (**1077**)
	Roger de Hauteville (**d. 1101**) conquers Sicily (**1072**)
Crusades:	First Crusade (**1095–1099**)
	Second Crusade (**1147–1149**)
	Third Crusade (**1189–1192**)

The coronation of 962 confirmed the close relations between Germany and Italy that lasted through the Middle Ages. Although the German emperors claimed to be the successors of the Caesars and of Charlemagne and thus the titular leaders of all Western Christendom, their effective power never extended beyond Germany and Italy and the small provinces contiguous to them—Provence, Burgundy, and Bohemia.

Ecclesiastics as Administrators Otto's problems of governing his far-flung territories were more formidable than the problems that confronted the English and French kings. Hoping to keep control over the powerful duchies, Otto relied, as had the Carolingians, on bishops and abbots as administrators of his realm. Otto could appoint loyal, educated, and clever clerical administrators and invest them with the fiefs associated with their office without being concerned about hereditary claims from these celibate priests.

The Ottonian Renaissance The dynasty that Otto established fostered the revival of learning in Germany. The examples of two scholars indicate the intellectual activity that characterized the "Ottonian Renaissance."

Roswitha of Gandersheim (ca. 937–1004) came from a noble family of Saxony and was put into a Benedictine nunnery at an early age. A Saxon duke had founded Gandersheim in 852 with the intention that women of the Saxon Dynasty would be its abbesses. Otto the Great's younger brother, a bishop, encouraged learning at the nunnery, and Roswitha had a series of learned nuns to teach her Latin. Her early writings were religious poetry, but, reading copies of Roman comedies that were in the nunnery library, she became fascinated by their language. Adapting the dramatic form, she wrote religious plays, the first plays to be written since Roman times. Toward the end of her life she wrote histories, including the *Deeds of Otto* about Otto the Great.

The other great figure was a monk, Gerbert of Auril-lac in France (d. 1003). Gerbert came from a peasant family, but local monks recognized his genius and educated him. He was sent to Spain, where he came into contact with the great learning of Arab and Hebrew scholars in Barcelona. Although he studied with Christian scholars because he did not know Arabic, he learned something of Arab mathematics and astronomy. He had an abacus with Arabic numerals, but he did not use the zero as the Arabs did. His fame in France brought patronage from the Ottonians, who first made him tutor to the young Otto III and then appointed him pope in Rome, where he served as Sylvester II. So great was his knowledge that people thought he was a necromancer or sorcerer. He was a man ahead of his time.

Salian House   The Ottonian line ended in 1024. The German nobles selected as emperor Henry III (r. 1039–1056), from another branch of the Saxon line. Some historians consider him to have been one of the strongest early medieval German emperors. Continuing the policy that was now well established in Germany, he relied on bishops and abbots that he had appointed as his administrators. But he also had a sincere interest in Church reform. In 1046 he crossed the Alps and called councils of clergy to reform the Church. He succeeded in nominating a series of able and educated popes to carry out reform programs that promoted clerical celibacy, forbade the sale of Church offices (simony), and restored the Benedictine Rule in monasteries.

Henry III left a six-year-old son, Henry IV (r. 1056–1106). During Henry IV's minority, he had time to observe the weaknesses of the German monarchy. His father had designated his mother as regent, but civil war broke out and Henry became a pawn in power shifts, living with first one faction and then another. This unsettling childhood made him a ruler adept at dealing with adversity. On becoming emperor, Henry IV realized that he needed to consolidate the royal demesne as the English and French kings were doing. He also had to suppress the overpowerful dukes. Because the largest block of demesne land was on the borders of Saxony, he annexed part of the land and deposed the Duke. The move alienated the nobles, who feared for their own estates.

Wanting to extend his authority through officials he could trust, Henry IV raised a number of lower-born men to the rank of *ministeriales* (bureaucrats and soldiers), equipping them with horses and armor. Again, he offended the nobility because he required them to take orders from these lowly soldiers and bureaucrats rather than from fellow nobles or bishops. Henry's nobles rebelled over these innovations. At this point,

Henry turned to the pope for help but encountered a pope—Gregory VII—who was a strict reformer. Their clash is called the *Investiture Controversy*, as will be explained shortly.

THE REFORM OF THE WESTERN CHURCH

The Church, like lay governments, was fundamentally transformed in the eleventh and twelfth centuries. The reform of the Church resulted from a renewal of monastic discipline, an upsurge of popular piety among the laity, and a clerical revolt against the traditional system of lay domination over ecclesiastical offices and lands.

The Church in Crisis

After the disintegration of the Carolingian Empire, a kind of moral chaos invaded the lives of the clergy. Since the fourth century, the Church had demanded that its clergy remain celibate, but this injunction was almost completely ignored in the post-Carolingian period. The sin of simony—the buying or selling of offices or sacraments—was also rampant. Many bishops and even some popes purchased their high positions, and parish priests frequently sold their sacramental services (baptisms, masses, absolutions of sins, marriages) to the people. A few reforming bishops in the tenth and eleventh centuries, some appointed by the German emperors, tried to suppress clerical marriage and the simony of their priests, but they could make little headway.

Monastic Reform

Cluniac Monasteries   Renewal of monastic discipline proved a more effective reform than the efforts of popes or bishops. The monastery of Cluny in Burgundy was the center of reform. Founded by a count in 910, the monastery was placed directly under the pope (neither lay lords nor bishops could interfere in its affairs). The monastic community elected the abbot directly. He administered not only Cluny but also the many dependent monastic communities that his monks had founded or reformed. The abbot of Cluny could visit these communities at will and freely correct abuses. The congregation of Cluny grew with extraordinary rapidity in the eleventh and twelfth centuries.

The Cluniac monks advocated a return to the strict observance of the Benedictine Rule (see chapter 6) and a new emphasis on the liturgy (services, songs, and prayers). The services were long, lasting most of the day and into the night. The monastery fostered a new architecture, Romanesque (discussed in chapter 9).

Papal Reform

The reforming popes began to take measures to rid the church of clerical abuses and seek alliances that would make them independent of the German emperor.

College of Cardinals   Tradition required that the clergy and people of the diocese elect all bishops and, by extension, the pope as bishop of Rome. In practice, however, either the emperor named the pope or, in the emperor's absence, the powerful noble families and factions of Rome did. A council in 1059, however, set up the election procedures for the pope, conferring this prerogative on the cardinals, the chief clergymen associated with the Church at Rome. This procedure ensured that the College of Cardinals, and the reformers who controlled it, could maintain continuity of papal policy. (Even today, all cardinals, no matter where they live in the world, hold a titular appointment to a church within the archdiocese of Rome and elect the pope.) The College of Cardinals simultaneously deprived both the emperor and the local Roman nobility of one of their strongest powers, the appointment of the pope.

Gregory VII   The climax of papal reform came with the pontificate of Pope Gregory VII (r. 1073–1085), a Cluniac monk named Hildebrand, who was instrumental in designing the College of Cardinals. Rather than being elected through the College of Cardinals, Gregory was proclaimed pope by the citizens and clergy of Rome. Gregory brought to the office a high regard for the papacy's powers and responsibilities and a burning desire for reform. With regard to Church matters, Gregory asserted that the pope wielded absolute authority—that he could, at will, overrule any local bishop in the exercise of his ordinary or usual jurisdiction.

Gregory believed that all Christian princes must answer to the pope in spiritual matters and that the pope himself had a weighty responsibility to guide those princes, including the rulers of the German Empire. Gregory's reforming ideals set up a direct conflict with the emperor Henry IV. In particular, he objected to the German emperor appointing the pope and bishops.

Investiture Controversy

As the name suggests, the principal issue in the **Investiture Controversy** was the practice of great laymen of "investing" bishops with their fiefs by using the spiritual symbols of office, the bishop's ring and the crozier or shepard's crook (indicating care of their flock). At its root, the struggle revolved around the claims of these powerful laymen to grant ecclesiastical offices and revenues as fiefs by their authority as lords. Laymen felt that they had a right to select loyal churchmen as well as warriors for vassals. The giving of the ring and staff was, in their view, similar to giving a clod of earth in passing on the fief. For the German emperors, selecting the bishop meant selecting an imperial administrator. Kings and emperors also argued that they had a right to select and invest a bishop with his office because kings also had sacred power because they were anointed during their coronation ceremony, in imitation of David's coronation in the Old Testament. The pope, they argued, was not the only one with spiritual power.

The Fight Is Joined   When Henry IV sent a letter in 1075 to Pope Gregory VII asking for help against his rebellious German nobles, Gregory, convinced that Henry was in a weak position, took advantage of the situation to condemn lay investiture and excommunicate some of Henry's advisers. Henry, who in the interval had defeated the rebellious nobles, reacted with fury; he summoned a meeting of loyal imperial bishops and declared Gregory not the true pope but a "false monk" (a reference to his elevation by acclamation rather than election in the College of Cardinals). His letter continued: "descend and relinquish the apostolic throne which thou hast usurped. . . . I Henry, king by the grace of God, do say unto thee, together with all my bishops: Down, down, to be damned through all the ages." Not one to pause in what he thought to be the work of God, Gregory excommunicated Henry, thereby freeing Henry's subjects from allegiance to him. These acts struck at the fundamental theory of the Christian empire, according to which the emperor was supreme head of the Christian people, responsible only to God.

Excommunication of Henry IV   The excommunication broke the feudal vows of loyalty, because fealty was sworn to a Christian lord and excommunication placed a Christian outside the Church. Henry's enemies demanded that he be judged, with Pope Gregory presiding, before an assembly of lords and prelates. Gregory readily accepted the invitation to meet at Augsburg in February 1077. Henry resolved to fight spiritual weapons with spiritual weapons. He slipped across the Alps and intercepted Gregory, then on his way to Germany, at the Apennine castle of Canossa near Modena. Henry came in the sackcloth of a penitent, radiating contrition, pleading for absolution. Gregory, who doubted the sincerity of the emperor's repentance, refused for three days to receive him, while Henry waited in the snow. Finally, in the face of such persistence, Gregory the suspicious pope had to give way to Gre-

Emperor Henry IV is shown at Canossa on his knees, begging Pope Gregory for readmission to the Church. Countess Matilda of Tuscany, a powerful supporter of the pope, appears on the right.
AKG London

gory the priest, who, like all priests, was obliged to absolve a sinner professing sorrow (see "Gregory VII's Letter to the German Nobility after Canossa," p. 238).

The incident at Canossa is one of the most dramatic events of medieval history. Henry was the immediate victor. He had divided his opponents and stripped his German enemies of their excuse for rebelling. Gregory died at Salerno in 1085, in apparent bitterness, avowing that his love of justice had brought him only death in exile. But the popes' claim of authority over kings and emperors was not dead.

Concordat of Worms   After years of argument and struggle, the papacy and lay rulers settled the Investiture Controversy through the Concordat of Worms in 1122. They agreed that the lay rulers, including the emperor, would no longer invest prelates with the symbols of their spiritual office. The pope would allow the elections of imperial bishops and abbots to be held in the presence of the emperor or his representative, thus permitting the emperor to influence the outcome of elections. In addition, the emperor retained the right of investing prelates with their temporalities—that is, their imperial fiefs. Although a compromise, the Concordat was a real victory for the papacy because it gave the popes more control over their bishops throughout Europe than they had previously enjoyed. Ultimately, lay leaders accepted papal approval as essential to a valid choice of bishops.

Consolidation of Papal Reform

In the twelfth century the popes continued to pursue and consolidate the Gregorian ideals of internal reform, freedom from lay domination, and centralization of papal authority over their bishops, abbots, and clergy. In their struggle to be free of lay authority, the reformers had insisted that members of the clergy, however minor their office, were to be tried in ecclesiastical courts.

Ecclesiastical Courts   The Church reserved the right to try any cases touching on the sacraments and breaches of dogma: sacrilege, heresy, marriage, testaments, contracts, and the like. Many aspects of ordinary people's moral lives, including fornication, taboos on marrying a person related by blood, legitimacy and bastardy, godparents, and grounds for anullment of a marriage, fell within the Church courts' business. A complex system of ecclesiastical courts developed throughout Europe to try people. These courts paralleled and at times rivaled the courts of the kings. Judicial decisions from the ecclesiastical courts could be appealed to Rome.

Canon Law   Legal scholars at this time were compiling and clarifying the canons of the Church—the authoritative statements from the Bible, Church councils, Church fathers, and popes, which constituted the law of the Church. The compilation that was ultimately recognized as official and binding was the *Decretum*, put together by the Italian jurist Gratian in about 1142. With his systematic compilation came trained canon lawyers to comment on, interpret, and apply canon law.

Papal Curia   Like the monarchs of Europe, the popes experimented with creating a stronger central bureaucracy in a **papal** *curia* (council). Among the most important branches was a centralized financial administration, the *camera*, or chamber. It handled moneys coming into the papacy from estates the papacy directly held around Rome, from the proceeds of administering justice in ecclesiastical courts, and from money bishops paid to the papacy. A judicial branch of the curia dealt with appeals on matters of canon law.

Gregory VII's Letter to the German Nobility after Canossa

Henry intercepted Gregory at a castle in Canossa in January of 1077, dressed as a penitent. Gregory explains why he gave in to Henry's contrition and removed the excommunication.

"When, after long deferring . . . and holding frequent consultations, we had, through all the envoys who passed, severely taken him to task for his excesses: he came at length of his own accord, with a few followers, showing nothing of hostility or boldness. . . . And there, having laid aside all the belongings of royalty, wretchedly, with bare feet and clad in wool, he continued for three days to stand before the gate of the castle. Nor did he desist from imploring with many tears the aid and consolation of the apostolic mercy until he moved all those who were present there, and whom the report of it reached, to such pity and depth of compassion that, interceding for him with many prayers and tears, all wondered indeed at the unaccustomed hardness of our heart, while some actually cried out that we were exercising, not the gravity of apostolic severity, but the cruelty, as it were of a tyrannical ferocity.

"Finally, conquered by the persistence of his compunction and by the constant supplications of all those who were present, we loosed the chain of the anathema and at length received him into the favor of communion and into the lap of the holy mother church."

From Norman Downs, *Basic Documents in Medieval History*, Melborne, FL: Kreiger, 1959, pp. 64–65.

Like monarchs, popes also had a chancery for sending out official letters to their clergy, legates, rulers, and laymen.

THE CRUSADES

In the eleventh century Western Europeans launched a series of armed expeditions to the East in an effort to free the Holy Land from Islamic rule. Known as **crusades,** these expeditions stimulated trade, encouraged the growth of towns, and contributed to the establishment of a stable political order in the West. Seen from a different perspective, the crusades were costly failures: They drained resources for what proved to be a temporary foothold in Palestine; they worsened relations not only with the Muslims but also with Eastern Christians; and they set in motion one of Europe's grimmest traditions, in which crusading zeal stimulated dreadful riots and pogroms against those most accessible non-Christians, the Jews.

Origins

The origins of the crusades must be sought in a double set of circumstances: social and religious movements in the West and the political situation in the East. Pilgrimage, a personal visit to a place made holy through the life of Christ or one of the saints or the presence of a sacred relic, was popular among Western Christians. Common since the fourth century, pilgrimages gained in popularity during the eleventh century. Bands of pilgrims, sometimes numbering in the thousands, set forth to visit sacred places; Palestine was the most holy.

The Turks   The pilgrim traffic was threatened when the Seljuk Turks, Muslim nomads, overran much of the Middle East in the eleventh century. The Seljuks apparently did not consciously seek to prevent pilgrims from reaching Palestine, but they did impose numerous taxes and tolls on them, and many Christians became angry at the domination of the holy places of Palestine by a strong, aggressive Islamic power.

Even more daunting to the West was the possibility that the Turks would overrun the Christian empire of Byzantium. The Seljuks had crushed a Byzantine army at the Battle of Manzikert in 1071, and the road to Constantinople seemed wide open. The fall of Byzantium would remove the traditional barrier to Islamic advance toward the West and would be a major disaster for the Christian world. When, therefore, a delegation from the emperor of Byzantium requested the help of Pope Urban II in 1095, he resolved to appeal to the Western knights and princes to go to the aid of their fellow Christians in the East.

The Byzantine Empire   Although severely threatened by the Turks, the Byzantine Empire was under able leadership once again with the Comnenus family. Alexius Comnenus (1081–1118) had some success against the Turks, but he needed mercenary soldiers to enlarge his army. Knowing of the Normans' successes in Sicily, he hoped to hire Norman mercenaries. When he wrote to Pope Urban II asking for assistance, he hoped to persuade the pope by suggesting that the schism between the Eastern and Western churches, which had occurred in 1054, might be brought to an end.

The Motives of the Crusaders

Religious Fervor Christians viewed the crusades as acts of religious devotion. Even before Urban made his appeal, the idea had gained currency in the West that God would reward those who fought in a good cause, that is, that wars could be holy. The crusaders also shared the belief expressed in the movement for Church reform that the good ought not simply to endure the evils of the world but should attempt to correct them. This active, confident spirit contrasted strongly with the withdrawal from the world that most Christian writers recommended in the Early Middle Ages.

Economic Motives for Expansion Social and economic motivations also contributed to the expeditions. The age of mass pilgrimages and crusades, from about 1050 to 1250, corresponds to the period in medieval history during which the European population was growing rapidly. The crusades may be considered one further example of the expansion of Europe, similar in motivation and character to the Spanish *Reconquista* or the German *Drang nach Osten*. Of course, the crusades differed in at least one significant way from these other ventures. The crusades were almost exclusively military expeditions of Europe's warrior classes; peasants did not settle in Palestine in significant numbers as they did in the lands of Eastern Europe and in the Iberian Peninsula. But the Italian merchants prospered from the crusades.

The Oversupply of Knights The younger sons of European knights were particularly aware of the pressures created by an expanding population. Trained for war, they used their skills to fight each other for land and castles. Pope Urban apparently observed the effects of land shortage, for he is reported to have told the knights of France: "This land which you inhabit is too narrow for your large population; nor does it abound in wealth; and it provides hardly enough food for those who farm it. This is the reason that you murder and consume one another." Urban urged them not to fight fellow Christians, but to go to the traditional land of milk and honey and fight Muslims for land instead. War against the Muslims thus offered constructive employment for Europe's surplus knights.

The First Crusade

In November 1095, Pope Urban II preached a sermon at Clermont in southern France, calling on the nobility to undertake an expedition to the Holy Land. The pope's sermon was intended for the upper classes, but its plea had sensational results at all levels of Western society.

The Popular Crusade In northern France and the Rhineland, influential preachers, such as Peter the Hermit and Walter the Pennyless, were soon rousing the people and organizing movements that historians now call the Popular Crusade. Bands of peasants and the poor (together with a few knights and clergy) set out for the East, miserably equipped and without competent leaders. They marched down the Rhine valley, attacking Jews as they went, and on through Hungary and Bulgaria to Constantinople. The emperor Alexius of Byzantium, who was shocked at the sight of this hapless army, gave them transport across the Bosporus. The Turks at once cut them to pieces.

The Crusading Army Far better organized was the official First Crusade, which was led by nobles. Robert of Normandy, son of William the Conqueror, headed a northern French army; Godfrey of Bouillon, his brother Baldwin, and Robert of Flanders commanded an army of Flemings; Raymond of Toulouse led the men of Languedoc; and Bohemund of Taranto and his nephew Tancred marshaled the Normans of southern Italy. These four armies moved by various overland and sea routes to Constantinople (see map 8.5) and arrived there in 1096 and 1097.

Although the leaders of the First Crusade had intended to conquer lands in the East in their own name, Emperor Alexius demanded from them an oath of fealty in exchange for provisioning the armies as they marched to Palestine. Grudgingly, the leaders agreed, promising to regard the emperor as the overlord of any lands they might reconquer from the Turks. Subsequently, both the emperor and the Western leaders accused each other of violating the terms of the oath. The failure of the crusaders and the Byzantines to find a firm basis for cooperating ultimately weakened, although it did not defeat, the enterprise. *The Alexiad*, written by Anna Comnena, daughter of Alexius, reflects the Greek viewpoint: "there were among the Latins such men as Bohemund and his fellow counselors, who, eager to obtain the Roman Empire for themselves, had been looking with avarice upon it for a long time."

Victories In 1097 the crusaders entered the Seljuk Sultanate of Rum, achieving their first major victory at Dorylaeum. Baldwin then separated his troops from the

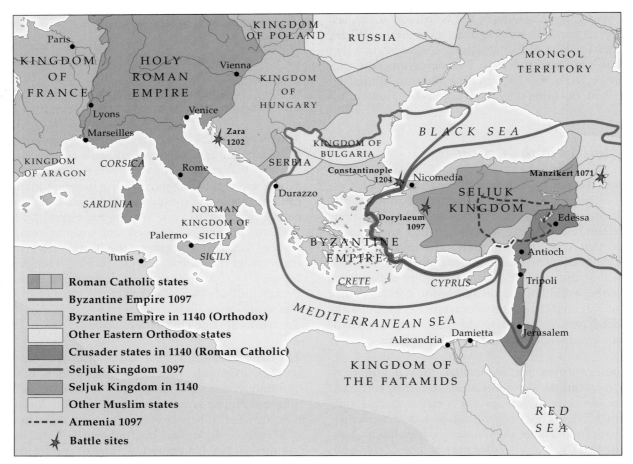

MAP 8.5 THE EASTERN MEDITERRANEAN DURING THE EARLY CRUSADES
This map of the eastern Mediterranean during the early Crusades shows the various states, including the crusader states, that had emerged in the East. What territories were the crusaders able to occupy? Identify the Roman Catholic, Eastern Orthodox, and Muslim territories. Locate the Mongols.
◆ For an online version, go to www.mhhe.com/chambers9 > chapter 8 > book maps

main body and conquered Edessa, where he established the first crusader state in the East. The decisive victory of the First Crusade came in the battle for the city of Antioch, which Bohemund claimed as his own. After that, the road to Jerusalem was open. On July 15, 1099, the crusaders stormed Jerusalem and slaughtered its population of Muslims, Jews, and Eastern Christians.

Besides a high level of organizational skill and their own daring, the Westerners had the advantage of facing an enemy that was politically divided. The Seljuk Turks had only recently risen to power and had not yet consolidated their rule. The Muslims' inability to present a united front against the crusaders was probably the decisive reason for the success of the First Crusade.

The Kingdom of Jerusalem

The crusaders now faced the problem of organizing a government for their conquered territory and its population of Muslims, Jews, and Eastern and Western

Christians. They chose as ruler Godfrey of Bouillon, but he died in 1100, and his younger brother Baldwin, the conqueror of Edessa, succeeded him.

Baldwin organized his realm through the application of feudal concepts and institutions. He kept direct dominion over Jerusalem and its surroundings, including a stretch of coast extending from modern Gaza to Beirut. To the north, three fiefs—the County of Tripoli, the Principality of Antioch, and the County of Edessa—were made subject to his suzerainty (see map 8.6). Although King Baldwin and his successors were able to exert a respectable measure of authority over all these lands, profound weaknesses undermined their power. The kings were never able to push their frontiers to an easily defensible, strategic border, such as the Lebanese mountains. With only a small garrison, the Kingdom of Jerusalem depended on a constant influx of men and money from Europe. Many knights and pilgrims came, but relatively few stayed as permanent settlers. The Westerners constituted a foreign aristocracy, small in number and set

WOMEN ASSISTING KNIGHTS
This manuscript illustration makes it clear that women took part in battles alongside the male crusaders. Here they wield picks and axes and throw stones in a siege. Moreover, it is clear that the woman in the foreground, just behind the ladder, who does not cower behind a shield like the man on the ladder, is about to be killed by an arrow.
The British Library, Ms Add. 15268 fol 101v

THE PILLAGE OF JERUSALEM BY ANTIOCHUS
Although the crusades were conducted in the name of Christ, the behavior of their armies was no different from that of soldiers throughout the ages. In this scene in front of Jerusalem from a fifteenth-century manuscript, the commander Antiochus watches as his troops pile up the spoils they have looted. Note the anachronism of the French royal symbol, the fleur-de-lis.
Bibliothèque Nationale de France, Paris

over a people of largely different faith, culture, and sympathies. The wonder is not that the crusader states ultimately fell but that some of their outposts survived on the mainland of Asia Minor for nearly 200 years, until 1291 when the port of Acre fell at last.

The Later Crusades

Although historians have traditionally assigned numbers to the later crusades, these expeditions were merely momentary swells in the steady current of Western people and treasures to and from the Middle East. The recapture of the city of Edessa by the Muslims in 1144 gave rise to the Second Crusade (1147–1149). Two armies, led by King Louis VII of France and the Emperor Conrad III of Germany, set out to capture Damascus to give the Kingdom of Jerusalem a more defensible frontier. They were soon forced to retreat ignominiously before superior Muslim forces.

The Third Crusade The unification of the Muslims under Saladin prompted the Third Crusade (1189–1192). Saladin already controlled Egypt and was able to conquer Syria as well so that the Latin Kingdom was surrounded. His capture of Jerusalem threatened to eliminate the Latin Kingdom of Jerusalem entirely. Emperor Frederick Barbarossa and kings Philip II of France and Richard I, the Lion-Hearted, of England all marched to the East. (Frederick drowned while crossing through Asia Minor, and most of his forces turned back.) Philip II left the campaign early. Richard I fought on and the crusaders captured Acre. The Kingdom of

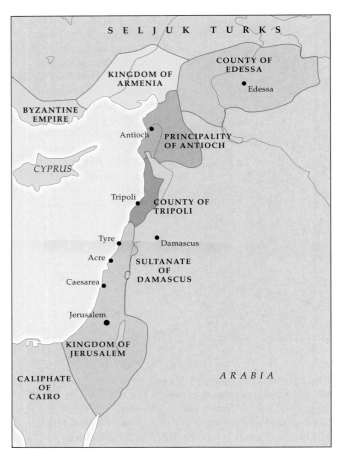

MAP 8.6 THE CRUSADER STATES AT THEIR HEIGHT
This map shows the Latin Kingdom of Jerusalem and the feudal principalities that the crusaders established. The crusader states proved vulnerable to further conquest: Edessa was lost in less than 50 years, and even Jerusalem fell in 1187. Did the crusader states have natural boundaries to protect them? Which peoples were to the north and east who could invade the crusader states?
◆ For an online version, go to www.mhhe.com/chambers9 > chapter 8 > book maps

Jerusalem remained limited to a narrow strip of the coast from Acre to Jaffa, but unarmed Christian pilgrims were given the right to visit Moslem-governed Jerusalem. These rights were paltry gains from so expensive a campaign.

The Fourth Crusade Pope Innocent III preached the Fourth Crusade (1202–1204), but events soon took it out of his hands. The response was limited, so the leaders negotiated with Venice to take them by sea, rather than going overland, and to supply them with provisions for a year. In addition the Venetians were to provide their own troops and receive half the conquests. The Venetians proposed that the crusaders cancel their

debt by aiding them in taking the trading port and Christian city of Zara, across the Adriatic from Venice. Although shocked at the proposal of attacking a Christian city, the crusaders were too far in debt to the Venetians to refuse. The Venetians and the crusade's leaders then persuaded the crusaders to attack Constantinople. The city, divided by factional strife, easily fell in 1204. Although Innocent III tried to stop the crusaders, they sacked the city and burned part of it. The Venetians and crusaders divided what remained of the Byzantine Empire into feudal principalities, but Western control lasted only until 1261.

Further Crusades With the Muslims of Egypt in control of Jerusalem, later crusaders tried new tactics. Emperor Frederick II married the heiress of the Latin Kingdom of Jerusalem and negotiated directly with the Muslim leaders to regain Jerusalem; the treaty did not long outlast him. King Louis IX of France tried two disastrous expeditions to North Africa (sometimes called the Sixth and Seventh Crusades), but neither succeeded and Louis died in the last attempt in Tunisia.

Military-Religious Orders Soon after the First Crusade, a new kind of institution, the military-religious order, was founded. The military-religious orders combined the dedication, discipline, and organizational experience of monasticism with the military purposes of the crusade. The orders offered armed escorts and safe lodgings to pilgrims on their way to Palestine. The orders became indispensable for the Latin Kingdom, assuming a major role in supplying the settlers with services, goods, defense, and means of communication back to Europe.

The Templars, or Knights of the Temple, assumed a major role in the maintenance of safe routes between Europe and the crusader states and in the defense of the Kingdom of Jerusalem. The Knights of the Hospital of St. John of Jerusalem, or Hospitalers, founded about 1130, made a major contribution to the defense of the Kingdom of Jerusalem. With the fall of Acre in 1291, the knights moved their headquarters to Cyprus, then to Rhodes, and finally to Malta. As the Knights of Malta, they ruled the island until 1798. This "sovereign order" of the Knights of Malta survives today as an exclusively philanthropic confraternity.

About 1190, German pilgrims organized the Teutonic Knights as a hospital order. Reorganized as a military order at the end of the twelfth-century, the Teutonic Knights defended the eastern frontiers in Prussia. There they became the armed vanguard of the German eastward expansion and conquered for themselves an extensive domain along the shores of the Baltic Sea. In 1525 the last grand master, Albert of

CITIZENS OF EDESSA IN HOMAGE TO BALDWIN I
To emphasize the crusaders' triumph, this manuscript illustration shows Baldwin I, who captured Edessa in 1099, asserting his authority over the conquered Muslims. He sits on the left, with his knights next to him, and receives the homage and tribute of his new subjects.
Bibliothèque Nationale de France, Paris

Hohenzollern, adopted Lutheranism and secularized the order and its territories.

Results of the Crusades

Although the crusades did not produce a permanent Western political presence in Asia Minor, the whole experience of the campaigns and the contact with the East had a profound effect on Europe. When the Ottoman Turks, successors to the Seljuks, finally seized the islands of Cyprus and Crete, the Europeans had already found new routes to the Far East and were in the midst of a far broader overseas expansion.

Warfare   The crusades had a powerful influence on military technology. After their initial invasions, the crusaders waged a largely defensive war, becoming particularly skilled in the art of constructing castles. The numerous remains of crusader castles in nearly all the Eastern lands reflect these advances in such features as the overhanging tower parapets, from which oil or missiles could be rained down on attackers, and the angular castle entranceways that prevented the enemy from shooting directly at the gates. Coincident with improvement of castle building was greater sophistication in siege engines to break down walls and gates.

Economy   Historians still cannot draw up an exact balance sheet that registers accurately the economic gains and losses of the crusades. Although the campaigns were expensive, they also put a considerable amount of money in circulation by paying for weapons, provisions, shipping, and accommodations. Some of the money was drained to the East and only partially

KNIGHTS IN COMBAT
This contemporaneous manuscript illustration is a splendid depiction, full of motion and action, of two knights jousting. The figure on the left is thought to be Richard the Lion-Hearted, battling with Saladin himself.
The British Library (1007628.011)

HOSPITALERS IN RHODES
This fifteenth-century manuscript depiction of the capture of the island of Rhodes commemorates an event in 1306, when the Hospitaler knights attacked this fortress from the neighboring island of Cyprus. Wearing their distinctive tunic with its white cross, the Hospitalers swarmed through Rhodes, which they were to control until it was conquered by the Ottomans in 1522.
Bibliothèque Nationale de France, Paris

recovered in booty. Nevertheless, the crusades stimulated trade in sugar, spices, and similar products from the East and encouraged the production of luxury goods, such as silk cloth, in Europe itself.

Explorations   The crusades encouraged a curiosity about exotic cultures. Starting from the crusader principalities in the East, first missionaries and then merchants penetrated deep into central Asia, and by the early thirteenth century they had reached China. Their reports, especially the memoirs of the Venetian Marco Polo at the close of the thirteenth century, gave Europe abundant information about East Asia and helped inspire Western navigators in the late fifteenth and sixteenth centuries to seek new ways to trade with China directly. The desire to explore, conquer other cultures, and spread Christianity that was part of the crusades inspired later imperialism.

Summary

The period from 1000 to 1200 was vigorously creative in every level of European life. Europe had changed substantially from what it was during the reign of Charlemagne. Its economy was more diversified and productive, its society more complex, its government more effective, its religion more organized. Europe had expanded its control into Spain, into the Slavic lands to the East, and even into Palestine. But the very innovations of the age posed severe problems for European society. How could the new forms of economic endeavor be reconciled with the older hostility and suspicion toward a life of buying and selling? How could the rising power of monarchs be reconciled with the self-consciousness and self-interest of the nobility, the reformed and independent Church, and the privileged towns? From about 1150 the West was trying to consolidate its recent advances and bring them into harmony with its older heritage. This effort at consolidation, reconciliation, and synthesis is the theme of Western history from 1150 to 1300.

QUESTIONS FOR FURTHER THOUGHT

1. It is said that the invasions of the Vikings, Magyars, and Muslims created the conditions that gave rise to feudalism. Do you agree with this statement, or would you point to other factors in the development of feudalism?
2. In a modern democracy, it is hard to imagine a strictly hierarchical society, but to understand the Middle Ages it is necessary to do so. How would you explain the medieval hierarchy to a fellow student?
3. What factors made the crusades possible? Do you think that the crusades would have been less violent if Western Christians had a greater understanding of Islam?

RECOMMENDED READING

Sources

Alexiad of Anna Comnena. Elizabeth A. S. Dawes (tr.). 1978. A Greek version of the First Crusade.

*Benton, John F. (ed.). *Self and Society in Medieval France: The Memoirs of Abbot Guibert of Nogent (1064?–c. 1125).* 1970. An autobiography.

*Fitz Stephen, William. *Norman London,* with an essay by Sir Frank Stenton and introduction by F. Donald Logan. 1990. A description of London.

The Life of Christina of Markyate. C. H. Talbot (tr.). 1987.

*Shinners, John (ed.). *Medieval Popular Religion, 1000–1500, A Reader.* 1997.

The Song of Roland. D. P. R. Owen (tr.). 1990. Many translations are available.

Stenton, Frank (ed.). *The Bayeux Tapestry.* 1957.

*Tierney, Brian (ed.). *The Crisis of Church and State, 1050–1300.* 1964. A selection of primary resources illustrating disputes between Church and state.

Whitelock, Dorothy (ed.). *The Anglo-Saxon Chronicle.* 1961.

Studies

*Arnold, Benjamin. *Medieval Germany, 500–1300: A Political Interpretation.* 1997.

*Barraclough, Geoffrey. *The Origins of Modern Germany.* 1963. Classic interpretation of medieval German history.

*Bloch, Marc. *Feudal Society.* L. A. Manyon (tr.). 1961. A classic work on the social, economic, and cultural institutions in feudal society.

Blumenthal, Uta-Renate. *The Investiture Controversy: Church and Monarchy from the Ninth to the Twelfth Century.* 1988. Discussion of the origins of the struggle between Church and state.

Clanchy, Michael T. *England and Its Rulers, 1066–1272.* 2nd ed. 1998. A brief political history of English monarchy.

*Douglas, David C. *William the Conqueror: The Norman Impact upon England.* 1966. Outstanding among many biographies.

*Duby, Georges. *The Knight, the Lady, and the Priest: The Making of Modern Marriage in Medieval France.* 1983.

*Ganshof, François. *Feudalism.* P. Grierson (tr.). 1961. Standard introduction to feudal institutions.

Hudson, John. *The Formation of the English Common Law: Law and Society in England from the Norman Conquest to Magna Carta.* 1996. Discussion of the development of common law and the English court system.

Morris, Colin. *The Papal Monarchy: The Western Church from 1050 to 1250.* 1989. Discussion of the growing power of the papacy.

Nicholas, David. *The Later Medieval City, 1300–1500.* 1997. An overview of the urban centers of Europe, including their economies and government.

*Phillips, J. R. S. *The Medieval Expansion of Europe.* 1988. Crusades, but also other contacts with the Orient and the first explorations.

*Reuter, Timothy. *Germany in the Middle Ages, 800–1056.* 1991. This is a modern survey, brief and suited to students.

*Riley-Smith, Jonathan. *The First Crusade and the Idea of Crusading.* 1986. Examines the idea of the First Crusade and its reinterpretations.

*Southern, Richard W. *The Making of the Middle Ages.* 1955. Classic essay on twelfth-century culture.

*Swanson, R. N. *Religion and Devotion in Europe, c. 1215–c. 1515.* 1995. An emphasis on medieval religious experiences such as the mass and pilgrimages. Good book for students.

* Available in paperback.

Giotto di Bondone
THE DREAM OF POPE INNOCENT III, **1298**
**Giotto di Bondone was the most important fourteenth-century Italian painter. His cycle on the life of Francis of
Assisi appears in the name of the upper church in Assisi dedicated to St. Francis. In this pane, Francis is shown
holding up St. Peter's cathedral while Pope Innocent III sleeps. Francis, dressed in the garb of the Franciscan Friars,
is depicted as the savior of the Church and the papacy.**
Erich Lessing/Art Resource, NY

Chapter Nine

THE FLOWERING OF MEDIEVAL CIVILIZATION

CULTURAL DEVELOPMENTS • THE STATES OF EUROPE • THE CHURCH

The period from 1150 to the beginning of the thirteenth century was one of creativity in Western Europe. The refinements in living that the nobility were beginning to experience led to the creation of an elaborate court culture and a French vernacular literature that accompanied it. Women had a profound influence on the themes of that literature and on court behavior. Intellectual revival, which far outstripped the Carolingian and Ottonian renaissances, led to new sophistication in philosophy and theology and to the establishment of universities. University-educated men found careers in the Church, with the increasingly powerful monarchies, and in urban centers. A unifying theme of the flowering of medieval civilization was the strong sense of community and class identity that was developing in universities, guilds, villages, and among the nobility.

Monarchies expanded their control over their populations through bureaucracy and law. In pursuing the unification of their governments, they formalized feudal principles into governmental ones. The Church also continued to press forward its control over its bishops, abbots, and the religious beliefs of all Christians. Its claim was not unchallenged during this period, because the Church was faced with two widespread heresies. With the help of two new mendicant orders, the Franciscans and Dominicans, the Church was able to suppress the heresies. The continued religious enthusiasm and devotions of the laity are dramatically evident in the great Romanesque and Gothic churches that they gave their money to build.

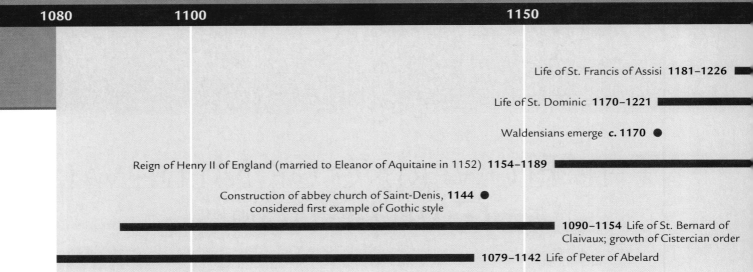

Life of St. Francis of Assisi **1181–1226** ∎

Life of St. Dominic **1170–1221** ∎

Waldensians emerge **c. 1170** ●

Reign of Henry II of England (married to Eleanor of Aquitaine in 1152) **1154–1189** ∎

Construction of abbey church of Saint-Denis, **1144** ●
considered first example of Gothic style

1090–1154 Life of St. Bernard of Claivaux; growth of Cistercian order

1079–1142 Life of Peter of Abelard

CULTURAL DEVELOPMENTS

The changes that were going on in European society in the twelfth and early thirteenth centuries brought about an intellectual revival that revolutionized education. Universities developed that offered bachelor of arts degrees and advanced degrees in theology, law, medicine, and science. The increased bureaucratization of monarchies, the commercial transactions in cities, and the development of canon (Church) and civil law in general increased the demand for educated men with university degrees. As society became wealthier and more expansive, the austere Romanesque architecture inspired by the Cluniac reform gave way to Gothic architecture.

The Rise of Universities

During the High Middle Ages, a new institution, the university, came to assume a role in intellectual life that it has not since relinquished. The university ranks as one of the most influential creations of the medieval world.

Monastic and Cathedral Schools Up to about 1050, monastic schools had dominated intellectual development in the West (see map 9.1). But the isolation of monasteries restricted the experiences of the monastic scholar and made difficult the exchange of ideas that intellectual progress requires.

From about 1050 to 1200, the cathedral, or bishop's, school assumed the intellectual leadership in Europe. These schools were at first very fluid in their structure. The bishop's secretary, the chancellor, was usually in charge of the school and was responsible for inviting learned men, or "masters," to lecture to the students. Both students and masters roamed from town to town, seeking either the best teachers or the brightest (or

MAP 9.1 GREAT MONASTIC CENTERS OF LEARNING
Monastic centers remained the repositories of manuscripts and the chief centers for training not only monks and nuns, but also some laymen and women. Where were the greatest concentrations of monasteries? Why did Spain have so few monasteries in this period?
◆ For an online version, go to www.mhhe.com/chambers9 > chapter 9 > book maps

best-paying) students and the most congenial atmosphere for their work. The twelfth century was the age of the wandering scholars, who have left us charming

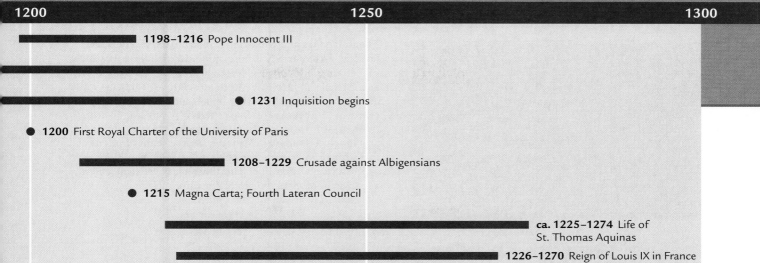

1198–1216 Pope Innocent III

1231 Inquisition begins

1200 First Royal Charter of the University of Paris

1208–1229 Crusade against Albigensians

1215 Magna Carta; Fourth Lateran Council

ca. 1225–1274 Life of St. Thomas Aquinas

1226–1270 Reign of Louis IX in France

traces of their spirit, or at least that of their more frivolous members in the form of "goliardic" verses,[1] largely concerned with such unclerical subjects as the joys of wine, women, and song.

Universities The throngs of masters and students, many of them strangers to the city in which they lectured and studied, eventually grouped themselves into guilds to protect their common interests. It was out of these spontaneously formed guilds of masters and students that the medieval university grew (*universitas* was a widely used Latin word for "guild.") The masters in Paris, for example, formed a guild and received a royal charter in about 1200 and sanction from the pope in 1231. These documents confirmed the guild's autonomy and authority to license teachers.

Italian Universities In Italy the students were older and professionally motivated, desiring degrees in canon law for a career in the church or in civil law (Justinian's *Corpus Juris Civilis*). Wishing to guarantee the quality of their training, the students rather than the professors constituted the dominant "university." At the oldest of these schools, the University of Bologna, the students established the fees to be paid to the professors and determined the hours and even the content of the lectures. Thomas Becket and Pope Innocent III, who are discussed in this chapter, attended Bologna.

The University of Paris The University of Paris became the model for northern Europe as professors founded schools at Oxford, Cambridge, Prague, and

---

[1] The exact etymology of the word *goliardic* remains unknown. It possibly derives from Goliath the Philistine, who was honored as a kind of antisaint by the boisterous students.

other cities throughout Europe (see map 9.2). These universities were run by the masters and granted the baccalaureate, or bachelor of arts degree. The curriculum was the *trivium* and *quadrivium* that Alcuin had developed in the Carolingian period (see p. 202). A master's degree involved further work and licensed the holder to teach. Higher degrees in theology, law, and medicine took five to seven years to complete. A candidate for a theology degree had to be thirty years old; the degree took seven years.

Students matriculated at a university in their early teens. They were expected to know Latin already and to have money for tuition and living expenses. At the University of Paris classes were in rented halls on the left bank of the river, and since the language of the lecturers was Latin, the area came to be—and still is—known as the Latin Quarter. Because the students were young, often poor, and undisciplined, Robert de Sorbonne founded a college, the first, in 1275 in Paris. Colleges provided meals, housing, and libraries for the students. Masters resided in the colleges and supervised student behavior. The system still exists at Oxford and Cambridge.

University Life Townspeople frequently protested to the bishops or the king against the students, whom they resented because of their boisterous ways and because their clerical status—all students automatically took minor orders of clergy—gave them immunity from the local courts. Students for their part resented the high prices that townspeople charged for rooms, food, and drink. Riots involving town and gown (as clerics, students wore ecclesiastical dress) were violent and commonplace.

Students listened to lectures and took notes. They took exams when they felt prepared. The exams, which

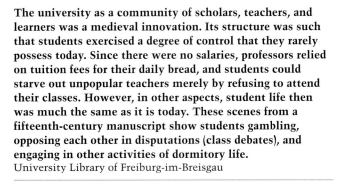

The university as a community of scholars, teachers, and learners was a medieval innovation. Its structure was such that students exercised a degree of control that they rarely possess today. Since there were no salaries, professors relied on tuition fees for their daily bread, and students could starve out unpopular teachers merely by refusing to attend their classes. However, in other aspects, student life then was much the same as it is today. These scenes from a fifteenth-century manuscript show students gambling, opposing each other in disputations (class debates), and engaging in other activities of dormitory life.
University Library of Freiburg-im-Breisgau

were oral and taken in front of an examining board of professors, were so difficult that students were forbidden to carry knives with them. If the student passed, he was required to give the professors a feast.

Scholasticism

Scholasticism was both a way of reasoning and a body of writings: Scholastics applied **dialectic** to Christian dogma. Dialectic is the art of analyzing the logical relationships among propositions in a dialogue or discourse. The method of presenting an argument was to state a proposition and then dispute its validity either orally or in writing. Scholasticism represented a shift from the humanistic studies of the early twelfth century. Cathedral schools emphasized familiarity with the classical authors, particularly Plato. But dialectic won out in the late twelfth century, partly because Aristotle's complete logic, brought to the West through Islamic Spain, became available to Western scholars.

Anselm of Canterbury The first thinker to explore, although still not rigorously, the theological applications of dialectic was St. Anselm of Canterbury (1033–1109). Anselm defined his own intellectual interests, using his faith in seeking to find logical consistency in Christian beliefs. He tried to show a necessary, logical connection between the traditional Judeo-Christian dogma that God is a perfect being and a logical proof that God exists.

Abelard Peter Abelard (1079–1142) brought a new rigor and popularity to dialectical theology. We know a great deal about Peter Abelard because he wrote an autobiography later in his life called *Historia calamitatum (Story of My Calamities).* Eldest son of a petty noble from Brittany, Abelard was destined for warfare and lordship, but his intellectual interests overrode this career. As a wandering scholar, he came to Paris, entered into a decisive disputation with the leading theologian, and began to give lectures. His brilliance

MAP 9.2 MEDIEVAL UNIVERSITIES
Starting in Bologna, Salerno, and Paris, universities spread throughout Europe. While some students became priests, many became administrators in various governments, or entered professions such as law and medicine. Where was the chief concentration of universities? What do the founding dates of the universities tell you?
◆ For an online version, go to www.mhhe.com/chambers9 > chapter 9 > book maps

attracted the attention of a clergyman attached to Notre Dame Cathedral, who engaged Abelard to tutor his niece, Héloïse (ca. 1100–ca. 1163). Despite an age difference of twenty-four years, Abelard tells his readers, they fell in love and conceived a child. They had a clandestine marriage because Héloïse knew that it would ruin his career if he, as a member of the clergy, were married. He would have had to give up his lecturing, an activity only clergy could do. Her uncle, betrayed and angry, had thugs castrate Abelard to punish him. Abelard and Héloïse then entered separate monasteries.

The child of their marriage, Astrolabe, was born at Abelard's sister's home. Héloïse became a respected abbess, but in her letters to Abelard, it is apparent that she continued to care about him with undiminished love. Abelard's replies admonish her to pray and to administer the nunnery.

Abelard continued his writing, and in *Sic et Non* ("Yes and No") he used what became the standard Scholastic method of argumentation, posing a formal question and citing authorities on both sides. Abelard assembled 150 theological questions and marshaled authorities from the Bible, Church councils, and Church fathers for arguments on either side. He made no effort to reconcile the discrepancies, but left the authorities standing in embarrassing juxtaposition (see "Abelard's

ABELARD'S SIC ET NON

Completed in 1138, Peter Abelard's Sic et Non *("Yes and No") explained the techniques for reconciling divergent opinions in theology and law. His approach reflects the ambition of Scholasticism to bolster faith through reason.*

"Among the many words of the holy fathers some seem not only to differ from one another but even to contradict one another. . . . Why should it seem surprising if we, lacking the guidance of the holy spirit, fail to understand them?

"Our achievement of understanding is impeded especially by unusual modes of expression and by the different significances that can be attached to one and the same word. We must also take special care that we are not deceived by corruptions of the text or by false attributions when sayings of the [Church] fathers are quoted that seem to differ from the truth or to be contrary to it; for many apocryphal writings are set down under names of saints to enhance their authority, and even the texts of the divine scripture are corrupted by the errors of scribes. If, in scripture, anything seems absurd, you are not permitted to say, 'The author of this book did not hold the truth,' but rather

that the book is defective or that the interpreter erred or that you do not understand. But if anything seems contrary to truth in the works of later authors, the reader or auditor is free to judge, so that he may approve what is pleasing and reject what gives offense, unless the matter is established by certain reason or canonical authority.

"In view of these considerations we have undertaken to collect various sayings of the fathers that give rise to questioning because of their apparent contradictions. Assiduous and frequent questioning is indeed the first key to wisdom. For by doubting we come to inquiry; and through inquiring we perceive the truth."

From *The Letters of Abelard and Heloise,* translated by C. K. Scott Moncrieff, copyright 1926 and renewed 1954 by Alfred A. Knopf, Inc. Used by permission of Alfred A. Knopf, a division of Random House, Inc.

HÉLOÏSE AND ABELARD, FROM *ROMAN DE LA ROSE*
Already a famous professor in Paris, Abelard began a secret relationship with Héloïse, and in revenge her relatives had him castrated. The two were then separated for decades, and their correspondence remains one of the most powerful human documents of medieval times. Despite the conventions of the day, Héloïse was clearly an equal partner in the relationship, as is indicated in this fifteenth- century depiction of the pair engaged in intense discussion.
Giraudon/Art Resource, NY

Sic et Non," above). *Sic et Non* implied that one must either enlist dialectic to reconcile the conflicts or concede that the faith was a tissue of contradictions. His book caused a furor of debate, and finally a Church council condemned it. To avoid charges of heresy, he was forced to throw it into the flames and submit to the Church. But the method of argument that he used, that of posing a question and then mustering arguments to support or refute it, became characteristic of medieval Scholasticism.

Reception of Aristotle   By the end of the twelfth century, dialectical argument was supreme in Paris and elsewhere. One reason it predominated was that, after the middle of the twelfth century, translators working chiefly in Spain and Sicily introduced European scholars to hitherto unknown works of Aristotle as well as to the great commentary that the Muslim Averroës had written on them (see chapter 7). Christian thinkers now had at their disposal the full Aristotelian corpus, and it confronted them with a philosophical system based solely on observation and human reason. Aristotle's logic drove Western scholars to examine his works and their own faith through Aristotelian logic.

Thomas Aquinas   The most gifted representative of Scholastic philosophy, and the greatest Christian theologian since Augustine, was St. Thomas Aquinas (ca. 1225–1274), whose career well illustrates the character of thirteenth-century intellectual life. At age seventeen Aquinas entered the new Dominican Order, perhaps attracted by its commitment to scholarship. He studied at the University of Naples and later, as a Dominican, at Cologne and Paris (see map 9.2). His most influential teacher was another Dominican, Albertus Magnus, a German who wrote extensively on theology and natural science, especially biology. Aquinas was no intellectual recluse; he lectured at Paris and traveled widely across Europe. His was such an active mind that when he dined with King Louis IX of France, the king provided him with scribes to keep notes on his brilliant discourse.

Aquinas produced a prodigious amount of writing. The *Summa contra Gentiles* was probably intended for Dominican missionaries working to convert heretics and infidels. His most important work, however, was one he did not live to finish. The *Summa Theologica* was meant to provide a comprehensive introduction to Christian theology and to present a systematic view of the universe that would do justice to all truth, ancient philosophers, and Christian theologians.

Aquinas brought to his task a subtle and perceptive intellect, and his system rests on several fundamental, delicate compromises. In regard to faith and reason, he taught that both are roads to a single truth. Reason is based ultimately on sense experience, as Aristotle argued. It is a powerful instrument, but insufficient to teach people all that God wishes them to know. Natural law governs many of our social institutions. But nature alone cannot carry them to ultimate understanding of matters such as the Trinity. These matters must be accepted on the basis of faith, not reason. In the final analysis, God's mind is infinite, while human beings' minds are finite.

The *Summa* shows certain characteristic weaknesses of Scholasticism. Aquinas affirmed that natural law and logic were based on observation, but in fact, he observed very little. He borrowed from Aristotle rather than doing his own observation or experimentation. Many later thinkers found his system too speculative, too elaborate. Nonetheless, the *Summa* remains an unquestioned masterpiece of Western theology. It offers comment on an enormous range of theological, philosophical, and ethical problems, and consistently demonstrates openness, insight, and wisdom.

Duns Scotus Aquinas' system fell under critical scrutiny in the generation following his death. Among his early critics, the most influential was a Scottish Franciscan, John Duns Scotus (ca. 1265–1308). Drawing inspiration from St. Augustine, Duns Scotus affirmed that faith was an essential ingredient to understanding reason. He rejected Aquinas' acceptance of observation of nature. He went back to an intellectual analysis of the concept of God as a necessary being, an argument

GOD AS ARCHITECT OF THE UNIVERSE
The notion of God creating the universe as an architect was common during the Middle Ages. In this manuscript illumination, God is depicted holding a compass and literally measuring the structure of the physical world.
Photo Archive, Nationalbibliotek Austria, Vienna

closer to Anselm before him and Descartes in the seventeenth century.

Spiritual Approaches to Knowledge

Many people who thought deeply about the nature of God and religion argued that the dialectic approach was not the best way to achieve knowledge. They argued that a spiritual approach based on prayer and humility would bring about a greater understanding of God. They emphasized the human side of the religion by encouraging worship of Mary.

Worship of Mary Mary, mother of Jesus, became an important figure in the dedication of churches and in popular worship. Her presence added a humanizing touch to the religion and invited prayers of intercession with Jesus and God. In the Early Middle Ages a stern, mature Jesus was depicted as a lawgiver in churches, but in the late twelfth century Mary with an infant Jesus on her hip came to dominate church dedications and sculpture.

Cistercians and St. Bernard   The **Cistercians** took their name from their first house at Cîteau. Although founded in 1098, their prominence came with the arrival of Bernard of Clairvaux (ca. 1090–1153) with thirty companions in 1112. Bernard played a major role in European politics, including the condemnation of Abelard's *Sic et Non.* He preached the Second Crusade and served as adviser to the monarchs of Europe.

The Cistercians advocated a greater simplicity than the Cluniacs. Their robes were made of white, undyed wool; for that reason they were called the "white monks." Their emphasis was on emotional devotion to Christ's and Mary's humility. All of their churches were dedicated to Mary. Bernard praised the human, nurturing quality of Mary in hymns as well as in devotional practices.

The Cistercian order spread rapidly both within the older borders of Europe and into frontier lands in northern England, along the newly reclaimed wasteland of Flanders, and in the newly conquered Slavic lands to the east. The order became identified with the expansion of Europe and the spread of efficient estate management and agriculture.

Women's Spirituality   Women could not attend universities in the Middle Ages, so their intellectual life centered in the nunnery or court. Perhaps because of the new emphasis on the worship of Mary, women became more prominent in the spiritual life of the Church. Hildegard of Bingen (d. 1179) was an abbess, musician, and writer. She wrote in Latin on scientific questions and revelations and corresponded with emperors and popes.

Other women became well known for their piety and their mystical visions. Marie D'Oignies (d. 1213) was a founding mother of the Beguines, a group of religious women to be discussed in chapter 10. Withdrawing to a cell connected to a monastery, she had a reputation as a healer and an ascetic. Women throughout the Middle Ages became anchorites, or holy women living in cells connected to churches or monasteries.

Romanesque Architecture

The increased prosperity and the revival of popular piety in the Early Middle Ages produced major new developments in architecture, sculpture, painting, and illustration. The austerity of the Cluniac period led to the sober Romanesque style—a style that took the Roman, rounded arch as its model. The Cistercian movement and the greater social, cultural, and technological exuberance of the mid-twelfth century expressed its piety with sunlit churches of the Gothic style (see p. 260).

The Romanesque Style   The architectural and artistic style of **Romanesque** (meaning "of Roman origins") took some elements from earlier models, but not exclusively; it also drew on other artistic traditions, such as Germanic, Byzantine, and Arabic. Thus, Romanesque buildings in different parts of western Europe had distinctive design features.

The most impressive artistic monuments left to us from the Romanesque period include churches, monasteries, and castles. One objective in the Romanesque style was to roof churches in stone rather than wooden beams and thatch roofs that were vulnerable to burning. Around the year 1000, small stone-roofed churches began to appear, especially in southern Europe. At first the builders used the simple barrel, or tunnel, vault (see p. 257). Because of the weight of the masonry roof, walls had to be thick and the windows small. Architects then developed and mastered the use of the groin vault, which is formed by the intersection of two barrel vaults. The area of intersection is called the bay, and the roof over the bay is supported at four points, not by the entire length of the lateral walls. Bays could be built next to bays, an entire church could be roofed with stone, windows could be enlarged, and the monotony of tunnel vaulting would be avoided.

Romanesque Decoration   Romanesque churches were decorated on the exterior with stone sculpture. Romanesque statues, which exist by the thousands, show a marked quality of antirealism, a refusal to allow visual accuracy to dominate portrayals. The artists were striving to present a world as seen by faith. Christ, for example, had to be shown larger than the other figures, in keeping with his dignity (see p. 258). Demons and monsters, many drawn from the popular imagination, abound in Romanesque sculpture. Romanesque statuary documents the exuberant spirit of this age of reform, when people seemed convinced that God was actively at work among them, setting right the world.

Other Characteristics of Romanesque Style   Nobles became consumers of art and architecture for building and furnishing their increasingly elaborate castles, but art remained, in most of its forms, the servant of the Church. The Cluniac monastic reform in the eleventh century brought with it a revival of church ceremony, which stimulated the art of metalwork (which produced chalices and other sacred vessels), glass making, and the weaving of fine fabrics for priests' vestments.

The Gregorian chant (named for Pope Gregory the Great, but in fact representing the traditional plainsong of the Church of Rome) became the common music of the Western Church in the Carolingian epoch. The eleventh and twelfth centuries witnessed the development of polyphonic music (part-singing). The

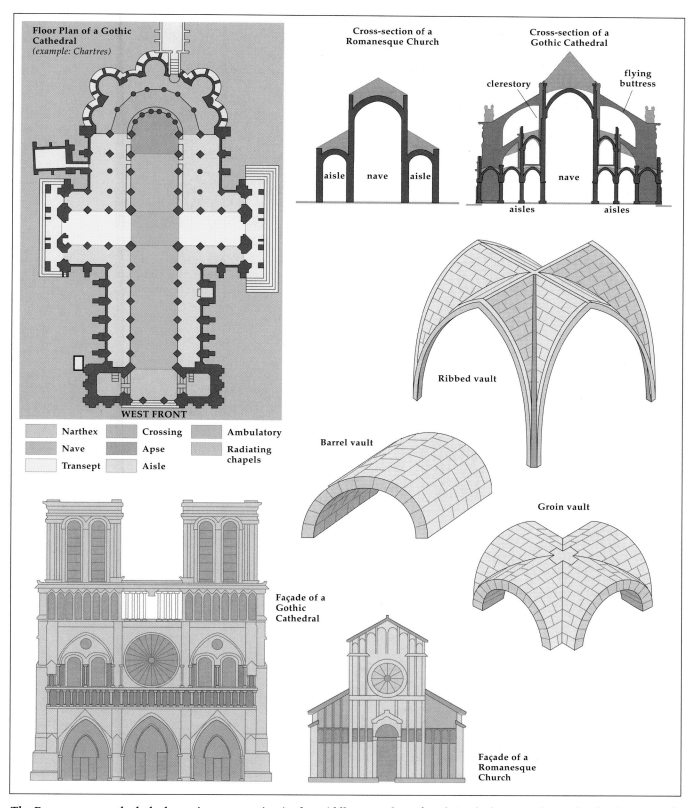

Floor Plan of a Gothic Cathedral (*example: Chartres*)

WEST FRONT

Narthex
Nave
Transept
Crossing
Apse
Aisle
Ambulatory
Radiating chapels

Cross-section of a Romanesque Church

aisle   nave   aisle

Cross-section of a Gothic Cathedral

clerestory   flying buttress

nave

aisles   aisles

Ribbed vault

Barrel vault

Groin vault

Façade of a Gothic Cathedral

Façade of a Romanesque Church

The Romanesque cathedral, shown in cross-section in the middle top and as a façade in the bottom, shows the simple nave and isle construction of the cathedral. The roof was either a barrel vault or a groin vault. The Gothic cathedral, shown in the floor plan and the façade, could be a more elaborate structure because of the use of flying buttresses, shown upper right, which formed an external skeleton supporting the walls. The buttresses permitted the walls to have great expanses of windows since they were not bearing all the weight of the stone roof. The ribbed vault permitted greater height in the Gothic cathedral.

PISA CATHEDRAL, CA. 1063–1272
One of the finest architectural ensembles in the new Romanesque styles of the eleventh and twelfth centuries is the cathedral and its surrounding buildings in Pisa, Italy. Although the famous leaning tower, which is now restored to nearly vertical, is the best known of these buildings, the huge marble-clad cathedral was in fact regarded as the supreme achievement of the Pisans and was widely influential in church building throughout Italy.
Casimir/eStock Photo

TYMPANUM OF SOUTH PORTAL OF ST. PIERRE, MOISSAC, CA. 1115–1135
The revival of sculpture is one of the noteworthy achievements of Romanesque art. Integrating architecture and sculpture, this tympanum (the semicircular space above a church portal) shows the Second Coming of Christ, attended by symbols of the evangelists and the kings of the world seated in rows divided by stylized clouds.
Giraudon/Art Resource, NY

ST. ETIENNE, CAEN, VAULTS, CA. 1115–1120
St. Etienne, Caen, was begun by William the Conqueror in 1067 and is considered a superb example of Norman Romanesque architecture. It was originally supposed to have a wooden roof, but it was vaulted in stone between 1115 and 1120. Each section of the roof is held up by six ribs that meet at the center and two arches, all of which rest on pillars at the side of the nave. The resultant pattern added to the sense of height and drew the eye ever upward toward heaven.
Foto Marburg/Art Resource, NY

coordination of the vocal parts in choral music also required systems of musical notation.

The Gothic Style

Artists as well as theologians were attempting to present a systematic view of the universe that was reflective of all truth. The artistic counterpart to the Scholastic *Summas* was the Gothic cathedral.

Gothic Architecture   Sixteenth-century critics coined the word *Gothic* as an expression of contempt for these supposedly barbarous medieval buildings. In fact, the Goths had disappeared some 500 years before any Gothic churches were built. As used today, **Gothic** refers to the style of architecture and art that initially developed in the royal lands in France, including Paris and its surroundings, from about 1150. The abbey church of Saint-Denis near Paris, built by the Abbot

Suger in 1144, is usually taken as the first authentic example of the Gothic style. In the thirteenth century the Gothic style spread widely through Europe and found special application in cathedrals and large monastic churches.

Technically, three engineering devices helped stamp the Gothic style: the pointed rather than rounded arch; ribbed vaulting, which concentrated support around the lines of thrust and gave the buildings a visibly delineated skeleton; and the flying buttress, an external support that allowed the walls to be made higher and lighter. The flying buttress also freed sections of the walls from the function of supporting the roof and therefore permitted the use of large areas for windows. The windows were filled with stained glass that depicted scenes from the Bible or from saints' lives. Romanesque architects had pioneered all three devices, but the Gothic architects combined them and used them with unprecedented vigor and boldness.

AMIENS CATHEDRAL, CA. 1220–1236
Built between 1220 and 1236, Amiens Cathedral exemplifies the structure of a Gothic cathedral. The weight of the walls is supported by a system of buttresses and ribbed vaults, which allowed medieval builders to break up the walls with luminous areas of stained glass. The colored light that poured into these massive structures gave them an otherworldly majesty never before achieved.
Scala/Art Resource, NY

In contrast to Romanesque sculpture, which overflows with great displays of emotion, Gothic sculpture evokes a sense of calm and orderly reality, as can be seen in the figures on the central portal of Chartres Cathedral.
Foto Marburg/Art Resource, NY

SAINTE-CHAPELLE, PARIS, INTERIOR, 1243–1248
Sainte-Chapelle, the private chapel attached to the French royal palace in Paris, was built between 1243 and 1248 to house relics brought back from the crusades by Louis IX. The building was deliberately designed to resemble a reliquary, and the enormous jewel-colored stained-glass windows make up three-quarters of its wall surface.
Giraudon/Art Resource, NY

The sculpture adorning buildings also represented innovation. Romanesque sculpture often conveyed great emotional power but did not reflect the natural world. Sculptors now wanted their works to emulate reality, or at least its handsomest parts (decorative foliage, for example, was carved with such accuracy that the botanical models can be identified). Their statues portray real and usually cheerful people, who subtly exert their own personalities without destroying the harmony of the whole.

The Gothic Spirit   These magnificent churches with their hundreds of statues took decades to construct and decorate, and many were never completed. The builders intended that the churches provide a comprehensive view of the universe and instruction in its sacred history. One principal element of the Gothic aesthetic is a strong sense of order. The naked ribs and buttresses and the intricate vaulting constitute a spectacular geometry that instills in the viewer a vivid impression of intelligence and logical relationships.

The most distinctive aspect of the Gothic style is its use of light in a manner unique in the history of architecture. Once within the church, the visitor has entered a realm defined and infused by a warm, colored glow. In Christian worship light is one of the most ancient, common, and versatile symbols. It suggests to the worshiper mystical illumination, spiritual beauty, grace, and divinity itself.

The thirteenth century was a great age of cathedral building. Gothic architecture reached its highest point with cathedrals in France, including those of Chartres, Paris, Amiens, and Rheims. England and Germany also produced fine Gothic cathedrals, such as Salisbury, Lincoln, and Cologne. Enhancing the style perfected in the thirteenth century, later additions came to be more elaborate, and by the fifteenth century the encrustation of the cathedrals with carvings and the height of the naves and towers have led historians to call them "wedding-cake Gothic."

Court Culture

At the same time that universities were being established and Gothic cathedrals were being built, the nobility was developing its own distinctive culture, influenced by wealth, leisure, and refinements in living learned from the Arabs and Greeks. A new code of behavior that included chivalry and courtly love became standard for all European nobility and was widely imitated by the urban elite as well.

Chivalry   A new code of behavior called **chivalry** (derived from *à cheval*, or "on horseback") refined the manners of knights. Added to bravery and loyalty, exemplified in *The Song of Roland* (see p. 221), were devotion to the Church and polite behavior, including rules at the table and in the lord's court. *Courtesy* means the manners appropriate to the noble court. The knight no longer was simply dubbed with a sword when he reached the age of twenty-one, but instead went through a religious ceremony that included a vigil and the blessing of his arms, a ritual cleansing, and an oath to protect women and the Church. In addition to using weapons, training for knighthood included learning to sing or play an instrument, to carve a roast and serve it to a lord and lady, to dance, and to dress appropriately. The etiquette of tournaments was elaborately established and taught to knights when they were young.

Courtly Love   **Courtly love,** or the polite relations between men and women, developed at the court of Eleanor of Aquitaine, of whom we shall speak presently. While married to Henry II of England, she and her sons and daughters spent much of their time at the seat of her duchy in Poitiers. One of the writers they patronized, Andreas Capellanus, updated Ovid's writings on love in a book called *The Art of Courtly Love.* The book instructs men on how to please and seduce women of different ranks, although when he refers to the love of a noble for a peasant he sanctions rape: "Do not hesitate to take what you seek and to embrace her by force." According to Andreas, Eleanor and her daughters set up a court to correct men who erred or to set tasks, such as fighting in a number of tournaments, for those wishing to win the love of a particular lady.

In an age of arranged marriages, in which love might or might not be present between the couples, courtly love permitted an atmosphere for flirtation. Historians debate whether adultery was widespread in these courts. Historians are also undecided about the influence courtly love had on the position of noblewomen in society: Did it trivialize them by making them mere objects of sexual desire, or did it make them more valued and respected?

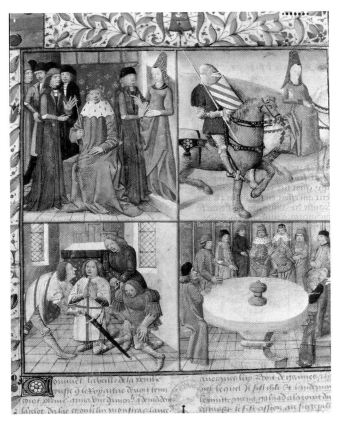

The most popular subject for courtly romance was the legends surrounding King Arthur. In the first picture, King Arthur is surrounded by his knights. His queen, Guinevere, is in the doorway. Below, the induction of a knight to the Round Table is shown. The altar in the background indicates the religious nature of the knighting ceremony. The upper right depicts the romance of Tristan, and the lower right displays the Holy Grail.
Musée Condé, Chantilly/Dagli Orti/The Art Archive

Noblewomen   As in the Early Middle Ages, women in the twelfth century spent much of their time in and around their castles. The castles had become much more comfortable, with pleasant quarters attached to gardens reserved for the women. Although noblewomen still faced the tasks of household and estate management in the absence of their husbands, the new luxury goods available and courtly manners provided more entertainment for them in their leisure hours. For noblewomen, as for knights, acquiring skill in singing, dancing, and playing musical instruments was important. With luxurious silks more available since the crusades, dress became more elaborate and noblewomen undertook embroidery with silk as well as woolen thread. Noblewomen learned to read and write vernacular poetry and prose, which was undergoing a great vogue in the twelfth century.

Vernacular Literature There were three principal genres of vernacular literature: the heroic epic, of which *The Song of Roland* is the best example; troubadour lyric poetry; and the courtly romance.

Very different from the heroic epic is **troubadour** lyric poetry. The novelty of this complex poetry is its celebration of women and of love, as opposed to heroic epics, which were written for the masculine society of the battle camp. The troubadours sang at courts, in which women exerted a powerful influence.

The troubadour usually addressed his poetry to a lady of superior social station, almost always someone else's wife, whom he had little chance of winning. Courtly love (at least as the troubadours present it) was not a dalliance but quite literally a means of rescuing the lover from despondency and introducing him into an earthly paradise of his imagination. This discovery and intensive exploration of the emotion of love represents one of the most influential creations of the medieval mind.

The *courtly romance*, which entered its great age after 1150, combines traits of both heroic epics and troubadour lyric poetry. It is a narrative, like the epic, but it allots a major role to women and love. Taking her stories from Celtic tales, Marie de France (d. 1210) wrote in the vernacular, composing brief romance narratives of love and adventure. Chrétien de Troyes wrote romances about King Arthur of Britain and his coterie of knights. Many of these tales are concerned with the tensions between adulterous love for a lord's wife and loyalty to the lord.

THE STATES OF EUROPE

Governments in the eleventh and early twelfth centuries had taken tentative steps toward expanding their control over their subjects and extending royal justice, as opposed to local justice, to everyone. The growth of universities and the use of academically trained lawyers helped define governmental and legal procedures. Subjects valued the more uniform law that royal justice provided. Merchants could travel from place to place under the rule of the same laws rather than the arbitrary administration of law that a feudal lord might apply. Lesser landholders appreciated a central court of appeal that could overcome the might of local overlords.

England

In England the kings were particularly aggressive in extending their control over the English countryside and their subjects by making royal justice the most important arbitrator in England. In doing so the kings clashed with the papacy and the English clergy, who claimed to be exempt from royal justice. Royal justice also undermined the prerogatives of the nobility and led to the rebellion that produced the *Magna Carta*.

Angevin Kingship Henry I had numerous bastard children, but the only legitimate child to survive him was a daughter, Matilda. Her first marriage was to the emperor of Germany, giving her the title of "Matilda Empress." Her second marriage was to the Count Geoffrey of Anjou. Rather than selecting a woman—and one who was married to a hostile and aggressive neighbor of the duchy of Normandy—the English nobility selected another descendent of William I's line, Stephen of Blois (r. 1135–1152), to be king. Civil war ensued, which was resolved with the compromise that the son of Matilda and the Count of Anjou would succeed to the throne at Stephen's death. In 1154 Henry of Anjou, grandson of Henry I, became the first Angevin king of England.

Henry II Through combined inheritances from his father and mother and his marriage to Eleanor of Aquitaine in 1152, Henry II ruled over a sprawling assemblage of territories that included England and nearly the entire west of France (see map 9.3). A man of great energy who carried to completion many of the reforms of Henry I, Henry II ranks among the most gifted statesmen of the twelfth century and among the greatest kings of England.

Itinerant Justices Henry II left a permanent mark on English government and law. He resurrected the "justices in eyre" (that is, on journey, or itinerant), who were endowed with all the authority of the king himself. The itinerant justices heard both criminal and civil pleas. In both cases, they relied on the testimony of a jury of "twelve good men." Called a "sworn inquest," the jury determined whether there was enough evidence for an indictment in a criminal case. It is the origin of our grand jury. After the Church condemned the ordeal in 1215, a small, or petty (*petite* in French), jury was used, as it is today, to judge the guilt or innocence of the alleged felon.

The itinerant justices did not forcibly interfere in civil disputes, but they did offer the services of the royal court in settling them. Barons receiving fiefs from the king had also been given the right to hold a court and judge the disputes of their own knights and dependents. Normally, therefore, litigants in a civil dispute appeared before a baronial court. As a result of Henry's reforms, a litigant could purchase a royal writ, which ordered the sheriff to bring the case under the scrutiny of the royal court presided over by the justice in eyre. Sworn inquest juries were composed of "good

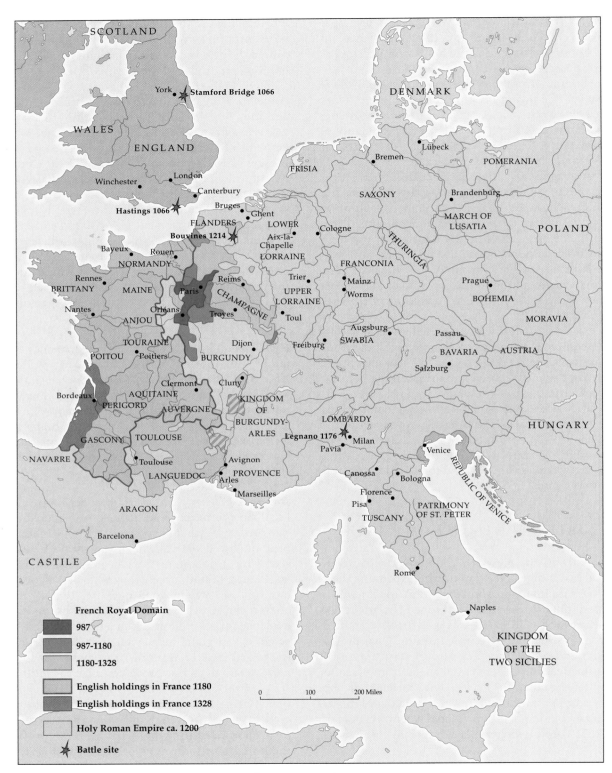

MAP 9.3   MEDIEVAL ENGLAND, FRANCE, AND GERMANY
The map indicates the areas belonging to the English kings, the French kings, and those of Germany. Although the Holy Roman Empire appears vast, it was really a collection of independent cities and duchies. Note the small extent of the territory that the French kings originally held and those territories that they gradually added. What was the period of greatest growth? Did English territory in France expand or contract over the centuries?
◆ For an online version, go to www.mhhe.com/chambers9 > chapter 9 > book maps

MURDER OF THOMAS BECKET
This depiction of the murder of Thomas Becket in Canterbury in 1170 was completed within a few years of the event. That it should have appeared as a wall painting in the church of Sts. Giovanni and Paolo in Spoleto, Italy, hundreds of miles away from Canterbury, suggests the intensity of the European reaction to the assassination.
André Held

men" from the neighborhood who were likely to know the facts at issue and were able to judge the truth or falsity of claims. They were put on oath to tell the truth of the case. While Henry made no effort to suppress baronial courts, the royal courts left them with a shrinking role in English justice.

Common Law   In time the justices built up a considerable body of decisions, which then served as precedents in similar cases. The result was the development of **common law**—common in that it applied to the entire kingdom and was thus distinct from the local customs. Precedent cases, used to decide later, similar cases, mark the beginning of the common law tradition under which most of the English-speaking world continues to live.

Thomas Becket   The judicial reforms of Henry II led him into a bitter conflict with the English Church,

which maintained its own ecclesiastical courts. Henry did not want a whole group of his subjects, members of the clergy, to fall outside his judicial system. In 1164 Henry claimed the right to retry clerics accused of crime in his royal courts. The archbishop of Canterbury, Thomas Becket, rejected this claim. He argued that both the Bible and canon law forbade what we now call "double jeopardy"—that is, a second trial and punishment for one crime.

Becket had been a personal friend of Henry and had served him ably and faithfully as Chancellor of the Exchequer, the chief financial official of the realm. After becoming archbishop of Canterbury in 1162, Becket seems to have undergone a conversion that made him devoted to the Church. When Henry tried to force Becket to agree to a document, the Constitutions of Clarendon, outlining the king's view of the relations of the church to the crown, Becket fled to France. He was

ELEANOR OF AQUITAINE EFFIGY
Eleanor was a worthy consort for Henry II, one of the most powerful and innovative rulers of the Middle Ages, and is buried next to him. The site, the splendid French abbey of Fontevrault, lies within the territories that Eleanor had inherited and added to the English kingdom. The crown and book in the effigy on her tomb are perfect symbols of the intelligence and power that characterized her life.
Giraudon/Art Resource, NY

ENGLISH KINGS: HENRY II, RICHARD I, JOHN I, HENRY III
A medieval illustrator captured three generations of Plantagenet kings. Henry II, who ruled England and a large part of France, is shown as a wise man. Richard I, his son, is depicted as a warrior with a sword and shield as befits a crusader. John I, also a son of Henry II, sits with his crown askew, indicative of his concessions in Magna Carta. Henry III, John's son, is a beardless youth because he was a child when he inherited the throne.
British Library, London. Cotton Claudius D. VI, f. 9v

reconciled with Henry once more in 1170, but a few months later he excommunicated the bishops who had supported the king.

Henry, then in France, demanded in fateful rhetoric, whether no man would free him of this pestilential priest. Four of the king's knights took the words to heart, journeyed to England, found Becket in his cathedral, and cut him down before the high altar on December 29, 1170. By popular acclaim Becket was regarded as a martyr and a saint. Canterbury became his shrine and a popular pilgrimage site. Henry had no choice but to revoke the objectionable reforms and perform an arduous personal penance for his unwise words, including a beating.

In a compromise, clerics suspected of crimes were tried first in the royal courts and, if convicted, surrendered their wealth to the king. They were then tried in ecclesiastical court, in which punishment was a penance rather than hanging.

Richard I, the Lion-hearted
Richard succeeded his father Henry in 1189. Growing up in Eleanor's court in Aquitaine, Richard acquired all the virtues of a model knight—boldness, military skill, stately bearing, even a flair for composing troubadour lyrics. He spent little time administering his realm, preferring fighting to ruling. In 1191 and 1192 he was fighting in the Holy Land on the Third Crusade. He died in 1199 from a neglected wound received while besieging a castle in a minor war in France. Richard spent less than ten months in England, but the English government continued to function efficiently even in the absence of its king—testimony to its fundamental strength.

John I
Richard was succeeded by his younger brother John, who, rightly or wrongly, is considered a wicked

king. Mostly his problems arose from misjudgments on his part.

Early in his reign he married a young woman who was already engaged to a vassal of King Philip II of France. Philip, upholding his feudal obligation to defend his vassal, used the incident as a pretext to seize the duchy of Normandy. John's wars to recapture Normandy were expensive. To pay for them, John abused the feudal contract by demanding payments rather than military service, marrying off heiresses to the highest bidder, selling off wardships, and even extorting money from his subjects.

In 1206 John defied Pope Innocent III by rejecting Stephen Langton as archbishop of Canterbury. Innocent retaliated and put England under interdict in 1208. An interdict meant that the English clergy were not to baptize

EXCERPTS FROM THE MAGNA CARTA

"John, by the grace of God, king of England, lord of Ireland, duke of Normandy and Aquitaine, and count of Anjou, to the archbishops, bishops, abbots, earls, barons, justiciars, foresters, sheriffs, stewards, servants, and to all his bailiffs and faithful subjects, greetings. Know that we, out of reverence for God and for the salvation of our soul and those of all our ancestors and heirs, for the honour of God and the exaltation of the holy church, and for the reform of our realm . . . :

"[6] Heirs may marry without disparagement; so nevertheless, that, before the marriage is contracted, it shall be announced to the relations by blood by the heir himself.

"[7] A widow, after the death of her husband, shall straightway, and without difficulty, have her marriage portion and her inheritance, nor shall she give anything in return for her dower, her marriage portion, or the inheritance which belonged to her. . . . And she may remain in the house of her husband, after his death, for forty days.

"[12] No scutage or aid shall be imposed in our kingdom unless by common counsel of our kingdom, except for ransoming our person, for making our eldest son a knight, and for once marrying our eldest daughter; and for these only a reasonable aid shall be levied. Be it done in like manner concerning aids from the city of London.

"[13] And the city of London shall have all its ancient liberties and free customs as well by land as by water. Furthermore, we will and grant that all other cities, boroughs, towns, and ports shall have all their liberties and free customs.

"[20] A free man shall not be amerced [fined] for a trivial offense except in accordance with the degree of the offense, and for a grave offense he shall be amerced in accordance with its gravity, yet saving his way of living; and a merchant in the same way, saving his stock-in-trade; and a villein shall be amerced in the same way, saving his means of livelihood—and none of the aforesaid amercements shall be imposed except by the oath of good men of the neighborhood.

"[21] Earls and barons shall not be amerced except by their peers, and only in accordance with the degree of the offense.

"[38] No bailiff shall in future put anyone to trial upon his own bare word, without reliable witnesses produced for this purpose.

"[39] No free man shall be arrested or imprisoned or disseised or outlawed or exiled or in any way victimized, neither will we attack him or send anyone to attack him, except by the lawful judgment of his peers or by the law of the land.

"[40] To no one will we sell, to no one will we refuse or delay right or justice.

"[52] If anyone has been disseised of or kept out of his lands, castles, franchises or his right by us without the legal judgment of his peers, we will immediately restore them to him: and if a dispute arises over this, then let it be decided by the judgment of the twenty-five barons who are mentioned below in the clause for securing the peace.

"[61] . . . the barons shall choose any twenty-five barons of the kingdom they wish, who must with all their might observe, hold and cause to be observed, the peace and liberties which we have granted and confirmed to them by this present charter of ours, so that if we, or our justiciar, or our bailiffs or any one of our servants offend in any way against anyone or transgress any of the articles of the peace or the security, and the offense be notified to four of the aforesaid twenty-five barons, those four barons shall come to us, or to our justiciar if we are out of the kingdom, and, laying the transgression before us, shall petition us to have that transgression corrected without delay. And if we do not correct the transgression . . . within forty days . . . , the aforesaid four barons shall refer that case to the rest of the twenty-five barons. And those twenty-five barons together with the community of the whole land shall distrain and distress us in every way they can . . . until, in their opinion, amends have been made; and when amends have been made, they shall obey us as they did before."

---

babies, marry couples, or bury the dead in public ceremony. When the interdict did not sway John, Innocent threatened to encourage Philip to invade. In 1213 John accepted Stephen Langton as archbishop of Canterbury.

Magna Carta   Already angry with John's abuses of the feudal contract and taxation, his enraged barons turned on him after a humiliating defeat at the Battle of Bouvines in 1214. Encouraged by Stephen Langton, they took to arms, and in June 1215 at Runnymede the barons forced John to grant them the "Great Charter." Archbishop Langton probably inspired, if not largely composed, the **Magna Carta** (so called because it was a large piece of parchment). The Magna Carta resembled coronation oaths that English kings since Henry I had taken. But no previous royal charter of liberties equaled it in length, explicitness, and influence (see "Excerpts from the Magna Carta," above).

The Magna Carta disappoints most modern readers. Unlike the American Declaration of Independence, it offers no grand generalizations about human dignity and rights. Its sixty-three clauses, arranged without apparent order, are largely concerned with technical problems of feudal law—rights of inheritance, feudal relief, wardship, and widow's rights. It granted the Church, barons, and all free subjects the peaceful exercise of their customary liberties. To all freemen it promised access to justice and judgment by known procedures. The king could impose new taxes only with the common consent of the realm. While these concessions were certainly significant, the Magna Carta addressed the concerns of only the elite. The rights of the unfree classes, the serfs and villeins who constituted 90 percent of the population at the time, are hardly mentioned.

The Magna Carta marked a major step toward government by recognized procedures that could be changed only with the consent of the realm. Future generations of English were to interpret the provisions of the Magna Carta in a much broader sense than its authors had intended.

John immediately renounced the Magna Carta as an oath sworn under duress, and the pope upheld this position. Fighting continued, but John died suddenly, leaving his son Henry, a nine-year-old boy, as heir. The barons reissued the Magna Carta and formed a council to rule in Henry's name.

France

In France the problems of consolidation were greater than they were in England. Unlike the English kings, who controlled the whole country, the Capetian kings of France held as their direct demesne (land they inherited) only the area around Paris (the Ile-de-France). Powerful dukes and counts controlled large provinces and were only nominally vassals to the kings of France.

Louis VII The able advisor to Louis VI, Abbot Suger (also patron of the first Gothic church), arranged the marriage of Louis VII (r. 1137–1180) to Eleanor of Aquitaine, heiress to the extensive lands of the Duchy of Aquitaine. This was Eleanor's first marriage; she later married Henry II of England. Her marriage to Louis more than doubled the lands under direct royal control, but the couple's incompatibility soon became clear. Louis had been raised for a career in the Church and became king only when his older brother died. He retained a monkish character that clashed with Eleanor's upbringing in Aquitaine, where her grandfather had been one of the first to write troubadour poetry. Having failed to produce a male heir, Eleanor accompanied Louis on the Second Crusade, hoping for better luck. She and her ladies dressed as Amazons and thoroughly enjoyed the jaunt. It was even rumored that she had an affair with her relative, Raymond of Antioch, while in the Holy Land. When the couple returned to France without a male heir, they agreed to have the Church annul their marriage on the grounds that they were too closely related. The dissolution of the marriage in 1152 meant that Eleanor resumed her duchy. In two months Henry II of England married her, although he was her junior by some ten years, and added the duchy of Aquitaine to his vast holdings in France (see map 9.3). Eleanor bore Henry four sons, two of whom (Richard and John) became kings of England.

Philip II Louis VII's son by a later marriage, Philip II Augustus (r. 1180–1223), was not a great warrior, but he was an aggressive politician and an able administrator. Forced to go on the Third Crusade with Richard the Lion-Hearted and Frederick I Barbarossa, he left the battle to Richard and returned home to harass Richard's possessions in France. It was Philip's intervention on behalf of his vassal that permitted him to confiscate Normandy from John I (see map 9.3). The victory over King John at Bouvines confirmed England's loss of Normandy and brought new prestige to the Capetian throne.

Strengthening the Administration In addition to increasing his lands, Philip strengthened the administration of his own properties, the royal demesne, although he still made no effort to interfere directly in the governments of the kingdom's fiefs. About 1190, apparently in imitation of the English itinerant justices, Philip began to appoint a new official, the *bailli*. The **bailli** supervised the collection of rents and taxes, the administration of justice, and all the king's interests within a certain prescribed circuit or area, but he never assumed the full range of functions and powers that the English justice in eyre had acquired. The baillinage system had some advantages, however, because the *bailli* was a paid official, increasingly university trained, and was moved from one place to another so that he could not build up local loyalties.

The central administration was also developing specialized bureaus, although less advanced than the English; the Chambre de Comptes, a special financial office, equivalent to the English Exchequer, gradually assumed responsibility for the royal finances.

St. Louis The successor of Philip Augustus, Louis VIII, ruled for only three years (r. 1223–1226). At Louis' death in 1226 the throne passed to Louis IX, St. Louis (r. 1226–1270), one of the great figures of the thirteenth century. Even during his life, Louis was considered

CHRONOLOGY
Political Events

d. 1106	Henry VI of Germany
1100–1135	Henry I of England
1108–1137	Louis VI of France
1137–1180	Louis VII of France
divorced 1152	Eleanor of Aquitaine
1154–1189	Henry II of England
married 1152	Eleanor of Aquitaine
1152–1190	Frederick I Barbarossa
1180–1223	Philip II Augustus of France
1189–1199	Richard I of England
1198–1216	Pope Innocent III
1199–1216	John I of England
1215	Magna Carta
1197–1250	Frederick II Hohenstaufen of Sicily
1141–1227	Pope Gregory IX Inquisition
1172–1216	Henry III of England
1226–1270	Louis IX of France

LOUIS IX, ST. LOUIS
In this fourteenth-century manuscript illumination, St. Louis hears the pleas of his humble and defenseless subjects, chiefly women and a monk. Note the hanged felons in the left panel. The picture illustrates the abiding reputation for justice that St. Louis earned for the French monarchy.

DEATH OF LOUIS IX
Louis IX of France died of the plague in Tunis during his last crusade. Attending his death bed in this manuscript illustration are his wife, Margaret of Provence, an unidentified bishop, and a mourner.
Master and Fellows of Corpus Christi College, Cambridge

saintly. He attended at least two masses a day, was sternly abstemious in food and drink, often washed the feet of the poor and the wounds of lepers, and was scrupulously faithful to his wife, Margaret of Provence, who, like her husband, bore an aura of sanctity. His personal asceticism did not preclude a grand conception of royal authority.

Legal Reforms   In his own realm Louis made no attempt to extend the royal power at the expense of his nobles or to deprive them of their traditional powers and jurisdictions, but he did expect them to be good vassals. He forbade wars among them, arbitrated their disputes, and insisted that his ordinances be respected; he was the first king to legislate for the whole of France. Although Louis did not suppress the courts of the great nobles, he and his judges listened to appeals from their decisions, so that royal justice would be available to all his subjects. The king liked to sit in the open under a great oak at Vincennes near Paris to receive personally the petitions of the humble. Louis also confirmed the Parlement of Paris—a tribunal for judicial cases rather than a representative assembly like the English Parliament—as the highest court in France, a position it retained until 1789.

The Iberian Kingdoms

The Christian *Reconquista* had achieved all but final victory by 1236, with only Granada still in Muslim hands. The principal challenge now was the consolidation of the earlier conquests under Christian rule and the achievement of a stable governing order.

The three major Christian kingdoms that emerged from the Christian offensive were Portugal, Castile (including Leon), and Aragon (including Catalonia and Valencia), but they were not really united within their own territories. The Christian kings had purchased the support of both old and new subjects through generous concessions during the course of the *Reconquista*.

Large communities of Jews and Muslims gained the right to live under their own laws and elect their own officials, and favored towns were granted special royal charters that permitted them to maintain their own court or forum. Barcelona and Valencia in the kingdom of Aragon and Burgos, Toledo, Valladolid, and Seville in the kingdom of Castile were virtually self-governing republics in the thirteenth century. Because women were scarce in the military society of the *Reconquista,* town laws gave them particular protection and property rights to encourage them to marry and have families. The military aristocracy, particularly in Castile, the largest of the Iberian kingdoms, held much of their lands not as fiefs but as properties in full, free title, which reinforced their independent spirit.

Strengthening the Monarchies   Holding all these elements together under a common government was a formidable task, but the kings also retained real advantages. The tradition of war against the Muslims gave kings a special prestige. And their rivals were too diverse and too eager to fight one another to be able to present a united challenge.

In order to impose a stronger, essentially feudal, sovereignty over their subjects, the Iberian kings set about systematizing the laws and customs of their realms, thus clarifying both their own prerogatives and their subjects' obligations. Alfonso X of Castile (r. 1252–1284) issued a code of law known as the *Siete Partidas* ("Seven Divisions"). It was thoroughly imbued with the spirit of Roman law and presented the king as the source of all justice. The code did serve to educate the people to the high dignity of kingship, even if the kings could not enforce it. Even more than in England and France, feudal government in the Iberian kingdoms rested on a delicate compromise between royal authority and private privilege, and this apparently fragile system worked tolerably well.

Cortes   Sooner than other Western monarchs, the Iberian kings recognized the practical value of securing the consent of their powerful subjects to major governmental decisions, particularly regarding taxes. By the end of the twelfth century the kings were frequently calling representative assemblies, called *Cortes.* Although they never achieved the constitutional position of the English Parliament because there were too many of them, the Cortes were the most powerful representative assemblies in Europe during the thirteenth century.

Germany: The Holy Roman Empire

For the German Empire, called the Holy Roman Empire in the late twelfth and early thirteenth centuries, the problems of unity as opposed to expansion remained unresolved. The lure of Italy and imperial aspirations diverted the attention of monarchs from unification of Germany. The German dukes managed to establish independent authority. Unlike France with Paris or England with London, Germany did not have a capital city, nor did the German emperor have a unified demesne of his own. Furthermore, the German kingship remained elective for much of the Middle Ages, rather than being based on hereditary claim, as was true in England and France.

Frederick I Barbarossa   The ruler who came closest to building a lasting foundation for the German Empire was Frederick I (r. 1152–1190) of the House of Hohenstaufen. He was called *Barbarossa,* meaning "red beard." Large, handsome, gallant, and courageous, Frederick, like Charlemagne before him, gained a permanent place in the memories and myths of his people. He much resembles in his policies, if not quite in his achievements, the other great statesmen of the twelfth century—Henry II of England and Philip II of France. Frederick showed a broad eclecticism in his political philosophy. He claimed to be the special protector of the Church and therefore a holy figure. He called his empire the Holy Empire; the later title, *Holy Roman Empire,* was used after 1254 and until Napoleon abolished this German Empire in 1806.

Frederick pursued three principal goals. First, he hoped to consolidate a strong imperial demesne consisting of Swabia, which he inherited; Burgundy, which he acquired by marriage; and Lombardy, which he hoped to subdue. These three contiguous territories would give him a central base of power that he could use for his second goal—to force the great German princes in the north and east to become his vassals. Finally, in Italy, he claimed, as successor of the Caesars, to enjoy the sovereignty that Roman law attributed to the emperors.

Italy and the Lombard League   Frederick's Italian ambitions disturbed the popes and the town communes, which from about 1100 had become the chief powers in the northern half of the peninsula. Both feared that a strong emperor would cost them their independence. With active papal support, the northern Italian towns, led by Milan, formed a coalition known as the Lombard League, which defeated the imperial forces at Legnano in 1176. The Battle of Legnano not only marked the failure of Frederick's efforts to establish full sovereignty over the Lombard cities but also was the first time in European history that an army of townsmen had bested the forces of an army under noble leadership. At the Peace of Constance in 1183, Frederick conceded to the towns almost full authority within their walls; the towns, in turn, recognized that their powers came from him, and they conceded to him sovereignty in the countryside. Frederick did not gain all that he had wished in Italy, but his position remained a strong one.

Germany and European Leadership

Forced to turn his attention to Germany, Frederick humiliated his most powerful vassal and took his land into his own hands (see map 9.3). Frederick now wanted to advance the empire's prestige in Europe and sought out a position of leadership in the Third Crusade. But the aged emperor drowned while trying to ford a small stream in Asia Minor, bringing to a pathetic end a crowded and brilliant career.

Henry VI (r. 1190–1197)

Barbarossa's son Henry VI married Constance, heiress to the Norman Kingdom of the Two Sicilies, so that their son would have a legal claim to southern Italy and to the German throne. The prospect of Italian unification under German auspices disturbed both the papacy and the free cities of Lombardy. The towns and the pope feared that the direct domination of the emperor would curtail their liberty. In his brief reign of seven years, however, Henry VI had little chance to unify Sicily, northern Italy, and Germany. He did come up with an unscrupulous way of raising money: by imprisoning Richard I on his way home from the Third Crusade and holding him for ransom.

Frederick II Hohenstaufen

Frederick II (r. 1212–1250), son of Henry and Constance, is one of the most fascinating personalities of the Middle Ages. A contemporary called him *stupor mundi* ("wonder of the world"). Later historians have hailed him as the first modern ruler, the prototype of the cold and calculating statesman. Frederick spoke six languages, loved learning, patronized poets and translators, founded a university, and, after a fashion, conducted scientific experiments.

The pope crowned Frederick emperor in 1219 on the double promise that he would renounce his mother's inheritance of southern Italy and lead a crusade to Palestine. Frederick procrastinated on both agreements.

Fragmentation of Germany

Frederick's policy toward Germany was to take as much profit as he could and devote his attention to Italy. To stabilize the political situation in Germany, he established on the empire's eastern frontier a military-religious order, the Teutonic Knights, who eventually created the Prussian state; he recognized Bohemia as a hereditary kingdom and Lübeck as a free imperial city; and he issued the earliest charter of liberties to the Swiss cantons. (Later in the century, in 1291, the cantons entered into a "Per-

FREDERICK II'S TREATISE ON FALCONRY
Frederick II was not only the dominant political leader of his age but also one of its most learned minds. He was an avid reader of classical texts and apparently used Aristotle's *Historia Animalium* as a guide in one of his favorite pursuits, a study of birds. Illustrated here is a page from his own copy of the treatise he wrote on falconry.
Città del Vaticano, Biblioteca Apostolica

petual Compact," or alliance, which marks the formal beginnings of the Swiss Confederation.) His most important policy, however, was to confer upon the German ecclesiastical princes and the lay nobles virtual sovereignty within their own territories. The emperor retained only the right to set the foreign policy of the empire, make war and peace, and adjudicate disputes between princes or subjects of different principalities. All other powers of government passed to the princes, and no later emperor could regain what Frederick gave away.

Attempt to Control Italy

In Italy Frederick pursued a much more aggressive policy. For the government of the Kingdom of the Two Sicilies, he relied on a trained lay bureaucracy. He rigorously centralized his administration, suppressed local privileges, imposed a universal tax on his subjects, recruited his army from all classes (from Muslims as well as Christians), and issued a constitution that, in the spirit of Roman law, interpreted all jurisdiction as stemming from the emperor. He encouraged trade and stabilized the currency, bringing prosperity to the port cities.

Frederick had to face the increasingly bitter opposition of the popes and the free cities of the north, because it was apparent he planned to pursue Frederick I's policies toward them. Pope Gregory IX excommunicated him in 1227 because of his failure to lead an Eastern crusade. Frederick then departed on the crusade, but he preferred to negotiate rather than fight and made a treaty with the Muslims that guaranteed unarmed Christian pilgrims access to Jerusalem. The more militant among the Western Christians believed that this treaty was dishonorable. Frederick returned to Italy in 1229 and came to terms with Pope Gregory a year later.

Frederick died before he could unify the Italian towns with Sicily. His sons did not long outlive him.

Sicily and Germany after 1250   Frederick II had reinforced a political fragmentation in Germany that had become ever more pronounced since the eleventh century. Wishing to keep their independent principalities, Germany elected a weak emperor who would not interfere with them.

In southern Italy Frederick II had completed the constitutional reorganization that the Norman kings, his forebears, had begun. With Frederick dead, the pope saw an opportunity to remove Sicily from German hands. With the pope's cooperation, in 1262 the brother of Louis IX, Charles of Anjou, defeated Manfred, Frederick's son, and won Sicily. Later, the native population rebelled in an incident known as the Sicilian Vespers. On Easter Monday 1282, while the church bells were ringing to call people for vespers, a massive insurrection occurred and the French were massacred. The forces loyal to Manfred's daughter had contacted her husband, the king of Aragon, and his fleet was already close at hand. The king of Aragon ousted the French, but the continued war left the Kingdom of the Two Sicilies impoverished.

THE CHURCH

Since the time of the Gregorian reform of the eleventh century, the papacy had sought to build in Europe a unified Christian commonwealth, one based on faith and on obedience to the pope. In the early thirteenth century the Church came close to achieving this grand design, but it still had to face powerful challenges to both Christian unity and its own deficiencies in leadership. At the same time, the continued involvement of the papacy in political affairs, the moral laxity of the clergy, and the wealth of bishops, abbots, and popes offended the laity.

The Growth of Heresy

The spread of heresy (adherence to religious views contrary to church dogma) in the eleventh and twelfth centuries can be traced to both criticism of the clergy and to new intellectual and spiritual demands on the part of the laity. The expansion of Europe meant that the population was more mobile and exposed to new ideas. Pilgrimage, crusade, and trade brought people into contact with the Greek Church, with Islam, and with Eastern heretical groups. The movement into new territories, the growth of towns, the appearance of new trades and industries—all created strong psychological tensions, which often found an outlet in heretical movements. The popes argued that the Church had the true interpretation of Christianity since their power derived from Peter through the Doctrine of the Petrine Succession (see chapter 6). The Church's charge was to save all Christian souls. People who became heretics were, in the Church's view, condemned to damnation. Heretics must be returned to the doctrines of the Church to save their souls.

Appeal of Heresies   Corruption in the Church played a role in the spread of heresy. Satirists poked fun at the money needed to get a case tried in ecclesiastical courts. Nobles saw that heresy offered an excuse to confiscate church property for themselves. Among the urban poor, heresy became a form of social protest against elite government. Because the Church condemned commercial wealth, rich townsmen, too, felt that heresy gave them assurance of reaching heaven.

Heresy had a particular appeal to women. Many women could not marry because of the large dowry demanded and could not enter a religious order because this also required a monetary contribution. The Church would not allow women to preach, to enter universities, or to have an active role in pastoral care. Church law upheld the legal subordination of women to men. Heretical groups welcomed women, teaching them to read the Scriptures and offering a spiritual equality that the established Church did not.

The age was one of spiritual and intellectual tension. Lay people wanted a more mystical and emotional reward from religion, and those with an education wanted a better educated clergy. Both wanted the Bible translated into vernacular languages so that they could read the word of God for themselves. The clergy resisted, maintaining that the laity would draw false conclusions from the Bible and that only trained readers should interpret it for the laity.

Waldensians   Around 1170 a rich merchant of Lyons, Peter Waldo, adopted a life of absolute poverty and began preaching. He soon attracted followers, who came to be known as "the poor men of Lyons," or Waldensians. The Waldensians attacked the moral laxness of the clergy and denounced the sacraments they administered. Women in the Waldensian movement could preach on a par with men. The group was declared heretical by the Lateran Council of 1215, but the Church never succeeded in suppressing the movement.

Albigensians, or Cathari   Far more powerful in their own day, though not destined to survive the Middle Ages, were the Cathari (Greek *katharos,* "pure"), or Albigensians, named for the town of Albi in Languedoc. The Albigensians, a dualistic sect, believed that two deities, a god of light and a god of darkness, were fighting for supremacy in the universe. The god of darkness was the god of the Old Testament, creator of the material world, and the god of light was the New Testament god who offered spiritual salvation. The good person must help the god of light vanquish the evil god of darkness.

The true Albigensians led lives of rigorous asceticism. They abstained from sexual intercourse, since procreation replenished the earth, the domain of the god of darkness. They abstained from meat, since it was sexually reproduced. Because a sect that preached against marriage and procreation risked bringing about its own extinction, the Albigensians reached a practical compromise: Those who abided by these stringent regulations, both women and men, were the "Perfects"(they formed the priesthood); those who did not live by this stern code were the believers.

The Albigensians, like the Waldensians, denied all value to the sacraments and priesthood with the established Church. A person's affiliation to the sect rested on the agreement to accept the *consolamentum* before death. The Perfect came to the death bed and performed a laying on of hands as a spiritual baptism. The person then spent the last few days before death fasting to preserve the spiritual state for salvation. Many otherwise Roman Catholics found spiritual reassurance from the *consolamentum,* admired the Perfects, and appreciated the Albigensians' willingness to preach in the vernacular. The Albigensians developed a strong organization, with councils and a hierarchy of Perfects that resembled that of bishops.

The Suppression of Heresy

The Church believed that the souls of Albigensians would be condemned to hell and that it was the responsibility of the Church, in its role as shepherd to its flock, to reclaim the Albigensians for the faith.

Crusade against Albigensians   Reconversion through preaching, persuasion, and example remained a slow and uncertain process. While a bishop had the right to try a suspected heretic before his own court, a heretic who was protected by important men in the community was virtually immune to prosecution. Since the nobility of Toulouse, including the count of Toulouse, were sympathetic to the Albigensians, protection was easy to find.

By the early thirteenth century, the Church began to suppress the Albigensians by force. Pope Innocent III, of whom more will be said later, favored peaceful solutions to heresy until his legate, who had excommunicated the count of Toulouse for tolerating heresy, was murdered. Innocent proclaimed a crusade (1208–1229) against the Albigensians and the nobles who supported them. Knights from the north of France responded with zeal, but more out of greed for plunder than concern for orthodoxy. They defeated the nobles of Toulouse, but the problem of suppressing heresy remained.

Beginnings of Inquisition   In 1231 Pope Gregory IX instituted a special papal court to investigate and punish heresy. This was the famous papal **Inquisition,** which was to play a large and unhappy role in European history for the next several centuries. Like the English justices in eyre, the inquisitors were itinerant justices who visited the towns within their circuit at regular intervals. Strangers to the locale, they were not subject to pressures from the important men of the region. They accepted secret denunciations and, to protect the accusers, would not reveal their names to those denounced; at times they used evidence that was not even revealed to the accused. The accused had no right of counsel and could be tortured. The suspected heretics were, in fact, considered guilty before even being summoned to the Inquisition. They could confess and repent, with the likely consequence of a heavy penance and usually the confiscation of their property. But they had little chance to prove their innocence. As an ecclesiastical court, the Inquisition was forbidden to shed blood, but here too its procedures were novel: It delivered relapsed or unrepentant heretics to the secular authority with full knowledge that they would be put to death (see "The Techniques of the Inquisition," p. 274).

The weaknesses of the inquisitorial process soon became apparent. Secret procedures protected incompetent and even demented judges. In addition, the Inquisition could function only where it had the close cooperation of the secular authority. It was never established in areas (for example, England) in which strong kings considered themselves fully competent to control heresy.

The number of heretics who were executed is not known exactly, but it was probably several hundred. The Inquisition had a terrible effect upon the medieval

THE TECHNIQUES OF THE INQUISITION

To combat heresy the Inquisition tried above all to get suspects to confess, repent, and thus save their souls. Bernard Gui, inquisitor at Toulouse in southern France between 1307 and 1323, left a vivid account of the psychological techniques used in interrogations.

"When a heretic is first brought up for examination, he assumes a confident air, as though secure in his innocence. I ask him why he has been brought before me. He replies, smiling and courteous, 'Sir, I would be glad to learn the cause from you.'

"I [Inquisitor]. You are accused as a heretic, and that you believe and teach otherwise than Holy Church believes.

"A [Answer]. (Raising his eyes to heaven, with an air of the greatest faith) Lord, thou knowest that I am innocent of this, and that I have never held any faith other than that of true Christianity. . . .

"I. I know your tricks. What the members of your sect believe you hold to be that which a Christian should believe. But we waste time in this fencing. Say simply, Do you believe in one God the Father, and the Son, and the Holy Ghost?

"A. I believe.

"I. Do you believe in Christ born of the Virgin, suffered, risen, and ascended to heaven?

"A. (Briskly) I believe.

"I. Do you believe the bread and wine in the mass performed by the priests to be changed into the body and blood of Christ by divine virtue?

"A. Ought I not to believe this?

"I. I don't ask if you ought to believe, but if you do believe.

"A. I believe whatever you and other good doctors order me to believe. . . .

"I. Will you then swear that you have never learned anything contrary to the faith which we hold to be true?

"A. (Growing pale) If I ought to swear, I will willingly swear.

"I. I don't ask you whether you ought, but whether you will swear.

"A. If you order me to swear, I will swear.

"I. I don't force you to swear, because as you believe oaths to be unlawful, you will transfer the sin to me who forced you; but if you will swear, I will hear it.

"A. Why should I swear if you do not order me to?

"I. So that you may remove the suspicion of being a heretic.

"A. Sir, I do not know how unless you teach me.

"I. If I had to swear, I would raise my hand and spread my fingers and say, 'So help me God, I have never learned heresy or believed what is contrary to the true faith.'

"Then trembling as if he cannot repeat the form, he will stumble along as though speaking for himself or for another, so that there is not an absolute form of oath, and yet he may be thought to have sworn. . . . Or he converts the oath into a form of prayer. . . . [And when further hard pressed he will appeal, saying] 'Sir, if I have done amiss in aught, I will willingly bear the penance, only help me to avoid the infamy of which I am accused.' But a vigorous inquisitor might not allow himself to be worked upon in this way, but proceed firmly until he makes these people confess their error, or at least publicly abjure heresy, so that if they are subsequently found to have sworn falsely, he can, without further hearing, abandon them to the secular arm."

From H. C. Lea, *A History of the Inquisition of the Middle Ages,* Vol. 1, 1887, pp. 411–414.

Church because it associated the papacy with persecution and bloodshed.

The Friars

Crusade and Inquisition could not alone preserve the unity of the medieval Church. A spiritual regeneration was needed; the Church had to reach lay people, especially those living in towns, and provide them with a spiritual message they could comprehend. The mendicant orders, or friars, met the needs of the laity.

St. Dominic   A priest from Castile named Dominic began to preach among the Albigensians of Languedoc in about 1205. Dominic insisted that his followers—

whose mission was to preach—live in poverty and support themselves by begging; they thus constituted a **mendicant,** or begging, order. Mendicant orders were known as friars rather than monks, because they were to live with the laity rather than in the seclusion of the monastery and did not follow the Benedictine Rule. Dominic's instruction to his followers was: "The world henceforth is your home. . . . Go you therefore into the whole world and teach all nations."

The new Order of Preachers grew with amazing rapidity; the bishop of Toulouse approved the order in Toulouse in 1215 and papal approval followed shortly afterward. To prepare its members for their work, the Dominican Order stressed education. Their preachers were all university trained and many became masters at the universities. They became the intellectual arm of the medieval Church, counting among the order Albertus Magnus, Thomas Aquinas, and many other important religious thinkers of the thirteenth century. Dominicans responded to the demands of educated laity for intellectually stimulating sermons and to the needs of the Church for missionaries to the Turks and Mongols in the East. The Dominicans also became the chief inquisitors.

Francis of Assisi   Francis (ca. 1182–1226) is probably the greatest saint of the Middle Ages and possibly the most sensitive poet of religious emotion. He succeeded in developing a style of piety that was both faithful to orthodoxy and abounding in new mystical insights. Since most of Francis' life is screened by legend, it is nearly impossible to reconstruct the exact course of his spiritual development. His father was a wealthy merchant in Assisi, but Francis as a young man fancied the life of a knight and the pleasures of courtly love and troubadour poetry. He tried the rowdy amusements of the city and the life of a knight. A severe illness after one of his nightlong parties led to a conversion. He turned to religion and adopted a life of poverty.

Franciscan Order   Disciples began to gather almost at once around the "little poor man" of Assisi. In 1215 Francis obtained papal approval for a new religious order. The papacy had some hesitation, since Francis' order resembled Peter Waldo's Poor Men of Lyons, but Francis recognized papal authority and the Church now realized the need for this sort of spiritual mission. His Order of Friars Minor (Lesser Brothers) grew with extraordinary rapidity: within ten years it included some five thousand members and spread from Europe to Palestine; before the end of the century it was the largest order in the Church. Although the problems of administering a huge order did not command Francis' deepest interests, he did write a brief rule for the Friars in which he stressed the importance of poverty and simplicity.

The success of the Friars Minor was an authentic triumph for the Church. Giving themselves to poverty and preaching, the Friars Minor came to include not only a second order of nuns but a third order of laypersons. Francis and his followers opened orthodox religion to delight in the natural world, to mystical and emotional experience, and to joy, which all people, they believed, including the ascetic and the pious, should be seeking.

Papal Government

The papacy recognized that in a period of social change and religious crisis they would have to clean their own house as well as address the problems of heresy. The

Giotto di Bondone
St. Francis Preaching to the Birds
This fresco from the basilica of St. Francis at Assisi, traditionally attributed to the Florentine painter Giotto, shows the saint preaching to the birds. He congratulates them on their bright plumage and bids them sing in praise of God. The implication is that if people too recognize God's providence over them, they will respond with gratitude and joy.
Scala/Art Resource, NY

pope whose reign best illustrates the aspirations and the problems of the medieval Church is Innocent III (r. 1198–1216).

Innocent III   Innocent was the product of twelfth-century education. He had a liberal arts degree from Paris and studied canon law at Bologna. Entering the papal government, he became a cardinal at age twenty-nine. As pope he sought with vigor and with remarkable, if always partial, success to achieve three major goals: the eradication of heresy, the hegemony of the papacy over Europe, and the clarification of Christian discipline and belief.

Within Europe, heresy was the greatest threat to Christian unity, and though he ordered the crusade against the Albigensians, Innocent primarily looked to the new mendicant orders, the Dominicans and Franciscans, to counter the appeal of the heretics.

The pope sought to exert his leadership over the princes of Europe in all spiritually significant affairs. Some of his efforts to bend kings to his will have already been mentioned, such as his struggle with King John to install Stephen Langton as archbishop of Canterbury. He also excommunicated Philip II of France for discarding his queen in order to cohabit with another woman. No prior pope had scrutinized princely behavior with so keen an eye.

The Fourth Lateran Council Innocent realized that problems and ambiguities within the Church were partly responsible for the problems it faced with heresy and dissent. In 1215 he summoned some 1,500 prelates to attend the Fourth Lateran Council. The Council defined the sacraments; imposed an obligation of yearly confession and communion; and defined the dogma of transubstantiation, according to which the priest, in uttering the words of consecration at Mass, transforms the substance of bread and wine into the body and blood of Christ. Transubstantiation unambiguously affirmed the Mass as miracle and thus conferred a unique power on the Catholic priesthood. The Council also addressed issues of church corruption and tried to provide corrections.

The Council's actions had implications for the broader population of Europe. Since it forbade priests to officiate at ordeals and trials by battle, these judicial tools were no longer valid for determining guilt or innocence of a person accused of crime. England adapted by extending the jury system to a trial, or petty jury, and France established panels of magistrates to examine the evidence in imitation of the Inquisition.

Summary

The achievements in architecture and art, in intellectual life, in vernacular culture, in the improved standard of living, and in government have led historians to give the period of the twelfth and early thirteenth century the title of "High Middle Ages." The growing consolidation of power by monarchs in France, England, and Germany, in addition to the strengthening of the papacy, produced a demand for more educated men. Universities trained both theologians and those who would staff the growing bureaucracies of monarchies and the papacy. Urban governments developed along lines that are still familiar, and they too began to hire university-trained lawyers and notaries. The continued agricultural prosperity permitted the building of fine cathedrals throughout Europe. The Romanesque style that was typical of the Cluniac reform movement was replaced in the twelfth century with the Gothic style. The Gothic arches and the increased emphasis on windows were much in tune with the expansive feeling of the period. The Church, threatened by heresies, licensed two new orders, the Dominicans and Franciscans, who responded to the needs of the laity. The next hundred years, however, began to see an unraveling of the success of the papacy, while monarchies and ideas of governing lay society by a rule of law continued to develop.

QUESTIONS FOR FURTHER THOUGHT

1. To what extent are contemporary universities similar to and different from medieval universities?
2. How did the Magna Carta reflect both continuity and change?
3. As you look at the buildings on your campus or in your town, what influences can you see of the Romanesque and Gothic architectural styles?

RECOMMENDED READING

Sources

Aquinas, Thomas. *Basic Writings.* Anton C. Pegis (ed.). 1945.

*Brown, Raphael (ed. and tr.). *The Little Flowers of St. Francis.* 1971. Legends collected in the early fourteenth century exemplifying the style of Franciscan piety.

*Chrétien de Troyes. *Yvain, The Knight of the Lion.* Burton Raffel (tr.). 1987. Recent translation of a great French romance.

*De Villehardouin, Geoffrey, and Jean De Joinville. *Chronicles of the Crusades.* Margaret R. Shaw (tr.). 1963. The Fourth Crusade to Constantinople and the crusades of Louis IX.

*Frisch, Teresa G. *Gothic Art, 1140–1450: Sources and Documents.* 1987.

Goldin, Frederick. *Lyrics of the Troubadours and Trouvères: Original Texts, with Translations.* 1973. Troubadour works in both the original and translated versions.

The Letters of Abelard and Héloïse. Betty Radice (tr.). 2003. Concise collection of the famous letters that the two lovers exchanged after their separation.

*Marie de France. *The Lais of Marie de France.* Glyn S. Burgess and Keith Busby (trs.). 1986.

*Otto of Freising. *The Deeds of Frederick Barbarossa.* Charles C. Mierow (tr.). 1953. Primary source regarding Frederick Barbarossa's life.

*Peters, Edward (ed. and tr.). *Heresy and Authority in Medieval Europe.* 1980. Contains sources regarding medieval heresies and the response.

Studies

*Abulafia, David. *Frederick II: A Medieval Emperor.* 1988.

Barlow, Frank. *Thomas Becket.* 1986. Balanced biography of the martyred archbishop.

*Boswell, John. *Christianity, Social Tolerance, and Homosexuality in Western Europe from the Beginning of the Christian Era to the Fourteenth Century.* 1980. A learned survey of the treatment of homosexuals in medieval Europe.

Bouchard, Constance Brittain. *"Strong of Body, Brave and Noble": Chivalry and Society in Medieval France.* 1998. Readable narrative of aristocracy aimed at general readers.

Calkins, Robert G. *Medieval Architecture in Western Europe: From A.D. 300 to 1500.* 1998. Accompanied by a PC-compatible CD-ROM. Calkins provides explanations of the transition from Romanesque buildings to Gothic.

Clanchy, M. T. *Abelard: A Medieval Life.* 1997. Abelard is placed within a medieval context with an emphasis on Héloïse's influence on him.

Costen, Michael. *The Cathars and the Albigensian Crusade.* 1997. A popular and accessible account of the Albigensians.

Fletcher, Richard. *Moorish Spain.* 1992. A concise survey of the Iberian Peninsula from the Muslim invasion to the fall of Granada.

*Furman, Horst. *Germany in the High Middle Ages, c. 1050–1200.* 1986. Readable survey of period.

Hallam, Elizabeth M. *Capetian France, 987–1328.* 1980. Survey of the period.

*Haskins, Charles H. *The Renaissance of the Twelfth Century.* 1927. A classic study.

———. *The Rise of Universities.* 1957.

*Holt, J. C. *Magna Carta.* 1965. Gives useful guidance to an extensive literature.

Lambert, Malcolm. *Medieval Heresy: Popular Movements from the Gregorian Reform to the Reformation.* 1992. Valuable summary of the heretical movements and the Church's response.

*LeRoy Ladurie, Emmanuel. *Montaillou: The Promised Land of Error.* Barbara Bray (tr.). 1978. Analysis of the inquisition records of one town's experience with Albigensianism. An engaging book.

*Moore, R. I. *The Formation of a Persecuting Society: Power and Deviance in Western Europe, 950–1250.* 1987. Examines the reasons for persecution in the Middle Ages.

*Morris, Colin. *The Discovery of the Individual, 1050–1200.* 1987. Looks not only at the intellectual movements of the twelfth century but also at the concept of the individual.

Munz, Peter. *Frederick Barbarossa: A Study in Medieval Politics.* 1969. A political biography.

*O'Callaghan, Joseph F. *A History of Medieval Spain.* 1975. Surveys medieval Spain.

*Peters, Edward M. *Inquisition.* 1988. The Inquisition in fact and imagination.

*Sayers, Jane. *Innocent III: Leader of Europe 1198–1216.* 1994. Readable account of Innocent and his historical context.

*Turner, Ralph V. *King John.* 1994. A political biography.

Turner, Ralph V., and Richard R. Heiser. *The Reign of Richard Lionheart: Ruler of the Angevin Empire, 1189–99.* 2000. A very accessible book on Richard I, his crusades, and his rule of England.

*Available in paperback.

VIEW OF VENICE
This elaborate depiction of Venice in a fourteenth-century manuscript shows the buying and selling that was characteristic of the citizens of this commercial and maritime center. Particularly notable at the upper left are the four bronze horses that the Venetians brought back to the city after the capture and looting of Constantinople in 1204 during the Fourth Crusade. The horses were placed on the facade of the cathedral of St. Mark's, and they have remained there ever since.
Snark/Art Resource, NY

Chapter Ten

THE URBAN ECONOMY AND THE CONSOLIDATION OF STATES

CITIES, TRADE, AND COMMERCE • MONARCHIES AND THE DEVELOPMENT OF
REPRESENTATIVE INSTITUTIONS • GOVERNMENT IN THE EAST • THE PAPACY AND THE
CHURCH • LEARNING AND LITERATURE

The period from roughly 1250 to the arrival of the Black Death in Europe in 1348 was one of urban development and intensified trade. Business practices became more sophisticated. Towns rebelled against the control of local lords and bishops, favoring instead self-government and charters of independence. Urban life entered into every aspect of medieval Europe. Europeans began to explore the Atlantic, the coast of Africa, and the Far East to establish trade and import new products.

Monarchs in Europe continued to consolidate control over their subjects, but they began to do so in consultation with representatives of their subjects in such bodies as the Parliament in England, the Estates General in France, and the Cortes in Spain. Eastern Europe and the Byzantine Empire went through another grim period of invasions, this time from the Mongols of central Asia. Ultimately the Byzantine Empire revived, and Moscow became the center of a newly reconstituted state of Russia.

With their power on the rise, monarchs' conflicts with the papacy intensified. The papacy increasingly did not have the resources to compete with secular states. Corruption of the Church's fiscal policies resulted in the laity's increased criticism of the papacy. But the laity, particularly laywomen, found spiritual comfort and even distinction in society through individual spiritual journeys. The greatest synthesis of medieval culture, Dante's *Divine Comedy*, is itself a poem of personal spiritual exploration.

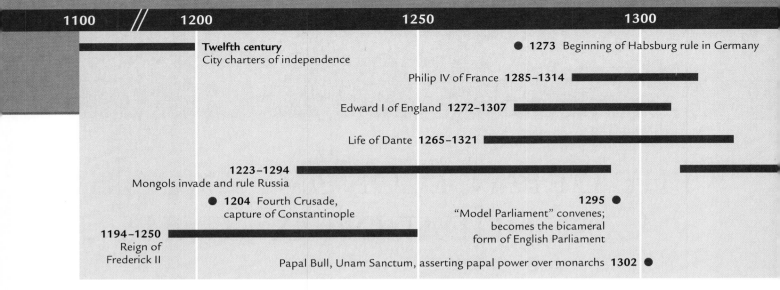

1100	1200	1250	1300

Twelfth century
City charters of independence

● **1273** Beginning of Habsburg rule in Germany

Philip IV of France **1285–1314**

Edward I of England **1272–1307**

Life of Dante **1265–1321**

1223–1294
Mongols invade and rule Russia

● **1204** Fourth Crusade,
capture of Constantinople

1295 ●
"Model Parliament" convenes;
becomes the bicameral
form of English Parliament

1194–1250
Reign of
Frederick II

Papal Bull, Unam Sanctum, asserting papal power over monarchs **1302** ●

CITIES, TRADE, AND COMMERCE

Urban development continued with the prosperity and population growth of the twelfth and thirteenth centuries. People who flocked into urban centers were a free population who did not fit easily into the old social divisions: peasants, or those who tilled the soil; nobility, or those who fought; and clergy, or those who prayed. The urban population also worked with their hands, but many made money in banking and trade. Increasingly the urban population felt that nobles and bishops, who were their overlords, were a hindrance to economic prosperity. Townsmen needed laws of commerce and contract and freedom from taxes.

Urban Government

Town Independence   The route to independent town government could be peaceful or violent. Some lords were eager to establish free towns in order to bring in wealth. In St. Omer's charter, dating from 1127, the count of Flanders granted the town freedom from taxes and the right of self-government. London won a similar charter from Richard I when its citizens agreed to pay a substantial portion of his ransom from imprisonment in Germany. In France, Philip II Augustus found that granting royal charters to towns was a way of securing their loyalty to the crown rather than to the counts and dukes, thus extending royal authority into the provinces.

At other times towns resorted to violence to free themselves of bishops and feudal lords. One of the most famous revolts was in Laon, where the bishop was found hiding in a wine cask. The finder "lifting his battle ax brutally dashed out the brains of that sacred, though sinner's head." The mob cut off his legs and one

man, seeing the bishop's ring on the dead man, cut the finger off and took the ring.

Communes, Oligarchs, and Consuls   One instrument by which medieval townsmen sought to govern themselves was the **commune,** a permanent association created by the oath of its members and under the authority of several elected officials. Communes first appeared in the eleventh century in northern Italy and Flanders, the two most heavily urbanized areas of Europe.

Few towns kept a communal form of government. For the most part, the wealthier elements, the long-distance merchants and knights, took control of town offices. Although revolts continued, the type of government that gradually evolved in urban centers was the oligarchy, in which the elite men of the city controlled government and its offices.

In Milan in 1097 the city set up a government of consuls, drawn from the city elite. Their function was both political and judicial. In order to control Milan after defeating it, Frederick I placed a city manager in Milan. The new city manager was an outsider with no local ties and proved to be more even-handed in justice than the communal officials. The institution became popular in northern Italy, and university-trained men entered the profession.

In northern Europe the model of a mayor and councilors or aldermen developed. The city wards elected them from the wealthier members of the city elite. They administered both the city and the judicial system.

Urban Population   Everywhere, the European urban population remained small compared to the rural population. In 1377 only 10 percent of the people in England lived in urban centers with a population greater than 3,200—a typical percentage for most of northern

Reign of Ivan III **1462–1505**

● **1356** Golden Bull on the rules for selecting the German Emperor

1347–1349 Plague in Europe

1309–1378 Avignon Papacy

YPRES GUILD HALL, CA. 1260–1380
The Flemish towns were renowned for their textiles, and the economic importance of this manufacture is reflected by the size of the thirteenth-century cloth hall at Ypres (destroyed in World War I). Rows of arched windows and a central tower puncture the massive square edifice that functioned as the headquarters of the guild as well as the place in which goods were marketed.
Roger-Viollet/Getty Images

Europe—whereas in Tuscany and Flanders about a quarter of the population lived in urban centers.

The largest medieval city was Paris, with a population of perhaps 210,000 in 1328. Venice probably had 120,000 inhabitants in 1338. Few cities surpassed 40,000.

Urban Regulation Growing towns needed considerable organization to regulate their concentrated populations. The total area of London within its walls was only a square mile; therefore its population of 60,000 was densely settled, with people living in rented rooms in houses three to four stories high.

One of the first concerns of city officials was the protection of the city. The walls protected the cities against possible external attack; the gates could be closed at night, keeping out undesirable criminal elements. Urban militias and guards watched the gates and patrolled the streets. To ensure order, many cities had curfews, rules about carrying weapons after dark, and ordinances on noise and nuisance (foul smells, obstruction of streets, and throwing slops out the window).

Sanitary measures included street cleaning, public latrines, wells and conduits to provide clean water, and segregation of the most noisome businesses, such as butchering, to places that were not upwind of the city.

Civic pride motivated a number of urban amenities. Guilds and citizens contributed money to performances of plays, processions, and tournaments. Hospitals were a frequent charity, as were foundling homes, free grammar schools, gardens, and chapels. In addition to a cathedral or large church, cities built a guildhall (town hall) where city officials held urban courts, private citizens met to transact business, and archives preserved records of both official business and private contracts.

Moral Regulation   Urban governments regulated the honesty and morality of their population. They maintained standard weights and measures and required those trading to use them. Prostitution was also regulated. While neither the Church nor urban governments condemned prostitution (they felt that it was better for men to seek sex with a prostitute than in adultery), they did not want its moral pollution in every part of the city. Some cities, such as London, limited the places that prostitutes could solicit. Other cities, such as Florence and Montpellier, set up official houses of prostitution, usually bathhouses, in which the city could regulate the trade and the health of the women practicing prostitution. People who used false weights, sold putrid food, or pimped or practiced prostitution outside the prescribed areas were fined and could be expelled from the cities for continuing offenses.

The Organization of Crafts and Trades

With the exception of mines, construction sites, and such enterprises as the arsenal in Venice, most work was performed in the home or in small shops. A merchant or manufacturer acquired raw materials, gave (or "put") it out in sequence to specialized artisans, and then sold the finished product. Usually called the putting-out system, this method of production remained characteristic of the Western economy until the Industrial Revolution of the late eighteenth century.

Wool Cloth Production   The making of woolen cloth, the largest industry in medieval towns, illustrates the complex character of thirteenth-century manufacturing. The raw wool—often coming from England, Spain, or North Africa—was first prepared by sorters, beaters, and washers. The cleaned and graded wool was then carded, or combed.

The next task, the spinning, was usually done by women who worked in their own homes with a distaff, a small stick to hold the wool, and a spindle, a weight to spin and twist the strands into thread. The spinning wheel, apparently first invented in India, adopted by the Arabs, and brought to Italy in the late thirteenth century, added speed and better quality to thread making. Since antiquity, women had been the primary weavers in society, but the invention of a larger, more expensive loom meant that the investment was beyond that of ordinary households. The weavers established guilds, purchased looms for their shops, and trained men to do the heavy work of manipulating the looms and large cloths they produced.

Weavers worked on large looms in shops and wove the thread into broadcloths that were 30 yards in length. The cloth was then fulled—that is, washed and worked with special earths that caused the wool to mat. This was arduous work and was often done at a water-driven fulling mill. The giant cloth was then stretched on a frame to dry properly and shrink evenly. Next, the dry cloth was rubbed with teasels to raise the nap, and the nap was then carefully cut. Several times repeated, this last operation gave the cloth a smooth, almost silky finish, but it was extremely delicate work; one slip of the scissors could ruin the cloth and the large investment it represented. Medieval people loved bright colors, and dyers used a great variety of animal, vegetable, and mineral dyes.

The medieval woolen industry came to employ a large, diversified labor force, which worked materials brought from all corners of the known world. Europe also developed a silk industry, largely run by women, as well as rug and tapestry weaving. In Florence in about 1300, wool shops numbered between two hundred and three hundred; they produced between 80,000 and 100,000 big broadcloths with a value surpassing 1.2 million gold florins. More than thirty thousand persons earned their living from this industry.

People took their surnames from their occupations. In England, *Weber* denoted a weaver, *Fuller* the one who fulled the cloth, *Shearer* the one who cut the nap, and *Dyer* and *Tailor* the obvious.[1]

---

[1] Surnames gradually became fixed in the late Middle Ages, and many reflect occupations. *Brewster*, for instance, indicates a female brewer. Trade names as surnames were common, but so too were place names of towns or places in towns, such as *Townsend*. Physical characteristics also became surnames, such as *Squint* and *Blond*.

CLOTH MARKET IN BOLOGNA
The manufacture and marketing of textiles was one of the main sources of wealth for the cities of northern Italy. This scene, from a manuscript dated 1411, gives us a sense of what the cloth market in Bologna must have been like as merchants examined, bought, and sold various fabrics.
Alinari/Art Resource, NY

Guilds   To defend and promote their interests, the merchants and master artisans formed associations known as **guilds.** (In chapter 9 we saw that university masters and students had also formed guilds.) Merchant guilds appeared in European cities in about 1000. From the twelfth century both master artisans (weavers, bakers, shoemakers) and merchants in special trades (dealers in wool, spices, or silk) had organized their own independent guilds to ensure the quality of the goods they produced and sold and to maintain a monopoly over their craft or trade. A large industrial town such as Florence had more than fifty professional guilds.

Guild Functions   Guilds elected masters to regulate methods of production and examine the finished product to maintain quality. Guild members who produced bad quality goods were fined and sometimes even publicly humiliated: A vintner who sold bad wine had to stand at the public stocks, drink a gallon of his worst, and have the rest poured over his head. The masters adjudicated disputes among members, administered properties of the guild, and supervised its expenditures. To protect the members from external competition, cities required all those who practiced a trade or craft within their walls to belong to the appropriate guild. Guilds reserved the right to examine and admit members (see "The Craft of Weavers of Silk Kerchiefs at Paris," p. 284).

Apprenticeship   One of the chief features of the guilds was the **apprenticeship** system. Boys entered apprenticeship at fourteen to eighteen years of age and stayed about seven to ten years. The apprenticeship of girls was of a shorter period and seemed to be designed to prepare the girl for marriage, bringing with her a useful craft. Apprentices lived in the master's home, a relationship that could be quasi-familial or terribly abusive.

Guilds stipulated what the apprentices had to be taught and what proof of skill they had to present to be admitted into the guild, how long they had to work in the master's shop, and what the master had to give them by way of lodging, food, and pocket money. To enter an apprenticeship, candidates or their family had to pay the master and the guild an entrance fee; the training was, therefore, not available to everyone. If, after finishing their training, they were too poor to open their own shop, they worked as paid laborers, or journeymen, in the shop of an established master. Apprentices with family capital or loans from their master could eventually become masters in a guild and have a shop.

Commercial Institutions

The growth of trade and manufacturing stimulated the development of sophisticated commercial institutions, but communication was slow. A person could travel on land between twenty and thirty miles per day: To get to Bruges by sea from Genoa took thirty days; from Venice, forty days.

Banks   Since each monarch, independent city, bishop, and lord minted their own coinage, specialists were needed to assay coins for their precious metal content. Banks (from the Old French *banc,* or bench) set up at the great European trade fairs in St. Denis, Champagne, St. Ives, and elsewhere to assay money for a fee. Gradually bankers offered more sophisticated services. By the late 1300s "book transfers" had become commonplace;

THE CRAFT OF WEAVERS OF SILK KERCHIEFS AT PARIS

In about 1270 Etienne de Goileau compiled a Book of Crafts recording guild regulations for Parisian guilds. Although the regulations here are for a woman's guild, the regulations were similar to those for other craft guilds.

"1. Any woman who wishes to weave silk kerchiefs in Paris may do so provided she knows how to practice the craft well and truly, according to the following usage and customs.

"2. First: it is ordered that no journeywoman of the craft may work on a feast day which the commune of the city celebrates and which is commanded by the Church.

"3. No one may work at night, because one cannot do as good work at night as during the day.

"4. It is ordered that no one may have more than one apprentice in the craft who is not related to her and one who is a relative; and she may not take an apprentice for fewer than seven years with a fee of twenty sous, or eight years without a fee. And if it happens that any mistress sells her apprentice for her need, she may not take another before her term is up; and if it happens that the apprentice buys her own freedom, the mistress may not take another

apprentice before the term of the one who bought her freedom is up.

"5. It is ordered that no mistress or journeywoman of the craft may buy silk from Jews, from spinsters or from any others, but only from the proper merchants.

"6. No woman may work on the premises of a man or woman if she does not know the craft.

"7. Whoever infringes any of these regulations, she must pay six sous as a fine for each time she is found at fault. . . .

"10. The aforesaid craft has three good women and true who will oversee the craft on behalf of the king, sworn and pledged at Chastelet, who will make known all the infringements against the craft, whenever they discover them."

From Emilie Amt, *Women's Lives in Medieval Europe: A Sourcebook*, Routledge, 1993, pp. 195–196.

---

that is, a depositor could pay a debt without using coin by ordering the bank to transfer credit from his own account to his creditor's. At first the depositor had to give the order orally, but by 1400 it was commonly written, making it an immediate ancestor of the modern check.

Loans and Usury   The Church condemned the practice of **usury,** which at the time meant any interest or profit on a loan, however tiny. In the Church's view, the only honest way to gain money was in exchange for work. Peasants and artisans worked with their hands, clergy prayed, and the nobility protected and governed society. Money could not make money, which is how the Church perceived the activity of bankers and merchants.

Because usury was prohibited, Christian merchants developed a variety of instruments of credit that disguised their profit. Most important for commercial purposes was the bill of exchange, in essence a loan, but one that required repayment at a specified time in another place with a higher valued currency. Thus, a merchant might borrow money in a lower valued currency and demand repayment in a higher valued currency. The rate of exchange thus concealed a substantial profit for the investor, who technically earned it for changing money, not for making the loan.

Partnerships   Business was risky, especially that which relied on sea trade, because a boat and its cargo could sink. Partnerships and business associations

were an important hedge against disaster. At Venice, Genoa, and Pisa, overseas ventures were most often financed through temporary partnerships, in which an investor gave a sum of money to a merchant traveling abroad in return for a share (usually three-quarters) of the eventual profits; the investor bore the entire loss if the ship sank or the venture failed.

Medici Bank

Merchant houses in the late fourteenth and fifteenth centuries learned to diversify their loans so that one default on the part of a royal borrower or the loss of a fleet did not ruin them. The Medici bank of Florence, which functioned from 1397 until 1498, for example, was not a single monolithic structure; rather, it rested on separate partnerships, which established branches at Florence, Venice, Rome, Avignon, Bruges, and London. Central control and unified management were ensured by having the senior partners—members of the Medici family—in all the contracts; but the branches had autonomy, and, most important, the collapse of one did not threaten others. This system of interlocked partnerships resembled a modern holding company.

Jewish Lenders

Jewish bankers, who were not under Church restrictions on usury, usually handled loans at high interest rates or rates above market value. Nobles going to war or paying a dowry for their daughters or financing the

EARLY BANKERS
This illustration from a printed Italian handbook, which gives instructions to merchants and is dated ca. 1496, shows the interior of a bank, or accounting house.

COLLECTING SILKWORMS AND PREPARING SILK
One of the new industries that appeared in Europe in the fourteenth century was the raising of silkworms. Since the spinning of silk was a craft usually associated with women, this scene, from a fifteenth-century manuscript, shows a woman gathering silk cocoons from the mulberry bushes on which the worms lived. The silk threads were unwound from those cocoons.
The British Library, London. Ms. Royal. 16GV, fol. 54v

Accounting and Insurance Double-entry bookkeeping was known in the ancient world but was not widely practiced in the West until the 1300s. In single-entry bookkeeping, only the debts owed were recorded, so that a person did not know whether the year represented a profit or loss until all debts and receipts were tallied at the end of the year. Double-entry bookkeeping recorded both output in terms of goods and services and the profits that these outputs earned or lost. Thus, an individual, company, or government knew where it stood immediately with each transaction and any arithmetical mistakes were corrected with each entry.

Insurance for land and sea transport developed in the fourteenth and fifteenth centuries. The first life insurance contracts appeared in fifteenth-century Italy and were limited to particular periods (the duration of a voyage) or particular persons (a wife during pregnancy).

Shipping and Navigation Before about 1325 there was still no regular sea traffic between northern and southern Europe by way of the Atlantic, but it grew rapidly thereafter. New, bigger ships increased profits because they carried more cargo with relatively smaller crews. Large ships were safer at sea, they could sail in uncertain weather when smaller vessels had to stay in port, they could remain at sea longer, and they did not have to sail close to the coastline in order to replenish their supplies.

Ocean navigation required a reliable means for estimating course and position. Scholars at the court of King Alfonso X of Castile compiled the Alfonsine

knighting of their sons mortgaged portions of their fiefs to Jews in return for loans. Since these loans were consumer rather than business loans and the nobles could not hope to raise the money to repay them, they lost the land to Jewish money lenders. Western European laws forbid Jews from actually having title to these lands, and the Jews sold the lands to other Christians at a profit. Some minor nobility overextended themselves on these loans and were ruined.

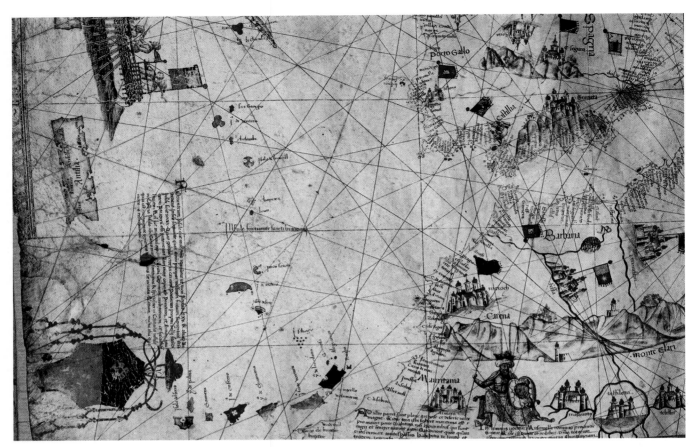

AN EARLY MAP OF THE WESTERN MEDITERRANEAN
Cartography benefited as sea voyages multiplied, as Europeans gained increased knowledge of the world, and as they improved
their skill in illustration. This map by the Italian cartographer Giovanni Benincasa describes in great detail the coasts of
Portugal, Spain, and North Africa.
Scala/Art Resource, NY

Tables, which accurately showed the position and movements of the heavenly bodies. Using such tables, captains could take the elevation of the sun or stars with an astrolabe and calculate a ship's latitude, or position on a north-south coordinate.[2]

The compass, whose origin is unclear, was common on Mediterranean ships by the thirteenth century. By 1300 Mediterranean navigators had remarkably accurate maps and port descriptions that minutely described harbors, coastlines, and hazards. All these technical developments gave European mariners a mastery of Atlantic coastal waters and helped prepare the way for the voyages of discovery in the fifteenth century.

[2] They could not tell their longitude, or position on an east-west coordinate, until they could carry accurate clocks that could compare their time with that of a basic reference meridian, such as Greenwich in England. Until the 1700s, when the first accurate clocks immune to a ship's swaying were developed, navigators who sailed across the Atlantic could not tell how far they had traveled.

Urban Life

Life in an urban environment was quite different from life in a village or a castle. Housing could be palatial, as evidenced by the surviving grand houses of Venice and Florence, but most people lived in cramped and overcrowded quarters. Without space to cook or relax, many people bought their food from street vendors (the fast food of the Middle Ages) or in taverns. Because so many people crowded into urban centers, cities were dirty and their populations prone to disease. Medieval and early modern urban populations did not replace themselves, but had to be augmented with immigration from the countryside. Thus, cities had to assimilate fresh groups of young people who came from the hinterland to be servants or apprentices.

Marital and Household Customs Cities were populous, but urban households tended to be small and unstable. The average household size in Florence in 1427

WOMAN SELLING POULTRY
Women worked at many trades during the Middle Ages. They contributed significantly to luxury crafts such as silk spinning and weaving, but they were also a major presence in the marketplace, selling such items as bread, beer, and poultry.
Bibliothèque Nationale de France, Paris

was only 3.8 persons, and in some other cities it was even smaller. The low numbers reflected the numerous deaths in a time of plagues, but marital customs also had an effect. Urban males who practiced crafts or were merchants were generally older than their brides. Because these men went through apprenticeships and started a business to accumulate capital, they postponed marriage. When they married, they tended to marry younger women: Florentine women were, on the average, less than eighteen years old when they married for the first time; women in London were more likely to be in their early twenties. Many young people, both men and women, came to the cities as servants and returned to their rural homes when they had enough money to marry. These young people did not form marriages in the urban centers at all.

Urban wives had considerable influence within their families. Merchants relied on their wives to run both the household and business in their absence. Artisans' wives helped with their craft. Some wives had occupations or businesses that they could do along with running the house and rearing children. Silk weaving, running an inn or tavern, selling prepared foods, dressmaking, and other such occupations added considerably to family incomes or could support a single woman who chose not to marry.

MONARCHIES AND THE DEVELOPMENT OF REPRESENTATIVE INSTITUTIONS

Monarchs in England and France in the late thirteenth century tried to concentrate more power and control over their subjects. The continual warfare between the two countries, however, was very expensive, and the kings could not pay for these wars without their subjects' financial and moral support. To raise money, monarchs enlisted the cooperation of the nobles, knights, and urban dwellers through representative institutions. In England, after the Magna Carta, these representatives often saw their role as a check on the monarchy. In France the monarch saw the representative institutions as bodies he could manipulate to achieve his own ends. The spread of royal justice and monarchical power meant increased bureaucracy. Middle-class, university-trained lawyers became justices and filled royal administrative posts.

England and the Development of Parliament

The death of John I so soon after the signing of the Magna Carta and the long minority of his son, Henry III, increased the power of the nobles and the free population of England and their demand for a role in government. In the late thirteenth century, their protests resulted in the development of **Parliament.**

Origins of Parliament Henry III (r. 1216–1272) had an uneasy relationship with his barons from the beginning. During his minority, the barons forced him to reissue the Magna Carta and appointed a regent who was to act on his behalf in consultation with a select council of barons.

Even after his majority in 1227, Henry III could raise taxes only through a grant from the Great Council of the barons and clergy. The meetings of the Great Council came to be called *parliaments*. (The word means

MAP 10.1 EUROPE, CA. 1250
By 1250 the map of Europe begins to resemble that of modern Europe. England, Scotland, Wales, and Ireland are named. The Scandinavian countries are demarked. But the map also shows that the Holy Roman Empire included northern Italy. Spain was not yet unified. What territory does the Mongol Empire include in Europe? What were the countries of Central Europe? What still remained of the Byzantine Empire?

◆ For an online version, go to www.mhhe.com/chambers9 > chapter 10 > book maps

"conversation" and, derivatively, an assembly in which discussion occurs.) Henry continued his father's policies of trying to regain Normandy. His wars and diplomatic efforts were expensive and unsuccessful, leading the barons to revolt against him under the leadership of Simon de Montfort (1208–1265). Simon de Montfort was the son of a French nobleman who came to England to pursue a claim to his English grandmother's estate. Henry befriended him, and de Montfort married Eleanor, Henry's sister. Like the other barons, however, de Montfort found Henry's ineptitude and expenditures too great. In 1258 the barons took control of the government, but dissensions within their own ranks rendered them unable to administer the realm. Henry regained power, but the barons under the leadership of de Montfort defeated him in 1264 at the battle of Lewes.

Because of continued divisions within the baronial ranks, Simon de Montfort sought to enlarge his power base by calling on the other constituents who had signed the Magna Carta, the knights and townsmen. In 1265 he summoned a parliament that included two knights elected from every shire and two townsmen from every town as well as the more powerful nobles, bishops, and abbots. Simon did not call these representatives to advise him, but rather sought to secure their loyalty for his policies. The representatives were to go back to their shires and towns and inform the population of the baronial policies. De Montfort was slain in battle in 1265, but kings continued to call parliaments. In 1295 Henry III's son and successor, Edward I (r. 1272–1307), called the "Model Parliament," in which it became the customary practice to invite representatives from the shires and towns.

THE ENGLISH PARLIAMENT
A meeting of the English Parliament before Edward I. To the left are the bishops and to the right are the barons. The judges are seated on wool sacks between them. The wool sacks are an indication of the importance of England's export trade in wool. To further enhance Edward's position, his chief vassals—the king of Scotland and the Prince of Wales—sit on either side of him. The two archbishops are on the extreme right and left.
© The Royal Collection; Her Majesty Queen Elizabeth II

Two Houses of Parliament   Historians cannot assign an exact date for the division of Parliament into separate houses: the House of Lords included the tenants-in-chief (the immediate vassals of the king, the upper-rank nobility), bishops, and the most powerful abbots, while the House of Commons was composed of two knights from each shire and two representatives of the towns. The meetings were officially called "Parliaments." Two unique features of the English Parliament helped enhance the influence of Commons. First, the knights and lower-ranked nobility sat with the burgesses (town representatives) and learned to act together in their mutual

interests. Second, though the bishops continued to sit in the House of Lords, they gradually became less interested in using Parliament as a vehicle for political representation. The bishops preferred to hold their own convocations to discuss Church affairs and to approve grants of money to the king. The functions of the House of Lords were thus reduced, which benefited the House of Commons.

Taxation and Representation   Parliament's role in levying taxes led to the development of a true system of representation. After the Magna Carta and the revolt of the barons, it was apparent the old levies on the nobility would not finance the king's wars. Edward I ordered the shires and the towns to elect representatives and to grant them "full power" to allow him to tax. These representatives, gathered in Parliament, had authority to consent to taxes that would be applicable to members of their shire and town. This maneuver vested considerable "power of the purse" in the hands of the House of Commons.

Edward I   Henry III's son Edward I (r. 1272–1307) took over governing the realm even before the death of his father. Edward was the sort of king that the English nobility respected. He was a bold fighter, a crusader, and a success in wars. His interest in effective administration left a strong mark on English law and institutions. In 1284 he defeated the Welsh, killed their king, and later gave their land to his eldest son. (Since 1301 the heir presumptive to the English throne has borne the title Prince of Wales.) He also pursued a war with Scotland in an effort to control the entire island. His victory was short-lived; Scotland regained independence under his son Edward II. He pursued a costly diplomatic war with France, which led to a breach with the Church and increased the importance of Parliament.

Legal Reforms   Edward produced no systematic codification of English law, like Justinian, but he sought to correct, codify, and enlarge the common law in certain critical areas and to give the system a new flexibility. He issued the first *Statutes of the Realm,* thereby setting a precedent for changing law only by legislation rather than by administrative decision. Edward's statutes restricted the rights of the nobility and clergy to exercise private justice in their own courts. They also limited the money that English bishops could send to Rome. In enacting these statutes and in governing the kingdom, Edward also placed a new emphasis on securing the consent of his subjects through Parliament.

At Edward's death in 1307 the English constitution had acquired certain distinctive features. The constitution was not contained in a single written document but was defined by both custom and statute law. The king was the chief of the state, but the nobility and the representatives from the shires and towns participated in the decision-making processes, especially regarding taxes.

France and the Consolidation of Rule

In France as well as England, representative institutions became a tool in the aid of royal government. As the French kings extended their power over the various provinces, meetings of representatives of their free subjects became valuable venues in which to announce policies. The turbulent struggles with England and with the papacy dominated Capetian policy in the late thirteenth and fourteenth centuries.

Philip IV   Louis IX's successors preserved the strength, but not the serenity, of his reign. His grandson Philip IV, the Fair (r. 1285–1314), is perhaps the most enigmatic of the medieval French kings; neither contemporaries nor later historians have agreed on his abilities. To some, Philip has seemed capable and cunning; to others, phlegmatic and uninterested, content to leave the business of government almost entirely to his ministers. If Philip lacked the personal ability to rule, he at least had the capacity to select strong ministers as his principal advisers. They were usually laymen trained in Roman law and possessing a high opinion of royal authority.

The greatest obstacle to Philip's power was Edward I of England, fiefholder of the Duchy of Aquitaine. Philip's resolve to drive England from the continent resulted in intermittent wars from 1294 to 1302. The woolen cloth weavers of the French county of Flanders relied on English wool. When Philip tried to block the importation of English wool into Flanders in order to hurt the English economy, the Flemish towns revolted against him. Philip's military campaign against them ended when the Flemish towns' militias defeated him at Courtrai in 1302.

These costly wars placed a heavy burden on the royal finances. Philip pursued a number of unscrupulous tactics to replenish the treasury. Following the lead of Edward I, who had confiscated Jewish property in England and expelled the Jews in 1290, Philip confiscated Jewish property in France and expelled them in 1306. He imprisoned foreign merchants to extort money from them. And he encouraged the pope to declare the wealthy Knights Templars heretics so that he could confiscate their property and treasure in France. Finally, Philip insisted on his right to demand from the Church "free gifts," which were actually taxes. The issue led to a protracted dispute with Pope Boniface VIII

CHRONOLOGY *Political Events*	
1194–1250	Frederick II of Germany and Sicily
r. 1226–1270	Louis IX of France
r. 1216–1272	Henry III of England
r. 1264–1265	Baronial wars of Simon de Montfort
r. 1272–1307	Edward I of England
r. 1273–1291	Rudolf of Habsburg, Germany
r. 1261–1282	Michael VIII Palaeologus, Byzantine Empire
1259–1294	Mongols
r. 1285–1314	Philip IV of France
1291	Origin of Swiss Confederation
r. 1294–1303	Boniface VIII
r. 1305–1314	Pope Clement V; beginning of Avignon papacy
r. 1309–1378	Charles IV of Luxemburg, emperor of Germany
1356	Golden Bull
r. 1462–1505	Ivan III of Russia

(see later in this chapter). In seeking to dominate these international powers—the Knights Templars and the Church itself—Philip showed his determination to become truly sovereign in his own lands.

Estates General   Seeking funds in his struggle against England and the pope, Philip used his royal bureaucrats to meet with provincial representative councils, the **Estates,** to grant taxation. The Estates were composed of three houses: representatives of the nobility (including the upper and lower nobility), of the clergy, and of the commoners (mostly urban middle class). The provincial Estates usually granted the taxes and did not dispute the king's policies.

Philip called the first meeting of the *Estates General,* with representatives of nobility, clergy, and commoners from all provinces, in 1302 and again in 1308. He used these meetings much as Edward I used the Parliament. He informed delegates about the insults that he and France had suffered at the hands of Pope Boniface VIII and his reasons for confiscating the property of the Templars. The Estates General met for Philip's propaganda purposes, not to deliberate on his policies.

In trying to achieve a powerful, centralized monarchy, Philip left France in a deeply disturbed condition.

BATTLE OF THE GOLDEN SPURS
In 1302, Flemish peasants, who had rebelled because Philip IV of France attempted to block the importation of wool from England, defeated the king at the battle of Courtrai. It was said that after the battle, seven hundred pairs of spurs were collected and displayed in the local cathedral. Some sense of the brutality of the fighting is conveyed by this illustration, with King Philip brandishing his sword at the center and the pile of bodies at the lower right.
Chroniques de France, fol. 333r. Bibliothèque Royale Albert 1er, Bruxelles

The Flemish towns remained defiant, and the king of England threatened to go to war. With the outbreak of the Hundred Years' War in the mid-fourteenth century, France under Philip's successors entered one of the darkest periods of its history.

The Holy Roman Empire and the Fragmentation of Rule

Frederick II's policy of granting away imperial rights in Germany left the vast territory a conglomeration of independent cities, bishoprics, dukedoms, and principalities. The king of Aragon's conquest of Sicily separated it from imperial ambitions. In the late Middle Ages the locus of power of the Holy Roman Empire shifted to the east, away from the Rhine and into central Europe.

The Habsburgs   The German territory went through a period of interregnum until 1273, when the German nobles met and elected Rudolph Habsburg (r. 1273–1291) emperor. He was selected in part because he was a minor noble with isolated lands near the Alps

and into Alsace. He took some initiatives that limited the outlawry of minor knights who were acting as tyrants over their territory, but he could not take on the more powerful nobles. He managed to take Austria by conquest from the king of Bohemia and add this territory to the family estates. The Habsburg's successes in acquiring territory alarmed the German nobles and bishops. In 1308 the German nobles and bishops elected a member of the house of Luxemburg in place of the Habsburgs.

The Luxemburgs and the Golden Bull   Like the Habsburgs, the Luxemburgs used the position of emperor to increase their personal holdings. Charles IV (r. 1346–1378) centered his power in Bohemia, a new acquisition of the Luxemburgs. To stabilize the process of electing the emperor, Charles promulgated the so-called Golden Bull of 1356, which fixed the number of electors at seven. The choice represented a balance of traditional parties: Three were ecclesiastics (the archbishops of Mainz, Trier, and Cologne) and four were powerful nobles (the king of Bohemia, the count palatine of the Rhine, the duke of Saxony, and the margrave of Brandenburg). The electors were to meet a month after the death of the king and elect a new one. The plan eliminated the papacy from the deliberations and future emperors broke the custom of having the pope bestow the imperial title. The Habsburgs once again gained control with the extinction of the Luxemburg line in 1437, thus joining Bohemia and Hungary with Austria and the Tyrol, which were already under Habsburg control.

Swiss Cantons   While Rudolph Habsburg was successfully adding to his territories, he lost three of the Swiss cantons that were part of his original patrimony. The cantons argued that they were granted independence under Frederick II. It was not until 1315 that the Habsburgs, with a large feudal force, tried to retake them. Swiss patriots rolled stones and tree trunks down on them as they marched through a mountain pass and then descended on them with their axes. Their success led other cantons to join them in a loose federation of independent cantons. The Swiss confederation was a new form of government for Europe—neither a monarchy nor a feudal principality. While retaining independence, they formed militias that cooperated in defending their territory.

GOVERNMENT IN THE EAST

While the West was secure from external invasions and able to continue its political, economic, and cultural development, the East was threatened by invasion from Asia once again. The East's defense against the new invaders meant that the West was sheltered, once again, from attack. The new threat came from the Mongols in the thirteenth century, followed by the Ottoman Turks in the fourteenth century.

The Byzantine Empire

When Greece and Constantinople fell in the Fourth Crusade in 1204, the Greeks rallied under descendants from the imperial line and established several principalities in Asia Minor and along the southern shore of the Black Sea. But it was the territory in Asia Minor, with its capital in Nicaea, that eventually dominated the political scene.

Michael VIII Palaeologus   Under the leadership of Michael VIII Palaeologus (r. 1261–1282), the Nicaean Empire managed to recapture Constantinople. By this time the Western attempt to establish an empire at Constantinople collapsed. Michael's general found the city unprotected and plundered of many of its treasures, which the crusaders had shipped back to Europe. The Greek population welcomed the return of Greek rule.

The Balkans   Michael VIII was an adept player in international politics and diplomacy. He needed to subdue a strong Bulgarian empire and negotiate with the rising Serb state. In the twentieth century we used the term "Balkanization" to refer to the splintering of a territory into a number of different states. Although the Byzantine emperors had settled various tribes in the Balkans, after the Fourth Crusade fights among these peoples became irreversible and are the root of modern tensions in the Balkans. The Bulgarians, taking advantage of the chaos after the Fourth Crusade, had established an empire (their leaders had taken the title of czar in imitation of the Roman "caesar") and threatened to invade Constantinople. Michael VIII managed to neutralize them through warfare and marriage with his female relatives. The Serbs had converted to Eastern Christianity in 1219. By Michael VIII's reign, they were beginning an ascendancy in the Balkans that allowed them to push into Byzantine territory.

Michael VIII left an empire that was again the Byzantine Empire, but warfare and taxation to defend the borders left it weak. Weakened as it was, it was still a major player, and the Palaeologus Dynasty remained on the throne to the final fall in 1453.

The Mongols

The Mongols (of Turkic origin and sometimes called Tartars in medieval sources) threatened Europe much as

COURT OF A MONGOL KING
The courts of the Mongol kings, as this illustration from a Persian manuscript suggests, were dazzlingly opulent. When Louis IX of France sent presents of liturgical objects (chalices and books), the Mongol king rejected the gift and suggested that a tribute of gold and silver would be more appropriate.
Bibliothèque Nationale de France, Paris

other groups from central Asia, such as the Huns, had. They were composed of nomadic tribes organized under a chief, who took the title of Genghis Khan, "Inflexible Emperor," in 1206. He turned eastward and took Beijing in 1216. Leaving his trusted lieutenants to subdue the rest of China, Genghis Khan turned his attention to the west and amassed the largest empire the world has ever known. Meeting little resistance from the Turks, his empire had expanded by 1225 to include central Asia, parts of Afghanistan, Persia, and the Caucasus.

The Golden Horde   In 1223 a Mongol army penetrated Eastern Europe in what seems to have been a reconnoitering expedition. The Mongols defeated the allied princes of Rus, and from 1237 to 1241 a Mongol army under the leadership of Batu, grandson of Genghis Khan, conducted raids throughout Eastern Europe, including Russia, Poland, and Hungary. The Mongols abandoned Poland and Hungary, but established the capital of a division of the Mongol Empire, called the **Golden Horde,** at Sarai, on the lower Volga River.

ONION DOMES AT KIZHI
Constructed entirely of wood, the remarkable churches of northern Russia, such as this eighteenth-century example from Kizhi, were made into magnificently elaborate structures even though they often served only small settlements. The onion domes were the characteristic symbol of the Russian Orthodox Church, and they were multiplied across the roofs of Russian churches.
Magnum Photos Inc.

The khans, or rulers, of the Golden Horde maintained suzerainty over the lands of what are now Ukraine and Belarus until the mid-1300s and over eastern Russia until the mid-1400s. The princes who were subject to the Golden Horde had to pay tribute to the khans, but otherwise they could rule their own people. As a result, despite the power they exercised over the East Slavs for centuries, the Mongols' influence on Slavic languages and cultures remained relatively slight.

Resettlement of the East Slavs   The devastation of the Mongol invasions and the formation of the Golden Horde led a chronicler to lament that Kiev, once proudly known as the "mother of Rus cities," had only two hundred houses left standing in the 1200s. Rus population dispersed. Some moved west, becoming known as White Russians. With a large Ukrainian population, these people developed their own literary languages and cultural traditions and remained under Polish or Austrian rule until 1944.

Other colonists moved north into a region ruled by the city of Novgorod. The Novgorod immigrants were the ancestors of the modern Russians, forming the largest group of East Slavic peoples.

Muscovite Russia

Historians call the period between the twelfth and fifteenth centuries the age of feudal Russia—the time during which Russia was divided into many princely domains. Nearly all the small towns within Russian

Mesopotamia had their own princes, their own citadels, or *kremlins,* and their own territories. All the princes were subject to the khan of the Golden Horde. Moscow gained preeminence primarily through the talents of its early princes.

Ivan I of Muscovy   Ivan I (r. 1328–1341) was the first Muscovite prince to raise Moscow to prominence. He extended his possessions along the entire course of the Moskva River and won enclaves of territory north of the Volga River. Ivan courted the favor of the still-powerful Mongol khan of the Golden Horde. In return for his loyalty and gifts, the khan made Ivan the chief representative of Mongol authority in Russia (the "grand duke"), with the right to collect the Mongol tribute from all Russian lands. Ivan increased his own treasury while collecting tribute for the Mongols.

With Ivan's encouragement, the primate (or chief bishop) of the Russian Church often visited Moscow, finally making the city his permanent residence. This move made Moscow the headquarters of the Russian Church even before it became the capital of the Russian people.

By the late 1300s the Mongols' power was declining, largely because of internal dissension. With the Mongols weakened, the princes of Moscow began to present themselves as leaders of the growing national opposition to Mongol rule.

Ivan III, Tsar   Ivan III (r. 1462–1505) completed the unification of Russian land and laid the foundations for

MAP 10.2 THE RISE OF MOSCOW, 1325–1533

This map shows the location of the Golden Horde and other countries surrounding Moscow. Despite its seeming backwoods location, Moscow was able to expand its power dramatically, especially in the reign of Ivan III. What was the original territory of Moscow? What territories were added in 1389, 1462, and 1533?

◆ For an online version, go to www.mhhe.com/chambers9 > chapter 10 > book maps

modern Russia. He acquired the prosperous city of Novgorod, which had developed strong trading and cultural links with Western Europe. Continuing his territorial expansion, he eventually ended two centuries of Mongol rule of Russia at the Oka River in 1480. No battle occurred, because neither side dared cross the river that separated them. Seeking to depict himself as the successor of the Byzantine emperors (Constantinople had fallen to the Ottoman Turks in 1453), Ivan adopted the title **tsar**, the Slavic equivalent of the Latin term *caesar*. Married to Sophia Palaeologus, who was the niece of the last Byzantine emperor and had been educated in Italy, Ivan added elaborate Byzantine pomp and etiquette to his court and adopted the Byzantine double-headed eagle as the seal and symbol of the new Russian empire. Under the influence of his wife, he invited Italian artists and architects to Moscow to help rebuild the Kremlin and make the city an impressive capital. In imitation of the Byzantine emperors, in 1497 Ivan promulgated a new code of laws known as the *Sudebnik*.

The Third Rome   The new strength and splendor of the tsar inspired several monastic scholars to propose the idea that Moscow was the third Rome. The first Rome, they said, had fallen into heresy, and the second, Constantinople, had been taken by the infidel. Moscow alone, the capital of the one Orthodox ruler, preserved the true religion.

Ivan's reforms were not completed until the reign of his grandson, Ivan IV, the Terrible (r. 1530–1584)—a tsar who brutally destroyed the *boyars* (hereditary nobility) and imposed on all landowners the status of servant to the tsar. Nonetheless, Ivan III can be seen as the founder of the Russian state. He finished the task of unifying the Russian land and its people, and he declared himself to be the autocrat of Russia. Ivan III bequeathed to his successors one of the most characteristic institutions of modern Russia: its centralized, autocratic government.

THE PAPACY AND THE CHURCH

While the monarchs of France and England were continuing to consolidate their rule over their subjects and while Russia was beginning to form a national identity around Moscow, papal administration also continued to expand. Often desperate for funds to carry on their ambitious political involvement in European affairs, the popes by the late thirteenth century exploited their spiritual powers to raise money for their political endeavors. In the past centuries new or reformed monastic orders had brought the Church back to its spiritual mission, but no new orders developed and existing ones had become increasingly corrupt.

The Papacy

Boniface VIII   The papal curia and the college of cardinals were aware that the papacy was losing its prestige, and they sought to remedy the situation by electing as pope a famous hermit, who took the name Celestine V (1294). They assumed that he would be a pious figurehead and that they could carry on business as usual. Celestine, however, observed the corruption and feared that his soul would be endangered if he continued as pope; he resigned in five months. His successor, Boniface VIII (r. 1294–1303), was rumored to have rigged up a speaking tube to the papal sleeping chamber through which he intoned that it was the will of God that Celestine resign.

Clash with Philip IV of France   By the late thirteenth century the papacy was facing a rising challenge from lay lords, who sought to tax the clergy within their own territories. Both Philip IV of France and Edward I of England had been taxing the clergy through the fiction of asking for, and always receiving, gifts or money for specific royal enterprises. In 1296, in the **papal bull** *Clericis laicos* (all solemn papal letters were called *bulls* because they were closed with a lead seal, or *bulla*, and they are usually identified by their first two words), Boniface forbade all clergy to make payments without papal permission. Such a restriction would have given the pope a powerful, if not controlling, voice in royal finances that no king could tolerate. The English simply ignored the order, but Philip retaliated by forbidding all exports of coin from his realm to Rome. Boniface issued another bull condemning Philip directly. Philip called a meeting of the Estates General in 1302 (the first such meeting) and presented the three Estates with an exaggerated description of Boniface's insults to the French king and people and revived the rumors surrounding the resignation of Celestine.

With both his personal character and the papal authority threatened, Boniface issued the bull *Unam Sanctam*, which declared that Philip must submit to his authority or risk the damnation of his immortal soul (see "Unam Sanctam," p. 296). Philip accused the pope of shocking crimes and demanded his arrest and trial at a general church council. To enforce his accusations, Philip sent one of his principal advisers to Italy. With the aid of a small army of Boniface's enemies, the French adviser broke into the papal palace at Anagni and arrested the pope in 1303. The citizens of Anagni rescued Boniface shortly afterward, but he died in Rome only a few months later.

Origin of the Avignon Papacy   Succeeding popes capitulated to the French king and revoked Unam Sanctam. Philip's victory was complete when a Frenchman,

Unam Sanctam

This statement of papal monarchy was issued by Pope Boniface VIII in 1302 to combat assertions of royal power by the kings of England and France against the authority of the universal Church. It did little, however, to deter the claims of such rulers to a growing sphere of authority.

"That there is one holy, Catholic and apostolic Church we are bound to believe and to hold, our faith urging us, and this we do firmly believe and simply confess; and that outside this Church there is no salvation or remission of sins. . . .

"We are taught by the words of the Gospel that in this Church and in her power there are two swords, a spiritual one and a temporal one. For when the apostles said 'Here are two swords' (Luke 22:38), meaning in the Church since it was the apostles who spoke, the Lord did not reply that it was too many but enough. Certainly anyone who denies that the temporal sword is in the power of Peter has not paid heed to the words of the Lord when he said, 'Put up thy sword into its sheath' (Matthew 26:52). Both then are in the power of the Church, the material sword and the spiritual. But the one is exercised for the Church, the other by the Church, the one by the hand of the priest, the other by the hand of kings and soldiers, though at the will and sufferance of the priest. One sword ought to be under the other and the temporal authority subject to the spiritual power. For, while the apostle says, 'There is no power but from God and those that are ordained of God' (Romans 13:1), they would not be ordained unless one sword was under the other and, being inferior, was led by the other to the highest things. . . . But that the spiritual power excels any earthly one in dignity and nobility we ought the more openly to confess in proportion as spiritual things excel temporal ones. Moreover we clearly perceive this from the giving of tithes, from benediction and sanctification, from the acceptance of this power and from the very government of things. For the truth bearing witness, the spiritual power has to institute the earthly power and to judge if it has not been good. . . .

"Therefore, if the earthly power errs, it shall be judged by the spiritual power, if a lesser spiritual power errs it shall be judged by its superior, but if the supreme spiritual power errs it can be judged only by God not by man. . . . Therefore we declare, state, define and pronounce that it is altogether necessary to salvation for every human creature to be subject to the Roman Pontiff."

From C. Warren Hollister et al., *Medieval Europe: A Short Sourcebook*, McGraw-Hill Companies, 1992, pp. 215–216.

Clement V, was elected pope in 1305. Clement V postponed going to Rome, preferring instead to settle in 1309 in the French-speaking city of Avignon (the city was in Burgundy, a German, not French, territory). Selecting a series of French cardinals, Clement V and his successors found Avignon congenial. For the next sixty-eight years the popes lived within the shadow of the French monarchy, executing its policies. In Rome revenues from the papal estates fell into the hands of competing factions of nobility. These nobles were so hostile to the French popes that return became impossible.

Papal Corruption Separated from the normal income derived from papal estates around Rome, the popes sought to finance their extravagant living in Avignon and the extensive church bureaucracy from other sources. The popes sold bishoprics (simony) and then extracted substantial payments from the first year that the bishop held his office; they imposed tithes (a tenth of income) on the clergy; and they sold to laypersons and clergy exemptions and dispensations from the regulations of canon law. Divorce or penances for sins could be purchased from the pope's representatives for a fee. The Dominicans and Franciscans, wandering through the world as they did, proved to be ideal agents for selling release from the strictures of canon law.

Monastic Orders In the past when the papacy had faced criticism and spiritual crisis, reforming monastic orders had come to its rescue. In the late thirteenth and fourteenth centuries, however, the monastic orders contributed to the Church's poor image. The Dominicans had become deeply implicated with the Inquisition, a role that cost them the trust of the laity. Rather than maintain their mendicant roots, both the Franciscans and Dominicans had become wealthy monastic orders. Within the Franciscans, a bitter fight developed between the Spiritual Franciscans, who wanted to return to the order as St. Francis had founded it, and the Conventual Franciscans, who favored monasteries and continued involvement in Church politics. The Conventuals won the fight, and the pope renounced the Spiritual Franciscans.

Lay Religious Observance

Whatever their discontent with the papacy, the laity were devoted to the Christian religion and found re-

THE BEGUINAGE OF SAINT ELIZABETH IN GHENT (1328)

The Beguines were religious women who chose to live not in nunneries but in communities such as that of Saint Elizabeth or in homes of their own family or others. They supported themselves with manual labor and tended to the poor and sick. Some became preachers, writers, and mystics.

"The Beguinage of Saint Elizabeth . . . is encircled by ditches and walls. In the middle of it is a church, and next to the church a cemetery and a hospital, which the aforesaid ladies endowed for the weak and infirm of that same Beguinage. Many houses were also built there for habitation of the said women, each of whom has her own garden, separated from the next by ditches or hedges; and two chaplains were established in this place by the same ladies.

"In these houses, indeed, many dwell together communally and are very poor, having nothing but their clothing, a bed and a chest, nor are they a burden to anyone, but by manual work, washing the wool and cleaning the pieces of cloth sent to them from the town, they earn enough money daily that, making thereby a simple living, they also pay their dues to the church and give a modest amount in alms. And in each convent there is one who is called the mistress of work, whose duty is to supervise the work and the workers, so that all things are faithfully carried through according to God's will.

"We shall not say much of their abstinence from food and drink but this: that many of them are satisfied for the whole day with the coarse bread and pottage which they have in common in each convent, and with a drink of cold water they lessen their thirst rather than increase their appetite. And many among them are accustomed to fast frequently on bread and water, and many of them do not wear linen on their bodies, and they use straw pallets instead of beds."

From Emilie Amt, *Women's Lives in Medieval Europe: A Sourcebook*, Routledge, 1993, pp. 264–265.

---

newed spiritual commitments in their parish churches, their individual salvation, and in lay organizations centered around religious observance.

Beguines and Beghars   Already in the twelfth century, pious groups of laity had formed quasi-monastic groups. The **Beguines,** pious laywomen, and their male counterparts, the Beghards, were popular in northern European cities. They lived together in houses or with families. While Beguines did not take vows of chastity and did not live by orders, they lived pious lives devoted to simple tasks such as spinning and caring for the sick, the old, and the bodies of the dead (see "The Beguinage of Saint Elizabeth in Ghent [1328]," above). They might spend their whole lives in this work or they might eventually marry. They were regarded with general suspicion by the Church, which tried to force them to become extensions of the Dominican order. The Franciscans and Dominicans had associated other laypersons, called the Third Order, or tertiaries to their orders. Tertiaries included widows or married people who worked in the world but spent time and money on charity and pious works. Many women found the tertiaries a refuge from household cares and an outlet for their spiritual drive.

Parish Guilds and Religious Practice   Married laypersons formed social-religious guilds within their parishes. The guilds celebrated the feast of their patron saint, helped maintain the parish church and perhaps even built a chapel within the church for their own use, provided candles for worship, and performed religious plays. In the early fourteenth century, a new theological emphasis on purgatory (the state in which the soul remained until it expiated the sins committed during life) encouraged the growth of guilds. The guild members prayed for the souls of dead brethren and sisters to release their souls from purgatory into heaven. Guilds also provided fellowship, including feasts, burial processions for members, and charity for those who had suffered illness.

Another theological and liturgical change influenced the practice of lay piety in the later Middle Ages. The emphasis on transubstantiation (the miraculous conversion of the bread and wine to the body and blood of Christ) and the requirement that the laity take Holy Communion (Eucharist) at least once a year elevated the importance of this liturgical practice. To aid the laity in understanding the importance of the Eucharist, a special day was set aside, Corpus Christi Day, on which the communion wafer, in a special box, was carried by the priest in religious procession. The procession won lay devotion, and popular religious plays were performed on Corpus Christi Day.

Anti-Semitism   Many of the Corpus Christi plays represented Jews dishonoring the Communion wafer by boiling it or nailing it to a piece of wood and being

WOMEN MYSTICS
During the fourteenth and fifteenth centuries, individuals sought salvation through meditation. Women were among the most famous mystics. Birgitta of Sweden (ca. 1302–1373) came from a noble family, married, and served in the royal household. Widowed in 1344, she retreated to a house near a Cistercian monastery and led a life of prayer and penance. She experienced a series of revelations, one of which is pictured here, which she recorded in Swedish. She was famous throughout Europe for her writings.
The Pierpont Morgan Library/Art Resource, NY

subsequently converted. Thus, an unintended result of the emphasis on the Eucharist was increased anti-Semitism in thirteenth-century Europe. The Church mandated that Jews wear special signs, the Star of David, on their clothing to indicate their religion. While these rules were not immediately enforced, they gradually became part of urban law. The participation of Jews in money lending led to feelings of competition and hostility on the part of the urban Christian population and the nobles and monasteries who had mortgaged their lands to borrow money from Jews. The hostility led to sporadic pogroms throughout Europe, such as the massacre of the Jews in London in 1264. The growing anti-Semitism in the thirteenth century was in marked contrast to the twelfth century, when

Jewish and Christian scholars exchanged theological ideas. The increased suspicion and hatred explains why Edward I and Philip IV were able to expel the Jews without public condemnation.

Individual Spiritualism A combination of the emphasis on the Eucharist and the Franciscans' encouragement of spiritual exercises that involved imaginative participation in scenes such as the Crucifixion led to individual quests for spiritual satisfaction. Women in particular took to this form of religious experience, imagining that they were at the Crucifixion and that the wounds of Christ could nourish them. These pious women might be nuns or Beguines, but many were lay-women who were wives, mothers, and daughters. They led lives of extreme abstinence, giving their food to the poor and refusing to eat or trying to live only on Communion wafers. In addition to fasting, some women performed extreme asceticism, beating themselves with whips and wearing hair shirts. Some became saints and were noted for their mystical visions.

LEARNING AND LITERATURE

The thirteenth- and early fourteenth-century developments in learning and literature brought new trends in Scholasticism. Just as the Franciscans profoundly influenced individual spirituality, so too they influenced philosophy. Although some of the radical new philosophers had their works condemned in their lifetimes, their thinking laid the foundation for modern scientific inquiry. In vernacular literature, Dante (1265–1321) made the greatest syntheses of medieval culture in *The Divine Comedy*, in which he included Scholasticism, courtly romance, spiritual journey, classical learning, and contemporary politics.

Philosophy

St. Bonaventure (1221–1274)   Born in central Italy, Bonaventure was cured of a childhood illness through the intercession of St. Francis of Assisi. He went on to become a leading member of the Franciscan order and a contemporary of Thomas Aquinas at the University of Paris. Rather than advocating rigorous logic for proving the existence of God, as Aquinas did, Bonaventure based his proof on intuited principles. To help humans understand the existence of God, Bonaventure emphasized spiritual exercises that began with looking at God's creations on Earth and seeing God in them. Contemplation would lead the believer to the revelation of God's existence. Bonaventure's theology and personal beliefs made him one of the great medieval mystics.

English Scholastics   Under the influence of two English Franciscans, Roger Bacon (1214–1294) and William of Ockham (ca. 1285–ca. 1349), philosophy began to investigate problems of natural laws. Both men were attracted to the emphasis in Aristotle's logic on empirical observation, and both are often considered the founders of Western scientific writing. Bacon argued that knowledge can be verified only through "experimental science," that is, he suggested establishing empirical hypotheses and developing ways of testing them.

William of Ockham did not attack Thomas Aquinas, but he did point out Aquinas' limitations. He argued that the articles of Christian faith could not be proved with logic and that they should be left to belief. Observation could be applied to nature, including the heav-

enly bodies and Earth. His guiding principle in logical argument is called Ockham's razor: "What can be explained on fewer principles is explained needlessly by more." Simplicity, or elegance of argument, became the basis for scientific explanation to the present day.

Medieval Science   Bacon and Ockham were medieval thinkers, but their students began to take their lessons to levels that we consider to be the beginnings of scientific thinking. Nicholas of Oresme (1320–1382), a student of Ockham, suggested that the movement of the planets could be better explained if Earth was in motion, like the planets, rather than stationary, which was the accepted view of the day. John Buridan (ca. 1300–ca. 1358) argued, following Ockham's razor, that there was no reason to assume that the celestial bodies were composed of a matter different from Earth. The work of Oresme later influenced Galileo's description of the uniform acceleration of falling bodies and Descartes' development of analytical geometry.

Dante

Literary output in most vernacular languages was abundant during the thirteenth century except in English, which was retarded in its development by the continued dominance of a French-speaking aristocracy. The masterpiece that best summarizes the culture of the age is the *Comedy* of Dante Alighieri.

Dante was born in Florence in 1265. Little is known of his education, but he seems to have been immersed in scholarship. The *Comedy* is one of the most learned, and hence most difficult, poems of world literature.

Two experiences in Dante's life profoundly influenced his attitudes and are reflected in his works. In 1274, when he was only nine years old, he fell deeply in love with a young girl named Beatrice. Much mystery surrounds her, but she seems to have been Beatrice Portinari, who later married into a prominent family and died in 1290. Dante could have seen her only rarely; we do not know if she ever returned his love.

In 1302 an experience of a much different sort shattered his life. For political reasons Dante was exiled from Florence. He spent the remaining years of his life wandering from city to city, a disillusioned, even bitter, man. He died in 1321 and was buried at Ravenna.

The Divine Comedy   Dante composed his masterpiece, the **Divine Comedy,** from 1313 to 1321. He called it a *commedia* in conformity with the classical notion that a happy ending made any story, no matter how serious, a comedy; the adjective *divine* was added to its title only after his death. The poem is divided into three parts, which describe the poet's journey through hell, purgatory, and heaven.

A detail from a fourteenth-century manuscript copy of Dante's *Divine Comedy* illustrates the section of hell reserved for usurers. The Church regarded usury as one of the many earthly sins that condemn people in the eyes of God. Dante appears three times in this scene, on two occasions accompanied by his bearded guide, Virgil. The British Library, London

The poem opens with Dante "in the middle of the way of this our life." An aging man, he has grown confused and disillusioned; he is lost in a "dark forest" of doubt, harassed by wild animals, symbols of his own untamed passions. The theme of the poem is Dante's rediscovery of a former sense of harmony and joy. Leading him back to his lost peace are two guides. The first, Virgil, who represents human reason, conducts Dante through hell and then up the seven-storied mountain of purgatory to the earthly paradise, the vanished Eden, at its summit. In hell Dante encounters people who have chosen as their supreme goal in life something other than the love of God—riches, pleasure, fame, or power. Virgil shows Dante that the good life cannot be built on such selfish choices. Reason, in other words, can enable humans to avoid the pitfalls of egoistic, material existence. In fact, reason can accomplish even more than that, for, as embodied by Virgil, it guides Dante through purgatory and shows him how to acquire the natural virtues that are the foundations of the earthly paradise—a full and peaceful earthly existence.

In the dignity and power given to Virgil, Dante shares the high regard for human reason characteristic of the thirteenth century. However, reason can take humans only so far. To enter heaven, Dante needs a new guide: Beatrice herself, representative of supernatural revelation and grace. She takes the poet through the heavenly spheres into the presence of God, "in Whom is our peace." The peace and joy of the heavenly court set the dominant mood at the poem's conclusion, in contrast to the confusion and violence of the dark forest with which it opens.

The poem reflects the great cultural issues that challenged Dante's contemporaries—the relations between reason and faith, nature and grace, human power and the divine will. Dante, like Aquinas, was trying to combine two opposed views of human nature and its ability to shape its own destiny. One, rooted in the optimism of the twelfth and thirteenth centuries and in the more distant classical heritage, affirmed that human beings were masters of themselves and the world. The other, grounded in the Judeo-Christian tradition, saw them, fundamentally, as lost children in a vale of tears. Dante's majestic panorama summarizes not only the medieval vision of the universe but also his estimation of what it meant to live a truly wise, truly happy, truly human life.

Summary

Medieval civilization attained a new stability in the thirteenth and early fourteenth centuries. Large-scale woolen cloth production, long-range commercial exchanges, and sophisticated business practices gave the economy a dynamic aura. In political life, feudal governments consolidated and clarified their constitutional procedures, and parliaments and representative assemblies came to play a recognized role in the processes of government. Urban institutions and the middle class became part of the political, economic, and social life of medieval Europe. The papacy energetically sought to lead the Western monarchs as their guide and conscience, but secular entanglements and fiscal problems threatened and gradually diluted its moral authority. While the papacy went into a serious decline, as did the Dominican and Franciscan orders, the laity remained deeply pious and increasingly sought communal or individual routes to salvation. Philosophy began to turn its attention to empirical science, and literature developed a new sophistication with the *Comedy* of Dante. The East, by contrast, suffered continual warfare and a devastating new invasion by the Mongols. Out of the ashes of this conquest, however, emerged a new state of Russia centered on Moscow. The fourteenth and fifteenth centuries brought radical new challenges to the stability achieved in the thirteenth century. Famines became common in the early fourteenth century, Philip IV and Edward I had sown the seeds of the Hundred Years' War, and the Byzantine Empire was so weakened by protracted warfare that the arrival of the Ottoman Turks would finally spell its doom.

QUESTIONS FOR FURTHER THOUGHT

1. In many ways the development of Parliament was a direct outgrowth of the Magna Carta. Who were the chief beneficiaries of the Magna Carta and of Parliament? How do these beneficiaries indicate a shift in the social class structure?
2. If you think of Dante's *Divine Comedy* as having intellectual roots in both medieval thought and the new "humanistic" thought, what elements of his writing would you use to make an argument that he was a bridge between the two?
3. Commerce assumed a larger and larger role in the European economy. What factors contributed to the success of trade and commerce? Think back to the early development of towns as well as the current chapter.

RECOMMENDED READING

Sources

*Alighieri, Dante. *The Divine Comedy*. Mark Musa (tr.). 1996.

*Amt, Emilie (ed.). *Women's Lives in Medieval Europe: A Sourcebook*. 1993.

The Chronicle of Novgorod. Robert Mitchell and Neville Forbes (trs.). 1914. Portrays social and political life of the principal commercial town of medieval Russia.

*Geary, Patrick J. (ed.). *Readings in Medieval History*. 1997. Collection of documents and texts covering the whole of the Middle Ages. Selections are long and representative of the writings of historical figures.

*Shinners, John (ed.). *Medieval Popular Religion, 1000–1500*. 1997. Valuable collection with generous selections from texts.

Studies

*Bynum, Caroline Walker. *Holy Feast and Holy Fast: The Religious Significance of Food to Medieval Women*. 1987. Discussion of female mystics in the later Middle Ages and their abstinence.

*Duby, Georges. *William Marshal: The Flower of Chivalry*. 1985. Sensitive biography of an Anglo-Norman lord.

Durham, Thomas. *Serbia: The Rise and Fall of a Medieval Empire*. 1989.

Fernández-Armesto, Felipe. *Before Columbus: Exploration and Colonization from the Mediterranean to the Atlantic, 1229–1492*. 1987. Discusses medieval exploration before Columbus, illustrating that later exploration grew out of the earlier tradition of navigating along the Atlantic coast.

*Hanawalt, Barbara. *Growing Up in Medieval London: The Experience of Childhood in History*. 1993. Childhood and adolescence in medieval London.

*Herlihy, David. *Opera Muliebria: Women and Work in Medieval Europe*. 1990. A survey of women's work with very good information on Paris.

*Jones, W. T. *A History of Western Philosophy: The Medieval Mind*. 1969. Very good survey with selections from the writings of major thinkers.

*Klapisch-Zuber, Christiane. *Women, Family, and Ritual in Renaissance Italy*. 1985. Collection of essays by

Klapisch-Zuber concerning her work on women and the family.

Leuschner, Joachim. *Germany in the Late Middle Ages.* 1980. Survey of the period.

Lynch, Katherine A., *Individuals, Families, and Communities in Europe, 1200–1800: The Urban Foundations of Western Society.* 2003. Provides a good summary of family and demographic history of the late medieval, early modern periods.

*Martin, Janet. *Medieval Russia 980–1584.* 1995. An accessible account of the development of medieval Russia.

Morgan, David. *The Mongols.* 1986. Emphasizes the impact of the Mongol conquests and empire on Eastern Europe.

Ozment, Steven. *The Age of Reform, 1250–1550: An Intellectual and Religious History of Late Medieval and Reformation Europe.* 1980. Survey of intellectual history for the period.

Simons, Walter. *Cities of Ladies: Beguine Communities in the Medieval Low Countries.* 2001. Provides a comprehensive study of the Beguines.

*Ward, Jennifer. *English Noble Women in the Later Middle Ages.* 1992. A valuable study of noble households and the women in them.

*Available in paperback.

THE HUNDRED YEARS WAR: THE BATTLE OF AGINCOURT
The war between England and France started in 1340 and continued off and on for over 100 years. Only three pitched battles were fought; most of the warfare consisted of plunder, minor skirmishes, and sieges of towns. In the skirmish shown here, Henry V of England crosses the Somme River. The English army is represented by the banner with the fleur-de-lis quartered with the lions of England, meant to illustrate the English claim to the French throne. The French banner is shown with the fleur-de-lis. The English use of the long bow and the French preference for the cross bow are apparent. The culmination of this encounter was the last major battle of the war fought at Agincourt in 1415.
Bibliothèque Nationale de France, Paris/The Art Archive

Chapter Eleven

BREAKDOWN AND RENEWAL IN AN AGE OF PLAGUE

POPULATION CATASTROPHES • ECONOMIC DEPRESSION AND RECOVERY •
POPULAR UNREST • CHALLENGES TO THE GOVERNMENTS OF EUROPE •
THE FALL OF BYZANTIUM AND THE OTTOMAN EMPIRE

In the fourteenth century, plague, famine, and recurrent wars decimated populations and snuffed out former prosperity. At the same time, feudal governments as well as the papacy struggled against mounting institutional chaos. But despite all the signs of crisis, the fourteenth and fifteenth centuries were not merely an age of breakdown. The failures of the medieval economy and its governments drove the Western peoples to repair their institutions. By the late fifteenth century the outlines of a new equilibrium were emerging. In 1500 Europeans were fewer in number than they had been in 1300, but they had developed a more productive economy and a more powerful technology than they had possessed two hundred years before. These achievements were to equip them for their great expansion throughout the world in the early modern period.

Some historians refer to the fourteenth and fifteenth centuries as the "autumn of the Middle Ages," emphasizing the decline and death of a formerly great civilization. People living at the time tended to think in terms of the Biblical passage in Revelation referring to the Four Horsemen of the Apocalypse—famine, disease, war, and the white horse of salvation. Constantinople, the last remnant of the Byzantine Empire, fell to the Ottoman Turks, providing a powerful symbol of decay. But the study of any past epoch requires an effort to balance the work of death and renewal. In few periods of history do death and renewal confront each other so dramatically as in the years between 1300 and 1500.

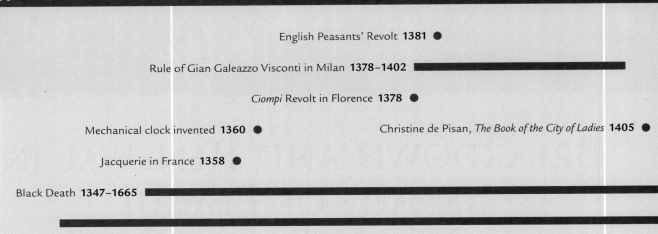

English Peasants' Revolt **1381** ●

Rule of Gian Galeazzo Visconti in Milan **1378–1402**

Ciompi Revolt in Florence **1378** ●

Mechanical clock invented **1360** ●   Christine de Pisan, *The Book of the City of Ladies* **1405** ●

Jacquerie in France **1358** ●

Black Death **1347–1665**

POPULATION CATASTROPHES

The famines and plagues that struck European society in the fourteenth and fifteenth centuries profoundly affected economic life. While the disasters disrupted the economy, Europeans recovered and reorganized to greatly changed demographic conditions. They significantly increased the efficiency of economic production.

Demographic Decline

A few censuses and other statistical records give us an insight into the size and structure of the European population in the 1300s. While incomplete, the figures show how population was changing.

Population Losses Almost every region of Europe shows an appalling decline of population between approximately 1300 and 1450. In Provence in southern France, the population seems to have shrunk after 1310 from between 350,000 and 400,000 to roughly one-third, or at most one-half, of its earlier size; only after 1470 did it again begin to increase. In Italy the decline of population was more severe.

For the larger kingdoms of Europe, the figures are less reliable, but they show a similar pattern. England had a population of about 3.7 million in 1347 and 2.2 million by 1377. France by 1328 may have reached 15 million; it was not again to attain this size for two hundred years. It can safely be estimated that all of Europe in 1450 had no more than one-half, and probably only one-third, of the population it had had around 1300. Population did not begin to recover until the end of the fifteenth century.

Famine and Hunger The first demographic catastrophe in late medieval Europe was **famine** and general food scarcities. In 1315, 1316, and 1317 a severe famine swept the north of Europe. Chroniclers described the incessant rainfall that rotted crops in the fields and prevented harvests; they spoke of people dying in the city streets and country lanes; cannibalism is another theme. In 1339 and 1340 a famine struck southern Europe. During famines, the starving people ate not only their reserves of grain but also most of the seed they had set aside for planting. Medieval Europe lacked a welfare system that could handle such massive crop failures.

Why was hunger so widespread in the early fourteenth century? Some historians see the root of trouble in the sheer number of people the lands had to support by 1300. The medieval population had been growing rapidly since about 1000, and by 1300 Europe, so this analysis suggests, was becoming the victim of its own success. Parts of the continent were crowded, even glutted, with people. Some areas of Normandy, for example, had a population in the early fourteenth century not much below what they supported six hundred years later. Thousands, millions even, had to be fed without chemical fertilizers, power tools, and fast transport. Masses of people had come to depend for their livelihood on infertile soils, and even in good years they were surviving on the margins of existence.

Although hunger did not always result in starvation, malnutrition raised the death rate from respiratory infections and intestinal ailments. While some parts of Europe returned to prosperity and good diets before the next disaster—plague—the experience of others demonstrated the dual impact of famine and

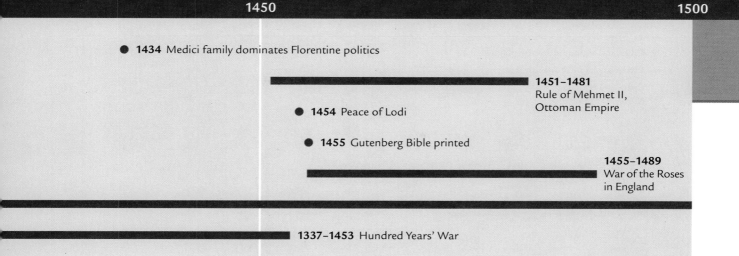

1434 Medici family dominates Florentine politics

1451–1481
Rule of Mehmet II,
Ottoman Empire

1454 Peace of Lodi

1455 Gutenberg Bible printed

1455–1489
War of the Roses
in England

1337–1453 Hundred Years' War

plague. Barceleona and its province of Catalonia experienced famine in 1333; plague in 1347–1351; famine in 1358–1359; and plague in 1362–1363, 1371, and 1397.

Plague

The great plague of the fourteenth century, known as the **Black Death,** provides a dramatic, but not a complete, explanation for the huge human losses. Plague is endemic (always present) in several parts of the world, including the southwestern United States, and occasionally spreads to become a pandemic. In the mid-fourteenth century it spread along caravan routes of central Asia and arrived at the Black Sea ports. Europe's active trade in luxury items from the East gave plague a route to Europe. In 1347 a merchant ship sailing from Caffa in the Crimea to Messina in Sicily seems to have carried rats infected with the plague. A plague broke out at Messina, and from there it spread rapidly throughout Europe (see map 11.1).

Nature of the Disease   The plague took several forms in Europe. The most identifiable one—the one that contemporary sources describe (see "Boccaccio on the Black Death," p. 309)—is the bubonic form. The pathogenic agent (not discovered until the late nineteenth century) is *Bacillus pestis.* While normally a disease of rodents, particularly house rats, it can spread to humans by fleas that carry the infection from rodents to humans through a flea bite. Bubonic plague has an incubation period of about two to ten days; its symptoms are chills, high fever, headache, and vomiting. The next symptoms are swellings (bubos) in lymph nodes of the groin and clotting blood under the skin, hence the

name "Black Death." Death is likely in 90 percent of the cases. Plague also spreads through a pneumonic variety in which the droplets containing the infection can spread directly from human to human. Infection is rapid and bubos may not form before the bacillus travels through the bloodstream to the lungs, causing pneumonia and death within three or four days. The real killer in the 1300s seems to have been pneumonic plague; it probably was spread through coughing and was almost always fatal.

What made plague so much more terrifying than famine was that it struck rich and poor, young and old, women and men, urban dwellers and villagers, nobles, peasants, monks, and clergy. Not knowing the cause of plague, physicians could do no more than lance the bubos to bring comfort, and many refused to treat plague patients at all. Those members of the clergy who went among the dying usually became infected themselves. Not knowing the true cause of the disease, people blamed the Jews for poisoning the wells; others (the Flagelants) thought it was the wrath of God and walked in procession beating themselves. Eventually, cities formed a contagion theory of the disease and refused admittance within their walls of anyone who came from a city in which the plague was prevalent.

Pandemic   The Black Death was not so much an epidemic as a pandemic (universal disease), striking an entire continent. The plague was the same one that had visited the Mediterranean and Western Europe in 542, during the reign of Justinian (see chapter 7). It struck not just once but repeatedly, until the last great outbreak in 1665, the Great Plague in London. Plague revisited every generation, and other diseases came into

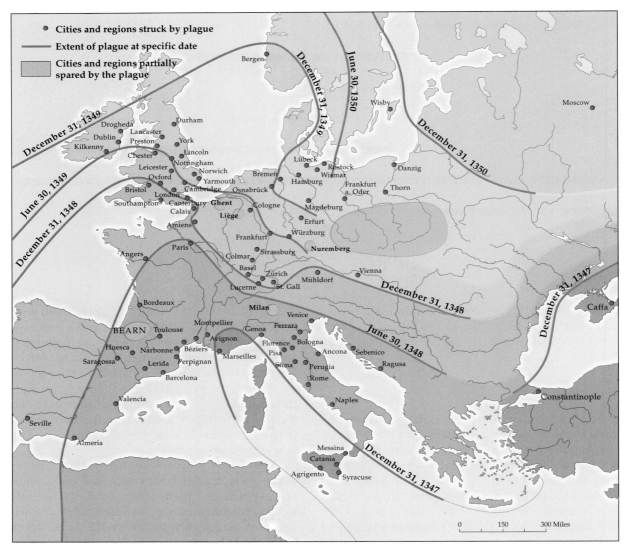

MAP 11.1 THE BLACK DEATH
The plague, as this map shows, took three years to move from Sicily to Sweden. Europe's poor travel conditions contributed to the gradual spread of plague. Where did plague appear first in Europe? Which cities and regions of Europe were partially spared by the plague?
◆ For an online version, go to www.mhhe.com/chambers9 > chapter 11 > book maps

Europe. Population did not begin to recover until the late fifteenth century.

Some of the horror of the plague can be glimpsed in this account by an anonymous cleric who visited the French city of Avignon in 1348: "To put the matter shortly, one-half, or more than a half, of the people at Avignon are already dead. Within the walls of the city there are now more than 7,000 houses shut up; in these no one is living, and all who have inhabited them are departed. . . . On account of this great mortality there is such a fear of death that people do not dare even to speak with anyone whose relative has died, because it

is frequently remarked that in a family where one dies nearly all the relations follow him."[1]

ECONOMIC DEPRESSION AND RECOVERY

A continent does not lose a third to a half of its population without feeling the effects immediately. After

[1] *Breve Chronicon clerici anonymi,* quoted in Francis Aidan Gasquet, *The Black Death of 1348 and 1349,* 1908, p. 46.

BOCCACCIO ON THE BLACK DEATH

The following eyewitness description of the ravages of the Black Death in Florence was written by one of its most famous citizens, the writer Giovanni Boccaccio. This passage comes from his masterpiece, The Decameron, *written during the three years following the plague.*

"In the year of our Lord 1348, there happened at Florence a most terrible plague, which had broken out some years before in the Levant, and after making incredible havoc all the way, had now reached the west. There, in spite of all the means that art and human foresight could suggest, such as keeping the city clear from filth and the publication of copious instructions for preservation of health, it began to show itself in the spring. Unlike what had been seen in the east, where bleeding from the nose is the fatal prognostic, here there appeared certain tumors in the groin or under the arm-pits, some as big as a small apple, others as an egg, and afterwards purple spots in most parts of the body—messengers of death. To the cure of this malady neither medical knowledge nor the power of drugs was of any effect; whether because the disease was in its own nature mortal, or that the physicians (the number of whom, tak-ing quacks and women pretenders into account, was grown very great) could form no just idea of the cause. Whichever was the reason, few escaped; but nearly all died the third day from the first appearance of the symptoms, some sooner, some later, without any fever or other symptoms. What gave the more virulence to this plague was that it spread daily, like fire when it comes in contact with combustibles. Nor was it caught only by coming near the sick, but even by touching their clothes. One instance of this kind I took particular notice of: the rags of a poor man just dead had been thrown into the street. Two hogs came up, and after rooting amongst the rags, in less than an hour they both turned around and died on the spot."

From C. Warren Hollister et al., *Medieval Europe: A Short Sourcebook,* McGraw-Hill Companies, 1992, pp. 248–249.

burying the dead, often in mass graves outside city walls, the survivors took stock of their economic position. According to contemporaries, survivors of the plague often gave up toiling in the fields or looking after their shops; presumably, they saw no point in working for the future when it was so uncertain. But in the long run Europeans adapted to the new conditions and prospered.

Agricultural Specialization

Perhaps the best indication of the changes in the European economy comes from the history of prices. The cost of most agricultural products—cereals, wine, beer, oil, and meat—shot up immediately after the Black Death and stayed high until approximately 1375 in the north and 1395 in Italy. High food prices in a time of declining population suggests that production was falling even more rapidly than the number of consumers. But high food prices mask the shift in agricultural production that led to greater specialization and, ultimately, improved diets.

Impact on the Peasantry Some historians have called the period following the depletion of population a golden age for peasantry. Conditions did change for the peasants, but these changes were not uni-formly for the better across Europe. The peasantry quickly realized that with labor in short supply they could demand higher wages for their labor, and that they could even break the bonds of their serfdom and move around the countryside to follow higher wages. The nobles and landlords were swift in their reaction to such gains.

In England, as elsewhere in Europe, the peasants had enjoyed a period of relative freedom from the labor demands of serfdom, but in the late thirteenth century landlords reimposed serfdom to take advantage of the money they could make from their crops in the period of high population and high demand for grain. With the sudden drop in population and demand for higher wages, Parliament passed the Statute of Laborers in 1351, which fixed prices and wages at what they were in 1347, the year before the plague. Like any law against supply and demand, the statute was hard to enforce, and during the course of the fifteenth century serfdom gradually disappeared in England, as the population moved away from the old manors or simply refused to pay any dues other than their rent.

Agricultural Specialization One branch of agriculture that enjoyed a remarkable period of growth in the fifteenth century was sheep raising. Since the prices

TRIUMPH OF DEATH
The great social disaster of the Black Death left few traces in the visual arts; perhaps people did not wish to be reminded of its horrors. One exception was the *Triumph of Death*, a mural painted shortly after 1348 in the Camposanto (cemetery) of Pisa in Italy. In this detail of the mural, an elegant party of hunters happens upon corpses prepared for burial. Note the rider who holds a handkerchief—scented, undoubtedly—to his nose, to ward off the foul odors.
Art Resource, NY

for wool, skins, mutton, and cheese remained high, English landlords sought to take advantage of the market by fencing large fields and converting them from plowland into sheep pastures and expelling the peasants or small herders who had formerly lived there. This process, called enclosure, continued for centuries and played an important role in English economic and social history. Other countries as well began to have agricultural specialization. The Netherlands did cheese and dairy while Spain developed Merino wool.

By the middle of the fifteenth century, agricultural prices stabilized, suggesting that production had become more dependable. Farms enjoyed the advantages of larger size, better location on more profitable soil, and increased capital investments in tools and animals. Agriculture was now more diversified, which benefited the soil, lowered the risk of famine from the failure of a single staple crop, and provided more nourishment for the people.

Gentry   The specialized agriculture brought prosperity to the land-owning nobility, but also to a new rural middle class. The middle-class urban dwellers, lawyers, bureaucrats, and wealthy peasants began to invest in land in the countryside. With capital to invest in either the purchase or lease of land, these people made considerable profits. New fortunes gave rise to a country middle class called the **gentry.**

Protectionism

The population decline caused wages to rise. The price of goods also increased, but not fast enough to offset wages. Between 1349 and 1351, England, France, Aragon, Castile, and other governments tried to fix prices and wages at levels favorable to employers. Such early experiments in a controlled economy failed.

Guilds on the Defensive   A related problem for businesses was that competition grew as population fell and markets contracted. Traders tried to protect themselves by creating restricted markets and establishing monopolies. Guilds limited their membership, and some admitted only the sons of established masters. To keep prices high, some guilds prohibited their members from hiring any women as workers, because their wages were low. Only wives and daughters of the household could work in the shops.

The Hanseatic League   Probably the best example of the monopolizing trend is the association of northern European trading cities, the **Hanseatic League.** Formed in the late thirteenth century as a defensive association, by the early fourteenth century it imposed a monopoly on cities trading in the Baltic and North seas. It excluded foreigners from the Baltic trade and could expel member cities who broke trade agreements. At its height, the Hanseatic League included seventy or eighty cities, stretching from Bruges to Novgorod and led by Bremen, Cologne, Hamburg, and especially Lübeck (see map 11.2). Maintaining its own treasury and fleet, the league supervised commercial exchange, policed the waters of the Baltic Sea, and negotiated with foreign princes. By the late fifteenth century, however, it began to decline and was unable to meet growing competition from the Dutch in northern commerce. Never formally

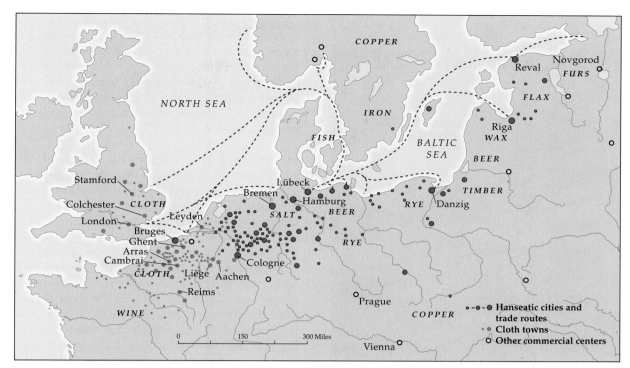

MAP 11.2 THE HANSEATIC LEAGUE AND THE GOODS IT TRADED IN THE FOURTEENTH CENTURY
Northern Europe developed a vigorous trade, mostly centered in cities around the Baltic Sea and along the rivers of Europe. The cities involved in the trade formed an association called the Hanseatic League, with its own regulations and requirements for membership. What would be the benefit of joining such a trade association? What types of goods did the Hanseatic League trade? Of these, which commodities seem to have been most in demand? Which cities predominated in the trade?

◆ For an online version, go to www.mhhe.com/chambers9 > chapter 11 > book maps

abolished, the Hanseatic League continued to meet—at lengthening intervals—until 1669.

Technological Advances

Attempts to raise the efficiency of workers proved to be far more effective than wage and price regulation in laying the basis for economic recovery. Employers were able to counteract high wages by adopting more rational methods of production and substituting capital for labor—that is, providing workers with better tools. Although hard times and labor shortages inspired most technical advances of the 1300s and 1400s, increased efficiency helped to make Europe a richer community.

Metallurgy Mining and metallurgy benefited from a series of inventions after 1460 that lowered the cost of metals and extended their use. Better techniques of digging, shoring, ventilating, and draining allowed mine shafts to be sunk several hundred feet into the earth, permitting the large-scale exploitation of the deep, rich mineral de-

posits of central Europe. During this period, miners in Saxony discovered a method for extracting pure silver from the lead alloy in which it was often found—an invention that was of major importance for the later massive development of silver mines in America.

By the late fifteenth century, European mines were providing an abundance of silver bullion for coinage. Money became more plentiful, which stimulated the economy. Exploitation also began in the rich coal deposits of northern Europe. Expanding iron production meant more and stronger pumps, gears and machine parts, tools, and iron wares.

Firearms and Weapons Europeans were constantly trying to improve the arts of war in the Middle Ages. The crossbow was cranked up and shot with a trigger; it was so powerful that it could penetrate conventional armor. The long bow came into widespread use during the Welsh wars of Edward I. It was light, accurate, and could be shot rapidly. In response to these two weapons, armor became more elaborate,

Mining, 1389
One does not normally associate miners with elegant decoration, but in this fourteenth-century manuscript, a miner provides the subject for the ornamentation of the capital *M* that starts the word *metalla* (metals). That the artist even considered such a subject is an indication of the growing importance of the industry in this period.
© Giancarlo Costa/Index

with exaggerated convex surfaces designed to deflect arrows from the chest, arms, and knees.

Siege weapons that hurled projectiles with great force and accuracy were also important. Adapting a Chinese invention for fireworks—consisting of an explosive mixture of carbon, sulfur, and saltpeter—the Europeans developed gunpowder and cannons to hurl boulders at an enemy. Firearms are first mentioned in 1328, and cannons were used in the early battles of the Hundred Years' War. With firearms, fewer soldiers could fight more effectively; capital, in the form of an efficient though expensive tool, was being substituted for labor.

Medieval architects and artists had long been interested in military engineering as well as building. Konrad Kyeser wrote and illustrated a book of weapons of war between 1395 and 1405. His work included cannons, siphons and wheels for raising water, pontoon bridges, hot-air balloons, and a device to pull horses across streams. He also made drawings of multiple guns arranged like a revolver.

Mechanical Clocks   Telling time in the Middle Ages was imprecise, based as it was on the position of the sun and the canonical hours for prayer at about three-hour intervals during the day. Times of meetings, for instance, were set within vague parameters of "at vesper," "at sunrise," or even within a few days. But in 1360 Henry De Vick designed the first mechanical clock with an hour hand for King Charles V of France, which was placed in the royal palace in Paris. Large astronomical clocks that showed the signs of the zodiac were the precursors of clocks that kept time and tolled the hours. Milan had a clock that struck a bell at every hour of the day. The regular ringing of the hours brought a new regularity to life, work, and markets and gave time itself a new value. Pocket watches, although cumbersome, had appeared by 1550 with the invention of the spring for running clocks.

Printing   The extension of literacy among laypeople and the greater reliance of governments and businesses on records created a demand for a cheap method of reproducing the written word. The introduction of paper from the East was a major step in reducing costs, for paper is far cheaper than parchment to produce. A substitute for the time-consuming labor of writing by hand was also necessary: Scribes and copiers were skilled artisans who commanded high salaries. To cut costs, printers first tried to press woodcuts—inked blocks with letters or designs carved on them—onto paper or parchment.

By the middle of the fifteenth century several masters were on the verge of perfecting the technique of printing with movable metal type. The first to prove this practicable was Johannes Gutenberg of Mainz, a former jeweler and stonecutter. Gutenberg devised an alloy of lead, tin, and antimony that would melt at a low temperature, cast well in the die, and be durable in the press; this alloy is still the basis of the printer's art. His Bible, printed in 1455, is the first major work reproduced through printing. The technique spread rapidly. By 1500 some 250 European cities had presses.

The Information Revolution   The immediate effect of the printing press was to multiply the output and cut

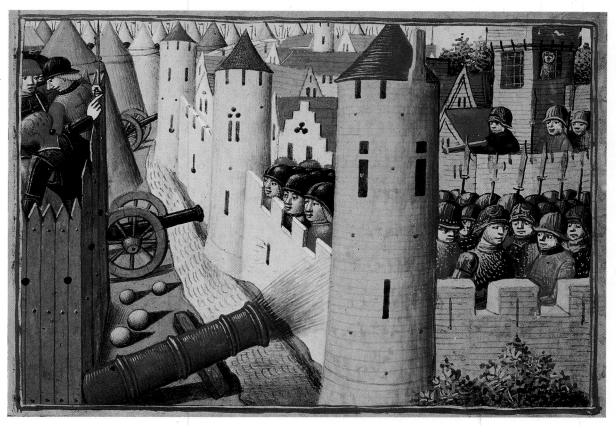

ENGLISH SIEGE OF ORLÉANS (1428–1429)
This piece shows the English soldiers behind a siege wall (left) firing cannons across the Loire River. The cannons at this stage were more frightening for their noise than for their destructive power because of design problems. The siege of Orléans was brought to an end by a French relief force led by Joan of Arc.
Bibliothèque Nationale de France, Paris

the costs of books (see map 11.3). It made information available to a much broader segment of the population, and libraries could store more information at lower cost. Printing helped disseminate and preserve knowledge in standardized form—a major contribution to the advance of technology and scholarship. Printing produced a revolution in what we would call information technology, and indeed it resembles in many ways the profound changes that computers are making in our own lives. Finally, printing could spread new ideas with unprecedented speed.

The Standard of Living

For those who survived the famine, plagues, and wars, the standard of living became better as the economy began to grow again in the late fifteenth century; but the pall of death and disease hung over the survivors.

Reduced Life Expectancy   The average life expectancy in the fifteenth century was thirty years of age. The principal victims of plague, other diseases, and famine were the very young. In many periods, between a half and a third of the babies born never reached age fifteen. Society swarmed with little children, but their deaths were common occurrences in almost every family.

The plague took a greater toll among young adults than among the aged. In effect, a person who survived one or more major epidemics had a good chance of living through the next onslaught. A mild attack of plague brought immunity rather than death as the population built up resistance to the disease; a favored few thus did reach extreme old age. The death toll of people in their child-bearing years slowed the demographic recovery.

Female Survival   Women seemed to be more robust than men in resisting or recovering from plague and the other diseases, and they became a disproportionately

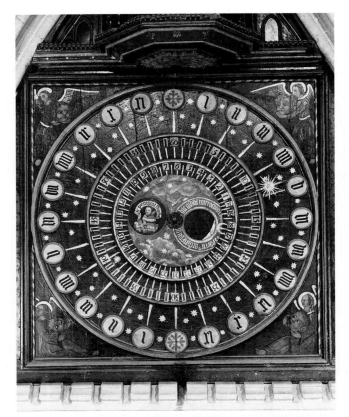

The mechanical clock, a medieval invention, was installed in major buildings. The Wells Cathedral clock was built in England. The face was decorated with the four winds and angels. The clock told the hours twenty-four hours a day and told the days in the lunar month. Bells tolled the hours.
(Top) Derek Bayes/Aspect Picture Library Ltd.
(Bottom) The Science Museum, London

larger part of the population. Historians have interpreted this fact in a number of ways. Some have argued that women took a greater role in urban and rural life and that this was a golden age for women. As historians find more evidence about women during this period, however, it appears that while more women found employment in urban centers, their roles were limited to household servants and unskilled labor. Women did not move into positions of power in government or guilds. Indeed, female guilds that had women as guild officers were forced to elect men.

Misogyny and the Debate over Women's Nature
Witchcraft charges against women were rare in the Middle Ages, but some historians have argued that the greater preponderance of women in the population contributed to the witch hunts of the sixteenth centuries. By the Late Middle Ages the intellectual debate about women's nature had become more pointed (see chapter 16). Both the ancient and the medieval world had relegated women to inferior positions, and some of the ancient and Christian authors had added strong negative invectives against women. The Church offered two images of women—Eve, the sinner who led Adam astray in the Garden of Eden, and the Virgin Mary, mother of Jesus. Neither image fit ordinary women's lives very well. As we saw in the last chapter, some very pious women commanded the respect of the Church through their asceticism.

Women were not without champions, however. Christine de Pisan, a widow with young children, turned to writing and translating to make a living. Among her books was *The Book of the City of Ladies.* She pointed to all the heroic women in history as examples of women's superior qualities, describing virtue in the most trying circumstances, heroism, self-sacrifice, wisdom, and leadership (see "The Status of Women in the Middle Ages," p. 317).

Knowledge of the Human Body   During the Late Middle Ages, some modest advances were made in medicine. Eyeglasses, invented in the thirteenth century, were perfected in the fourteenth century. For the most part they were designed for reading rather than distance vision.

Until the later part of the Middle Ages, religious prohibitions against dissecting the human cadaver meant that medicine had not advanced much beyond the Hellenistic and Arabic contributions. By the end of the thirteenth century, a teacher of medicine at the University of Bologna wrote a textbook on dissections with illustrations of human anatomy. With a superior knowledge of the human body, physicians' ability to diagnose illnesses advanced, but their knowledge of cures did not. Surgery remained the practice of barber-surgeons, guildsmen whose sharp knives could shave beards and perform surgery and whose supply of leeches could draw blood.

ꭑꝺꞃꞇ

et reumptaueuet me iam p decem vices
nec obedierunt voti mee · no videbut
terram pro qua iuraui patribus eorū:
nec quiſqz eʒ illis qui detraxit michi
intuebitur eam. Seruū meū chaleb q
pletus alio ſpiritu ſecut⁹ eſt me indu-
cam in terram hanc quā circuiuit · et
ſemen eius poſſidebit eam : quoniam
amalechites ʒ chananeus habitat in
vallibus. Cras mouere caſtra: ʒ reuer-
timini in ſolitudinē p viam maris ru-
bri . Locutuſqz ē dūs ad moyſen ʒ aaron dicens. Uſquequo multitudo hec
peſſima murmurat contra me ? Que-
relas filiorū iſrahel audiui. Dic ergo
eis. Uiuo ego ait dominus: ſicut lo-
cuti eſtis audiente me · ſic faciā vobis.
In ſolitudine hac iacebunt cadauera
veſtra . Omnes qui numerati eſtis a
viginti ānis ʒ ſupra · ʒ murmuraſtis
contra me · non intrabitis terram ſup
quā leuaui manū meam ut habitare
vos facerem: preter chaleb filiū iephone · ʒ ioſue filiū nun. Paruulos aute
veſtros de quibʒ dixiſtis quod prede
hoſtibus forent introducam: ut vide-
ant terram que vobis diſplicuit : veſtra
cadauera iacebūt in ſolitudine . Filij
veſtri erunt vagi in deſerto ānis qua-
draginta : ʒ portabunt fornicationē
veſtram · donec conſumetur cadauera
patrū in deſerto : iuxta numerū qdra-
ginta dierū quibus conſideraſtis terrā.
Ann⁹ pro die imputabitur . Et qua-
draginta ānis recipietis iniquitates
veſtras: ʒ ſcietis ultionem meā. Quoniam ſicut locut⁹ ſum · ita faciā omni
multitudini huic peſſime· que conſur-
rexit aduerſum me: in ſolitudine hac
deficiet ʒ morietur. Igitur omnes viri
quos miſerat moyſes ad contemplan-
dam terram · ʒ qui reuerſi murmurare

fecerant contra eū omnē multitudinē.
Detrahentes terre qd eſſet mala: mor-
tui ſunt atqz percuſſiqz in conſpectu domini . Ioſue aut filius nun ʒ chaleb
filius iephone vixerunt eʒ omnibus
qui pergerant ad conſiderandā terrā.
Locutuſqz eſt moyſes vniuerſa verba
hec ad omnes filios iſrahel: et luxit
popul⁹ nimis . Et ecce mane primo
ſurgentes · aſcenderūt verticem montis
atqz dixerunt. Parati ſum⁹ aſcendere
ad locum de quo dominus locutus
eſt: quia peccauimus . Quibus moyſes. Cur inquit tranſgredimini verbū
dūi · quod vobis non redet in proſpe-
rum ? Nolite aſcendere · non enim eſt
dūs vobiſcum : ne corruatis corā ini-
micis veſtris. Amalechites ʒ chananeus ante vos ſunt quos gladio corru-
etis: eo ꝙ nolueritis acquieſcere dūo:
nec erit dominus vobiſcū. At illi con-
tenebrati· aſcenderūt in verticem montis. Archa autem teſtamenti domini
et moyſes non receſſerūt de caſtris. De-
ſcenditqz amalechites ʒ chananeus q
habitabat i monte: et percutiens eos atqz
concidens · perſecut⁹ ē eos uſqz horma. XV
Locutus eſt domin⁹ ad moyſen
dicens. Loquere ad filios iſrl· ʒ
dices ad eos. Cum ingreſſi fueritis terram habitationis veſtre quā ego dabo
vobis · ʒ feceritis oblationē domino
in olocauſtum · aut victimam pacifi-
cam vota ſoluetes· vel ſponte offeretes
munera · aut in ſolennitatibʒ veſtris a-
dolentes odorem ſuauitatis dūo: de
bubus ſiue de ouibʒ offeret quicunqz
immolauerit victimam: ſacrificiū ſic
decimam partem ephi conſperſam oleo-
quod menſurā habebit quartā parte
hin: et vinum ad liba fundenda eiuſ-
dem menſure dabit in olocauſtū ſiue

Housing and Diets The revitalized economy brought improvements in housing, dress, and diet and increased spending on art and decorative objects. Housing was generally improving for most people in the Late Middle Ages. The increasing use of brick and tile meant that buildings were more substantial and more spacious. The nobility, gentry, and wealthy urban dwellers built large town houses and country houses with gardens and large windows rather than defensive walls. The fireplace on the wall replaced the hearth in the center of the room even in peasant houses.

The European diet had been largely based on cereal products, and when population was dense, all land had to be devoted to raising grain, even if the land was not particularly well suited for it. Reduced population meant that land could be devoted to other crops or to

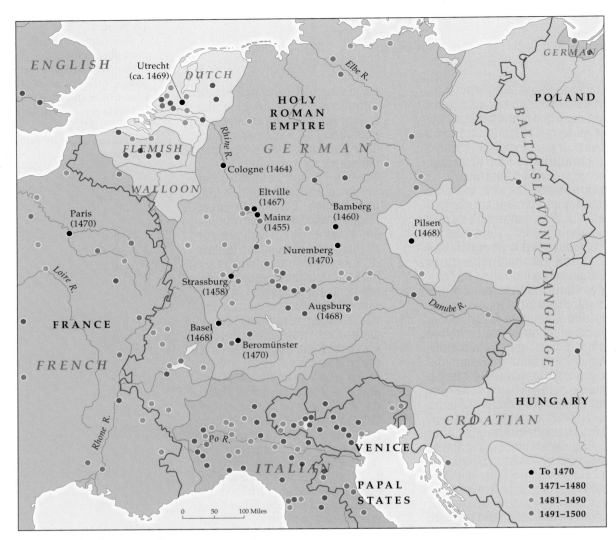

MAP 11.3 THE SPREAD OF PRINTING BEFORE 1500
After the invention of printing in the Rhineland, printing presses sprang up along the rivers of Europe. How quickly did the printing technology spread? In which countries were the printing presses concentrated?
◆ For an online version, go to www.mhhe.com/chambers9 > chapter 11 > book maps

CHRISTINE DE PISAN PRESENTS POEMS TO ISABEAU OF BAVARIA
Christine de Pisan (1364–1439) was the author of several important historical and literary works including a biography of King Charles V of France and *The Book of the Three Virtues*, a manual for the education of women. She is here depicted presenting a volume of her poems to the queen of France, who is surrounded by ladies-in-waiting and the symbol of the French royal family, the fleur-de-lis. It is significant that there were such scenes of elegance and intellectual life even amidst the chaos and destruction of the Hundred Years' War.
The British Library, London; Harly Ms. 4431, fol. 3

HISTORICAL ISSUES: THE STATUS OF WOMEN IN THE MIDDLE AGES

The study of medieval women has become a major area of historical research in the past thirty-five years. Scholars have raised a number of unresolved questions about women's lives and their experiences. The questions discussed here suggest ongoing areas of research.

1. Does the periodization of political history apply to women's history or to the history of ordinary people? Historians have used watersheds in political history such as the Battle of Bosworth Field in 1485 to define the end of medieval England and the beginning of early modern England. But did women or peasants wake up after the battle and declare that a new era had begun and life was going to change for them? Intellectual movements, since they largely involved men, may have had little influence on women's lives, as Joan Kelly asked in her famous essay, "Did Women Have a Renaissance?"*

2. To what extent did the Church's misogyny influence the way women lived? In Church writings, women were either saintly like the Virgin Mary or sinners like Eve. The Church blessed women's roles only as virgins or as wives and mothers. The general misogyny was also prevalent in medieval lay society and appeared in jokes, in literary pieces such as the Romance of the Rose, and in various regulations regarding women. But did women consciously take these strictures to heart when they lived their everyday lives? Some women did move into positions of power as regents and queens; powerful female saints and mystics became a part of late medieval religious life; women joined the tertiaries and the Beguinages. Individual peasant and urban women farmed their plots or ran their own businesses. Many other women moved into business and administrative capacities when their husbands were away or when they became widows. But women who took these initiatives generally worked within a framework of acceptable female behavior. Joan of Arc, on the other hand, offended the Church perhaps more because she adopted male dress and role than because of the heresy and witchcraft charges the Inquisitors brought.

3. Understanding the role of patriarchy is important for understanding women's freedom in marriage and widowhood. Customs varied greatly depending on the availability of women for marriage, on local laws covering dower and dowry, and on economic necessity. Some marriage arrangements, particularly among the peasantry, assumed that the household was the unit of economic production and that the sex roles were equally important for the survival of the family. In urban Florence the age differences between spouses seemed to preclude a strong voice for a young bride. Other studies will, no doubt, show other patterns.

4. Women's participation in intellectual and political life continues to be researched. Women could not attend universities, be ordained as priests, or participate in legal and magisterial roles. On the other hand, nunneries, courts, and individual experiences did permit them to write, engage in intellectual debate, and contribute to the cultural enrichment of the Middle Ages. Much women's writing and artistic work has been lost, but enough survives to indicate the ways women participated in the cultural life of the Middle Ages. Christine de Pisan is an example of a writer who was so well-known that Richard II of England offered to be her patron.

*From "Did Women Have a Renaissance?" by Joan Kelly from Renate Bridenthal, Claudia Koonz, and Susan Stuard, *Becoming Visible: Woman in European History*, 2nd ed. Copyright © 1987 by Houghton Mifflin Company. Adapted with permission.

---

animal rearing. Diet generally improved, with more meat, cheese, oil, butter, fruit, wine, and beer.

Courtesy and Dress   Refinements in living brought a new emphasis on polite behavior, particularly at the table. Guild ordinances began to include instructions about manners at the annual feast, and books of advice for young people moving up in social station proliferated in every language. Silver forks replaced fingers as a tool for polite dining among the upper class.

Dress for the upper classes became very grand, with the tall pointed caps and the long pointed shoes that we associate with medieval Europe. That the fine dress was not limited to the upper classes is obvious from the sumptuary legislation that cities and kingdoms passed, which tried to regulate who was allowed to wear fine cloth with furs and who was prohibited from doing so.

POPULAR UNREST

The demographic collapse and economic troubles of the fourteenth century deeply disturbed the social peace of Europe. European society had been remarkably stable and mostly peaceful from the Early Middle Ages until around 1300, and there is little evidence of uprisings or social warfare. The fourteenth and fifteenth

Dress became very elaborate, with tall headdresses for women and pointed shoes and tights for men. The most elaborate court was that of the Duke of Burgundy, which is pictured here with courtiers dancing.
Bibliothèque Nationale de France, Paris

centuries, however, witnessed numerous revolts of peasants and artisans against what they believed to be the oppression of the propertied classes.

Rural Revolts

One of the most spectacular fourteenth-century rural uprisings was the English Peasants' Revolt of 1381. This revolt originated in popular resentment against both the policies of the royal government and the practices of the great landlords. Although the Statute of Laborers (1351), which tried to fix prices and wages at the preplague level, had little practical success, the mere effort to implement it aggravated social tensions, especially in the countryside, where it would have reimposed serfdom on the peasants. Concurrent attempts to collect poll taxes (a flat tax on each member of the population), which by their nature burdened the prosperous less than the humble, crystallized resentment against the government.

Under leaders of uncertain background—Wat Tyler, Jack Straw, and a priest named John Ball—peasant bands, enraged by the latest poll tax, marched on London in 1381. They called for the abolition of serfdom, labor services, and tithes and demanded an end to the poll taxes. The workers of London, St. Albans, York, and other cities who had similar grievances rose in support of the peasants. After mobs killed the king's advis-

ers and burned the houses of prominent lawyers and royal officials, King Richard II, then age fifteen, bravely met with the peasants in person at Mile End, outside the walls of London. One of his followers killed Wat Tyler as he negotiated with the king. Thinking quickly, Richard told the peasants that he was their leader and promised to give them charters of freedom. But as the peasants dispersed, the great landlords reorganized their forces and violently suppressed the last vestiges of unrest in the countryside; the young king also reneged on his promises and declared the charters invalid.

The peasant uprising in England was only one of many rural disturbances between 1350 and 1450, including revolts near Paris, called the **Jacquerie,** and in Languedoc, Catalonia, and Sweden. Germany also experienced such disturbances in the fifteenth century and a major peasant revolt in 1524, which was to feed into the tensions of the early days of the Protestant Reformation.

Urban Revolts

The causes of social unrest within the cities were similar to those in the countryside—wages and taxes. In the 1300s and early 1400s Strasburg, Metz, Ghent, Liège, and Paris were all scenes of riots. Though not entirely typical, one of the most interesting of these urban revolts was the Ciompi uprising at Florence in 1378.

Florence was one of the wool manufacturing centers of Europe; the industry employed probably one-third of the working population of the city, which shortly before the Black Death may have risen to 120,000 people. The wool industry, like most, entered bad times immediately after the plague. To protect themselves, employers cut production, thereby spreading unemployment.

The poorest workers—mainly the wool carders, known as *Ciompi*—rose in revolt. They demanded, and for a short time got, several reforms: The employers would produce at least enough cloth to ensure work, they would refrain from monetary manipulations considered harmful to the workers, and they would allow the workers their own guild and representation in communal government. Because the Ciompi did not have the leaders to maintain a steady influence on government policy, the great families regained full authority in the city by 1382 and quickly ended the democratic concessions. Although the Ciompi revolt was short-lived and ultimately unsuccessful, the incident is one of the first signs of the urban class tensions that would be a regular disturbance in future centuries.

The Seeds of Discontent

While local and unique circumstances shaped each of the social disturbances of the 1300s and 1400s, the so-

Jehan Froissart
PEASANTS' REVOLT,
CA. 1460–1480
One of the leaders of the peasant revolt was a preacher, John Ball, who is shown on the horse. One of his messages was a simple egalitarian rhyme: "When Adam delved and Eve span, where then were all the gentlemen?" Wat Tyler, another leader, is in the foreground holding a banner with the English coat of arms. Rather than a rabble with pitchforks, many peasants had trained in the militia that defended the English coast against French raids. Loyal to the king, the peasants did not want to kill him, but rather to get rid of his bad advisers.
British Library, London/Bridgeman Art Library

cial movements had common elements. With the standard of living generally rising after the Black Death, misery was not the main cause of unrest. Rather, the peasants and workers, now reduced in number, were better able to bargain for lower rents, higher wages, and a fairer distribution of social benefits.

With the possible exception of the Ciompi, the people who revolted were rarely the desperately poor. In England, for example, the centers of the peasant uprising of 1381 were in the lower Thames valley—a region with more fertility, more prosperity, less oppression, and less serfdom than other parts of the kingdom had. Also, the immediate provocation for the revolt was the imposition of a poll tax, and poll taxes (or any taxes) do not alarm the truly destitute who cannot be forced to pay what they do not have, but they do anger people who have recently made financial gains and are anxious to hold on to them.

The principal goad to revolt in both town and country, therefore, seems to have been the effort of the propertied classes to retain their old advantages and deny the workers their new ones. Peasants and workers felt that their improving social and economic status was being threatened.

The impulse to revolt also drew strength from the psychological tensions of this age of devastating plagues, famines, and wars. The nervous temper of the times predisposed people to take action against real or imagined enemies. When needed, justifications for re-volt could be found in Christian belief, for the Christian fathers had taught that neither the concept of private property nor social inequality had been intended by God. In John Ball's words: "When Adam delved and Eve span, where then were all the gentlemen?" The emotional climate of the period turned many of these uprisings into efforts to attain the millennium, to reach that age of justice and equality that Christian belief saw in the past, expected in the future, and put off for the present.

CHALLENGES TO THE GOVERNMENTS OF EUROPE

War, the third horseman of the Apocalypse, joined famine and disease. War was frequent throughout the Middle Ages but was never so widespread or long lasting as in the conflicts of the 1300s and 1400s. The Hundred Years' War between England and France is the most famous of these struggles, but there was fighting in every corner of Europe. The inbred violence of the age indicated a partial breakdown in governmental systems, which failed to maintain stability at home and peace with foreign powers.

The governmental systems of Europe were founded on multiple partnerships: feudal ties with vassals, relations with the Church, representative institutions, and subjects in general. Out of the crises of the fourteenth and fifteenth centuries many of the new governments that came to dominate the European political scene in the late 1400s conceded far more power to a king, prince, despot, or oligarchy.

Roots of Political Unrest

Dynastic Instability   In a period of demographic instability, dynasties suffered, as did the population as a whole. The Hundred Years' War, or at least the excuse for it, arose from the failure of the Capetian kings of France, for the first time since the tenth century, to produce a male heir. The English War of the Roses resulted from the uncertain succession to the crown of England and the claims of the two rival houses of Lancaster and York. In Portugal, Castile, France, England, Naples, Hungary, Poland, and the Scandinavian countries, the reigning monarchs of 1450 were not the direct, male, legitimate descendants of those reigning in 1300. Most of the founders of new lines had to fight for their positions.

Changes in Warfare   War grew more expensive as well as more frequent. Better-trained armies were needed to fight for longer periods of time and with more complex weaponry. Above all, the increasing use of firearms added to the costs of war. To replace the traditional, undisciplined, unpaid, and poorly equipped feudal armies, governments came to rely on mercenaries, who were better trained and better armed. Many mercenaries were organized into associations known as companies of adventure, whose leaders were both good commanders and good businessmen.

Seeking Revenue   While war went up in price, the traditional revenues on which governments depended sank. Until the fourteenth century, the king or prince met most of the expenses of government from ordinary revenues, chiefly rents from his properties; but his rents, like everyone else's, were falling in the late Middle Ages. Individuals, movable property, salt, prostitutes, and a variety of products were taxed to raise revenue. Surviving fiscal records indicate that governments managed to increase their incomes hugely through taxes. For example, the English monarchy never collected or spent more than £30,000 per year before 1336; thereafter, the budget rarely sank below £100,000 and at times reached £250,000 in the late fourteenth century.

The Nobility and Factional Politics   The nobility that had developed nearly everywhere in Europe also entered a period of instability in the Late Middle Ages. Birth was the main means of access to this class, and membership offered legal and social privileges such as exemption from most taxes, immunity from certain juridical procedures (such as torture), and hunting privileges. The nobles saw themselves as the chief counselors of the king and his principal partners in the conduct of government.

By the 1300s, however, the nobles began to experience economic instability. Their wealth was chiefly in land, and they, like all landlords, faced the problem of declining rents. Unlike the gentry, they often lacked the funds needed for the new agricultural investments, and they continued to have the problem of finding income and careers for their younger sons.

As the social uncertainties intensified, the nobles tended to coalesce into factions that disputed with one another over the control of government and the distribution of its favors. From England to Italy, factional warfare constantly disturbed the peace. A divided and grasping nobility added to the tensions of the age and to its violence. Characteristically, a faction was led by a great noble house and included people of varying social station—great nobles in alliance with the leading royal house, poor knights, retainers, servants, sometimes even artisans and peasants.

A good example of liveried retainers of these great nobles are the Pastons of England. The family originated from wealthy peasant stock who prospered in the agricultural opportunities of the fifteenth century. The founder of the family fortune, William, managed to marry up socially, taking a knight's daughter as wife. He educated his sons in law because land could be gained by legal maneuverings as well as through advantageous marriages. He was also careful about the local patronage system and placed his eldest son, John, in the Duke of Norfolk's household. John was part of the duke's retinue on ceremonial occasions. Sir John Fastolf, a soldier who made a fortune in the Hundred Years' War and was the model for Shakespeare's Falstaff, relied on John for legal advice and eventually made him his heir. The Pastons continually defended their lands either in court or in actual sieges. At one point John's wife, Margaret, organized the defense of one of their manors from armed attack. The people trying to obtain their property had the support of other great lords in the district, particularly the Duke of Suffolk. The family managed to survive the War of the Roses to emerge in the sixteenth century as nobility.

England, France, and the Hundred Years' War

All the factors that upset the equilibrium of feudal governments—dynastic instability, fiscal pressures, and factional rivalries—helped to provoke the greatest struggle of the epoch, the **Hundred Years' War.** The war had distinctive characteristics. It was not fought continually for one hundred years, but in different phases. The great battles were of less significance for determin-

Ambrogio Lorenzetti
ALLEGORY OF GOOD GOVERNMENT, **1338–1339**
**The effects of good government, seen in this idealized representation of a peaceful city by Ambrogio Lorenzetti, include
flourishing commerce, dancing maidens, and lavish residences, as opposed to the protective towers of feudal warfare. This
fresco in the city hall of Siena was a constant reminder to the citizens of the advantages of living in their city.**
Scala/Art Resource, NY

ing the outcome than was the war of attrition against
the population. Economic embargo and interruption of
trade became weapons of states in winning wars.

Causes   The issue that is alleged to have started the
Hundred Years' War was a dispute over the French royal
succession. While most noble families had direct father-
to-son succession for only three generations, the
Capetians had produced male heirs for three hundred
years. The last three Capetian kings (the sons of Philip
IV, the Fair) all died without male heirs. In 1328, when
the last Capetian died, the nearest surviving male relative was King Edward III of England, son of Philip's
daughter Isabella. The Parlement of Paris—the supreme
court of France—discovered that the laws of the Salian
Franks precluded women from inheriting or transmitting
a claim to the crown. Philip of Valois, a first cousin of the
previous kings, became king. Edward did not at first dispute this decision, and, as holder of the French fiefs of
Aquitaine and Ponthieu, he did homage to Philip VI.

More important than the dynastic issue was the
clash of French and English interests in Flanders, an
area whose cloth-making industry relied on England
for wool. In 1302 the Flemings had rebelled against
their count, a vassal of the French king, and had remained virtually independent until 1328, when Philip
VI defeated their troops and restored the count. At
Philip's insistence, the count ordered the arrest of all
English merchants in Flanders; Edward retaliated by

cutting off the export of wool, which spread unemployment in the Flemish towns. The Flemings revolted once more and drove out the count. To give
legal sanction to their revolt, they persuaded Edward
to assert his claim to the French crown, which held
suzerainty over Flanders.

The most serious point of friction, however, was the
status of Aquitaine and Ponthieu. Philip began harassing the frontiers of Aquitaine and declared Edward's
fiefs forfeit in 1337. The attack on Aquitaine pushed
Edward into supporting the Flemish revolt and was
thus the main provocation for the Hundred Years' War.

Economic maneuvers by both sides aggravated tensions. The French king encouraged French pirates and
shippers to interfere with the wine trade from English
Gascony. Edward began to tax wool leaving England
and encouraged the Flemish weavers to come to England under his special protection to set up workshops
with their superior craftsmanship. Incidentally, this
move was the beginning of the woolen cloth weaving
tradition in England.

The Tides of Battle

The confused struggle of the Hundred Years' War may
be divided into three periods: initial English victories
from 1338 to 1360; French resurgence, then stalemate,
from 1369 to 1415; and a wild denouement with tides
rapidly shifting from 1415 to 1453 (see map 11.4).

MAP 11.4 THE HUNDRED YEARS' WAR
In reading this map, one must keep in mind that control of these territories shifted for centuries (see map 9.3, p 264). In the tenth century, French royal domain was concentrated in the areas around Paris. While the French kings extended their territory through marriage alliances and conquest, so, too, did England increase its holdings in France. For example, Henry II of England acquired the extensive lands of the duchy of Aquitaine through his marriage to Eleanor of Aquitaine in 1152. England later lost much of its territory in France and by 1339 had only a small fraction of its earlier holdings. English monarchs tried continually to repossess the lands that they lost and the French monarchs tried to push the English entirely out of French territory. What areas did England and France control outright in 1339 and what areas were contested? After its victory at Agincourt, which areas did England attempt to control?

◆ For an online version, go to www.mhhe.com/chambers9 > chapter 11 > book maps

CHRONOLOGY
The Hundred Years' War

1328	Charles IV, last Capetian king in direct line, dies; Philip of Valois is elected king of France as Philip VI; Philip defeats Flemings at Cassel; unrest continues in Flemish towns.
1329	Edward III of England does simple homage to Philip for continental possessions but refuses liege homage.
1336	Edward embargoes wool exports to Flanders.
1338	Philip's troops harass English Guienne; Edward, urged on by the Flemings, claims French crown; war begins.
1346	Major English victory at Crécy.
1347–1351	Black Death ravages Europe.
1356	Black Prince defeats French at Poitiers.
1358	Peasants' uprising near Paris.
1360	Peace of Brétigny; English gain major territorial concessions but abandon claim to French crown.
1369	Fighting renewed in France.
1370	Bertrand du Guesclin, constable of France, leads French resurgence.
1381	Peasants' Revolt in England.
1392	Charles VI of France suffers first attack of insanity; Burgundians and Armagnacs contend for power over king; fighting wanes as both sides are exhausted.
1399	Henry IV of Lancaster takes English throne, deposing Richard II.
1415	Henry V wins major victory at Agincourt.
1420	Treaty of Troyes; Charles VI recognizes Henry V as legitimate heir to French crown; high-water mark of English fortunes.
1429	Joan of Arc relieves Orléans from English siege; Dauphin is crowned king at Reims as Charles VII.
1431	Joan is burned at the stake at Rouen.
1435	Peace of Arras; Burgundy abandons English side.
1436	Charles retakes Paris.
1453	Bordeaux falls to French; English retain only Calais on continent; effective end of war, though no treaty is signed.

First Period An English naval victory at Sluys in 1340 ensured English communications across the channel and determined that France would be the scene of the fighting. Six years later Edward landed in France on what was more a marauding expedition than a campaign of conquest. Philip pursued the English and finally overtook them at Crécy in 1346. The English were on a hill, and Edward positioned his troops so that the longbowmen could shoot into the advancing French line. The French knights had arrived after a long journey but decided to attack without waiting for their crossbowmen, who were coming on foot. Charging up the hill, the French knights met a rain of arrows that cut their horses from under them. The English knights came down to finish the fight. The victory ensured the English possession of Calais, which they took in 1347.

The plague interrupted the war until 1356. At Poitiers, John II, who had succeeded Philip, attacked an English army led by Edward's son, the Black Prince, and suffered an even more crushing defeat. John was captured and died, unransomed by his son and vassals. English victories, the Black Death, and mutual exhaustion led to the Peace of Brétigny in 1360. The English were

granted Calais and an enlarged Aquitaine, and Edward, in turn, renounced his claim to the French crown.

Second Period The French were not willing to allow so large a part of their kingdom to remain in English hands. In 1369, under John's successor, Charles V, the French opened a second phase of the war. Their strategy was to avoid full-scale battles and instead wear down the English forces, and they succeeded. By 1380 they had pushed the English nearly into the sea, confining them to Calais and a narrow strip of the Atlantic coast from Bordeaux to Bayonne. Fighting was sporadic from 1380 until 1415, with both sides content with a stalemate. During this war of attrition, mercenaries on both sides devastated the countryside, plundering villages, ruining crops and vineyards, and driving the population to seek refuge. It was a type of warfare that reappeared in the Thirty Years' War and in World War II.

Third Period The last period of the war, from 1415 to 1453, was one of high drama and rapidly shifting fortunes. Henry V of England invaded France and shattered the French army at Agincourt in 1415. The battle was a replay of Crécy and Poitiers. The English

JOAN OF ARC, 1484
Surrounded by the clerics who had condemned her, Joan of
Arc is bound to the stake in this scene from a manuscript
that was prepared half a century after she was executed in
1431. Despite Joan's own preference for short hair and manly
costume, she is shown here as a conventionally idealized
female figure.
Bibliothèque Nationale de France, Paris

longbowmen shot at the French knights in full armor as they charged downhill into a marshy area. Henry's success was confirmed by the Treaty of Troyes in 1420, an almost total French capitulation. King Charles VI of France declared his son the Dauphin (the future Charles VII) illegitimate, named Henry his successor and regent of France, and gave him direct rule over all French lands as far south as the Loire River (see map 11.4). Charles also gave Henry his daughter Catherine in marriage, with the agreement that their son would become the next king of France.

The Dauphin could not accept this forced abdication, and from his capital at Bourges he led an expedition across the Loire River. The English drove his forces back and systematically took the towns and fortresses north of the river that were loyal to him. In 1428 they finally laid siege to Orléans, a city whose fall would have given them a commanding position in the Loire valley and would have made the Dauphin's cause desperate.

Joan of Arc   The intervention of a young peasant girl, Joan of Arc, saved the Valois Dynasty. Convinced that heavenly voices were ordering her to rescue France, Joan persuaded several royal officials, and finally the Dauphin himself, of the authenticity of her mission and was given command of an army. In 1429 she marched to Orléans and forced the English to raise the siege. She then escorted the Dauphin to Reims, the historic coronation city of France, where his coronation confirmed his legitimacy and won him broad support

as the embodiment of French royalist sentiment. The tide had turned.

Joan passed from history as quickly and as dramatically as she had arrived. The Burgundians, allies of the English, captured her in 1430 and sold her to the English. They turned her over to a church court which put her on trial for witchcraft and heresy (see "The Trial of Joan of Arc," p. 325). She was burned at the stake at Rouen in 1431. Yet Joan's commitment was one sign of an increasingly powerful feeling among the people. They had grown impatient with continuing destruction and had come to identify their own security with the expulsion of the English and the establishment of a strong Valois monarchy. This growing loyalty to the king finally saved France from its long agony. A series of French successes followed Joan's death, and by 1453 only Calais was left in English hands. No formal treaty ended the war, but both sides accepted the outcome: England was no longer a continental power.

The Effects of the Hundred Years' War

Like all the disasters of the era, the Hundred Years' War accelerated change. It stimulated the development of firearms and the technologies needed to manufacture them, and it helped establish the infantry—armed with longbow, crossbow, pike, or gun—as superior in battle to mounted knights. It also introduced wars of attrition in which the countryside was devastated in an effort to bring the enemy to submission. The war had a major effect on government institutions in England and France.

English Government   The expense of fighting forced the English king to request more revenue through taxation. In England the king willingly gave Parliament a larger political role in return for grants of new taxes. The tradition became firmly established that Parliament had the right to grant or refuse new taxes, to agree to legislation, to channel appeals to the king, and to offer advice on important decisions such as peace and war. The House of Commons gained the right to introduce all tax legislation, since the Commons, unlike the Lords, were representatives of shires and boroughs. Parliament also named a committee to audit tax records and supervise payments. Equally important, the Commons could impeach high royal officials, a crucial step in establishing the principle that a king's ministers were responsible to Parliament as well as to their royal master. By the end of the Hundred Years' War, Parliament had been notably strengthened at the expense of royal power.

French Government   The need for new taxes had a rather different outcome in France, where it enhanced

THE TRIAL OF JOAN OF ARC

The records of the trial of Joan of Arc in Rouen in 1431 give us a rare opportunity to hear her directly, or at least the words a secretary heard. Whether recorded accurately or not, her testimony does give us a glimpse of her extraordinary spirit and determination.

"When she had taken the oath the said Jeanne was questioned by us about her name and her surname. To which she replied that in her own country she was called Jeannette. She was questioned about the district from which she came.

"She said she was born in the village of Domrémy. Asked if in her youth she had learned any craft, she says yes, to sew and spin; and in sewing and spinning she feared no woman in Rouen.

"Afterwards she declared that at the age of 13 she had a voice from God to help her and guide her. And the first time she was much afraid. And this voice came towards noon, in summer, in her father's garden. Asked what instruction this voice gave her for the salvation of her soul, she said it taught her to be good and to go to church often; and the voice told her that she should raise the siege of the city of Orléans.

"Asked whether, when she saw the voice coming to her, there was a light, she answered that there was a great deal of light on all sides. She added to the examiner that not all the light came to him alone!

"Asked whether she thought she had committed a sin when she left her father and mother, she answered that since God commanded, it was right to do so. She added that since God commanded, if she had had a hundred parents, she would have gone nevertheless.

"Jeanne was admonished to speak the truth. Many of the points were read and explained to her, and she was told that if she did not confess them truthfully she would be put to the torture, the instruments of which were shown to her.

"To which Jeanne answered in this manner: 'Truly if you were to tear me limb from limb and separate my soul from my body, I would not tell you anything more; and if I did say anything, I should afterwards declare that you had compelled me to say it by force.'"

From G. G. Coulton and Eileen Power (eds.), *The Trial of Jeanne d' Arc*, W. P. Barrett (trans.), Routledge, 1931.

the power of the monarchs while weakening the Estates General, the national representative assembly. In 1343 Philip VI established a monopoly over the sale of salt, fixing in many areas of France its cost and the amount each family could have to consume. The tax on salt, called the *gabelle,* was to be essential to French royal finance until 1789. In gaining support for this and other taxes, Philip and his successors sought the agreement of regional assemblies of estates as well as the national Estates General. The kings' reliance on the local estates hindered the rise of a centralized assembly that could speak for the entire kingdom. By the reign of Charles VII, during the last stages of the war, the monarchy obtained the right to impose national taxes (notably the *taille,* a direct tax from which nobles and clerics were exempt) without the consent of the Estates General. By then, too, the royal government was served by a standing professional army—the first in any European country since the fall of the Roman Empire.

The War of the Roses   Both England and France experienced internal dissension during the Hundred Years' War. Both countries suffered from a brutalization of life, with groups of former fighters and thugs pillaging the countryside. After the death of Edward III in 1377, England faced more than a century of turmoil, with nobles striving to maintain their economic fortunes through factional conflicts. The powerful magnates and their liveried followers used law and brute force to gain lands of competitors, as we have seen in the case of the Pastons. The son of Henry V and Catherine of France, Henry VI, went through periods of insanity, which led to a civil war for succession to the throne. Two factions, the Lancastrians and the Yorkists, laid claim to the throne, and the English nobles aligned themselves on one side or the other. The civil war that followed is known to historians as the War of the Roses (the Lancastrians' emblem was a red rose; the Yorkists', a white rose).

The civil war lasted some thirty-five years. While not bloody for the population as a whole, the war did decimate the ranks of the nobility. It also gave rise to the allegations that Richard III, a Yorkist, killed his two young nephews in the Tower of London because they had a clearer title to the kingship than he had. Finally, the Lancastrian Henry Tudor defeated Richard III at Bosworth Field in 1485. Henry VII Tudor married Elizabeth of York to heal the breech between the factions. By the end of the fifteenth century, prosperity had relieved the pressures on the English nobles, and the people in general, weary of war, welcomed the strong and orderly regime that Henry established.

Burgundy　In France, too, the power of the monarchy was threatened by rival factions of nobles, the Armagnacs and the Burgundians. The Armagnacs wanted the war with England vigorously pursued, while the Burgundians favored accommodation. The territorial ambitions of the Burgundians also posed a threat to the French monarchy. King John II of France had granted the huge Duchy of Burgundy to his younger son, Philip the Bold, in 1363. Philip and his successors greatly enlarged their possessions in eastern France, the Rhone and Rhine valleys, and the Low Countries (see map 11.3). They were generous patrons of literature and the arts, and they made their court at Dijon the most brilliant in Europe.

The dukes seem to have sought to establish a Burgundian "middle kingdom" between France and the Holy Roman Empire; such a state would have affected the political geography of Europe permanently and undermined the position of the French monarch. But the threat vanished in 1477 when the last duke, Charles the Bold, was killed in battle with the Swiss at Nancy. His daughter and heir, Mary of Burgundy, could not hold her scattered inheritance together, and a large part of it came under French control.

The English and French States　With the loss of most of its continental possessions, England emerged from the war geographically more consolidated. It was also homogeneous in its language (English gradually replaced French and Latin as the language of the law courts and administration) and more conscious of its cultural distinctiveness and national identity. Although the French had made some incursions in coastal areas, England had not been invaded, and the woolen industry began to be very profitable. Freed from its continental entanglements, England was ready for its expansion beyond the seas and for a surge in national pride and self-consciousness.

France did not immediately achieve quite the territorial consolidation of England, but the expulsion of the English from French lands and the disintegration of the Duchy of Burgundy left the French king without a major rival among his feudal princes. The monarchy emerged from the war with a permanent army, a rich tax system, and no clear constitutional restrictions on its exercise of power. Most significantly, the war gave the French king high prestige and confirmed him as the chief protector and patron of the people. Although ravaged by warfare, the land was so rich that, when the peasants returned and began cultivating, the French economy quickly recovered.

In both France and England, government at the end of the Middle Ages was still decentralized and "feudal," meaning here that certain privileged persons and institutions (nobles, the Church, towns, and the like) continued to hold and to exercise some form of private jurisdiction. They retained, for example, their own courts. But the king had unmistakably emerged as the dominant partner in the feudal relationship. Moreover, he was prepared to press his advantages in the sixteenth century.

The States of Italy

Free cities, or communes, dominated the political life of central and northern Italy in the early fourteenth century. The Holy Roman Empire claimed a loose sovereignty over much of the peninsula north of Rome, and the papacy governed the area around Rome; but most of the principal cities, and many small ones too, had gained the status of self-governing city-states.

The new economic and social conditions of the 1300s, however, worked against the survival of the smaller communes. Regional states, dominated politically and economically by a single metropolis, replaced the numerous, free, and highly competitive communes.

Milan　Perhaps the most effective Italian despot was the ruler of Milan, Gian Galeazzo Visconti (r. 1378–1402), who set about enlarging the Visconti inheritance of twenty-one cities in the Po valley. Through shrewd negotiations and opportune attacks, he secured the submission of cities to his east, which gave him an outlet to the Adriatic Sea. He then seized Bologna, purchased Pisa, and through a variety of methods was accepted as ruler of Siena, Perugia, Spoleto, Nocera, and Assisi. In the course of this advance deep into central Italy, Gian Galeazzo kept his chief enemies, the Florentines and the Venetians, divided, and he seemed ready to create a united Italian kingdom.

To establish a legal basis for his power, Gian Galeazzo secured from the emperor an appointment as imperial vicar in 1380 and then as hereditary duke in 1395. This move made him the only duke in all Italy, which seemed a step closer to a royal title. He revised the laws of Milan, but the chief administrative foundation of his success was his ability to wring enormous tax revenues from his subjects. Gian Galeazzo was also a generous patron of the new learning of his day; with his conquests, wealth, and brilliance, he seemed to be awaiting only the submission of the Florentines before adopting the title of king. But he died unexpectedly in 1402, leaving two minor sons who were incapable of defending their inheritance.

Florence　Florence by the mid-1300s was the principal banking center in Europe and one of the most impor-

tant producers of luxury goods. Its silks, textiles, fine leather, and silver and gold objects were much prized. The florin, the city's gold coin, had international standing as one of the most reliable currencies of the time.

By the 1300s Florence had been a self-governing commune for two centuries, but it had rarely enjoyed political stability. It was ruled by a series of councils, whose members were drawn from the leading families.

The rich Medici banking family gained control of the city's government in 1434 and made sure that only people they favored were defined as eligible for government positions. While retaining a facade of republican government, Cosimo de Medici established a form of boss rule over the city. His tax policies favored the lower and middle classes, and he also gained the support of the middle classes by appointments to office and other forms of political patronage. He secured peace for Florence and started his family's brilliant tradition of patronage of learning and the arts.

This tradition was enhanced by Cosimo's grandson, Lorenzo the Magnificent (r. 1469–1492), who beat back the plots of other powerful Florentine families and strengthened centralized control over the city. Lorenzo's Florence came to set the style for Italy, and eventually for Europe, in the splendor of its festivals, the elegance of its social life, the beauty of its buildings, and the lavish support it extended to scholars and artists.

Venice Already independent for more than five hundred years, the city of Venice by 1400 controlled a far-flung empire in northern Italy and the eastern Mediterranean and kept a large army and navy. Venice's wealth came from its dominance of the import of goods from Asia, notably spices like black pepper and cloves, which were probably the most expensive commodities, per ounce, sold in Europe. Its wealthiest citizens also controlled its government. Unlike Florence, Venice was ruled by a cohesive, rather than faction-ridden, oligarchy of some 150 families who inherited this dominance from generation to generation. From among their number they elected the *doge*, the head of the government, who held that position for life. (To increase turnover, older men were usually elected.)

Venice enjoyed remarkable political stability. There were occasional outbursts of discontent, but usually the patricians—who stayed united, relied on informers, made decisions in secret, and were ready to punish troublemakers severely—were able to maintain an image of orderliness and justice in government. They were also careful to show a concern for public welfare. The chief support of the navy, for instance—an essential asset for a city that, though containing more than 100,000 people, was built on a collection of islands in a lagoon—was a unique shipbuilding and arms manufacturing facility, the Arsenal. This gigantic complex, which employed more than 5 percent of the city's adult population, was not only the largest industrial enterprise in Europe but also a crucial source of employment. The Arsenal could build a fully equipped warship, starting from scratch, in just one day, and the skills it required helped maintain Venice's reputation as a haven for the finest artisans of the day. Not only men but entire families came to work there; one visitor described a "hall where about fifty women were making sails for ships" and another where one hundred women were "spinning and making ropes and doing other work related to ropes."

Because of its location and its easy openness to all who wished to trade, Venice was a meeting ground for Slavs, Turks, Germans, Jews, Muslims, Greeks, and other Italians. It was a favorite tourist spot for travelers and for pilgrims on the way to the Holy Land, a major center for the new international art of printing, and famous for its shops and entertainments. By the mid-1400s, its coin, the ducat, was replacing the florin as a standard for all Europe; and its patrons, often interested in more earthy themes than the Florentines, were promoting a flowering of literature, learning, and the arts that made Venice a focus of Renaissance culture.

From the early fifteenth century onward, Venice initiated a policy of territorial expansion on the mainland. By 1405, Padua, Verona, and Vicenza had become Venetian dependencies (see map 11.5).

Papal States The popes, like the leaders of the city-states, worked to consolidate their rule over their possessions in central Italy, but they faced formidable obstacles because the papacy was now located in Avignon in southern France. The difficult terrain of the Italian Papal States—dotted with castles and fortified towns—enabled communes, petty lords, and brigands to defy papal authority. Continuing disorders discouraged the popes from returning to Rome, and their efforts to pacify their tumultuous lands were a major drain on papal finances. Even after its return to Rome in 1378, the papacy had difficulty maintaining authority. Not until the pontificate of Martin V (r. 1417–1431) was a stable administration established, and Martin's successors still faced frequent revolts throughout the fifteenth century.

Kingdom of Naples and Sicily The political situation was equally confused in the Kingdom of Naples and Sicily with competing factions. In 1435 the king of Aragon, Alfonso V, the Magnanimous, reunited Sicily and southern Italy and made the kingdom the center of an Aragonese Empire in the Mediterranean. Alfonso sought to suppress the factions of lawless nobles and to reform taxes and strengthen administration. His efforts were not completely successful, for southern Italy and Sicily were rugged, poor lands and difficult to subdue; but he was at least able to overcome the chaos that had prevailed earlier. Alfonso thus extended to the Mediter-

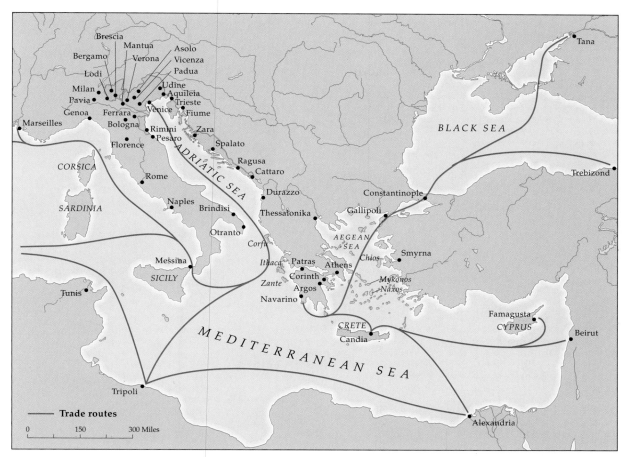

MAP 11.5 THE VENETIAN EMPIRE IN THE 1400S
The Venetian trade routes, as this map shows, moved Venice to a position of major power. How far did Venice's rule extend? Which cities did it control? Who were its trading partners in the eastern Mediterranean?
◆ For an online version, go to www.mhhe.com/chambers9 > chapter 11 > book maps

ranean the strengthening of central governments that took place elsewhere in Europe in the 1400s. The court he created at Naples was one of the most brilliant centers of art and literature of the age.

Balance of Power   Relations between the city-states on the Italian peninsula were tense as they clashed over trade and the acquisition of surrounding territory. The Peace of Lodi in 1454 ended a war among Milan, Florence, and Venice. Cosimo de Medici sought to make the peace a lasting one by creating an alliance system between Milan, Naples, and Florence on one side and Venice and the Papal States on the other (see map 11.6). During the next forty years, until the French invaded the peninsula in 1494, the balance was occasionally rocked but never overturned. This system represents one of the earliest appearances in European history of a diplomatic **balance of power** for maintaining peace.

THE FALL OF BYZANTIUM AND THE OTTOMAN EMPIRE

Although the Byzantine Empire revived under Michael VIII Palaeologus, by the mid-fifteenth century the empire's control was effective only in Greece, the Aegean, and the area around Constantinople. The Ottoman Turks eventually fell heir to Byzantium's former power and influence, and by the early sixteenth century they were the unquestioned masters of southeast Europe and the Middle East.

The Fall of Constantinople

The Rising Threat   Turkish peoples had been assuming a large military and political role in the Middle East since the late tenth century. The Seljuk Turks dominated western Asia Minor since the late 1000s.

MAP 11.6 THE ITALIAN STATES IN 1454
As this map shows, after the Peace of Lodi in 1454, five major states dominated Italy. For forty years they maintained a balance of power among themselves. What were the five major states of Italy? What forms of government did these states represent?
◆ For an online version, go to www.mhhe.com/chambers9 > chapter 11 > book maps

Antonio Natale
VENICE ARSENAL
This eighteenth-century depiction of the huge complex that made up the Arsenal in Venice indicates some of the specialized buildings that formed the production line around the pools in which the ships were built. At the back, hulls are being laid, and in the foreground, a ship is being scuttled. At the very front are the two towers that flanked the entrance gate to the Arsenal.
© Giancarlo Costa/Index

Although Turks survived the attacks of Western crusaders, they were defeated by the Mongols in the thirteenth century. The Ottoman Turks, who had converted to Islam, followed the Mongol invasions and took over Asia Minor. They took their name from Osman, or Othman (r. 1290–1326), who founded a dynasty of sultans that survived for six centuries.

Establishing themselves at Gallipoli on the European side of the Straits in 1354, the Ottomans completely surrounded the Byzantine territory. The Byzantine emperors, fearing the worst for their small and isolated realm, tried desperately but unsuccessfully to persuade the West to send military help. At the council of Florence in 1439, Emperor John VII even accepted reunion with Rome, largely on Roman terms, in return for aid, but he had no power to impose the reunion of the churches on his people; in fact, many Eastern Christians preferred Turkish rule to submission to the hated Westerners.

The Capture of the City The Ottomans were unable to mount a major campaign against Constantinople until 1453, when Sultan Mehmet II, the Conqueror, finally attacked by land and water. The city fell after a heroic resistance, and Emperor Constantine XI Palaeologus, whose imperial lineage stretched back more than 1,400 years to Augustus Caesar, died in this final agony of the Byzantine Empire.

The fall of Constantinople had little military or economic effect on Europe and the Middle East. The Byzantine Empire had not been an effective barrier to Ottoman expansion for years, and Constantinople had dwindled commercially as well as politically. The shift to Turkish dominion did not, as historians once believed, substantially affect the flow of trade between the East and West. Nor did the Turkish conquest of the city provoke an exodus of Byzantine scholars and manuscripts to Italy. Scholars from the East, recognizing the decline and seemingly inevitable fall of the Byzantine Empire, had been emigrating to Italy since the late fourteenth century; the revival of Greek letters was well under way in the West by 1453.

The End of an Era The impact of the fall was largely psychological; although hardly unexpected, it shocked the Christian world. The end of the Byzantine Empire and the rise of the **Ottoman Empire** had great symbolic importance for contemporaries and, perhaps even more, for later historians. In selecting Byzantium as his capital in 324, Constantine had founded a Christian Roman empire that could be considered the first authentically medieval state. For more than 1,000 years this Christian Roman empire played a major political and cultural role in the history of both Eastern and Western peoples. In some respects, the years of its existence mark the span of the Middle Ages, and its passing symbolizes the end of an era.

The Ottoman Empire

Under Mehmet II (r. 1451–1481), who from the start of his reign committed his government to a policy of conquest, the Ottomans began a century of expansion (see

THE SULTAN MEHMET II

One of the first histories of the Ottomans by a Westerner was written by an English schoolmaster named Richard Knolles and published in 1603. It is obvious that a great deal of research went into his work, which is marked by vivid portraits such as this one of the Sultan Mehmet II, known as the Conqueror because of his capture of Constantinople, who had lived a century before Knolles wrote.

"He was of stature but low, square set, and strongly limbed; his complexion sallow and melancholy; his look and countenance stern, with his eyes piercing, and his nose so high and crooked that it almost touched his upper lip. He was of a very sharp and apprehending wit, learned especially in astronomy, and could speak the Greek, Latin, Arabic, Chaldee, and Persian tongues. He delighted much in reading of histories, and the lives of worthy men, especially the lives of Alexander the Great and Julius Caesar, whom he proposed to himself as examples to follow. He was of an exceeding courage, and a severe punisher of injustice. Men that excelled in any quality, he greatly favored and honorably entertained, as he did Gentile Bellini, a painter of Venice, whom he purposely caused to come from thence to Constantinople, to draw the lively counterfeit of himself for which he most bountifully rewarded him. He so severely punished theft, as that in his time all the ways were safe. He was altogether irreligious, and most perfidious, ambitious above measure, and in nothing more delighted than in blood: insomuch that he was responsible for the death of 800,000 men; craft, covetousness and dissimulation were in him accounted tolerable, in comparison of his greater vices. In his love was no assurance, and his least displeasure was death; so that he lived feared of all men, and died lamented of none."

From Richard Knolles, in John J. Saunders (ed.), *The Muslim World on the Eve of Europe's Expansion*, Prentice Hall, 1966, adapted by T. K. Rabb.

Gentile Bellini
MEHMET II
Mehmet II, here shown in a painting attributed to the Venetian artist Gentile Bellini, was the conqueror of Constantinople in 1453.
The Granger Collection, New York

"The Sultan Mehmet II," above). After the fall of Constantinople, which became his capital under the name of Istanbul (though the name was not officially adopted until 1930), Mehmet subjugated Morea, Serbia, Bosnia, and parts of Herzegovina. He drove the Genoese from their Black Sea colonies, forced the khan of the Crimea to become his vassal, and fought a lengthy naval war with the Venetians. At his death the Ottomans were a power on land and sea, and the Black Sea had become a Turkish lake (see map 11.7).

Early in the following century, under the leadership of Suleiman II, the Magnificent (r. 1520–1566), the Ottoman Empire came to the height of its power. Turkish domination was extended over the heart of the Arab lands through the conquest of Syria, Egypt, and the western coast of the Arabian peninsula. (The Arabs did not again enjoy autonomy until the twentieth century.) With the conquest of the sacred cities of Mecca and Medina, the sultan assumed the title of caliph, "successor of the Prophet," claiming to be Islam's supreme religious head as well as its mightiest sword. Suleiman II also extended Turkish conquests into the Balkan peninsula and Hungary. His attempts to conquer Austria failed when Vienna withstood the onslaught of the Ottomans in 1529. (For more on Suleiman II and the Ottomans see chapter 14.)

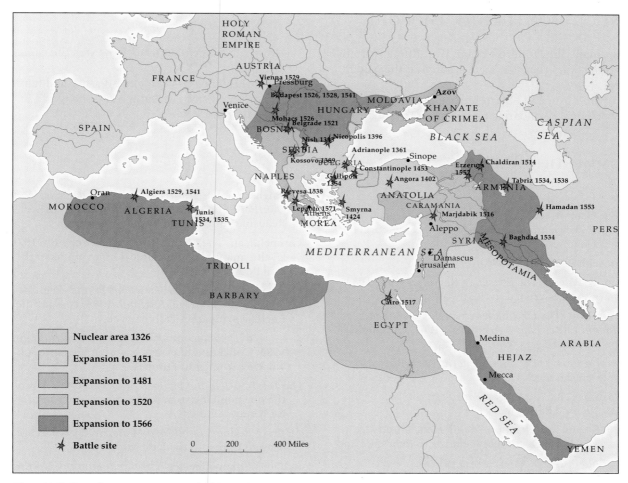

MAP 11.7 THE OTTOMAN EMPIRE, 1300–1566
This map shows the gradual expansion of the Ottoman Empire from 1300 to 1566. What areas of Europe did the Ottoman Empire include? What was the decisive battle that stopped further advances into Europe?
◆ For an online version, go to www.mhhe.com/chambers9 > chapter 11 > book maps

Summary

While the fall of Constantinople had a strong psychological effect on Europe, the threat of the Ottoman invasion initially meant little except to the Austrians, Hungarians, Balkan states, and the Knights Hospitalers. The West was preoccupied with the reality of the Four Horsemen of the Apocalypse. Early fourteenth-century famines, recurrent plague, and wars, including the Hundred Years' War, diverted their attention. By the end of the fifteenth century, peace was generally restored. England emerged as a government that would come to be described as a constitutional monarchy, the French king was on his way to a control over his subjects that would be called absolutism, and Italy had established a balance-of-power politics. The economy was strengthened by new inventions, such as the printing press, that would change the way people spread and received information to the present day. Europe was on the verge of new expansions. The explorations of the late fifteenth century introduced new concepts of power and wealth to the competing countries; the problems of the Church intensified with major splits; and the economy, although plagued with problems of overpopulation once again, was expanding in new directions and with new products from the conquests in America.

QUESTIONS FOR FURTHER THOUGHT

1. What made the Hundred Years' War different from the other wars that you have studied in the Middle Ages?
2. Compare Europe in 800 to Europe in 1450. What new political boundaries had been established?

How had society changed? How was the economy different?
3. What influence has epidemic disease and famine had on the history of Europe and the world in general?

RECOMMENDED READING

Sources

*Brucker, Gene A. (ed.) *The Society of Renaissance Florence: A Documentary Study.* 1971. Collection of primary sources.

Byrne, Joseph P. *The Black Death.* 2004.

*Dobson, R. B. (ed.). *The Peasant's Revolt of 1381.* 1983. Primary sources related to the revolt.

*Froissart, Jean. *The Chronicles of England, France, Spain and Other Places Adjoining.* 1961. Chronicles of the Hundred Years' War.

*Horrox, Rosemary. *The Black Death.* 1994. Primary sources on the Black Death.

The Pastons: The Letters of a Family in the War of the Roses. Richard Barber (ed.). 1981.

Pernoud, Regine (ed.). *Joan of Arc: By Herself and Her Witnesses.* 1966. Documents relating to Joan's life and trial.

*Pisan, Christine de. *The Book of the City of Ladies.* Earl Jeffrey Richards (tr.). 1982. The author was a court writer who wrote this book on women's virtues in response to the debate of the time on women.

Studies

*Allmand, Christopher. *The Hundred Years' War: England and France at War, c. 1300–1450.* 1988. An account of the military aspects.

*Bennett, Judith M. *Women in the Medieval English Countryside.* 1987. An assessment of peasant women's status.

*Brucker, Gene A. *Giovanni and Lusanna: Love and Marriage in Renaissance Florence.* 1986.

Cohn, Samuel K. *The Black Death Transformed: Disease and Culture in Early Renaissance Europe.* 2002. Cohn has provided a new interpretation of possible diseases that may not be the plague described by previous historians.

Eisenstein, Elizabeth L. *The Printing Press as an Agent of Change in Early-Modern Europe.* 2 vols. 1979. Provocative interpretation of the place of printing in European history.

Gillingham, John. *The Wars of the Roses: Peace and Conflict in Fifteenth-Century England.* 1981. Readable political and military history.

Gimpel, Jean. *The Medieval Machine.* Penguin, 1976. Useful analysis of mechanical innovations in the Middle Ages.

*Hanawalt, Barbara. *The Ties That Bound: Peasant Families in Medieval England.* 1986. Peasant life in England sympathetically viewed.

*——— (ed.). *Women and Work in Preindustrial Europe.* 1986. Collection of essays covering the issues of working women in Europe.

Harvey, L. P. *Islamic Spain 1250–1500.* 1990. A survey of the one non-Christian territory in Western Europe and its steady decline.

*Hilton, Rodney. *Bond Men Made Free.* 1979. A study of peasant unrest in the Late Middle Ages.

Jordan, William Chester. *The Great Famine: Northern Europe in the Early Fourteenth Century,* 1996. An overview of the famines and their climatic causes and effects in northern Europe.

Kaeuper, Richard W. *War, Justice, and Public Order: England and France in the Late Middle Ages.* 1988. Assessment of the intersection of war and justice in two countries.

Oakley, Francis. *The Western Church in the Later Middle Ages.* 1979.

*Perroy, Edouard. *The Hundred Years' War.* 1965. Classic; excellent survey.

Unger, Richard W. *The Ship in the Medieval Economy.* 1980. The evolution of medieval ship design.

Warner, Marina. *Joan of Arc: The Image of Female Heroism.* 1981. Examination of Joan's life and legend.

Wittek, Paul. *The Rise of the Ottoman Empire.* 1971.

*Ziegler, Philip. *The Black Death.* 1970. Synthesis of plague studies.

*Available in paperback.

Jan Van Eyck

PORTRAIT OF GIOVANNI ARNOLFINI AND HIS WIFE, 1434

The symbolism that permeates this depiction of a husband and wife has led to the suggestion that it is a wedding picture. The bed and seeming pregnancy are symbols of marriage, and the husband blesses his wife as he bestows the sacrament of marriage (for which the Church did not yet require a priest). On the back wall, the mirror reflects the witnesses attending the wedding. Van Eyck's use of the new medium of oil paint allowed him to reproduce vividly the texture of the fur-edged robe and the glimmer of the mirror's glass.

Chapter Twelve

TRADITION AND CHANGE IN EUROPEAN CULTURE, 1300–1500

THE NEW LEARNING • ART AND ARTISTS IN THE ITALIAN RENAISSANCE •
THE CULTURE OF THE NORTH • SCHOLASTIC PHILOSOPHY AND RELIGIOUS THOUGHT
• THE STATE OF CHRISTENDOM

By 1300 the civilization of Europe appeared to have settled into stable and self-assured patterns. Society as a whole shared assumptions about religious beliefs, about the appropriate way to integrate faith with the heritage of the ancient world, about the purposes of scholarship, and about the forms of literature and art. These shared assumptions have led historians to describe the outlook of the age as "the medieval synthesis." But such moments of apparent stability rarely last long. Within a few generations, profound doubts had arisen on such fundamental questions as the nature of religious faith, the authority of the Church, the aims of scholarship, the source of moral ideals, and the standards of beauty in the arts. As challenges to old ideas arose, especially in the worlds of religion and cultural expression, there was an outpouring of creativity: a "golden age" comparable to those which, five hundred years earlier, had transformed the cultures of China and the Tang Dynasty or the Muslim world under the Abbassids. Like those flowerings, it has dazzled us ever since. Because those seeking new answers in Europe tended to look for guidance to what they considered to be a better past—in this case classical antiquity or the early days of Christianity—and sought to revive long-lost values, their efforts, and the times in which they lived, have been called an age of rebirth, or **Renaissance.**[1]

[1] The creator of the modern view of the Renaissance as one of the formative periods of Western history, and the single most influential historian of the subject, was Jacob Burckhardt (see Recommended Reading).

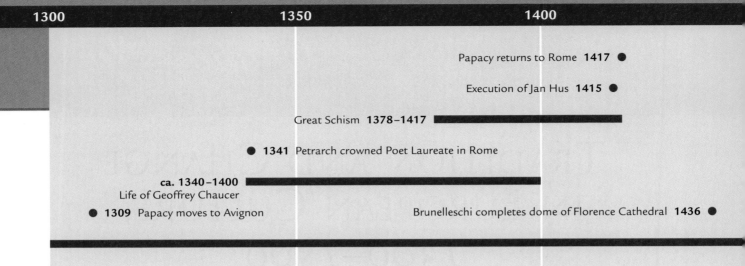

Papacy returns to Rome **1417** ●

Execution of Jan Hus **1415** ●

Great Schism **1378–1417** ▬▬▬▬▬▬▬▬▬▬▬

● **1341** Petrarch crowned Poet Laureate in Rome

ca. 1340–1400 ▬▬▬▬▬▬▬▬▬▬▬
Life of Geoffrey Chaucer

● **1309** Papacy moves to Avignon

Brunelleschi completes dome of Florence Cathedral **1436** ●

THE NEW LEARNING

Although traditional forms of learning remained vital in the fourteenth and fifteenth centuries, medieval Scholasticism, with its highly refined forms of reasoning, had little to offer Europe's small but important literate lay population. The curriculum was designed mainly to train teachers and theologians, whereas the demand was increasingly for practical and useful training, especially in the arts of persuasion and communication: good speaking and good writing. For many, the Scholastics also failed to offer moral guidance. As Petrarch emphasized, education was meant to help people lead a wise, pious, and happy life. A central aim of the Renaissance was to develop new models of virtue and a system of education that would do exactly that.

The Founding of Humanism

One minor branch of the medieval educational curriculum, rhetoric, was concerned with the art of good speaking and writing. More and more, its practitioners in Italy began to turn to the Latin classics for models of good writing. Their interest in the Classical authors was helped by the close relationship between the Italian language and Latin, by the availability of manuscripts, and by the presence in Italy of countless Classical monuments. It was rhetoricians who first began to argue, in the late thirteenth century, that education should be reformed to give more attention to the classics and to help people lead more moral lives.

These rhetoricians were to found an intellectual movement known as **Humanism.** The term *Humanism* was not coined until the nineteenth century. In fifteenth-century Italy, *humanista* signified a professor of humane studies or a Classical scholar, but eventually Humanism came to mean Classical scholarship—the ability to read, understand, and appreciate the writings of the ancient world. Humanists wanted to master the classics so as to learn both the right way to conduct their lives and the eloquence to persuade others to follow that same way. The modern use of the word *humanism* to denote a secular philosophy that denies an afterlife has no basis in the Renaissance. Most Renaissance humanists read the Church fathers as avidly as they read pagan authors and believed that the highest virtues were rooted in piety. Humanism sought far more to enrich than to undermine traditional religious attitudes.

Petrarch   The most influential early advocate of Humanism was Francesco Petrarca, known as Petrarch (1304–1374). He was a lawyer and cleric who practiced neither of those professions but rather devoted his life to writing poetry, scholarly and moral treatises, and letters. He became famous for his Italian verse—his sonnets inspired poets for centuries—but he sought above all to emulate Virgil by writing a Latin epic poem. A master of self-promotion, he used that work as the occasion for reviving the ancient title of "poet laureate" and having himself crowned in Rome in 1341. But he was also capable of profound self-examination. In a remarkable work, which he called *My Secret*—a dialogue with one of his heroes, St. Augustine—he laid bare his struggles to achieve spiritual peace despite the temptations of fame and love. Increasingly, he became concerned that nowhere in the world around him could he find a model of virtuous behavior that he could respect. The leaders of the Church he considered poor examples, for they seemed worldly and materialistic. Convinced that no guide from his own times or the immediate past would serve, Petrarch concluded that he had to turn to the Church fathers and the ancient

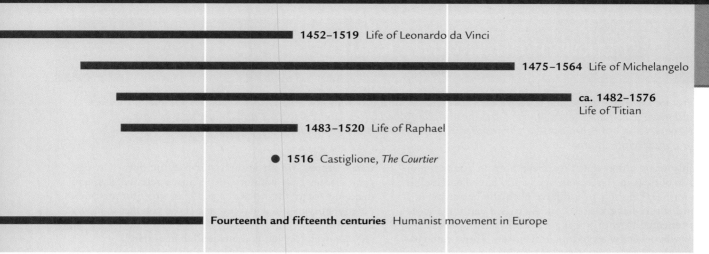

Romans to find worthy examples of the moral life (see "Petrarch on Ancient Rome," p. 340).

How could one be a good person? By imitating figures from antiquity, such as Cicero and Augustine, who knew what proper values were and pursued them in their own lives, despite temptations and the distractions of public affairs. The period between their time and his own—which Petrarch regarded as the "middle" ages—he considered contemptible. His own world, he felt, would improve only if it tried to emulate the ancients, and he believed that education ought to teach what they had done and said. In particular, like the good rhetorician he was, he believed that only by restoring the mastery of the written and spoken word that had distinguished the great Romans—an imitation of their style, of the way they had conveyed their ideas—could his contemporaries learn to behave like the ancients.

Boccaccio The program Petrarch laid out soon caught fire in Florence, the city from which his family had come and in which he found influential friends and disciples. The most important was the poet and writer Giovanni Boccaccio (1313–1375), famous for a collection of short stories known as *The Decameron*. The first prose masterpiece in Italian, *The Decameron* created new aims in Western Literature with its frank treatment of sex and vivid creation of ordinary characters. But in his later years Boccaccio grew increasingly concerned with the teaching of moral values, and he became a powerful supporter of Petrarch's ideas.

The Spread of Humanism In the generation after Petrarch and Boccaccio, Humanism became a rallying cry for the intellectual leaders of Florence. They argued that, by associating their city with the revival of antiquity, Florentines would be identified with a distinctive

vision that would become the envy of their rivals elsewhere in Italy. And that was indeed what happened. The campaign for a return to the classics started a revolution in education that soon took hold throughout Italy; the writing and speaking skills the humanists emphasized came to be in demand at every princely court (including that of the papacy); and the crusade to study and imitate the ancients transformed art, literature, and even political and social values.

Led by the chancellor of Florence, Coluccio Salutati (whose position, as the official who prepared the city's official communications, required training in rhetoric), a group of humanists began to collect ancient manuscripts and form libraries, so as to make accessible virtually all the surviving writings of Classical Latin authors. These Florentines also wanted to regain command of the Greek language, and in 1396 they invited a Byzantine scholar to lecture at the University of Florence. In the following decades—troubled years for the Byzantine Empire—other Eastern scholars joined the exodus to the West, and they and Western visitors returning from the East brought with them hundreds of Greek manuscripts. By the middle of the fifteenth century, Western scholars had both the philological skill and the manuscripts to establish direct contact with the most original minds of the Classical world, and they were making numerous Latin and Italian translations of Greek works. Histories, tragedies, lyric poetry, the dialogues of Plato, many mathematical treatises, and the most important works of the Greek fathers of the Church fully entered Western culture for the first time.

Civic Humanism Salutati and his contemporaries and successors in Florence are often called civic humanists because they stressed that participation in public affairs is essential for full human development.

339

PETRARCH ON ANCIENT ROME

Petrarch was so determined to relive the experience of antiquity that he wrote letters to famous Roman authors as if they were acquaintances. In one letter, he even described Cicero coming to visit him. While he was passing through Padua in February 1350, he recalled that the city was the birthplace of the Roman historian Livy, and he promptly wrote to him.

"I only wish, either that I had been born in your time or you in ours. If the latter, our age would have benefited; if the former, I myself would have been the better for it. I would surely have visited you. As it is, I can merely see you reflected in your works. It is over those works that I labor whenever I want to forget the places, times, and customs around me. I am often filled with anger at today's morals, when people value only gold and silver, and want nothing but physical pleasures.

"I have to thank you for many things, but especially because you have so often helped me forget the evils of today, and have transported me to happier times. As I read you, I seem to be living with Scipio, Brutus, Cato, and many others. It is with them that I live, and not with the ruffians of today, among whom an evil star had me born. Oh, the great names that comfort me in my wretchedness, and make me forget this wicked age! Please greet for me those older historians like Polybius, and those younger than you like Pliny.

"Farewell forever, you unequalled historian!

"Written in the land of the living, in that part of Italy where you were born and buried, in sight of your own tombstone, on the 22nd of February in the 1350th year after the birth of Him whom you would have seen had you lived longer."

Petrarch, *Epistolae Familiares*, 24.8. Passages selected and translated by Theodore K. Rabb.

Petrarch had wondered whether individuals should cut themselves off from the larger world, with its corruptions and compromises, and focus only on what he called the contemplative life, or try to improve that world through an active life. Petrarch's models had offered no clear answer. Cicero had suggested the need for both lives, but Augustine had been fearful of outside temptations. In the generations following Petrarch, however, the doubts declined, and the humanists argued that only by participating in public life, seeking higher ends for one's society as well as oneself, could an individual be truly virtuous. Republican government was the best form, they argued, because unless educated citizens made use of their wisdom for the benefit of all, their moral understanding would not benefit their societies. These were lessons exemplified by the ancient classics, and thus in one connected argument the civic humanists defended the necessity of studying the ancients, the superiority of the active life, and the value of Florentine republican institutions.

Humanism in the Fifteenth Century

As the humanist movement gained in prestige, it captured all of Italy. Pope Nicholas V (1447–1455), for example, founded a library in the Vatican that was to become the greatest repository of ancient manuscripts in Italy. And princely courts, such as those of the Gonzaga family at Mantua and the Montefeltro family at Urbino, gained fame because of their patronage of humanists. Moreover, the influence of antiquity was felt in all areas of learning and writing. Literature was profoundly influenced by the ancients, as a new interest in Classical models reshaped the form and content of both poetry and drama, from the epic to the bawdy comedy. Purely secular themes, without religious purpose, became more common. And works of history grew increasingly analytic, openly acknowledging inspiration from ancient writers such as Livy.

Education Perhaps the most direct effect was on education itself. Two scholars from the north of Italy, Guarino da Verona and Vittorino da Feltre, succeeded in turning the diffuse educational ideas of the humanists into a practical curriculum. Guarino argued for a reform of traditional methods of education, and Vittorino brought the new methods to their fullest development in the various schools he founded, especially his Casa Giocosa ("Happy House") at Mantua. The pupils included boys and girls, both rich and poor (the latter on scholarships). All the students learned Latin and Greek, mathematics, music, and philosophy; in addition—because Vittorino believed that education should aid physical, moral, and social development—they were taught social graces, such as dancing and courteous manners, and received instruction in physical exercises like riding and fencing. Vittorino's school attracted pupils from all over Italy, and his methods were widely imitated.

Raphael
PORTRAIT OF BALDASSARE CASTIGLIONE, CA. **1514**
**Raphael painted this portrait of his friend, the count
Baldassare Castiglione, around 1514. Castiglione's solemn
pose and thoughtful expression exude the dignity and
cultivation that were described as essential attributes of the
courtier in Castiglione's famous book on courtly behavior.**
Giraudon/Art Resource, NY

Thus, a new image of fine behavior, which included the qualities that Guarino fostered—a commitment to taste and elegance as well as to courage—became widely accepted. This new lifestyle was promoted in a book, *The Courtier*, written in 1516 by Baldassare Castiglione, which took the form of a conversation among the sophisticated men and women at the court of Duke Federigo Montefeltro of Urbino, Castiglione's patron. *The Courtier* became a manual of proper behavior for gentlemen and ladies for centuries.

Humanism Triumphant   By the mid-1400s Humanism dominated intellectual life in much of Italy, and by 1500 it was sweeping all of Europe, transmitted by its devotees and also by a recent invention, printing, which made the texts of both humanists and ancients far more easily available. Dozens of new schools and universities were founded, and no court of any significance was without its roster of artists and writers familiar with the latest ideas. Even legal systems were affected, as the principles of Roman law (which tended to endorse the power of the ruler) were adopted in many countries. But in the late fifteenth century the revival of antiquity took a direction that modified the commitment to the active life that had been the mark of the civic humanists. A new movement, **Neoplatonism,** emphasized the interest in spiritual values that was the heart of the contemplative life.

The Florentine Neoplatonists

The turn away from the practical concerns of the civic humanists toward a renewed exploration of grand ideals of truth and perfection was a result of the growing interest in Greek as well as Roman antiquity—especially the works of Plato. A group of Florentine philosophers, active in the last decades of the fifteenth century and equally at home in Greek and Latin, led the way. They were known as "Neoplatonists," or "new" followers of Plato.

Ficino   The most gifted of these Neoplatonists was the physician Marsilio Ficino. His career is a tribute to the cultural patronage of the Medici family, which spotted his talents as a child and gave him the use of a villa and library near Florence. In this lovely setting, a group of scholars and statesmen met frequently to discuss philosophical questions. Drawn to the idealism of Plato, Ficino and his colleagues argued that Platonic ideas demonstrated the dignity and immortality of the human soul. To spread these views among a larger audience, Ficino translated into Latin all of Plato's dialogues and the writings of Plato's chief followers. Another member of the group, Giovanni Pico della Mirandola, tried to reconcile all philosophies, including

Ultimately, a humanist education was to give the elite throughout Europe a new way of measuring social distinction. It soon became apparent that the ability to quote Virgil or some other ancient writer was not so much a sign of moral seriousness as a badge of superiority. What differentiated people was whether they could use or recognize the quotations, and that was why the new curriculum was so popular—even though it seemed to consist, more and more, of endless memorizations and repetitions of Latin texts.

New Standards of Behavior   The growing admiration for the humanists and their teachings also gave an important boost to the patronage of arts and letters. In the age of gunpowder, it was no longer easy to claim that physical bravery was the supreme quality of noblemen. Instead, nobles began to set themselves apart not just by seeking a humanist education but also by patronizing artists and writers whose praise made them famous.

MAP 12.1 THE SPREAD OF UNIVERSITIES IN THE RENAISSANCE
This map charts the growing importance of education and the emergence of new universities throughout Europe during the Renaissance. Even where earlier universities existed, as at Oxford, many new colleges were founded, and the number of graduates increased rapidly in the fifteenth and sixteenth centuries. How do you suppose that Humanism is related to the growing number of universities?
◆ For an online version, go to www.mhhe.com/chambers9 > chapter 12 > book maps

those of Asia, in order to show that there was a single truth that lay behind every quest for the ideal.

Both Ficino and Pico started from two essential assumptions. First, the entire universe is arranged in a hierarchy of excellence, with God at the summit. Second, each being in the universe, with the exception only of God, is impelled by "natural appetite" to seek perfection; to try to achieve—or at least contemplate—the beautiful. As Pico expressed it, humans are placed in the middle of the universe, linked with both the spiri-

tual world above and the material world below. Their free will enables them to seek perfection in either direction; they are free to become all things. The good life should thus be an effort to achieve personal perfection, and the highest human value is the contemplation of the beautiful.

These writers believed that Plato had been divinely illuminated and, therefore, that Platonic philosophy and Christian belief were two wholly reconcilable faces of a single truth. Because of this synthesis, and also its passionate idealism, Neoplatonic philosophy was to be a major influence on artists and thinkers for the next two centuries.

The Heritage of the New Learning

Although its scholarship was often arid and difficult, fifteenth-century Italian Humanism left a deep imprint on European thought and education. The humanists greatly improved the command of Latin; they restored a large part of the Greek cultural inheritance to Western civilization; their investigations led to a mastery of other languages associated with great cultural traditions, most notably Hebrew; and they laid the basis of modern textual criticism. They also developed new ways of examining the ancient world—through archaeology, numismatics (the study of coins), and epigraphy (the study of inscriptions on buildings, statues, and the like), as well as through the study of literary texts. As for the study of history, while medieval chroniclers had looked to the past for evidence of God's providence, the humanists used the past to illustrate human behavior and provide moral examples. They also helped standardize spelling and grammar in vernacular languages; and the Classical ideals of simplicity, restraint, and elegance of style that they promoted helped reshape Western literature.

No less important was the role of the humanists as educational reformers. The curriculum they devised spread throughout Europe in the sixteenth century, and until the twentieth century it continued to define the standards by which the lay leaders of Western society were trained. The fact that men and women throughout Europe came to be steeped in the same classics meant that they thought and communicated in similar ways. Despite Europe's divisions and conflicts, this common humanistic education helped preserve the fundamental cultural unity of the West.

ART AND ARTISTS IN THE ITALIAN RENAISSANCE

The most visible effect of Humanism and its admiration for the ancients was on the arts. Because the movement first took hold in Florence, it is not surprising that its first artistic disciples appeared among the Florentines. They had other advantages. First, the city was already famous throughout Italy for its art, because the greatest painters of the late 1200s and 1300s, Cimabue (1240–1302) and his pupil Giotto (1276–1336), were identified with Florence. Giotto, in particular, had decorated buildings from Padua to Naples and thus gained a wide audience for the sense of realism, power-

Giotto di Bondone
PIETÀ (LAMENTATION)
The Florentine Giotto di Bondone (ca. 1267–1337) was the most celebrated painter of his age. He painted fresco cycles in a number of Italian cities, and this segment from one of them indicates the qualities that made him famous: the solid bodies, the expression of human emotion, and the suggestion of landscape, all of which created an impact that was without precedent in medieval art.
Scrovegni Chapel, Padua, Italy. Alinari/Art Resource, NY

ful emotion, and immediacy that he created (in contrast to the formal, restrained styles of earlier artists). Second, Florence's newly wealthy citizens were ready to patronize art; and third, the city had a tradition of excellence in the design of luxury goods such as silks and gold objects. Many leading artists of the 1400s and 1500s started their careers as apprentices to goldsmiths, in whose workshops they mastered creative techniques as well as aesthetic principles that informed their painting, sculpture, and architecture.

Three Friends

The revolution in these three disciplines was started by three friends, who were united by a determination to apply the humanists' lessons to art. They wanted to break with the styles of the immediate past and create paintings, statues, and buildings that would not merely imitate the glories of Rome but actually bring them back to life. All three went to Rome in the 1420s, hoping by direct observation and study of ancient masterpieces to re-create their qualities and thus fulfill the

Masaccio
***THE EXPULSION OF ADAM AND EVE*, 1425–1428**
Masaccio shows Adam and Eve expelled from paradise through a rounded archway that recalls ancient architecture. Also indicative of the influence of Roman art is the attempt to create what we would consider realistic (rather than stylized) human beings and to portray them nude, displaying powerful, recognizable emotions. This was one of the paintings that made the Brancacci Chapel an inspiration to generations of artists.
Brancacci Chapel, S. Maria del Carmine, Florence, Italy. Erich Lessing/Art Resource, NY

humanists' goal of reviving the spirit of Classical times. The locals thought the three very strange, for they went around measuring, taking notes, and calculating sizes and proportions. But the lessons they learned enabled them to transform the styles and purposes of art.

Masaccio Among the three friends, the painter Masaccio (1401–1428) used the inspiration of the ancients to put a new emphasis on nature, on three-dimensional human bodies, and on perspective. In showing Adam and Eve, he not only depicted the first nudes since antiquity but showed them coming through a rounded arch that was the mark of Roman architecture, as opposed to the pointed arch of the Middle Ages. The chapel he decorated in a Florentine church, the Carmine, became a place of pilgrimage for painters, because here the values of ancient art—especially its emphasis on the individual human figure—were reborn.

Donatello Masaccio's friend Donatello (1386–1466) was primarily a sculptor, and his three-dimensional figures had the same qualities as Masaccio's in paint. Once again the focus was on the beauty of the body itself, because that had been a notable and distinctive concern of the ancients. The interest in the nude, accurately displayed, transformed the very purpose of art, for it led to an idealized representation of the human form that had not been seen in centuries. Because the biblical David—shown by Donatello in contemplation after his triumph over Goliath—symbolized vigor, youth, and the weak defeating the strong, he became a favorite hero for the Florentines.

Brunelleschi The most spectacular of these three pioneers was the architect Brunelleschi (ca. 1377–1446). For decades, his fellow citizens had been building a new cathedral, which, as a sign of their artistic superiority, was going to be the largest in Italy. Seen from above, it was shaped—as was traditional—like a cross. The basic structure was in place, but the huge space at which the horizontal and vertical met, the crossing, had not yet been covered. In response to a competition for a design to complete the building, Brunelleschi, inspired by what he had learned in Rome, proposed covering the crossing with the largest dome built in Europe since antiquity. Although the first reaction was that it was impossible, eventually he got the commission. In an extraordinary feat of engineering, which required that he build the dome in rings, without using scaffolding, he erected a structure that became not only a fitting climax to the cathedral but also the hallmark of Renaissance Florence and an inspiration for all archi-

Brunelleschi
DOME OF FLORENCE CATHEDRAL, 1420–1436
Brunelleschi's famous dome—the first built in Italy since the fall of the Roman Empire—embodied the revival of Classical forms in architecture. The contrast with the bell tower designed a century earlier by Giotto, with its suggestion of pointed Gothic arches, is unmistakable. The dome was a feat of engineering as well as design: Its 135-foot diameter was spanned without scaffolding, and Brunelleschi himself invented the machines that made the construction possible.
© David Ball/Corbis Stock Market

Donatello
DAVID, CA. **1430–1432**
Like Masaccio, Donatello imitated the Romans by creating idealized nude bodies. His David has just killed and decapitated Goliath, whose head lies at his feet. Goliath's helmet recalls those worn by Florence's enemies, which makes this sculpture a work of patriotism as well as art. It happens also to have been the first life-size bronze figure cast since antiquity.
Alinari/Art Resource, NY

and drapery, so as to recapture the ancients' mastery of depth, and they made close observations of nature. Sculptors created monumental figures, some on horseback, in imitation of Roman models. And architects perfected the use of the rounded arches and symmetrical forms they saw in antique buildings. Subject matter also changed, as artists produced increasing numbers of portraits of their contemporaries and depicted stories out of Roman and Greek myths as well as traditional religious scenes. By the end of the 1400s, the leading Florentine painter of the day, Botticelli (ca. 1444–1510), was presenting ancient subjects like the *Birth of Venus*, goddess of love, in exactly the way a Roman might have fashioned them.

The High Renaissance

The artists at work in the early years of the 1500s are often referred to as the generation of the High Renaissance. Four in particular—Leonardo, Raphael, Michelangelo, and Titian—are thought of as bringing the new movement that had begun a hundred years before to a climax.

Leonardo The oldest, Leonardo (1452–1519), was the epitome of the experimental tradition. Always seeking new ways of doing things, whether in observing

tects. The symmetrical simplicity of his other buildings shaped a new aesthetic of harmony and balance that matched what Masaccio and Donatello accomplished in painting and sculpture. In all three, the imitation of ancient Rome inspired subjects and styles that broke decisively with their immediate medieval past.

New Creativity During the remaining years of the 1400s, a succession of artists, not just in Florence but increasingly in other parts of Italy as well, built on the achievements of the pioneer generation. They experimented with perspective and the modeling of bodies

Leonardo da Vinci
MONA LISA, CA. **1503–1505**
This is probably the most celebrated image in Renaissance art. The famous hint of a smile and the calm and solid pose are so familiar that we all too easily forget how striking it seemed at the time and how often it inspired later portraits. As in his *Last Supper*, however, Leonardo was experimenting with his materials, and the picture has therefore faded over the years.
Louvre, Paris, France. Réunion des Musées Nationaux/Art Resource, NY

CHRONOLOGY
A Century and a Half of Renaissance Art

1420s	Masaccio, Donatello, and Brunelleschi visit Rome and begin transforming painting, sculpture, and architecture
1430s	Donatello's *David;* completion of Brunelleschi's dome; Van Eyck's *Arnolfini Marriage*
1440s	Botticelli born; death of Brunelleschi
1450s	Leonardo da Vinci born
1460s	Death of Donatello
1470s	Dürer, Michelangelo, and Titian born
1480s	Raphael born; Botticelli's *Birth of Venus*
1490s	Dürer's *Apocalypse*
1500s	Leonardo's *Mona Lisa;* Michelangelo's *David;* Cellini born
1510s	Raphael and Michelangelo decorate the Vatican; Titian's *Bacchanal*
1520s	Deaths of Raphael and Dürer
1530s	Michelangelo's *Last Judgement* in the Sistine Chapel
1540s	Cellini's *Salt Cellar;* Titian's *Charles V at Mülberg*
1550s	Giorgio Vasari begins publishing *Lives of the Artists,* the first study of the achievements of Renaissance art
1560s	Death of Michelangelo
1570s	Deaths of Cellini and Titian

anatomy or designing fortifications, he was unable to resist the challenge of solving practical problems, even in his paintings. They are marvels of technical virtuosity, which make difficult angles, tricks of perspective, and bizarre geological formations look easy. His portrait of the Mona Lisa, for example, is famous not only for her mysterious smile but for the incredible rocky landscape in the background. Unfortunately, Leonardo also experimented with methods of painting; as a result, one of his masterpieces, the *Last Supper*, has almost completely disintegrated.

Raphael By contrast, Raphael (1483–1520) used the mastery of perspective and ancient styles that had been achieved in the 1400s to produce works of perfect harmony, beauty, and serenity. His paintings give an impression of utter relaxation, of an artist in complete command of his materials and therefore able to create sunny scenes that are balanced and at peace. His tribute to the ancient world, *The School of Athens*, places

in a Classical architectural setting the great philosophers of Greece, many of whom are portraits of the artists of the day: Plato, for instance, has Leonardo's face. If the philosophers were the chief glory of Athens, Raphael seems to be saying, then the artists are the crowning glory of the Renaissance.

Michelangelo For Michelangelo (1475–1564), painting was but one means of expression. Equally at home in poetry, architecture, and sculpture, he often seems the ultimate embodiment of the achievements of his age. Constantly seeking new effects, he once said that no two of the thousands of figures he depicted were the same, and one might add that just about every one of them conveys the sense of latent strength, of striving, that was Michelangelo's signature. In *The Creation of*

Raphael
SCHOOL OF ATHENS
Painted in 1510 and 1511, this fresco celebrating the glories of Greek philosophy represents the triumph of the Renaissance campaign to revive antiquity. That the classical setting and theme could have been accepted as appropriate for a wall of the Vatican suggests how completely Humanism had captured intellectual life. A number of the figures are portraits of artists whom Raphael knew: Plato, pointing to heaven at the back, has the face of Leonardo, and the notoriously moody Michelangelo broods, with his head on his arm, at the front.
Scala/Art Resource, NY

Man Adam, shown at the moment of his creation, has not yet received the gift of life from God, but he already displays the vigor that Michelangelo gave to every human body. The same is true of Michelangelo's version of David, seemingly tranquil but showing his potential power in his massive, oversized hand. The human being is shown in full majesty, as an independent and potent individual.

Titian   In Venice, developments in art took a slightly different form. This was also a rich trading city, sophisticated, with broad international connections. But here Humanism was not so central, and the art—as befitted this most down-to-earth and cosmopolitan of Europe's cities—was more sensuous. The most famous Venetian painter, Titian (ca. 1482–1576), depicted rich velvets, lush nudes, stormy skies, and dogs with wagging tails

with a directness and immediacy that enable the viewer almost to feel them. His friend Aretino said of one of his pictures: "I can say nothing of the crimson of the garment nor of its lynx lining, for in comparison real crimson and real lynx seem painted, and these seem real." Titian was Europe's most sought-after portraitist, and to this day we can recognize the leading figures of his time, and sense their character, because of the mastery of his depictions.

Status and Perception

Art as Craft   To the generation of Masaccio, a painter was merely one of the many people engaged in a craft, not inherently more admired than a skilled clothworker or mason. Like them, he was a member of a guild, he had to pass a carefully regulated apprenticeship, and he was

◄ **Michelangelo**
THE CREATION OF MAN
Michelangelo worked on the ceiling of the Sistine Chapel in the Vatican from 1508 to 1512 and painted hundreds of figures. None has come to symbolize the rebirth associated with the Renaissance and the power of creative genius so forcefully as the portrayal of God extending a finger to bring the vigorous body of Adam to life. Tucked under God's other arm is the figure of Eve, ready to join Adam in giving birth to humankind.
Detail of the Sistine ceiling. Scala/Art Resource, NY

◄ **Titian**
BACCHANAL (THE ANDRIANS), 1518–1519
The earthy realism of Venice contrasted sharply with the idealization common in Florentine art. The setting and even the sky seem more tangible, and Titian's lush nude in the foreground (who was to be much copied) is the essence of sensuality. It has been suggested that the painting represents the different stages of life, from the incontinent child through the vigorous youths and adults to the old man who has collapsed in the back.
Museo del Prado, Madrid, Spain. Scala/Art Resource, NY

Joos van Wassenhove and Pedro Berruguete
FEDERICO DA MONTEFELTRO WITH HIS SON GUIDOBALDO
This remarkable painting embodies the new ideal of the gentleman that emerged in the Renaissance. Federico da Montefeltro was both one of the most notable warriors and one of the most distinguished patrons of learning of the age, and this portrait captures both sides of his princely image. Sitting in his study with his richly clothed son, Guidobaldo, Duke Federico is reading a book but is also dressed in armor.
Galleria Nazionale delle Marche, Urbino, Italy. Scala/Art Resource, NY

subject to the rules that controlled his trade. Both Donatello and Brunelleschi were trained as goldsmiths, and the latter was even briefly imprisoned by his guild for not paying his dues while he was working on the cathedral dome—as an independent person, so he thought, and thus outside the guild structure. Given the Florentines' interest in gaining fame by beautifying their city, it was not surprising that the work of these artists should have attracted considerable attention. But it rarely occurred to anyone in the early 1400s—as Brunelleschi discovered from his guild—that they might deserve special respect or be considered more elevated than tradesmen. It was true that some of them were becoming famous throughout Italy, but would that lead to a change in their social status?

Humanism and the Change in Status The answer was that it did, and again the impetus came from the humanist movement. Three consequences of the revival of antiquity, in particular, began to alter the position of the artist. First was the recognition that the most vivid and convincing re-creations of the achieve-

ments of the ancient world were being produced in the visual arts. No letter written like Cicero's could compare with a painting, a statue, or a building as a means of bringing Rome back to life for all to see.

A second influence was the humanists' new interest in personal fame. This had been an acceptable aspiration in antiquity, but during the Middle Ages spiritual

ISABELLA D'ESTE'S QUEST FOR ART

As the passion for art took hold, the great patrons of the Renaissance became relentless in their search for new works. None was more avid than Isabella d'Este (1474–1539), who became the wife of the Gonzaga prince of Mantua at the age of sixteen and made her private suite of rooms (which she called her studio) a gathering place for artists, musicians, and poets for nearly fifty years. Her passion for art shines through her letters; in these extracts, she is pursuing both the Venetian painter Bellini and Leonardo da Vinci.

"To an agent, 1502: 'You may remember that many months ago we gave Giovanni Bellini a commission to paint a picture for the decoration of our studio, and when it ought to have been finished we found it was not yet begun. We told him to abandon the work, and give you back the 25 ducats, but now he begs us to leave him the work and promises to finish it soon. As till now he has given us nothing but words, tell him that we no longer care to have the picture, but if instead he would paint a Nativity, we should be well content, as long as he does not keep us waiting any longer.'

"Two months later: 'As Bellini is resolved on doing a picture of the Madonna and Child and St. John the Baptist in place of the Nativity scene, I should be glad if he would also include a St. Jerome; and about the price of 50 ducats we are content, but above all urge him to serve us quickly and well.'

"Three years later, to Bellini himself: 'You will remember very well how great our desire was for a picture painted by your hand, to put in our studio. We appealed to you for this in the past, but you could not do it on account of your many other commitments. (We recently heard you might be free,) but we have been ill with fever and unable to attend to such things. Now that we are feeling better it has occurred to us to write begging you to consent to painting a picture, and we will leave the poetic invention for you to make up if you do not want us to give it to you. As well as the proper payment, we shall be under an eter-

nal obligation to you. When we hear of your agreement, we will send you the measurements of the canvas and an initial payment.'

"In the meantime, in May 1504, she wrote to Leonardo da Vinci: 'Hearing that you are staying in Florence, we have conceived the hope that something we have long desired might come true: to have something by your hand. When you were here and drew our portrait in charcoal, you promised one day to do it in color. Since it would be inconvenient for you to move here, we beg you to keep your good faith with us by substituting for our portrait a youthful Christ of about twelve years old, executed with that sweetness and soft ethereal charm which is the peculiar excellence of your art.'

"Five months later she wrote again: 'Some months ago we wrote to you that we wanted to have a young Christ, about twelve years old, by your hand. You replied that you would do this gladly, but owing to the many commissioned works you have on your hands, we doubt whether you remembered ours. Wherefore it has occurred to us to send you these few lines, begging you that you will turn to doing this little figure for us by way of recreation, which will be doing us a very gracious service and of benefit to yourself.'"

From D. S. Chambers (ed.), *Patrons and Artists in the Italian Renaissance,* London: Macmillan, 1970, pp. 128–130 and 147–148.

concerns encouraged a disdain for worldly matters. It was still a problem for Petrarch to admit that, like the ancients he admired, he wanted to be famous. Among later humanists, the doubts receded, and the princes who valued their ideas eagerly accepted the notion that they should devote their lives to attaining fame. That was what nobles previously had won as warriors, but now there was a more reliable way to ensure that one's name lived forever.

The New Patrons　That way was provided by the third of the humanists' lessons: that the truly moral person had to combine the contemplative with the active life. A prince, therefore, ought to cultivate the fine as well as the martial arts. No aristocratic court could be complete without its poets and painters, who sang their pa-

tron's praises while fashioning the masterpieces that not only brought prestige but also endured forever. As a result, if an aristocrat wanted immortality, it was no longer enough to be a famous warrior; now it became essential to build a splendid new palace or have one's portrait done by a famous painter. To be most like the virtuous heroes of Rome who were the society's ideal, vigorous leadership had to be linked to patronage of culture, and this outlook was not confined to noblemen. Noblewomen, whose chief role had long been to offer an idealized object of chivalric devotion and who continued to struggle to gain access to education, occasionally won that struggle, and the result was a refined patronage that could be crucial in fashioning a princely image. Without Isabella d'Este, for example, the court in Mantua would not have achieved its fame as a center of

Sandro Botticelli
THE BIRTH OF VENUS
Sandro Botticelli was a member of the intellectual circle of Lorenzo de Medici, and this painting is evidence of the growing interest in Neoplatonism at the Medici court. The wistful, ethereal look on Venus' face reflects the otherworldliness that was emphasized by the Neoplatonists; moreover, their belief in the analogies that link all ideas suggests that Botticelli may have been implying that Venus resembled the Virgin Mary as a source of divine love. In depicting an ancient myth as ancient painters would have shown it, Botticelli represents the triumph of Renaissance ambitions, and the idealized beauty of his work helped shape an aesthetic standard that has been admired ever since.
Erich Lessing/Art Resource, NY

painting, architecture, and music. That both Leonardo and Titian did her portrait was a reflection not of her husband's importance but of her own independent contribution to the arts. Her rooms, surrounding a lovely garden, remain one of the wonders of the palace at Mantua and a worthy testimony to her fame as a patroness (see "Isabella d'Este's Quest for Art," p. 350).

The effect of this new attitude was to transform the status of artists. They became highly prized at the courts of aristocrats, who saw them as extraordinarily effective image makers. Perhaps the most famous family of patrons in Italy, the Medici of Florence, were envied throughout Europe mainly because, for generations, they seemed always to be surrounded by the finest painters, sculptors, and architects of the age. And soon the richest princes in Italy, the popes, followed suit. The Church had been the main sponsor of art in the Middle Ages, but now it was the papacy in particular that promoted and inspired artistic production. In their determination to rebuild and beautify Rome as a worthy capital of Christendom, the popes gave such artists as Raphael and Michelangelo their most famous commissions—notably Michelangelo's Sistine Chapel within the Vatican. It was thus as a result of shifting patterns in the commissioning and buying of art that, as honored members of papal as well as princely courts, Renaissance artists created both a new aesthetic and a new social identity.

THE CULTURE OF THE NORTH

North of the Alps the transformations of the 1300s and 1400s were not as dramatic as in Italy, but they had consequences after 1500 that were no less dramatic than the effects of Humanism, Neoplatonism, and the other changes in the south. This area of Europe did not have the many large cities and the high percentages of

Benozzo Gozzoli
Procession of the Three Kings to Bethlehem (detail), **1459**
This enormous fresco in the Medici palace in Florence, completed in 1459, gives place of honor in the biblical scene of the procession of the Magi to the future ruler of Florence, the ten-year-old Lorenzo de Medici, riding a white horse, and to his grandfather Cosimo de Medici, the founder of the dynasty's power, who is behind Lorenzo, also on a white horse.
Palazzo Medici Riccardi, Florence, Italy. Erich Lessing/Art Resource, NY

urban dwellers that were crucial to the humanist movement in Italy. Nor did the physical monuments and languages of northern Europe offer ready reminders of the Classical heritage. Humanism and the revival of classical learning—with its literate, trained laity—did not come to the north until the last decade of the fifteenth century. But in these territories, where cultural life was dominated by the princely court rather than the city, and by the knight rather than the merchant, there were other vital shifts in outlook.

Chivalry and Decay

In 1919 a Dutch historian, Johan Huizinga, described northern European culture in the 1400s and 1500s not as a renaissance but as the decline of medieval civiliza-tion. His stimulating book, *The Waning of the Middle Ages*, focused primarily on the court of the dukes of Burgundy, who were among the wealthiest and most powerful princes of the north. Huizinga found tension and frequent violence in this society, with little of the serenity that had marked the thirteenth century.

Its uneasiness and inclination to escape from reality was reflected in its extravagant cultivation of the notion of chivalry. Militarily, the knight was becoming less important than the foot soldier armed with longbow, pike, or firearms. But the noble classes of the north continued to pretend that knightly virtues governed all questions of state and society; they discounted such lowly consid-erations as money, arms, recruitment, and supplies in deciding the outcome of wars. For example, before the Battle of Agincourt, one knight told the French king

Benvenuto Cellini
SALT CELLAR FOR FRANCIS I
Benvenuto Cellini, a Florentine goldsmith who challenged the common distinction between artisan and artist in his lively *Autobiography* (1562), executed this work for the French king Francis I in 1543. Juxtaposing allegorical images of the Earth and the Sea, which he presented as opposing forces, Cellini created figures as elegant as any sculpture and set them on a fantastic base of gold and enamel. His extraordinary skills indicate why so many Renaissance artists began their careers in goldsmiths' workshops.
Erich Lessing/Art Resource, NY

Charles that he should not use contingents from the Parisian townsfolk because that would give his army an unfair numerical advantage; the battle should be decided strictly on the basis of chivalrous valor.

Bravery and Display   This was the age of the perfect knight and the "grand gesture." King John of Bohemia insisted that his soldiers lead him to the front rank of battle, so that he could strike at the enemy even though he was blind. The feats of renowned knights won the admiration of chroniclers but hardly affected the outcome of battle. And the reason for the foundation of new orders of chivalry—notably the Knights of the Garter in England and the Burgundian Knights of the Golden Fleece—was that these orders would reform the world by cultivating knightly virtues.

Princes rivaled one another in the sheer glitter of their arms and the splendor of their tournaments. They waged wars of dazzlement, seeking to confound rivals with spectacular displays of gold, silks, and tapestries. Court ceremony was marked by excess, as were the chivalric arts of love. A special order was founded for the defense of women, and knights frequently took lunatic oaths to honor their ladies, such as keeping one eye closed for weeks. Obviously, people rarely made love or war in this artificial way. But they still found satisfaction in dreaming about the possibilities for love and war if this sad world were only a perfect place.

The Cult of Decay   Huizinga called the extravagant lifestyle of the northern courts the "cult of the sublime," or the impossibly beautiful. But he also noted that both knights and commoners showed a morbid fascination with death and its ravages. Reminders of the ultimate victory of death and treatments of decay are frequent in both literature and art. One popular artistic motif was the *danse macabre*, or dance of death, depicting people from all walks of life—rich and poor, clergy and laity, good and bad—dancing with a skeleton. Another melancholy theme favored by artists across Europe was the *Pietà*—the Virgin weeping over her dead son.

This morbid interest in death and decay in an age of plague was not the result of lofty religious sentiment. The obsession with the fleetingness of material beauty in fact indicated how attached people were to earthly pleasures; it was a kind of inverse materialism. Above all, the gloom reflected a growing religious dissatisfaction. In the 1200s Francis of Assisi addressed death as a sister; in the fourteenth and fifteenth centuries people apparently regarded it as a ravaging, indomitable fiend. Clearly (as Petrarch, too, had noted) the Church was failing to provide consolation to many of its members, and a religion that fails to console is a religion in crisis.

Devils and Witches   Still another sign of the unsettled religious spirit of the age was a fascination with the devil, demonology, and witchcraft. The most enlightened scholars of the day wondered whether witches could ride through the air on sticks. One of the more notable witch trials of Western history was held at Arras in 1460, when scores of people were accused of participating in a witches' sabbath, giving homage to the devil, and having sexual intercourse with him. In 1486 two inquisitors who had been authorized by the pope to prosecute witches published the *Malleus Maleficarum* ("hammer of witches"), which defined witchcraft as heresy and became the standard handbook for prosecutors. Linked to the fear of the devil was a fear of women. They were the most frequent victims of witchcraft accusations, easy scapegoats in an age of social upheaval. Any hint of change in their traditional subordination to men, such as learning to read, combined with their vulnerability to make them targets of denunciation.

Relics   There was also a growing fascination with concrete religious images. The need to have immediate, physical contact with the objects of religious devotion added to the popularity of pilgrimages and stimulated the obsession with the relics of saints. These were usually fake, but they became a major commodity in international trade. Some princes accumulated collections of relics numbering in the tens of thousands.

Huizinga saw these aspects of northern culture as signaling the disintegration of the cultural synthesis of the Middle Ages. Without a disciplined and unified view of the world, attitudes toward war, love, and religion lost balance, and disordered behavior followed. The culture was not young and vigorous but old and dying. Yet the concept of decadence must be used with caution. Certainly this was a disturbed world that had lost the self-confidence of the thirteenth century; but these supposedly decadent people, though dissatisfied, were also passionately anxious to find solutions to the tensions that unsettled them. We need to recall that passion when trying to understand the appeal and the power behind other cultural movements—lay piety and efforts of religious reform.

Literature, Art, and Music

Literature   In addition to the fascination with the chivalric and the supernatural, there was also a fascination with the everyday, the equivalent in the North of the down-to-earth work of Boccaccio. His most famous disciple was an Englishman, Geoffrey Chaucer (ca. 1340–1400), who was a soldier, diplomat, and government official. His *Canterbury Tales*, written in the 1390s, recounts the pilgrimage of some thirty men and women to the tomb of St. Thomas Becket at Canterbury. For entertainment on the road, each pilgrim agrees to tell two stories. Chaucer's lively portraits are a rich tapestry of English society, especially in its middle ranges. The stories also sum up the moral and social ills of the day. His robust monk, for example, ignores the Benedictine rule; his friar is more interested in donations than in the cure of souls; his pardoner knowingly hawks fraudulent relics; and the wife of Bath complains of prejudice against women. Apart from the grace of his poetry, Chaucer had the ability to delineate character and spin a lively narrative. The *Canterbury Tales* is a masterly portrayal of human personalities and human behavior that can delight readers in any age.

Art   The leaders of the transformation in both the style and the status of artists in the 1400s were mainly Italians. But there were also major advances in northern Europe. Indeed, oil painting—on wood or canvas—was invented in the Netherlands, and its first great exponent, Jan Van Eyck, a contemporary of Donatello, revealed both the similarities and the differences between North and South. Van Eyck was less interested in idealization than were the Florentines and more fascinated with the details of the physical world. One sees almost every thread in a carpet. But his portrait of an Italian couple, the Arnolfinis, is shot through with religious symbolism as well as a sly sense of humor about

Albrecht Dürer
The Riders on the Four Horses from the Apocalypse,
CA. 1496
The bestseller that Düer published in 1498, *The Apocalypse*, has the text of the biblical account of the apocalypse on one side and full-page woodcuts on the other. The four horsemen who will wreak vengeance on the damned during the final Day of Judgment are Conquest holding a bow, War holding a sword, Famine, or Justice, holding scales, and Death, or Plague, riding a pale horse and trampling a bishop.
Woodcut. The Metropolitan Museum of Art, Gift of Junius S. Morgan, 1919. (19.73.209). Photograph © 2002 The Metropolitan Museum of Art, New York

sex and marriage. The dog is a sign of fidelity, and the carving on the bedpost is of St. Margaret, the patron saint of childbirth; but the single candle is what newlyweds are supposed to keep burning on their wedding night, and the grinning carved figures behind their clasped hands are a wry comment on their marriage. The picture displays a combination of earthiness and piety that places it in a tradition unlike any in the Italy of this time (see p. 336).

The leading northern artist of the period of the High Renaissance was a German, Albrecht Dürer, who deliberately sought to blend southern and northern styles. He made two trips to Venice, and the results were clear in a self-portrait that shows him as a fine gentleman, painted in the Italian style. But he continued, especially in the engravings that made him famous, to emphasize the detailed depiction of nature and the religious purposes that were characteristic of northern art.

Dürer refused to break completely with the craft origins of his vocation. He knew, from his visits to Venice, that Italian painters could live like lords, and he was invited by the Holy Roman Emperor to join his court. But he preferred to remain in his home city of Nuremberg, earning his living more through the sale of his prints than from the stipends he was offered by patrons. Eventually he became a highly successful **entrepreneur,** creating different kinds of prints for different markets—the elite liked elegant and expensive copper engravings, while others preferred cruder but cheaper woodcuts—and producing a best seller in a book of illustrations of the Apocalypse. His wife was a highly effective seller of his prints, and she preferred running her stall in the marketplace to fine entertainments by city fathers. Indeed, the couple can be seen as pioneers in the business of art.

Developments in Music   The process that was at work in the visual arts had similar effects in music, which again had developed primarily for liturgical purposes in the Middle Ages. In the Renaissance, musicians became as prized as artists at princely courts, and their growing professionalism was demonstrated by the organists and choir singers hired by churches, the trumpeters employed by cities for official occasions, and the composers and performers who joined the households of the wealthy. Musical notation became standardized, and instruments became more diverse as old ones were improved and new ones—such as the viol, the oboe, and the clavichord—were invented. Moreover, unlike the practice of art, which usually required apprenticeship to guilds that were closed to women, musical performance, whose patron saint was St. Cecilia, relied on the talents of both men and women.

Unlike the visual arts, the chief musical center of Europe around 1500 was in the Low Countries, not Italy. The choirmasters of cathedral towns like Bruges employed professional singers who brought to new levels the traditional choral form of four-part polyphony (that is, four different lines playing against one another). This complex vocal harmony had no need of instrumental accompaniment; as a result, freed from their usual subservience to the voice, instruments could be developed in new ways. The greatest masters of the time, Guillaume Dufay and Josquin des Prez, excelled in secular as well as religious music, and theirs was one field of creativity in which new techniques and ideas flowed mainly from the north to Italy, not the other way around.

SCHOLASTIC PHILOSOPHY AND RELIGIOUS THOUGHT

In theology, Scholasticism retained its hold even as Humanism swept the literary world. But it was not the thirteenth-century Scholasticism of Thomas Aquinas, which asserted that human reason could fashion a universal philosophy that embraced all truths and reconciled all apparent conflicts. Nor did the traditional acceptance of ecclesiastical law continue, with its definition of the Christian life in terms of precise rules of behavior rather than interior spirit. The style of thinking changed as the Scholastics of the 1400s and 1500s were drawn to analysis (breaking apart) rather than synthesis (putting together) as they examined philosophical and theological statements. Many of them no longer shared Aquinas' confidence in human reason, and they hoped to repair his synthesis or to replace it with new systems that, though less comprehensive, could at least be more easily defended in an age growing doubtful about reason. Discussions of faith changed too, as more and more Christian leaders sought ways to deepen the interior, sometimes mystical, experience of God.

The "Modern Way"

The followers of Aquinas remained active in the schools, but the most original of the Scholastics in the fourteenth century took a different approach to their studies. They were known as **nominalists,** because they focused on the way we describe the world—the names (in Latin, *nomina*) that we give to things—rather than on its reality. The nominalists denied the existence, or at least the knowability, of the universal forms that supposedly make up the world—"manness," "dogness," and the like. The greatest among them was the English Franciscan William of Ockham (ca. 1300– ca. 1349), and his fundamental principle came to be called Ockham's razor. It states essentially that, between alternative explanations for the same phenomenon, the simpler is always to be preferred.

Ockham   On the basis of this "principle of parsimony," Ockham attacked the traditional focus of philosophy on universal, ideal forms. These concepts had led Aquinas to argue, for instance, that all individual beings must be understood as reflections of their universal forms. By contrast, Ockham argued that the simplest way to explain the existence of any specific object is just to say it exists. The mind can find resemblances among objects and make generalizations about them, which can then be examined in coherent and logical ways. But these offer no certainty of the actual existence of Aquinas' ideal forms—the universal principles like "manness" that all beings and objects reflect.

The area of reality that the mind can grasp is thus severely limited. The universe, as far as human reason can detect, is a collection of separate beings and objects, not a hierarchy of ideal forms. The proper way to deal with this universe is by direct experience, not by speculating about abstract natures. Such a philosophy, based on observation and reason, sought limited, not universal, truths. Ockham believed that one could still prove the existence of some general principles, but he thought human beings could know very little about the ultimate necessary principle, God.

Nominalist Theology   Ockham and many of his contemporaries insisted on the total power of God and humanity's absolute dependence on him. If he chose, God could reward vice, punish virtue, and act erratically; which raised the question, how could there be a stable system of theology or ethics? The nominalists' answer was that, instead of using his absolute power, God relied on his ordained power: through a covenant, or agreement, God assures people that he will act in consistent and predictable ways. Thus, theology becomes the study not of metaphysics but of God's will and covenant with the human race.

Nominalists rejected Aquinas' high assessment of human powers and his confident belief in the ordered and knowable structure of the natural world. Living in a disturbed, pessimistic age, they reflected the crisis of confidence in natural reason and human capability that is a major feature of the cultural history of the North in these years. Nominalists were popular in the universities, and Ockhamite philosophy, in particular, came to be known as the *via moderna* ("modern way"). Although nominalists and humanists were frequently at odds, they did share a dissatisfaction with aspects of the medieval intellectual tradition, especially the speculative abstractions of medieval thought; and both advocated approaches to reality that concentrated on the concrete and the present and demanded a strict awareness of method.

Social and Scientific Thought

Marsilius   The belief of the nominalists that reality was to be found not in abstract forms but in concrete objects had important implications for social thought. The most remarkable of these social thinkers was Marsilius of Padua, an Italian lawyer who served at the French royal court. In 1324 he wrote a book, *Defender of Peace*, which attacked papal authority and supported lay sovereignty within the Church. His purpose was obviously to endorse the independent authority of his patron, the king of France, who pursued a running battle with the pope. But his work had wider implications. Using nominalist principles, Marsilius argued that the reality of the Christian community, like the reality of the universe, consists of the sum of all its parts. The sovereignty of the Church thus belongs to its members, who alone can define the collective will of the community.

Marsilius was one of the first theorists of the modern concept of sovereignty. Emphasizing secular authority, he maintained that only regulations supported by force are true law and that, therefore, the enactments of the Church do not bind because they are not supported by coercive force. The Church has no right to power or to property and is entirely subject to the sovereign will of the state, which is indivisible, absolute, and unlimited. *Defender of Peace* is noteworthy not only for its radical ideas but also for its reflection of deep dissatisfactions. Marsilius and others revealed a hostile impatience with the papal and clerical domination of Western political life. They wanted laypersons to guide the Church and the Christian community. In this respect at least, the book was a prophecy of things to come.

New Explanations of Nature   In studies of nature, a few nominalists at Paris and Oxford in the fourteenth century took the first hesitant steps toward a criticism of the Aristotelian world system that had dominated European studies of physics ever since they had been recovered through translations by Muslim scholars. At the University of Paris, for example, Jean Buridan proposed an important revision in Aristotle's theory of motion. If, as Aristotle had said, all objects are at rest in their natural state, what keeps an arrow flying after it leaves the bow? Aristotle had reasoned rather lamely that the arrow disturbs the air through which it passes and that it is this disturbance that keeps pushing the arrow forward. Buridan suggested, instead, that the movement of the bow lends the arrow a special quality of motion, an "impetus," that stays with it permanently unless removed by the resistance of the air. In addition, Buridan and other fourteenth-century nominalists theorized about the acceleration of falling objects and made some attempt to describe this phenomenon in mathematical terms. Although they were often inadequate or inaccurate, these attempts at new explanations started the shift away from an unquestioned acceptance of ancient systems (such as Aristotle's) that was to climax, three hundred years later, in the scientific revolution.

Humanism and Science   Humanists also helped prepare the way for scientific advance. They rediscovered important ancient writers whose works had been forgotten, and their skills in textual and literary criticism taught people to look with greater precision at works inherited from the past. As more of the classics became available, it became apparent that ancient authors did not always agree. Could they, therefore, always be correct? Furthermore, the idealism of Plato and the number mysticism of Pythagoras suggested that unifying forms and harmonies lay behind the disparate data of experience and observation. Once this assumption took hold, it was soon being argued that perhaps the cosmic harmonies might be described in mathematical terms.

THE STATE OF CHRISTENDOM

The Church as an institution also experienced major transformations in the 1300s and 1400s. It continued to seek a peaceful Christendom united in faith and obedience to Rome. But the international Christian community was in fact beset by powerful forces (reflected by Marsilius) that undermined its cohesiveness and weakened papal authority and influence. Although the culmination of these disruptions did not come until the Reformation in the 1500s, the history of the previous two centuries made it clear that the institution was profoundly troubled.

The Avignon Exile   The humiliation of Pope Boniface VIII by the agents of Philip IV of France at Anagni in 1303 opened the doors to French influence at the curia. In 1305 the College of Cardinals elected a French pope, Clement V, who because of the political disorders in the Papal States eventually settled at Avignon (1309). Though technically a part of the Holy Roman Empire, Avignon was in language and culture a French city. The popes who followed Clement hoped to return to Rome but remained at Avignon, claiming that the continuing turmoil of central Italy would not permit papal government to function effectively. These popes were skilled administrators who expanded the papal bureaucracy enormously—especially its fiscal machinery—but the long absence from Rome clearly harmed papal prestige.

Fiscal Crisis   Like many secular governments, the papacy at Avignon faced an acute fiscal crisis. But unlike the major powers of Europe, its territorial base could not supply it with the funds it needed, because controlling the Papal States usually cost more money than they produced. As a result, the papacy was drawn into the unfortunate practice of exploiting its ecclesiastical powers for financial gain. Thus, the popes insisted that candidates appointed to high ecclesiastical offices pay a special tax, which usually amounted to a third or a half of the first year's revenues. The popes also claimed the income from vacant offices and even sold future appointments to office when the incumbents were still alive. Dispensations, which were also sold, released a petitioner from the normal requirements of canon law.

A monastery or religious house, for example, might purchase an exemption from visitation and inspection by the local bishop. The pope received in tithes one-tenth of the revenues of ecclesiastical benefices or offices throughout Christendom. And the Church offered indulgences, remissions of the temporal punishment for sin, in return for monetary contributions to the papacy.

These fiscal practices enlarged the popes' revenues, but they had deplorable results. Prelates who paid huge sums to Avignon tended to pass on the costs to the lower clergy. Parish priests, hardly able to live from their incomes, were more easily tempted to lower their moral standards. The flow of money to Avignon angered rulers and prompted demands for a halt to such payments and even for the confiscation of Church property. Dispensations gravely injured the authority of the bishops, since an exempt person or house all but escaped their supervision. The bishops were frequently too weak, and the pope too distant, to deal effectively with abuses on the local level. The fiscal measures thus helped sow chaos in many parts of the Western Church.

The Great Schism   The end of the seventy-year Avignon exile led to a controversy that almost split the Western Church. In 1377 Pope Gregory XI returned reluctantly to Rome and died there a short time later. The Roman people, fearing that Gregory's successor would once more remove the court to Avignon and thereby deprive Rome of desperately needed revenues, agitated for the election of an Italian pope. Responding to this pressure, the College of Cardinals found a compromise candidate who satisfied both French and Italian interests, but the new pope, Urban VI (1378–1389), soon antagonized the French cardinals by trying to limit their privileges and by threatening to pack the College with his own appointments. Seven months after choosing Urban, a majority of the cardinals declared that his election had taken place under duress and was invalid; they then named a new pope, who returned to Avignon. Thus began the **Great Schism** of the West (1378–1417), the period when two, and later three, popes fought over the rule of the Church.

Christendom now had two pretenders to the throne of Peter, one in Rome and one in Avignon. Princes and peoples quickly took sides (see map 12.2), and the troubles of the papacy multiplied. Each pope had his own court and needed yet more funds, both to meet ordinary expenses and to pay for policies that he hoped would defeat his rival. And since each pope excommunicated the other and those who supported him, everyone in Christendom was at least technically excommunicated.

The Conciliar Movement   Theologians and jurists had long speculated on who should rule the Church if

MAP 12.2 THE GREAT SCHISM, 1378–1417
The antagonisms in Europe during the Great Schism set neighboring regions against one another and created divisions from which the Church never fully recovered. One of the problems that made the Great Schism particularly acute was the presence of different papal candidates in different cities. Avignon was a long way from Rome, and it easy for the "pope" in one city to ignore his rival in the other. Which countries and regions recognized the pope at Rome? Which recognized the pope at Avignon? What were the areas of shifting obedience? What do you notice about the location of the councils that tried to end the schism? Where were they in relation to Avignon and Rome?
◆ For an online version, go to www.mhhe.com/chambers9 > chapter 12 > book maps

the pope were to become heretical or incompetent; some concluded that it should be the College of Cardinals or a general council of Church officials. Since the College of Cardinals had split into two factions, each backing one of the rival popes, many prominent thinkers supported the theory that a general council should rule the Church. These **conciliarists,** as they were called, went further. They wanted the Church to have a new constitution to confirm the supremacy of a general council. Such a step would have reduced the pope's role to that of a limited monarch, but the need to correct numerous abuses strengthened the

idea that a general council should rule and reform the Church.

Pisa and Constance   The first test of the conciliarists' position was the Council of Pisa (1409), convened by cardinals of both Rome and Avignon. This council asserted its supremacy within the Church by deposing the two popes and electing another. But this act merely added to the confusion, for it left Christendom with three rivals claiming to be the lawful pope. A second council finally resolved the situation. Some four hundred ecclesiastics assembled at the Council of Constance (1414–1418), the greatest international gathering of the Middle Ages. The council was organized in a new way, with the delegates voting as nations to offset the power of the Italians, who made up nearly half the attendance. This procedure reflected the new importance of national and territorial churches. It enabled the delegates to depose both the Pisan pope and the Avignon pope and persuade the Roman pope to resign. In his stead they elected a Roman cardinal, who took the name Martin V. Thus, the Great Schism was ended, and the Western Church was once again united under a single pope.

As the meetings continued, the views of the conciliarists prevailed. The delegates formally declared that a general council was supreme within the Church. To ensure continuity in Church government, they also directed that new councils be summoned periodically.

The Revival of the Papacy

In spite of this assertion of supremacy, the council made little headway in reforming the Church. The delegates, mostly great prelates, were the chief beneficiaries of the fiscal system and were reluctant to touch their own privileges and advantages. The real victims of the fiscal abuses, the lower clergy, were poorly represented. As a result, the council could not agree on a general program of reform, because it was too large, too cumbersome, and too divided to maintain effective ecclesiastical government. The restored papacy soon reclaimed its position as supreme head of the Western Church.

The practical weaknesses of the conciliar movement were revealed at the Council of Basel (1431–1449). Because disputes broke out almost at once with the pope, the council deposed him and elected another, Felix V. The conciliar movement, designed to heal the schism, now seemed responsible for renewing it. Recognizing the futility of its actions, the council tried to rescue its dignity when Felix died by endorsing the cardinals' election of a new pope, Nicholas V, in 1449 and then disbanding. This action ended efforts to give supreme authority to councils. But the idea of government by representation that they advanced was to have an important influence on later political developments in Europe.

Territorial Independence
Although the popes remained suspicious of councils, they had much more serious rivals to their authority in the powerful lay princes, who were exerting ever tighter control over territorial churches. Both England and France issued decrees that limited papal powers within their kingdoms, and this policy was soon imitated in Spain and the stronger principalities of the Holy Roman Empire. Although such decrees did not establish national or territorial churches, they do document the decline of papal control over the international Christian community.

The Revival of Rome
When Martin V returned to Rome in 1417, the popes faced the monumental task of rebuilding their office and their prestige as both political and cultural leaders of Europe. They wanted Rome to be a major capital, a worthy home for the papacy, and not dependent on French rulers or culture, as they had been for the past century. To this end, they adopted the new literary and artistic ideas of the Renaissance, and the result was a huge rebuilding program that symbolized the restored authority of the popes. They sought, as one contemporary put it, "by the construction of grand and lasting buildings to increase the honor of the Roman Church and the glory of the Apostolic see, and widen and strengthen the devotion of all Christian people." One of the popes even proclaimed that if any city "ought to shine by its cleanliness and beauty, it is above all that which bears the title of capital of the universe." The building of a new St. Peter's Church in the 1400s was but the climax of this campaign of beautification, designed to assert a cultural supremacy that went along with the supremacy of the pope's authority. At the same time, vigorous military campaigns in the Papal States subdued that difficult territory and established the papacy as a major Italian power.

It could be argued, however, that in identifying itself so closely with Rome and with Italian politics, the papacy became less universal. For all its splendor and its renewed control over the institution of the Church, it was failing to retain the spiritual allegiance of Europe, especially in the North. The popes may have succeeded in reshaping the Church into a powerful and centralized body, and in making Rome once again a cultural capital of the Western world, but the new cultural and intellectual forces that were at work in the 1400s ultimately undermined the centrality of the papacy to the life of Europe.

Styles of Piety

Partly in response to the disorder of the Church as an institution, new forms of piety and religious practice began to appear. Whereas praying for the salvation of the community had once been considered the clergy's responsibility, many now felt that it was up to each individual to seek the favor of God.

Lay Mysticism and Piety
One consequence was that mysticism—an interior sense of the direct presence and love of God—which previously had been seen only in monastic life, began to move out of the monasteries in the thirteenth century. The prime mission of the Franciscans and the Dominicans was preaching to the laity, and they were now communicating some of the satisfactions of mystical religion. Laypersons wishing to remain in the outside world could join special branches of the Franciscans or Dominicans known as

third orders. **Confraternities,** which were religious guilds founded largely for laypersons, grew up in the cities and, through common religious services and programs of charitable activities, tried to deepen the spiritual lives of their members. Humanism had strong overtones of a movement for lay piety. And hundreds of devotional and mystical works were written to teach laypersons how to feel repentance, not just how to define it. Translations of the Scriptures into vernacular languages also appeared, though the Church disapproved of such efforts, and the high cost of manuscripts before the age of printing severely limited their circulation.

This growth of lay piety was, in essence, an effort to give everyone access to forms of faith that hitherto had been restricted to a spiritual elite. Frightened by the disasters of the age, people hungered for emotional reassurance, for evidence of God's love and redeeming grace within themselves. Also, the spread of education among the laity, at least in the cities, made people discontented with empty forms of religious ritual.

Female Piety   The commitment to personal piety among the laity was particularly apparent among women. It is significant that in the years between 1000 and 1150 male saints outnumbered females by 12 to 1, but in the years 1348 to 1500 the ratio dropped to 2.74 to 1. Moreover, the typical female saints of the later Middle Ages were no longer queens, princesses, and abbesses. They were mystics and visionaries, ordinary yet charismatic people who gained the attention of the Church and the world by the power of their message and the force of their own personalities. Catherine of Siena (1347–1380), for example, was the youngest of the twenty-five children of a humble Italian dyer. Her reputation for holiness attracted a company of followers from as far away as England, and she wrote (or dictated, for she probably couldn't write) devotional tracts that are monuments of Italian literature. Similar charismatic qualities made a simple Englishwoman, Margery Kempe, famous for her visions and her piety.

Women who out of poverty or preference lived a religious life outside convents became numerous, especially in towns. Some lived with their families, and others eked out a living on the margins of society. Still others lived in spontaneously organized religious houses—called *Beguines* in northern Europe—where they shared all tasks and property. The Church was suspicious of these women professing a religious life outside convents, without an approved rule. But the movement was too large for the Church to suppress or control. And many of them came to be particularly identified with one of the most powerful forms of lay piety in this period, mysticism.

Pisan Artist of XIV Century
The Mystic Marriage of Catherine of Siena
Catherine of Siena was a nun who was known for her efforts to return the papacy to Rome. Part of the reason for her sainthood was that, like Joan of Arc, she experienced visions from an early age. She is shown here with her symbol, the lily, in a scene from one of her visions. About to enter into a mystic marriage with Christ, she is accepting the wedding ring directly from him. Note that in the Renaissance, wedding rings were often placed on the middle finger of the right hand.
Soprintendenza B.A.A.A.S., Pisa. Museo Nazionale di S. Matteo

The Mystics   Among the most active centers of the new lay piety was the Rhine valley, a region that was especially noted for its remarkable mystics. The most famous was the Dominican Meister Eckhart (ca. 1260–ca. 1327), a spellbinding preacher who sought to bring his largely lay listeners into a mystical confrontation with God. Believers, he maintained, should cultivate the "divine spark" that is in every soul by banishing all thought and seeking to attain a state of pure passivity. If they succeeded, the divine presence would dwell within them. God is too great for dogma, he taught, and cannot be moved by conventional piety.

Brethren of the Common Life   Just as the nominalists argued for philosophical reasons that God is unknowable, so the mystics dismissed the value of formal knowledge and stressed the need for love and an emotional commitment to God. Perhaps the most influential of the mystics was Gerhard Groote of Holland.

Groote wrote sparingly, exerting his influence over his followers largely through his personality. After his death in 1384, his disciples formed a religious congregation known as the Brethren of the Common Life. The Brethren founded schools in Germany and the Low Countries that imported a style of lay piety known as the *devotio moderna* ("modern devotion). This emphasized interior experience as essential to faith. The believer needed no fasting, pilgrimages, or other acts of piety, but only imitation of the life of Jesus. Later reformers, such as Erasmus of Rotterdam and Martin Luther, were to be among the pupils of the Brethren.

Features of Lay Piety   The new lay piety was by no means a revolutionary break with the medieval Church, but it implicitly discounted the importance of many traditional institutions and practices. In this personal approach to God, there was no special value in the monastic vocation. As Erasmus would later argue, what was good in monasticism should be practiced by every Christian. Stressing simplicity and humility, the new lay piety reacted against the pomp and splendor that surrounded popes, prelates, and religious ceremonies. Likewise, the detailed rules for fasts, abstinences, and devotional exercises; the cult of the saints and their relics; and the traffic in indulgences and pardons all seemed peripheral to true religious needs. Without the proper state of the soul, these traditional acts of piety were meaningless; with the proper state, every act was worship. This new lay piety, emerging as it did out of medieval religious traditions, was clearly a preparation for the reformations of faith that took place in the sixteenth century among both Protestants and Catholics. It helped produce a more penetrating faith at a time when the formal beliefs of the Middle Ages, for all their grandeur and logical intricacies, no longer fully satisfied the religious spirit and were leaving hollows in the human heart.

Although the *devotio moderna* was a religious movement with little regard for humanist learning, it shared the humanists' distaste for the abstractions and intellectual arrogance of Scholasticism, and their belief that a wise and good person will cultivate humility and will maintain a "learned ignorance" toward the profound questions of religion. Moreover, both movements directed their message primarily to laypersons, in order to help them lead a higher moral life. The humanists, of course, drew their chief inspiration from the works of pagan and Christian antiquity, whereas the advocates of the new lay piety looked almost exclusively to Scripture. But the resemblances were close enough for scholars like Erasmus and Thomas More, writing in the early 1500s, to combine elements from both in the movement known as Christian Humanism.

Movements of Doctrinal Reform

The effort to reform the traditions of medieval Christianity also led to open attacks on the religious establishment—fueled, of course, by antagonism toward the papacy and Church corruption and by the larger tensions of this troubled epoch. Above all, these attacks gained support because the Church remained reluctant to adapt its organization and teachings to the demands of a changing world. In two prominent cases, moreover, the critiques arose at a university, where the basic method of instruction, the disputation, encouraged the discussion of unorthodox ideas. At disputations, students learned by listening to arguments for and against standard views. It was not impossible for someone taking the "wrong" side in such a debate to be carried away and cross the line between a theoretical discussion and open dissent.

Wycliffe   Whatever its origins, the most prominent of the assaults of the 1300s was launched by an Englishman, John Wycliffe (ca. 1320–1384), who taught at Oxford University. Wycliffe argued that the Church had become too remote from the people, and he wanted its doctrines simplified. To this end, he sought less power for priests and a more direct reliance on the Bible, which he hoped would be translated into English to make it easier to understand. Beyond his unease over the Church's remoteness from ordinary believers, he may have had political reasons (and thus support) for his stand. He was close to members of the royal court, who were increasingly resistant to papal demands and who were troubled that, in the midst of England's war with France, the papacy should have come under French influence when it moved from Rome to Avignon. In 1365 Wycliffe denounced the payment of Peter's pence, the annual tax given by English people to the papacy, and shortly thereafter he publicly denounced the papal curia, monks, and friars for their vices.

Wycliffe argued that the Scriptures alone declared the will of God and that neither the pope and the cardinals nor the Scholastic theologians could tell Christians what they should believe. In particular, he questioned one of the central dogmas of the Church that emphasized the special power of the priest: **transubstantiation,** which asserts that priests at the Mass work a miracle when they change the substance of bread and wine into the substance of Christ's body and blood. Besides attacking the exalted position and privileges of the priesthood in such rites as transubstantiation, Wycliffe denied the authority of the pope and the hierarchy to exercise jurisdiction or to hold property. He claimed that the true Church was that of the predestined—that is, those whom God would save and

HUS AT CONSTANCE

A few weeks before he was executed, Jan Hus wrote to his Czech followers to tell them how he had responded to his accusers at the Council of Constance:

"Master Jan Hus, in hope a servant of God, to all faithful Czechs who love God: I call to your attention that the proud and avaricious Council, full of all abomination, condemned my Czech books having neither heard nor seen them; even if it had heard them, it would not have understood them. O, had you seen that Council which calls itself the most holy, and that cannot err, you would have seen the greatest abomination! I have heard it commonly said that Constance would not for thirty years rid itself of the sins which that Council has committed. That Council has done more harm than good.

"Therefore, faithful Christians, do not allow yourselves to be terrified by their decrees, which will profit them nothing. They will fly away like butterflies, and their decrees will turn into a spiderweb. They wanted to frighten me, but could not overcome God's power in me. They did not dare to oppose me with Scripture.

"I am writing this to you that you may know that they did not defeat me by any Scripture or any proof, but that they sought to seduce me by deceits and threats to recant and abjure. But the merciful Lord God, whose law I have extolled, has been and is with me, and I hope that He will be with me to the end and will preserve me in His grace until death.

"This letter was written in chains, in the expectation of death."

From Matthew Spinka (ed.), *The Letters of John Hus*, Manchester: University Press, 1972, pp. 195–197.

were thus in a state of grace. Only these elect could rule the elect; therefore, popes and bishops who had no grace could have their properties removed and had no right to rule. Responsibility for ecclesiastical reform rested with the prince, and the pope could exercise only as much authority as the prince allowed.

The Lollards   Many of Wycliffe's views were branded heretical, but even though he was forced to leave Oxford when he offended his protectors at the royal court, they did keep him unharmed until he died. His followers, mostly ordinary people known as **Lollards**—a name apparently derived from lollar ("idler")—were not so lucky. They managed to survive as an underground movement in the countryside until the Protestant Reformation exploded more than a century later, but they were constantly hounded, and in 1428 the Church had Wycliffe's remains dug up, burned, and thrown into a river.

Hus   An even harsher fate awaited Wycliffe's most famous admirer, a Bohemian priest named Jan Hus (1369–1415), who started a broad and even more defiant movement in his homeland. Hus was a distinguished churchman and scholar. He served as rector (the equivalent of president) of the Charles University in Prague, one of Europe's best-known institutions, and he was the main preacher at a fashionable chapel in Prague. Like Wycliffe, whose ideas he had first heard expounded at a disputation, he argued that priests were not a holy and privileged group, set apart from laypersons, but that the Church was made up of all the faithful. To emphasize this equality, he rejected the division that allowed the congregation at a Mass to consume the wafer that symbolized Christ's body but not the wine that symbolized his blood, which only the priest could drink. In a dramatic gesture, Hus shared the cup of wine with all worshipers, thus reducing the distinctiveness of the priest. His followers adopted a chalice, or cup, as the symbol of their movement.

Hus did not hesitate to defy the leadership of the Church. Denounced for the positions he had taken, he replied by questioning the authority of the pope himself: "If a Pope is wicked, then like Judas he is a devil and a son of perdition and not the head of the Church militant. If he lives in a manner contrary to Christ, he has entered the papacy by another way than through Christ." In 1415 Hus was summoned to defend his views before the Church Council at Constance. Although he had been guaranteed safe passage if he came to answer accusations of heresy, the promise was broken. He was condemned, handed over to the secular authorities, and executed (see "Hus at Constance," above). But his followers, unlike the Lollards who stayed out of sight in England, refused to retreat in the face of persecution.

The Hussites   A new leader, Jan Žižka, known as John of the Chalice, raised an army and led a successful campaign against the emperor, who was also king of Bohemia and the head of the crusade that was now mounted against the **Hussites.** The resistance lasted twenty years, outliving Žižka, but sustained by Bohemian nobles, and eventually the Hussites were allowed to establish a special church, the Utraquist Church, in which both cup and wafer were shared by all worshipers at Mass. But Hus's other demands, such as the surrender of all personal possessions by the clergy (an echo of St. Francis), were rejected. Those who tried to fight on for these causes were defeated in battle, and after a long struggle the resistance came to an end, having made only a minor dent in the unity of the Church.

Summary

The popular appeal of Wycliffe and Hus reflected widespread dissatisfaction with official teachings in the late 1300s and 1400s—a dissatisfaction that Petrarch, too, had shared, though he did not challenge traditional doctrine but simply looked elsewhere for moral guidance. The movement that he launched, Humanism, transformed education and the arts, but others were determined to bring change to Europe's spiritual leadership as well. When, in pursuit of this ideal, Wycliffe and Hus chose to risk open confrontation, they demonstrated that reform ideas, advanced by charismatic leaders, could find a following among those who resented the authoritarian and materialistic outlook of the Church. At the same time, however, it became clear that such dissent could not survive without support from nobles, princes, or other leaders of society. Even with such help, the Hussites had to limit their demands; without it, they would have gained nothing. It was one hundred years after Hus's death before a new reformer arose who had learned these lessons, and he was to transform Western Christianity beyond recognition.

QUESTIONS FOR FURTHER THOUGHT

1. Why is it, when we think of the "golden ages" of history, that it is not just new ideas, but great art, that makes them seem such special times?

2. How do dominant cultural institutions like the medieval Church lose their hold over people's loyalty and respect?

RECOMMENDED READING

Sources

*Brucker, Gene A. (ed.). *The Society of Renaissance Florence: A Documentary Study.* 1971.

*Cassirer, Ernst, P. O. Kristeller, and J. H. Randall, Jr. (eds.). *The Renaissance Philosophy of Man.* 1953. Selections from Petrarch, Ficino, Pico, and others.

*Chambers, David, and Brian Pullan (eds.). *Venice: A Documentary History,* 1450–1630. 1992.

Kempe, Margery. *The Book of Margery Kempe* (1436). B. A. Windeatt (tr.). 1985. The autobiography of an extraordinary woman.

*Kohl, Benjamin G., and Ronald G. Witt (eds.). *The Earthly Republic: Italian Humanists on Government and Society.* 1978.

*Marsilius of Padua. *Defender of Peace.* Alan Gerwith (tr.). 1986.

Studies

*Berenson, Bernard. *The Italian Painters of the Renaissance.* 1968. Classic essays on the history of art.

Brown, Judith, and Robert Davis (eds.). *Gender and Society in Renaissance Italy.* 1998.

*Burckhardt, Jacob. *The Civilization of the Renaissance in Italy.* 1958. One of the pioneering works of European history, first published in 1860.

Campbell, Gordon (ed.). *The Oxford Dictionary of the Renaissance.* 2003.

*Hale, John. *The Civilization of Europe in the Renaissance.* 1993. The best overview.

*Hollingsworth, Mary. *Patronage in Renaissance Italy from 1400 to the Early Sixteenth Century.* 1994.

*Huizinga, Johan. *The Waning of the Middle Ages.* 1954.

Klapisch-Zuber, Christiane. *Women, Family, and Ritual in Renaissance Italy.* 1985. Collected essays.

Martin, John, J. *The Renaissance: Italy and Abroad.* 2003.

*Rabb, Theodore K. *Renaissance Lives.* 1993.

*Available in paperback.

Pieter Brueghel the Elder
THE PEASANT DANCE, **1568**
The most vivid images of life in the village during the sixteenth century were created by the Flemish artist Pieter Brueghel. The different human types, and the earthiness of country life, are captured in scenes that show the villagers both at work and, as here, at ease and relaxed. But the world of these ordinary Europeans was transformed during these very years by massive campaigns of religious reform: the Reformation and the Counter-Reformation. Even a villager unable to read would have been aware of the competing claim of these two movements, which swept through Europe from the 1520s onward.
Erich Lessing/Art Resource, NY

Chapter Thirteen

REFORMATIONS IN RELIGION

PIETY AND DISSENT • THE LUTHERAN REFORMATION •
THE SPREAD OF PROTESTANTISM • THE CATHOLIC REVIVAL

Although it may have seemed monolithic and all-powerful, the Roman Church in the fifteenth century was neither a unified nor an unchallenged institution. It had long permitted considerable variety in individual beliefs, from the analytic investigations of canon lawyers to the emotional outpourings of mystics. There were local saints, some of whom were recognized as holy only by a few villages; and for many Europeans the papacy remained a distant and barely comprehensible authority. To assume that its theological pronouncements were understood by the average illiterate Christ-

ian is to misrepresent the loose, fragmentary nature of the medieval Church. Moreover, the political disputes and reform movements of the fourteenth and fifteenth centuries had raised doubts about the central structure and doctrines of the Church. That the papacy had weathered these storms by 1500 indicated both how flexible and how powerful it was. What was to be remarkable in the years that followed was the sudden revelation of the Church's fragility, as a protest by a single monk snowballed into a movement that shattered the thousand-year unity of Western Christendom.

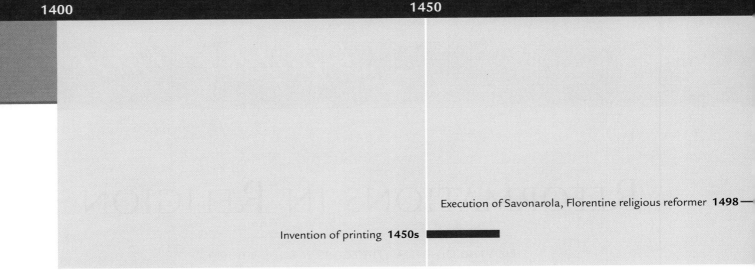

Execution of Savonarola, Florentine religious reformer **1498**—

Invention of printing **1450s**

PIETY AND DISSENT

The Roman Church may have held sway throughout Western Europe in 1500, but it was proving less and less able to meet the increasingly varied needs of the faithful. Different ideas about the ways an individual might achieve salvation were spreading, and some were turning into criticisms that the Church hierarchy could neither refute nor silence.

Doctrine and Reform

Two Traditions   A fundamental question that all Christians face is: How can sinful human beings gain salvation? In 1500, the standard official answer was that the Church was an essential intermediary. Only through participation in its rituals, and particularly through the seven **sacraments** its priests administered—baptism, confirmation, matrimony, the **Eucharist,** ordination, penance, and extreme unction—did the believer have access to the grace that God offered as an antidote to sin. But there was another answer, identified with distinguished Church fathers such as St. Augustine: People can be saved by their faith in God and love of him. This view emphasized inward and personal belief and focused on God as the source of grace.

The two traditions were not incompatible; for centuries they had coexisted without difficulty. Yet the absence of precise definition in many areas of doctrine was a major problem for theologians, because it was often difficult to tell where orthodoxy ended and heresy began. The position taken by the papacy, however, had grown less inclusive and adaptable over the years; by 1500 it seemed to be stressing the outward and institutional far more than the inward and personal route to salvation. Reformers for over a century had tried to reverse this trend, and it was unclear whether change

would come from within or would require a revolution and split in the Church.

The Quest for Reform   The root of the demand for change, as Hus had known, was the need of many laypersons for a way to express their piety that was more personal than official practices allowed. Church rituals meant little, they felt, unless believers could cultivate a sense of the love and presence of God. Rejecting the theological subtleties of Scholasticism, they sought divine guidance in the Bible and the writings of the early Church fathers, especially St. Augustine. Lay religious fraternities dedicated to private forms of worship and charitable works proliferated in the cities, especially in Germany and Italy. The most widespread in Germany, the Brotherhood of the Eleven Thousand Virgins, consisted of laypersons who gathered together, usually in a church, to sing hymns. In the mid-fifteenth century, more than one hundred such groups had been established in Hamburg, a city of slightly more than ten thousand inhabitants. Church leaders, unhappy about a development over which they had no control, had tried to suppress them, to no avail.

Savonarola   The most spectacular outburst of popular piety around 1500 occurred in seemingly materialist Florence, which embraced Girolamo Savonarola, a zealous friar who wanted to banish the irreligion and materialism he saw everywhere about him. The climax of his influence came in 1496, when he arranged a tremendous bonfire in which the Florentines burned cosmetics, light literature, dice, and other such frivolities. Savonarola embodied the desire for personal renewal that had long been a part of Western Christianity but seemed to be gaining intensity in the 1400s. His attempts at reform eventually brought him into conflict with the papacy, which rightly saw him as a threat to

● **1509** Erasmus, *The Praise of Folly*

● **1516** More, *Utopia*

● **1517** Luther's ninety-five theses; start of Reformation

■ **1524–1525** Peasants' Revolt in Germany

● **1534** King Henry VIII has himself proclaimed head of the Church of England

■ **1534–1549** Pope Paul III launches Counter-Reformation

■ **1545–1563** Council of Trent

Anonymous
The Martyrdom of Savonarola, ca. 1500
This painting still hangs in the monastery of San Marco where Savonarola lived during his years of power. It shows the city's central square—a setting that remains recognizable to anyone who visits Florence today—where the bonfire of the "vanities" had been held in 1496, and where Savonarola was executed in 1498. The execution is depicted here as an event that the ordinary citizens of Florence virtually ignore as they go about their daily routines.
Erich Lessing/Art Resource, NY

its authority. The Church therefore denounced him and gave its support to those who resented his power in Florence. His opponents had him arrested in 1498 and then executed on a trumped-up charge of treason.

Reform in Spain The widespread search for a more intense devotional life was a sign of spiritual vitality. But Church leaders in the age of Savonarola gave little encouragement to ecclesiastical reform and the evangelization of the laity. Only in Spain were serious efforts launched to eradicate abuses and encourage religious fervor, and they were led not by Rome but by Queen Isabella herself and by the head of the Spanish Church, Cardinal Ximenes de Cisneros. In other countries the hierarchy reacted harshly when such movements threatened its authority.

Causes of Discontent

Although its power over the Church had been restored by 1500, the papacy was still struggling to assert spiritual authority in the wake of the blows it had received in the previous two centuries. The move to Avignon, the Great Schism, and the conciliar movement had challenged its aura of moral and doctrinal superiority, and now its troubles multiplied.

Secular Interests Of major concern to many Christians were the papacy's secular interests. Increasingly, popes conducted themselves like princes. With skillful diplomacy and military action, they had consolidated their control over the papal lands in the Italian peninsula; Julius II (1503–1513) was even known as the Warrior Pope. An elaborate court arose in Rome, famous for its lavish patronage of the arts and symptomatic of a commitment to political power and grandeur that seemed to eclipse religious duties. Matters had reached such a point that some popes used their spiritual powers to raise funds for their secular activities. The fiscal measures developed at Avignon had expanded the papacy's income, but the enlarged revenues led to widespread abuses. High ecclesiastical offices were bought and sold, and men (usually sons of nobles) were attracted to these positions by the opportunities they provided for wealth and power, not by a religious vocation.

Abuse was widespread at lower levels in the Church as well. Some prelates held several offices at a time and could not give adequate attention to any of them. The ignorance and moral laxity of the parish and monastic clergy also aroused antagonism. Even more damaging was the widespread impression that the Church was failing to meet individual spiritual needs because of its remoteness from the day-to-day concerns of the average believer, its elaborate and incomprehensible system of canon law and theology, and its formal

Hans Baldung Grien
THE THREE AGES OF WOMAN AND DEATH, 1510
The preoccupation with the transitoriness of life and the vanity of earthly things took many forms in the sixteenth century. Here the point is hammered home unmistakably, as the central figure—a young woman at the height of her beauty between infancy and old age—is reminded of the passage of time (the hourglass) and the omnipresence of death even as she admires herself in a convex mirror.
Kunsthistorisches Museum, Vienna, Austria. Erich Lessing/Art Resource, NY

ceremonials. Above all, there was a general perception that priests, monks, and nuns were profiting from their positions, exploiting the people, and offering minimal moral leadership or religious guidance in return.

Anticlericalism These concerns provoked anticlericalism (hostility to the clergy) and calls for reform, which went unheeded except in the Spain of Cardinal Ximenes. For increasing numbers of deeply pious people, the growing emphasis on ritual and standardized practices seemed irrelevant to their personal quest for salvation.

Hans Sebald Beham
Large Peasant Holiday, Woodcut, 1535
The celebration of the anniversary of a church's consecration was one of the most important holidays in a village. Not everyone, however, used this opportunity for spiritual ends, like the couple getting married in front of the church. Some overindulged at the tavern (lower right); some had a tooth extracted (center left); and some, as the chickens in the center and various couples in the scene suggest, used the occasion for pleasure alone.
Photograph © 1998. The Art Institute of Chicago. Potter Palmer Collection, 1967. 491. All rights reserved

And their reaction was symptomatic of the broad commitment to genuine piety that was apparent not only in the followers of Wycliffe, Hus, and Savonarola but in many segments of European society in the early 1500s.

Popular Religion

The Spread of Ideas   It was not only the educated elite and the city dwellers (a minority of Europe's inhabitants) who sought to express their faith in personal terms. The yearning for religious devotion among ordinary villagers, the majority of the population, was apparent even when the local priest—who was often hardly better educated than his parishioners—did little to inspire spiritual commitments. People would listen avidly to news of distant places brought by travelers who stopped at taverns and inns (a major source of information and ideas), and increasingly the tales they told were of religious upheaval. In addition, itinerant preachers roamed some regions, notably Central Europe, in considerable numbers, and they drew crowds when they started speaking—on street corners in towns or out in the fields—and described the power of faith. They usually urged direct communication between believers and God, free from ritual and complex doctrine. To the vast crowds they often drew, many of them seemed to echo the words of St. Augustine: "God and the soul I want to recognize, nothing else."

Equally important as a means of learning about the latest religious issues were the gatherings that regularly brought villagers together. Throughout the year, they would assemble to celebrate holidays—not only the landmarks of the Christian calendar like Christmas and Easter but also local festivals. Religion was always essential to these occasions. When, for example, the planting season arrived, the local priest would lead a procession into the countryside to bless the fields and pray for good crops. Family events, too, from birth to death, had important religious elements.

The Veillée   The most common occasion when the community's traditional beliefs and assumptions were aired, however, was the evening gathering—generally referred to by its French name, *veillée*, which means staying up in the evening. Between spring and autumn, when the weather was not too cold, a good part of the village came together at a central location after each day's work was done. There was little point in staying in one's own home after dark, because making a light with candles or oil was too expensive. Instead, sitting around a communal fire, people could sew clothes, repair tools, feed babies, resolve (or start) disputes, and discuss news. It was one of the few times when women were of no lesser status than men; the views they expressed were as important as any in shaping the common outlook of the villagers.

A favorite occupation at the *veillée* was listening to stories. Every village had its storytellers, who recounted wondrous tales of local history, of magical adventures, or of moral dilemmas, as the mood required. Biblical tales and the exploits of Christian heroes like the Crusaders had always drawn an attentive audience. Now, however, in addition to entertainment and general moral uplift, peddlers and travelers who attended the *veillée* brought news of challenges to religious traditions. They told of attacks on the pope and Church practices and of arguments for a simpler and more easily understood faith. In this way the ideas of religious reformers spread, and those with unorthodox views, such as the Lollards, kept their ideas alive. In some cases, the beliefs that were described made converts of those who heard them. Traveling preachers came to regard the *veillée* as a ready-made congregation; they were usually far more knowledgeable, better trained, and more effective than local priests.

The Role of the Priest   The response of the traditional Church to this challenge, after decades of indifference, was to insist that the local priest be better educated and more aware of what was at stake in the religious struggles of the day. As long as he had the support of the local authorities, he could make sure that his views dominated the *veillée*. Whichever way the discussions at these communal gatherings went, however, they demonstrated the power of popular piety in the tens of thousands of villages that dotted the European countryside.

The Impact of Printing   The expression of this piety received unexpected assistance from technology: the invention of a printing press with movable type in the mid-1400s. At least a hundred years earlier, Europeans had known that by carving words and pictures into a wood block, inking them, and pressing the block onto paper, they could make an image that could be repeated on many sheets of paper. We do not know exactly when they discovered that they could speed up this cumber-

Jost Amman
"THE PRINTER" FROM *DAS STÄNDEBUCH* (*THE BOOK OF TRADES*), 1568
This illustration is the first detailed depiction of a printer's shop, showing assistants taking type from large wooden holders in the back, the press on the right, the pages of type being prepared and inked in the foreground, and the sheets of paper before and after they are printed.

some process and change the text from page to page if they used individual letters and put them together within a frame. We do know, however, that a printer named Johannes Gutenberg, who lived in the city of Mainz on the Rhine, was producing books this way by the 1450s. The technique spread rapidly (see table on next page) and made reading material available to a much broader segment of the population.

It has been estimated that some nine million books had been printed by 1500. As a result, new ideas could travel with unprecedented speed. Perhaps a third of the men (and half that percentage of women) among the trading and upper classes—townspeople, the educated, and the nobility—could read, but books could reach a much wider audience, because peddlers began to sell printed materials throughout Europe. They were bought everywhere and became favorite material for reading out loud at *veillées*. Thus, people who had had

	German-	Italian-	French-					
Period	Speaking Areas			Spain	England*	Netherlands	Other	Total
Before 1471	18	4	1	1	—	—	—	14
1471–1480	22	36	9	6	3	12	5	93
1481–1490	17	13	21	12	—	5	4	72
1491–1500	9	5	11	6	—	2	8	41
Total by 1500	56	58	42	25	3	19	17	220

THE SPREAD OF PRINTING THROUGH 1500
Number of towns in which a printing press was established for the first time, by period and country

*In an attempt to try to control the printers, the English government ordered that they work only in London and at Oxford and Cambridge universities.

Adapted from Lucien Febvre and Henri-Jean Martin, *The Coming of the Book: The Impact of Printing 1450–1800*, David Gerald (tr.), London: NLB, 1976, pp. 178–179, 184–185.

little contact with written literature in the days of manuscripts now gained access to the latest ideas of the time.

Printing and Religion   Printers quickly took advantage of the popular interest in books by publishing almanacs filled with home-spun advice about the weather and nature that were written specifically for simple rural folk. Even the almanacs, however, carried religious advice. More importantly, translations of the Bible made it available to ordinary people in a language that, for the first time, they could understand. Books thus became powerful weapons in the religious conflicts of the day. Devotional tracts, lives of the saints, and the Bible were the most popular titles—often running to editions of around one thousand copies. They became means of spreading new ideas, and the ready markets they found reflected the general interest of the age in spiritual matters.

Printing lessened the dependence of ordinary people on the clergy; whereas traditionally the priest had read and interpreted the Scriptures for his congregation, now people could consult their own copies. By 1522, eighteen translations of the Bible had been published. Some fourteen thousand copies had been printed in German alone, enough to make it easy to buy in most German-speaking regions. The Church frowned on these efforts, and governments tried to regulate the numbers and locations of presses; but in the end it proved impossible to control the effects of printing.

Piety and Protest in Literature and Art

Literature   The printing press broke the Church's monopoly over the dissemination of religious teachings. The most gifted satirist of the sixteenth century, for

Matthias Grünewald
THE TEMPTATION OF ST. ANTHONY, CA. 1515
This detail from a series of scenes Grünewald painted for the Isenheim Altar suggests the power that the devil held over the imagination of sixteenth-century Europeans. The gentle, bearded St. Anthony is not seated in contemplation, as in Dürer's portrayal (see plate on p. 372). Instead, he is surrounded by the monsters the devil has sent to frighten him out of his faith. This fear was a favorite subject of the period and provided artists like Bosch and Grünewald the opportunity to make vivid and terrifying the ordinary Christian's fear of sin.
A panel from the Isenheim Altar. Musée d'Unterlinden, Colmar, France. Erich Lessing/Art Resource, NY

Albrecht Dürer
ENGRAVING OF ST. ANTHONY,
CA. 1600
The ease and mastery that Dürer brought to the art of engraving made it as powerful and flexible a form as painting. Here the massive figure of the saint, deep in study, is placed in front of a marvelously observed city. The buildings display Dürer's virtuosity—their shapes echo the bulk and solidity of the figure—and they may have symbolized the temptations of city life for a saint who was revered for his solitary piety in the desert.
Victoria & Albert Museum,
London/Art Resource, NY

instance, the French humanist François Rabelais, was able to ridicule openly the clergy and the morality of his day.

But the attacks came from many directions. Scurrilous **broadsides**, usually anonymous, became very popular during the religious disputes of the 1500s. These single sheets often contained vicious assaults on religious opponents and were usually illustrated by cartoons with obscene imagery. The broadsides were examples of partisan hostility, but their broader significance should not be ignored. Even the most lowly of hack writers could share with a serious author like Rabelais a sense of outrage at indifference in high places and find an audience for attacks on the inadequate spiritual leadership of the time.

Piety in Art The emphasis on religious belief, so evident in European literature, also permeated the work of northern artists (see plates on p. 354 and p. 371). The gruesome paintings of Hieronymus Bosch, for example, depicted the fears of devils and hell that troubled his contemporaries at all times. He put on canvas the demons, the temptations, the terrible punishments for sin that people considered as real as their tangible surroundings. His paintings explored the darker side of faith, taking inspiration from the fear of damnation and the hope for salvation—the first seen in the demons, the second in the redeeming Christ.

The depth of piety, conveyed by an artist such as Bosch, reflected the temper of Europe. In art and literature, as in lay organizations and the continuing popularity of itinerant preachers, people showed their concern for individual spiritual values and their dissatisfaction with a Church that was not meeting their needs.

Christian Humanism

No segment of society expressed the strivings and yearnings of the age more eloquently than the northern humanists. The salient features of the Humanist movement in Italy—its theory of education, its emphasis on eloquence, its reverence for the ancients, and its endorsement of active participation in affairs of state—began to win wide acceptance north of the Alps in the late 1400s. But the northerners added a significant religious dimension to the movement by devoting considerable attention to early Christian literature: the Bible and the writings of the Church fathers. As a result, they have been called *Christian humanists.*

The Northern Humanists By the end of the fifteenth century the influence of Humanism, carried by the printing press, was Europe-wide. The northern Humanists were particularly determined to probe early Christianity for the light it could throw on the origins and accuracy of current religious teachings. Indeed, northern Humanism's broad examination of religious issues in the early 1500s helped create an atmosphere in which much more serious criticism of the Church could flourish.

The Christian humanists did not abandon the interest in classical authors or the methods for analyzing ancient texts, language, and style that had been developed by Italian Humanism. But they put these methods to a new use: analysis of the Bible in order to explain more clearly the message of Jesus and his apostles, and thus to provide a better guide to true piety and morality. This deeply religious undertaking dominated the writings of the two most famous Christian humanists, one English and one Dutch.

More   Sir Thomas More (1478–1535), a lawyer and statesman, was the central figure of English Humanism. His reputation as a writer rests primarily on a short work, *Utopia*, published in Latin in 1516, which describes an ideal society on an imaginary island. In it, More condemned war, poverty, intolerance, and other evils of his day and defined the general principles of morality that he felt should underlie human society. The first book of *Utopia* addresses the conflict between the active and the contemplative life that Petrarch had emphasized and asks whether a learned person should withdraw from the world to avoid the corruptions of politics or participate in affairs of state so as to guide policy. In his own career, More chose the latter path, with fatal results. The second, more famous, book of *Utopia* leaves such practical issues aside and describes what an ideal commonwealth might be like. Utopia's politics and society are carefully regulated, an almost monastic community that has succeeded in abolishing private property, greed, and pride—and thus has freed its inhabitants from some of the worst sins of More's day. Well-designed institutions, education, and discipline are his answer to human failings: Weak human nature can be led to virtuousness only if severely curbed.

Deeply devout and firmly attached to the traditional Church, More entered public life as a member of Parliament in 1504. He rose high in government service, but eventually he gave his life for remaining loyal to the pope and refusing to recognize the decision of his king, Henry VIII, to reject papal authority and become head of the English Church. When Henry had him beheaded for treason, More's last words revealed his unflinching adherence to the Christian principles he pursued throughout his life: "I die the King's good servant, but God's first."

Erasmus   The supreme representative of Christian Humanism was the Dutchman Desiderius Erasmus (ca. 1466–1536). Erasmus early acquired a taste for ancient writers, and he determined to devote himself to classical studies. For the greater part of his life, he wandered through Europe, writing, visiting friends, and occasionally working for important patrons. He always retained his independence, however, for unlike More, he answered the question of whether a scholar should enter public life by avoiding the compromises a ruler might demand.

Erasmus was so famous for his learning that he dominated the intellectual world of letters of his time. Con-

Hans Holbein the Younger
***PORTRAIT OF ERASMUS OF ROTTERDAM*, 1523**
The leading portraitist of the age, Hans Holbein, painted his friend Erasmus a number of times. Here he shows the great scholar at work, possibly writing one of the many elegantly constructed letters that he sent to colleagues throughout Europe. The richness of the scene bears noting: the gold ring, the fine coat with a fur collar, and the splendid tapestry hanging over the paneled wall.
Louvre, Paris, France. Scala/Art Resource, NY

stantly consulted by scholars and admirers, he wrote magnificently composed letters that reflected every aspect of the culture of his age. He became known throughout Europe, however, as a result of a little book, *The Praise of Folly* (1509), which was one of the first best-sellers created by the printing press. Some of it is lighthearted banter that pokes fun at the author himself, his friends, and the follies of everyday life and suggests that a little folly is essential to human existence. The book also points out that Christianity itself is a kind of folly, a belief in "things not seen." In many passages, though, Erasmus launches sharply satirical attacks against monks, the pope, meaningless ceremonies, and the many lapses from what he perceived to be the true Christian spirit.

The Philosophy of Christ At the heart of Erasmus' work was the message that he called the "philosophy of Christ." He believed that the life of Jesus and especially his teachings in the Sermon on the Mount should be models for Christian piety and morality. For the Church's ceremonies and for rigid discipline, he had only censure: Too often, he said, they served as substitutes for genuine spiritual concerns. People lit candles, for instance, but forgot that true devotion, meant far more than such practices. By simply following the precepts of Jesus, he argued, a Christian could lead a life guided by sincere faith. Because of his insistence on ethical behavior, Erasmus could admire truly moral people even if they were pagans. "I could almost say, 'Pray for me, St. Socrates!'" he once wrote.

Erasmus believed that the Church had lost sight of its original mission. In the course of fifteen centuries, traditions and practices had developed that obscured the intentions of its founder, and purity could be restored only by studying the Scriptures and the writings of the early Church fathers. Here, the literary and analytic tools of the humanists became vitally important because they enabled scholars to understand the meaning and intention of ancient manuscripts. Practicing what he preached, Erasmus spent ten years preparing a new edition of the Greek text of the New Testament so as to correct errors in the Latin **Vulgate**, which was the standard version, and he revised it repeatedly for another twenty years. But the calm, scholarly, and tolerant moderation Erasmus prized was soon left behind by events. The rising intensity of religious reformers and their opponents destroyed the effort he had led to cure the ills of the Church quietly, from within. Erasmus wanted a revival of purer faith, but he would never have dreamed of rejecting the traditional authority of the Church. As Europe entered an age of confrontation, he found it impossible to preserve a middle course between the two sides, and he was swept aside by revolutionary forces that he himself had helped build but that Martin Luther was to unleash.

THE LUTHERAN REFORMATION

The disputes over doctrine and the yearning for piety helped undermine the authority of the Roman Church. But it took a charismatic individual of extraordinary determination to break apart an institution that had survived for a thousand years. And without political support, even he could not have succeeded.

The Conditions for Change

That a major religious conflict should have erupted in the Holy Roman Empire is not surprising. In this territory of fragmented government, with hundreds of independent local princes, popular piety was noticeably strong. Yet anyone who was unhappy with Church leadership had all the more reason to resent the power of bishops, because in the empire they were often also princes—such as the aristocratic bishop who ruled the important city of Cologne on the Rhine. There were few strong secular princes who could protect the people from the fiscal demands of the Church, and the popes therefore regarded the empire as their surest source of revenue.

This situation was made more volatile by the ambitions of the secular princes. Their ostensible overlord, the emperor, had no real power over them, and they worked tirelessly to strengthen their control over their subjects and to assert their independence from all outside authority. A number of them were, in fact, to see the religious upheavals of the 1500s as a means of advancing their own political purposes. Their ambitions help explain why a determined reformer, Martin Luther, won such swift and widespread support.

Martin Luther

Martin Luther (1483–1546) was born into a miner's family in Saxony in central Germany. The household was dominated by the father, whose powerful presence some modern commentators have seen reflected in his son's vision of an omnipotent God. The boy received a good education and decided to become a lawyer, a profession that would have given him many opportunities for advancement. But in his early twenties, shortly after starting his legal studies, he had an experience that changed his life. Crossing a field during a thunderstorm, he was thrown to the ground by a bolt of lightning, and in his terror he cried out to St. Anne that he would enter a monastery.

Luther in the Monastery Although the decision may well have been that sudden, it is clear that there was more to Luther's change of direction than this one incident, however traumatic. A highly sensitive, energetic, and troubled young man, he had become obsessed with his own sinfulness, and he joined a monastery as an Augustinian friar in the hope that a penitential life would help him overcome his sense of guilt. Once in the monastery, he pursued every possible opportunity to earn worthiness in the sight of God. He overlooked no means of discipline or act of contrition or self-denial, and for added merit he endured austerities, such as self-flagellation, that went far beyond normal requirements. But it was all useless: When officiating at his first Mass after his ordination in 1507, he was so terrified at the idea of a sinner like himself administering the sacrament of the Eucharist—that is, transforming

LUTHER'S "EXPERIENCE IN THE TOWER"

The following passage was written by Luther in 1545, at least twenty-five years after the experience it describes. As a result, scholars have been unable to decide (a) whether the breakthrough was in fact as sudden as Luther suggests; (b) when it took place—possibly as early as 1512, five years before the indulgence dispute, or as late as 1519, when Luther was already under attack for his views; or (c) how it should be interpreted—as a scholar's insight, as a revelation from God, or as Luther's later crystallization into a single event of a process that had taken many years.

"I wanted very much to understand Paul's Epistle to the Romans, but despite my determination to do so I kept being stopped by the one word, 'the righteousness of God.' I hated that word, because I had been taught to understand it as the active righteousness by which a just God punishes unjust sinners. The trouble was that, although I may have been an impeccable monk, I felt myself to be a sinner before God. As a result, not only was I unable to love, but I actually hated this just God, who punishes all sinners. And so I raged, yet I still longed to understand St. Paul.

"At last, as I grappled with the words day and night, God had mercy on me, and I saw the connection between the words 'the righteousness of God' and 'The righteous shall live by faith' (Romans 1:17). I understood that the righteousness of God refers to the gift by which God enables the just to live—that is, by faith. A merciful God justifies us by faith, as it is written: 'The righteous shall live by faith.' At that point, I felt as if I had been reborn and had passed through open doors into paradise. The whole of Scripture took on new meaning. As I had previously hated the phrase, 'the righteousness of God,' so now I lovingly praised it."

Translation from the Latin by Theodore K. Rabb of Luther's preface to the 1545 edition of his writings, in Otto Scheel (ed.), *Dokumente zu Luthers Entwicklung*, Tübingen: Mohr, 1929, pp. 191–192.

the wafer and wine into the body and blood of Christ—that he almost failed to complete the ritual.

Fortunately for Luther, his superiors took more notice of his intellectual gifts than his self-doubts, and in 1508 they assigned him to the faculty of a new university in Wittenberg, the capital of Saxony. It was from his scholarship, which was excellent, and especially from his study of the Bible, that he was able at last to draw comfort and spiritual peace.

Justification by Faith   This second crucial change in Luther's life, as important as the entry into the monastery, happened while he was preparing his university lectures. Until this event, which is known as "the experience in the tower," Luther could see no way that he, a despicable mortal, could receive anything but the fiercest punishments from a God of absolute justice. Now, however, he had an insight that led him to understand that he needed only to rely on God's mercy, a quality as great as divine justice (see "Luther's 'Experience in the Tower,'" above). The many advances in Luther's thinking thereafter came from this insight: that justification—which removes sin and bestows righteousness through a gift of grace—is achieved by faith alone.

The Break with Rome

In 1517 an event occurred that was ultimately to lead Luther to an irrevocable break with the Church. In the spring, a friar, Johann Tetzel, began to peddle **indulgences** a few miles from Wittenberg as part of a huge fund-raising effort to pay for the new Church of St. Peter in Rome. Originally, an indulgence had been granted to anyone going on a crusade. It was then extended to those who, though unable to join a crusade, gave enough money for a poor crusader to be able to reach the Holy Land. Indulgences released sinners from a certain period of punishment in purgatory before they went on to heaven; the theory was that they drew on a sort of credit from the treasury of merit built up by Jesus and the saints. But neither the theory nor the connection with money had been fully defined, and clerics had taken advantage of this vagueness simply to sell indulgences. Tetzel, an expert peddler, was offering complete releases from purgatory without bothering to mention the repentance that, according to Church teachings, was essential if a sinner was to be forgiven or absolved.

The Ninety-Five Theses   The people of Wittenberg were soon flocking to Tetzel to buy this easy guarantee of salvation. For Luther, a man groping toward an evangelical solution of his own doubts, it was unforgivable that people should be deprived of their hard-earned money for worthless promises. On October 31, 1517, he published in Wittenberg ninety-five theses, or statements, on indulgences that he offered to debate with experts in Christian doctrine.

Jörg Breu
ENGRAVING DEPICTING THE SALE OF INDULGENCES, CA. 1530
This scene would have been a familiar one in Europe until Luther's attacks brought it to an end. The clerics on their fine horses on the right bring a cross and the papal bull, which is authenticated by the elaborate seals and ribbons that hang from it. The faithful put money in the barrel in the middle or hand it to the dispenser of certificates on the left, who sits near the large locked chest that will hold the revenues from the sales.
Bildarchiv Preussischer Kulturbesitz, Berlin/Art Resource, NY

This was no revolutionary document. It merely described, in Latin, what Luther believed to be correct teachings on indulgences: that the pope could remit only the penalties that he himself or canon law imposed; that, therefore, the promise of a general pardon was damnable; and that every true believer shared in the treasury of merit left by Jesus and the saints, whether or not he or she obtained an indulgence. Within a few weeks, the story was all over the empire that a monk had challenged the sale of indulgences. The proceeds of Tetzel's mission began to drop off; and other members of his order, the Dominicans, rallied to their brother by attacking his presumptuous critic, Luther, of the rival order of the Augustinians.

Luther Elaborates   The controversy soon drew attention in Rome. At first, Pope Leo X regarded the affair as merely a monks' quarrel. But, in time, Luther's responses to the Dominicans' attacks began to deviate radically from Church doctrine, and by 1520 he had gone so far as to challenge the authority of the papacy itself.

In three pamphlets published that year, he outlined where he stood. He asked Emperor Charles V to call a council to end the abuses of the Church. He attacked the belief that the seven sacraments, the basis of the Church's authority, were the only means of attaining grace and thus salvation By accepting only two, baptism and the Eucharist, he asserted that justification was by faith alone. And, though he did not reject good works, he insisted that only the individual believer's faith could bring salvation from an all-powerful, just, and merciful God. These views had an overwhelming impact on Luther's fellow Germans. His appeal to their resentment of Church power and their wish for a more personal faith made him, almost overnight, the embodiment of a widespread yearning for religious reform.

The Diet of Worms   There could no longer be any doubt that Luther was breaking with the Church, and in 1520 Pope Leo X issued a bull excommunicating him. Luther publicly tossed the document into a bonfire, defending his action by calling the pope an Antichrist. In 1521 Emperor Charles V, who was officially the papacy's secular representative, summoned the celebrated monk to offer his defense against the papal decree at a **Diet** of the empire (a meeting of princes, city leaders, and churchmen) at Worms, a city on the Rhine.

The journey across Germany was a triumphant progress for Luther, who now seemed a heroic figure. Appearing before the magnificent assembly dressed in his simple friar's robe, he offered a striking contrast to the display of imperial and princely grandeur. First in German and then in Latin, he made the famous declaration that closed the last door behind him: "I cannot and will not recant anything, since it is unsafe and wrong to go against my conscience. Here I stand. I cannot do otherwise. God help me. Amen." On the following day the emperor gave his reply: "A single friar who goes counter to all Christianity for a thousand years must be wrong."

Luther Protected   Charles added legality to the papal bull by issuing an imperial edict calling for Luther's arrest and the burning of his works. At this point, however, the independent power of the German princes and their resentment of foreign ecclesiastical interference came to the reformer's aid. The Elector Frederick III of Saxony, who had never met Luther and who was never to break with the traditional Church, nonetheless determined to protect the rebel, who lived in his territory. A fake kidnapping brought Luther to the Wartburg castle, one of Frederick's strongholds, and here Luther remained for almost a year, safe from his enemies.

Lutheran Doctrine and Practice

While at the Wartburg castle, Luther, together with his friend Philipp Melanchthon, developed his ideas and shaped them into a formal set of beliefs that influenced most of the subsequent variations of Protestant Christianity. Codified in 1530 in a document known as the Augsburg Confession, these doctrines have remained the basis of Lutheranism ever since.

Faith and the Bible   The two fundamental assertions of Luther's teachings derive from the emphasis on God's power and mystery that Luther learned in his nominalist monastery. First, faith alone—not good works or the receiving of the sacraments—justifies the believer in the eyes of God and wins redemption. People themselves are helpless and unworthy sinners who can do nothing to cooperate in their own salvation; God bestows faith on those he chooses to save. Second, the Bible is the sole source of religious authority. It alone carries the word of God, and Christians must reject all other authorities: Church tradition, commentaries on the Bible, or the pronouncements of popes and Church councils.

These two doctrines had far-reaching implications. According to Luther, all people are equally capable of understanding God's word as expressed in the Bible and can gain salvation without the help of intermediaries; they do not need a priest endowed with special powers or an interceding church. Luther thus saw God's faithful as a "priesthood of all believers," a concept totally foreign to the traditional Church, which insisted on the distinction between clergy and laity. The distinction disappeared in Luther's doctrines, because all the faithful shared the responsibilities formerly reserved for priests.

Sacraments and the Mass   True to his reliance on biblical authority, Luther retained only two sacraments—baptism and the Eucharist—as means by which God distributes grace. Moreover, the ceremony of the Eucharist was now called *communion* (literally, "sharing") to emphasize that all worshipers, including the officiating clergy, were equal; all shared both wafer and wine. Luther also reduced the distinctiveness of priests by giving them the right to marry.

Luther's teachings on the sacraments transformed the Mass, the ceremony that surrounds the Eucharist. According to traditional dogma, when the priest raises

Lucas Cranach the Elder
PORTRAIT OF MARTIN LUTHER, **1529**
One of the first faces made familiar by portraits, but not belonging to a nobleman, was Luther's. Cranach painted the reformer a number of times, so we can see what he looked like at various periods of his life. Luther here is in his early forties, a determined figure who four years earlier had made his stand at the Diet of Worms.
Uffizi, Florence, Italy. Scala/Art Resource, NY

the wafer, the host, during the Mass and recites the words *Hoc est corpus meum* ("This is my body"), the sacrifice of Jesus on the cross is reenacted. The wafer and the wine retain their outward appearance, their "accidents," but their substance is transformed into the body and blood of Christ—in other words, transubstantiation takes place.

Luther asserted that the wafer and wine retain their substance as well as their accidents at the moment the priest says, "This is my body." The real presence of Christ and the natural substance coexist within the wafer and wine. Nothing suddenly happens; there is no miraculous moment. Instead, the believer is simply

CARTOON FROM LUTHERAN WOODCUT BROADSIDE
Vicious cartoons were a favorite device of religious propaganda during the Age of Religious Reformation. They were especially popular for an illiterate audience, which had to get the message from pictures. The more vivid the image, the easier it was to understand. Here the Protestants show the enemies of Luther as vicious animals. One theologian is a cat eating a mouse; another is a dog holding a bone. The pope is in the middle, reaching out to Eck.
Germanisches Nationalmuseum, Nürnberg

made aware of the real presence of God, who is everywhere at all times. Again, it is the faith of the individual, not the ceremony itself, that counts. Moreover, by allowing the congregation to drink the wine—as Hus had demanded—Luther further reduced the mystery of the Lord's Supper and undermined the position of the priest. And by abolishing the use of Latin, processions, incense, and votive candles, he simplified services and gave ordinary people a greater role in worship.

Translation of the Bible   With the priest reduced in stature, it was vital to make God's word more readily available to the faithful, so that they could read or hear the Bible for themselves. To this end, Luther began the long task of translating the Bible. He completed the work in 1534, creating a text that is a milestone in the history of the German language. Families were encouraged to read Scripture on their own, and the reformed faith stimulated rising literacy among women as well as men. This was Luther's last major contribution to the religious changes of the sixteenth century. Although he lived until 1546, henceforth the progress of the revolution he had launched would rely on outside forces: its popular appeal and the actions of political leaders.

The Spread of Lutheranism

It is usually said that Lutheranism spread from above, advancing only when princes and rulers helped it along. Although this view has some merit, it does not adequately explain the growth of the movement. The response to Luther's stand was immediate and widespread. Even before the Diet of Worms, preachers critical of the Church were drawing audiences in many parts of the Holy Roman Empire, and in 1521 there were

waves of image smashing, reports of priests marrying, and efforts to reform and simplify the sacraments.

Soon there were congregations following Luther's teachings throughout the empire and neighboring countries. Broadsides and pamphlets fresh from the printing presses rapidly disseminated the reformer's message, and they stimulated an immediate response from thousands who welcomed the opportunity to renew their faith.

Radical Preachers   As long as his own doctrines remained unaltered, Luther was naturally delighted to see his teachings spread. But from the start, people drew inferences that he could not tolerate. Early in 1522, for example, three men from the nearby town of Zwickau appeared in Wittenberg claiming to be prophets who enjoyed direct communication with God. Their ideas were, in Luther's eyes, damnable. When he returned from Wartburg castle, therefore, he preached eight sermons to expose their errors—a futile effort, because the movement to reform the Church was now too dispersed to control. Capitalizing on mass discontent, radical preachers incited disturbances in the name of faith, and soon social as well as religious protest exploded, posing a new challenge for Luther as he struggled to keep his reform movement under control.

Social and Religious Protest   The first trouble arose in the summer of 1522, started by the weakest independent group in the empire, the imperial knights. The knights occupied a precarious social position, because they rarely owned more than a single castle. They accepted no authority but the emperor himself, and they resented the growing power of cities and princes (rulers of large territories) in the empire. Calling themselves true representatives of the imperial system—that is, loyal supporters of the emperor, unlike the cities and princes who wanted to be more independent—and using Lutheranism as further justification, the knights launched an attack on one of the leading ecclesiastical rulers, the archbishop of Trier. They were crushed within a year, but the Lutherans' opponents could now suggest that the new religious teachings undermined law and order.

Peasant Revolt   The banner of the new faith rose over popular revolts as well. A peasant uprising began in Swabia in 1524 and quickly engulfed the southern and central parts of the empire. Citing Luther's inspiration, and especially his teaching that faith was all the individual needed, the peasants published a list of twelve demands in 1525. Admittedly, ten of their grievances concerned social, not religious, injustices: They wanted an end to the restrictions and burdens imposed by their overlords, including prohibitions on hunting and fishing, excessive rents and services, and unlawful punishments. But they also had two religious aims: They wanted the right to choose their own pastors, and they refused to accept any authority other than Scripture to determine whether their demands were justified.

Luther sympathized with the last two claims, and at first he considered the peasants' demands reasonable. But when it became apparent that they were challenging all authority, he ignored the oppressions they had suffered and wrote a vicious pamphlet, *Against the Rapacious and Murdering Peasants,* calling on the nobility to cut them down without mercy so as to restore peace. A few months later the rebels were defeated in battle, and thereafter Luther threw his support unreservedly on the side of the princes and the established political and social order. He also grew more virulent in his attacks on Catholics and Jews and became as insistent as the Roman Church he was defying that his doctrines were not to be questioned.

Lutheranism Established

The advance of Lutheranism thus far had depended largely on its appeal to the ordinary believer, and it continued to enjoy wide support. But when Luther was forced to choose between the demands of his humblest followers and the authority of the princes who had protected him, he opted for the princes. It was a decision that enabled his movement to survive and may well have saved him from the fate of Hus a century before. Had Luther not condemned the disorders, he would doubtless have been abandoned by the princes, and without their backing he and his followers could not have stood up to the traditional Church or been safe from the power of Charles V.

Luther's Conservatism   One of the reasons the new set of beliefs attracted these princes was its conservatism. Any person who adopted the basic doctrines of justification by faith alone and Scripture as the sole authority could be accepted as a Lutheran. Consequently, the new congregations could retain much from the old religion: most of the liturgy, the sacred music, and, particularly important, a structured church that, though less hierarchical than before, was still organized to provide order and authority.

The Lutheran Princes   Some rulers were swept up by the same emotions that moved their subjects, but others were moved by more material interests. Since the Church lost all its property when reform was introduced, princes could confiscate the rich and extensive ecclesiastical holdings in their domains. Furthermore, they now had added reason for flaunting their independence from Emperor Charles V, an unwavering upholder of orthodoxy. It was risky to adopt this policy, for Charles could strip a prince of his title. And if a prince promised to remain loyal to the Church, he could blackmail the pope into offering him almost as many riches as he could win by confiscation.

Nevertheless, the appeal of the new faith eventually tipped the balance for enough princes to create a formidable party capable of resisting Charles's power. While they were attending an imperial Diet at Speyer in 1529, they signed a declaration "protesting" the Diet's decree that no religious innovations were to be introduced in the empire. Thereafter, all who accepted religious reform, including the Lutherans, were known as Protestants; and adherents of the traditional Church, led from Rome, which continued to claim that it was universal (or catholic), came to be known as Roman Catholics.

The following year, at another imperial Diet, the Lutheran princes announced their support of the Augsburg Confession, the official statement of Lutheran doctrines that had been prepared by Melanchthon and Luther. Charles V now threatened to use military force to crush the heresy, and in the face of this danger, the Lutherans formed a defensive league in 1531 at the small Saxon town of Schmalkalden. Throughout the 1530s this alliance consolidated Protestant gains, brought new princes into the cause, and, in general, amassed sufficient strength to deter Charles, who was repeatedly distracted by foreign wars, from decisive military action.

War over Religion   The reform party became so solidly established that it negotiated with the Catholics on equal terms about the possibility of reconciliation in 1541, but the talks collapsed, and the chances for a reunification of Christendom evaporated. Not until 1546, the year of Luther's death, however, did

ENGRAVING OF THE DIET OF AUGSBURG, 1530
At the Diet—the meeting of the princes and cities of the Holy Roman Empire—in Augsburg in 1530, the Lutherans presented to the emperor, Charles V, a statement, or "confession," of their faith. This "Confession of Augsburg" became the founding doctrine of the Lutheran Church. It was rejected as heretical by Charles, but he could not suppress it. One of the Lutheran princes told him in 1530 that he would rather have his head cut off than attend a Catholic mass. Charles was unable to crush such defiance.
Bibliothèque Nationale de France, Paris

open war begin. Then, after a brief campaign, Charles won a crushing victory over the Lutherans in 1547. But matters had advanced too far for their movement to collapse merely because of a single defeat on the battlefield. The new faith had won the devotion of a large part of the German people, particularly in the north and the east, farthest away from the center of imperial power. Some of the great cities of the south, such as Nuremberg, which had been centers of Humanism, had also come over to the Lutheran side. By the 1550s Lutheranism had captured about half the population of the empire.

The Catholic princes also played a part in ensuring the survival of the new faith. Fearful of Charles V's new power, they refused to cooperate in his attempt to establish his authority throughout the empire, and he had to rely on Spanish troops, who further alienated him from his subjects. The Lutherans regrouped after their 1547 defeat, and in 1555 the imperial Diet at Augsburg drew up a compromise settlement that exposed the decline of the emperor's power. Henceforth,

each prince was allowed to determine the religion of his own territory, Lutheran or Catholic, and his subjects could leave (a major concession) if they were of the other faith. Religious uniformity was at an end, and the future of Lutheranism was secure.

The Heritage of Lutheranism The influence that this first Protestant Church was to exert on all of European life was immense. The idea that all believers were equal in the eyes of God inspired revolutionary changes in thought and society. It justified antimonarchical constitutional theories, it allowed people to feel that all occupations were equally worthy and that there was nothing wrong with the life of the merchant or even the moneylender, and it undermined the hierarchic view of the universe. One can easily overstate the notion that Lutheranism made people more self-reliant, because independent and pioneering behavior was far from new. Nevertheless, there is no question that, by condemning the traditional reliance on priests and the Church and by making individuals responsible for their own salvation, Luther did encourage his followers to act on their own. Yet the new faith had its most immediate effect on religious life itself: Before the century was out, the dissent started by Luther inspired a multitude of sects and a ferment of ideas without precedent in the history of Europe.

THE SPREAD OF PROTESTANTISM

Hardly had Luther made his protest in 1517 when religious dissent in many different forms suddenly appeared. It was as if no more was needed than one opening shot before a volley of discontent broke out—testimony to the deep and widespread desire for individual piety of the times.

Zwingli and the Radicals

Zwingli's Reforms   The most influential of the new initiatives began in the Swiss city of Zurich, where reform was led by Ulrich Zwingli (1484–1531), a priest, humanist, and disciple of Erasmus. The doctrines he began to develop between 1519 and 1522 were similar to Luther's in that Zwingli based his ideas entirely on Scripture and emphasized faith alone. Suspicious of any reliance on Church rituals, Zwingli, even more than Luther, wanted to simplify religious belief and practice. In his view, none of the sacraments bestowed grace; they were merely signs of grace already given. Thus, baptism is symbolic, not a ceremony that regenerates the recipient; and communion is no more than a memorial and thanksgiving for the grace given by God, who is present only symbolically—not in actuality, as Luther believed.

Despite his obvious debt to Luther, Zwingli diverged significantly from the German. His new form of Protestantism was more thoroughly dependent on the individual believer and more devoid of mystery and ritual than anything Luther could accept. Zwingli saw a need for constant correction if people were to lead godly lives, and he established a tribunal of clergy and secular officials to enforce discipline among the faithful. They supervised all moral issues, from compulsory church attendance to the public behavior of amorous couples. They could excommunicate flagrant transgressors, and they maintained constant surveillance—through a network of informers—to keep the faithful moral and godly. Because Zwingli considered education vital for discipline, he founded a theological school and authorized a new translation of the Bible. He also insisted on lengthy sermons at each service. Worship was stripped bare, as were the churches, and preaching began to assume tremendous importance as a means of instructing believers and strengthening their faith. Zwingli also revived the ancient Christian practice of public confession of sin—yet another reinforcement of discipline.

Zwingli's Church   Zwingli's ideas spread rapidly in the Swiss Confederation, helped by the virtual autonomy of each canton, or region. By 1529 a number of cantons had accepted Zwinglianism. As a result, two camps formed in the country, and a war broke out in 1531 in which Zwingli himself was killed. Thereafter, the Swiss Confederation remained split between Catholics and reformers. Zwinglianism never grew into a major religion, but it had a considerable effect on later forms of Protestantism, particularly Calvinism.

The Anabaptists   Both Luther and Zwingli wanted to retain Church authority, and both therefore insisted that infant baptism was the moment of entry into the Church, even though this belief had no scriptural sanction. Some radical reformers, however, insisted on taking the Bible literally and argued that, as in biblical times, baptism should be administered only to mature adults who could make a conscious choice to receive grace, not to infants who could not understand what was happening. Soon these reformers were being called **Anabaptists** ("rebaptizers") by their enemies. The term is often applied to all radicals, though in fact it described only one conspicuous group.

Radical Sects   Diversity was inevitable among the radical reformers, most of whom refused to recognize church organization, rejected priests, and gave individual belief free rein, sometimes to the point of recognizing only personal communication with God and disregarding Scripture. Many groups of like-minded radicals formed small sects—voluntary associations that rarely included more than one hundred or so adults—in an effort to achieve complete separation from the world and avoid compromising their ideals. They wanted to set an example for others by adhering fervently to the truth as they saw it, regardless of the consequences. Some sects established little **utopian** communities, holding everything in common, including property and spouses. Others disdained all worldly things and lived only for the supreme ecstasy of a trance in which they made direct contact with God himself. Many, believing in the imminent coming of the Messiah, prepared themselves for the end of the world and the Day of Judgment.

Persecution of the Radicals

Such variety in the name of a personal search for God was intolerable to major reformers like Luther and Zwingli, who believed that their own doctrines were the only means of salvation. Once these branches of Protestantism were firmly entrenched, they, like the

Catholic Church, became deeply committed to the status quo and to their own hierarchies and traditions.
The established reformers thus regarded the radicals'
refusal to conform as an unmistakable sign of damnation, and they were just as ready as Catholics to persecute those who rejected their particular brand of
salvation.

Münster and the Melchiorites   The assault on the radicals began in the mid-1520s and soon spread through
most of Europe. The imperial Diet in 1529, for instance, called for the death penalty against all Anabaptists. Finally, in the northwest German city of
Münster, a particularly fiery sect, inspired by a
"prophet" named Melchior and known as Melchiorites,
provoked a reaction that signaled doom even for less
radical dissenters.

The Melchiorites had managed to gain considerable
influence over the ordinary workers of Münster and
over the craft guilds to which many belonged. They
gained political control of the city early in 1534 and began to establish their "heavenly Jerusalem" on earth.
They burned all books except the Bible, abolished private property, introduced polygamy, and in an atmosphere of abandon and chaos, dug in to await the
coming of the Messiah. Here was a threat to society
sufficient to force Protestants and Catholics into an alliance, and they captured the city and brutally massacred the Melchiorites. Thereafter, the radicals were
savagely persecuted throughout the empire. To survive,
many fled, first to Poland, then to the Low Countries
and England, and eventually to the New World.

John Calvin

During the 1530s, Protestantism began to fragment.
Neither Lutherans nor Zwinglians expanded much beyond the areas in which their reforms had begun; sects
multiplied but gained few followers; and it might have
seemed that the original energy had left the movement.
In the early 1540s, however, a new dynamism and also
a more elaborate and systematic body of doctrine were
brought to Protestantism by a second-generation reformer, John Calvin (1509–1564). Born in Noyon, a
small town in northern France, Calvin studied both
law and the humanities at the University of Paris. In
his early twenties he apparently had a shattering spiritual experience that he later called his "sudden conversion," an event about which he would say almost
nothing else. Yet from that moment on, all his energy
was devoted to religious reform.

In November 1533 Calvin was indicted by French
Church authorities for holding heretical views, and after
more than a year in hiding, he took refuge in the Swiss
city of Basel. There, in 1536, he published a little treatise, *Institutes of the Christian Religion*, outlining the
principles of a new system of belief. He would revise and
expand the *Institutes* for the remainder of his life, and it
was to become the basis of Calvinism, the most vigorous
branch of Protestantism in the sixteenth century.

Geneva Later in 1536, Calvin settled in Geneva, where, except for a brief period, he was to remain until his death and where he was to create a new church in the 1540s. The citizens of this prosperous market center had just overthrown their prince, a Catholic bishop. In achieving their independence, they had allied with other Swiss cities, notably Bern, a recent convert to Zwinglianism. Rebels who, with the help of Protestants, had just freed themselves from an ecclesiastical overlord were understandably receptive to new religious teachings, though Calvin's beliefs were also supported by persecution and intolerance.

Calvinism

Outwardly, Calvinism seemed to have much in common with Lutheranism. Both emphasized people's sinfulness, lack of free will, and helplessness; both rejected good works as a means of salvation; both accepted only two sacraments, baptism and communion; both regarded all occupations as equally worthy in the sight of God; both strongly upheld established political and social authority; and both had similar views of faith, people's weaknesses, and God's omnipotence. But the emphases in Calvinism were very different.

Predestination In arguing for justification by faith alone, Luther assumed that God can predestine a person to be saved but rejected the idea that damnation can also be preordained. Calvin's faith was much sterner. He recognized no such distinction: If people are damned, they should praise God's justice, because their sins certainly merit such a judgment; if people are saved, they should praise God's mercy, because their salvation is not a result of their own merits. Either way, the outcome is predestined, and nothing can be done to affect an individual's fate. It is up to God to save a person; he then perseveres in his mercy despite the person's sins; and finally, he alone decides whether to receive the sinner into the small band of saints, or elect, whom he brings into heaven. Calvin's was a grim but powerful answer to the age-old Christian question: How can sinful human beings gain salvation?

Calvin believed that our behavior here on earth, whether good or bad, is no indication of our fate. He did suggest that someone who is to be saved by God is likely to be upright and moral, but such conduct is not necessarily a sign of salvation. However, because we should try to please God at all times, and because our communities ought to be fitting places for the elect to live, we must make every effort to lead lives worthy of one of the elect.

Morality and Discipline Calvin therefore developed a strict moral code for the true believer that banned frivolous activities, like dancing, in favor of constant self-examination, austerity, and sober study of the Bible. To help the faithful observe such regulation, he reestablished public confessions, as Zwingli had, and required daily preaching. He made services starkly simple: Stripped of ornaments, worship concentrated on uplifting sermons and the celebration of communion. His doctrine of communion occupied a middle ground between Luther's and Zwingli's. He rejected Zwingli's interpretation, saying instead that Christ's body and blood were actually and not just symbolically present. But unlike Luther, he held that they were present only in spirit and were consumed only spiritually, by faith.

To supervise the morals of the faithful and ensure that the community was worthy of the elect, Calvin gave his church a strict hierarchical structure. It was controlled by church officials called deacons and by lay elders, who were able to function even in the hostile territories where many Calvinists found themselves. A body of lay elders called the *consistory* served as the chief ecclesiastical authority. These elders enforced discipline and had the power of excommunication, though local officials imposed the actual punishments—most notoriously in 1553, when a radical who denied the Trinity, Michael Servetus, was invited to Geneva and then executed for heresy.

Church Organization Calvin's system produced a cohesiveness and organization achieved by no other Protestant church. The *Institutes* spelled out every point of faith and practice in detail—an enormous advantage for Calvin's followers at a time when new religious doctrines were still fluid. The believer's duties and obligations were absolutely clear, as was his or her position in the carefully organized hierarchy of the church. In France, for example, there was a small community (or cell) in each town, a governing synod (or council) in each local area, a provincial synod in each province, and a national synod at the top of the pyramid. Tight discipline controlled the entire system, with the result that Calvinists believed they were setting a moral and religious example that the entire world would eventually have to follow. They were part of a privileged community from whom the elect would be drawn. Thus, they could be oppressive when they had power, yet holy rebels when they were a minority. After all, since they were freed of responsibility for their own salvation, they were acting selflessly at all times. Like the children of Israel, they had a mission to live for God, and this sense of destiny was to be one of Calvinism's greatest strengths.

Preachers from Geneva traveled through Europe to win adherents and organize the faithful wherever they could. In 1559 the city opened a university for the purpose of training preachers, because Calvin regarded education as an essential means of instilling faith. From Geneva flowed a stream of pamphlets and books, which strengthened the faith of all believers and made sure that none who wished to learn would lack the opportunity. A special target was Calvin's homeland, France, where his preachers had their first successes, especially in the cities. Calvinism also won important support in the nobility, notably among women aristocrats, who often influenced their families to adopt the new beliefs.

By 1564, when Calvin died, his church was well established: more than a million adherents in France, where they were called Huguenots; the Palatinate converted; Scotland won by his fiery disciple, John Knox; and considerable groups of followers in England, the Low Countries, and Hungary. Despite its severity, Calvin's coherent and comprehensive body of doctrine proved to have wide appeal in an age of piety that yearned for clear religious answers.

The Appeal of Calvinism   Certain groups seemed especially open to Protestant, and particularly Calvinist, teachings. All the reformed faiths did particularly well in cities, and it has been suggested that the long history of independence among townspeople made them more inclined to challenge traditional authorities. In addition, they tended to be more literate, and thus were drawn to beliefs that emphasized reading the Bible for oneself. Moreover, Calvinism put an emphasis on sobriety, discipline, and communal responsibility that appealed strongly to the increasingly self-confident merchants and artisans of the cities. That the Calvinists were also successful in the areas of southern France farthest away from central authority in Paris only reinforces the connection with an inclination toward independence and self-reliance. Geneva itself became a determinedly independent place—morals were strictly supervised, and there was an aura of public discipline that all visitors noted. Gradually in the seventeenth century the atmosphere of austerity softened, but the city continued to be seen as a model community for all Calvinists.

Women and Reform   Cities were not the only centers of religious reform. In some parts of Europe, such as Scotland, new beliefs flourished outside towns because they won political support. But in all areas, the importance of women to the spread of Protestantism was unmistakable. Calvin's earliest significant converts were aristocratic women, whose patronage helped his faith take root at the highest levels of society. Like the literate women of the cities, they saw in its message an opportunity to express themselves and to work for others in ways that had not been possible before. They were often the main readers of the Bible in family gatherings; they took the lead in demanding broader access to education, especially for girls; and they were regularly prominent in radical movements.

One theologian who despaired at the results of Luther's translation of the New Testament reserved his most bitter complaints for the women who were studying the Bible for themselves. And the results were apparent not only among the literate. The records of the **Inquisition**, the Catholic tribunal charged with rooting out heresy, are full of the trials and executions of women who were martyrs for their beliefs and who died defending doctrines they had learned from preachers or other women. Again and again, they rejected the authority of priests and asserted their right to individual faith. It was determination like this that enabled the **Reformation** to establish itself and to spread until it posed a major challenge to the traditional Church (see "The Trial of Elizabeth Dirks," p. 385). Yet the encouragement of female piety by the major reformers should not be overdrawn, for (unlike the radicals) they insisted that women remain silent in services. Moreover, the abolition of nunneries, of the veneration of the Virgin, and of prayers to female saints narrowed the opportunities for spiritual expression among all Protestant women and reduced their roles in their faiths.

The Anglican Church

In England, which created its own version of the Protestant Church, the role of the prince was crucial. There was a local tradition of dissent, represented by the Lollards, but it was severely repressed in the early days of the Reformation. King Henry VIII even wrote an attack on Luther that persuaded the pope to grant him the title "Defender of the Faith" that British monarchs still use. But by the late 1520s this loyalty was in peril because Henry's wife was clearly not going to produce the male heir he needed to continue his dynasty, and the traditional solution—to have the pope annul the marriage—was unavailable. The result was another advance for the Reformation.

The King's Divorce   The case Henry made to the pope was that he had married his brother's widow, Catherine of Aragon, under a special papal dispensation from the biblical law that prohibited a union between such close relatives. He argued that the lack of an heir proved the dispensation to have been sinful, and the marriage no marriage. Henry did not mention that he had become infatuated with a young lady at court, Anne Boleyn, but under normal circumstances the papacy would not have hesitated to comply. At this very moment, however, the pope was in the power of the Emperor Charles V, who had invaded Italy. Charles, it happened, was

THE TRIAL OF ELIZABETH DIRKS

In radical groups, women often occupied central roles they never achieved in the larger churches. Since the most important attributes of a believer in these groups were faith, commitment, and the presence of the Holy Spirit, there was frequently an egalitarianism not found elsewhere in sixteenth-century society. Thus it was that the radical "teacher" (or leader) whom the Inquisition in the Netherlands interrogated in January 1549 was a woman named Elizabeth Dirks. Her replies give us a vivid sense of the beliefs the Reformation was stimulating among ordinary people—though in this case they were put forward with a clarity and a conviction that would lead to Elizabeth's execution two months later.

"Examiner: We understand you are a teacher and have led many astray. Who are your friends?

"Elizabeth: Do not press me on this point. Ask me about my faith and I will answer you gladly.

"Examiner: Do you not consider our Church to be the house of the Lord?

"Elizabeth: I do not. For it is written that God said 'I will dwell with you.'

"Examiner: What do you think of our mass?

"Elizabeth: I have no faith in your mass, but only in the word of God.

"Examiner: What do you believe about the Holy Sacrament of the Eucharist?

"Elizabeth: I never in my life read in Scripture about a Holy Sacrament, but only of the Supper of the Lord.

"Examiner: You speak with a haughty tongue.

"Elizabeth: No. I speak with a free tongue.

"Examiner: Do you not believe that you are saved by baptism?

"Elizabeth: No: all the water in the sea cannot save me. My salvation is in Christ, who commanded me to love my God and my neighbor as myself.

"Examiner: Do priests have the power to forgive sins?

"Elizabeth: How should I believe that? Christ is the only priest through whom sins are forgiven.

"As torture was applied:

"Examiner: You can recant everything you have said.

"Elizabeth: No, I will not, but I will seal it with my blood."

Adapted from Thieleman von Bracht, *The Bloody Theater or Martyr's Mirror*, Daniel Rupp (tr.), Lancaster, PA: David Miller, 1837, pp. 409–410.

Catherine's nephew, and he refused to allow this blot on her honor.

Stymied by Rome, Henry summoned England's Parliament in 1529 and gave it free rein to express bitter anticlerical sentiments. He sought opinions in European universities in favor of the divorce, and he even extracted a vague recognition from England's clergy of his position as "supreme lord" of the Church. Finally, one of his ministers, Thomas Cromwell, suggested a radical but simple solution: that Henry break with the pope, declare himself head of the Church, and divorce Catherine on his own authority. The king agreed, and in 1534 Parliament declared him supreme head of the newly independent Church of England. By joining Europe's Protestants in opposition to Rome, Henry gave his subjects a cause that was increasingly to stimulate their patriotic pride.

The English Church   The Reformation gave the monarchy a huge financial boost. Henry took over the ecclesiastical fees that the pope had collected, and he confiscated the immensely valuable property of all monasteries. When a revolt erupted against the Reformation in 1536, he crushed it easily. But in doctrine and the structure of the Church, Henry was deeply conservative; he allowed few changes in dogma or liturgy and seems to have hoped that he could continue the old ways, changing only the person at the head of the institution. He even tried to restrain the spread of Reformation beliefs, brought to England from the Continent by travelers and books, and he persecuted heresy.

But it proved impossible to stop the momentum. Although many English men and women clung to tradition, others were drawn to the new religious ideas, and they pressured Henry to accept Protestant doctrines. Lollards had kept Wycliffe's ideas alive, and they now joined forces with Protestants inspired by continental reformers to demand services in English and easier access to Scripture. New translations of the Bible appeared in the 1530s, as did echoes of the opposition to clerical privilege that had swept Protestant areas on the Continent. Perhaps realizing that the pressure would only grow, Henry had his son, Edward, tutored by a committed reformer. Edward VI ruled for only six years (1547–1553). He was followed by a committed Catholic, Mary, the daughter of Catherine of Aragon, but her attempt to turn back the clock failed. When her five-year reign ended, the English Church became firmly Protestant under the rule of Elizabeth I, the child Henry had with Anne Boleyn after the divorce (see chapter 15).

THE CATHOLIC REVIVAL

Those with Protestant sympathies usually refer to the Catholic revival that started in the 1530s as the **Counter-Reformation,** implying that the Roman Church acted only as a result of criticisms by Luther and others. Catholic historians call it the Catholic Reformation, implying that the movement began within the Church and was not merely a reaction to Protestantism. There is justification for both views. Certainly the papacy was aware of its loss of control over millions of Christians, but a great deal of the effort to put the Church's house in order was a result of strong faith and a long-standing determination to purify belief and practice.

Strengths and Weaknesses

Although the institution faced serious problems of doctrine and organization, and a major reform effort was certainly needed, it is important to remember that the Church had a vast reserve of loyalty and affection. In the long run, many more Europeans remained Catholic than converted to Protestantism. They took comfort from tradition and from priests who, rather than demanding that believers achieve salvation on their own, offered the Church's mediation, beautiful ceremonies, and rituals to help people overcome their sins. Catholicism had a long history of charity for the poor, which it strengthened during the sixteenth century. For ordinary Christians, the familiarity, support, and grandeur they found in the Church were often reason enough to resist the reformers.

Losses and Difficulties   There was no doubt, however, that the first half of the sixteenth century was the lowest point in the history of the Catholic Church and that few could have expected the recovery that followed. By 1550 many areas of Europe had been lost to the Protestants, and even in regions that were still loyal the papacy was able to exercise little control. The French Church, for example, had a well-established tradition of autonomy, exemplified by the right France's kings had held since 1516 to make ecclesiastical appointments. In Spain, too, the monarchy retained its independence and even had its own Inquisition. In the Holy Roman Empire, those states that had rejected Protestantism gave the pope no more than token allegiance.

Moreover, there was still no comprehensive definition of Catholic doctrine on justification, salvation,

Titian
POPE PAUL III FARNESE WITH HIS NEPHEWS OTTAVIO FARNESE, DUKE OF PARMA, AND CARDINAL ALESSANDRO FARNESE, 1546
The psychological tension Titian created in this family portrait is extraordinary. The shrewd seventy-seven-year-old pope who had launched the Church's vigorous response to Protestantism looks benignly on Ottavio, whose seemingly calculated gesture of deference hints at the aggressiveness that was soon to cause a major family quarrel over land and money. And Cardinal Alessandro, standing apart, was already a famous patron of art with little concern for Church affairs. Perhaps because of its revelation of character, the painting was never finished.
Museo Nazionale di Capodimonte, Naples, Italy. Erich Lessing/ Art Resource, NY

and the sacraments. Worse yet, the Church's leadership was far from effective. Although one pope, Leo X, had attempted to correct notorious abuses such as simony (the sale of church offices) in the early sixteenth century, Rome simply did not have the spiritual authority to make reform a vital force in the Catholic Church.

Paul III   The situation changed with the pope elected in 1534: Paul III, a man not renowned for saintliness but a genius at making the right decisions for the Church. By the end of his reign, in 1549, the Catholic revival was under way.

The heart of Paul's strategy was his determination to assert papal responsibility throughout the Church. Re-

Titian
THE COUNCIL OF TRENT, CA. **1564**
The splendor of the gathering of representatives of the Catholic Church from all of Europe is conveyed by this scene, attributed to Titian. The ranks of bishops in their miters, listening to one of their number address the assembly from the pulpit on the right, visibly embodied a Church putting itself in order as it faced the challenge of Protestantism.
Giraudon/Art Resource, NY

alizing that uncertainties in Catholic doctrine could be resolved only by reexamining traditional theology, he decided within a few months of taking office to call a Church council for that purpose, despite the danger of rekindling the conciliar movement. It took ten years to overcome resistance to the idea, but in the meantime Paul attacked abuses throughout the Church, disregarding both vested interests and tradition. He aimed his campaign at all levels of the hierarchy, undeterred by powerful bishops and cardinals long used to a lax and corrupt regime. In addition, he founded a Roman Inquisition, a decision that reflected the era's growing reliance on persecution as a means of destroying dissent.

Paul realized that, in the long run, the revival of Catholicism would depend on whether his successors maintained his efforts. During his fifteen-year reign, therefore, he made a series of superb appointments to the College of Cardinals (the body that elects the popes); the result was the creation of possibly the most illustrious College in history. Many of its members were famous for their piety, others for their learning.

They came from all over Europe, united by their devotion to the Church and their resolve to see it once again command admiration and reverence. The result of Paul's farsighted policy was to be a succession of popes through the early seventeenth century who would fully restore the atmosphere of spirituality and morality that had long been missing from the papacy.

The Council of Trent

The ecumenical, or general, council of Church leaders called by Paul finally assembled at Trent, a northern Italian city, in 1545, and met irregularly until the delegates managed to complete their work in 1563. The council's history was one of stormy battles between various national factions. The non-Italians pressed for decentralization of religious authority; the Italians, closely tied to the papacy, advocated a consolidation of power. For both sides, the divisions were political as well as ecclesiastical, because at issue was the independence not only of bishops but also of local princes and kings. A large majority of the delegates were Italians, however, and their conclusions almost always reinforced the dominance of the pope. The threat of a revival of conciliarism never materialized.

Defining Doctrine   In keeping with Paul's instructions, the Council of Trent gave more of its time to the basic issue of Church doctrine than to the problem of reform. Nearly all its decisions were intended to establish clear definitions of practice and belief and to end long-standing theological uncertainties or differences of opinion. The main sources for these decisions were the interpretations put forward by Thomas Aquinas, who now became the central theologian of the Catholic Church. At the same time, Trent's decrees were designed to affirm precisely those teachings that the Protestants had rejected. Catholicism from then on would be committed primarily to the outward, sacramental heritage of Christianity. In this view, the Bible is not the exclusive authority for the believer: Church tradition holds an equal place in establishing religious truth. Human will is free, good works as well as faith are a means of salvation, all seven sacraments are channels of grace, and Christ's sacrifice is reenacted in every Mass. The Council of Trent endorsed the special position of the priest and insisted that God be worshiped with appropriately elaborate ceremonies and rites.

These were the main decisions at Trent, but many minor matters were also settled: For the first time, the priest's presence became essential at the sacrament of marriage, a further reinforcement of his importance; the Vulgate, the Latin translation of the Bible prepared chiefly by St. Jerome, was decreed to be a holy text, a decision which rebutted humanists and other scholars who had found mistranslations of Greek and Hebrew in Jerome's work; and in direct contrast to the Protestants, gorgeous ritual was heavily stressed, which encouraged artists to beautify church buildings and ceremonies.

Restoring the Church   The achievement of the council was to adjust the Church to the world. Many ordinary people, troubled by the stern self-denial and predestination taught by most Protestant churches and sects, preferred the traditional comfort, ceremony, and support Catholicism had long offered. They were ready to champion their old faith as soon as its leadership restored its sense of purpose by removing abuses and defining doctrines. And the new discipline of the Church was apparent in the council's effort to deal with morality as thoroughly as with belief. When it gave its approval to the Inquisition and to the "Index of Forbidden Books," which informed all Catholics of the heretical works they were not allowed to read, the council signaled the determination of the Church to recover the ground it had lost.

The Aftermath of Trent

The new atmosphere of dedication swept through the Catholic Church, inspiring thinkers and artists throughout Europe to lend their talents to the cause. Painters, architects, and musicians caught up by the new moral fervor in Catholicism expressed their faith in brilliant and dramatic portrayals of religious subjects and in churches that were designed to dazzle the observer in a way that most Protestants could not allow. This artistic outpouring was, of course, far more than a reflection of the decisions of a few hundred prelates assembled in a council. It was also one of many indicators of the new vigor of Catholicism. In France, for example, a new generation of Church leaders appeared in the late sixteenth century who were distinguished for their austerity, learning, and observance of duties.

Women in the Church   Moreover, the crucial contribution of women to Protestantism was echoed in the revival of Catholicism. There was a remarkable flowering of new religious orders for women in the sixteenth and seventeenth centuries, many of which became identified with charitable works. Since one of the most important ways the Church set about winning back the faithful was by expanding its philanthropic activities—through new hospitals and expanded assistance to the poor, to orphans, and to other unfortunates—its female orders played an essential role in the Counter-Reformation. And nowhere was their devout spirituality more apparent than in Spain, the most fiercely Catholic of all European countries.

The Spaniards expressed their religious passion in many ways—by insisting on converting the native peoples they conquered overseas, by giving great power to the Inquisition that guarded orthodoxy from large Muslim and Jewish communities at home, by encouraging lay as well as clerical piety, and by founding the most famous new order of the age, the Jesuits (see below). But no indication of their devotion was as distinctive as the great flowering of mysticism, which was most famously represented by St. Teresa (1515–1582).

St. Teresa   The mystic seeks to worship God directly and immediately, in an encounter that usually takes place in a trance and without the intervention of a priest. Because this religious experience is entirely personal and does not require the mediation of the Church, it has always been looked on with suspicion by the authorities. St. Teresa was no exception. As a rich and spoiled young girl, she had led a rather loose life, and her concerned father had sent her to a convent to instill some discipline. Perhaps because the family had only recently converted from Judaism, considerable attention was also given to Teresa's religious edu-

St. Teresa's Visions

These two passages are among the most famous from the autobiography that St. Teresa began writing in 1562, when she was forty-seven years old. The book is essentially the story of a spiritual journey, as a restless young woman gains purpose and strength through mystical visions and unwavering faith. Her account of a mystical transport in the second passage quoted here was the inspiration for a famous sculpture by Gian Lorenzo Bernini, The Ecstasy of St. Teresa, *in the seventeenth century.*

"I: One day, when I was at prayer, the Lord was pleased to reveal to me nothing but His hands, whose beauty was so great as to be indescribable. This made me very fearful. A few days later I also saw the Divine face. On St. Paul's Day, I saw a complete representation of his sacred Humanity. If there were nothing else in Heaven to delight the eyes but the extreme beauty of the glorified bodies there, that alone would be the greatest bliss. If I were to spend years and years imagining how to invent anything so beautiful, I could not do it. In its whiteness and radiance, it exceeds all we can imagine. It is a soft whiteness which, without wearying the eyes, causes them the greatest delight. By comparison with it, the brightness of our sun seems quite dim."

"II: It pleased the Lord that I sometimes saw beside me an angel in bodily form. He was not tall, but short, and very beautiful, his face aflame. In his hands I saw a long golden spear, and at the end of the iron tip I seemed to see a point of fire. With this he seemed to pierce my heart several times. When he drew it out, he left me completely afire with a great love for God. During the days when this continued, I went about as if in a stupor."

From E. Allison Peers, *The Life of Teresa of Jesus,* London: Sheed & Ward, 1944; New York: Doubleday, 1960, pp. 258–260, 273–274.

cation. Soon she began to experience visions of God, which gradually convinced her that she had a special religious mission (see "St. Teresa's Visions," above).

Church authorities became worried when, after becoming a nun, Teresa began to attract a following as a spiritual adviser to a number of women in her native city of Avila. Some churchmen suggested that her visions were the work of the devil, not God. After many examinations, however—and finally an interview with the king of Spain himself, who was deeply impressed by her holiness—the doubts evaporated. Teresa founded a strict new order of nuns and traveled all over Spain establishing convents. She soon became a legendary figure and was made a saint only forty years after her death.

The Revitalized Papacy   The most conspicuous embodiments of the new energy of the Church, however, were the popes themselves. Paul III's successors used their personal authority and pontifical resources not to adorn their palaces but to continue the enormous cleansing operation within the Church and to lead the counterattack against Protestantism. If a king or prince refused to help, the popes would try to persuade one of his leading subjects (for example, the Guise family in France or the dukes of Bavaria in the empire) to organize the struggle. Their diplomats and agents (often friars) were everywhere, urging Catholics to stamp out Protestantism. And the pontiffs insisted on strict personal morality so as to restore their reputation for piety and set a proper example to the faithful.

With the leaders of the Church thus bent on reform, the restoration of the faith and the reconquest of lost souls could proceed with maximum effect. And the popes had at their disposal a religious order established by Ignatius Loyola in 1540 specifically for these purposes: the Society of Jesus.

Ignatius Loyola

The third of the great religious innovators of the sixteenth century, after Luther and Calvin, was Ignatius Loyola (1491–1556); unlike his predecessors, however, he sought to reform the Catholic Church from within. Loyola was the son of a Basque nobleman, raised in the chivalric and intensely religious atmosphere of Spain, and he was often at the royal court. In his teens he entered the army, but when he was thirty, a leg wound ended his military career. While convalescing, he was deeply impressed by a number of popular lives of the saints he read, and soon his religious interests began to take shape in chivalric and military terms. He visualized Mary as his lady, the inspiration of a Christian quest in which the forces of God and the devil fight in mighty battle. This was a faith seen from the perspective of the knight, and though the direct parallel lessened as Loyola's thought developed, it left an unmistakable stamp on his future work.

Peter Paul Rubens
THE MIRACLE OF ST. IGNATIUS, **1617–1618**
Loyola quickly became one of the major heroes of the Catholic revival. Within less than sixty years of his death (1556), he was to become a saint of the Church. He was one of the heroes of Baroque art, as is apparent in this painting by Peter Paul Rubens, which creates a powerful image of Loyola at the moment when he cures a man and a woman who have been possessed by the devil.
Kunsthistorisches Museum, Vienna, Austria. Erich Lessing/Art Resource, NY

In 1522 Loyola gave up his knightly garb and swore to go on a pilgrimage to Jerusalem. He retired to a monastery for ten months to absolve himself of the guilt of a sinful life and to prepare spiritually for the journey to the Holy Land. At the monastery he had a momentous experience that, like Luther's and Calvin's, dominated the rest of his life. According to tradition, he had a vision lasting eight days, during which he saw in detail the outline of a book, the *Spiritual Exercises,* and a new religious order, the Society of Jesus.

The Spiritual Exercises   The first version of the *Spiritual Exercises* certainly dated from this period, but like Calvin's *Institutes,* it was to be thoroughly revised many times. The book deals not with doctrines or theology but with the discipline and training necessary for

a God-fearing life. Believers must undertake four weeks of contemplation and self-examination that culminate in a feeling of union with God, when they surrender their minds and wills to Christ. If successful, they are then ready to submit completely to the call of God and to pursue the Church's commands without question.

The manual was the heart of the organization of the Society of Jesus, and it gave those who followed its precepts (known as Jesuits) a dedication and determination that made them seem the Church's answer to the Calvinists. But while the end might be similar to Luther's and Calvin's—the personal attainment of grace—the method, with its emphasis on individual effort and concentration, could not have been more different. For the *Spiritual Exercises* emphasize that believers can act for themselves; they do not have to depend on faith alone to gain salvation, as Protestants assert. One can prepare for grace through a tremendous act of will and not rely solely on a gift from God. Loyola makes immense demands precisely because he insists that the will is free and that good works are efficacious.

Loyola's Followers   During the sixteen years after he left the monastery, Loyola led a life of poverty and study. Though lame, he traveled to Jerusalem and back barefoot in 1523–1524, and two years later, at the University of Alcala, he attracted his first disciples, three fellow students. Suspected by the Inquisition of being rather too independent in their beliefs, the little band walked to Paris, where six more disciples joined them. In 1537 Loyola and his followers became ordained as priests. With their activities beginning to take definite shape, they decided to seek the pope's blessing for their work. They saw Paul III in 1538, and two years later, despite opposition from those who saw it as a threat to the authority of local bishops, the pope approved a plan Loyola submitted for a new religious order that would be supervised directly by the papacy.

The Jesuits

Jesuit Activities   The Society, or Company, of Jesus had four principal functions: preaching, hearing confessions, teaching, and missionary work. The first two were the Jesuits' means of strengthening the beliefs of individual Catholics or converting Protestants. The third became one of their most effective weapons. The Christian humanists he encountered convinced Loyola of the tremendous power of education. The Jesuits therefore set about organizing the best schools in Europe and were so successful that some Protestants sent their children to the Society's schools despite the certainty that the pupils would become committed Catholics. The instructors followed humanist principles and taught the latest ideas, including the most re-

MAP 13.1 RELIGIOUS DIVISIONS IN EUROPE AT THE END OF THE SIXTEENTH CENTURY
By the late sixteenth century, the division of Europe into distinct areas, each committed primarily to one church, was virtually complete. Now that they were solidly established, the major faiths became associated with universities that elaborated and promoted their beliefs. Where were the major Roman Catholic universities? Where were the major Protestant universities?
◆ For an online version, go to www.mhhe.com/chambers9 > chapter 13 > book maps

cent advances in science. The Jesuits' final activity, missionary work, brought them their most spectacular successes among both non-Christians and Protestants.

Jesuit Campaigns   A number of qualities combined to make the Jesuits extraordinarily effective in winning converts and turning Catholics into militant activists.

First, the order demanded high intellectual abilities. It selected recruits carefully (rejecting many applicants) and gave them a superb education. Jesuits were famous for their knowledge of Scripture and traditional teachings and their ability to out-argue opponents. In addition, they were highly effective preachers and excellent educators. Their discipline, determination, and awareness of the contemporary world soon won them a fearsome reputation. They had no equal in the forcefulness with which they advanced the aims of the Council of Trent and the papacy.

The Jesuits can be regarded as the striking arm of the Counter-Reformation; indeed, their organization was to some extent modeled on the medieval military orders. A Jesuit at a royal court was often the chief inspiration for a ruler's militant support of the faith, and in many areas the Society was the main conqueror of rival beliefs—for example in Poland, where Jesuits in the late sixteenth century led a campaign that eradicated widespread Protestantism and created a devoted Catholic country. Yet it must be noted that in an age that took persecution for granted, the Jesuits always opposed execution for heresy; they far preferred to win a convert than to kill a heretic. Their presence was soon felt all over the world: As early as the 1540s, one of Loyola's first disciples, Francis Xavier, conducted a mission to Japan. Despite the many enmities they aroused by their single-mindedness and their self-assurance, their unswerving devotion was a major reason for the revival of the Roman Church.

Religion and Politics

As a revived Catholic Church confronted the Protestants, religious warfare of unprecedented ferocity erupted throughout Europe (see chapter 15). More people seemed to feel more passionately about faith than at any other time in Western history. But the conflict would not have continued as long as it did without the armies and resources provided by princes and monarchs. Both sides drew crucial support from rulers who were determined either to suppress any sign of heresy in their territories or to overthrow heretical regimes in neighboring lands. For these rulers, the struggle over religion was a means of establishing their authority in their own realms and a justification for aggression abroad.

CHRONOLOGY
The Reformation and Counter-Reformation

1517	Luther's protest begins: the ninety-five theses on indulgences.
1521	Diet of Worms: Luther condemned by Emperor Charles V.
1524–1525	Peasants' Revolt in Germany.
	Zürich adopts Zwingli's Reformation.
1531	Protestant League of Schmalkalden formed in Germany.
	Death of Zwingli.
1534	Paul III becomes pope.
	Anabaptists take over the city of Münster in Germany.
	King Henry VIII is proclaimed head of the Church of England.
1535	Thomas More executed for not accepting Henry VIII as head of the Church of England.
1536	Calvin comes to Geneva; first edition of his *Institutes.*
	Death of Erasmus.
1540	Pope Paul III approves the Jesuit Order.
1541	Calvin settles in Geneva permanently.
1545	Council of Trent begins.
1546	Death of Luther.
1556	Death of Loyola.
1559	First "Index of Forbidden Books" published.
	Execution of Protestants after Inquisition trials in Spain.
1564	Publication of the Decrees of the Council of Trent.
	Death of Calvin.

Summary

The strong connection between politics and belief, and its dire consequences, was the result of a transformation that was almost as far-reaching as the Reformation itself. Just as Western Christianity was changed forever in the sixteenth century, so too were the power and the ambition of the territorial state. At the same time as a handful of reformers, building on powerful social and intellectual forces, reshaped religious structures and practices, a handful of political leaders—building on no less powerful military, social, and economic forces—created armies, systems of taxation, and bureaucratic organizations that reshaped the structures and practices of central governments throughout Europe.

QUESTIONS FOR FURTHER THOUGHT

1. If spiritual yearning has often changed individuals, why are outside forces such as politics necessary before large-scale changes in faith can take hold?

2. Is religious belief best understood as personal or as communal?

RECOMMENDED READING

Sources

*Calvin, John. *On God and Political Duty.* J. T. McNeill (ed.). 1950.

*Erasmus, Desiderius. *Essential Works of Erasmus.* W. T. H. Jackson (ed.). 1965.

Loyola, Ignatius. *The Spiritual Exercises of St. Ignatius.* R. W. Gleason (ed.). 1964.

*Luther, Martin. *Martin Luther: Selections from His Writings.* John Dillenberger (ed.). 1961.

Studies

*Bossy, John. *Christianity in the West, 1400–1700.* 1985. An overview of the religious history of Europe by one of the leading historians of Catholic thought and practice.

*Bouwsma, William J. *John Calvin: A Sixteenth-Century Portrait.* 1988. The standard biography.

*Davis, Natalie Zemon. *Society and Culture in Early Modern France.* 1975. A collection of essays about popular beliefs and attitudes, particularly on religious matters, during the sixteenth century.

*Huizinga, Johan. *Erasmus and the Age of Reformation.* 1957. A warm and sympathetic biography, beautifully written.

Jones, M. D. W. *The Counter Reformation.* 1995.

*Kenny, Anthony. *Thomas More.* 1983. An excellent brief introduction to More's life and work.

Kittelson, James M. *Luther the Reformer: The Story of the Man and His Career.* 1986. The best introduction to Luther's life and thought.

*Mullett, Michael A. *The Catholic Reformation.* 1999.

O'Malley, John. *The First Jesuits.* 1993.

Scribner, Robert. *For the Sake of Simple Folk: Popular Propaganda for the German Reformation.* 1981. A pathbreaking analysis of how the Reformation was spread.

Tracy, James. *Europe's Reformations, 1450–1650.* 1999. A recent overview.

Wiesner, Merry. *Women and Gender in Early Modern Europe.* 1993.

Williams, George H. *The Radical Reformation.* 1962. The most comprehensive account of the sects and their founders.

*Available in paperback.

Hans Holbein the Younger
THE AMBASSADORS, **1533**
Hans Holbein the Younger's *The Ambassadors* shows the worldliness that was expected of diplomats (many of whom were also soldiers) in the sixteenth century. The two men are surrounded by symbols of the skills, knowledge, and refinement their job required—geography, mathematics, literature, and music. But despite this emphasis on material concerns, Holbein reminds us (in the optically distorted skull across the bottom of the painting) that death and spiritual needs cannot be forgotten.

Chapter Fourteen

ECONOMIC EXPANSION AND A NEW POLITICS

EXPANSION AT HOME • EXPANSION OVERSEAS • THE CENTRALIZATION OF POLITICAL POWER • THE SPLINTERED STATES • THE NEW STATECRAFT

Europe in 1400 was a poor, technologically backward, and politically disorganized area compared to the realms of the Indian moguls or Chinese emperors. And yet within little more than a century, Europeans were expanding aggressively into Asia and the Americas. Their numbers were growing, their economy was booming, their technological advances were making possible the creation of new markets and new empires, and their political leaders were developing structures of government and authority more elaborate than any that had been seen since the fall of the Roman Empire.

The emergence of this new world power was one of the most astonishing transformations in Western history, and historians have long debated its causes. Their suggestions have ranged from the initiatives of specific kings or explorers to such forces as demographic change or climatic warming. Like the fall of the Roman Empire, however, this was so profound a reshaping of Europe's economy and politics that no definitive explanation seems possible. Yet a survey of the main individual changes can help explain how far the reordering had progressed by the late sixteenth century.

Cortès lands in Mexico; Magellan's voyage around the world (to 1522); Charles V Holy Roman Emperor (to 1556) **1519** ●

Machiavelli, *The Prince* **1513** ●

Vasco da Gama sails to India **1497** ●

Treaty of Tordesillas; Italian wars begin (to 1559) **1494** ●

1492 ●
Columbus' first voyage; capture of Muslim
Granada by Spanish; expulsion of Jews from Spain

Dias rounds the Cape of Good Hope **1488** ●

● **1469** Marriage of Ferdinand of Aragon and Isabella of Castile

EXPANSION AT HOME

During the last third of the fifteenth century, signs of change appeared in the demographic, economic, and political history of Europe. Some argue that the causes were political: that trade quickened and populations grew because of rising confidence as assertive regimes restored order and authority in a number of states. Others regard either economic or demographic advance as the source of change. In fact, though, all three were connected and all three reinforced one another. What is unmistakable is the increase in the number of Europeans after more than one hundred years of decline and the social and economic consequences of that increase.

Population Increase

Exact measurements are not possible, but it seems likely that the loss of population that began with the Black Death in the 1340s had run its course by the 1460s. Plagues, though recurrent, began to take less of a toll (perhaps because immunities developed); bad harvests became less frequent (perhaps because of a warming climate); and families were thus able to produce more surviving children. As a result, Europe's population rose by some 50 percent between 1470 and 1620. And cities expanded even faster: London had fewer than 50,000 inhabitants in the early sixteenth century but over 200,000 a hundred years later. There was also extensive reoccupation of marginal farmland, which had been abandoned in the fourteenth and fifteenth centuries because of a shrinking population. Now there were more mouths to feed, and the extra acres again became profitable.

Consequences of the Increase The rise in population was followed by a staggering jump in food prices. By the early 1600s wheat cost approximately five times more than in the late 1400s, an increase that far outpaced the movement of prices in general. It is not surprising, therefore, that this period witnessed the first wave of enclosures in England: Major landowners put up fences around common tilling or grazing ground, traditionally open to all the animals of the locality, and reserved it for their own crops or their sheep, whose wool was also in increasing demand. By 1600 about one-eighth of England's arable land had been enclosed. The only answer, when changes like these made a village incapable of supporting its growing population, was for people to move to towns and cities.

Economic Growth

As markets began to grow in response to population pressures, the volume of trade also shot upward; commercial profits thus kept pace with those of agriculture. Customs receipts rose steadily, as did the yield of tolls from ships entering the Baltic Sea, one of the main routes of European trade. In many areas, too, shipbuilding boomed. This was the heyday of the English cloth trade and the great Spanish sheep farms, of the central German linen industry and the northern Italian silk industry. Printing became a widespread occupation, and gun making and glassmaking also expanded rapidly. Glassmaking had a major effect on European society because the increasing use of windows allowed builders to divide houses into small rooms, thus giving many people a little privacy for the first time.

The Growth of Banking Leading financiers who invested in the growing volume of trade accumulated large fortunes. For centuries the Italians had led economic advance, but in the sixteenth century firms of other nations were achieving international prominence. The most successful of the new enterprises was

1520–1566 Suleiman the Great expands the Ottoman Empire

● 1529 Reformation Parliament assembles

● 1545 Silver discovered in South America

run by a family descended from a fourteenth-century weaver, Johannes Fugger of Augsburg. The sixteenth-century Fuggers financed the Spanish King Charles I's quest for the throne of the Holy Roman Empire and his later wars after he became the Emperor Charles V. Great bankers were thus often closely allied with monarchs, and like all merchants, they gained from the growing power of central governments. Rulers encouraged commerce in the hope of larger revenues from customs duties and taxes, and they gave leading entrepreneurs valuable privileges. Such alliances were eventually the undoing of some firms, which were ruined when kings went bankrupt, but until the late sixteenth century, Italian and German bankers controlled Europe's finances.

New Kinds of Businesses

Almost every level of commercial activity offered opportunities for advancement. The guild system expanded in the sixteenth century to incorporate many new trades, and the structure of merchant enterprises became more elaborate. The idea took hold that a business firm was an impersonal entity—larger than the person who owned it—with an identity, legal status, permanence, and even profits that were not the same as those of its members. Here was yet another indication of major economic change.

Inflation

The surest sign of growth, however, was the slow inflation of prices, which began around 1500 after some one hundred fifty years of either stagnant or falling prices. By modern standards, the increase was tiny—1 or 2 percent a year, totaling 75 percent in Spain by 1600 and slightly less elsewhere in Europe—but it prompted bitter protests from those who thought a loaf of bread had a "just" price and that any increase was mere exploitation by the baker. In general, however, the modest inflation was an indication that demand

was rising, and it not only boosted profits but also reduced people's debts (because the amount that had been borrowed was worth less each year).

Silver Imports

A major reason for the inflation was the growth of the population, but it was also propelled by the huge quantities of silver the Spaniards imported from the New World, which made money more readily available (see accompanying table). Most of the silver passed from Spain to the Italian and German merchants who financed Spanish wars and controlled the American trade, and thus it affected all of Europe. The flow of New World silver was the main reason for the end of the crippling shortage of precious metals and coins that had plagued Europe for centuries. By the middle of the seventeenth century, the continent's holdings in gold had increased by one-fifth and, more important, its stock of silver had tripled.

IMPORTS OF TREASURE TO SPAIN FROM THE NEW WORLD, 1511–1600	
Decade	*Total Value**
1511–1520	2,626,000
1521–1530	1,407,000
1531–1540	6,706,000
1541–1550	12,555,000
1551–1560	21,437,000
1561–1570	30,418,000
1571–1580	34,990,000
1581–1590	63,849,000
1591–1600	85,536,000

*In ducats.

Adapted from J. H. Elliott, *Imperial Spain, 1469–1716*, New York, 1964, p. 175.

Anonymous
MERCHANTS CLEARING ACCOUNTS, FRENCH MINIATURE
This sixteenth-century depiction of a group of people in a fine house calculating accounts gives a sense of the increasingly complicated exchanges that became necessary as commerce expanded. Books had to be checked and money counted. It is noteworthy that the transactions involve the monk on the left and the woman holding her purse on the right.
Bettmann/Corbis

With money circulating more freely and markets growing, the profits of traders and financiers improved dramatically. They could invest more widely (for example, in overseas ventures) and thus achieve new levels of wealth.

The Commercial Revolution As the volume of trade rose, new mechanisms for organizing large-scale economic activity were put in place—a process that has been called Europe's commercial revolution. Bookkeepers devised new, standardized principles for keeping track of a firm's accounts, bankers created elaborate systems of agents and letters of credit to transfer funds across large distances, merchants developed more effective means of forming broad partnerships that were capable of major investments and of ensuring against losses, and governments gave increased support to new

ventures and to the financial community in general. Essential to these activities was an attitude and a way of conducting business that is known as *capitalism*.

Capitalism Capitalism was both a product of economic change and a stimulus to further change. It is often thought of as a system, but it refers primarily to the distinct outlook and kinds of behavior displayed by certain people as they make, buy, and sell goods. At its root, capitalism means the accumulation of capital—that is, tangible wealth—for its own sake. In practice, this requires taking risks and also reinvesting whatever one earns so as to enlarge one's profits. Those who undertook long-distance trade had many capitalist traits: They took great risks, and they were prepared to wait months and even years in order to make as large a financial gain as possible. Similarly, bankers were prepared to lend their capital, despite the danger that the loan might not be repaid, in the hope of profit; and if they succeeded, they continually plowed their earnings back into their businesses to make them ever larger. The fortunes that these capitalists accumulated, and the desire for worldly riches that they displayed, became an essential stimulus to economic growth. Far from the rural world where food was grown primarily for survival, not for profit, they were forging a new way of thinking about money and wealth. Although their outlook had existed before, only in the sixteenth century did it come to dominate Europe's economy. As a result, traditional religious prohibitions on the charging of interest began to weaken, and materialist ambitions became more open and accepted.

Unease over this new outlook did not disappear. Shakespeare's play *The Merchant of Venice*, written in the 1590s, attacked the values that capitalism was coming to represent. He contrasted unfavorably the quest for profit with more traditional commitments, such as charity and mercy. But criticism had no effect on the relentless spread of capitalism.

Social Change

Unequal Impacts in the Countryside Not everyone shared in the new prosperity of the sixteenth century. Landowners, food producers, artisans, and merchants benefited most from the rising population and could amass fortunes. Tenants who were able to harvest a surplus beyond their own needs did well, because for a while rents did not keep pace with food prices. But the wages of ordinary laborers lagged miserably. By the early 1600s, a laborer's annual income had about half the purchasing power it had had at the end of the 1400s, a decline that had its most drastic impact in Eastern Europe, where serfdom reappeared.

In the West, the large numbers of peasants who were forced off the land as the population rose turned to beg-

Jost Amman
ALLEGORY OF TRADE, WOODCUT
This late-sixteenth-century celebration of the world of the merchant shows, around the sides, the shipping of goods, the keeping of accounts, and the exchange of money that were transforming economic life. In the center, the virtues of the merchant are symbolized: integrity (a man looking over his shoulder), taciturnity (two men on his right), and a knowledge of languages (two men in turbans) in front of judiciousness on a throne and a book representing invention.

ging and wandering across country, often ending up in towns, where crime became a serious problem. Peasant uprisings directed at tax collectors, nobles, or food suppliers were almost annual affairs in one region or another of France after the mid-sixteenth century, and in England the unending stream of vagrants gave rise to a belief that the country was overpopulated. The extreme poverty was universally deplored, particularly as it promoted crime and disorder.

Relief of Distress   Nobody could understand, much less control, the forces that were transforming society. Some governments tried to relieve the economic distress, but their efforts were not always consistent. English legislation in the sixteenth century, for example, treated beggars sometimes as shirkers who should be punished and at other times as unfortunates who needed to be helped. Not until the enactment of the English Poor Law of 1601, which provided work for the poor, did the less severe view begin to prevail. In the years that followed, governments in a number of countries began to create institutions that offered basic welfare benefits.

The traditional source of food for the hungry and care for the ill, the monastery, had lost its importance because of the Reformation and because governments were now considered responsible for the needy. Among the remedies governments offered were the workhouses established by the English Poor Law where, although conditions could be horrible, the destitute could at least find work, food, and shelter. Other governments founded hospitals, often staffed by nuns, which were especially important as places that looked after abandoned women or children. But these institutions were few and far between, and it was exceptional for a poor person to find such relief. The conditions were especially harsh for women forced off the land, because few trades were open to them even if they got to a town; their choice might be either continued vagrancy or prostitution.

The Hazards of Life in the Town   Vagrancy was only one of the signs that Europeans were witnessing the beginnings of modern urbanization with all its dislocations. Major differences also developed between life in the country and life in the town. Rural workers may have led a strenuous existence, but they escaped the worst hazards of their urban counterparts. Whole sections of most large cities were controlled by the sixteenth-century equivalent of the underworld, which offered sanctuary to criminals and danger to most citizens. Plagues were much more serious in towns— the upper classes soon learned to flee to the country at

Petrus Christus
ST. ELIGIUS AS A GOLDSMITH, **1449**
**Goldsmiths played a vital financial role in the
early days of capitalism. Because of the value of
the merchandise they made and sold, their
shops—like the one here, with customers
looking in the window, reflected in the convex
mirror on the right—were sources of capital as
well as goods. In addition to providing such
items as the ring he is handing to the young
woman, the goldsmith might well have provided
investments for the traders in his city.**
The Metropolitan Museum of Art, Robert Lehman
Collection, 1975. (1975.1.110) Photography © 1993
The Metropolitan Museum of Art, New York

Quentin Metsys
THE MONEY CHANGER AND HIS WIFE, **1514**
**That people engaged in this business could be the subject of
a respectful portrait by a leading artist is an indication that
money lending and currency dealing had come to be taken
for granted in European cities. It was a family enterprise,
with the wife helping her husband, and it is worth noting
that in business circles a literate woman—she has here
interrupted the reading of a book—was not that unusual.**
Erich Lessing/Art Resource, NY

the first sign of disease—and famines more devastating
because of the far poorer sanitation in urban areas and
their remoteness from food supplies.

New Opportunities Nevertheless, it was in towns
and cities that the economic advances of the age were
most visible. As cities grew, they stimulated construction, not only of houses but also of public buildings and
city walls. Anyone skilled in bricklaying, in carpentry,
or even in carrying heavy loads found ready employment. Townsfolk needed endless services, from sign
painting to transportation, which created jobs at all levels. Given the demand for skills, guilds increasingly

allowed the widows of members to take over their husbands' trades, and women shopkeepers were not un-
common. Nobody would have been taken aback, for
example, to see an artisan's daughter or wife (like

Pieter Brueghel the Elder
Fight Between Carnival and Lent, **1559**
This detail from a huge scene shows one of the customary practices during the season of Lent: giving alms to the poor. Beggars were a common subject for Brueghel, who used them to convey a vivid sense of the appearance and behavior of the unfortunate as well as the more comfortable members of his society.
Erich Lessing/Art Resource, NY

Agnes Dürer, the wife of the famous German artist) take charge of a market stall or a shop. In some trades, such as oil making and baking, women were often essential to production as well as sales, and there is also evidence of their growing importance as the keepers of the paperwork and the accounts in family businesses. The expansion of opportunity in the cities, in other words, had social as well as economic consequences.

At the top levels of society—at princely courts and in royal administrations, in the law, among the leaders of the burgeoning cities, and in growing empires overseas— the economic expansion enabled ambitious families to win fortunes and titles and to found new aristocratic dynasties. The means of advancement varied. Once a family had become rich through commerce, it could buy the lands that, in Protestant countries, rulers had confiscated from the Church, or the offices that many governments sold to raise revenue and build bureaucracies. In addition, the New World offered the possibility of acquiring vast estates. Since the possession of land or high office was the key to noble status, the newly rich were soon able to enter the ranks of the nobility. The long boom in commerce thus encouraged broad social change. By the 1620s, when the growth in the economy came to an end, a new aristocracy had been born that was destined to dominate Europe for centuries.

Daily Life   The expanding resources changed many aspects of daily life. The availability (and affordability) of books, for example, helped promote literacy. Evidence is scarce, but the ability to sign documents, for example, tripled in many areas during the two centuries following the early 1500s. And many more could

read than could write, though on both counts women lagged far behind. In Molière's play *The School for Wives* (1661), the lead character hopes his new wife can read, so that she can study the "Rules for Marriage" that he has written, but he is mortified when he discovers she can also write. With money, too, came broadening access to such consumer goods as household utensils, which transformed behavior at the table: by the late seventeenth century, meals in polite society required individual place settings, with plates, napkins, knives, and forks.

At the same time, an enormous boom in house building, and the dividing off of rooms within these houses, created new atmospheres in the homes of the well-to-do. Private spaces were created whose names reflected their purposes: thus, the place where one studied became the study; in French, the word *cuisine* still refers both to the kitchen and to the food that is cooked there. People began to collect souvenirs for decoration, to spend significant sums on furnishings and art, and to make the bedroom a special place. By the mid-1600s the dressing-gown was a popular item of clothing, and the room in which it might be worn could have suggestive overtones.

EXPANSION OVERSEAS

Long before Europe's demographic and economic recovery began in the late 1400s, pioneer explorers had taken the first steps toward creating huge empires overseas. Extending the voyages beyond Europe of the crusaders and such travelers as Marco Polo, sailors had been

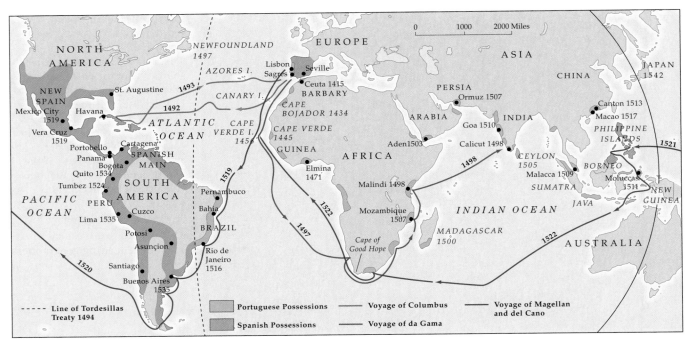

MAP 14.1 EXPLORATION AND CONQUEST IN THE FIFTEENTH AND SIXTEENTH CENTURIES
The division of the world between the Portuguese and the Spaniards led to distinct areas of exploration and settlement, demarcated by the line that both sides accepted at the Treaty of Tordesillas. Notice the extraordinary range of voyages and discoveries that were made in just a few decades after 1492. Which nation dominated exploration and settlement in the New World? What were other key areas of exploration and settlement?

◆ For an online version, go to www.mhhe.com/chambers9 > chapter 14 > book maps

inching around Africa seeking a route to the Far East. As they moved farther afield, they began conquering territory and peoples. The riches in goods and lands they eventually found would help fuel the boom of the sixteenth century.

The Portuguese

Henry the Navigator   Among the Portuguese, who began these voyages in the 1410s, there was little expectation of world-shattering consequences. The Portuguese lived in an inhospitable land whose seafarers had always been essential to the country's economy. The need for better agricultural opportunities had long drawn them to Atlantic islands like the Canaries and to territories held by the Muslims (Moors) in North Africa. But this ambition had to be organized into a sustained effort if it was to achieve results. In the early fifteenth century, Prince Henry the Navigator, a younger son of the king, undertook that task.

Henry participated in the capture of the North African port of Ceuta from the Muslims in 1415, a crusading expedition that only whetted his appetite for more such victories. At Ceuta he probably heard stories about lost Christians and mines of gold somewhere in the interior of Africa. A mixture of motives—profit, re-

ligion, and curiosity—spurred him on; and in 1419 he began patronizing sailors, mapmakers, astronomers (for their help in celestial navigation), shipbuilders, and instrument makers who were interested in discovery. They were mainly Italians, and their aim was not merely to make contact with Africans but to find an alternative route to India and the Far East around Africa (in order to avoid the Ottoman Empire, which was coming to dominate the eastern Mediterranean). The early adventurers did not succeed, but during their gradual advance down the West African coast, they opened a rich new trade in ivory, gold, and slaves.

To India and Beyond   Then, in 1488, a Portuguese captain, Bartholomeu Dias, returned to Lisbon after making a landfall on the east coast of Africa, beyond the Cape of Good Hope, which previously no one had been able to pass. The way to India now seemed open, but before the Portuguese sent out their first expedition, the news arrived that a sailor employed by the Spaniards, one Christopher Columbus, had apparently reached India by sailing west. To avoid conflicting claims that might interfere with their trade, Portugal and Spain signed the **Treaty of Tordesillas** in 1494. This gave Portugal possession of all the lands to the east of an imaginary line about 300 miles west of the Azores and Spain a monopoly of everything to the west. Portugal thus kept the only practical route to India (as well as the rights to Brazil, which one of its sailors may already have discovered). Three years later Vasco da Gama took the first Portuguese fleet across the Indian Ocean.

At first, he found it hard to trade, because the Arabs, who had controlled these waters for centuries, tried to keep out all rivals. Within fourteen years, however, the Portuguese merchants had established themselves. The key to their success was naval power. In addition to improving the design of sails to increase speed and maneuverability, the Portuguese were the first to emphasize firepower, realizing that cannon, not soldiers, won battles at sea. In addition, they deployed their ships in squadrons rather than individually, a tactic that further increased their superiority. The result was overwhelming military success. A series of victories reduced Arab naval strength, and bombardments quieted stubborn cities. By 1513 Portugal's trading posts extended beyond India to the rich Spice Islands, the Moluccas.

The Portuguese Empire   The empire Portugal created remained dependent on sea power, not overseas colonies. Except in Brazil, which was virtually unpopulated and where the settlers were able to establish huge estates worked by slave labor, the Portuguese relied on a chain of small trading bases that stretched from West Africa to China. They supplied and defended these bases, which usually consisted of little more than a few warehouses and a fort, by sea; and they tended to keep contacts with the local people to a minimum, so as to maintain friendly relations and missionary and trading rights. The one exception to the isolation was caused by the small numbers of Portuguese women who traveled to the settlements: In these early years there were more marriages with local women than there were in other European empires. But even though their effort remained relatively small-scale, the Portuguese soon profited from their explorations. Between 1442 and 1446 the Portuguese brought almost one thousand slaves from Africa. In the 1500s their wealth grew as they became major importers of luxuries from the East, such as spices, which were in great demand as medicines, preservatives, and tasty delicacies.

By dominating commerce with Eastern civilizations, which were not only richer but also more sophisticated than their own, Portugal's merchants controlled Europe's most valuable trade. But their dominance was to last less than a century, for their success spurred a competition for empire that was to stimulate new waves of overseas expansion. First, Spain determined to emulate its neighbor; and later, the Dutch, English, and French sought to outdo their predecessors and one another. This competition gave the Europeans the crucial stimulus that other peoples lacked, and it projected them into a dominance over the rest of the globe that would last for more than 450 years.

The Spaniards

Inspired by the same centuries-old crusading ambitions as the Portuguese, the Spaniards rode the second wave of expansion overseas. Because Spain was much larger than Portugal and directed its attention toward a more sparsely populated continent, the Spaniards founded their empire on conquest and colonization, not trade. But they got their start from a stroke of luck.

Columbus   Christopher Columbus—an experienced Genoese sailor who was widely read, well-versed in Atlantic sailing, and familiar with the leading geographers of his day—seems to have believed (we do not know for certain, because he was a secretive man) that Asia lay only 3,500 miles beyond the Canary Islands. Thus, convinced that sailing west across the Atlantic to the Far East was perfectly feasible, Columbus sought support from the Portuguese government. It refused, but he persisted and eventually gained the financial backing of Ferdinand V and Isabella I of Spain that enabled him to set sail in 1492. He was an excellent navigator (one of his discoveries on the voyage was the difference between true and magnetic north), and he kept his men going despite their horror of being so long at sea without sight of land. After thirty-three days, he reached the Bahamas. He was disappointed that he found no

Columbus Landing, Woodcut
This picture, by a contemporary, shows King Ferdinand, back in Spain, pointing to Columbus' three ships and the natives greeting the explorer in the New World.
New York Public Library

HISTORICAL ISSUES: TWO VIEWS OF COLUMBUS

The following two passages suggest the enormous differences that have arisen in interpretations of the career of Christopher Columbus. The first, by Samuel Eliot Morison, a historian and a noted sailor, represents the traditional view of the explorer's achievements that held sway until recent years. The second, by Kirkpatrick Sale, a writer and environmentalist, indicates how radically the understanding of the effects of exploration has changed in recent years.

1. "Columbus had a Hellenic sense of wonder at the new and strange, combined with an artist's appreciation of natural beauty. Moreover, Columbus had a deep conviction of the sovereignty and the infinite wisdom of God, which enhanced all his triumphs. One only wishes that the Admiral might have been afforded the sense of fulfillment that would have come from foreseeing all that flowed from his discoveries. The whole history of the Americas stems from the Four Voyages of Columbus, and as the Greek city-states looked back to the deathless gods as their founders, so today a score of independent nations unite in homage to Christopher the stout-hearted son of Genoa, who carried Christian civilization across the Ocean Sea."

   From S. E. Morison, *Admiral of the Ocean Sea: A Life of Christopher Columbus*, Boston: Little, Brown, 1942, pp. 670–671.

2. "For all his navigational skill, about which the salty types make such a fuss, and all his fortuitous headings, Admiral Colón [Christopher Columbus] could be a wretched mariner. The four voyages, properly seen, quite apart from bravery, are replete with lubberly mistakes, misconceived sailing plans, foolish disregard of elementary maintenance, and stubborn neglect of basic safety—all characterized by the assertion of human superiority over the natural realm. Almost every time Colón went wrong, it was because he had refused to bend to the inevitabilities of tide and wind and reef or, more arrogantly still, had not bothered to learn about them.

   "Many of those who know well the cultures that once existed in the New World have reason to be less than enthusiastic about [the 1992 celebrations of] the event that led to the destruction of much of that heritage and the greater part of the people who produced it; others are planning to protest the entire goings-on as a wrongful commemoration of an act steeped in bloodshed, slavery, and genocide."

   From Kirkpatrick Sale, *The Conquest of Paradise: Christopher Columbus and the Columbian Legacy*, New York: Knopf, 1990, pp. 209–210, 362.

Chinese or Japanese as he investigated Cuba and the west coast of Hispaniola (today's Haiti), but he was certain that he had reached Asia, even though the few natives he saw did not resemble those whom travelers such as Marco Polo had described.

Columbus crossed the Atlantic Ocean three more times, but he made no other significant discoveries. Yet he did also start the tradition of violence against local people that was to characterize the European conquest of the New World. During his first stay in the Caribbean, his men killed some of the natives they encountered. From the very beginning, therefore, it became clear that the building of empires in the Americas would be a process of destruction as well as creation, of cruelty as well as achievement (see "Two Views of Columbus," above). For the victims, the effect of the brutality, soon intensified by the devastating diseases that accompanied the Europeans, was to undermine their ancient civilizations.

The Limits of Westward Voyages By the end of Columbus' life in 1506, it was becoming apparent that he had found islands close by a new continent, not Asia. The last hope of a quick journey to the riches of East Asia was dashed in 1522, when the one surviving ship from a fleet of five that had set out under Ferdinand Magellan three years before returned to Spain after the ordeal of having sailed around the world.

Magellan's 98-day crossing of the Pacific was the supreme accomplishment of seamanship in the age of discovery. But the voyage persuaded the Spaniards that Portugal had the fastest route to the East, and in 1529 they renounced all attempts to trade with the Spice Islands. Spain could now concentrate on the Americas, those unexpected continents that were to become not an obstacle on the way to the Spice Islands but possessions of unbelievable richness.

The Conquistador Volunteers for empire building were amply available. When the last Muslim kingdom in southern Spain was conquered by the Castilians in 1492, soldiers with long experience of military service found themselves at loose ends. Many were the younger sons of noble families, who were often kept from inheriting land because Spanish law usually allowed only the eldest son to inherit. The prospect of unlimited land

and military adventure across the Atlantic appealed to them, as it did to ambitious members of Castile's lower classes, and thus the **conquistador,** or conqueror, was born. There were not many of them—fewer than one thousand—but they overran much of the Americas in search of wealth and glory.

The first and most dramatic was Hernando Cortès, who in 1519 landed on the Mexican coast and set out to overcome the rich Aztec civilization in the high plateau of central Mexico. His army consisted of only six hundred troops, but in two years, with a few reinforcements, he had won a complete victory. Guns alone made no important difference, because Cortès had only thirteen muskets and some unwieldy cannons. More effective were his horses, his manipulation of the Aztecs' beliefs (especially after he murdered their ruler) to make them regard him as invincible, and the unshakable determination of his followers. The conquest of the Mexican Mayas also began under Cortès, while the Incas of Peru fell to Francisco Pizzaro. Other conquistadors repeated these successes throughout Central and South America. By 1550 the conquest was over, and the military leaders gave way to administrators who began organizing the huge empire they had won.

The First Colonial Empires

The Spanish government established in the New World the same pattern of political administration that it was setting up in its European territories. Representatives of the throne, viceroys, were sent to administer each territory and to impose centralized control. They were advised by the local *audiencia,* a kind of miniature council that also acted as a court of law, but the ultimate authority remained in Spain.

Real growth did not begin, however, until women pioneers came out to the settlements. In this empire, unlike Portugal's, intermarriage was strongly discouraged. Indeed, the indigenous peoples were treated with a brutality and disdain that set a dismal model for overseas empires. Their labor was cruelly exploited on farms and especially in silver mines that the Spaniards discovered, where working conditions were dreadful. Families were split apart so that men could be put to work, and local beliefs and traditions were actively suppressed (though many survived despite the oppression). Over the years, intermarriage between Europeans and natives increased, and a more united society evolved, but this transformation took centuries to achieve. In the meantime, Spain's colonies were an object of envy because of their mineral wealth. In 1545 Spaniards discovered a major vein of silver at Potosì, in Bolivia, and from those mines came the treasure that made fortunes for the colonists, sustained Spain's many wars, and ultimately enriched much of Europe.

For the balance of the sixteenth century, however, despite the efforts of other countries, Portugal and Spain remained the only conspicuous participants in Europe's overseas expansion.

The Perilous Life of the Settlers   It took a great deal of determination to board one of the ships that set off across the oceans from Europe. Life at sea offered discomfort and peril: horrible overcrowding, inadequate and often rotting food, disease, dangerous storms, poor navigation, and threats from enemy ships. One cannot determine numbers precisely, but it has been estimated that in some decades of the sixteenth and seventeenth centuries, fewer than two-thirds of those who embarked reached their destination. And their troubles did not end when they came off the ships. Unfamiliar countries, famine, illness, and attacks by natives and European rivals made life precarious at best. Although five thousand people sailed for Virginia between 1619 and 1624, for instance, disease and massacre kept the colony the same size at the end of that period—about one thousand inhabitants—as it had been at the beginning. And yet, despite the difficulties and dangers, people found reasons to keep coming.

The Aims of the Colonists   For a few leaders, like the Spanish minor nobles known as *hidalgos* who commanded most of Spain's first missions, the attraction was partly adventure, partly the chance to command a military expedition of conquest, and partly the hope of making a fortune that seemed unlikely at home. For another fairly small group, the clergy, the aim was to bring the word of God to people who had never encountered Christianity before. And government officials and traders hoped they might advance more rapidly than in their native lands. For these middle and upper levels of society, however, survival was rarely an issue: They might die in battle or from illness, and life may not have been as comfortable as it would have been at home, but the opportunities to exercise power or to make a fortune were far greater. The outlook was very different for the vast majority of the new settlers.

Finding Ordinary Settlers   For most of them, leaving Europe was a fairly desperate act, an indication that almost any alternative seemed preferable to the bleak prospects in their homeland. If it had not been for the growth of population in the sixteenth century—and the many thousands it made homeless, unable to remain in their villages or make a living in towns—it is unlikely that enough emigrants would have been found to do the work in ports and on the land that was crucial to building empires in Asia and America. It is significant that fewer people moved from a rich country like France than from the less prosperous Spain and Portugal. Despite the pressures that persuaded thousands of

SLAVE SHIP
This picture, made aboard a slave ship, shows the dangerously crowded conditions in which Africans were brought to the New World. It is small wonder that so many died of disease even before the end of this miserable voyage.
National Maritime Museum, Greenwich, London

people to leave their homelands, therefore, additional means had to be found to populate the empires.

Long before the English colonized Australia with convicts in the eighteenth century, for example, they were taking people out of prison to send overseas to places desperate for settlers. Another tactic was to offer land to anyone who was willing to work for others for seven years. The English, and to a lesser extent the French, permitted religious minorities who feared persecution at home to start a new and more independent existence in America. In general, powerful inducements like poverty or persecution were needed to drive Europeans to accept the hazards of the journey and the subsequent struggles of the pioneer. Some, such as the religious refugees, set out as families, but usually many more men than women made the voyage. In pioneer communities all labor was essential and difficult, but there is no question that women, not only more vulnerable to violence but also regarded as subordinate to males, had far more to risk by emigrating; the chronic imbalance between sexes thus became yet another hardship of life overseas.

Exploitation of Settlers and Natives   When even distress at home provided too few volunteers, the coloniz-

ers relied on force to obtain the workers they needed. Just as captains often kidnapped men for a ship's crew, so, too, did the suppliers of settlers. Many persons woke up at sea surprised to find where they were. And once in the colonies, wage earners could expect their employment to be harsh.

Indigenous populations, however, faced the most ruthless treatment: In Central and South America millions died (estimates vary between 25 and 90 percent of the native peoples, with the worst devastations in Mexico) as a result mainly of the new diseases the Europeans brought, though their susceptibility may have been heightened by the terrible forced labor to which they were subjected. Even exploitation, however, was not enough to feed the insatiable need for miners, laborers, servants, and farmhands.

The Commerce in Slaves   The solution the colonizers found was slavery, familiar since ancient times but virtually nonexistent among Europeans by 1500. To find the slaves, ships began visiting the west coast of Africa, where the local inhabitants were either captured or purchased from local rulers and then transported to the New World under the most ghastly conditions. They were thrown together in cramped, filthy quarters, often bound, barely fed, and beaten at the slightest provocation. Nor was there much improvement for those—often fewer than half—who survived the crossing. The slaves sustained the empires and made it possible for their white masters to profit from the silver, tobacco, cotton, and other goods they produced; but the grim conditions of their lives, and their high rates of mortality, would have wiped them out if there had not been a constant stream of slaves from Africa to replenish their numbers.

Long-Term Effects   For those settlers who reaped rewards from the mines and the agricultural products of America, or from the trade with Europe that enriched all the colonies, the hardships did not last long. They created flourishing cities and universities and made huge fortunes. Their commercial networks began to link the entire world together for the first time in history. But for the many who struggled to expand these empires, life on the frontier, despite the promise of new opportunities, remained hard and dangerous for centuries. And for the slaves, there was not the slightest improvement in conditions or even hope of improvement, until revolts and civil wars finally abolished slavery in the nineteenth century. This was the context in which European institutions and culture came to dominate the rest of the world, though the encounter was by no means a one-way process.

One historian has described the interaction that followed Columbus as the Columbian Exchange, because ideas, people, microbes, plants, and animals flowed in both directions between the Old and New Worlds. Although the Spaniards saw themselves as converting natives from paganism to Catholicism, local cultures often tailored Western ideas to their own needs and managed to retain ancient practices and attitudes. In India, both the Portuguese and the English adopted customs and language from the local population, thus confirming what the Frenchman Michel de Montaigne had said as early as the 1580s, when he had compared the greed and violence of the Europeans unfavorably with the simplicity and harmonious lives of those whom they had conquered. For all that they learned, however, there is no question that the Europeans saw themselves mainly as teachers: their military and technological might entitled them, so they believed, to bring their "civilization" to the rest of the world.

THE CENTRALIZATION OF POLITICAL POWER

The economic and social transformations that began around 1500 gained important support from the actions of central governments. Especially in England, France, and Spain, rulers gave vital encouragement to the growth of trade, overseas expansion, and attempts to relieve social distress. At the same time, the growing prosperity of the age enhanced the tax revenues that were essential to their power. Both of these mutually reinforcing developments had long-term effects, but it could be argued that the creation of well-organized states, built around strong central governments, was even more decisive than the economic boom in shaping the future of Western Europe.

The rulers of England, France, and Spain in the late fifteenth and early sixteenth centuries were especially successful in accumulating and centralizing power, and historians have therefore called them "new monarchs." The reigns of Henry VII, Louis XI, and Ferdinand and Isabella, in particular, have come to be regarded as marking the end of more than a century of political fragmentation. They set in motion a revival of royal authority that eventually weakened all rivals to the crown and created the bureaucracies characteristic of the modern state.

Tudor England

The English monarchs had relied for centuries on local cooperation to run their kingdom. Unlike other European countries, England contained only fifty or sixty families who were legally nobles out of a population of perhaps 2.5 million. But many other families, though not technically members of the nobility, had large estates and were dominant figures at the parish, county, and even national levels. They were known as gentry, and it was from their ranks that the crown appointed the local officers who administered the realm—notably the justices of the peace (usually referred to as JPs). These voluntary unpaid officials served as the principal public servants in the more than forty counties of the land.

For reasons of status as well as a feeling of responsibility, the gentry had always sought such appointments. From the crown's point of view, the great advantage of the system was its efficiency: Enforcement was in the hands of those who could enforce. As a "great man" in his neighborhood, the JP rarely had trouble exerting his authority. Thus, the king had at his disposal an administrative structure without rival in Europe because, unlike other rulers, he could count on the cooperation of the leaders of each locality. Since the gentry had so much responsibility, they developed a strong sense of duty over the centuries, and the king increasingly sought their advice.

Parliament and Common Law   In the sixteenth century an institution that had developed from this relationship, the consultative assembly known as **Parliament,** began to take on a general importance as the chief representative of the country's wishes; it was increasingly considered the only body that could give a

HENRY VIII CLAIMS INDEPENDENCE FROM THE POPE

One of the crucial acts of Parliament through which Henry VIII made the Church of England independent of Rome was the so-called Act in Restraint of Appeals, which became law in 1533. This law forbade English subjects from appealing court decisions to Rome, which they had been allowed to do when the pope was accepted as the supreme authority. To justify this action, the preamble of the act made a claim for the independence of England and the authority of the king that was typical of the new monarchs of the age.

"Where by divers sundry old authentic histories and chronicles it is manifestly declared that this realm of England is an empire, governed by one supreme head and king, having the dignity and royal estate of the imperial crown of the same, unto whom a body politic be bound and owe next to God a natural and humble obedience; he being also furnished by the goodness of Almighty God with whole and entire power, preeminence, authority, prerogative and jurisdiction to render justice and final determination in all causes, debates and contentions, without restraint to any foreign princes, [and] without the intermeddling of any exterior person, to declare and determine all such doubts. In consideration whereof the King's Highness, his Nobles and Commons, enact, establish and ordain that all causes, already commenced or hereafter coming into contention within this realm or within any of the King's dominions, whether they concern the King our sovereign lord or any other subject, shall be from henceforth heard, examined, discussed, finally and definitely adjudged and determined within the King's jurisdiction and authority and not elsewhere."

From 24 Henry VIII, c. 12, as printed in *Statutes of the Realm*, Vol. 3, London, 1810–1828, pp. 427–429.

ruler's actions a broad stamp of approval. Although Parliament remained subordinate to the crown for a long time, England's kings already realized that without parliamentary consent they could not take measures such as raising extraordinary taxes.

Just as Parliament served to unify the country, so too did another ancient institution: the common law. This was a system of justice based on precedent and tradition that was the same, or "common," throughout England. In contrast to the Roman law that prevailed on the Continent, common law grew out of the interpretations of precedent made by individual judges and the decisions of juries. A court could be dominated by local leaders, but in general this was a system of justice, administered by judges who traveled from area to area, that helped bind England together. Like Parliament, the common law would eventually be regarded by opponents of royal power as an independent source of authority with which the crown could not interfere. In the late 1400s, however, it was an important help to a king who was trying to overcome England's political fragmentation and forge a more unified realm.

Henry VII and the Revival of Royal Power
Henry VII (1485–1509), who founded the Tudor Dynasty, came to the throne as a usurper in the aftermath of more than thirty years of civil conflict, the Wars of the Roses. England's nobles had caused chaos in these wars, and they had consistently ignored the wishes of the monarchy. The situation hardly looked promising for a reassertion of royal power. Yet Henry both extended the authority of the crown and restored order with extraordinary speed.

With a combination of fiscal caution and the determined collection of revenues, he put royal finances on a sound footing. At the same time, by relying on JPs and exerting his own authority in both political and legal matters, he began to tame England's nobles. He increased the authority of the royal Council, and had his councillors serve on a new, powerful court (known as Star Chamber from the decorations on the ceiling of the room where they met). Here there was no jury, local lords had no influence, and decisions were quick and fair. Eventually, Star Chamber and other royal courts came to be seen as threats to England's traditional common law. Under the Tudors, however, they were accepted as highly effective means of restoring order and asserting the power of the central government.

Henry's son and successor, Henry VIII (1509–1547), was an arrogant, dazzling figure, a strong contrast to his careful father. In 1513 he removed a long-standing threat from England's north by inflicting a shattering defeat on an invading Scots army at Flodden. With his prestige thus enhanced, he spent the next fifteen years consolidating royal power.

The Transformation of Parliament
The turning point in the reign came when Henry decided to break with the Roman Church (see chapter 13). The creation of an independent English Church had major political consequences, notably its strengthening of the institution of Parliament. The Reformation Parliament, summoned in 1529, remained in existence for seven years and acted on more matters of importance than a Parliament had ever considered before. The laws it passed gave it

Anonymous
EDWARD VI AND THE POPE
The anti-Catholic feelings that began to grow in England during the reign of Edward VI are expressed in this painting. The young king sits on his throne. His father, Henry VIII, who started the Reformation in England, points to him as the victor over Catholicism. The crushing of the old faith is symbolized by Christ's conquering of the pope and monks (below) and the destruction of Roman churches and images (through the window).
By courtesy of The National Portrait Gallery, London (NPG4165)

new responsibilities, and the length of its sessions also enhanced its stature.

Previously, election to Parliament had been considered a chore by the townsmen and landed gentry in the House of Commons, who found the expense of unpaid attendance and the time it took more irksome than did the wealthy nobles in the House of Lords. But this attitude changed in the 1530s as members of the Commons met again and again; they came to know one another and to regard themselves as guardians of Parliament's traditions and privileges. Eventually, they were to make the Commons the dominant house in Parliament.

Royal Power   After guiding Henry through the break with Rome, Thomas Cromwell became the king's chief minister. He was a tireless bureaucrat who reorganized the administration of the country and used the newly created Privy Council, consisting of the king's principal advisers, to coordinate and direct royal government. The principal beneficiary of these events was the crown. Royal income rose markedly with the appropriation of

Church fees and possessions, many of which were sold, making fortunes for speculators and new families of landowners. For all the stimulus he gave to parliamentary power and the landed class, Henry now had a much larger, wealthier, and more sophisticated administration at his disposal; and no one doubted where ultimate authority lay. He did not establish a standing army, as some of the continental kings did, because he could crush all opposition without it. And this strong central administration even survived the eleven years of uncertainty that followed Henry's death in 1547.

Edward VI and Mary I   During the reign of Edward VI (1547–1553), who died while still a minor, the nobility attempted to regain control of the government. There was a relaxation of central authority, and the Reformation advanced rapidly. But even when Edward's half-sister, Mary I (1553–1558), briefly reestablished Roman Catholicism, forced many of her subjects into exile, and provoked two major revolts, royal power was strong enough to survive. The next monarch, Henry VIII's last surviving child, Elizabeth, demonstrated that the growth of the monarchy's authority had hardly been interrupted under Edward and Mary.

Valois France

The rulers of France in the fifteenth century, members of the Valois family, were unlike the English kings in that they lacked a well-formed organization for local government. Aristocrats dominated many regions, particularly those farthest from Paris, and great nobles had become virtually independent rulers. With their own administrations and often their own courts and taxation, they left the crown little say in their affairs. The size of the kingdom also limited royal power; it took more than a week to travel from Paris to the remoter parts of the realm—almost double the time for the equivalent English journey. The monarchy had tried to resolve the problem of ruling distant provinces by granting to close relatives large blocs of territory that the crown seized or inherited. Theoretically, these relatives would execute royal wishes more effectively than the king could from Paris. In practice, however, an ambitious family member often became just as difficult to handle as any powerful noble. After 1469 the crown kept control over such acquisitions—an indication that it now had the resources to exercise authority even in areas far from the capital.

Royal Administration   The administrative center of the government was the royal council in Paris. The greatest court of law in the land was the Parlement of Paris, which had remained a judicial body, unlike the English Parliament, and whose members were appointed by the crown. As the central administration grew in the fifteenth and early sixteenth centuries, various provinces received their own **parlements,** a recognition of the continuing strength of the demand for local autonomy. But there was a countervailing force: the dominance of Roman law, which (unlike England's common law) was based on royal decree and which allowed the monarch to govern by issuing ordinances and edicts. These had to be registered by the parlements in order to take effect, but usually that was a formality.

Estates and Finance   Representative assemblies, known as **Estates,** also limited the power of the throne. A number of provinces had such Estates, and they had to approve the level of taxation and other royal policies. Negotiations with these bodies were essential for the support of the king's income and his army. But France's chief representative body, the Estates General—consisting of clergy, nobles, and townsmen from every region—never attained the prestige of the English Parliament and was never able to bind the country together or function as a vital organ of government. The French kings thus had a degree of independence that English monarchs did not achieve, particularly in the area of finance. For centuries they had supplemented their main sources of income, from lands and customs duties, with a sales tax (*aide*), a hearth tax (*taille*), and a salt tax (*gabelle*). In earlier days the consent of the localities had been required for such levies, but after 1451 the taxes could be collected on the king's authority alone, though he still had to negotiate the exact rate with provincial Estates and be careful not to go beyond what would seem reasonable to his subjects.

The Standing Army   The most decisive source of power available to the French king (unlike the English king) was his standing army. The upkeep of the troops accounted for more than half the royal expenditures in Louis XI's reign, mainly because their numbers grew as revenues increased. In the 1480s a force of at least fifteen thousand men, chiefly professional mercenaries and military-minded nobles, was kept in readiness every campaigning season from spring to fall. Because of the rising costs associated with the development of gunpowder weapons, only the central government could afford to maintain such an army. And the troops had to be billeted in various provinces, with support from the local Estates. As a result, the entire French population eventually bore the indirect burden of heavier taxation, while many regions of France had direct contact with royal soldiers. Although frequently short of pay, the troops were firmly under royal control and hence a vital device—rarely used, but always a threat—in the strengthening of royal authority.

Louis XI   When Louis XI (1461–1483) began his reign, he faced a situation as unpromising as that of Henry VII at his succession, for the country had just emerged from the Hundred Years' War and royal authority was generally ignored. English troops, which had been in France for most of the war, had finally departed in the 1450s; but a new and equally dangerous menace had arisen in the east: the dukedom of Burgundy.

Extending Control   By the 1460s the duke of Burgundy was among the most powerful lords in Western Europe. He ruled a loosely organized dominion that stretched from the Low Countries to the Swiss Confederation, and his capital, Dijon, had become a major cultural and political center. In 1474 Louis XI put together a coalition against Charles the Bold, Duke of Burgundy, who had been at war with him for some seven years, and in 1477 Charles was killed in battle. Louis then annexed the duchy of Burgundy itself, though Mary, the duke's daughter, retained the Low Countries, which would later form part of the inheritance of her grandson, the Holy Roman Emperor Charles V.

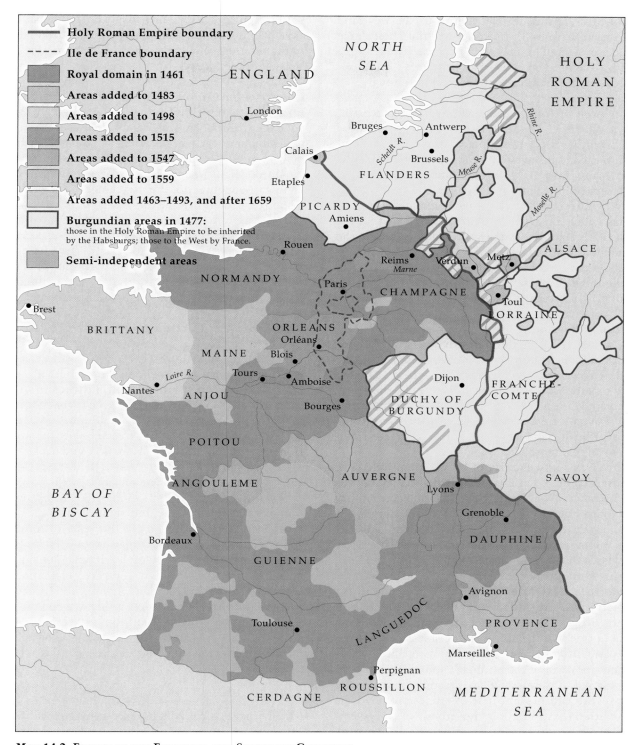

MAP 14.2 FRANCE IN THE FIFTEENTH AND SIXTEENTH CENTURIES
This map shows in detail the successive stages whereby the monarchy extended its control throughout France.
Note the territory that the king controlled directly in 1461. What were the largest new areas added after 1461?
Which Burgundian areas did France acquire?

◆ For an online version, go to www.mhhe.com/chambers9 > chapter 14 > book maps

Louis also expanded his authority to the west and south, because in 1481 he inherited the three large provinces of Anjou, Maine, and Provence. Thus, by the end of his reign, royal power had penetrated into massive areas where previously it had been unknown.

The Invasion of Italy   Louis XI's son and successor, Charles VIII (1483–1498), was only thirteen years old when his father died. When he came of age, he determined to expand his dynasty's territory, and in 1494 he led an army into Italy. After some successes, the French settled into a prolonged struggle with the Habsburgs for control of the rich Italian peninsula. The conflicts lasted for sixty-five years, ending in defeat for the French. Although the Italian wars failed to satisfy the monarchy's territorial ambitions, they provided an outlet and distraction for the restless French nobility and gave the kings, as commanders in time of war, an opportunity to consolidate royal power at home.

Increasing Revenues   After Charles VIII's reign, France's financial and administrative machinery grew in both size and effectiveness, largely because of the demands of the Italian wars. There was rarely enough money to support the adventure; the kings, therefore, relied heavily on loans from bankers, who sometimes shaped France's financial policies. At the same time, the crown made a determined effort to increase traditional royal revenues.

France was a rich country of 15 million people with the most fertile land in Europe; yet the financial needs of the monarch always outstripped his subjects' ability to pay. With exemptions from the *taille* and the *gabelle* for nobles, many towns, royal officeholders, and the clergy, the bulk of the taxes had to be raised from the very classes that had the least to give. Other means of raising revenue were therefore needed, and one solution was the sale of offices. Positions were sold in the administration, the parlements, and every branch of the bureaucracy to purchasers eager to obtain both the tax exemption and the considerable status (sometimes a title of nobility) that the offices bestowed. From modest and uncertain beginnings under Louis XII (1498–1515), the system widened steadily; by the end of the sixteenth century, the sale of offices provided the crown with one-twelfth of its revenues.

Many other rulers were adopting this device, and everywhere it had similar effects: It stimulated social mobility, creating dynasties of noble officeholders and a new administrative class; it caused a dramatic expansion of bureaucracies; and it encouraged corruption. The system spread most rapidly and the effects were most noticeable in France, where the reign of Francis I (1515–1547) witnessed a major increase in the government's power as its servants multiplied. Francis tried hard to continue expanding royal control by launching expeditions into Italy, but in fact, he contributed more to the development of the crown's authority by his actions at home.

Control of the Church   One of the most remarkable of Francis' accomplishments was the power he gained over the Church. He was highly successful in his Italian campaigns early in his reign, and he used the power he won in Italy to persuade the pope in 1516 to give the crown the right to appoint all of France's bishops and abbots. According to this agreement, the income a bishop earned during his first year in office still went to the Vatican, but, in effect, Francis now controlled the French Church. Its enormous patronage was at his disposal, and he could use it to reward servants or raise money. By making an agreement with the pope, he did not need to break with Rome in order to obtain authority over the clergy, as did Henry VIII in England.

The Advance of Centralization   In the 1520s Francis also began a major reorganization of the government. He legalized the sale of offices and formed an inner council, more manageable than the large royal council, to act as the chief executive body of the realm. Against the parlements, meanwhile, the king invoked the *lit de justice*, a prerogative that allowed him to appear in person before an assembly that was delaying the registration of any of his edicts or ordinances and declare them registered and therefore law. As for the Estates General, they did not meet between 1484 and 1560.

By the end of Francis' reign, royal power was stronger than ever before; but signs of disunity had appeared that would intensify in the years to come. The Reformation was under way, and one of its movements, Calvinism, soon caused religious divisions and social unrest in France. As the reign of Francis' son Henry II (1547–1559) came to a close, the Italian wars finally ended in a French defeat, badly damaging royal prestige. The civil wars that followed came perilously close to destroying all that France's kings had achieved during the previous one hundred years.

United Spain

The Iberian Peninsula in the mid-fifteenth century was divided into three very different kingdoms. Portugal on the west, with some 1.5 million inhabitants, looked overseas. Castile, in the center, with a population of more than 8 million, was the largest and richest area. Sheep farming was the basis of its prosperity, and its countryside was dominated by powerful nobles. Castile was the last kingdom still fighting Muslims on its southern frontier, and in this ceaseless crusade the nobles played a leading part. They had built up both a

Anonymous
FRANCIS I AND HIS COURT
The splendor and the patronage of learning for which the new monarchs were known are evoked by this tiny painting of the French king. He sits at a table with his three sons, surrounded by his courtiers and listening to the author reading the very manuscript (a translation of an ancient Greek historian) that this picture illustrates.
From Les Trois Premiers Livres de Diodore de Sicile, translated by A. Macault, 1534. Parchment, Ms. 721, f. lv, frontispiece. Musée Condé, Chantilly, France. Réunion des Musées Nationaux/ Art Resource, NY

great chivalric tradition and considerable political strength as a result of their exploits, and their status was enhanced by the religious fervor that the long struggle had inspired. To the east, Aragon, slightly larger than Portugal, consisted of three areas: Catalonia, the heart of the kingdom and a great commercial region centered on the city of Barcelona; Aragon itself, which was little more than a barren hinterland to Catalonia; and Valencia, a farming and fishing region south of Catalonia along the Mediterranean coast.

In October 1469, Isabella, future queen of Castile, married Ferdinand, future king of Sicily and heir to the throne of Aragon. Realizing that the marriage would strengthen the crown, the Castilian nobles opposed the

union, precipitating a ten-year civil war. But the two monarchs emerged victorious, and they created a new political entity: the Kingdom of Spain. They and their successors were to be as effective as the kings of England and France in centralizing power and establishing royal control over their realms.

Ferdinand and Isabella   When Ferdinand and Isabella jointly assumed the thrones of Castile in 1474 and Aragon five years later, they made no attempt to create a monolithic state. Aragon remained a federation of territories, administered by viceroys who were appointed by the king but who allowed local customs to remain virtually intact. The traditions of governing by consent and preserving the subjects' rights were particularly strong in this kingdom, where each province had its own representative assembly, known as the **Cortes.** In Castile, however, the two monarchs were determined to assert their superiority over all possible rivals to their authority. Their immediate aims were to restore the order in the countryside that had been destroyed by civil war, much as it had been in England and France, and to reduce the power of the nobility.

The first objective was accomplished with the help of the Cortes of Castile, an assembly dominated by urban representatives who shared the wish for order because peace benefited trade. The Cortes established special tribunals to pursue and try criminals, and by the 1490s it had succeeded in ending the widespread lawlessness in the kingdom.

The Centralization of Power   To reinforce their authority, Ferdinand and Isabella sharply reduced the number of great nobles in the royal council and overhauled the entire administration, particularly the financial agencies, applying the principle that ability, rather than social status, should determine appointments. As the bureaucracy spread, the *hidalgo,* a lesser aristocrat who depended heavily on royal favor, became increasingly important in government. Unlike the great nobles, whose enormous wealth was little affected by reforms that reduced their political role, the hidalgos were hurt when they lost their tax exemptions. The new livelihood they found was in serving the crown, and they became essential figures in the centralization of power in Castile as well as in the overseas territories.

The monarchs achieved greater leverage over their nobles in the 1480s and 1490s, when they gained control of the aristocracy's rich and powerful military orders. These wealthy organizations, run by Castile's most important aristocratic families, gave allegiance primarily to their own elected leaders. To take over their leadership required assertiveness and determination, especially by Isabella, Castile's ruler. At one point she rode on horseback for three straight days in order to get to one of the order's elections and control the outcome. The great nobles could not be subdued completely; nor did the monarchs seek to destroy their power, for they were essential servants of the crown in the army and the higher levels of government. But like the kings of England and France, Ferdinand and Isabella wanted to reduce the nobles' autonomy to a level that did not threaten central authority, and it was thus crucial that they overcame the independence of the military orders by 1500.

Independence of the Church   They also succeeded in weakening Spain's bishops and abbots, who were as strong and wealthy as leading nobles. When Ferdinand and Isabella finally destroyed the power of the Muslims in southern Castile in 1492, the pope granted the monarchy the right to make major ecclesiastical appointments in the newly won territory, and this right was extended to the **New World** shortly thereafter. During the reign of Ferdinand and Isabella's successor, Charles I, the monarchy gained complete control over Church appointments, making Spain more independent of Rome than any other Catholic state.

Royal Administration   Mastery over the towns and the Cortes of Castile proved easy to achieve. Where local rule was concerned, a minor royal official, the *corregidor,* was given new powers and a position of responsibility within the administrative hierarchy. He was usually a hidalgo, and he became the chief executive and judicial officer in his region, rather like the justice of the peace in England; he also supervised town affairs. The Cortes did not seriously restrict the crown, because Spanish taxes, like French, could be raised without consent. The Castilian assembly met frequently and even provided additional funds for foreign wars, but it never challenged royal supremacy during this reign.

The justice system the monarchs supervised directly, hearing cases personally once a week. As in most Roman law systems, all law was considered to come from the throne, and the monarchs had full power to overrule the decisions of local courts, often run by nobles. Centralized judicial machinery began to appear, and in a few decades Castilian law was organized into a uniform code—always a landmark in the stabilization of a state. The code remained in effect for centuries and was a tribute to the determination and effectiveness with which the crown had centralized its dominions.

The Increase in Revenues   Considering the anarchy at the start of their reign and the absence of central institutions, Ferdinand and Isabella performed greater wonders in establishing royal power than any of the other new monarchs. Thanks to their takeover of the military orders and their growing bureaucracy, their finances soon improved. After the main administrative reforms were completed in the 1490s, the yield of the sales tax (the *alcabala*), the mainstay of royal income, rose dramatically. Total annual revenue is estimated to have soared from 80,000 ducats in 1474 to 2.3 million by 1504, the year Isabella died.

Religious Zeal   Religious affairs, too, helped the consolidation of royal authority. After the civil wars in Castile ended in 1479, the two monarchs sought to drive the Muslims from southern Castile. The reasons for the aggressive policy were clear: First, it complemented the drive for centralized power; second, war was a traditional interest for ambitious rulers, and it helped keep restless nobles occupied; and finally, the crusade stimulated the country's religious fervor, which in turn promoted enthusiasm for its rulers.

The religious zeal aroused by the fight with the Muslims intensified Spaniards' loyalty toward their rulers, and it is not surprising that the monarchy sought religious uniformity as a means of strengthening political uniformity. Nor did the campaign come to an end when the last Muslim stronghold in the south, Granada, capitulated in 1492. Later that year, all Jews were expelled from Spain. Some 150,000 of the country's most enterprising people—including prominent physicians, government officials, and other leaders of economic and cultural life—were given four months to leave. Targeting a visible and often persecuted minority was a popular move, and it also fed a religious passion that indirectly enhanced the crown's authority.

The Inquisition   The same drive to consolidate their strength prompted Ferdinand and Isabella to obtain permission from the pope in 1478 to establish their own Inquisition. Beginning in 1483 this body was run by a royal council and given a mandate to root out those *Conversos* and *Moriscos*—converted Jews and former Muslims—who were suspected of practicing their old beliefs in secret. After the fall of Granada, the Church tried to convert the conquered Muslims, and in 1502 those who had not accepted Christianity were expelled from the country. Eventually, in 1609, the Moriscos too were exiled from Spain. The persecution helped foster a religious unity that only enhanced the political centralization that the monarchy had achieved.

Military and Diplomatic Achievements   Ferdinand focused heavily on foreign affairs during the twelve years he ruled on his own after Isabella's death in 1504. He regained two provinces on the French border, and then, worried by France's Italian invasion, Ferdinand entered the war in Italy.

His achievements in the next two decades were due to a combination of military and diplomatic skills unusual even among the highly capable rulers of the age. A reorganization of Spain's standing army made it the most effective in Europe, and it soon dominated Italy. Ferdinand also founded the finest diplomatic service of the sixteenth century, centered on five permanent embassies: at Rome, Venice, London, Brussels, and the Habsburg court. The ambassadors' reports and activities made him the best-informed and most effective maneuverer in the international politics of his reign. By the time of his death in 1516, the united Spain that he and Isabella created had gained both territory and authority at home and international power abroad.

Charles V, Holy Roman Emperor

To bolster their dynasty, Ferdinand and Isabella had married their children to members of the leading families of Europe. Their daughter Joanna became the wife of the Habsburg Archduke Philip of Austria, and her son Charles became heir to the royal throne of Spain as well as the Habsburg dukedom.

The Revolt of the Communes   Early in his reign as King of Spain, however, Charles (1516–1556) had to withstand a major onslaught on the crown's position. Educated in Flanders, he spoke no Castilian, and when he arrived in Spain late in 1517, he soon aroused the resentment of the local nobility, particularly when members of the large Flemish entourage he brought with him were given positions in the government. The young king stayed for two and a half years, during which time he was elected emperor of the Holy Roman Empire (1519). This enhanced his prestige, but it also intensified his subjects' fears that he would become an absentee ruler with little interest in their affairs. As he left for Germany in 1520, revolts began to break out in Spain's towns, and the risings of these communes racked the country for two years. The troubles Charles now endured were among the first of many major clashes during the next 150 years between the traditional dynastic aims of the leading European monarchs and the jealous sense of distinctiveness felt by their subjects.

Fortunately for the crown, the communes lacked clear aims; their resentments and hopes were deep but vague. They wanted to reverse the growth of royal power and restore their traditional autonomy—a grievance central governments were bound to encounter as they extended their authority. At first they had the strong sympathy of the Spanish nobles, who particularly disliked the foreign ruler. But the movement soon revealed other aims, with social overtones: The communes launched attacks on the privileged orders of society, especially the nobility, and this lost the revolt its only chance for success. For the nobles then turned against the communes and defeated them in battle even before Charles returned to Spain.

Imperial Ambitions   The king took warning from the uprisings and made sure that his administration was now kept entirely Spanish. As calm returned, his subjects could channel their energies into imperial missions overseas, where the conquest of Mexico was under way, and against the Ottoman Turks in the Mediterranean. The large empire the Spaniards established in Central and South America was the most notable extension of royal power during Charles's reign. Closer to home, however, there was little that pleased his Spanish subjects. As Holy Roman Emperor, Charles was the official ruler of almost all of continental Europe west of Poland and the Balkans, with the major exception of France; and although his real power in the Empire was limited, he was almost ceaselessly at war defending his territories. In the Spaniards' view, most of the wars helped Charles's ambitions as emperor and were thus irrelevant to Spain. As far as they were concerned, aside from the widening acquisitions in the New World, Charles did little to further the expansion started by Ferdinand and Isabella.

Royal Government   The recurrent crises and wars kept Charles away from Spain for more than two-thirds of his forty-year reign. In his absence, his representatives confirmed the supremacy of the crown by enlarging the bureaucracy and elaborating a system of councils that Ferdinand and Isabella had begun. In the 1520s this structure, which was to survive for centuries, received its final form. There were two types of council, one for each department of government—finance, war, the Inquisition, and so on—the other for each territory the crown ruled: Aragon, Castile, Italy, the Indies, and (later in the century) the Low Countries. At the head of this system was the Council of State, the principal advisory group, consisting of leading officials from the lower councils. All councils reported to the king or to his chief ministers, but since they all controlled their own bureaucracies, they were perfectly capable of running the empire in the monarch's absence.

What emerged was a vast federation, with Castile at its heart but with the parts, though directed from the center, allowed considerable autonomy. A viceroy in every major area (there were nine altogether, from Naples to Peru) ran the administration under the supervision of an *audiencia*, a territorial council, and while on the whole these officials were left to do as they wished, they had to report to Castile in minute detail at regular intervals and refer major decisions to the central government.

MAP 14.3 THE EMPIRE OF CHARLES V
This map indicates both the vastness of Charles's empire and the extent of the fighting in which he became involved. Almost every battle his troops fought—against Spanish communes, German Protestants, the Turks, and the French—is included here to show the full measure of the emperor's never-ending ordeal. When he abdicated in 1556, Charles decided to divide his realm between his brother and his son. What characteristics of his empire seem to have shaped his decision to divide his territories?

◆ For an online version, go to www.mhhe.com/chambers9 > chapter 14 > book maps

Control through the Bureaucracy   Although corruption was widespread and communications slow (it took over eight months to send a message from Castile to Peru), the centralization gave the monarch considerable power. Spain's administrative machine was one of the most remarkably detailed (if not always efficient) structures ever devised for ruling so vast an empire.

The Financial Toll of War   The only serious strain on Charles's monarchy was financial, the result of the Habsburgs' constant wars. Much of the money for the fighting came from Italy and the Low Countries, but Spain had to pay a growing share of the costs, and Spaniards increasingly resented the siphoning away of their funds into foreign wars. It was the tragedy of their century of glory that so much of the wealth they discovered in South America was exported for hostilities that brought them little benefit.

The burden was by no means equally distributed. The more independent Cortes of Aragon was able to prevent substantial increases in taxation, which meant that Castile had to assume the brunt of the payments.

Pieter Brueghel the Elder
CENSUS AT BETHLEHEM
Although ostensibly a religious scene, the *Census at Bethlehem* gives us a glimpse of the growing intrusion into daily life of expanding governments. In their hardest season, winter, the people of this Flemish village have to line up in front of the bureaucrat at the table, who takes his fee even as he records the names of the villagers.
Art Resource, NY

To some extent this was balanced by a monopoly of trade with the New World that was granted to the inhabitants of Castile, but in the next century the basic inequality among different Spanish regions would lead to civil war.

New World Trade Charles's finances were saved from disaster only by the influx of treasure—mainly silver—from America. Approximately 40 percent of the bullion went into the royal coffers, while the rest was taken by merchants (mainly Genoese) in the Castilian port of Seville, which was the only city where ships carrying goods to and from America were permitted to load and unload. Charles was receiving some 800,000 ducats' worth of treasure each year by the end of his reign. Unfortunately, it was always mortgaged in ad-

vance to the Italian and German bankers whose loans sustained his armies.

The difficulties mounted as the wars continued for over a century and a half. Seville's monopoly on shipping prevented the rest of the nation from gaining a share of the new wealth, and foreigners—notably Italian and German financiers—came to dominate its economy and its commerce. Spain was squeezed dry by the king's financial demands, yet he only just kept his head above water. In 1557, early in the reign of Charles's successor, Philip II, the monarchy had to declare itself bankrupt, a self-defeating evasion of its mammoth debts that it had to repeat seven times in the next 125 years. There has never been a better example of the way that ceaseless war can sap the strength of even the most formidable nation.

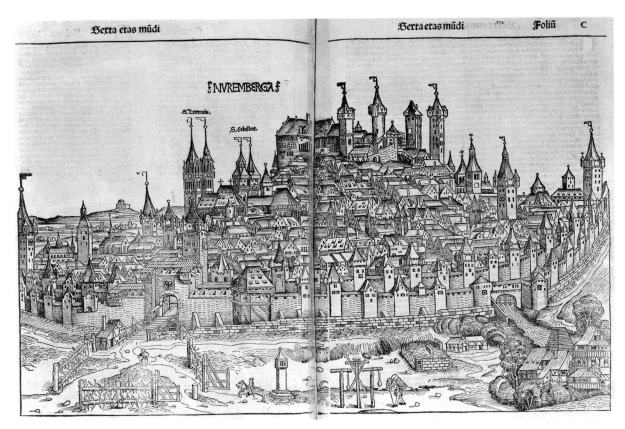

Hartmann Schedel
THE NUREMBERG CHRONICLE, **1493**
This lavishly illustrated book, a history of the world since the creation, is one of the earliest masterpieces of the printer's art. It took about four years to produce and contains dozens of elaborate woodcuts, most of which are recognizable views of European cities. This one depicts the proud and independent German city in which the book was printed, Nuremberg, a major center of art and craft work.
Rare Books and Manuscripts Division, New York Public Library, Astor, Lenox, and Tilden Foundations

THE SPLINTERED STATES

Whereas in England, France, and Spain the authority of kings had begun to replace that of the local lord, to the east of these three kingdoms such centralization advanced fitfully and only within small states.

The Holy Roman Empire In the largest of these territories, the Holy Roman Empire, weak institutions prevented the emergence of a strong central government. Members of the leading family of Central Europe, the Habsburgs, had been elected to the imperial throne since the thirteenth century, but they lacked the authority and machinery to halt the fragmentation of this large territory; indeed, except for their own personal domain in the southeast of the empire, they ruled most areas and princes in name only. In addition to about two thousand imperial knights, some of whom owned no more than four or five acres, there were fifty ecclesi-

astical and thirty secular princes, more than one hundred counts, some seventy prelates, and sixty-six cities—all virtually independent politically, though officially subordinate to the emperor.

Local Independence The princes, whose territories comprised most of the area of the Holy Roman Empire, rarely had any trouble resisting the emperor's claims; their main concern was to increase their own power at the expense of their subjects, other princes, and the cities. The cities themselves also refused to remain subordinate to a central government. In 1500, fifty of them contained more than two thousand inhabitants—a sizable number for this time—and twenty had over ten thousand. Their wealth was substantial because many were situated along a densely traveled trade artery, the Rhine River, and many were also political powers. But their fierce independence meant that the emperor could rarely tap their wealth or the services of

Titian
EMPEROR CHARLES V AT THE BATTLE OF MÜHLBERG, **1547**
**Because a statue of an ancient Roman emperor showed him
in this pose, it was thought in the sixteenth century that a
ruler appeared at his most magnificent on a horse and in full
armor. Remarkable equestrian sculptures appeared in the
fifteenth century, but this is the most famous such painting.**
Museo del Prado, Madrid, Spain. Erich Lessing/Art Resource, NY

their inhabitants. The only central institution along-side the emperor was the Diet, which consisted of three assemblies: representatives of the cities, the princes, and the seven electors who elected each new emperor. Given this makeup, the Diet became in effect the instrument of the princes; with its legislation, they secured their position against the cities and the lesser nobility within their domains.

By the late fifteenth century, most princes had gained considerable control over their own territories. Their success paralleled the achievements of monarchs in England, France, and Spain except that the units were much smaller. Although the Habsburgs tried to develop strong central authority, they exercised significant control only over their personal domain, which in 1500 consisted of Austria, the Low Countries, and Franche-Comtè.

Attempts at Centralization   Nevertheless, the need for effective central institutions was recognized. In 1495 the emperor created a tribunal to settle disputes among local powers. Controlled and financed by the princes, the chief beneficiaries of its work, it made considerable headway toward ending the lawlessness that had marked the fifteenth century—an achievement similar to the restoration of order in France, Spain, and England at the same time. The tribunal's use of Roman law had a wide influence on legislation and justice throughout the empire, but again only to the advantage of the princes, who interpreted its endorsement of a leader's authority as referring only to themselves.

Other attempts at administrative reform had little effect, as ecclesiastical and secular princes tightened their hold on the many individual territories within the empire. The religious dissensions of the Reformation worsened the rivalries, dividing the princes and making Charles V no more than the leader of one party, incapable of asserting his authority over his opponents. The sheer number of Charles's commitments repeatedly diverted him, but even when he won decisive military victories, he could not break the long tradition of local independence. His dream had been to revive the imperial grandeur of an Augustus or a Charlemagne, and his failure brought to an end the thousand-year ambition to restore in Europe the power of ancient Rome.

Power and Decline in Hungary   In the late fifteenth century, the dominant force in Eastern and Central Europe was the Kingdom of Hungary, ruled by Matthias Corvinus (1458–1490). He was in the mold of the other new monarchs of the day: He restrained the great nobles, expanded and centralized his administration, dramatically increased the yield of taxation, and established a standing army. The king's power grew spectacularly both at home and abroad: He gained Bohemia and German and Austrian lands, and he made Vienna his capital in 1485.

Immediately after Matthias' death, however, royal authority collapsed. To gain Habsburg recognition of his right to the throne, his successor, Ladislas II (1490–1516), gave up the conquests of Austrian and German lands and married his children to Habsburgs. This retreat provided the nobles of Hungary with the excuse to reassert their position. They refused the king essential financial support and forced him to dissolve the standing army. Then, after a major peasant revolt against increasing repression by landowners, the nobles imposed serfdom on all peasants in 1514 at a meeting of the Hungarian Diet, which they controlled. Finally, they became the major beneficiaries of the conquest of Hungary by the Ottoman Empire over the next thirty years. That empire always supported leaders who promised allegiance to Constantinople; declaring loyalty to their new masters, the nobles were able to strengthen their power at the expense of both the

Christoph Paudiss
Peasants in a Hut
**The sadness in the eyes of these two figures, even in a
relaxed moment—the old man smoking a pipe, the boy
playing the bagpipes—reflects the hardships of the peasants
who were at the lowest level of European society and in
Eastern Europe were bound to the land as serfs.**
Kunsthistorisches Museum, Vienna

old monarchy and the peasantry. By the mid-sixteenth
century, a revival of central authority had become impossible.

The Fragmentation of Poland

Royal power in Poland
began to decline in the 1490s, when the king was
forced to rely on the lesser nobles to help him against
the greater nobility. In return, he issued a statute in
1496 that strengthened the lower aristocrats against
those below them, the townsmen and the peasants.
The latter became virtual serfs, forbidden to buy land
and deprived of freedom of movement. Once that was
accomplished, the nobles united against the king. In
1505 the national Diet, consisting only of nobles, was
made the supreme body of the land, and shortly thereafter it established serfdom officially. Since no law
could now be passed without the Diet's consent, the
crown's central authority was severely limited.

Royal and noble patronage produced a great cultural
flowering around 1500 in Poland, which became an active center of Renaissance humanism and scholarship,
most famously represented by the astronomer Nicolaus
Copernicus. Yet the monarchy was losing influence
steadily, as was apparent from the failure of its attempts to found a standing army. At the end of Sigis-
mund II's reign (1548–1572), his kingdom was the
largest in Europe; but his death ended the Jagellon
Dynasty, which had ruled for centuries. The Diet then
made sure that succession to the crown, which had always been elective and controlled by nobles, would depend entirely on their approval—thus confirming the
aristocracy's dominance and the ineffectiveness of
royal authority.

Aristocracies

The political and social processes at
work in Eastern and Central Europe thus contrasted
starkly with developments in England, France, and
Spain in this period. Nevertheless, although the trend
was toward fragmentation in the East, one class, the
aristocracy, did share the vigor and organizational ability that in the West was displayed by kings and queens.
To that extent, therefore, the sense of renewed vitality
in Europe during these years, spurred by economic and
demographic growth, was also visible outside the borders of the new monarchies. But where nobles dominated, countries lost ground in the fierce competition
of international affairs.

The Ottoman Empire

Only in one state in Eastern
Europe was strong central authority maintained in the
sixteenth century: the Ottoman Empire. From his capital in Constantinople, the sultan exercised unparalleled powers throughout the eastern Mediterranean
and North Africa, and the Ottomans prevented any serious challenges to their empire until they began to
lose ground to the Habsburgs in the eighteenth century.

The first signs of weakening at the center began to
appear after the death in 1566 of the sultan whose conquests brought the empire to its largest size, Suleiman
II. Suleiman had gained control of the Balkans with a
victory at Mohacs in 1526, and he had even briefly laid
siege to Vienna in 1529 (see "Suleiman the Magnificent
Invades Europe," pp. 422–424). Under his successors,
the determined exercise of authority that had marked
his rule began to decline; harem intrigues, corruption
at court, and the loosening of military discipline became increasingly serious. Yet the Ottomans remained
an object of fear and hostility throughout the West—
a constant threat to Central Europe from the Balkans
and, despite naval setbacks, a formidable force in the
eastern Mediterranean.

Republics in Italy

Italy, the cultural and economic
leader of Europe, had developed a unique political struc-

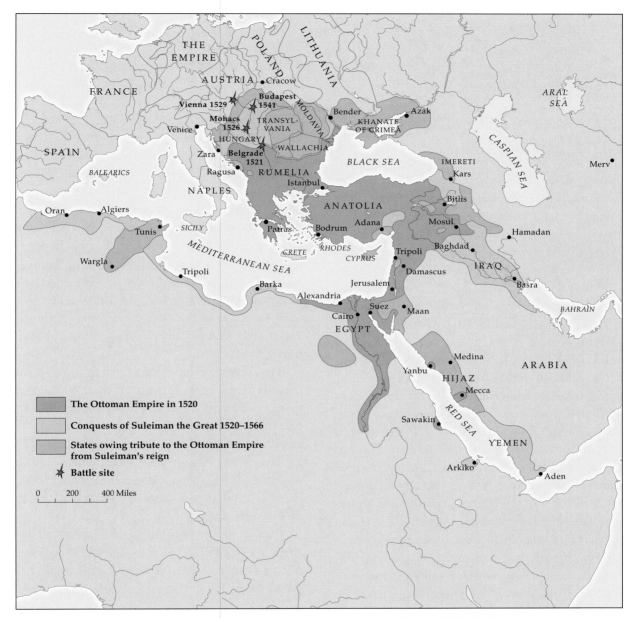

MAP 14.4 THE GROWTH OF THE OTTOMAN EMPIRE UNDER SULEIMAN THE GREAT, 1520–1566
The Ottoman Empire had expanded greatly during the fifteenth and sixteenth centuries (see map 11.7, p. 333). Note the area of Ottoman control in 1520. What were the key areas the Ottomans conquered under Suleiman the Great? Why would rulers of Central and Eastern Europe be alarmed at these advances? What key battle halted the Ottoman advance into Europe?

◆ For an online version, go to www.mhhe.com/chambers9 > chapter 14 > book maps

ture during the Renaissance. In the fifteenth century the five major states—Naples, the Papal States, Milan, Florence, and Venice—established a balance among themselves that was preserved without serious disruption from the 1450s to the 1490s. This long period of peace was broken in 1494, when Milan, abandoning a long tradition of the Italians settling problems among themselves, asked Charles VIII of France to help protect it against Florence and Naples. Thus began the Italian

wars, which soon revealed that these relatively small territories were totally incapable of resisting the force that newly assertive monarchies could bring to bear.

Venice and Florence had long been regarded by Europeans as model republics—reincarnations of Classical city-states and centers of freedom governed with the consent of their citizens. In truth, Venice was controlled by a small oligarchy and Florence by the Medici family, but the image of republican virtue was still

Global Moment

SULEIMAN THE MAGNIFICENT INVADES EUROPE

In the age of the Crusades and the Christian reconquest of Spain, Europeans seemed to be on the march against their Muslim neighbors. But there was widespread fear that the tables might be turned after Constantinople, the capital of the Byzantine Empire, fell to the Ottoman Turks in 1453. A crucial decade was the 1520s, when it looked as though the Ottoman Sultan, Suleiman II (known to his people as "The Lawgiver" but to the West as "The Magnificent") might sweep through Europe.

Ambitious, and the ruler of a rich and powerful empire that surrounded the eastern and southern Mediterranean, Suleiman was determined to earn eternal glory both for himself and for his faith at the expense of the Christians who ruled the lands to his west. He drew on Islamic traditions of governmental authority, particularly the notion that the Sultan was the successor of Muhammad, the legitimate ruler of all true believers. Like every member of the Islamic community, he was subject to the sacred law. But he was also the supreme judge of that law. Also influenced by Byzantine traditions that gave total control of society to the emperor, the Sultan united in his own person supreme civil, military, and religious power, and used elaborate Court ceremonies (as in Byzantium) to emphasize the aura of sanctity that surrounded him.

The chief source of his power was a superbly trained army, divided into two major sections: unpaid holders of lands that were granted by the Sultan in exchange for military service; and paid soldiers, technically considered slaves, who were permanently in the Sultan's service. As in the West, the landholder had to provide the military with armed men. The number was determined by the revenues raised from his lands, but it was always in his interest to expand his holdings, and thus for the Ottoman Empire to keep growing. Among the paid soldiers, the most important were the Janissaries, an elite corps of troops dedicated to Islam, who were feared by all who encountered the Ottomans. The Janissaries became an influential force in Ottoman politics and a major source of the Sultan's power. These were well-disciplined and thoroughly professional soldiers, but legally they were slaves—often captives from conquered peoples. Slave armies had been common in Islamic states, but the Ottomans did not adopt the practice until the 1430s, when they began converting war captives to Islam, teaching them Turkish, and training them as a tough, military contingent. Thereafter, the tribute the Ottomans demanded from the Christian parts of their empire was the handing over of young boys who would be trained to join this elite military corps.

With this superb fighting force at his disposal, and presiding over a government in which he held unquestioned authority, Suleiman drove to expand Ottoman rule into Europe. In 1521 he captured the citadel of Belgrade in the Balkan Peninsula, and the next year he conquered the island of Rhodes, home of an order of Christian knights who had been harassing his shipping. He was now in complete command of the eastern Mediterranean.

Then came the Ottomans' major overland advance. After the death of the Hungarian ruler Matthias Corvinus in 1490, domestic rivalries had drained the European kingdom of its former strength. When landowners and the Janissaries sought new lands to conquer after the fall of Rhodes, Suleiman decided to invade vulnerable Hungary. In April 1526 he left Constantinople and headed west. Four months later, on August 29, he met the Hungarian army in the plain of Mohacs. What followed was one of the decisive battles of world history. An opening charge by the Hungarian cavalry seemed to sweep all before them, but it was a trap. The Janissaries halted the charge and their artillery shattered the cavalry. As a contemporary Ottoman historian put it:

> At the order of the sultan the fusiliers of the Janissaries, directing their blows at the cruel panthers who opposed us, caused thousands of them, in the space of a moment, to descend into hell.

SULEIMAN AND OTTOMAN FORCES AT BATTLE OF MOHACS, 1526
Topkapi Palace Museum, Istanbul, Turkey. Giraudon/Art Resource

It has been estimated that some 30,000 men—three-quarters of the Hungarian army—not to mention their king, the leaders of their church, and their most prominent aristocrats, were all killed.

By September 10 the Ottomans were in the Hungarian capital, Buda, which they burned to the ground. Suleiman was now master of the Balkans, and he took the next three years to consolidate his position. When, finally, he decided to advance again, toward the Habsburg capital of Vienna, his communications were becoming stretched, and he had given his enemy time to prepare. The summer of 1529 happened to be extremely rainy, which meant that Suleiman was unable to bring his heavy artillery to the siege of Vienna, and his army had to move slowly. As a result, the garrison had time to assemble heavy reinforcements, and was ready to hold out against light artillery. After a few months of indecisive skirmishing, therefore, the Ottomans decided to withdraw. Their advance into Europe had been halted. The Balkans would be prize enough.

For the rest of his reign Suleiman turned his attention toward the East, where his armies overran Mesopotamia and southern Arabia. But the long-term effect of his conquest of the Balkans can be seen in the religious divisions that continue to trouble the area to this day. This came to be a major fault line in the boundary between Europe and the rest of the world, a perennial source of upheaval and discontent for centuries to come.

continued

What was remarkable about Suleiman's rule, however, was that he was able to hold together his huge empire in a way that avoided the local challenges to his power that were common in the West. The Sultan gained the loyalty of subject populations by allowing them to live by their own laws under their own officials, requiring them only to pay taxes and supply men for the Ottoman army and administration. Trade, for example, which remained vigorous in the Black Sea and the eastern Mediterranean, was still largely in the hands of Greeks, Armenians, and Jews. The Ottomans themselves remained aloof from commercial undertakings and confined their careers to government service and the army.

Although Ottoman power was to wane over the centuries that followed, hastened by corruption at court and the loosening of military discipline, the expansive days of Suleiman's reign were never forgotten. To this day, the mosque that he built, which houses his elegantly decorated tomb, dominates the Istanbul skyline.

widely accepted. Indeed, the political stability Venice had maintained for centuries was the envy of Europe. Tourists came not only to enjoy its many relaxations and entertainments but also to marvel at the institutions that kept the city calm, powerful, and rich. Venice's leaders were thought of as the heirs of Roman senators, and throughout Europe, the Italians were regarded as masters not only of politics but also of culture and manners.

The Italian Wars It was a considerable shock, therefore, when the Italian states crumbled before the onslaught of French and then Spanish and Habsburg armies. Charles VIII's invasion led to the expulsion of the Medici from Florence in 1494 and the establishment of a new Florentine republic. In 1512 the family engineered a return to power with the help of Ferdinand of Aragon, and eventually the Habsburgs set up the Medici as hereditary dukes of Tuscany. Ferdinand annexed Naples in 1504, and Emperor Charles V took over Milan in 1535. When the fighting ended in 1559, the Habsburgs controlled Italy and would do so for the next century. Only Venice, Tuscany under the Medici, and the Papal States remained relatively independent—though Venice was no longer a force in European affairs. The one major local beneficiary of the Italian wars was the papacy, whose army carved out a new papal territory in central and eastern Italy.

The critical lesson of these disastrous events was that small political units could not survive in an age when governments were consolidating their authority in large kingdoms. No matter how brilliant and sophisticated, a compact city-state could not withstand such superior force. Italy's cultural and economic prominence faded only slowly, but by the mid-sixteenth century, except for the papacy, the international standing of its states was fading.

THE NEW STATECRAFT

The Italian states of the fifteenth century, in their intense political struggles and competition with one another, developed various new ways of pursuing foreign policy. During the Italian wars, these techniques spread throughout Europe and caused a revolution in diplomacy. Any state hoping to play a prominent role in international affairs worked under a serious disadvantage if it did not conform. And an Italian observer, Machiavelli, suggested radically new ways of understanding the nature of politics and diplomacy.

New International Relations

The Italians' essential innovation was the resident ambassador. Previously, rulers had dispatched ambassadors to other states only for specific missions, such as to arrange an alliance, declare war, or deliver a message; but from the sixteenth century on, important states maintained representatives in every major capital or court at all times. The permanent ambassador could keep the home government informed of the latest local and international developments and could also move without delay to protect his country's interests.

Titian
THE VENDRAMIN FAMILY, **1547**
The magnificence of the patrician families who ruled Venice is celebrated in this group portrait. Ostensibly, they are worshiping a relic of the true cross, but in fact they are displaying the hierarchy that rules their lives. Only men appear, dominated by the head of the family and his aged father, followed by his eldest son and heir, all of whom convey an image of wealth and power.
Reproduced by courtesy of the Trustees, © The National Gallery, London (NG4452)

The New Diplomacy   As states established embassies, procedures and organization became more sophisticated. A primitive system of diplomatic immunities (including freedom from prosecution for ambassadors and their households) evolved, and formal protocol developed. Many advances were still to come, but by 1550 the outlines of the new diplomacy were already visible—yet another reflection of the growing powers and ambitions of central governments.

The new diplomacy took hold in the Italian wars, a Europe-wide crisis that involved rulers as distant as the English King Henry VIII and the Ottoman Sultan Suleiman the Great. Gradually, all states recognized that it was in everybody's interest not to allow one power to dominate the rest. In later years this prevention of excessive aggression was to be known as the balance of power, but by the mid-sixteenth century the idea was already affecting alliances and peace treaties.

Machiavelli

As the Italian wars unfolded, political commentators began to seek explanations for the new authority and aggressiveness of rulers and the collapse of the Italian city-states. Turning from arguments based on divine will or contractual law, they treated effective government as an end in itself. The most disturbing assessment came from an experienced Florentine diplomat, Niccolò Machiavelli, who was exiled when the Medici took control of Florence in 1512. Barred from politics and bitter over the collapse of Italy, he set about analyzing exactly how power is won, exercised, and lost.

The result, *The Prince,* is one of the few radically original books in history. To move from his predecessors to Machiavelli is to see legal and moral thought transformed. Machiavelli swept away conventions as he attempted, in an age of collapsing regimes, to understand how states function and how they affect their subjects. If he came out of any tradition, it was the Renaissance fascination with method that had produced manuals on cooking, dancing, fencing, and manners. But he wrote about method in an area that had never previously been analyzed in this way: power. Machiavelli showed not why power does or should exist, but how it works. Without reference to divine, legal, or natural justification, the book explains what a ruler needs to do to win and maintain complete control over his subjects. Machiavelli did not deny the force of religion or law; what concerned him was how they ought to be used in the tactics of governing—religion for molding unity and contentment, and devotion to law for building the ruler's reputation as a fair-minded person. *The Prince* outlines the methods to be used to deal with insurrection and the many other problems that rulers encounter. Fear and respect are the bases of their authority, and they must exercise care at all times not to relax their control over potential troublemakers or over their image among the people.

Few contemporaries of Machiavelli dared openly to accept so harsh a view of politics, but he did not hesitate to expand his analysis in his other masterpiece, the *Discourses*. This book developed a cyclical theory of every government moving inexorably from tyranny to democracy and back again. His conclusion, drawn mainly from a study of Roman history, is that healthy government can be preserved only by the active participation of all citizens in the life of the state. He also suggested that the state is the force that keeps people civilized—a notable testimony to the new importance of effective government.

Summary

It was appropriate that theorists emphasized the obsession with power that dominated this age. The relentless pragmatism and ambition of kings and princes as they extended their authority both at home and abroad reshaped institutions and governments throughout Europe. Given the assertiveness of these rulers and the rising fanaticism generated by religious dispute, it is not surprising that there should have begun in the mid-sixteenth century a series of wars of a ferocity and destructiveness that Europe had never before seen.

Questions for Further Thought

1. Is there some reason that major economic changes and major political changes always seem to go hand in hand?

2. Is it inevitable that rapid economic advance will have both favorable and unfavorable effects on ordinary people?

Recommended Reading

Sources

*Guicciardini, Francesco. *The History of Italy and Other Selected Writings.* Cecil Grayson (tr.). 1964.

*Machiavelli, Niccolò. *The Prince and the Discourses.* Luigi Ricci (tr.). 1950.

*Parry, J. H. (ed.). *The European Reconnaissance: Selected Documents.* 1968.

Studies

*Anderson, M. S. *The Origins of the Modern European State System, 1494–1618.* 1998.

*Bonney, Richard. *The European Dynastic States, 1494–1660.* 1991. An excellent overview.

*Crosby, Alfred W. *The Columbian Exchange: Biological and Cultural Consequences of 1492.* 1972. A fascinating study of plants, diseases, and other exchanges between the Old World and the New World.

Dewald, Jonathan. *The European Nobility, 1400–1800.* 1996.

*Elliott, J. H. *The Old World and the New, 1492–1650.* 1970. A survey of the impact on Europe of the overseas discoveries.

*Femia, Joseph V. *Machiavelli Revisited.* 2004.

*Mattingly, Garrett. *Renaissance Diplomacy.* 1971. An elegant account of the changes that began in international relations during the fifteenth century.

*Rady, Martin. *The Emperor Charles V.* 1988. An excellent overview, with illustrative documents, of the reign of the most powerful ruler in Europe.

*Richardson, Glenn. *Renaissance Monarchy: The Reigns of Henry VIII, Francis I and Charles V.* 2002.

Scammell, G. V. *The First Imperial Age: European Overseas Expansion c. 1400–1715.* 1989. An excellent survey.

*Skinner, Quentin. *Machiavelli.* 1981. An excellent brief introduction to the man and his thought.

Wilford, John Noble. *The Mysterious History of Columbus: An Exploration of the Man, the Myth, the Legacy.* 1991. A judicious account, both of Columbus' career and of the ways it has been interpreted.

*Wrigley, E. A. *Population and History.* 1969. An introduction to the methods and findings of historical demography by one of the pioneers of the field.

*Available in paperback.

Francois Dubois
THE MASSACRE OF ST. BARTHOLOMEW'S DAY
Although it makes no attempt to depict the massacre realistically, this painting by a Protestant does convey the horrors of religious war. As the victims are hanged, disemboweled, decapitated, tossed from windows, bludgeoned, shot, or drowned, their bodies and homes are looted. Dubois may have intended the figure dressed in widow's black and pointing at a pile of corpses near the river at the back to be a portrait of Catherine de Medici, who many thought inspired the massacre.
Musée Cantonal des Beaux-Arts, Lausanne

Chapter Fifteen

WAR AND CRISIS

RIVALRY AND WAR IN THE AGE OF PHILIP II • FROM UNBOUNDED WAR TO
INTERNATIONAL CRISIS • THE MILITARY REVOLUTION • REVOLUTION IN ENGLAND •
REVOLTS IN FRANCE AND SPAIN • POLITICAL CHANGE IN AN AGE OF CRISIS

In the wake of the rapid and bewildering changes of the early sixteenth century—the Reformation, the rises in population and prices, the overseas discoveries, and the dislocations caused by the activities of the new monarchs—Europe entered a period of fierce upheaval. So many radical alterations were taking place that conflict became inevitable. There were revolts against monarchs, often led by nobles who saw their power dwindling. The poor launched hopeless rebellions against their social superiors. And the two religious camps struggled relentlessly to destroy each other. From Scotland to Russia, the century following the Reformation, from about 1560 to 1660, was dominated by warfare; and the constant military activity had widespread effects on politics, economics, society, and thought. The fighting, in fact, helped bring to an end the long process whereby Europe came to terms with the revolutions that had begun about 1500. As we will see, two distinct periods of ever more destructive warfare—the age of Philip II from the 1550s to the 1590s, and the age of the Thirty Years' War from the 1610s to the 1640s, with a decade of uneasy peace in between—led to a vast crisis of authority throughout Europe in the mid-1600s. From the struggles of that crisis there emerged fundamental economic, political, social, and religious changes, as troubled Europeans at last found ways to accept their altered circumstances. Interestingly, there were peasant revolts in Russia and China at the same time as those in Western Europe in the mid-seventeenth century, and they, too, reflected unease with state power, which was growing in Russia, but declining in China as the Ming Dynasty came to an end.

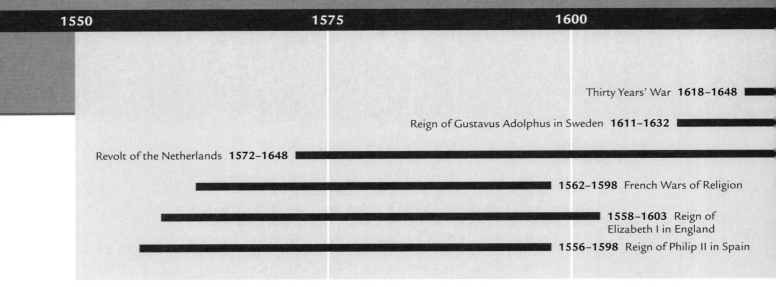

1550	1575	1600

Thirty Years' War **1618–1648**

Reign of Gustavus Adolphus in Sweden **1611–1632**

Revolt of the Netherlands **1572–1648**

1562–1598 French Wars of Religion

1558–1603 Reign of Elizabeth I in England

1556–1598 Reign of Philip II in Spain

RIVALRY AND WAR IN THE AGE OF PHILIP II

The wars that plagued Europe from the 1560s to the 1650s involved many issues, but religion was the burning motivation, the one that inspired fanatical devotion and the most vicious hatred. A deep conviction that heresy was dangerous to society and hateful to God made Protestants and Catholics treat one another brutally. Even the dead were not spared: Corpses were sometimes mutilated to emphasize how dreadful their sins had been. These emotions, which shaped politics in this period, especially the decades dominated by Philip II, gave the fighting a brutality unprecedented in European history.

Philip II of Spain

During the second half of the sixteenth century, international warfare was ignited by the leader of the Catholics, Philip II of Spain (r. 1556–1598), the most powerful monarch in Europe. A stern defender of the Catholic faith, who is looked back on by Spaniards as a model of prudence, self-discipline, and devotion, he was also a tireless administrator, building up and supervising a vast and complex bureaucracy. It was needed, he felt, because of the far-spreading territories he ruled: the Iberian Peninsula, much of Italy, the Netherlands, and a huge overseas empire. Yet his main concern was to overcome the two enemies of his church, the Muslims and the Protestants.

Against the Muslims in the Mediterranean area, Philip's campaigns seemed to justify the financial strains they caused. In particular, his naval victory over the Ottomans at Lepanto, off the Greek coast, in 1571 made him a Christian hero at the same time that it re-

duced Muslim power. Although the Ottomans remained a considerable force in the eastern half of the Mediterranean, and indeed were able to besiege Vienna again in 1683, Philip was unchallenged in the west. He dominated the rich Italian peninsula; in 1580 he inherited the kingdom of Portugal; and his overseas wealth, passing through Seville, made this the fastest-growing city in Europe. The sixteenth century was the last age in which the Mediterranean was the heart of the European economy, but its prosperity was still the chief pillar of Philip's power.

Further north, Philip fared less well. He tried to prevent a Protestant, Henry IV, from inheriting the French crown and continued to back the losing side in France's civil wars even though Henry converted to Catholicism. Philip's policy toward England and the Netherlands was similarly ineffective. After the Protestant Queen Elizabeth I came to the English throne in 1558, Philip remained uneasily cordial toward her for about ten years. But relations deteriorated as England's sailors and explorers threatened Philip's wealthy New World possessions. Worse, in 1585 Elizabeth began to help the Protestant Dutch, who were rebelling against Spanish rule. Though their countries were smaller than Spain, the English and Dutch were able to inflict on Philip the two chief setbacks of his reign; and in the years after his death they were to wrest the leadership of Europe's economy away from the Mediterranean.

Elizabeth I of England

In a struggle with Spain, England may have seemed an unlikely victor: a relatively poor kingdom that had lost its continental possessions and for some time had played a secondary role in European affairs. Yet its people were united by such common bonds as the institution of Parliament and a commitment to the international Protes-

1640–1668
Revolts by Catalonia, Portugal, Sicily, and Naples against Spain

1642–1660 Revolution in England

1648–1653 *Fronde* revolt in France

tant cause that was carefully promoted by Queen Elizabeth I (r. 1558–1603).

Elizabeth is an appealing figure because she combined shrewd hardheadedness with a disarming appearance of frailty. Her qualities were many: her dedication to the task of government; her astute choice of advisers; her civilizing influence at court, where she encouraged elegant manners and the arts; her tolerance of religious dissent as long as it posed no political threat; and her ability to feel the mood of her people, to catch their spirit, to inspire their enthusiasm. Although social, legal, and economic practices usually subordinated women to men in this age, inheritance was respected; thus, a determined woman with a recognized claim to authority could win complete acceptance. Elizabeth was the most widely admired and most successful queen of her time, but she was by no means alone; female rulers also shaped the histories of France, Sweden, and the southern Netherlands in the sixteenth and seventeenth centuries.

Royal Policy   Elizabeth could be indecisive, notably where the succession was concerned. Her refusal to marry caused serious uncertainties, and it was only the shrewd planning of her chief minister, Robert Cecil, that enabled the king of Scotland, James Stuart, to succeed her without incident in 1603. Similar dangers arose from her indecisive treatment of England's remaining Catholics. They hoped that Mary Queen of Scots, a Catholic, would inherit the throne; and since she was next in line, they were not above plotting against Elizabeth's life. Eventually, in 1587, Elizabeth had Mary executed and the plots died away. Despite her reluctance to take firm positions, Elizabeth showed great skill in balancing policy alternatives, and her adroit maneuvering assured her of her ministers' loyalty at all times. She also inspired the devotion of her subjects by traveling

throughout England to make public appearances; by delivering brilliant speeches (see "Queen Elizabeth's Armada Speech," p. 433); and by shaping her own image, even regulating how she was to be depicted in portraits. She thus retained her subjects' allegiance despite the profound social changes that were eroding traditional patterns of deference and order. England's nobility, for instance, no longer dominated the military and the government; nearly all Elizabeth's ministers were new in national life; and the House of Commons was beginning to exert more political influence within Parliament than the House of Lords. All groups in English society, however, shared a resentment of Spanish power, and Elizabeth cultivated this sentiment astutely as a patriotic and Protestant cause.

The Dutch Revolt

The same cause united the people living in the provinces in the Netherlands that Philip inherited from his father, the Emperor Charles V. Here his single-minded promotion of Catholicism and royal power provoked a fierce reaction that grew into a successful struggle for independence: the first major victory in Western Europe by subjects resisting royal authority.

Causes of Revolt   The original focus of opposition was Philip's reorganization of the ecclesiastical structure so as to gain control over the country's Catholic Church, a change that deprived the aristocracy of important patronage. At the same time, the **billeting** of troops aroused the resentment of ordinary citizens. In this situation, the local nobles, led by William of Orange, warned of mass disorder, but Philip kept up the pressure: He put the Inquisition to work against the Calvinists, who had begun to appear in the Netherlands, and also summoned the Jesuits to combat the

El Greco
THE DREAM OF PHILIP II, 1578
Characteristic of the mystical vision of El Greco is this portrayal of the devout, black-clad figure of Philip II. Kneeling alongside the doge of Venice and the pope, his allies in the victory of Lepanto over the Turks, Philip adores the blazing name of Jesus that is surrounded by angels in heaven, and he turns his back on the gaping mouth to hell.
Reproduced by courtesy of the Trustees, © The National Gallery, London (NG6260)

William Segar (attrib.)
PORTRAIT OF ELIZABETH I, 1585
Elizabeth I was strongly aware of the power of propaganda, and she used it to foster a dazzling public image. Legends about her arose in literature. And in art she had herself portrayed in the most elaborate finery imaginable. Here, she is every inch the queen, with her magnificent dress, the trappings of monarchy, and the symbol of virginity, the ermine.
By courtesy of The Marquess of Salisbury

heretics. These moves were disastrous because they further undermined local autonomy and made the Protestants bitter enemies of the king.

Philip's aggressiveness provoked violence in 1566. Although the Protestants were still a tiny minority, they formed mobs in a number of cities, assaulted Catholics, and sacked churches. In response, Philip tightened the pressure, appointing as governor the ruthless duke of Alba, who used his Spanish troops to suppress opposition. Protestants were hanged in public, rebel groups were hunted down, and two nobles who had been guilty of nothing worse than demanding that Philip change his policy were executed.

Full-Scale Rebellion Organized revolt broke out in 1572, when a small group of Dutch sailors flying the flag of William of Orange seized the fishing village of Brill, on the North Sea. The success of these "sea beggars," as the Spaniards called them, stimulated uprisings in towns throughout the Low Countries. The banner of William of Orange became the symbol of resistance, and under his leadership full-scale rebellion erupted. By 1576, when Philip's troops mutinied and rioted in Antwerp, sixteen of the seventeen provinces in the Netherlands had united behind William. The next

Queen Elizabeth's Armada Speech

Elizabeth's ability to move her subjects was exemplified by the speech she gave to her troops as they awaited the fight with the Spanish Armada. She understood that they might have doubts about a woman leading them in war, but she turned that issue to her own advantage in a stirring cry to battle that enhanced her popularity at the time and her legendary image thereafter.

"My loving People: We have been persuaded by some that are careful of our safety, to take heed how we commit ourselves to armed multitudes, for fear of treachery; but I assure you, I do not desire to live to distrust my faithful and loving people.

"Let tyrants fear; I have always so behaved myself, that, under God, I have placed my chiefest strength and safeguard in the loyal hearts and good will of my subjects, and therefore I am come amongst you, as you see, at this time, not for my recreation . . . but being resolved in the midst and heat of the battle, to live or die amongst you all, to lay down for my God, and for my kingdoms, and for my people, my honour and my blood, even in the dust.

"I know I have the body of a weak and feeble woman; but I have the heart and stomach of a king, and of a king of England too; and think foul scorn that . . . Spain, or any prince of Europe should dare to invade the borders of my realm; to which rather than any dishonour shall grow by me, I myself will take up arms, I myself will be your general, judge, and rewarder of every one of your virtues in the field. . . . By your concord in the camp, and your valour in the field, we shall shortly have a famous victory over those enemies of my God, of my kingdoms, and of my people."

Walter Scott (ed.), *A Collection of Scarce and Valuable Tracts, on the Most Interesting and Entertaining Subjects: But Chiefly Such as Relate to the History and Constitution of These Kingdoms*, Vol. 1, London, 1809, pp. 429–430.

Anonymous
Engraving of the Spaniards in Haarlem
This engraving was published to arouse horror at Spanish atrocities during the Dutch revolt. As the caption indicates, after the Spanish troops (on the right) captured the city of Haarlem, there was a great bloodbath (*ein gross bluit batt*). Blessed by priests, the Haarlemites were decapitated or hung, and then tossed in a river so that the city would be cleansed of them. The caption states that even women and children were not spared.
New York Public Library

Pieter Brueghel the Elder
THE MASSACRE OF THE INNOCENTS, **1565**
Probably to avoid trouble, Brueghel hid his critique of the Spanish rulers of the Netherlands in this supposed portrayal of a biblical event. It would have been clear to anyone who saw it, however, that this was a scene of Spanish cruelty toward the local inhabitants in the harsh days of winter, as soldiers tear babies from their mothers and kill them.
Erich Lessing/Art Resource, NY

year, however, Philip offered a compromise to the Catholic nobles, and the ten southern provinces returned to Spanish rule.

The United Provinces   In 1579 the remaining seven provinces formed the independent United Provinces. Despite the assassination of William in 1584, they managed to resist Spain's army for decades, mainly because they could open dikes, flood their country, and thus drive the invaders back. Moreover, Philip was often diverted by other wars and, in any case, never placed total confidence in his commanders. The Calvinists formed the heart of the resistance; though still a minority, they had the most to lose, because they sought freedom for their religion as well as their country. William never showed strong religious commitments, but his son, Maurice of Nassau, a brilliant military commander who

won a series of victories in the 1590s, embraced Calvinism and helped make it the country's official religion. Unable to make any progress, the Spaniards agreed to a twelve-year truce in 1609, but they did not recognize the independence of the United Provinces until the Peace of Westphalia in 1648.

The Armada   In 1588 Philip tried to end his troubles in northern Europe with one mighty blow. Furious that the English were interfering with his New World empire (their traders and raiders had been intruding into Spain's American colonies for decades) and that Elizabeth was helping Dutch Protestants, he sent a mammoth fleet—the Armada—to the Low Countries. Its task was to pick up a Spanish army, invade England, and thus undermine Protestant resistance. By this time, however, English mariners were among the best in the world, and their

MAP 15.1 THE NETHERLANDS, 1579–1609
The seventeen provinces making up the Netherlands, or the Low Countries, were detached from the Holy Roman Empire when Charles V abdicated in 1556. As the map indicates, their subsequent division into two states was determined not by the linguistic differences between French-speaking people of the south and Dutch-speaking people of the north but rather by geography. The great river systems at the mouth of the Rhine eventually proved to be the barrier beyond which the Spaniards could not penetrate. Notice the shifting boundaries. Did the United Provinces gain more between 1590 and 1648 than they lost after 1579?
◆ For an online version, go to www.mhhe.com/chambers9 > chapter 15 > book maps

ships had greater maneuverability and firepower than did the Spaniards'. After several skirmishes in the Channel, the English set fire to a few of their own vessels with loaded cannons aboard and sent them drifting toward the Spanish ships, anchored off Calais. The Spaniards had to raise anchor in a hurry, and some of the fleet was lost. The next day the remaining Spanish ships retreated up the North Sea. The only way home was around Ireland; and wind, storms, and the pursuing English ensured that less than half the fleet returned safely to Spain. This shattering reversal was comparable in scale and unexpectedness only to Xerxes' disaster at Salamis more than two thousand years earlier. More than any other single event, it doomed Philip's ambitions in England, the Netherlands, and France and signaled a northward shift in power in Europe.

Civil War in France

The other major power of Western Europe, France, was rent apart by religious war in this period, but it too felt the effects of the Armada's defeat. By the 1550s Calvinism was gaining strength among French peasants and in the towns of the south and southwest, and its leaders had virtually created a small semi-independent state. To meet this threat, a great noble family, the Guises, assumed the leadership of the Catholics; in response, the Bourbons, another noble family, championed the Calvinists, about a twelfth of the population. Their struggle split the country apart.

It was ominous that in 1559—the year that Henry II, France's last strong king for a generation, died—the Calvinists (known in France as Huguenots) organized their first national synod, an indication of impressive strength. During the next thirty years, the throne was occupied by Henry's three ineffectual sons. The power behind the crown was Henry's widow, Catherine de Medici (see "The Kings of France in the Sixteenth Century," p. 436), who tried desperately to preserve royal authority. But she was often helpless because the religious conflict intensified the factional struggle for power between the Guises and the Bourbons, both of whom were closely related to the monarchy and hoped one day to inherit the throne.

The Wars Fighting started in 1562 and lasted for thirty-six years, interrupted only by short-lived peace agreements. Catherine switched sides whenever one party became too powerful; and she may have approved the notorious massacre of St. Bartholomew's Day—August 24, 1572—which started in Paris, spread through France, and destroyed the Huguenots' leadership. Henry of Navarre, a Bourbon, was the only major figure who escaped. When Catherine switched sides again and made peace with the Huguenots in 1576, the Guises formed the Catholic League, which for several years dominated the eastern half of the country. In 1584 the league allied with Spain's Philip II to attack heresy in France and deny the Bourbon Henry's legal right to inherit the throne.

The defeat of the Armada in 1588 proved to be the turning point in the French civil wars, for Spain could not continue helping the duke of Guise, who was soon assassinated, and within a few months Henry of Navarre inherited the throne as Henry IV (r. 1589–1610). He had few advantages as he began to reassert royal authority, because the Huguenots and Catholics ran almost independent governments in large sections of France. In addition, the royal administration was in a sorry state because the crown's oldest rivals, the great nobles, could now resist all outside interference in their domains.

Anonymous
THE ARMADA
This depiction suggests the sheer splendor of the scene as Philip II's fleet sailed through the Channel on its way to invading England. The opposing ships were never this close, but the colorful flags (red cross English, yellow cross Spanish) and the elaborate coats of arms must have been dazzling. The firing cannon and the sinking ship remind us that, amidst the display, there was also death and destruction.
National Maritime Museum, Greenwich, London

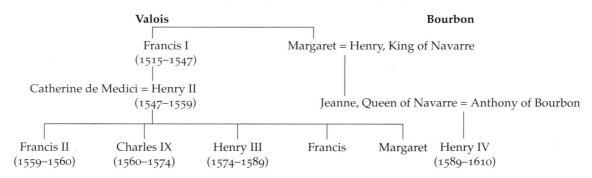

THE KINGS OF FRANCE IN THE SIXTEENTH CENTURY

Peace Restored　Yet largely because of the assassination of the duke of Guise, Henry IV was able to restore order. The duke had been a forceful leader and a serious contender for the throne. His replacement was a Spanish candidate for the crown who had little chance of success. The distaste for a possible foreign ruler, combined with war weariness, destroyed much of the support for the Catholic League, which finally collapsed as a result of revolts against it in eastern France in the 1590s. These up-

risings, founded on a demand for peace, increased in frequency and intensity after Henry IV renounced Protestantism in 1593 in order to win acceptance by his Catholic subjects. The following year Henry had himself officially crowned, and all of France rallied to the king as he beat back a Spanish invasion—Spain's final, rather weak, attempt to put its own candidate on the throne.

When Spain finally withdrew and signed a peace treaty in 1598, the fighting came to an end. To complete

MAP 15.2 CATHOLIC AND PROTESTANT POWERS IN THE LATE SIXTEENTH CENTURY
The heart of the Catholic cause in the wars of religion was the Spain of Philip II. Spanish territories surrounded France and provided the route to the Netherlands, where the Protestant Dutch had rebelled against the Spaniards (see map 15.1). The Armada was launched to help that cause by crushing the ally of the Dutch, Protestant England. In the meantime, the surrounded French had problems of their own with the Huguenots, who protected their Protestantism in a network of fortified towns. Why did the Armada follow the route shown on the map?
◆ For an online version, go to www.mhhe.com/chambers9 > chapter 15 > book maps

the reconciliation, Henry issued (also in 1598) the Edict of Nantes, which granted limited toleration to the Huguenots. Although it did not create complete religious liberty, the edict made Calvinist worship legal, protected the rights of the minority, and opened public office to Huguenots.

FROM UNBOUNDED WAR TO INTERNATIONAL CRISIS

During the half century after Philip II's death, warfare spread throughout Europe. There was a brief lull in the early 1600s, but then the slaughter and the devastations began to multiply. For a while it seemed that nothing could bring the fighting to an end, and a feeling of irresolvable crisis descended on international affairs. Not until an entirely new form of peacemaking was devised, in the 1640s, was the fighting brought under control.

The Thirty Years' War

The new arena in which the warfare erupted was the Holy Roman Empire. Here religious hatreds were especially disruptive because the empire lacked a central authority and unifying institutions. Small-scale fighting broke out repeatedly after the 1550s, always inspired by religion. Although elsewhere the first years of the seventeenth century were a time of relative peace that seemed to signal a decline of conflict over faith, in the empire the stage was being set for the bloodiest of all the wars fired by religion.

Known as the Thirty Years' War, this ferocious struggle began in the Kingdom of Bohemia in 1618 and continued until 1648. The principal battleground, the empire, was ravaged by the fighting, which eventually involved every major ruler in Europe. At first it was a renewed struggle between local Protestants and Catholics, but eventually it became a fight among political rivals who were eager to take advantage of the fragmentation of the empire to advance their own ambitions. As the devastation spread, international relations seemed to be sinking into total chaos; but the chief victims were the Germans, who, like the Italians in the sixteenth century, found themselves at the mercy of well-organized states that used another country as a place to settle their quarrels.

The First Phase, 1618–1621   The immediate problem was typical of the situation in the empire. In 1609 the Habsburg Emperor Rudolf II promised toleration for Protestants in Bohemia. When his cousin Ferdinand, a pious Catholic, succeeded to the Bohemian throne in 1617, he refused to honor Rudolf's promise, and the Bohemians rebelled in 1618. They declared Ferdinand deposed, replacing him with the leading Calvinist of the empire, Frederick II of the Palatinate. Frederick accepted the crown, an act of defiance whose only possible outcome was war.

The first decade or so of the war was a time of victories for the Catholics. When Ferdinand became emperor (r. 1619–1637), the powerful Catholic Maximilian

"THE HANGING TREE," ENGRAVING FROM JACQUES CALLOT'S *MISERIES OF WAR*, 1633
An indication of the growing dismay over the brutality of the Thirty Years' War was the collection of sixteen prints produced by the French engraver Callot depicting the life of the soldier and the effects of armies on civilian populations. His soldiers destroy, loot, and rape, and only a few of them receive the punishments they deserve, like this mass hanging.
Anne S. K. Brown Military Collection, Brown University Library

"HEADS OF THE BOHEMIAN REBELS," ENGRAVING FROM MATHAUS MERIAN, *THEATRUM EUROPAEUM*, CA. 1630
Since the scene had not changed when the engraving was made, this illustration is probably a fairly accurate representation of the punishment in 1621 of the leaders of the Bohemian rebellion. Twenty-four rebels were executed, and the heads of twelve of them were displayed on long poles at the top of the tower (still standing today) on the bridge over Prague's river. The heads were kept there for ten years.

of Bavaria put an army at his disposal. Within a year, the imperial troops won a stunning victory over the Bohemians. Ferdinand II confiscated all of Frederick's lands. Maximilian received half as a reward for his army, and the remainder went to the Spaniards, who occupied it as a valuable base for their struggle with the Dutch. In this first round, the Catholic and imperial cause had triumphed.

The Second Phase, 1621–1630 When the truce between the Spaniards and the Dutch expired in 1621 and warfare resumed in Germany as well as in the Netherlands, the Protestants made no progress for ten years. A new imperial army was raised by Albrecht von Wallenstein, a minor Bohemian nobleman and remarkable opportunist who had become one of the richest men in the empire. By 1627 Wallenstein's army had begun to conquer the northern region of the empire, the last major center of Protestant strength. To emphasize his supremacy, Ferdinand issued the Edict of Restitution in 1629, ordering the restoration to Catholics of all the territories they had lost to Protestants since 1552.

But these Habsburg successes were more apparent than real, because it was only the extreme disorganization of the empire that permitted a mercenary captain like Wallenstein to achieve such immense military power. Once the princes realized the danger he posed to their independence, they united (Catholic as well as Protestant) against the Habsburgs, and in 1630 they forced the dismissal of Wallenstein by threatening to keep Ferdinand's son from the imperial succession. This concession proved fatal to the emperor's cause, for

Jan Asselyn
THE BATTLE OF LÜTZEN
Although it is not an accurate rendition of the scene, this painting of Gustavus Adolphus (the horseman in a brown coat with sword raised) shot by a gunman in red does give the flavor of seventeenth-century battle. Because of the chaos, the smoke, and the poor visibility that often obscured what was happening, Gustavus' escort did not notice when Gustavus was in fact hit by a musket shot that shattered his left arm and caused his horse to bolt. Further shots killed him, and not until hours after the battle was his seminaked body found, stripped of its finery.
Herzog Anton Ulrich-Museum, Braunschweig. Museum photo, B. P. Keiser

Sweden and France were preparing to unleash new aggressions against the Habsburgs, and Wallenstein was the one military leader who might have been able to resist the onslaught.

The Third Phase, 1630–1632   The year 1630 marked the beginning of a change in fortune for the Protestants and also a drift toward the purely political aim (of resisting the Habsburgs) that was coming to dominate the war. Although France's king was a Catholic, he was ready to join with Protestants against other Catholics so as to undermine Habsburg power. In 1631, the French allied with Gustavus Adolphus of Sweden, who, dismayed by Ferdinand's treatment of Protestants and fearing a Habsburg threat to Swedish lands around the Baltic Sea, had invaded the empire in 1630. The following year Gustavus destroyed an imperial army in a decisive battle that turned the tide against the Habsburgs.

Ferdinand hastily recalled Wallenstein, whose troops met the Swedes in battle at Lützen in 1632. Although Gustavus' soldiers won the day, he himself was killed, and his death saved the Habsburg Dynasty. Nothing, however, could restore Ferdinand's former position. The emperor was forced by the princes to turn against Wallenstein once more; a few months later Ferdinand had Wallenstein assassinated. The removal of the great general marked the end of an era, because Wallenstein was the last leader for more than two centuries who was capable of establishing unified authority in what is now Germany.

Gerard Terborch
THE PEACE OF WESTPHALIA, **1648**
The artist was an eyewitness to this scene, the formal signing of peace between the United Provinces and Spain in Münster on May 15, 1648. The two leaders of the Spanish delegation on the right put their hands on a Bible as they swear to uphold the terms of the treaty, and the Dutch on the left all raise their hands as they declare "So help me God." Terborch himself, dressed in brown, is looking out at the viewer on the far left.
Reproduced by courtesy of the Trustees, © The National Gallery, London (NG896)

The Fourth Phase, 1632–1648 Gustavus' success opened the final phase of the war, as political ambitions—the quest of the empire's princes for independence and the struggle between the Habsburgs and their enemies—almost completely replaced religious aims. The Protestant princes began to raise new armies, and by 1635 Ferdinand had to make peace with them. In return for their promise of assistance in driving out the Swedes, Ferdinand agreed to suspend the Edict of Restitution and to grant amnesty to all but Frederick of the Palatinate and a few Bohemian rebels. Ferdinand was renouncing most of his ambitions, and it seemed that peace might return at last.

But the French could not let matters rest. In 1635 they finally declared war on Ferdinand. For the next thirteen years, the French and Swedes rained unmitigated disaster on Germany. Peace negotiations began in 1641, but not until 1648 did the combatants sign the treaties of Westphalia. Even thereafter the war between France and Spain, pursued mainly in the Spanish Netherlands, continued for another eleven years; and hostilities around the Baltic among Sweden, Denmark, Poland, and Russia, which had started in 1611, did not end until 1661.

The Effect of War The wars and their effects (such as the diseases spread by armies) killed off more than a third of Germany's population. The conflict caused serious economic dislocation because a number of princes—

already in serious financial straits—sharply debased their coinage. Their actions worsened the continent-wide trade depression that had begun around 1620 and had brought the great sixteenth-century boom to an end, causing the first drop in prices since 1500. Few contemporaries perceived the connection between war and economic trouble, but nobody could ignore the drain on men and resources, the crisis in international relations, or the widespread destruction caused by the conflict.

The Peace of Westphalia

By the 1630s it was becoming apparent that the fighting was getting out of hand and that it would not be easy to bring the conflicts to an end. There had never been such widespread or devastating warfare, and many diplomats felt that the settlement had to be of far greater scope than any negotiated before. And they were right. When at last the treaties were signed in 1648, after seven years of negotiation in the German province of Westphalia, a landmark in international relations was passed—remarkable not only because it brought an anarchic situation under control but because it created a new system for dealing with wars.

The most important innovation was the gathering at the peace conference of all the participants in the Thirty Years' War, rather than the usual practice of bringing only two or three belligerents together. The presence of delegations from 109 interested parties

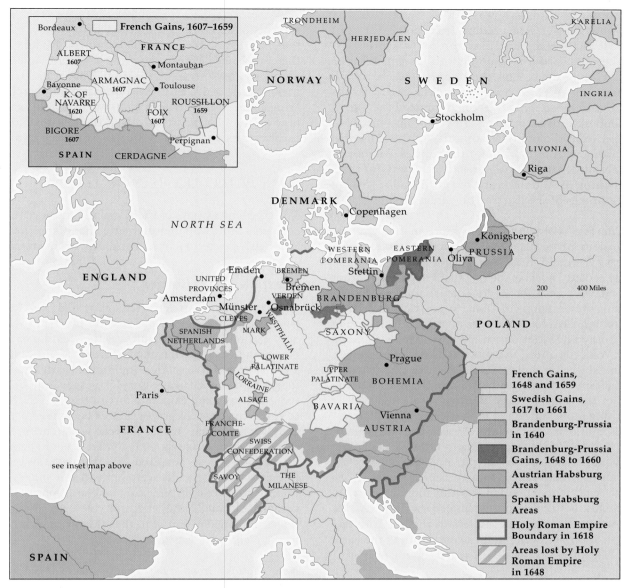

MAP 15.3 TERRITORIAL CHANGES, 1648–1661
This map shows the territorial changes that took place after the Thirty Years' War. The treaties of Westphalia (1648) and the Pyrenees (1659) arranged the principal transfers, but the settlements in the Baltic were not confirmed until the treaties of Copenhagen, Oliva (both 1660), and Kardis (1661). Who were the main winners and losers in the territorial changes of this period?
◆ For an online version, go to www.mhhe.com/chambers9 > chapter 15 > book maps

made possible, for the first time in European history, a series of all-embracing treaties that dealt with nearly every major international issue at one stroke. Visible at the meetings was the emergence of a state system. These independent states recognized that they were creating a mechanism for controlling their relations with one another. Although some fighting continued, the Peace of Westphalia in 1648 became the first comprehensive rearrangement of the map of Europe in modern times.

Peace Terms The principal beneficiaries were France and Sweden, the chief aggressors during the last decade of the war. France gained the provinces of Alsace and Lorraine, and Sweden obtained extensive territories in the Holy Roman Empire. The main loser was the House of Habsburg, since both the United Provinces and the Swiss Confederation were recognized as independent states, and the German princes, who agreed not to join an alliance against the emperor, were otherwise given almost complete independence.

The princes' autonomy was formally established in 1657, when they elected as emperor Leopold I, the head of the House of Habsburg, in return for two promises. First, Leopold would give no help to his cousins, the rulers of Spain; and second, the empire would be a state of princes, in which each ruler would be free from imperial interference. This freedom permitted the rise of Brandenburg-Prussia and the growth of absolutism—the belief that the political authority of the ruler was unlimited—within the major principalities. Moreover, the Habsburgs' capitulation prepared the way for their reorientation toward the east along the Danube River—the beginnings of the Austro-Hungarian Empire.

The Effects of Westphalia For more than a century, the settlement reached at Westphalia was regarded as the basis for all international negotiations. Even major new accords, such as the one that ended yet another series of wars in 1713, were seen mainly as adjustments of the decisions of 1648. In practice, of course, multinational conferences were no more effective than brief, limited negotiations in reducing tensions among states. Wars continued to break out, and armies grew in size and skill. But diplomats did believe that international affairs were under better control and that the chaos of the Thirty Years' War had been replaced by something more stable and more clearly defined.

This confidence was reinforced as it became clear after 1648 that armies were trying to improve discipline and avoid the excesses of the previous thirty years. As religious passions waned, combat became less vicious and the treatment of civilians became more orderly. On battlefields, better discipline reduced the casualty rate from one death per three soldiers in the 1630s to one death in seven, or even one in twenty, during the early 1700s. The aims of war also changed significantly.

Changed International Relations The most obvious differences after the Peace of Westphalia were that France replaced Spain as the continent's dominant power and that northern countries—especially England and the Netherlands, where growth in population and in commerce resumed more quickly than elsewhere—took over Europe's economic leadership. But behind this outward shift a more fundamental transformation was taking place. What had become apparent in the later stages of the Thirty Years' War was that Europe's states were prepared to fight only for economic, territorial, or political advantages. Dynastic aims were still important, but supranational goals like religious causes could no longer determine a state's foreign policy.

The Thirty Years' War was the last major international conflict in Europe in which two religious camps organized their forces as blocs. After 1648 such connections gave way to purely national interests; it is no surprise that the papacy denounced the peace vehemently. For this shift marked the decisive stage of a process that had been under way since the Late Middle Ages: the emergence of the state as the basic unit and object of loyalty in Western civilization. That it had taken a major crisis, a descent into international anarchy, to bring about so momentous a change is an indication of how profoundly the upheavals of the mid-seventeenth century, this age of crisis, affected European history.

THE MILITARY REVOLUTION

The constant warfare of the sixteenth and seventeenth centuries brought about dramatic changes in the ways that battles were fought and armies were organized.

Weapons and Tactics

The Use of Gunpowder Though it had been known since the 1330s, gunpowder became central to warfare only around 1500. The result was the creation of a new type of industry, cannon and gun manufacture, and also a transformation of tactics. Individual castles could no longer be defended against explosives; even towns had to build heavy and elaborate fortifications if they were to resist the new firepower. Sieges became expensive, complex operations whose purpose was to bring explosives right up to a town wall so that it could be blown up. This process required an intricate system of trenches, because walls were built in star shapes so as to multiply angles of fire and make any approach dangerous. Although they became increasingly costly, sieges remained essential to the strategy of warfare until the eighteenth century.

New Tactics In open battles, the effects of gunpowder were equally expensive. The new tactics that appeared around 1500, perfected by the Spaniards, relied on massed ranks of infantry, organized in huge squares, that made the traditional cavalry charge obsolete. Interspersed with the gunners were soldiers carrying pikes. They fended off horses or opposing infantry while the men with guns tried to mow the enemy down. The squares with the best discipline usually won, and for more than a century after the reign of Ferdinand of Aragon, the Spaniards had the best army in Europe. Each square had about three thousand troops, and to maintain enough squares to fight all of Spain's battles required an army numbering approximately forty thousand. The cost of keeping that many men clothed, fed, and housed, let alone equipped and paid, was enormous. But worse was to come: New tactics emerged in the early seventeenth century that required even more soldiers.

Anonymous
WAFFENHANDLUNG, ENGRAVING AFTER JACQUES DE GHEYN
The expansion of armies and the professionalization of war in the seventeenth century were reflected in the founding of military academies and in the growing acceptance of the notion that warfare was a science. There was now a market for published manuals, especially if they had illustrations like this one, which shows how a pikeman was supposed to crouch and hold his weapons (stabilizing his pike against his foot) when facing a cavalry charge.
Deutsches Historisches Museum, Berlin, Germany

Since nobody could outdo the Spaniards at their own methods, a different approach was developed by their rivals. The first advance was made by Maurice of Nassau, in the Dutch revolt against Spain. He relied not on sheer weight and power but on flexibility and mobility. Then Sweden's Gustavus Adolphus, one of the geniuses of the history of warfare, found a way to achieve mobility on the field without losing power. His main invention was the salvo: Instead of having his musketeers fire one row at a time, like the Spaniards, he had them all fire at once. What he lost in continuity of shot he gained in a fearsome blast that, if properly timed, could shatter enemy ranks. Huge, slow-moving squares were simply no match for smaller, faster units that riddled them with well-coordinated salvos.

The Organization and Support of Armies

These tactical changes brought about steady increases in the size of armies, because the more units there were, the better they could be placed on the battlefield. Although the Spanish army hardly grew between 1560 and 1640, remaining at 40,000 to 60,000 men, the Swedes had 150,000 by 1632; and at the end of the century, Louis XIV considered a force of 400,000 essential to maintain his dominant position in Europe.

This growth had far-reaching consequences. One was the need for **conscription,** which Gustavus introduced in the late 1620s. At least half his army consisted of his own subjects, who were easier to control than foreign mercenaries. Because it also made sense not to disband such huge forces each autumn, when the campaigning season ended, most armies were kept permanently ready. To strengthen discipline, new mechanisms were developed: drilling, combat training, uniforms, and the various officer ranks we still have. And the need to maintain so many soldiers the year round caused a rapid expansion of supporting administrative personnel. Taxation mushroomed. All levels of society felt the impact, but especially the lower classes, who paid the bulk of the taxes and provided most of the recruits.

The Life of the Soldier

Some soldiers genuinely wanted to join up. They had heard stories of adventure, booty, and comradeship, and they were tempted by free food and clothing. But many "volunteers" did not want to go, for they had also heard of the hardship and danger. Unfortunately for them, recruiting officers had quotas, and villages had to provide the numbers. Community pressure, bribery, enlistment of drunken men, and even outright kidnapping helped fill the ranks.

Joining an army did not necessarily mean cutting oneself off from friends or family. Men from a particular area enlisted together and, in some cases, wives and even children came along. There were dozens of jobs to do aside from fighting, because soldiers needed cooks, launderers, peddlers, and other tradespeople. An army in the field often needed five people for every soldier. Few barracks were built, and therefore, unless they were on the march or out in the open on a battlefield, troops were housed (or billeted) with ordinary citizens. Since soldiers almost never received their wages on time—delays could be as long as a year or more—they rarely could pay for their food and housing. Local civilians, therefore, had to supply their needs or risk the thievery that was universal. It was no wonder that the approach of an army was a terrifying event.

Discomforts of Military Life Military life was not easy. Soldiers suffered constant discomfort. A garrison might be able to settle into a town in reasonable conditions for a long stretch, but if it was besieged, it became hungry, fearful, and vulnerable. Days spent on the march could be grim, exhausting, and uncertain; even in camps soldiers were often filthy and wet. Real danger

Sebastian Vrancx
A MILITARY CAMP
Vrancx was himself a soldier, and the many military scenes he painted during the Thirty Years' War give us a sense of the life of the soldier during the long months when there were no campaigns or battles. Conditions could be grim, but there were many hours during which a soldier could simply nap, chat, or play dice.
Hamburg/Hamburger Kunsthalle/The Bridgeman Art Library

was not common, though it was intense during battles and occasionally during sieges. Even a simple wound could be fatal, because medical care was generally appalling. Despite traditional recreations—drink, gambling, and the brawls common among soldiers—the attractions of army service were limited; most military men had few regrets when they returned to civilian life.

REVOLUTION IN ENGLAND

In the 1640s and 1650s the growing burdens of war and taxation, and the mounting assertiveness of governments, sparked upheavals throughout Europe that were the equivalent in domestic politics of the crisis in international relations. In country after country, people rose up in vain attempts to restore the individual and regional autonomies that were being eroded by power-

ful central governments. Only in England, however, did the revolt become a revolution—an attempt to overturn the social and political system and create a new structure for society.

Pressures for Change

The Gentry   The central figures in the drama were the gentry, a social group immediately below the nobles at the head of society. They ranged from people considered great in a parish or other small locality to courtiers considered great throughout the land. Although in Elizabeth's reign there were never more than sixty nobles, the gentry numbered close to twenty thousand. Most of the gentry were doing well economically, profiting from agricultural holdings and crown offices. A number also became involved in industrial activity, and hundreds invested in new overseas trading and colonial ventures. The gentry's participation in commerce made them unique among the landed classes of Europe, whose members were traditionally contemptuous of business affairs, and it testified to the enterprise and vigor of England's social leaders. Long important in local administration, they flocked to the House of Commons to express their views on public matters. Their ambitions eventually posed a serious threat to the monarchy, especially when linked with the effects of rapid economic change.

Economic Advance   In Elizabeth's reign, thanks to a general boom in trade, England's merchants, aided by leading courtiers, had begun to transform the country's economy. They opened commercial links throughout Europe and parts of Asia and promoted significant industrial development at home. Mining and manufacture developed rapidly, and shipbuilding became a major industry. The production of coal increased fourteen-fold between 1540 and 1680, creating fortunes and an expertise in industrial techniques that took England far ahead of its neighbors.

The economic vigor and growth that ensued gave the classes that benefited most—gentry and merchants—a cohesion and a sense of purpose that made it dangerous to oppose them when they felt their rights infringed. They were coming to see themselves as leaders of the nation, almost alongside the nobility. They wanted respect for their wishes, and they bitterly resented the economic interference and political high-handedness of Elizabeth's successors.

The Puritans   Heightening this unease was the sympathy that many of the gentry felt toward a small but vociferous group of religious reformers, the **Puritans.** Puritans believed that the Protestant Anglican Church established by Elizabeth was still too close to Roman Catholicism, and they wanted further reductions in ritual and hierarchy. Elizabeth refused, and although she tried to avoid a confrontation, in the last years of her reign she had to silence the most outspoken of her critics. As a result, the Puritans became a disgruntled minority. By the 1630s, when the government tried to repress religious dissent more vigorously, many people in England, non-Puritan as well as Puritan, felt that the monarchy was leading the country astray and was ignoring the wishes of its subjects. Leading parliamentarians in particular soon came to believe that major changes were needed to restore good government in England.

Parliament and the Law

The place where the gentry made their views known was Parliament, the nation's supreme legislative body.

Three-quarters of the House of Commons consisted of gentry. They were better educated than ever before, and nearly half of them had legal training. Since the Commons had to approve all taxation, the gentry had the leverage to pursue their grievances.

The monarchy was still the dominant force in the country when Elizabeth died in 1603, but Parliament's demand to be heard was gathering momentum. Although the queen had been careful with money, in the last twenty years of her reign her resources had been overtaxed by war with Spain and an economic depression. Thus, she bequeathed to her successor, Scotland's James Stuart, a huge debt—£400,000, the equal of a year's royal revenue; his struggle to pay it off gave the Commons the means to seek changes in royal policy.

James I's Difficulties   Trouble began during the reign of James I (r. 1603–1625), who had a far more exalted view of his own powers than Elizabeth and who did not hesitate to tell his subjects that he considered his authority almost unlimited. In response, gentry opposed to royal policies dominated parliamentary proceedings, and they engaged in a running battle with the king. They blocked the union of England with Scotland that James sought. They drew up an "Apology" explaining his mistakes and his ignorance, as a Scotsman, of English traditions. They forced two of his ministers to resign in disgrace. And they wrung repeated concessions from him, including the unprecedented right for Parliament to discuss foreign policy.

Conflict over the Law   The Commons used the law to justify their resistance to royal power. The basic legal system of the country was the common law—justice administered on the basis of precedents and parliamentary statutes and relying on the opinions of juries. This system stood in contrast to Roman law, prevalent on the Continent, where royal edicts could make law and decisions were reached by judges without juries. Such practices existed in England only in a few royal courts of law, such as Star Chamber, which, because it was directly under the crown, came to be seen as an instrument of repression.

The common lawyers, whose leaders were also prominent in the Commons, resented the growing business of the royal courts and attacked them in Parliament. Both James and his successor were accused of pressuring judges, particularly after they won a series of famous cases involving a subject's right to criticize the monarch. Thus, the crown could be portrayed as disregarding not only the desires of the people but the law itself. The king still had broad powers, but when he exercised them contrary to Parliament's wishes, his actions seemed to many to be taking on the appearance of tyranny.

Rising Antagonisms

The confrontation between Parliament and king grew worse during the 1620s, especially in the reign of James's son, Charles I (r. 1625–1649). At the Parliament of 1628–1629, the open challenge to the crown reached a climax in the Petition of Right, which has become a landmark in constitutional history. The petition demanded an end to imprisonment without cause shown, to taxation without the consent of Parliament, to martial law in peacetime, and to the billeting of troops among civilians. Charles agreed, in the hope of gaining much-needed subsidies, but then broke his word. To many, this betrayal seemed to threaten Parliament's essential role in government alongside the king. Seeking to end discussion of these issues in the Commons, Charles ordered Parliament dissolved.

Resentful subjects were clearly on the brink of openly defying their king. Puritans, common lawyers, and disenchanted country gentry had taken over the House of Commons; Charles avoided further trouble only by refusing to call another session of Parliament. This he managed to do for eleven years, all the while increasing the repression of Puritanism and using extraordinary measures (such as reviving crown rights to special taxes that had not been demanded for a long time) to raise revenues that did not require parliamentary consent. But in 1639, the Calvinist Scots took up arms rather than accept the Anglican prayer book, and the parliamentarians had their chance. To pay for an army to fight the Scots, Charles had to turn to Parliament, which demanded that he first redress its grievances. When he resisted, civil war followed.

Civil War

By the summer of 1640, the Scots occupied most of northern England, and Charles, after quarrelling with and dismissing one assembly, was forced to summon a new Parliament. This sat for thirteen years, earning the appropriate name of the Long Parliament.

In its first year, the House of Commons abolished the royal courts, such as Star Chamber, and made mandatory the writ of habeas corpus (which prevented imprisonment without cause shown); it declared taxation without parliamentary consent illegal; and it ruled that Parliament had to meet at least once every three years. Meanwhile, the Puritans in the Commons prepared to reform the church. Oliver Cromwell, one of their leaders, demanded abolition of the Anglican Book of Common Prayer and strongly attacked the authority and very existence of bishops. The climactic vote came the next year, when the Commons passed a Grand Remonstrance, which outlined for the king all the legislation they had passed and asked that bishops be deprived of votes in the House of Lords.

The Two Sides This demand was the prelude to a more revolutionary Puritan assault on the structure of the Church, but in fact the Grand Remonstrance passed by only eleven votes. A moderate group was detaching itself from the Puritans, and it was to become the nucleus of a royalist party. The nation's chief grievances had been redressed, and there was no longer a uniform desire for change. Still, Charles misjudged the situation and tried to arrest five leaders of the Commons, supposedly for plotting treason with the Scots. But Parliament resisted, and the citizens of London, openly hostile to Charles, sheltered the five. England now began to split in two. By late 1642 both the royalists and the antiroyalists had assembled armies, and the Civil War was under way.

What made so many people overcome their habitual loyalty to the monarchy? We know that the royalists in Parliament were considerably younger than their opponents, which suggests that it was long experience with the Stuarts and nostalgia for Elizabeth that created revolutionaries. Another clear divide was regional. The south and east of England were primarily antiroyalist, while the north and west were mostly royalist. These divisions indicated that the more cosmopolitan areas, closer to the Continent and also centers of Puritanism, were largely on Parliament's side. The decision was often a personal matter: A prominent family and its locality chose one side because its rival, a nearby family, had chosen the other. The Puritans were certainly antiroyalist, but they were a minority in the country and influential in the House of Commons only because they were so vocal and determined. Like all revolutions, this one was animated by a small group of radicals (in this case, Puritans) who alone kept the momentum going.

Independents and Presbyterians As the fighting began, a group among the Puritans known as Independents urged that the Anglican Church be replaced by a congregational system in which each local congregation, free of all central authority, would decide its own form of worship. The most important leader of the Independents in Parliament was Oliver Cromwell. Opposed to them, but also considered Puritans, were the Presbyterians, who wanted to establish a strictly organized Calvinist system, like the one in Scotland in which local congregations were subject to centralized authority. Since both the Scots, whose alliance was vital in the war, and a majority of the Puritans in the Commons were Presbyterians, Cromwell agreed to give way, but only for the moment. The two sides also quarreled over the goals of the war. The Independents were in general more determined to force Charles into total submission, and eventually they had their way.

As the fighting continued, Cromwell persuaded the Commons to allow him to reorganize the antiroyalist troops. His New Model Army—whipped to fervor by

sermons, prayers, and the singing of psalms—became unbeatable. At Naseby in 1645, it won a major victory, and a year later Charles surrendered. The next two years were chaotic. The Presbyterians and Independents quarreled over what to do with the king, and finally civil war resumed. This time the Presbyterians and Scots backed Charles against the Independents. But even with this alliance the royalists were no match for the New Model Army; Cromwell soon defeated his opponents and captured the king.

The King's Fate At the same time, in 1647, the Independents abolished the House of Lords and removed all Presbyterians from the House of Commons. This "Rump" Parliament tried to negotiate with Charles but discovered that he continued to plot a return to power. With Cromwell's approval, the Commons decided that their monarch, untrustworthy and a troublemaker, would have to die. A trial of dubious legality was held, and though many of the participants refused to sign the death warrant, the "holy, anointed" king was executed by his subjects in January 1649, to the horror of all Europe and most of England.

England under Cromwell

Oliver Cromwell was now master of England. The republic established after Charles's execution was officially ruled by the Rump Parliament, but a Council of State led by Cromwell controlled policy with the backing of the army. And they had to contend with a fer-

ment of political and social ideas. One group, known as the Levellers, demanded the vote for nearly all adult males and parliamentary elections every other year. The men of property among the Puritans, notably Cromwell himself, were disturbed by the egalitarianism of these proposals and insisted that only men with an "interest" in England—that is, land—should be qualified to vote.

Radical Ideas Even more radical were the Diggers, a communistic sect that sought to implement the spirit of primitive Christianity by abolishing personal property; the Society of Friends, which stressed personal inspiration as the source of faith and all action; and the Fifth Monarchists, a messianic group who believed that the "saints"—themselves—should rule because the Day of Judgment was at hand. People of great ability, such as the famous poet John Milton, contributed to the fantastic flood of pamphlets and suggestions for reform that poured forth in these years, and their ideas inspired future revolutionaries. But at the time, they merely put Cromwell on the defensive, forcing him to maintain control at all costs.

Cromwell's Aims Cromwell himself fought for two overriding causes: religious freedom (except for the Anglican and Catholic churches) and constitutional government. But he achieved neither, and he grew increasingly unhappy at the Rump Parliament's refusal to enact reforms. He dissolved the assembly in 1653 (the final end of the Long Parliament), and during the remaining five

OLIVER CROMWELL'S AIMS

When Parliament in late 1656 offered to make Oliver Cromwell the king of England as a way of restoring political stability, he hesitated before replying. When he finally came to Parliament with his response on April 13, 1657, he turned down the offer of a crown and explained in a long speech—from which a passage follows—why he felt it would be wrong to reestablish a monarchy in England.

"I do think you ought to attend to the settling of the peace and liberties of this Nation. Otherwise the Nation will fall in pieces. And in that, so far as I can, I am ready to serve not as a King, but as a Constable. For truly I have, before God, often thought that I could not tell what my business was, save comparing myself to a good Constable set to keep the peace of the parish. And truly this hath been my content and satisfaction in the troubles I have undergone . . . I was a person who, from my first employment, was suddenly lifted up from lesser trusts to greater. . . . The Providence of God hath laid aside this Title of King; and that not by sudden humor, but by issue of ten or twelve years Civil War,

wherein much blood hath been shed. I will not dispute the justice of it when it was done. But God in His severity hath eradicated a whole Family, and thrust them out of the land. And God hath seemed providential not only in striking at the family but at the Name [of king]. It is blotted out. God blasted the very Title. I will not seek to set up that which Providence hath destroyed, and laid in the dust: I would not build Jericho again."

From Thomas Carlyle (ed.), *Oliver Cromwell's Letters and Speeches,* Vol. 3, London, 1908, pp. 230, 231, and 235.

years of his life he tried desperately to lay down a new constitutional structure for his government.

Cromwell was driven by noble aspirations, but in the end he had to rule by military dictatorship. From 1653 on he was called lord protector and ruled through eleven major generals, each responsible for a different district of England and supported by a tax on the estates of royalists. To quell dissent, he banned newspapers; to prevent disorder, he took such measures as enlisting innkeepers as government spies. Cromwell was always a reluctant revolutionary; he hated power and sought only limited ends. Some revolutionaries, like Lenin, have a good idea of where they would like to be carried by events; others, like Cromwell, move painfully, hesitantly, and uncertainly to the extremes they finally reach. It was because he sought England's benefit so urgently and because he considered the nation too precious to abandon to irreligion or tyranny that Cromwell remained determinedly in command to the end of his life.

The End of the Revolution   Gradually, more traditional political forms reappeared. The Parliament of 1656 offered Cromwell the crown, and, though he refused, he took the title of "His Highness" and ensured that the succession would go to his son. Cromwell was monarch in all but name, yet only his presence ensured stability (see "Oliver Cromwell's Aims," above). After he died, his quiet, retiring son Richard proved no match

for the scheming generals of the army, who created political turmoil. To bring an end to the uncertainty, General George Monck, the commander of a well-disciplined force in Scotland, marched south in 1660, assumed control, and invited the son of Charles I, Charles II, to return from exile and restore the monarchy.

Results of the Revolution   Only the actions taken during the first months of the Long Parliament—the abolition of royal courts, the prohibition of taxation without parliamentary consent, and the establishment of the writ of habeas corpus—persisted beyond the revolution. Otherwise, everything seemed much the same as before: Bishops and lords were reinstated, religious dissent was again repressed, and Parliament was called and dissolved by the monarch. But the tone and balance of political relations had changed for good.

Henceforth, the gentry could no longer be denied a decisive voice in politics. In essence, this had been their revolution, and they had succeeded. When in the 1680s a king again tried to impose his wishes on the country without reference to Parliament, there was no need for another major upheaval. A quiet, bloodless coup reaffirmed the new role of the gentry and Parliament. The crisis of authority that had arisen from a long period of growing unease and open conflict had been resolved, and the English could settle into a system of rule that with only gradual modification remained in force for some two centuries.

Anonymous
THE SEINE FROM THE PONT NEUF, CA. 1635
Henry IV of France, celebrated in the equestrian statue overlooking the Seine that stands in Paris to this day, saw the physical reshaping of his capital as part of the effort to restore order after decades of civil war. He laid out the first squares in any European city, and under the shadow of his palace, the Louvre, he built the Pont Neuf (on the right)—the first open bridge (without houses on it) across the Seine.
Giraudon/Art Resource, NY

REVOLTS IN FRANCE AND SPAIN

The fact that political upheaval took place not only in England but in much of Europe in the 1640s and 1650s is the main reason that historians have come to speak of a "general crisis" during this period. Political institutions and political authority were being challenged in many countries, and although only England went through a revolution, the disruptions and conflicts were also significant in the two other major states of the age, France and Spain.

The France of Henry IV

In the 1590s Henry IV resumed the strengthening of royal power, which had been interrupted by the civil wars that had begun in the 1560s. He mollified the traditional landed aristocracy, known as the nobility of the sword, with places on his Council of Affairs and with large financial settlements. The principal bureaucrats, known as the nobility of the robe, controlled the country's administration, and Henry made sure to turn their interests to his benefit. Because all crown offices had to be bought, he used the system both to raise revenues and to guarantee the loyalty of the bureaucrats. He not only accelerated the sales of offices but also invented a

new device, an annual fee known as the *paulette,* which ensured that an officeholder's job would remain in his family when he died. This increased royal profits and also reduced the flow of newcomers, thus strengthening the commitment of existing officeholders to the crown.

By 1610 Henry had imposed his will throughout France, and he was secure enough to plan an invasion of the Holy Roman Empire. Although he was assassinated before he could join his army, and the invasion was called off, his heritage, especially in economic affairs, long outlived him. France's rich agriculture may have had one unfortunate effect—successful merchants abandoned commerce as soon as they could afford to move to the country and buy a title of nobility (and thus gain exemption from taxes)—but it did ensure a solid basis for the French economy. Indeed, agriculture suffered little during the civil wars, though the violence and the rising taxes did cause uprisings of peasants (the main victims of the tax system) almost every year from the 1590s to the 1670s.

Mercantilism   By restoring political stability, Henry ended the worst economic disruptions, but his main legacy was the notion that his increasingly powerful government was responsible for the health of the country's economy. This view was justified by a theory

RICHELIEU ON DIPLOMACY

The following passages are taken from a collection of the writings of Cardinal Richelieu that was put together after his death and published in 1688 under the title Political Testament. *The book is presented as a work of advice to the king and summarizes what Richelieu learned of politics and diplomacy as one of Europe's leading statesmen during the Thirty Years' War.*

"One cannot imagine how many advantages States gain from continued negotiations, if conducted wisely, unless one has experienced it oneself. I admit I did not realize this truth for five or six years after first being employed in the management of policy. But I am now so sure of it that I say boldly that to negotiate everywhere without cease, openly and secretly, even though one makes no immediate gains and future gains seem unlikely, is absolutely necessary for the good of the State. . . . He who negotiates all the time will find at last the right moment to achieve his aims, and even if he does not find it, at least it is true that he can lose nothing, and that through his negotiations he knows what is happening in the world, which is of no small consequence for the good of the State. . . . Important negotia-tions must not be interrupted for a moment. . . . One must not be disheartened by an unfortunate turn of events, because sometimes it happens that what is undertaken with good reason is achieved with little good fortune. . . . It is difficult to fight often and always win. . . . It is often because negotiations are so innocent that one can gain great advantages from them without ever faring badly. . . . In matters of State one must find an advantage in everything; that which can be useful must never be neglected."

From Louis Andrè (ed.), *Testament Politique* (Editions Robert Laffont, 1947), pp. 347–348 and 352; translated by T. K. Rabb.

developed mainly in France: **mercantilism,** which became an essential ingredient of absolutism. Mercantilism was more a set of attitudes than a systematic economic theory. Its basic premise—an erroneous one—was that the world contained a fixed amount of wealth and that each nation could enrich itself only at the expense of others. To some thinkers, this theory meant hoarding bullion (gold and silver); to others, it required a favorable balance of trade—more exports than imports. All mercantilists, however, agreed that state regulation of economic affairs was necessary for the welfare of a country. Only a strong, centralized government could encourage native industries, control production, set quality standards, allocate resources, establish tariffs, and take other measures to promote prosperity and improve trade. Thus, mercantilism was as much about politics as economics and fit perfectly with Henry's restoration of royal power. In line with their advocacy of activist policies, the mercantilists also approved of war. Even economic advance was linked to warfare in this violent age.

Louis XIII

Unrest reappeared when Henry's death left the throne to his nine-year-old son, Louis XIII (r. 1610–1643). The widowed queen, Marie de Medici, served as regent and soon faced revolts by Calvinists and disgruntled nobles. In the face of these troubles, Marie summoned the Es-tates General in 1614. This was their last meeting for 175 years, until the eve of the French Revolution; and the weakness they displayed, as various groups within the Estates fought one another over plans for political reform, demonstrated that the monarchy was the only institution that could unite the nation. The session revealed the impotence of those who opposed royal policies, and Marie brought criticism to an end by declaring her son to be of age and the regency dissolved. In this absolutist state, further protest could be defined as treason.

Richelieu   For a decade, the monarchy lacked energetic direction; but in 1624, one of Marie's favorites, Armand du Plessis de Richelieu, a churchman who rose to be a cardinal through her favor, became chief minister and took control of the government. Over the next eighteen years, this ambitious and determined leader resumed Henry IV's assertion of royal authority (see "Richelieu on Diplomacy," above).

The monarchy had to manage a number of vested interests as it concentrated its power, and Richelieu's achievement was that he kept them under control. The strongest was the bureaucracy, whose ranks had been swollen by the sale of offices. Richelieu always paid close attention to the views of the bureaucrats, and one reason he had such influence over the king was that he acted as the head and representative of this army of royal servants. He also reduced the independence of traditional nobles by giving them positions in the regime as diplomats, soldiers, and officials without significant administrative responsibility. Finally, he took on the Huguenots in a military campaign. After he defeated them, he abolished most of the guarantees in the Edict of Nantes and ended the Huguenots' political independence.

Royal Administration   Under Richelieu the sale of offices broke all bounds: By 1633 it accounted for approximately one-half of royal revenues. Ten years later more than three-quarters of the crown's direct taxation was needed to pay the salaries of the officeholders. It was a vicious circle, and the only solution was to increase the taxes on the lower classes. As this financial burden grew, Richelieu had to improve the government's control over the realm to obtain the revenue he needed. He increased the power of the **intendants,** the government's chief agents in the localities, and established them (instead of the nobles) as the principal representatives of the monarchy in each province of France. Unlike the nobles, the *intendants* depended entirely on royal favor for their position; consequently, they enthusiastically recruited for the army, arranged billeting, supervised the raising of taxes, and enforced the king's decrees. They soon came to be hated figures, both because of the rising taxes and because they threatened the power of the nobles. The result was a succession of peasant uprisings, often led by local notables who resented the rise of the *intendants* and of royal power.

Political and Social Crisis

France's foreign wars made the discontent worse, and it was clear that eventually the opponents of the central government would reassert themselves. But the centralization of power by the crown had been so successful that when trouble erupted, in a series of revolts known as the *Fronde* (or "sling," the simple weapon of the rebels), there was no serious effort to reshape the social order or the political system. The principal actors in the Fronde came from the upper levels of society: nobles, townsmen, and members of the regional courts and legislatures known as parlements. Only rarely were these groups joined by peasants, who may have been resentful of taxes and other government demands and vulnerable to starvation when harvests failed, but the Fronde never raised issues that connected with the peasants' uprisings. These focused on issues like food scarcities, which often brought women into prominent roles, especially since soldiers were reluctant to shoot them. But without noble support, such disorders remained fairly low-scale; they never reached the level of disruption that was to overtake France in the Revolution.

Mazarin   The death of Louis XIII in 1643, followed by a regency because Louis XIV was only five years old, offered an opportunity to those who wanted to reverse the rise of absolutism. Louis XIII's widow, Anne of Austria, took over the government and placed all the power in the hands of an Italian, Cardinal Giulio Mazarin. He used his position to amass a huge fortune, and he was therefore a perfect target for the anger caused by the encroachment of central government on local authority.

Early in 1648 Mazarin sought to gain a respite from the monarch's perennial financial trouble by withholding payment of the salaries of some royal officials for four years. In response, the members of various institutions in Paris, including the Parlement, drew up a charter of demands. They wanted the office of *intendant* abolished, no new offices created, power to approve taxes, and enactment of a habeas corpus law.

The Fronde   Mazarin reacted by arresting the Paris Parlement's leaders, thus sparking a popular rebellion in the city that forced him and the royal family to flee from the capital—an experience the young Louis XIV never forgot. In 1649 Mazarin promised to redress the *parlementaires'* grievances, and he was allowed to return to Paris. But the trouble was far from over; during that summer, uprisings spread throughout France, particularly among peasants and in the old Huguenot stronghold, the southwest.

The next three years were marked by political chaos, mainly as a result of intrigues and shifting alliances among the nobility. As it became clear that the perpetual unrest was producing no results, Mazarin was able to take advantage of disillusionment among nobles and *parlementaires* to reassert the position of the monarchy. He used military force and threats of force to subdue Paris and most of the rebels in the countryside, and he brought the regency to an end by declaring the fourteen-year-old Louis of age in 1652. Although the nobles were not finally subdued until the following year, and peasants continued their occasional regional uprisings for many years to come, the crown now established its authority as the basis for order in the realm. As surely as England, France had surmounted its crisis and found a stable solution for long-standing conflicts.

Sources of Discontent in Spain

For Spain the crisis that swept much of Europe in the mid-seventeenth century—with revolt in England and France and war in the empire—meant the end of the country's international power. Yet the difficulties the monarchy faced had their roots in the sixteenth century. Philip II had already found it difficult to hold his sprawling empire together despite his elaborate bureaucracy. Obsessively suspicious, he maintained close

Anonymous
ENGRAVING OF THE SPANISH INQUISITION, 1560
The burning of heretics was a major public event in sixteenth-century Spain. Aimed mainly at people who practiced Judaism or Islam secretly and in a few cases at Protestants, the Inquisition's investigations usually led to imprisonment or lesser punishments. The occasional executions of those who determinedly refused to accept Catholic teachings, even after torture, were carried out by secular authorities, and they attracted huge crowds.
Bibliothèque Nationale de France, Paris

control over all administrative decisions, and government action was, therefore, agonizingly slow. Moreover, the bureaucracy was run by Castilian nobles, who were resented as outsiders in other regions of the empire. And the standing army, though essential to royal power, was a terrible financial drain.

Philip did gain wide admiration in Spain for his devoutness. His commitment to religion undoubtedly promoted political cohesion, but the economic strains caused by relentless religious warfare eventually undermined Spanish power.

Economic Difficulties   Spain was a rich country in Philip's reign, but the most profitable activities were monopolized by limited groups. Because royal policy valued convenience above social benefit, the city of Seville (dominated by foreign bankers) received a monopoly over shipping to and from the New World; other lucrative pursuits, such as wool and wine production, were also controlled by a small coterie of insiders. The

only important economic activities that involved large numbers of Spaniards were shipping and the prosperous Mediterranean trade, centered in Barcelona, which brought wealth to much of Catalonia. Thus, the influx of silver into Spain was not profitably invested within the country. Drastically overextended in foreign commitments, Philip had to declare himself bankrupt three times. For a while it seemed that the problems might ease because there was peace during the reign of Philip's son, Philip III (r. 1598–1621). But in fact, Philip III's government was incompetent and corrupt, capable neither of dealing with the serious consequences of the spending on war nor of broadening the country's exports beyond wool and wine. And when the flow of treasure from the New World began to dwindle after 1600, the crown was deprived of a major source of income that it was unable to replace (see "Imports of Treasure to Spain . . . ," p. 453). The decline was caused partly by a growing use of precious metals in the New World colonies but also by depletion of the mines.

IMPORTS OF TREASURE TO SPAIN FROM THE NEW WORLD, 1591–1660	
Decade	Total Value*
1591–1600	85,536,000
1601–1610	66,970,000
1611–1620	65,568,000
1621–1630	62,358,000
1631–1640	40,110,000
1641–1650	30,651,000
1651–1660	12,785,000

*In ducats.

Adapted from J. H. Elliott, *Imperial Spain, 1469–1716*, Edward Arnold, Hodder Neadling PLC Group, 1964, p. 175.

In the meantime, tax returns at home were shrinking. The most significant cause of this decrease was a series of severe plagues, which reduced the population of Castile and Aragon from 10 million in 1590 to 6 million in 1700. No other country in Europe suffered a demographic reversal of this proportion during the seventeenth century. In addition, sheep farming took over huge tracts of arable land, and Spain had to rely increasingly on imports of expensive foodstuffs to feed its people. When Spain resumed large-scale fighting against the Dutch and French under Philip IV (r. 1621–1665), the burdens became too much to bear. The effort to maintain the commitment to war despite totally inadequate finances was to bring the greatest state in Europe to its knees.

Revolt and Secession

The final crisis was brought about by the policies of Philip IV's chief minister, the count of Olivares. His aim was to unite the realm so that all the territories shared equally the burden of maintaining Spanish power. Although Castile would no longer dominate the government, it would also not have to provide the bulk of the taxes and army. Olivares' program was called the Union of Arms, and while it seemed eminently reasonable, it caused a series of revolts in the 1640s that split Spain apart.

The reason was that Castile's dominance had made the other provinces feel that local independence was being undermined by a centralized regime. They saw the Union of Arms, imposed by Olivares, as the last straw. Moreover, the plan appeared at a time when Spain's military and economic fortunes were in decline. France had declared war on the Habsburgs in 1635, the funds to support an army were becoming harder to raise, and in desperation Olivares pressed

more vigorously for the Union of Arms. But all he accomplished was to provoke revolts against Castile in the 1640s by Catalonia, Portugal, Naples, and Sicily. By 1641 Catalonia and Portugal had declared themselves independent republics and placed themselves under French protection. Plots began to appear against Olivares, and Philip dismissed the one minister who had understood Spain's problems but who, in trying to solve them, had made them worse.

The Revolts   The Catalonian rebellion continued for another eleven years, and it was thwarted in the end only because the peasants and town mobs transformed the resistance to the central government into an attack on the privileged and wealthy classes. When this happened, the Catalan nobility abandoned the cause and joined the government side. About the same time, the Fronde forced the withdrawal of French troops from Catalonia. When the last major holdout, Barcelona, fell to a royal army in 1652, the Catalan nobles could regain their rights and powers, and the revolt was over.

The Portuguese had no social upheaval; as a result, though not officially granted independence from Spain until 1668, they defended their autonomy easily and even invaded Castile in the 1640s. But the revolts that the people of Sicily and Naples directed at their Castilian rulers in 1647 took on social overtones. In Naples the unrest developed into a tremendous mob uprising led by a local fisherman. The poor turned against all representatives of government and wealth they could find, and chaos ensued until the leader of the revolt was killed. The violence in Sicily, the result of soaring taxes, was aimed primarily at government officials. But in both Naples and Sicily the government was able to reassert its authority by force within a few months.

Consequences   The effect of this unrest was to end the Spanish government's international ambitions and, thus, the worst of its economic difficulties. Like England and France, Spain found a new way of life after its crisis: It became a stable second-level state, heavily agricultural, run by its nobility.

POLITICAL CHANGE IN AN AGE OF CRISIS

Although the level of violence was highest in England and Spain, almost all of Europe's countries experienced the political upheavals of this era of "general crisis." In some cases—for instance, Sweden—the conflict was minor and did little to disturb the peace of the land. But everywhere the basic issue—Who should hold political authority?—caused some degree of strife. And

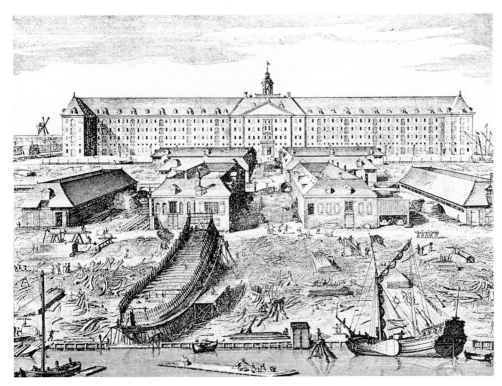

Anonymous
ENGRAVING OF A DUTCH SHIPYARD
The Dutch became the best shipbuilders in Europe in the seventeenth century; the efficiency of their ships, which could be manned by fewer sailors than those of other countries, was a major reason for their successes in trade and commerce.
The Granger Collection, New York

each state had to find its own solutions to the competing demands of governments and their subjects.

The United Provinces

The Dutch did not escape the struggles against the power of centralized governments that created an atmosphere of crisis in much of Europe during the middle decades of the seventeenth century. Despite the remarkable fluidity of their society, the Dutch, too, became embroiled in a confrontation between a ruling family seeking to extend its authority and citizens defending the autonomy of their local regions. The outcome determined the structure of their government for more than a century.

The United Provinces were unique in a number of ways. Other republics existed in Europe, but they were controlled by small oligarchies; the Dutch, who had a long tradition of a strong representative assembly, the Estates General, had created a nation in which many citizens participated in government through elected delegates. Although powerful merchants and a few aristocrats close to the House of Orange did create a small elite, the social differentiation was less than elsewhere in Europe. The resulting openness and homogeneity underlay the economic mastery and cultural brilliance of the United Provinces.

Commerce and Tolerance   The most striking accomplishment of the Dutch was their rise to supremacy in the world of commerce. Amsterdam displaced Antwerp as the Continent's financial capital and gained control of the trade of the world's richest markets. In addition, the Dutch rapidly emerged as the cheapest international shippers. As a result, by the middle of the seventeenth century they had become the chief carriers of European commerce.

The openness of Dutch society permitted the freest exchange of ideas of the time. The new state gave refuge to believers of all kinds, whether extreme Protestant radicals or Catholics who wore their faith lightly, and Amsterdam became the center of a brilliant Jewish community. This freedom attracted some of the greatest minds in Europe and fostered remarkable artistic creativity. The energy that produced this outpouring reflected the pride of a tiny nation that was winning its independence from Spain.

Two Political Parties   There was, however, a basic split within the United Provinces. The two most urbanized and commercial provinces, Holland and Zeeland, dominated the Estates General because they supplied a majority of its taxes. Their representatives formed a mercantile party, which advocated peace abroad so that their trade could flourish unhampered, government by the Estates General so that they could make their influence felt, and religious toleration so that their cities could attract enterprising people of all faiths. In opposition to this mercantile interest was the House of Orange: the descendants of William of Orange, who sought to establish their family's leadership of the Dutch. They were supported by the more rural provinces and stood for war because their authority and popularity derived from their command of the army, for centralized power to enhance the position of the family, and for the strict Calvinism that was upheld in the rural provinces.

The differences between the two factions led Maurice of Nassau to use religion as a pretext to execute his chief opponent, Jan van Oldenbarneveldt, the representative of the province of Holland, in 1618. Oldenbarneveldt was against war with Spain, and his removal left the House of Orange in control of the country. Maurice resumed the war in 1621, and for more than twenty years, his family remained in command, unassailable because it led the army in wartime. Not until 1648—when a new leader, William II, tried to prolong the fighting—did the mercantile party reassert itself by insisting on peace. As a result, the Dutch signed the Treaty of Westphalia, which recognized the independence of the United Provinces. It now seemed that Holland and Zeeland had gained the upper hand. But their struggle with the House of Orange continued (there was even a threat by Orange troops to besiege Amsterdam) until William II suddenly died in 1650, leaving as his successor a baby son, William III.

Jan De Witt   The mercantile interest now assumed full power, and Jan De Witt, the representative of the province of Holland, took over the government in 1653. De Witt's aims were to leave as much authority as possible in the hands of the provinces, particularly Holland; to weaken the executive and prevent a revival of the House of Orange; to pursue trading advantage; and to maintain peace so that the economic supremacy of the Dutch would not be endangered. For nearly twenty years he guided the country in its golden age. But in 1672 French armies overran the southern provinces, and De Witt lacked the military instinct to fight a dangerous enemy. The Dutch at once turned to the family that had led them to independence; a mob murdered De Witt; and the House of Orange, under William III, resumed the centralization that henceforth was to characterize the political structure of the United Provinces. The country had not experienced a midcentury upheaval as severe as those of its neighbors, but it had nevertheless been forced to endure unrest and violence before the form of its government was securely established.

CHRONOLOGY
An Age of Crisis
1618–1660

1618	Revolt in Bohemia, beginning of Thirty Years' War.
1621	Resumption of war between Spanish and Dutch.
1629	Edict of Restitution—high point of Habsburg power.
1630	Sweden enters war against Habsburgs.
1635	France declares war on Habsburgs.
1639	Scots invade England.
1640	Revolts in Catalonia and Portugal against Spanish government.
1642	Civil War in England.
1647	Revolts in Sicily and Naples against Spanish government.
1648	Peace of Westphalia ends Thirty Years' War. Outbreak of *Fronde* in France. Coup by nobles in Denmark. Revolt of Ukraine against Poland. Riots in Russian cities.
1650	Constitutional crisis in Sweden. Confrontation between William of Orange and Amsterdam in Netherlands.
1652	End of Catalan revolt.
1653	End of *Fronde*.
1655	War in Baltic region.
1659	Peace of the Pyrenees between France and Spain.
1660	End of English revolution. Treaties end war in Baltic.

Sweden

The Swedes, too, settled their political system in the mid-seventeenth century. In 1600 Sweden, a Lutheran country of a million people, was one of the backwaters of Europe. A feudal nobility dominated the countryside, a barter economy made money almost unknown, and both trade and towns were virtually nonexistent. Moreover, the country lacked a capital, central institutions, and government machinery. The royal administration consisted of the king and a few courtiers; other officials were appointed only to deal with specific problems as they arose.

Gustavus Adolphus (r. 1611–1632) transformed this situation. He won over the nobles by giving them dominant positions in a newly expanded bureaucracy, and he reorganized his army. Thus equipped both to govern and to fight, Gustavus embarked on a remarkable series of conquests abroad. By 1629 he had made Sweden the most powerful state in the Baltic area. He then entered the Thirty Years' War, advancing victoriously through the Holy Roman Empire until his death, in 1632, during the showdown battle with Wallenstein. Without their great general, the Swedes could do little more than hang on to their gains, but they were now a force to be reckoned with in international affairs.

Government and Economy   The highly efficient system of government established by Gustavus and his chief adviser, Axel Oxenstierna, was to be the envy of other countries until the twentieth century. At the heart of the system were five administrative departments, each led by a nobleman, with the most important—the Chancellery, for diplomacy and internal affairs—run by Oxenstierna. An administrative center emerged in Stockholm, and the new bureaucracy proved that it could run the nation, supply the army, and implement policy even during the last twelve years of Gustavus' reign, when the king himself was almost always abroad.

A major cause of Sweden's amazing rise was the development of the domestic economy, stimulated by the opening up of copper mines and the development of a major iron industry. The country's traditional tar and timber exports were also stepped up, and a fleet was built. By 1700 Stockholm had become an important trading and financial center, growing in the course of the century from fewer than five thousand to more than fifty thousand inhabitants.

The Nobles   The one source of tension amidst this remarkable progress was the position of the nobles. After Gustavus died, they openly challenged the monarchy for control of government and society. Between 1611 and 1652 they more than doubled the proportion of land they owned in Sweden, and much of this growth was at the expense of the crown, which granted away or sold lands to help the war effort abroad. Both peasants and townspeople viewed these developments with alarm, because the nobility usually pursued its own, rather than public, interests. The concern intensified when, in 1648, the nobles in neighboring Denmark took advantage of the death of a strong king to gain control of their government. Two years later the showdown came in Sweden.

Political Confrontation   The monarch now was Gustavus' daughter Christina, an able but erratic young queen who usually allowed Oxenstierna to run the government. For some time, she had hoped to abdicate her throne, become a Catholic, and leave Sweden—an ambition she fulfilled in 1654. She wanted her cousin Charles recognized as her successor, but the nobles threatened to create a republic if she abdicated. The queen, therefore, summoned the Riksdag, Sweden's usually weak representative assembly, in 1650; she encouraged the townspeople and peasants to raise their grievances and allowed them to attack the aristocracy. Soon these groups were demanding the return of nobles' lands to the crown, freedom of speech, and real power; under this pressure, the nobility gave way and recognized Charles X as successor to the throne.

The political upheaval of 1650 was short-lived. Once Christina had her way, she turned against the Riksdag and rejected the lower estates' demands. Only gradually did power shift away from the great nobles toward a broader elite of lesser nobles and bureaucrats, but the turning point in Sweden, as elsewhere, was during the crisis years of the mid-seventeenth century.

Eastern Europe and the Crisis

In Eastern Europe, too, long-term patterns became clear in this period. The limits of Ottoman rule were reconfirmed when an attack on Vienna failed in 1683. Although the Ottomans' control of the Balkans did not immediately waver, their government was increasingly beset by internal problems, and their retreat from Hungary was under way by 1700. Further north, Poland's weak central government lost all claim to real authority in 1648 when it proved unable to stop a group of nobles in the rich province of the Ukraine from switching allegiance from the king of Poland to the tsar in Moscow. And in Russia, following a period of disorder known as the Time of Troubles (1584–1613), the new Romanov **Dynasty** began consolidating its power. The nobility was won over; the last possibilities for escaping serfdom were closed; the legal system was codified; the church came under the tsar's control; and the revolts that erupted against these changes between 1648 and 1672—involving peasants and Cossacks (marauding horsemen, mainly from the South), and often looking like rural revolts in the West, especially France—were brutally suppressed. As elsewhere in Europe, long-standing conflicts between centralizing regimes and their opponents were resolved, and a new political system, supported by the government's military power, was established for centuries to come. Further east, the Ming Dynasty of China was overthrown by the new Ch'ing Dynasty in 1644, a shift that was also accompanied by peasant revolts. That parallel suggests that this was a time of upheaval throughout much of the world, possibly because of a cooling in climate that affected food crops. But everywhere the outcome was a return to stability: crisis there may have been, but the restoration of order was a worldwide phenomenon, too.

Summary

Because these struggles were so widespread, historians have called the midcentury period an age of "general crisis." In country after country, people tried to resist the growing ambitions of central governments. These confrontations reached crisis proportions in almost all cases during the 1640s and 1650s and then subsided at the very time that the anarchy of warfare and international relations was resolved by the Peace of Westphalia. As a result, the sense of settlement after 1660 contrasted sharply with the turmoil of the preceding decades. Moreover, the progression in politics from turbulence to calm had its analogs in the cultural and social developments of the sixteenth and seventeenth centuries.

QUESTIONS FOR FURTHER THOUGHT

1. Are the social benefits of warfare so minimal, compared to its destructive effects, that one can dismiss them as unimportant?

2. Why are there differences in the ways warfare changes domestic politics?

RECOMMENDED READING

Sources

Bodin, Jean. *On Sovereignty.* Julian H. Franklin (ed. and tr.). 1992. An abridgment of Bodin's *Six Books of the Republic.*

Kossmann, E. H., and A. E. Mellink. *Texts Concerning the Revolt of the Netherlands.* 1974. A collection of Spanish and Dutch documents that reveal the different political and religious goals of the two sides.

Studies

*Aston, Trevor (ed.). *Crisis in Europe, 1560–1660: Essays from Past and Present.* 1965. This is a collection of the essays in which the "general crisis" interpretation was initially put forward and discussed.

Braudel, Fernand. *The Mediterranean and the Mediterranean World in the Age of Philip II.* S. Reynolds (tr.). 2 vols. 1972 and 1973. A pioneering and far-ranging work of social history.

Coward, Barry. *The Cromwellian Protectorate.* 2002.

*Duplessis, Robert R. *Transitions to Capitalism in Early Modern Europe.* 1997.

*Elliott, J. H. *Richelieu and Olivares.* 1984. A comparative study of the two statesmen who dominated Europe in the 1620s and 1630s; also analyzes the changing nature of political authority.

*Hale, J. R. *War and Society in Renaissance Europe, 1450–1620.* 1985. A vivid account of what it meant to be a soldier.

Kishlansky, Mark A. *A Monarchy Transformed: Britain, 1603–1714.* 1997.

MacCaffrey, Wallace. *Elizabeth I.* 1994.

*Mattingly, Garrett. *The Armada.* 1959. This beautifully written book, which was a best seller when it first appeared, is a gripping account of a major international crisis.

Moote, A. Lloyd. *The Revolt of the Judges: The Parlement of Paris and the Fronde, 1643–1652.* 1971. The most detailed account of the causes of the Fronde and its failures.

Parker, Geoffrey. *The Army of Flanders and the Spanish Road, 1567–1659: The Logistics of Spanish Victory and Defeat in the Low Countries' Wars.* 2004.

———. *The Dutch Revolt.* 1977. This brief book gives a good introduction to the revolt of the Netherlands and the nature of Dutch society in the seventeenth century.

———. *The Thirty Years' War.* 1984. The most up-to-date history of the war.

Parker, Geoffrey, and Lesley M. Smith (eds.). *The General Crisis of the Seventeenth Century.* 1997.

Pierson, Peter. *Philip II of Spain.* 1975. A clear and lively biography of the dominant figure of the second half of the sixteenth century.

*Rabb, Theodore K. *The Struggle for Stability in Early Modern Europe.* 1975. An assessment of the "crisis" interpretation, including extensive bibliographic references.

Rogers, Clifford, J. *The Military Revolution Debate: Readings on the Military Transformation of Early Modern Europe.* 1995.

*Available in paperback.

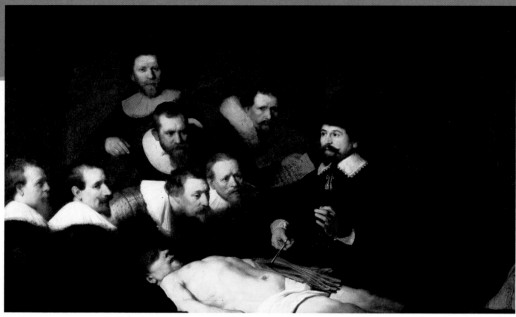

Rembrandt van Rijn
THE ANATOMY LESSON OF DR. NICOLAAS TULP, 1632
Among the many representations of the public anatomy lessons so popular in seventeenth-century Holland, the most famous is one of Rembrandt's greatest paintings, *The Anatomy Lesson of Dr. Nicolaas Tulp.* Here art reflects the new fascination with science.
Mauritshuis, The Hague

Chapter Sixteen

Culture and Society in the Age of the Scientific Revolution

Scientific Advance from Copernicus to Newton • The Effects of the Discoveries • The Arts and Literature • Social Patterns and Popular Culture

Of all the many changes of the sixteenth and seventeenth centuries, none had a more far-reaching impact than the scientific revolution. By creating a new way of understanding how nature worked—and by solving long-standing problems in physics, astronomy, and anatomy—the theorists and experimenters of this period gave Europeans a new sense of confidence and certainty. They also began to set their civilization apart from those of the rest of the world, where the outlook of the scientist did not take hold for centuries. Although the revolution began with disturbing questions, but few clear answers, about the physical world, it ended by offering a promise of knowledge and truth that was eagerly embraced by a society racked by decades of religious and political turmoil and uncertainty. Indeed, it is remarkable how closely intellectual and cultural patterns paralleled the progression from struggle and doubt to stable resolution that marked the political developments of these years. In the mid-seventeenth century, just as Europe's states were able to create more settled conditions following a major crisis, so in the realms of philosophy and the study of nature a long period of searching, anxiety, and dispute was resolved by scientists whose discoveries and self-assurance helped restore a sense of order in intellectual life. And in literature, the arts, and social relations, a time of insecurity and doubt also gave way to an atmosphere of confidence and calm.

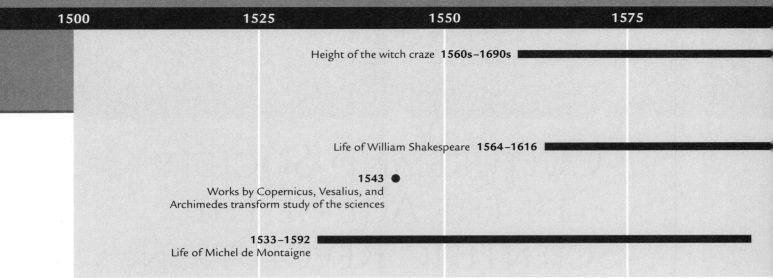

Height of the witch craze **1560s–1690s**

Life of William Shakespeare **1564–1616**

1543 ●
Works by Copernicus, Vesalius, and
Archimedes transform study of the sciences

1533–1592
Life of Michel de Montaigne

SCIENTIFIC ADVANCE FROM COPERNICUS TO NEWTON

Fundamental to the transformation of Europe in the seventeenth century were advances in the knowledge of how nature worked. At first the new discoveries added to the uncertainties of the age, but eventually the scientists were seen as models of orderly thought, who had at last solved ancient problems in convincing fashion.

Origins of the Scientific Revolution

The Importance of Antiquity   Until the sixteenth century, the study of nature in Europe was inspired by the ancient Greeks. Their work shaped subsequent research in three main fields: Aristotle in physics, Ptolemy in astronomy, and Galen in medicine. The most dramatic advances during the **scientific revolution** came in these fields, to some extent because it was becoming evident that the ancient theories could not account for new observations without highly complicated adjustments. For instance, Ptolemy's picture of the heavens, in which all motion was circular around a central earth, did not readily explain the peculiar motion that observers noticed in some planets, which at times seemed to be moving backward. Similarly, dissections often showed Galen's anatomical theories to be wrong.

Despite these problems, scientists (who in the sixteenth and seventeenth centuries were still known as "natural philosophers," or seekers of wisdom about nature) preferred making adjustments rather than beginning anew. And it is unlikely they would have abandoned their cherished theories if it had not been for other influences at work in this period. One such stimulus to rethinking was the Humanists' rediscovery of a number of previously unknown ancient scientists, who had not always agreed with the theories of Aristotle or Ptolemy. A particularly important rediscovery was the work of Archimedes, whose writings on dynamics helped inspire new ideas in physics.

The Influence of "Magical" Beliefs   Another influence was a growing interest in what we now dismiss as "magic," but which at the time was regarded as a serious intellectual enterprise. There were various avenues of magical inquiry, many of which had been pursued in other civilizations, as well as Europe, for centuries. Alchemy was the belief that matter could be understood and transformed by mixing substances and using secret formulas. A famous sixteenth-century alchemist, Paracelsus, suggested that metals as well as plants might have medicinal properties, and he helped demonstrate that mercury (if carefully used) could cure syphilis. Another favorite study was astrology, which claimed that natural phenomena could be predicted if planetary movements were properly interpreted.

What linked these "magical" beliefs was the conviction that the world could be understood through simple, comprehensive keys to nature. The theories of Neoplatonism—an influential school of thought during the Renaissance, based on Plato's belief that truth lay in essential but hidden "forms"—supported this conviction, as did some of the mystical ideas that attracted attention at this time. One of the latter, derived from a system of Jewish thought known as *cabala*, suggested that the universe might be built around magical arrangements of numbers. The ancient Greek mathematician Pythagoras had also suggested that numerical patterns might connect all of nature, and his ideas now gained new attention. For all its irrational elements, it

1606–1669 Life of Rembrandt van Rijn

1607 Premier of Monteverdi's opera *Orfeo*

1633 Condemnation of Galileo by the Inquisition

1637 Descartes, *Discourse on Method*

1660 Founding of the Royal Society in London

1687 Newton, *Principia*

was precisely this interest in new and simple solutions for long-standing problems that made natural philosophers capable, for the first time, of discarding the honored theories they had inherited from antiquity, trying different ones, paying greater attention to mathematics, and eventually creating an intellectual revolution.

Observations, Experiments, and Instruments Two other influences deserve mention. The first was Europe's fascination with technological invention. The architects, navigators, engineers, and weapons experts of the Renaissance were important pioneers of a new reliance on measurement and observation that affected not only how domes were built or heavy cannons were moved but also how problems in physics were addressed. A second, and related, influence was the growing interest in experiment among anatomists. In particular, the medical school at the University of Padua became famous for its dissections and direct observations of nature; many leading figures in the scientific revolution were trained there.

It was not too surprising, therefore, that during the sixteenth and seventeenth centuries important new instruments were invented, which helped make scientific discovery possible: the telescope, the vacuum pump, the thermometer, the barometer, and the microscope. These instruments encouraged the development of a scientific approach that was entirely new in the seventeenth century: It did not go back to the ancients, to the practitioners of magic, or to the engineers. This approach rested on the belief that in order to make nature reveal its secrets, it had to be made to do things it did not do normally. What this meant was that one did not simply observe phenomena that occurred normally in nature—for instance, the way a stick seems to bend when it is placed in a glass of water—but created

Pieter Brueghel the Elder
THE ALCHEMIST
This down-to-earth portrayal, typical of Brueghel's art, shows the alchemist as an undisciplined figure. He is surrounded by a chaos of instruments and half-finished experiments, and his helpers resemble witches. Like Brueghel, most people thought it unlikely that this disorganized figure would make a major contribution to the understanding of nature.
Pen and brown ink on paper, Kd Z 4399. Kupferstichkabinett, Staatliche Museen zu Berlin, Germany. Bildarchiv Preussischer Kulturbesitz/Art Resource, NY

461

conditions that were not normal. With the telescope, one saw secrets hidden to the naked eye; with the vacuum pump, one could understand the properties of air.

The Breakthroughs

Vesalius The earliest scientific advances came in anatomy and astronomy, and by coincidence they were announced in two books published in 1543, which was also the year when the earliest printed edition of Archimedes appeared. The first book, *The Structure of the Human Body* by Andreas Vesalius (1514–1564), a member of the Padua faculty, pointed out errors in the work of Galen, the chief authority in medical practice for over a thousand years. Using dissections, Vesalius produced anatomical descriptions that opened a new era of careful observation and experimentation in studies of the body.

Copernicus The second book, *On the Revolutions of the Heavenly Spheres* by Nicolaus Copernicus (1473–1543), a Polish cleric who had studied at Padua, had far greater consequences. A first-rate mathematician, Copernicus believed that the calculations of planetary movements under Ptolemy's system had grown too complex. In Ptolemaic astronomy, the planets and the sun, attached to transparent, crystalline spheres, revolved around the earth. All motion was circular, and irregularities were accounted for by **epicycles**—movement around small revolving spheres that were attached to the larger spheres. Influenced by Neoplatonic ideas, Copernicus believed that a simpler picture would reflect more accurately the true structure of the universe. In sound Neoplatonic fashion, he argued that the sun, as the most splendid of celestial bodies, ought rightfully to be at the center of an orderly and harmonious universe. The earth, no longer immobile, would thus circle the sun.

Copernicus' system was, in fact, scarcely simpler than Ptolemy's—the spheres and epicycles were just as complex—and he had no way of demonstrating the superiority of his theory. But he was such a fine mathematician that his successors found his calculations of planetary motions indispensable. His ideas thus became part of intellectual discussion, drawn on when Pope Gregory XIII decided to reform the calendar in 1582. The Julian calendar, in use since Roman times, counted century years as leap years, thus adding extra days that caused Easter—whose date is determined by the position of the sun—to drift farther and farther away from its normal occurrence in late March. The reform produced the Gregorian calendar, which we still use. Ten days were simply dropped: October 5, 1582, became October 15; and since then only one out of every four century years has been counted as a leap year (1900 had no February 29, but 2000 did). The need

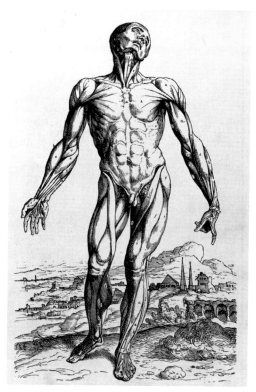

Titian (attrib.)
Engraving Illustrating The Structure of the Human Body by Andreas Vesalius, 1543
Almost as remarkable as the findings themselves were these illustrations of the results of Vesalius' dissections. Traditionally, professors of anatomy read from textbooks to their students while lowly barber-surgeons cut up a cadaver and displayed the parts being discussed. Vesalius did his dissections himself and thus could observe directly such structures as the musculature. Here his illustrator displays the muscles on a gesturing figure and places it in a stretch of countryside near Padua, where Vesalius taught.

for calendar reform had been one of the motives for Copernicus' studies, which thus proved useful even though his theories remained controversial.

Theories in Conflict For more than half a century, the effect of *Revolutions* was growing uncertainty, as the scholarly community argued over the validity of the new ideas. The leading astronomer of the period, the Dane Tycho Brahe (1546–1601), produced the most remarkable observations of the heavens before the invention of the telescope by plotting the paths of the moon and planets every night for decades. But the only theory he could come up with was an uneasy compromise between the Ptolemaic and Copernican systems. There was similar indecision among anatomists, who admired Vesalius but were not ready to discard Galen.

Kepler and Galileo Address the Uncertainties

As late as 1600, it seemed that scientists were creating more problems than solutions. But then two brilliant discoverers—the German Johannes Kepler (1571–1630) and Galileo Galilei, an Italian professor of mathematics—made major advances on the work of Copernicus and helped resolve the uncertainties in the field of astronomy.

Kepler and the Laws of Planetary Motion   Like Copernicus, Kepler believed that only the language of mathematics could describe the movements of the heavens. He was a famous astrologer and an advocate of magical theories, but he was also convinced that Copernicus was right. He threw himself into the task of confirming the sun-centered (heliocentric) theory, and by studying Brahe's observations, he discovered three laws of planetary motion (published in 1609 and 1619) that opened a new era in astronomy. Kepler was able to prove that the orbits of the planets are ellipses and that there is a regularity, based on their distance from the sun, which determines the movements of all planets. So revolutionary were these laws that few astronomers accepted them until Isaac Newton used them fifty years later as the basis for a new system of the heavens.

Galileo and a New Physics   A contemporary of Kepler's, the Italian Galileo Galilei (1564–1642), made further advances when he became the first to perceive the connection between planetary motion and motion on earth. His studies revealed the importance to astronomy not only of observation and mathematics but also of physics. Moreover, Galileo's self-consciousness about technique, argument, and evidence marks him as one of the first investigators of nature to approach his work in essentially the same way as a modern scientist.

The study of motion inspired Galileo's most fundamental scientific contributions. When he began his investigations, the Aristotelian view that a body is naturally at rest and needs to be pushed constantly to keep moving dominated the study of dynamics. Galileo broke with this tradition, developing instead a new type of physical explanation that was perfected by Isaac Newton half a century later. Much of Galileo's work was based on observation. From watching how workers at the Arsenal in Venice used pulleys and other devices to lift huge weights, he gained insights into physics; adapting a Dutch lens maker's invention, he built a primitive telescope that was essential to his studies of the heavens; and his seemingly mundane experiments, such as swinging a pendulum or rolling balls down inclined planes, were crucial means of testing his theo-

CHRONOLOGY
The Scientific Revolution

1543	Publication of Copernicus' *On the Revolutions of the Heavenly Spheres.*
	Publication of Vesalius' *The Structure of the Human Body.*
	First printing of the work of Archimedes.
1582	Pope Gregory XIII reforms the calendar.
1609	Publication of Kepler's first two laws of planetary motion.
1610	Publication of Galileo's *Starry Messenger.*
1619	Publication of Kepler's third law of planetary motion.
1627	Publication of Bacon's *New Atlantis.*
1628	Publication of Harvey's *On the Motion of the Heart.*
1632	Publication of Galileo's *Dialogue on the Two Great World Systems.*
1633	Condemnation of Galileo by the Inquisition.
1637	Publication of Descartes' *Discourse on Method.*
1639	Pascal's theorem concerning conic sections.
1660	Founding of the Royal Society of London for Improving Natural Knowledge.
1666	Founding of the French Royal Academy of Sciences.
1687	Publication of Newton's *Mathematical Principles of Natural Philosophy.*

ries. Indeed, it was by moving from observations to abstraction that Galileo arrived at the first wholly new way of understanding motion since Aristotle: the principle of inertia.

This breakthrough could not have been made by observation alone, for the discovery of inertia depended on mathematical abstraction, the ability to imagine a situation that cannot be created experimentally: the motion of a perfectly smooth ball across a perfectly smooth plane, free of any outside forces, such as friction. Galileo's conclusion was that "any velocity once imparted to a moving body will be rigidly maintained as long as external causes of acceleration and retardation are removed. . . . If the velocity is uniform, it will not be diminished or slackened, much less destroyed." This insight overturned the Aristotelian view. Galileo had demonstrated that only mathematical language could describe the underlying principles of nature.

A New Astronomy   Galileo's most celebrated work was in astronomy. He first became famous in 1610, when he published his discoveries, made with the telescope, that Jupiter has satellites and the moon has mountains. Both these revelations were further blows to traditional beliefs, which held that the earth is changing and imperfect while the heavens are immutable and unblemished. Now, however, it seemed that other planets had satellites, just like the earth, and that these satellites might have the same rough surface as the earth. This was startling enough, but Galileo also argued that the principles of terrestrial physics could be used to explain phenomena in the heavens. He calculated the height of the mountains on the moon by using the geometric techniques of surveyors, and he described the moon's secondary light—seen while it is a crescent—as a reflection of sunlight from the earth. Galileo was treating his own planet simply as one part of a uniform universe. Every physical law, he was saying, is equally applicable on earth and in the heavens, including the laws of motion. As early as 1597 Galileo had admitted that some of his discoveries in physics could be explained only if the earth were moving, and during the next thirty years he became the most famous advocate of Copernicanism in Europe (see "Galileo and Kepler on Copernicus," p. 465).

Galileo Galilei
The Moon, 1610
This sketch of the moon's surface appeared in Galileo's *Starry Messenger* (1610). It shows what he had observed through the telescope and had interpreted as proof that the moon had a rugged surface because the lighted area within the dark section had to be mountains. These caught the light of the setting sun longer than surrounding lower terrain and revealed, for example, a large cavity in the lower center of the sketch.
New York Public Library

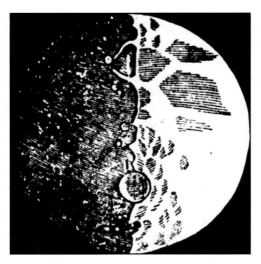

Galileo made a powerful case. Why, he asked, was it necessary to say that the entire universe revolved around the earth when all celestial motions could be explained by the rotation of a single planet, the earth? When academic and religious critics argued that we would feel the earth moving or pointed out that the Bible said Joshua made the sun stand still, he reacted with scorn. In response to religious objections, he asserted that "in discussions of physical problems we ought to begin not from the authority of scriptural passages, but from sense experience and necessary demonstrations."

Conflict with the Church   For all the brilliance of his arguments, Galileo was now on dangerous ground. Although traditionally the Catholic Church had not concerned itself with investigations of nature, in the early seventeenth century the situation was changing. The Church was deep in the struggle with Protestantism, and it responded to the challenge to its authority by trying to control potentially questionable views. And Galileo's biting sarcasm toward other scientists antagonized Jesuit and Dominican astronomers. These two orders were the chief upholders of orthodoxy in the Church. They referred Galileo's views to the Inquisition and then guided the attack on Copernicanism by seeking to condemn the brilliant advocate who had made the theory famous throughout Europe.

The Book and the Trial   In 1616 the Inquisition forbade Galileo, within certain limits, to teach the heretical doctrine that the earth moves. When one of his friends was elected pope in 1623, however, Galileo thought he would be safe in writing a major work on astronomy. The result was his *Dialogue on the Two Great World Systems*, published in 1632 (with the approval, probably accidental, of the Church). A marvelously witty, elegant book, the *Dialogue* is one of the few monuments in the history of science that the layperson can read with pleasure. And so it was intended. Galileo wrote it in Italian, not the Latin that had always been used for scholarly works, because he wanted to reach the widest possible audience.

In April 1633 he was brought before the Inquisition for having defied the order not to teach Copernicanism. In a trial that has caused controversy ever since, the aged astronomer, fearing excommunication, abjured the "errors and heresies" of believing that the earth moved. But he did not remain docile for the remainder of his life, though he was kept under house arrest and progressively lost his eyesight. Many of his letters ridiculed his opponents, and in 1638 he published (in tolerant Holland) his principal work on physics, the *Two New Sciences.*

GALILEO AND KEPLER ON COPERNICUS

In 1597 Kepler sent Galileo a copy of his New Astronomy, *which argued for the Copernican theory of the heavens, and asked the Italian for his opinion. The exchange of letters that followed, with Galileo cautious and Kepler urging him on, reflects an age when the new ideas were not yet proved and also gives a hint, in Kepler's last comments, of the troubles that lay ahead.*

Galileo to Kepler: "Like you, I accepted the Copernican position several years ago. I have written up many reasons on the subject, but have not dared until now to bring them into the open. I would dare publish my thoughts if there were many like you; but, since there are not, I shall forbear."

Kepler's Reply: "I could only have wished that you, who have so profound an insight, would choose another way. You advise us to retreat before the general ignorance and not to expose ourselves to the violent attacks of the mob of scholars. But after a tremendous task has been begun in our time, first by Copernicus and then by many very learned mathematicians, and when the assertion that the Earth moves can no longer be considered something new, would it not be much better to pull the wagon to its goal by our joint efforts, now that we have got it under way, and gradually, with powerful voices, to shout down the common herd? Be of good cheer, Galileo, and come out publicly! If I judge correctly, there are only a few of the distinguished mathematicians of Europe who would part company with us, so great is the power of truth. If Italy seems a less favorable place for your publication, perhaps Germany will allow us this freedom."

From Giorgio de Santillana, *The Crime of Galileo,* Chicago: University of Chicago Press, 1955, pp. 11, 14–15.

Galileo's Legacy   The condemnation of Galileo discouraged further scientific activity by his compatriots. Italy had been a leader of the new investigations, but now major further advances were made by the English, Dutch, and French. Yet this shift showed merely that the rise of science, once begun, could not be halted for long. By the late 1630s, no self-respecting astronomer could deny the correctness of the Copernican theory.

Assurance Spreads   The new studies of nature may have caused tremendous bewilderment at first, as scientists struggled with the ideas of pioneers like Copernicus and Vesalius. But in the end these investigations created a renewed sense of certainty about the physical world, which was to have a far-reaching influence. This was true not only in physics and astronomy but also in anatomy, where, in 1628, another genius of the scientific revolution, the English doctor William Harvey, revolutionized the understanding of the human body when he identified the function of the heart and proved that the blood circulates.

The Climax of the Scientific Revolution: Isaac Newton

The culmination of the scientific revolution was the work of Isaac Newton (1642–1727), who made decisive contributions to mathematics, physics, astronomy, and optics and brought to a climax the changes that had begun with Copernicus. He united physics and astronomy into a single system to explain all motion, he helped transform mathematics by developing the calculus, and he established some of the basic laws of modern physics.

Part of the explanation of his versatility lies in the workings of the scientific community at the time. Newton was a retiring man who nevertheless got into fierce arguments with prominent contemporaries, such as the learned German scholar and scientist Wilhelm von Leibniz, who was working on the calculus. If not for his active participation in meetings of scientists at the recently founded Royal Society of London (see p. 468), Newton might never have pursued his researches to their conclusion. He disliked the give-and-take of these discussions, but he felt forced, in order to prove that he had solved various problems, to prepare some of his most important papers for the Royal Society. Such institutions were now being established throughout Europe to promote the advance of science, and their creation indicates how far the scientific community had come since the days of Copernicus, who had worked largely in isolation.

The Principia   Newton's masterpiece, *The Mathematical Principles of Natural Philosophy* (1687)— usually referred to by the first word of its Latin title, the *Principia*—was the last widely influential book to be written in Latin, the traditional language of scholarship. Latin was still useful to Newton, who wanted as many experts as possible to read the book, which claimed that everything he said was proved by experiment or by mathematics.

The most dramatic of Newton's findings was the solution to the ancient problem of motion. Building on Galileo's advances and overturning Aristotle's theories once and for all, Newton defined his system in three laws: first, in the absence of force, motion continues in a straight line; second, the rate of change of the motion is determined by the forces acting on it (such as friction); and third, action and reaction between two bodies are equal and opposite. To arrive at these laws, he defined the concepts of mass, inertia, and force in relation to velocity and acceleration as we know them today.

Newton extended these principles to the entire universe by demonstrating that his laws govern the motions of the moon and planets too. Using the concept of gravity, he provided the explanation of the movement of objects in space that is the foundation for current space travel. There is a balance, he said, between the earth's pull on the moon and the forward motion of the satellite, which would continue in a straight line were it not for the earth's gravity. Consequently, the moon moves in an elliptical orbit in which neither gravity nor inertia gains control. The same pattern is followed by the planets around the sun (as Kepler had shown).

The Influence of Newton   The general philosophical implication of the uniformity that Newton described—that the world was stable and orderly—was as important as his specific discoveries in making him one of the idols of his own and the next centuries. The educated applauded Newton's achievements, and he was the first scientist to receive a knighthood in England. Only a few decades after the appearance of the *Principia*, the poet Alexander Pope summed up the public feeling:

> Nature and nature's law lay hid in night;
> God said, "Let Newton be!" and all was light.

So overpowering was Newton's stature that in physics and astronomy the remarkable advances of 150 years slowed down for more than half a century after the publication of the *Principia*. There was a general impression that somehow Newton had done it all, that no important problems remained. There were other reasons for the slowdown—changing patterns in education, an inevitable lessening of momentum—but none was so powerful as the reverence for Newton, who became the intellectual symbol of his own and succeeding ages.

THE EFFECTS OF THE DISCOVERIES

The scientists' discoveries about the physical universe made them famous. But it was the *way* they proved their case that made them so influential. The success of their reasoning encouraged a new level of confidence in human powers that helped end the doubts and uncertainties of the previous age.

A New Epistemology

Galileo had stressed that his discoveries rested on a way of thinking that had an independent value, and he refused to allow traditional considerations, such as common sense or theological teachings, to interfere with his conclusions. Scientists were now moving toward a new **epistemology,** a new theory of how to obtain and verify knowledge. They stressed experience, reason, and doubt; they rejected all unsubstantiated authority; and they developed a revolutionary way of determining what was a true description of physical reality.

Scientific Method   The process the scientists said they followed, after they had formulated a hypothesis, consisted of three parts: first, observations; second, a generalization induced from the observations; and third, tests of the generalization by experiments whose outcome could be predicted by the generalization. A generalization remained valid only as long as it was not contradicted by experiments specifically designed to test it. The scientist used no data except the results of strict observation—such as the time it took balls to roll down Galileo's inclined planes—and scientific reasoning uncovered the laws, principles, or patterns that emerged from the observations. Since measurement was the key to the data, the observations had a numerical, not a subjective, value. Thus, the language of science came to be mathematics.

In fact, scientists rarely reach conclusions in the exact way this idealized scheme suggests. Galileo's perfectly smooth balls and planes, for instance, did not exist, but Galileo understood the relevant physical theory so well that he knew what would happen if one rolled across the other, and he used this "experiment" to demonstrate the principle of inertia. In other words, experiments as well as hypotheses can occur in the mind; the essence of scientific method is a special way of looking at and understanding nature.

The Wider Influence of Scientific Thought

The principles of scientific inquiry received attention throughout the intellectual community only gradually; it took time for the power of the scientists' method to be recognized. If the new methods were to be accepted, their effectiveness would have to be demonstrated to more than a few specialists. This wider understanding was eventually achieved by midcentury, as much through the efforts of ardent propagandizers as through the writings of the great innovators themselves. Gradually, they convinced a broad, educated public that science, after first causing doubts by challenging ancient truths, now offered a promise of certainty that was not to be found anywhere else in an age of general crisis.

Bacon and Descartes

Bacon's Vision of Science   Although he was not an important scientist himself, Francis Bacon was the greatest of science's propagandists, and he inspired a whole generation with his vision of what it could accomplish for humanity. His description of an ideal society in the *New Atlantis*—published in 1627, the year after his death—is a vision of science as the savior of the human race. It predicts a time when those doing research at the highest levels will be regarded as the most important people in the state and will work on vast government-supported projects to gather all known facts about the physical universe. By a process of gradual **induction**, this information will lead to universal laws that, in turn, will enable people to improve their lot on earth. Bacon's view of research as a collective enterprise inspired a number of later scientists, and by the mid-seventeenth century, his ideas had entered the mainstream of European thought.

Descartes and the Principle of Doubt   The Frenchman René Descartes (1596–1650) made the first concentrated attempt to apply the new methods of science to theories of knowledge, and, in so doing, he laid the foundations for modern philosophy. The impulse behind his work was his realization that, for all the importance of observation and experiment, people can be deceived by their senses. In order to find some solid truth, therefore, he decided to apply to all knowledge the principle of doubt—the refusal to accept any authority without strict verification. He began with the assumption that he could know unquestionably only one thing: that he was doubting. This assumption allowed him to proceed to the observation "I think, therefore I am," because the act of doubting proved he was thinking, and thinking, in turn, demonstrated his existence.

From the proof of his own existence he derived a crucial statement: That whatever is clearly and distinctly thought must be true. This assertion in turn enabled him to construct a proof of God's existence. We cannot fail to realize that we are imperfect, he argued, and we must therefore have an idea of perfection

Frans Hals
***PORTRAIT OF DESCARTES*, 1649**
The increasingly common portraits of scientists in the seventeenth century testify to their growing fame. In this case, Descartes sat for one of the Netherlands' most renowned artists, and because the painting was copied in a number of engravings, his face became as well known as that of many kings and princes.
Erich Lessing/Art Resource, NY

against which we may be measured. If we have a clear idea of what perfection is, then it must exist; hence, there must be a God.

The Discourse on Method   Descartes' proof may have served primarily to show that the principle of doubt did not contradict religious belief, but it also reflected the emphasis on the power of the mind in his major work, *Discourse on the Method of Rightly Conducting the Reason and Seeking Truth in the Sciences* (1637). Thought is a pure and unmistakable guide, he said, and only by relying on its operations can people hope to advance their understanding of the world. Descartes developed this view into a fundamental proposition about the nature of the world—a proposition that philosophers have been wrestling with ever since. He stated that there is an essential divide between thought and extension (tangible objects) or, put another way, between spirit and matter. Bacon and Galileo had insisted that science, the study of nature, is separate from and unaffected by faith. But Descartes turned this distinction into a far-reaching principle, dividing not only science from faith but even the reality of the world from our perception of that reality. There is a difference, in other words, between a chair and how we think of it as a chair.

The Influence of Descartes   Descartes' emphasis on the operations of the mind gave a new direction to epistemological discussions. A hypothesis gained credibility not so much from external proofs as from the logical tightness of the arguments used to support it. Descartes thus applied what he considered the methods of science to all of knowledge. Not only the phenomena of nature but all truth had to be investigated according to the methods of the scientist.

Descartes' contributions to scientific research were theoretical rather than experimental. In physics, he was the first to perceive the distinction between mass and weight; and in mathematics, he was the first to apply algebraic notations and methods to geometry, thus founding analytic geometry. Above all, his emphasis on the principle of doubt undermined forever traditional assumptions such as the belief in the hierarchical organization of the universe.

Pascal's Protest Against the New Science

At midcentury only one important voice still protested against the new science and, in particular, against the philosophy of Descartes. It belonged to a Frenchman, Blaise Pascal, a brilliant mathematician and experimenter. Pascal's investigations of probability in games of chance produced the theorem that still bears his name, and his research in conic sections helped lay the foundations for integral calculus. He also helped discover barometric pressure and invented a calculating machine. In his late twenties, however, Pascal became increasingly dissatisfied with scientific research, and he began to wonder whether his life was being properly spent. Moved by a growing concern with faith, Pascal had a mystical experience in November 1654 that made him resolve to devote his life to the salvation of his soul.

The Pensées   During the few remaining years of his life, Pascal wrote a collection of reflections—some only a few words long, some many pages—that were gathered together after his death and published as the *Pensées* (or "Reflections"). These writings revealed not only the beliefs of a deeply religious man but also the anxieties of a scientist who feared the growing influ-

ence of science. He did not wish to put an end to research; he merely wanted people to realize that the truths uncovered by science were limited and not as important as the truths perceived by faith. As he put it in one of his more memorable *pensées*, "The heart has its reasons that reason cannot know."

Pascal's protest was unique, but the fact that it was put forward at all indicates how high the status of the scientist and his methods had risen by the 1650s. Just a quarter-century earlier, such a dramatic change in fortune would have been hard to predict. But now the new epistemology, after its initial disturbing assault on ancient views, was offering one of the few promises of certainty in an age of upheaval and general crisis. In intellectual matters as in politics, turmoil was gradually giving way to assurance.

Science Institutionalized

Many besides Bacon realized that scientific work should be a cooperative endeavor and that information should be exchanged among all its practitioners. A scientific society founded in Rome in 1603 made the first major effort to apply this view, and it was soon followed up in France, where in the early seventeenth century a friar named Marin Mersenne became the center of an international network of correspondents interested in scientific work. He also spread news by bringing scientists together for discussions and experiments. Contacts that were developed at these meetings led eventually to a more permanent and systematic organization of scientific activity.

The Royal Society   In England, the first steps toward such organization were taken at Oxford during the Civil War in the 1640s, when the revolutionaries captured the city and replaced those at the university who taught traditional natural philosophy. A few of the newcomers formed what they called the Invisible College, a group that met to exchange information and discuss each other's work. The group included only one first-class scientist, the chemist Robert Boyle; but in 1660 he and eleven others formed an official organization, the Royal Society of London for Improving Natural Knowledge, with headquarters in the capital. In 1662 it was granted a charter by Charles II—the first sign of a link with political authority that not only boosted science but also indicated the growing presence of central governments in all areas of society.

The Royal Society's purposes were openly Baconian. Its aim for a few years—until everyone realized it was impossible—was to gather all knowledge about nature, particularly if it had practical uses. For a long time the members offered their services for the public good, helping in one instance to develop for the government

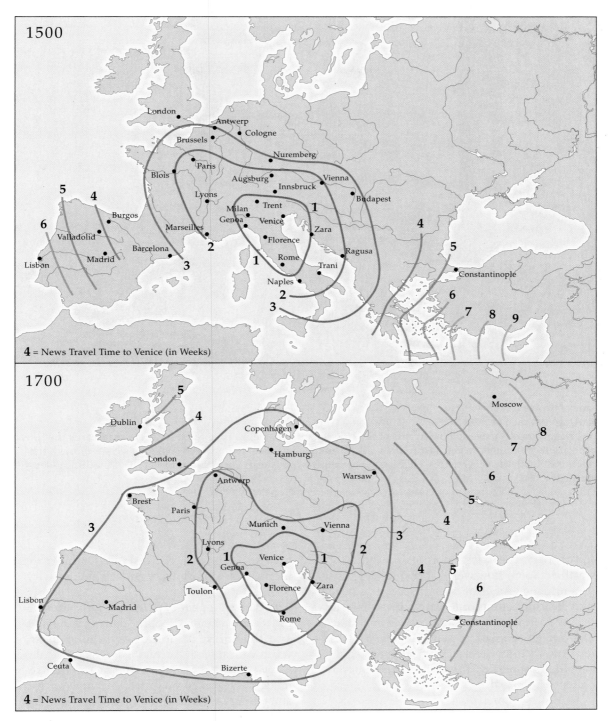

MAP 16.1 SPEED OF NEWS TRAVELING TO VENICE IN 1500 AND 1700
Although the dramatic advances in communications lay in the future, by 1700 improved roads and canals and more efficient shipping did bring about significant advances in the distance news could travel in two or three weeks. How much faster could news get from Madrid to Venice in 1700 than in 1500? What about from Constantinople to Venice? Why might communication across Western Europe have speeded up more than across Eastern Europe?

◆ For an online version, go to www.mhhe.com/chambers9 > chapter 16 > book maps

Charles-Nicolas Cochin
The Académie Royale des Sciences, Paris, Engraving, **1698**
This celebration of the work done by one of the first scientific societies suggests the variety of research that these organizations promoted. In contrast to the students of theology, who merely read books (as we see through the arch on the right), the geographers, engineers, astronomers, physicists, and anatomists of the scientific academy examine the real world.
© British Museum, Department of Prints and Drawings ([C292] Neg # N/N R8-85)

the science of social statistics ("political arithmetic," as it was called). Soon, however, it became clear that the society's principal function was to serve as a headquarters and clearing center for research. Its secretaries maintained an enormous correspondence to encourage English and foreign scholars to send in news of their discoveries. And in 1665 the society began the regular publication of *Philosophical Transactions,* the first professional scientific journal.

Other Scientific Societies Imitators soon followed. In 1666 Louis XIV gave his blessing to the founding of a French Royal Academy of Sciences, and similar organizations were established in Naples and Berlin by 1700. Membership in these societies was limited and highly prized, a sign of the glamour that was beginning to attach itself to the new studies. By the 1660s there could be no doubt that science, secure in royal patronage, had become a model for all thought. Its practitioners were extravagantly admired, and throughout intellectual and

high social circles, there was a scramble to apply its methods to almost every conceivable activity.

The Wider Appeal of Science Descartes had applied the ideas of science to philosophy in general; Bacon had said they must be useful. And the applications soon were widespread. Formal gardens were designed to show the order, harmony, and reason that science had made such prized qualities. Methods of fortification and warfare were affected by the new emphasis on accurate measurement. As the scientists' activities became more popular and fashionable, even aristocrats began to spend time playing at science. Herbariums and small observatories were added to country estates, and parties featured an evening of star gazing. Science also fascinated the general populace. Among the most eagerly anticipated occasions in seventeenth-century Holland was the public anatomy lesson. The body of a criminal would be brought to an enormous hall that was packed with students and a fascinated public. A famous surgeon would dissect the cadaver, announcing and displaying each organ as he removed it.

On the whole, the reverence for science and its methods did not develop from an understanding of its actual accomplishments or its potential consequences. Rather, it was caused by the fame of the spectacular discoveries that had offered new and convincing solutions to centuries-old problems in astronomy, physics, and anatomy. Here was a promise of certainty and order in a world that otherwise was bedeviled by conflict and doubt. As a result, the protests of Pascal could be ignored, and the new discipline could be given unblemished admiration. The entire world was coming to be viewed through the scientist's eyes—a striking achievement for a recently minor member of the intellectual community—and the qualities of regularity and harmony associated with science began to appear in the work of artists and writers.

THE ARTS AND LITERATURE

We have seen that in the mid-seventeenth century a more settled Europe emerged from the political turbulence and crisis of the late 1500s and early 1600s. And we have seen that the development of science followed a similar pattern—with decades of uncertainty as old truths were challenged, and then a new sense of assurance in the mid-seventeenth century. Not surprisingly, so too did the concerns of the arts and literature.

Unsettling Art

Mannerism   One response that was provoked by the upheavals of the sixteenth century was the attempt to escape reality, an effort that was echoed by some of the painters of the age, known as *Mannerists*. The Mannerists and their patrons reacted against the serenity and idealization of the High Renaissance by cultivating artificial and esoteric images of the world; they undermined perspective, distorted human figures, and devised unnatural colors and lighting to create startling effects.

El Greco   Mannerism was embodied in El Greco (1541–1614), a Greek who was trained in Italy and settled in Spain. His compelling and almost mystic canvases created an otherworldly alternative to the troubles of his time. El Greco's cool colors, eerie lighting, and elongated and often agonized human beings make him one of the most distinctive painters in the history of art (see p. 432). After 1600, though, painters increasingly rejected the Mannerists' flight from reality; eventually the arts, too, reflected the sense of settlement that descended over European civilization in the mid-seventeenth century.

Unsettling Writers

Michel de Montaigne   In the world of literature, the concerns of the age were most vividly expressed by the Frenchman Michel de Montaigne (1533–1592). Obsessed by the death he saw all around him and determined to overcome his fears, he retired in 1570 to his country home in order to "essay," or test, his innermost feelings by writing short pieces of prose even about subjects he did not fully comprehend. In the process he created a new literary form, the essay, that also helped shape the modern French language. But his chief influence was philosophical: He has inspired the search for self-knowledge ever since.

At first Montaigne's anxieties led him to radical doubt about the possibility of finding truth; known as **skepticism**, this preoccupation inspired the total uncertainty of his motto, "Que sais-je?" ("What do I know?"). Eventually, however, Montaigne struggled toward a more confident view, taking as his model the ancient saying "Know thyself." By looking into one's own person, one can find values that hold true at least for oneself, and these will reflect the values of all humanity. Montaigne came close to a morality without theology, because good and self-determination were more important to him than doctrine, and he saw everywhere religious people committing inhuman acts. Trying to be an angel is wrong, he said; being good is enough.

Montaigne was also one of the first writers to use non-Western models to criticize Europeans. He met a cannibal who had been brought to France, and he suggested that those who kill for food were more moral than those who kill for other purposes, such as religious beliefs.

Neostoicism   A more general approach to morality was a theory known as **Neostoicism**, inspired by the ancient Stoics' emphasis on self-knowledge and a calm acceptance of the world. The most influential of the Neostoics, a Dutch writer named Justus Lipsius, argued that public leaders ought to be guided by profound self-examination. Lipsius urged rulers to be restrained and self-disciplined, and he was much admired by the kings and royal ministers of the seventeenth century.

Cervantes   In Spain the disillusionment that accompanied the political and economic decline of Europe's most powerful state was perfectly captured by Miguel de Cervantes (1547–1616). Cervantes saw the wide gap between the hopes and the realities of his day—in religion, in social institutions, in human behavior—and made the dichotomy the basis of scathing social satire in his novel *Don Quixote*.

At one level, Cervantes was ridiculing the excessive chivalry of the Spanish nobility in his portrayal of a knight who was ready to tilt at windmills, though he obviously admired the sincerity of his well-meaning hero and sympathized with him as a perennial loser. On another level, the author brought to life the Europe of the time—the ordinary people and their hypocrisies and intolerances—with a liveliness rarely matched in literature. Cervantes avoided politics, but he was clearly directing many of his sharpest barbs at the brutality and disregard for human values that were characteristic of his fanatical times. And in England another towering figure was grappling with similar problems.

Shakespeare For the English-speaking world, the most brilliant writer of this and all other periods was William Shakespeare (1564–1616), whose characters bring to life almost every conceivable mood: searing grief, airy romance, rousing nationalism, uproarious humor. Despite his modest education, his imagery shows a familiarity with subjects ranging from astronomy to seamanship, from alchemy to warfare. It is not surprising, therefore, that some have doubted that one man could have produced this amazing body of work. During most of his writing career, Shakespeare was involved with a theatrical company, where he often had to produce plays on short notice. He thus had the best of all possible tests—audience reactions—as he gained mastery of theatrical techniques.

Shakespeare's plays made timeless statements about human behavior: love, hatred, violence, sin. Of particular interest to the historian, however, is what he tells us about attitudes that belong especially to his own era. Again and again, legality and stability are shown as fundamental virtues amidst turbulent times. Shakespeare's expressions of patriotism are particularly intense; when in *Richard II* the king's uncle, John of Gaunt, lies dying, he pours out his love for his country in words that have moved the English ever since:

> This royal throne of kings, this scepter'd isle,
> This earth of majesty, this seat of Mars,
> This other Eden, demi-paradise, . . .
> This happy breed of men, this little world,
> This precious stone set in the silver sea, . . .
> This blessed plot, this earth,
> This realm, this England.
>
> *Richard II*, act 2, scene 1

As in so much of the art and writing of the time, instability is a central concern of Shakespeare's plays. His four most famous tragedies—*Hamlet, King Lear, Macbeth,* and *Othello*—end in disillusionment: The heroes are ruined by irresoluteness, pride, ambition, and jealousy. Shakespeare was exploring a theme that had absorbed playwrights since Euripides—the fatal flaws that destroy the great—and producing dramas of revenge that were popular in his day; but the plays also

demonstrate his deep understanding of human nature. Whatever one's hopes, one cannot forget human weakness, the inevitability of decay, and the constant threat of disaster. The contrast appears with compelling clarity in a speech delivered by Hamlet:

> What a piece of work is man! How noble in reason! how infinite in faculties! in form and moving how express and admirable! in action how like an angel! in apprehension how like a god! the beauty of the world, the paragon of animals! And yet to me what is this quintessence of dust? Man delights not me.
>
> *Hamlet*, act 2, scene 2

Despite such pessimism, despite the deep sense of human inadequacy, the basic impression Shakespeare gives is of immense vigor, of a restlessness and confidence that recall the many achievements of the sixteenth century. Yet a sense of decay is never far absent. Repeatedly, people seem utterly helpless, overtaken by events they cannot control. Nothing remains constant or dependable, and everything that seems solid or reassuring, be it the love of a daughter or the crown of England, is challenged. In this atmosphere of ceaseless change, where landmarks easily disappear, Shakespeare conveys the tensions of his time.

The Return of Assurance in the Arts

The Baroque After 1600, the arts began to move toward the assurance and sense of settlement that was descending over other areas of European civilization. A new style, the **Baroque,** sought to drown the uneasiness of Mannerism in a blaze of grandeur. Passion, drama, mystery, and awe were the qualities of the Baroque: Every art form—from music to literature, from architecture to opera—had to involve, arouse, and uplift its audience.

The Baroque style was closely associated with the Counter-Reformation's emphasis on gorgeous display in Catholic ritual. The patronage of leading Church figures made Rome a magnet for the major painters of the period. Elsewhere, the Baroque flourished primarily at the leading Catholic courts of the seventeenth century, most notably the Habsburg courts in Madrid, Prague, and Brussels, and remained influential well into the eighteenth century in such Catholic areas as the Spanish Empire. Few styles have conveyed so strong a sense of grandeur, theatricality, and ornateness.

Caravaggio The artist who first shaped the new aesthetic, Caravaggio (1571–1610), lived most of his life in Rome. Although he received commissions from high Church figures and spent time in a cardinal's household, he was equally at home among the beggars and petty criminals of Rome's dark back streets. These

Caravaggio
THE SUPPER AT EMMAUS, CA. 1597
By choosing moments of high drama and using sharp contrasts of light, Caravaggio created an immediacy that came to be one of the hallmarks of Baroque painting. Here he shows the moment during the supper at Emmaus when his disciples suddenly recognized the resurrected Christ. The force of their emotions and their almost theatrical gestures convey the intensity of the moment, but many at the time objected to the craggy, tattered appearance of the disciples. These were not idealized figures, as was expected, but ordinary people at a humble table.
Reproduced by courtesy of the Trustees, © The National Gallery, London (NG172)

ordinary people served as Caravaggio's models, which shocked those who believed it inappropriate for such humble characters to represent the holy figures of biblical scenes. Yet the power of Caravaggio's paintings—their depiction of highly emotional moments, and the drama created by their sharp contrasts of light and dark—made his work much prized. He had to flee Rome after he killed someone in a brawl, but he left behind an outpouring of work that influenced an entire generation of painters.

Rubens   Among those who came to Rome to study Caravaggio's art was Peter Paul Rubens (1577–1640), the principal ornament of the brilliant Habsburg court at Brussels. His major themes typified the grandeur that came to be the hallmark of Baroque style: glorifi-

cations of great rulers and also of the ceremony and mystery of Catholicism. Rubens' secular paintings convey enormous strength; his religious works overwhelm the viewer with the majesty of the Church and excite the believer's piety by stressing the power of the faith.

Velázquez   Other artists glorified rulers through idealized portraiture. The greatest court painter of the age was Diego Velázquez (1599–1660). His portraits of members of the Spanish court depict rulers and their surroundings in the stately atmosphere appropriate to the theme. Yet occasionally Velázquez hinted at the weakness of an ineffective monarch in his rendering of the face, even though the basic purpose of his work was always to exalt royal power. And his celebration of a notable Habsburg victory, *The Surrender of Breda,*

Artemisia Gentileschi
JUDITH SLAYING HOLOFERNES, CA. **1620**
Female artists were rare in the seventeenth century because they were not allowed to become apprentices. But Artemisia (1593–1652) was the daughter of a painter who happened to be a friend of Caravaggio, and she had the opportunity to become a gifted exponent of Baroque style. Known throughout Europe for her vivid portrayals of dramatic scenes (she painted the murder of Holofernes by the biblical heroine Judith at least five times), she practiced her chosen profession with considerable success, despite the trauma of being raped at age seventeen by a friend of her father's—an act of violence that may be reflected (and avenged) in this painting.
Uffizi, Florence, Italy. Scala/Art Resource, NY

Peter Paul Rubens
DESCENT FROM THE CROSS, **1612**
This huge altarpiece was one of the first pictures Rubens painted upon returning to his native Antwerp after spending most of his twenties developing his art in Italy. The ambitious scale, the strong emotions, the vivid lighting, and the dramatic action showed the artist's commitment to the Baroque style that had recently evolved in Italy. The powerful impact of the altarpiece helped make him one of the most sought-after painters of the day.
Center panel. Scala/Art Resource, NY

Diego Velázquez
THE SURRENDER OF BREDA, 1635
The contrasting postures of victory and defeat are masterfully captured by Diego Velázquez in *The Surrender of Breda*. The Dutch soldiers droop their heads and lances, but the victorious Spaniards hardly show triumph, and the gesture of the victorious general, Ambrogio Spinola, is one of consolation and understanding.
Oroñoz

managed to suggest the sadness and emptiness as much as the glory of war.

Bernini   GianLorenzo Bernini (1598–1680) brought to sculpture and architecture the qualities that Rubens brought to painting, and like Rubens he was closely associated with the Counter-Reformation. Pope Urban VIII commissioned him in 1629 to complete both the inside and the outer setting of the basilica of St. Peter's in Rome. For the interior, Bernini designed a splendid papal throne that seems to float on clouds beneath a burst of sunlight. For the exterior, he created an enormous plaza, surrounded by a double colonnade, that is the largest such plaza in Europe. Similarly, his dramatic religious works reflect the desire of the Counter-

Reformation popes to electrify the faithful. The sensual and overpowering altarpiece dedicated to the Spanish mystic St. Teresa makes a direct appeal to the emotions of the beholder that is the epitome of the excitement and confidence of the Baroque.

New Dimensions in Music   The seventeenth century was significant, too, as a decisive time in the history of music. New instruments, notably in the keyboard and string families, enabled composers to create richer effects than had been possible before. Particularly in Italy, which in the sixteenth and seventeenth centuries was the chief center of new ideas in music, musicians began to explore the potential of a form that first emerged in these years: the opera. Drawing on the

GianLorenzo Bernini
ST. PETER'S SQUARE AND CHURCH, ROME
The magnificent circular double colonnade that Bernini created in front of St. Peter's is one of the triumphs of Baroque architecture. The church itself was already the largest in Christendom (markers in the floor still indicate how far other famous churches would reach if placed inside St. Peter's), and it was topped by the huge dome Michelangelo had designed. The vast enclosed space that Bernini built reinforced the grandeur of a church that was the pope's own.
Joachim Messerschmidt/Corbis Stock Market

Gian Lorenzo Bernini
THE ECSTASY OF ST. TERESA, **1652**
Bernini's sculpture is as dramatic an example of Baroque art as the paintings of Caravaggio. The moment that St. Teresa described in her autobiography at which she attained mystic ecstasy, as an angel repeatedly pierced her heart with a dart, became in Bernini's hands the centerpiece of a theatrical tableau. He placed the patrons who had commissioned the work on two walls of the chapel that houses this altarpiece, sitting in what seem to be boxes and looking at the stage on which the drama unfolds.
Scala/Art Resource, NY

resources of the theater, painting, architecture, music, and dance, an operatic production could achieve splendors that were beyond the reach of any one of these arts on its own. The form was perfectly attuned to the courtly culture of the age, to the love of display among the princes of Europe, and to the Baroque determination to overwhelm one's audience.

The dominant figure in seventeenth-century music was the Italian Claudio Monteverdi (1567–1643), one of the most innovative composers of all time. He has been called with some justification the creator of both the operatic form and the orchestra. His masterpiece, *Orfeo* (1607), was a tremendous success, and in the course of the next century operas gained in richness and complexity, attracting composers, as well as audiences, in ever-increasing numbers.

Stability and Restraint in the Arts

Classicism **Classicism,** the other major style of the seventeenth century, attempted to recapture (though on a much larger scale than Renaissance imitations of antiquity) the aesthetic values and the strict forms that had been favored in ancient Greece and Rome. Like the Baroque, Classicism aimed for grandiose effects, but unlike the Baroque, it achieved them through restraint and discipline within a formal structure. The gradual rise of the Classical style in the seventeenth century echoed the trend toward stability that was taking place in other areas of intellectual life and in politics. In the arts, the age of striving and unrest was coming to an end.

Poussin The epitome of disciplined expression and conscious imitation of Classical antiquity was Nicolas Poussin (1594–1665), a French artist who spent much of his career in Rome. Poussin was no less interested than his contemporaries in momentous and dramatic subjects, but the atmosphere is always more subdued than in the work of Velázquez or Rubens. The colors are muted, the figures are restrained, and the settings are serene. Peaceful landscapes, men and women in togas, and ruins of Classical buildings are features of his art.

The Dutch Style In the United Provinces different forces were at work, and they led to a style that was much more intimate than the grandiose outpourings of a Rubens or a Velázquez. Two aspects of Dutch society, Protestantism and republicanism, had a particular influence on its painters. The Reformed Church frowned on religious art, which reduced the demand for paintings of biblical scenes. Religious works, therefore, tended to express personal faith. And the absence of a court meant that the chief patrons of art were sober merchants, who were far more interested in precise, dignified portraits than in ornate displays. The result,

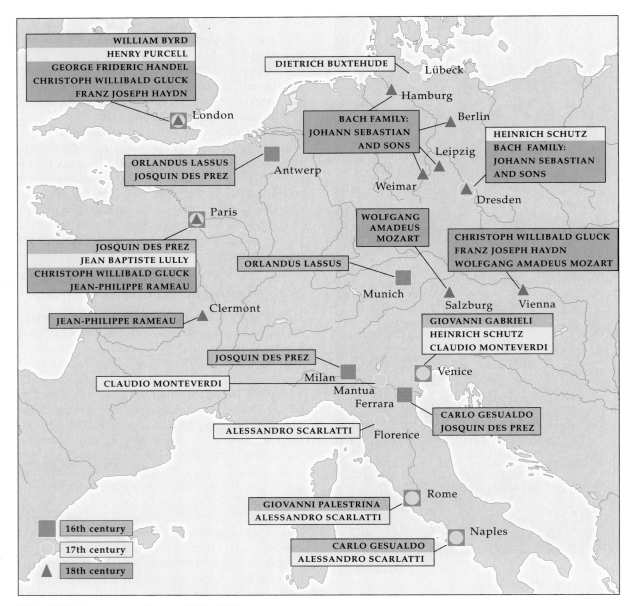

MAP 16.2 CENTERS OF MUSIC, 1500–1800
This map indicates the shifting centers of new ideas in music from Flanders and Italy in the sixteenth century, to Italy in the seventeenth, and on to Germany in the eighteenth. Where, outside of Germany, were other key centers of creativity in music in the eighteenth century?

◆ For an online version, go to www.mhhe.com/chambers9 > chapter 16 > book maps

notably in the profound and moving works of Rembrandt, was a compelling art whose beauty lies in its calmness and restraint.

Rembrandt Rembrandt van Rijn (1606–1669) explored an amazing range of themes, but he was particularly fascinated by human character, emotion, and self-revelation. Whether children or old people, simple servant girls or rich burghers, his subjects are presented without elaboration or idealization; always the person-

ality speaks for itself. Rembrandt's most remarkable achievement in portraiture—and one of the most moving series of canvases in the history of art—is his depiction of the changes in his own face over his lifetime. The brash youth turns into the confident, successful, middle-aged man, one of the most sought-after painters in Holland. But in his late thirties the sorrows mounted: He lost his beloved wife, and commissions began to diminish. Sadness fills the eyes in these pictures. The last portraits move from despair to a final,

Nicolas Poussin
THE INSPIRATION OF THE POET,
CA. **1628**
**Whereas Baroque art emphasized
emotion, the Classical style
sought to embody reason. Poussin,
the leading Classical artist of his
time, believed that painting, like
poetry, had to elevate the minds
of its audience. The poet was thus
a particularly apt subject for
him—a noble and serious theme
that could be presented as a scene
from antiquity, with formal
figures, muted colors, and ancient
symbols like the laurel wreath.
Poussin's views became the
official doctrine of the academy of
art founded in France with royal
approval, and they influenced
generations of painters.**
Louvre, Paris, France. Scala/Art Resource, NY

quiet resignation as his sight slowly failed. Taken together, these paintings bear comparison with Montaigne's essays as monuments to the exploration of
one's own spirit—a searching appraisal that brings all
who see it to a deeper understanding of human nature.

Like the advocates of Classicism, Rembrandt in his
restraint seems to anticipate the art of the next generation. After his death in 1669, serenity, calm, and elegance became the watchwords of European painting.
An age of repose and grace was succeeding a time of upheaval as surely in the arts as in other spheres of life.

Rembrandt van Rijn
SELF-PORTRAIT WITH PALETTE, **1660**
**More than sixty self-portraits by Rembrandt have survived;
though all are penetrating explorations of human character,
those from his last years are especially moving. We see him
here in his mid-fifties with the tools of his trade. Adapting
Caravaggio's interest in light, he uses different shades of
brown and the illumination of the face to create a somber
and reflective mood. The very act of thinking is captured in
this canvas, not to mention the full life that is etched in
Rembrandt's wrinkles.**
Louvre, Paris, France. Scala/Art Resource, NY

Classicism in Drama　By the middle of the seventeenth century, the formalism of the Classical style was also being extended to literature, especially drama. This change was most noticeable in France, but it soon moved through Western Europe, as leading critics insisted that new plays conform to the structure laid down by the ancients. In particular, they wanted the three Classical unities observed: unity of place, which required that all scenes take place without change of location; unity of time, which demanded that the events in the play occur within a twenty-four-hour period; and unity of action, which dictated simplicity and purity of plot.

Corneille　The work of Pierre Corneille (1606–1684), the dominant figure in the French theater during the midcentury years, reflects the rise of Classicism. His early plays were complex and involved, and even after he came into contact with the Classical tradition, he did not accept its rules easily. His masterpiece, *Le Cid* (1636), based on the legends of a medieval Spanish hero, technically observed the three unities, but only by compressing an entire tragic love affair, a military campaign, and many other events into one day. The play won immediate popular success, but the critics, urged on by the royal minister Cardinal Richelieu, who admired the regularity and order of Classical style, condemned Corneille for imperfect observance of the three unities. Thereafter, he adhered to the Classical forms, though he was never entirely at ease with their restraints.

Passion was not absent from the Classical play; the works of Jean Racine (1639–1699), the model Classical dramatist, generate some of the most intense emotion ever seen on the stage. But the exuberance of earlier drama was disappearing. Nobody summed up the values of Classicism better than Racine in his eulogy of Corneille:

> You know in what a condition the stage was when he began to write. . . . All the rules of art, and even those of decency and decorum, broken everywhere. . . . Corneille, after having for some time sought the right path and

struggled against the bad taste of his day, inspired by extraordinary genius and helped by the study of the ancients, at last brought reason upon the stage.

　Paul Mesnard (ed.), *Oeuvres de J. Racine*, Vol. 4, 1886, p. 366, trans. T. K. Rabb.

This was exactly the progression—from turbulence to calm—that was apparent throughout European culture in this period.

SOCIAL PATTERNS AND POPULAR CULTURE

The new sense of orderliness, of upheaval subdued, was visible throughout European society in the last years of the seventeenth century. After decades of political and religious conflict, of expressions of uneasiness in philosophy, literature, and the arts, stability and confidence were on the rise. Similarly, the end of population decline, the restoration of social order, and the suppression of disruptive forces like witchcraft indicated that the tensions were easing at all levels of society.

Population Trends

The sixteenth-century rise in Europe's population was succeeded by a period of decline that in most areas lasted long after the political and intellectual upheavals subsided. The rise had been fragile, because throughout these centuries only one child in two reached adulthood. Each couple had to give birth to four children merely to replace themselves, and since they had to wait until they were financially independent to marry—usually in their mid-twenties—they rarely had the chance to produce a big family. Before improvements in nutrition in the nineteenth century, women could bear children only until their late thirties; on average, therefore, a woman had some twelve years in which to give birth to four children to maintain the population. Because lactation delayed ovulation, the

EUROPE'S POPULATION, 1600–1700, BY REGIONS			
Region	*1600**	*1700*	*Percentage Change*
Spain, Portugal, Italy	23.6	22.7	−4
France, Switzerland, Germany	35.0	36.2	+3
British Isles, Low Countries, Scandinavia	12.0	16.1	+34
Total	70.6	75.0	+6

*All figures are in millions.
From Jan de Vries, *The Economy of Europe in an Age of Crisis, 1600–1750*, Cambridge, 1976, p. 5.

mean interval between births was almost two and a half years, which meant that most couples were capable of raising only two children to adulthood. As soon as there was outside pressure—such as plague, famine, or war—population growth became impossible.

The worst of these outside pressures in the seventeenth century was the Thirty Years' War, which alone caused the death of more than 5 million people. It also helped plunge Europe into a debilitating economic depression, which, in turn, decreased the means of relieving the regular famines that afflicted all areas. Disasters like these were not easily absorbed, despite government efforts to distribute food and take other measures to combat natural calamities. Only when better times returned could population increase resume. Because England and the Netherlands led in economic recovery, they experienced a demographic revival long before their neighbors; indeed, the rise in their numbers, which began in the 1660s, accounted for most of the slight population increase the whole of Europe was able to achieve in this difficult century. By 1700, though, prosperity and population were again on the rise—both a reflection and a cause of Europe's newfound assurance and stability.

Social Status

The determinants of status in modern times—wealth, education, and family background—were viewed rather differently in the seventeenth century. Wealth was significant chiefly to merchants, education was important mainly among professionals, and background was vital primarily to the nobility. But in this period the significance of these three social indicators began to shift. Wealth became a more general source of status, as ever-larger numbers of successful merchants bought offices, lands, and titles that allowed them to enter the nobility. Education was also becoming more highly prized; throughout Europe attendance at institutions of higher learning soared after 1550, bringing to universities the sons of artisans as well as nobles. And although background was being scrutinized ever more defensively by old-line nobles, who regarded family lineage as the only criterion for acceptance into their ranks, their resistance to change was futile as the "new" aristocrats multiplied.

In general, it was assumed that everyone occupied a fixed place in the social hierarchy and that it was against the order of nature for someone to move to another level. The growing social importance of wealth and education, however, indicates that mobility was possible. Thanks to the expansion of bureaucracies, it became easier to move to new levels, either by winning favor at court or by buying an office.

Contradictions in the Status of Women   At each level of society, women were usually treated as subordinate

by the legal system: In many countries, even the widows of aristocrats could not inherit their husbands' estates; an abbess could never become prominent in Church government; and the few women allowed to practice a trade were excluded from the leadership of their guild. Yet there were notable businesswomen and female artists, writers, and even scientists among the growing numbers of successful self-made people in this period. Widows often inherited their husbands' businesses and pursued thriving careers in their own right, from publishing to innkeeping. One of Caravaggio's most distinguished disciples was Artemisia Gentileschi; the Englishwoman Aphra Behn was a widely known playwright; and some of the leading patrons of intellectual life were the female aristocrats who ran literary circles, particularly in Paris. In fiction and drama, female characters often appeared as the equals of males, despite the legal restrictions of the time and the warnings against such equality in sermons and moral treatises.

Mobility and Crime

The Peasants' Plight   The remarkable economic advances of the sixteenth century helped change attitudes toward wealth, but they brought few benefits to the lower levels of society. Peasants throughout Europe were, in fact, entering a time of increasing difficulty at the end of the sixteenth century. Their taxes were rising rapidly, but the prices they got for the food they grew were stabilizing. Moreover, landowners were starting what has been called the "seigneurial reaction"—making additional demands on their tenants, raising rents, and squeezing as much as they could out of the lands they owned. The effects of famine and war were also more severe at this level of society. The only escapes were to cities or armies, both of which grew rapidly in the seventeenth century. Many of those who fled their villages, however, remained on the road, part of the huge bodies of vagrants and beggars who were a common sight throughout Europe.

A few of those who settled in a town or city improved their lot, but for the large majority, poverty in cities was even more miserable and hungry than poverty on the land. Few could become apprentices, and day laborers were poorly paid and usually out of work. As for military careers, armies were carriers of disease, frequently ill fed, and subject to constant hardship.

Crime and Punishment   For many, therefore, the only alternative to starvation was crime. One area of London in the seventeenth century was totally controlled by the underworld. It offered refuge to fugitives and was never entered by respectable citizens. Robbery and violence—committed equally by desperate men,

women, and even children—were common in most cities. As a result, social events like dinners and outings, or visits to the theater, took place during the daytime because the streets were unsafe at night.

If caught, Europe's criminals were treated harshly. In an age before regular police forces, however, catching them was difficult. Crime was usually the responsibility of local authorities, who depended on part-time officials (known in England as constables) for law enforcement. Only in response to major outbreaks, such as a gang of robbers preying on travelers, would the authorities recruit a more substantial armed band (rather like a posse in the American West) to pursue criminals. If such efforts succeeded in bringing offenders to justice, the defendants found they had few rights, especially if they were poor, and punishments were severe. Torture was a common means of extracting confessions; various forms of maiming, such as chopping off a hand or an ear, were considered acceptable penalties; and repeated thefts could lead to execution. Society's hierarchical instincts were apparent even in civil disputes, where nobles were usually immune from prosecution and women often could not start a case. If a woman was raped, for example, she had to find a man to bring suit.

Change in the Villages and Cities

Loss of Village Cohesiveness   Over three-quarters of Europe's population still lived in small village communities, but their structure was changing. In Eastern Europe, peasants were being reduced to serfdom; in the West—our principal concern—familiar relationships and institutions were changing.

The essence of the traditional village had been its isolation. Cut off from frequent contact with the world beyond its immediate region, it had been self-sufficient and closely knit. Everyone knew everyone else, and mutual help was vital for survival. There might be distinctions among villagers—some more prosperous, others less so—but the sense of cohesiveness was powerful. It extended even to the main "outsiders" in the village, the priest and the local lord. The priest was often indistinguishable from his parishioners: almost as poor and sometimes hardly more literate. He adapted to local customs and beliefs, frequently taking part in semipagan rituals so as to keep his authority with his flock. The lord could be exploitative and demanding; but he considered the village his livelihood, and he therefore kept in close touch with its affairs and did all he could to ensure its safety, orderliness, and well-being.

Forces of Change   The main intrusions onto this scene were economic and demographic. As a result of the boom in agricultural prices during the sixteenth century, followed by the economic difficulties of the seventeenth, differences in the wealth of the villagers became more marked. The richer peasants began to set themselves apart from their poorer neighbors, and the feeling of village unity began to break down. These divisions were exacerbated by the rise in population during the sixteenth century—which strained resources and forced the less fortunate to leave in search of better opportunities in cities—and by the pressures of taxation, exploitation, plague, and famine during the more difficult times of the seventeenth century.

Another intrusion that undermined the traditional cohesion of the community was the increased presence of royal officials. For centuries, elected councils, drawn from every part of the population, had run village affairs throughout Europe. In the late seventeenth century, however, these councils began to disappear as outside forces—in some cases a nearby lord, but more often government officials—asserted their control over the localities. Tax gatherers and army recruiters were now familiar figures throughout Europe. Although they were often the target of peasant rebellions, they were also welcomed when, for example, they distributed food during a famine. Their long-term influence, however, was the creation of a new layer of outside authority in the village, which was another cause of the division and fragmentation that led many to flee to the city.

As these outside intrusions multiplied, the interests of the local lord, who traditionally had defended the village's autonomy and had offered help in times of need, also changed. Nobles were beginning to look more and more to royal courts and capital cities, rather than to their local holdings, for position and power. The natural corollary was the "seigneurial reaction," with lords treating the villages they dominated as sources of income and increasingly distancing themselves from the inhabitants. Their commitment to charitable works declined, and they tended more and more to leave the welfare of the local population to church or government officials.

City Life   As village life changed, the inhabitants who felt forced to leave headed for the city—an impersonal place where, instead of joining a cohesive population, they found themselves part of a mingling of peoples. The growing cities needed ever wider regions to provide them with food and goods, and they attracted the many who could not make ends meet in the countryside. Long-distance communications became more common, especially as localities were linked into national market and trade networks, and in the cities the new immigrants met others from distant villages.

A city was a far more chaotic place than a rural community. Urban society in general was fragmentary and

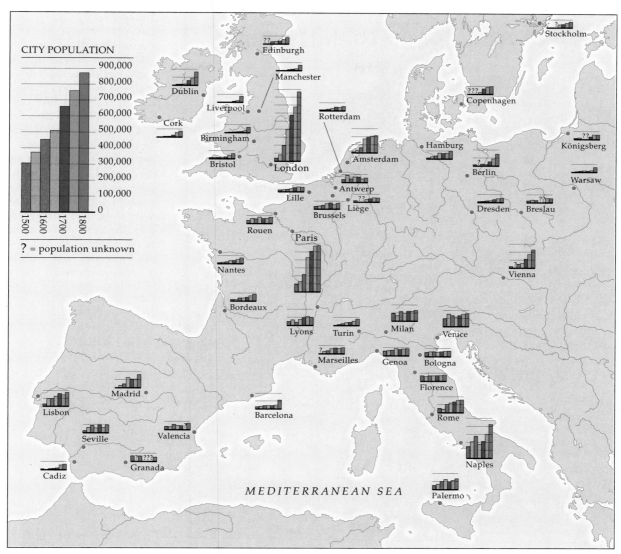

MAP 16.3 THE GROWTH OF CITIES, 1500–1800
In addition to the remarkable rise in the population of Europe's cities, particularly after 1550, this map reveals the northward shift in the distribution of the largest cities: in 1500, three of the four largest were in Italy; in 1700, only one. When did London overtake Paris as the largest city in Europe?
◆ For an online version, go to www.mhhe.com/chambers9 > chapter 16 > book maps

disorganized, even if an individual area, such as a parish, seemed distinct and cohesive—some parishes, for example, were associated with a single trade. A city's craft guilds gave structure to artisans and shopkeepers, regulating their lives and providing welfare, but less than half the population could join a guild. The rest did odd jobs or turned to crime. The chief attraction of cities was the wide variety of economic opportunity: for women, in such areas as selling goods and processing food; for men, in construction, on the docks, and in delivery services. But employment was unpredictable, and citizens did not have community support to fall back on in hard times as they did in the village. Even forms of recreation and enjoyment were different in the city.

Popular Culture in the City One major difference between country and town was the level of literacy. Only in urban areas were there significant numbers of people who could read: It has been estimated that in cities perhaps a third of adult males were literate by 1700. Not only was reading necessary for commerce but it had been strongly encouraged by the Reformation, with its insistence that the faithful read the Bible for themselves.

Der Kramer vnd der newe Zeittung.

Ihr liebe gütte fromme Herren,
Die ihr hört neuwe Zeittung gern.
Hie bring ich euch ein gantzen hauffen,
Die wil ich euch al bar verkauffen.
It alles war vnd nichts erlogen.
Wird kewer keiner nit betrogen.
Groß wunder sag euch meine Zeittung,
Von der arm ababorder seitten.
Auß Frauckreich vnd auß Engellandt.
Geb ich bericht euch aller handt.

Ich trag nicht brieff wie andre botten,
Die euch verierrn vnd euwer spotten,
Was ich hab ist nach allem lust,
Drey tag er logen vor der vist.
Dieß müß ir alles glauben frey,
Weill alles noch ist frisch vnd new.
Auch geb ich euch so wolfeil hin,
Weil ich des geldsbenötiget bin.
Mein wawarart ist sehr bös vnd schwach,
Ist zeit das ist ein anders mach.

Auff das ab geht die Neuwe mehr,
Von der Hertzog von gaisen sehr.
Hab ich mit gantzem fleiß gethan,
Nar auch frantzoisch hosen an.
Vnd das ir wist so wil nit ich.
Die bleiben seen, langsamen nach,
Drumb sorch mein sachschwantz gesellt.
Kaufft ihn das ich loß euwer gelt.
An sedderin ist der augen schein.
Was ich müß für ein vogel sein.

Gedruckt bey Jacob Kempner

Anonymous
***The Newsvendor,* Woodcut**
The ancestor of the regularly published newspaper was the occasional single sheet describing the latest news or rumors. Printers would produce a few hundred copies and have them sold by street vendors whenever they had an event of some importance to describe: a battle, the death of a ruler, or some fantastic occurrence like the birth of a baby with two heads. As cities and the potential readership grew, the news sheets expanded; by the seventeenth century they had distinctive names and began to appear every week.
Bibliothèque Nationale de France, Paris

This stimulus ensured that literacy also rose among women, who increasingly became pupils at the growing number of schools in Europe (although they were still not admitted to universities). As many as 25 percent of the adult women in cities may have been able to read.

These changes had a notable effect on urban life. There was now a readership for newspapers, which became common by the mid-seventeenth century, as did the coffeehouses in which they were often read. Although newspaper stories were regularly inaccurate or untrue, and their writers (relying on informants at courts) could find themselves prosecuted for showing the authorities in a bad light, they were avidly consumed, and they made politics for the first time a subject of wide interest and discussion. Theater and opera also became popular entertainments, with women for the first time taking stage roles and obtaining performances for plays they had written. Sales of books surged, often because they had a popular audience, and they gave broad circulation to traditional favorites, such as travel stories and lives of saints, as well as to the latest ideas of science.

Belief in Magic and Rituals

Although in the countryside cultural patterns looked different—with lower literacy, simpler recreations, and more visible religiosity—there was one area of popular culture in which the outlook of the city and the village was remarkably similar: the belief in magic. The townspeople may have seemed more sophisticated, but the basic assumption they shared with their country cousins was that mysterious forces controlled nature and their own lives and that there was little they could do to ensure their own well-being. The world was full of spirits, and all one could do was encourage the good, defend oneself against the evil, and hope that the good would win. Nothing that happened—a calf dying, lightning striking a house—was accidental. Everything had a purpose. Any unusual event was an omen, part of a larger plan, or the action of some unseen force.

Charivari   To strengthen themselves against trouble, people used whatever help they could find. They organized special processions and holidays to celebrate good times such as harvests, to lament misfortunes, to complain about oppression, or to poke fun at scandalous behavior. These occasions, known as "rough music" in England and *charivari* in France, often used the theme of "the world turned upside down" to make their point. In the set pieces in a procession, a fool might be dressed up as a king, a woman might be shown beating her husband, or a tax collector might appear hanging from a tree. Whether ridiculing a dominating wife or lamenting the lack of bread, the community was expressing its solidarity in the face of difficulty or distasteful behavior through these rituals. They were a form of public opinion, enabling people to let off steam and express themselves.

The potential for violence was always present at such gatherings, especially when religious or social differences became entangled with other resentments. The viciousness of ordinary Protestants and Catholics toward one another revealed a frustration and aggressiveness that was not far below the surface. When food was scarce or new impositions had been ordered by their rulers, peasants and townspeople needed little excuse to show their anger openly. Women often took the

lead, not only because they had firsthand experience of the difficulty of feeding a family but also because troops were more reluctant to attack them.

Magical Remedies   Ordinary people also had other outlets for their frustrations. Recognizing their powerlessness in the face of outside forces, they resorted to their version of the magic that the literate were finding so fashionable at this very time. Whereas the sophisticated patronized astrologers, paying handsomely for horoscopes and advice about how to live their lives, the peasants and the poor consulted popular almanacs or sought out "cunning men" and wise women for secret spells, potions, and other remedies for their anxieties. Even religious ceremonies were thought of as being related to the rituals of the magical world, in which so-called white witches—the friendly kind—gave assistance when a ring was lost or when the butter would not form out of the milk.

Witches and Witch-Hunts   Misfortunes were never just plain bad luck; rather, there was intent behind everything that happened. Events were willed, and if they turned out badly, they must have been willed by the good witch's opposite, the evil witch. Such beliefs often led to cruel persecutions of innocent victims—usually helpless old women, able to do nothing but mutter curses when taunted by neighbors, and easy targets if someone had to be blamed for unfortunate happenings.

This quest for scapegoats naturally focused on the most vulnerable members of society, such as Jews or, in the case of witches, women. Accusations were often directed at a woman who was old and alone, with nobody to defend her. She was feared because she seemed to be an outsider or not sufficiently deferential to her supposed betters. It was believed that witches read strange books and knew magic spells, an indication of what many regarded as inappropriate and dangerous levels of literacy for a woman.

In the sixteenth and seventeenth centuries, the hunt for witches intensified to levels never previously reached. This period has been called the era of the "great witch craze," and for good reason. There were outbursts in every part of Europe, and tens of thousands of the accused were executed. Dozens of men, most of them clerics, made witch-hunting a full-time profession and persuaded civic and other government authorities to devote their resources to stamping out this threat to social and religious stability. Suspects were almost always tortured, and it is not too surprising that they usually "confessed" and implicated others as servants of the devil. The practices that were uncovered varied—in some areas witches were said to dance with the devil, in others to fly on broomsticks, in

Hans Baldung Grien
WITCHES, WOODCUT
This woodcut by the German artist Grien shows the popular image of witches in early modern Europe. One carries a potion while flying on a goat. The others put together the ingredients for a magic potion in a jar inscribed with mystical symbols. The fact that witches were thought to be learned women who could understand magic was another reason they were feared by a Europe that expected women to be uneducated.

others to be possessed by evil spirits who could induce dreadful (and possibly psychosomatic) symptoms—but the punishment was usually the same: burning at the stake. And the hysteria was infectious. One accusation could trigger dozens more until entire regions were swept with fear and hatred.

Forces of Restraint

By the middle of the seventeenth century, the wave of assaults on witches was beginning to recede (see "A Witness Analyzes the Witch Craze," p. 487). Social and political leaders came to realize that the campaigns

A Witness Analyzes the Witch Craze

Although for most Europeans around 1600 witchcraft was real—a religious problem caused by the devil—there were a few observers who were beginning to think more analytically about the reasons for the rapid spread of accusations. One such observer was a clergyman named Linden, who was attached to the cathedral of the great city of Trier in western Germany. His description of a witch-hunt in the Trier region ignored the standard religious explanations.

"Inasmuch as it was popularly believed that the continued sterility of many years was caused by witches, the whole area rose to exterminate the witches. This movement was promoted by many in office, who hoped to gain wealth from the persecution. And so special accusers, inquisitors, notaries, judges, and constables dragged to trial and torture human beings of both sexes and burned them in great numbers. Scarcely any of those who were accused escaped punishment. So far did the madness of the furious populace and the courts go in this thirst for blood and booty that there was scarcely anybody who was not smirched by some suspicion of this crime. Meanwhile, notaries, copyists and innkeepers grew rich. The executioner rode a fine horse, like a noble of the court, and dressed in gold and silver; his wife competed with noble dames in the richness of her array. A direr pestilence or a more ruthless invader could hardly have ravaged the territory than this inquisition and persecution without bounds. Many were the reasons for doubting that all were really guilty. At last, though the flames were still unsated, the people grew poor, rules were made and enforced restricting the fees and costs of examinations, and suddenly, as when in war funds fail, the zeal of the persecutors died out."

From George L. Burr (ed.), "The Witch Persecutions," *Translations and Reprints from the Original Sources of European History,* Vol. 3, Philadelphia: University of Pennsylvania, 1902, pp. 13–14.

against witches could endanger authority, especially when accusations were turned against the rich and privileged classes. Increasingly, therefore, cases were not brought to trial, and when they were, lawyers and doctors (who treated the subject less emotionally than the clergy) cast doubt on the validity of the testimony. Gradually, excesses were restrained and control was reestablished; by 1700 there was only a trickle of new incidents.

The decline in accusations of witchcraft reflected not only the more general quieting down of conflict and upheaval in the late seventeenth century but also the growing proportion of Europe's population that was living in cities. Here, less reliant on the luck of good weather, people could feel themselves more in control of their own fates. If there were unexpected fires, there were fire brigades; if a house burned down, there might even be insurance—a new protection for individuals that was spreading in the late 1600s. A process that has been called the "disenchantment" of the world—growing skepticism about spirits and mysterious forces, and greater self-reliance—was under way.

Religious Discipline   The churches played an important part in suppressing the traditional reliance on magic. In Catholic countries the Counter-Reformation produced better-educated priests who were trained to impose official doctrine instead of tolerating unusual local customs. Among Protestants, ministers were similarly well educated and denounced magical practices as idolatrous or superstitious. And both camps treated passion and enthusiasm with suspicion. Habits did not change overnight, but gradually ordinary people were being persuaded to abandon old fears and beliefs. There were still major scares in midcentury. An eclipse in 1654 prompted panic throughout Europe; comets still inspired prophecies of the end of the world; and in the 1660s a self-proclaimed messiah named Shabtai Zvi attracted a massive following among the Jews of Europe and the Middle East. Increasingly, though, such visions of doom or the end of time were becoming fringe beliefs, dismissed by authorities and most elements of society. Eclipses and comets now had scientific explanations, and the messiah came to be regarded as a spiritual, not an immediate, promise.

Summary

Even at the level of popular culture, therefore, Europeans had reason to feel, by the late seventeenth century, that a time of upheaval and uncertainty was over. A sense of confidence and orderliness was returning, and in intellectual circles the optimism seemed justified by the achievements of science. In fact, there arose a scholarly dispute around 1700, known as the "battle of the books," in which one side claimed, for the first time, that the "moderns" had outshone the "ancients." Using the scientists as their chief example, the advocates of the "moderns" argued—in a remarkable break with the reverence for the past that had dominated medieval and Renaissance culture—that advances in thought were possible and that one did not always have to accept the superiority of antiquity. Such self-confidence made it clear that, in the world of ideas as surely as in the world of politics, a period of turbulence had given way to an era of renewed assurance and stability.

QUESTIONS FOR FURTHER THOUGHT

1. Are there similarities in the creativity that marks the scientist and the artist?

2. Is it fair to ask whether popular beliefs and rituals do more harm than good?

RECOMMENDED READING

Sources

*Drake, Stillman (tr. and ed.). *Discoveries and Opinions of Galileo.* 1957. The complete texts of some of Galileo's most important works.

*Hall, Marie Boas (ed.). *Nature and Nature's Laws: Documents of the Scientific Revolution.* 1970. A good collection of documents by and about the pioneers of modern science.

Studies

Biagioli, Mario. *Galileo, Courtier: The Practice of Science in the Culture of Absolutism.* 1993. A fascinating study of the political forces at work in Galileo's career.

Braudel, Fernand. *Capitalism and Material Life, 1400–1800.* Miriam Kochan (tr.). 1973. A classic, pioneering study of the structure of daily life in early modern Europe.

*Burke, Peter. *Popular Culture in Early Modern Europe.* 1978. A lively introduction to the many forms of expression and belief among the ordinary people of Europe.

Fara, Patricia. *Newton: The Making of a Genius.* 2002.

*Gutmann, Myron P. *Toward the Modern Economy: Early Industry in Europe, 1500–1800.* 1988. A clear survey of recent work on economic development in this period.

*Ladurie, Emmanuel Le Roy. *The Peasants of Languedoc.* John Day (tr.). 1966. A brilliant evocation of peasant life in France in the sixteenth and seventeenth centuries.

*Levack, Brian P. *The Witch-Hunt in Early Modern Europe.* 1987. An excellent survey of the belief in witchcraft and its consequences.

Oppenheimer, Paul. *Rubens: A Portrait.* 2002.

Rabb, Theodore K. *Renaissance Lives.* 1993. Brief biographies of fifteen people, both famous and obscure, who lived just before and during this period.

*Shapin, S. *The Scientific Revolution.* 1996.

*Shearman, John. *Mannerism.* 1968. The best short introduction to a difficult artistic style.

*Thomas, Keith. *Religion and the Decline of Magic.* 1976. The most thorough account of popular culture yet published, this enormous book, while dealing mainly with England, treats at length such subjects as witchcraft, astrology, and ghosts in a most readable style.

Wiesner, Merry E. *Women and Gender in Early Modern Europe.* 1993.

*Available in paperback.

Nicolas de Largilliére
LOUIS XIV AND HIS FAMILY
Louis XIV (seated) is shown here in full regal splendor surrounded by three of his heirs. On his right is his eldest son, on his left is his eldest grandson, and, reaching out his hand, is his eldest great-grandson, held by his governess. All three of these heirs died before Louis, and thus they never became kings of France.
Reproduced by Permission of the Trustees of the Wallace Collection, London

Chapter Seventeen

THE EMERGENCE OF THE EUROPEAN STATE SYSTEM

ABSOLUTISM IN FRANCE • OTHER PATTERNS OF ABSOLUTISM • ALTERNATIVES TO
ABSOLUTISM • THE INTERNATIONAL SYSTEM

The acceptance of strong central governments that emerged out of the crisis of the mid-seventeenth century was a victory not merely for kings but for an entire way of organizing society. As a result of huge increases in the scale of warfare and taxation, bureaucracies had mushroomed, and their presence was felt throughout Europe. Yet no central administration, however powerful, could function without the support of the nobles who ruled the countryside. Regional loyalties had dominated European society for centuries, and only a regime that drew on those loyalties could hope to maintain the support of its subjects. The political structures that developed during the century following the 1650s were, therefore, the work not only of ambitious princes but also of a nobility long accustomed to exercising authority and now prepared to find new ways of exerting its influence. To the leaders of society during the century following the crisis of the 1640s and 1650s, it was clear that state building and the imposition of their power on the rest of the world were now ever more central to rulers' ambitions, and required a common effort to establish stronger political, social, military, financial, and religious structures that would support effective government. The institutions and practices they created have remained essential to the modern state ever since.

Locke, *Second Treatise of Civil Government* **1690** ●

"Glorious" Revolution in England **1689** ●

Reign of Peter the Great in Russia **1682–1725** ▬▬▬

Hobbes, *Leviathan* **1651** ●

Reign of Louis XIV in France **1643–1715** ▬▬▬

ABSOLUTISM IN FRANCE

One way of creating a strong, centralized state was the political system known as **absolutism:** the belief that power emanated from the monarch's unlimited authority. Absolutism was based on a theory known as the **divine right of kings,** derived from the fact that kings were anointed with holy oil at their coronations; it asserted that the monarch was God's representative on earth.

The Rule of Louis XIV

The most famous absolutist state was the Kingdom of France, which became the most powerful regime in Europe. Taken to an extreme, as it was by Louis XIV (1643–1715), absolutism justified unlimited power and treated treason as blasphemy. The leading advocate of the theory, Bishop Bossuet, called Louis God's lieutenant and argued that the Bible itself endorsed absolutism. In reality, the king worked in close partnership with the nobles to maintain order, and he often (though not always) felt obliged to defend their local authority as a reinforcement of his own power. Nevertheless, the very notion that the king not only was supreme but could assert his will with armies and bureaucracies of unprecedented size gave absolutism both an image and a reality that set it apart from previous systems of monarchical rule. Here at last was a force that could hold together and control the increasingly complex interactions of regions and interest groups that made up a state.

Versailles   The setting in which a central government operated often reflected its power and its methods. Philip II in the late 1500s had created, at the Escorial outside Madrid, the first isolated palace that controlled a large realm. A hundred years later, Louis XIV created at Versailles, near Paris, a far more elaborate court as the center of an even larger and more intrusive bureaucracy than Philip's. The isolation of government and the exercise of vast personal power seemed to go hand in hand.

The king moved the court in the 1680s to Versailles, 12 miles from Paris, where, at a cost of half a year's royal income, he transformed a small chateau his father had built into the largest building in Europe. There, far from Parisian mobs, he enjoyed the splendor and the ceremonies, centered on himself, which exalted his majesty. His self-aggrandizing image as "Sun King" was symbolized by coins that showed the sun's rays falling first on Louis and only then, by reflection, onto his subjects. Every French nobleman of any significance spent time each year at Versailles, not only to maintain access to royal patronage and governmental affairs but also to demonstrate the wide support for Louis' system of rule. Historians have called this process the domestication of the aristocracy, as great lords who had once drawn their status from their lineage or lands came to regard service to the throne as the best route to power. But the benefits cut both ways. The king gained the services of influential administrators, and they gained privileges and rewards without the uncertainties that had accompanied their traditional resistance to central control.

Court Life   The visible symbol of Louis' absolutism was Versailles. Here the leaders of France assembled, and around them swirled the most envied social circles of the time. From the court emanated the policies and directives that increasingly affected the lives of the king's subjects and also determined France's relations with other states.

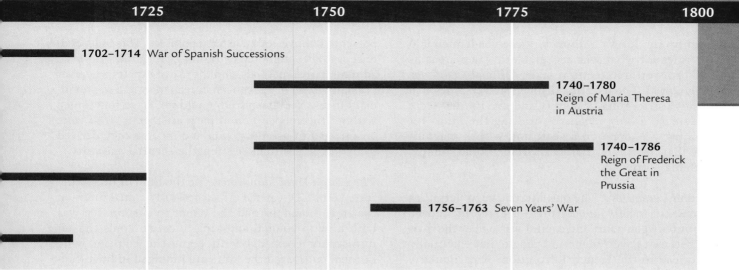

1725 1750 1775 1800

1702–1714 War of Spanish Successions

1740–1780
Reign of Maria Theresa
in Austria

1740–1786
Reign of Frederick
the Great in
Prussia

1756–1763 Seven Years' War

At Versailles, too, French culture was shaped by the king's patronage of those artists and writers who appealed to the royal taste. For serious drama and history, Louis turned to the playwright and writer Racine (1639–1699); for comedy, to the theatrical producer and playwright Molière (1622–1673); and for opera and the first performances of what we now call ballet, to the composer Lully (1632–1687). Moreover, all artistic expression, from poetry to painting, was regulated by royal academies that were founded in the 1600s;

PERSPECTIVE VIEW OF VERSAILLES FROM THE PLACE D'ARMES, 1698
This painting shows Versailles not long before Louis decided to move there; he was soon to begin an enormous expansion into the gardens at the back that more than doubled the size of the buildings. In this scene, the royal coach, with its entourage, is just about to enter the château.
Giraudon/Art Resource, NY

backed by the king's authority, these academies laid down rules for what was acceptable in such areas as verse forms or architectural style. Official taste was what counted. The dazzling displays at Versailles had to observe strict rules of dignity and gravity that were considered the only means of exalting the king. Yet everything was done on a scale and with a magnificence that no other European ruler could match, though many tried.

Paris and Versailles The one alternative to Versailles as a center of society and culture was Paris, and indeed the split between court and capital was one of the divisions between government and people that eventually was to lead to the French Revolution. A particularly notable difference was in the role of women. Versailles was overwhelmingly a male society. Women achieved prominence only as royal mistresses in Louis' early years or as the creators of a rigidly pious atmosphere in his last years. They were also essential to the highly elaborate rituals of civility and manners that developed at Versailles. But they were allowed no independent initiative in social or cultural matters.

In Paris, by contrast, women established and dominated the gatherings known as **salons** that promoted easy conversation, a mixture of social backgrounds, and forms of expression—political discussion and ribald humor, for example—that were not acceptable at the staid and sober court. Yet the contrasts were not merely between the formal palace and the relaxed salon. Even before Louis moved to Versailles, he banned as improper one of Molière's comedies, *Tartuffe*, which mocked excessive religious devoutness. It took five years of reworking by Molière before Louis allowed the play to be performed (1669), and it then became a major hit in Paris, but it was never a favorite at court.

Government

Absolutism was more than a device to satisfy royal whims, for Louis was a gifted administrator and politician who used his power for state building. By creating and reorganizing government institutions, he strengthened his authority at home and increased his ascendancy over his neighbors. The longest-lasting result of his absolutism was that the French state won control over three crucial activities: the use of armed force, the formulation and execution of laws, and the collection and expenditure of revenue. These functions, in turn, depended on a centrally controlled bureaucracy responsive to royal orders and efficient enough to carry them out in distant provinces over the objections of local groups.

Nobody could suppress all vested interests and local loyalties, but the bureaucracy was supposed to be insulated from outside pressure by the absolute monarch's power to remove and transfer appointees. This independence was also promoted by training programs, improved administrative methods, and the use of experts wherever possible—both in the central bureaucracy and in provincial offices. Yet the system could not have functioned without the cooperation of local aristocrats, who were encouraged to use the power and income they derived from official positions to strengthen central authority.

The King's Dual Functions At the head of this structure, Louis XIV carried off successfully a dual function that few monarchs had the talent to sustain: He was both king in council and king in court. Louis the administrator coexisted with Louis the courtier, who hunted, cultivated the arts, and indulged in huge banquets. Among his many imitators, however, the easier side of absolutism, court life, consumed an excessive share of a state's resources and became an end in itself. The effect was to give prestige to the leisure pursuits of the upper classes while sapping the energies of influential figures. Louis was one of the few who avoided sacrificing affairs of state to regal pomp.

Like court life, government policy under Louis XIV was tailored to the aim of state building. As he was to discover, the resources and powers at his disposal were not endless. But until the last years of his reign, they served his many purposes extremely well (see "Louis XIV on Kingship," p. 495). Moreover, Louis had superb support at the highest levels of his administration—ministers whose viewpoints differed but whose skills were carefully blended by their ruler.

Competing Ministers Until the late 1680s the king's two leading advisers were Jean-Baptiste Colbert and the marquis of Louvois. Colbert was a financial wizard who regarded a mercantilist policy as the key to state building. He believed that the government should give priority to increasing France's wealth. As a result, he believed that the chief danger to the country's well-being was the United Provinces, Europe's great trader state, and that royal resources should be poured into the navy, manufacturing, and shipping. By contrast, Louvois, the son of a military administrator, consistently emphasized the army as the foundation of France's power. He believed that the country was threatened primarily by land—by the Holy Roman Empire on its flat, vulnerable northeast frontier—and thus that resources should be allocated to the army and to border fortifications.

Foreign Policy

Louis tried to balance these goals within his overall aims—to expand France's frontiers and to assert his superiority over other European states. Like the magnifi-

LOUIS XIV ON KINGSHIP

From time to time, Louis XIV put on paper brief accounts of his actions: For example, he wrote some brief memoirs in the late 1660s. These reflections about his role as king were intended as a guide for his son and indicate both his high view of kingship and the seriousness with which he approached his duties. The following are extracts from his memoirs and other writings.

"Homage is due to kings, and they do whatever they like. It certainly must be agreed that, however bad a prince may be, it is always a heinous crime for his subjects to rebel against him. He who gave men kings willed that they should be respected as His lieutenants, and reserved to Himself the right to question their conduct. It is His will that everyone who is born a subject should obey without qualification. This law, as clear as it is universal, was not made only for the sake of princes: it is also for the good of the people themselves. It is therefore the duty of kings to sustain by their own example the religion upon which they rely; and they must realize that, if their subjects see them plunged in vice or violence, they can hardly render to their person the respect due to their office, or recognize in them the living image of Him who is all-holy as well as almighty.

"It is a fine thing, a noble and enjoyable thing, to be a king. But it is not without its pains, its fatigues, and its troubles. One must work hard to reign. In working for the state, a king is working for himself. The good of the one is the glory of the other. When the state is prosperous, famous, and powerful, the king who is the cause of it is glorious; and he ought in consequence to have a larger share than others do of all that is most agreeable in life."

From J. M. Thompson, *Lectures on Foreign History, 1494–1789*, Oxford: Blackwell, 1956, pp. 172–174.

Antoine Watteau
***FÊTE IN THE PARK*, 1718**
The luxurious life of the nobility during the eighteenth century is captured in this scene of men and women in fine silks, enjoying a picnic in a lovely park setting.
Reproduced by Permission of the Trustees of the Wallace Collection, London

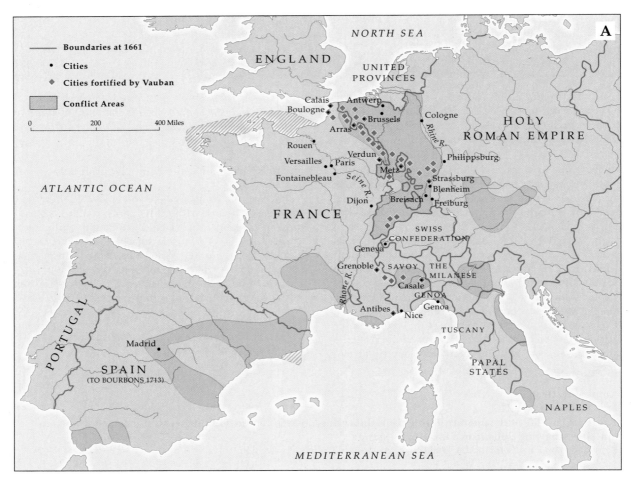

MAP 17.1A THE WARS OF LOUIS XIV
Louis XIV's aggressive aims took his troops to many areas of Europe.
◆ For an online version, go to www.mhhe.com/chambers9 > chapter 17 > book maps

cence of his court, his power on the international scene served to demonstrate *la gloire* (the glory) of France. But his effort to expand that power prompted his neighbors to form coalitions and alliances of common defense, designed to keep him in check. From this response was to emerge the concept of a state system and the notion of a **balance of power** among the states of Europe.

In his early years Louis relied heavily on Colbert, who moved gradually toward war with the Dutch when he was unable to undermine their control of French maritime trade. But the war (1672–1678) was a failure, and so the pendulum swung toward Louvois' priorities. In the early 1680s Louis adopted the marquis's aims and claimed a succession of territories on France's northeast border. No one claim seemed large enough to provoke his neighbors to fight, especially

since the Holy Roman Emperor, Leopold I, was distracted by a resumption in 1682 of war with the Turks in the east. The result was that France was able to annex large segments of territory until, in 1686, a league of other European states was formed to restrain Louis' growing power (see maps 17.1A and 17.1B).

Louis versus Europe   The leaders of the league were William III of the United Provinces and Emperor Leopold. Leopold was prepared to join the struggle because his war with the Turks turned in his favor after 1683, when his troops broke a Turkish siege of Vienna. And six years later William became a far more formidable foe when he gained the English throne. In 1688 the league finally went to war to put an end to French expansion. When Louis began to lose the territories he had gained in the 1680s, he decided to seek peace and

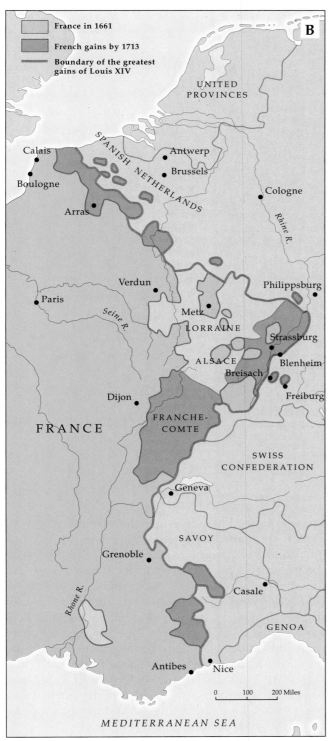

MAP 17.1B
THE WARS OF LOUIS XIV
The main conflict was on France's eastern border, where Louis made small but significant gains. Why was there so much conflict along this border?

◆ For an online version, go to www.mhhe.com/chambers9 > chapter 17 > book maps

remove Louvois from power in 1690, though the war did not end until 1697. But the respite did not last long. Four years later France became involved in a bitter war that brought famine, wretched poverty, and humiliation. This was a war to gain the Spanish throne for Louis' family, regardless of the devastating consequences of the fighting. This final, ruinous enterprise revealed both the new power of France and its limits. By launching an all-out attempt to establish his supremacy in Europe, Louis showed that he felt capable of taking on the whole of the continent; but by then he no longer had the economic and military base at home or the weak opposition abroad to ensure success.

Economic strains had begun to appear in the 1690s, when shattering famines throughout France reduced tax revenues and the size of the workforce, even as enemies began to unite abroad. Louis had the most formidable army in Europe—400,000 men by the end of his reign—but both William and Leopold believed he could be defeated by a combined assault, and they led the attack in the final showdown when the Habsburg king of Spain, Charles II, died without an heir in 1700.

The War of Spanish Succession   There were various claimants to the Spanish throne, but Charles's choice was Philip, Louis XIV's grandson (see "The Spanish Succession, 1700," p. 498). Had Louis been willing to agree not to unite the thrones of France and Spain and to allow the Spanish empire to be opened (for the first time) to foreign traders, Charles's wish might have been respected. But Louis refused to compromise, and in 1701 William and Leopold created the so-called Grand Alliance, which declared war on France the following year. The French now had to fight virtually all of Europe in a war over the Spanish succession, not only at home but also overseas, in India, Canada, and the Caribbean.

Led by two brilliant generals—the Englishman John Churchill, duke of Marlborough, and the Austrian Prince Eugène—the Grand Alliance won a series of smashing victories. France's hardships were increased by a terrible famine in 1709. Although the criticism of his policies became fierce and dangerous rebellions erupted, the Sun King retained his hold over his subjects. Despite military disaster, he was able to keep his nation's borders intact and the Spanish throne for his grandson (though he had to give up the possibility of union with France and end the restrictions on trade in the Spanish empire) when peace treaties were signed at Utrecht in 1713 and 1714. When it was all over, Louis' great task of state building, both at home and abroad, had withstood the severest of tests: defeat on the battlefield.

THE SPANISH SUCCESSION, 1700

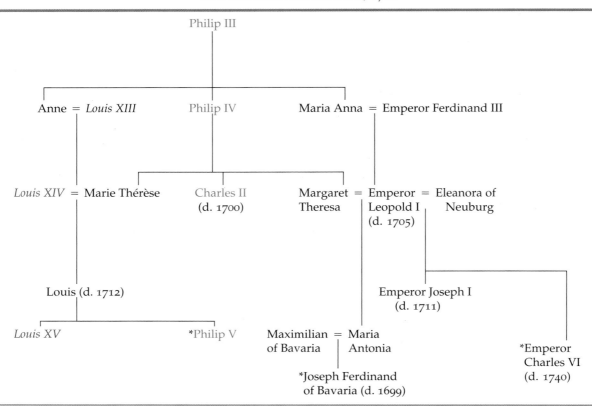

Note: Names in blue = kings of Spain; names in red = kings of France.
*People designated at various times as heirs of Charles II.

Domestic Policy

Control and Reform The assertion of royal supremacy at home was almost complete by the time Louis came to power, but he extended centralized control to religion and social institutions. Both the Protestant Huguenots and the Catholic Jansenists interfered with the religious uniformity that Louis considered essential in an absolutist state. As a result, pressures against these groups mounted steadily. In 1685 Louis revoked the Edict of Nantes, now almost a century old, which had granted Protestants limited toleration, and he forced France's 1 million Huguenots either to leave the country (four-fifths did) or to convert to Catholicism. This was a political rather than a religious step, taken to promote unity despite the economic consequences that followed the departure of a vigorous, productive, and entrepreneurial minority.

Jansenism was more elusive. It had far fewer followers, and it was a movement that emphasized spiritual values within Catholicism. But the very fact that it challenged the official Church emphasis on ritual and

was condemned by Rome made it a source of unrest. Even more unsettling was its success in gaining support among the magistrate class—the royal officers in the parlements, who had to register all royal edicts before they became law. The Parlement of Paris was the only governmental institution that offered Louis any real resistance. The issues over which it caused trouble were usually religious, and the link between *parlementaire* independence and Jansenism gave Louis more than enough reason for displeasure. He razed the Jansenists' headquarters, the Abbey of Port-Royal, and persuaded the pope to issue a bull condemning Jansenism. He was prevented from implementing the bull only by his death in 1715.

The drive toward uniformity that prompted these actions was reflected in all of domestic policy. Louis kept in check what little protest arose in the parlements and either forbade or overruled their efforts to block his decrees; major uprisings by peasants in central France in the 1690s and 1700s were ruthlessly suppressed; Parisian publishers came under bureaucratic supervision; and the *intendants*, the government's chief provincial officers, were given increased authority, especially to supply the ever-growing money and recruitment needs of the army.

At the outset of his rule, Louis also used his power to improve France's economy. In these early years, under Colbert's ministry, major efforts were made to stimulate manufacturing, agriculture, and home and foreign trade. Some industries, notably those involving luxuries, like the silk production of Lyons, received considerable help and owed their prosperity to royal patronage. Colbert also tried, not entirely effectively, to reduce the crippling effects of France's countless internal tolls. These were usually nobles' perquisites, and they could multiply the cost of shipped goods. The government divided the country into a number of districts, within which shipments were to be toll-free, but the system never removed the worst abuses. Louis also hoped to boost foreign trade, at first by financing new overseas trading companies and later by founding new port cities as naval and commercial centers. He achieved notable success only in the West Indies, where sugar plantations became a source of great wealth.

The End of an Era

Louis' success in state building was remarkable, and France became the envy of Europe. Yet ever since the Sun King's reign, historians have recalled the famines and wars of his last years and have contrasted his glittering court with the misery of most French people. Taxes and rents rose remorselessly, and in many regions the hardships were made worse by significant declines in the population. Particularly after the famines of the 1690s and 1709, many contemporaries remarked on the dreadful condition of France's peasants.

The reign of Louis XIV can thus be regarded as the end of an era in the life of the lower classes. By pushing his need for resources to its limits, he inflicted a level of suffering that was not to recur, because governments increasingly came to realize that state building depended on the welfare and support of their people. In the eighteenth century, although there was still much suffering to come, the terrible subsistence crises, with their cycles of famine and plague, came to an end, largely because of official efforts to distribute food in starving areas and to isolate and suppress outbreaks of plague. Thus, although the hand of the central government was heavier in 1715 than a hundred years before, it was becoming more obviously a beneficent as well as a burdensome force. The Counter-Reformation Church, growing in strength since the Council of Trent, also had a more salutary influence as religious struggles died away, for it brought into local parishes better-educated and more dedicated priests who, as part of their new commitment to service, exerted themselves to calm the outbreaks of witchcraft and irrational fear that had swept the countryside for centuries. Despite the strains Louis had caused, therefore, his absolutist authority was now firmly in place and could ensure a dominant European role for a united and powerful France.

France after Louis XIV

The Sun King had created a model for absolutism in partnership with his nobility, but the traditional ambitions of the nobles reasserted themselves after he died in 1715, leaving a child as his heir. The duke of Orlèans, Louis XIV's nephew, who became regent until 1723, sought to restore the aristocrats' authority. He also gave the parlements political power and replaced royal bureaucrats with councils composed of leading members of the nobility. The councils were unable to govern effectively, but the parlements would never again surrender their power to veto royal legislation. They became a rallying point for those who opposed centralization and wished to limit the king's powers.

Finance was also a serious problem for the government, because of the debts left by Louis XIV's wars. A brilliant Scottish financier, John Law, suggested an answer: a government-sponsored central bank that would issue paper notes, expand credit, and encourage investment in a new trading company for the French colonies. By tying the bank to this company, the Company of the Occident, a venture that promised subscribers vast profits from the Louisiana territory in North America, Law set off an investment boom. But the public's greed soon pushed prices for the company's stock to insanely high levels. A bust was inevitable, and when it came, in 1720, the entire scheme of bank notes and credit collapsed.

Louis XV and Fleury   Political and financial problems were to plague France throughout the eighteenth century, until the leaders of the French Revolution sought radical ways to solve them in the 1790s. Yet the uncertainties of the regency did give way to a long period of stability after 1726, when Louis XV gave almost unlimited authority to his aging tutor and adviser, Cardinal Fleury. Cautious, dedicated to the monarchy, and surrounded by talented subordinates, Fleury made absolutism function quietly and effectively and enabled France to recover from the setbacks that had marked the end of Louis XIV's reign. Fleury's tenure coincided with abundant harvests, slowly rising population, and increased commercial activity.

Political Problems   Fleury contained the ambitions of the governing class, but when he died in 1743 at the age of 90, the pressures exploded. War hawks plunged

HISTORICAL ISSUES: TWO VIEWS OF LOUIS XIV

Implicit in any assessment of the reign of Louis XIV in France is a judgment about the nature of absolutism and the kind of government the continental European monarchies created in the late seventeenth and eighteenth centuries. From the perspective of Frenchman Albert Sorel, a historian of the French Revolution writing at the end of the nineteenth century, the Revolution had been necessary to save France from Louis' heritage. For the American John Rule, a historian who concerned himself primarily with the development of political institutions during the seventeenth century, the marks of Louis XIV's rule were caution, bureaucracy, and order.

Sorel: "The edifice of the state enjoyed incomparable brilliance and splendor, but it resembled a Gothic cathedral in which the height of the nave and the arches had been pushed beyond all reason, weakening the walls as they were raised ever higher. Louis XIV carried the principle of monarchy to its utmost limit, and abused it in all respects to the point of excess. He left the nation crushed by war, mutilated by banishments, and impatient of the yoke which it felt to be ruinous. Men were worn-out, the treasury empty, all relationships strained by the violence of tension, and in the immense framework of the state there remained no institution except the accidental appearance of genius. Things had reached a point where, if a great king did not appear, there would be a great revolution."

From Albert Sorel, *L'Europe et la révolution française,* 3rd ed., Vol. 1, Paris, 1893, p. 199, as translated in William F. Church (ed.), *The Greatness of Louis XIV: Myth or Reality?,* Boston: D. C. Heath, 1959, p. 63.

Rule: "As Louis XIV himself said of the tasks of kingship, they were at once great, noble, and delightful. Yet Louis' enjoyment of his craft was tempered by political prudence. At an early age he learned to listen attentively to his advisers, to speak when spoken to, to ponder evidence, to avoid confrontations, to dissemble, to wait. He believed that time and tact would conquer. Despite all the evidence provided him by his ministers and his servants, Louis often hesitated before making a decision; he brooded, and in some instances put off decisions altogether. As he grew older, the king tended to hide his person and his office. Even his officials seldom saw the king for more than a brief interview. And as decision-making became centralized in the hands of the ministers, [so] the municipalities, the judges, the local estates, the guilds and at times the peasantry contested royal encroachments on their rights. Yet to many in the kingdom, Louis represented a modern king, an agent of stability whose struggle was their struggle and whose goal was to contain the crises of the age."

From John C. Rule, "Louis XIV, *Roi-Bureaucrate,*" in Rule (ed.), *Louis XIV and the Craft of Kingship,* Columbus: Ohio State University Press, 1969, pp. 91–92.

France into the first of several unsuccessful wars with its neighbors that strained French credit to the breaking point. At home royal authority also deteriorated. Having no one to replace Fleury as chief minister, Louis XV put his confidence in a succession of advisers, some capable, some mediocre. But he did not back them when attacks arose from court factions. Uninterested in government, he avoided confrontation, neglected affairs of state, and devoted himself instead to hunting and to court ceremony.

Although Louis XV provided weak leadership, France's difficulties were structural as well as personal. The main problems—special privileges and finance—posed almost impossible challenges. Governments that levy new taxes arbitrarily seem despotic, even if the need for them is clear and the distribution equitable. One of France's soundest taxes was the *vingtième,* or twentieth, which was supposed to tap the income of all

parts of French society roughly equally. But the nobility and clergy evaded most of the tax. Naturally, aggressive royal ministers wanted to remedy that situation. In the 1750s, for example, an effort was made to put teeth into the *vingtième's* bite on the clergy's huge wealth. But the effort failed. The clergy resisted furiously; and the parlements denounced the "despotism" of a crown that taxed its subjects arbitrarily. Thus, the privileged groups not only blocked reforms but also made the monarch's position more difficult by their opposition and rhetoric of liberty.

The Long Term   Despite these special interests, the 1700s were a time of notable advance for Europe's most populous and wealthy state. France enjoyed remarkable expansion in population, in the rural economy, in commerce, and in empire building. No one knew at the time that the failures of reforming royal ministers in

Pierre Denis Martin
Procession after Louis XV's Coronation at Rheims, 26 October 1722, ca. 1724
This magnificent scene, in front of the cathedral in which French kings traditionally were crowned, provides a sense of the throngs who came to celebrate the day in 1722 when Louis XV officially came of age and received his crown. Paintings depicting royal virtue were erected around the cathedral, and Louis himself (in red on a white horse just to the right of center) was preceded by a flag covered with his symbol, the fleur-de-lis. The other flags remind us that this event was an occasion for international pageantry.
Giraudon/Art Resource, NY

the mid-1700s foretold a stalemate that would help bring the old regime crashing down.

Other Patterns of Absolutism

Four other monarchies pursued state building through absolutist regimes in this period, often in imitation of the French model. The governments they created in Vienna, Berlin, Madrid, and St. Petersburg differed in strengths and weaknesses, but all were attempts to centralize power around a formidable ruler.

The Habsburgs at Vienna

The closest imitation of Versailles was the court of the Habsburg Leopold I, the Holy Roman emperor (1658–1705). Heir to a reduced inheritance that gave him control over only Bohemia, Austria, and a small part of

Hungary, Leopold still maintained a splendid establishment. His plans for a new palace, Schönbrunn, that was supposed to outshine Versailles were modified only because of a lack of funds. And his promotion of the court as the center of all political and social life turned Vienna into what it had never been before: a city for nobles as well as small-time traders.

Nevertheless, Leopold did not display the pretensions of the Sun King. He was a younger son and had come to the throne only because of the death of his brother. Indecisive, retiring, and deeply religious, he had no fondness for the bravado Louis XIV enjoyed. He was a composer of some talent, and his patronage laid the foundation for the great musical culture that was to be one of Vienna's chief glories. But he did inherit considerable royal authority, which he sought to expand—though unlike Louis XIV he relied on a small group of leading nobles to devise policy and run his government.

Government Policy   The Thirty Years' War that ended in 1648 had revealed that the elected head of the Holy Roman Empire could no longer control the princes who nominally owed him allegiance. In his own domains, however, he could maintain his control with the cooperation of his nobility. The Privy Council, which in effect ran Leopold's government, was filled largely with members of aristocratic families, and his chief advisers were always prominent nobles. To make policy, he consulted each of his ministers and then, even when all agreed, came to decisions with agonizing slowness.

Unlike the other courts of Europe, Schönbrunn did not favor only native-born aristocrats. The leader of Austria's armies during the Turks' siege of Vienna in 1683 was Charles, duke of Lorraine, whose duchy had been taken over by the French. His predecessor as field marshal had been an Italian, and his successor was to be one of the most brilliant soldiers of the age, Prince Eugène of Savoy. They became members of the Austrian nobility only when Leopold gave them titles within his own dominions, but they all fitted easily into the aristocratic circles that controlled the government and the army.

Eugène and Austria's Military Success   Prince Eugène (1663–1736) was a spectacular symbol of the aristocracy's continuing dominance of politics and society. A member of one of Europe's most distinguished families, he had been raised in France but found himself passed over when Louis XIV awarded army commissions, perhaps because he had been intended for the Church. Yet he was determined to have a military career, and he volunteered to serve the Austrians in the war with the Turks that, following the siege of Vienna, was to expand Habsburg territory in the Balkans by the time peace was signed in 1699 (see map 17.2). Eugène's talents quickly became evident: He was field marshal of Austria's troops by the time he was 30. Over the next forty years, as intermittent war with the Turks continued, he became a decisive influence in Habsburg affairs. Though foreign-born, he was the minister primarily responsible for the transformation of Vienna's policies from defensive to aggressive.

Until the siege of Vienna by the Turks in 1683, Leopold's cautiousness kept Austria simply holding the line, both against Louis XIV and against the Turks. In the 1690s, however, at Eugène's urging, he tried a bolder course and in the process laid the foundations for a new Habsburg empire along the Danube River: Austria-Hungary. He helped create the coalition that defeated Louis in the 1700s, he intervened in Italy so that his landlocked domains could gain an outlet to the sea, and he began the long process of pushing the Turks out of the Balkans. Although Leopold did not live to see the advance completed, by the time of Eugène's death, the Austrians' progress against the Turks had brought them within a hundred miles of the Black Sea.

The Power of the Nobility   Yet the local power of the nobility tempered the centralization of Leopold's dominions. Unlike Louis XIV, who supported his nobles only if they worked for him, Leopold gave them influence in the government without first establishing control over all his lands. The nobles did not cause the Habsburgs as much trouble as they had during the Thirty Years' War, but Leopold had to limit his centralization outside Austria. Moreover, as Austrians came increasingly to dominate the court, the nobles of Hungary and Bohemia reacted by clinging stubbornly to their local rights. Thus, compared to France, Leopold's was an absolutism under which the nobility retained far more autonomous power.

The Hohenzollerns at Berlin

The one new power that emerged to prominence during the age of Louis XIV was Brandenburg-Prussia, and here again state building was made possible by a close alliance between a powerful ruler and his nobles. Frederick William of Hohenzollern (r. 1640–1688), known as the "great elector," ruled scattered territories that stretched seven hundred miles from Cleves, on the Rhine, to a part of Prussia on the Baltic. That so fragmented and disconnected a set of lands could be shaped into a major European power was a testimony to the political abilities of the Hohenzollerns. The process began when, taking advantage of the uncertainties that followed the Thirty Years' War, Frederick William made his territories the dominant principality in northern Germany and at the same time strengthened his power over his subjects.

Foreign Policy   His first task was in foreign affairs, because when he became elector, the troops of the various states that were fighting the Thirty Years' War swarmed over his possessions. Frederick William realized that even a minor prince could emerge from these disasters in a good position if he had an army. With some military force at his disposal, he could become a useful ally for the big powers, who could then help him against his neighbors; while at home he would have the strength to crush his opponents.

By 1648 Frederick William had eight thousand troops, and he was backed by both the Dutch and the French in the Westphalia negotiations that year as a possible restraint on Sweden in northern Europe. With-

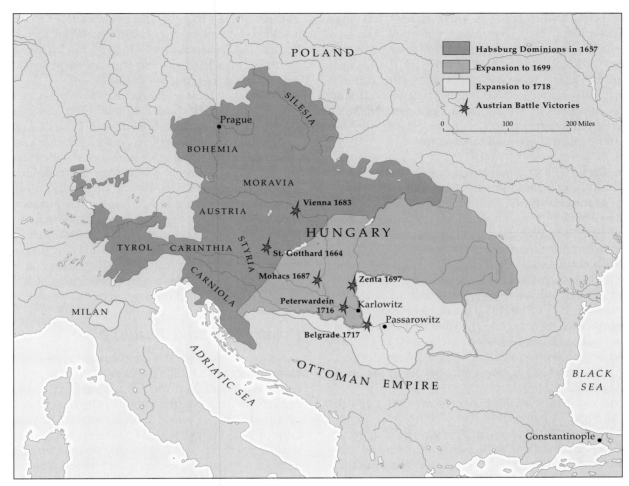

MAP 17.2 THE AUSTRIAN EMPIRE, 1657–1718
The steady advance of the Habsburgs into the Balkans was marked by a succession of victories; their gains were confirmed by treaties with the Turks at Karlowitz (1699) and Passarowitz (1718). How much bigger were Habsburg dominions in 1718 than they were in 1657?

◆ For an online version, go to www.mhhe.com/chambers9 > chapter 17 > book maps

out having done much to earn new territory, he did very well in the peace settlement, and he then took advantage of wars around the Baltic in the 1650s to confirm his gains by switching sides at crucial moments. In the process, his army grew to twenty-two thousand men, and he began to use it to impose his will on his own lands. The fact that the army was essential to Frederick William's success—at home and abroad—was to influence much of Prussia's and thus also Germany's subsequent history.

Domestic Policy   The role of the military in establishing the elector's supremacy was apparent throughout Brandenburg-Prussia's society. In 1653 the Diet of Brandenburg met for the last time, sealing its own fate by giving Frederick William the right to raise taxes without its consent. The War Chest, the office in charge of financing the army, took over the functions of a treasury department and collected government revenue even when the state was at peace. The implementation of policies in the localities was placed in the hands of war commissars—who originally were responsible for military recruitment, billeting, and supply but now became the principal agents of all government departments.

Apart from the representative assemblies, Frederick William faced real resistance only from the long-independent cities of his realm. Accustomed to going their own way because authority had been fragmented in the empire for centuries, and especially during the Thirty Years' War, city leaders were dismayed when the elector began to intervene in their affairs. Yet once again sheer intimidation overcame opposition. The last determined effort to dispute his authority arose in the rich city of Königsberg, which allied with the Estates General of Prussia to refuse to pay taxes. But this resistance was crushed in 1662, when Frederick William marched into the city with a few thousand troops. Similar pressure brought the towns of Cleves into submission after centuries of proud independence.

The Junkers The main supporters and beneficiaries of the elector's state building were the Prussian nobles, known as **Junkers** (from the German for "young lord," *jung herr*). In fact, it was an alliance between the nobility and Frederick William that undermined the Diet, the cities, and the representative assemblies. The leading Junker families saw their best opportunities for the future in cooperation with the central government, and both in the representative assemblies and in the localities, they worked to establish absolutist power—that is, to remove all restraints on the elector. The most significant indicator of the Junkers' success was that by the end of the century, two tax rates had been devised, one for cities and one for the countryside, to the great advantage of the latter.

As the nobles staffed the upper levels of the elector's army and bureaucracy, they also won new prosperity for themselves. Particularly in Prussia, the support of the elector enabled them to reimpose serfdom and consolidate their land holdings into vast, highly profitable estates. This area was a major grain producer, and the Junkers maximized their profits by growing and distributing their produce themselves, thus eliminating middlemen. Efficiency became their hallmark, and their wealth was soon famous throughout the Holy Roman Empire. These Prussian entrepreneurs were probably the most successful group of European aristocrats in pursuing economic and political power.

Frederick III Unlike Louis in France, Frederick William had little interest in court life. The Berlin court became the focus of society only under his son, Elector Frederick III, who ruled from 1688. The great elector had begun the development of his capital, Berlin, into a cultural center—he founded what was to become one of the finest libraries in the world, the Prussian State Library—but this was never among his prime concerns. His son, by contrast, had little interest in state building, but he did enjoy princely pomp and encouraged the arts with enthusiasm.

Frederick III lacked only one attribute of royalty: a crown. When Emperor Leopold I, who still had the right to confer titles in the empire, needed Prussia's troops during the War of the Spanish Succession, he gave Frederick, in return, the right to call himself "king in Prussia"; the title soon became "king of Prussia." At a splendid coronation in 1701, Elector Frederick III of Brandenburg was crowned King Frederick I, and thereafter his court felt itself the equal of the other monarchical centers of Europe.

Frederick determinedly promoted social and cultural glitter. He made his palace a focus of art and polite society that competed, he hoped, with Versailles. A construction program beautified Berlin with new churches and huge public buildings. He also established an Academy of Sciences and persuaded the most famous German scientist and philosopher of the day, Gottfried Wilhelm von Leibniz, to become its first president. All these activities obtained generous support from state revenues, as did the universities of Brandenburg and Prussia. By the end of his reign in 1713, Frederick had given his realm a throne, celebrated artistic and intellectual activity, and an elegant aristocracy at the head of social and political life.

Rivalry and State Building

Europe's increasingly self-confident states were in constant rivalry with their neighbors during the eighteenth century. The competition intensified their state building, because the conflicts forced rulers to expand their revenues, armies, and bureaucracies. The counterexample was Poland, which failed to centralize and was partitioned three times by Russia, Austria, and Prussia, until in 1795 it ceased to exist as a sovereign state. Political consolidation, by putting a premium on military and economic power, shaped both the map of modern Europe and the centralization of the major states.

The relationship between international rivalry and internal development is well illustrated by Prussia and Austria. In the mid-eighteenth century these two powers sought to dominate central Europe, and they launched reforms to wage their struggle more effectively. Their absolute rulers built their states by increasing the size of their armies, collecting larger revenues, and developing bureaucracies for the war effort. Whether the ruler was a modern pragmatist like Frederick II of Prussia or a pious traditionalist like Maria Theresa of Austria, both understood the demands of the state system.

The Prussia of Frederick William I

Prussia's Frederick William I (r. 1713–1740) relentlessly pursued a strengthened absolutism at home and Europe-wide influence abroad. Strikingly different from his refined father, this spartan ruler approached affairs of state as all business and little pleasure. He disdained court life, dismissed numerous courtiers, and cut the salaries of those who remained. Uncluttered by royal cere-

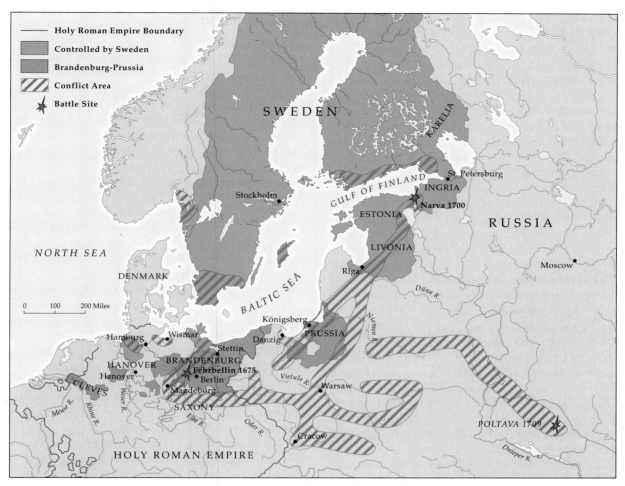

MAP 17.3 CONFLICT IN THE BALTIC AREA, 1660–1721
The fighting around the Baltic eventually destroyed Sweden's power in northern Europe; the new powers were to be Brandenburg-Prussia and Russia. At what point did Sweden no longer dominate the Baltic?
◆ For an online version, go to www.mhhe.com/chambers9 > chapter 17 > book maps

monies, his days were strictly regulated as he attempted to supervise all government activities personally.

Emphasis on the Military   It has been said that Frederick William I organized his state to serve his military power. During his reign the army grew from 38,000 to 83,000, making it the fourth largest in Europe, behind France, Russia, and Austria. And all his soldiers had to undergo intensive drilling and wear standardized uniforms. Determined to build an effective force, he forbade his subjects to serve in foreign armies and compelled the sons of nobles to attend cadet schools to learn martial skills and attitudes. But Frederick William did not intend to die in battle. For all his involvement with military life, he avoided committing his army to battle and was able to pass it on intact to his son.

Centralization kept pace with the growth of the army. In 1723 the General Directory of Finance, War, and Do-

mains took over all government functions except justice, education, and religion. A super-agency, it collected revenues and oversaw expenditures (mostly military) and local administration. Even education was seen merely as a way to encourage people to serve the state. Frederick made education compulsory for all children, ordering local communities to set up schools where there were none, though he never enforced these decrees. Uninterested in intellectual pursuits for their own sake, the king allowed the universities to decline; they did not fit his relentless vision of how to build his state.

Frederick the Great

Frederick William I's most notable triumph, perhaps, was the grooming of his successor. This was no mean task. Frederick II (r. 1740–1786) seemed opposite in temperament to his father and little inclined to follow in his footsteps. The father was a God-fearing German Protestant. The son disdained German culture and was a deist (see p. 558). Sentimental and artistically inclined, Frederick II was a composer of music who played the flute, wrote poetry, and greatly admired French culture. He even wrote philosophical treatises and corresponded with leading European intellectuals.

But the young prince was not exempt from the effort to draw all Prussians into the task of state building. On the contrary: His father forced him to work at all levels of the state apparatus so as to experience them directly, from shoveling hay on a royal farm to marching with the troops. The father trained his son for kingship, reshaping his personality, giving him a sense of duty, and toughening him for leadership. Despite Frederick's resistance, this hard apprenticeship succeeded.

Frederick's Absolutism

When he assumed the throne in 1740, Frederick II was prepared to lead Prussia in a ruthless struggle for power and territory. While his intellectual turn of mind caused him to agonize over moral issues and the nature of his role, he never flinched from exercising power. But he did try to justify absolutism at home and aggression abroad. He claimed undivided power for the ruler, not because the dynasty had a divine mission but because only absolute rule could bring results. The king, he said, was the first servant of the state, and in the long run an enlightened monarch might lead his people to a more rational and moral existence. Some of his objectives, such as religious toleration and judicial reform, he could reach at once, and by putting them into effect Frederick gained a reputation as an **"enlightened" absolutist.**

But these were minor matters. The paramount issue, security, provided the best justification for absolutism. Success here required Prussia to improve its vulnerable geographic position by acquiring more territory, stronger borders, and the power to face other European states as an equal. Until that was achieved, Frederick would not consider the domestic reforms that might disrupt the flow of taxes or men into the army, or provoke his nobility. The capture of territory was his most singular contribution to the rise of Prussia and what earned him his title of Frederick the Great. As it happened, a suitable task for his army presented itself in the year Frederick II came to the throne, 1748—an attack on the province of Silesia, which the Habsburgs controlled but were unable to defend. Prussia had no claim to the province; it was simply a wealthy neighboring domain that would expand Prussia's territory. Yet the conquest of Silesia brought to a new level the state building that the great elector had begun in 1648; the reaction also shaped state building in the Habsburg Empire.

The Habsburg Empire

The Habsburg Empire was like a dynastic holding company of diverse territories under one crown: Austria, Bohemia, Hungary, and other possessions such as the Austrian Netherlands, Lombardy, and Tuscany. The emperors hoped to integrate Austria, Bohemia, and Hungary into a Catholic, centralized, German-speaking super-state. But the traditional representative assemblies in these provinces resisted such centralization.

International Rivalry

In the reign of Leopold's successor, Charles VI (r. 1711–1740), yet another problem complicated the destiny of this multinational empire, for his only heir was his daughter, Maria Theresa. In 1713 Charles drafted a document known as the Pragmatic Sanction, declaring that all Habsburg dominions would pass intact to the eldest heir, male or female; and for the next twenty-five years he sought recognition of the Pragmatic Sanction from the European powers. By making all kinds of concessions and promises, he won this recognition on paper. But when he died in 1740, his daughter found that the commitments were worthless: The succession was challenged by force from several sides. Concentrating on diplomacy alone, Charles had neglected the work of state building, leaving an empty treasury, an inadequately trained army, and an ineffective bureaucracy.

In contrast to Austria, Prussia had a full treasury, a powerful army, and a confident ruler, Frederick II, who seized the Habsburg province of Silesia without qualm. His justification was simply **"reasons of state,"** combined with the Habsburgs' faltering fortunes. And Maria Theresa had her hands more than full, because the French declared war on her to support their ally Bavaria's claim to the Habsburg throne. Meanwhile, Spain hoped to win back control of Austria's Italian possessions. Worse yet, Maria Theresa faced a rebellion by the Czech nobles in Bohemia. Her position would probably have been hopeless if Hungary's Magyar nobles had followed suit. But Maria Theresa promised them autonomy within the Habsburg Empire, and they offered her the troops she needed to resist the invaders.

The War of Austrian Succession

In the War of Austrian Succession (1740–1748) that followed, Maria Theresa learned the elements of state building. With her Hungarian troops and with financial help from her one ally, Britain, she fought her opponents to a stalemate. Frederick's conquest of Silesia proved to be the only significant territorial change produced by the war. Even for England and France, who fought the war mainly in overseas colonies, it was a standoff. But Maria Theresa was now determined to recover Silesia

E. F. Cunningham
THE RETURN OF FREDERICK II FROM A MANEUVRE, **1787**
Were it not for the richly embroidered saddle cover and the fine white horse, Frederick the Great would be hard to spot among his officers. Nor is there anything to indicate that the two men on the black and brown horses behind him are his nephew and grandnephew. This sober evocation of a king as a professional soldier contrasts strikingly with earlier glorifications (see painting, p. 419).
Staatliche Museen Preussischer Kulturbesitz Nationalgalerie/BPK Berlin

and humiliate Prussia, and this required a determined effort of state building.

Maria Theresa   The woman whose authority was established not by her father's negotiations but by force of arms was a marked contrast to her archenemy, Frederick. The Prussian king was practical and irreligious; Maria Theresa was moralistic and pious. Her personality and her ruling style were deceptively traditional, however, for she was a shrewd innovator in the business of building and reasserting the power of her state.

Unlike Frederick, Maria Theresa had a strong regard for her dynasty. In this respect, being a woman made no difference to the policies or government of the empire. She believed in the divine mission of the Habsburgs and conscientiously attended to the practical needs of her realm.

Reform in Church and State   It was because she put the state's interests first that this most pious of Catholic sovereigns—who disdained religious toleration and loathed atheists—felt obliged to reform the Church. Responding to waste and self-interest in her monasteries, she forbade the founding of new establishments. She also abolished the clergy's exemptions from taxes, something the French king found impossible to do.

A new bureaucratic apparatus was constructed on the models of French and Prussian absolutism. In Vienna, reorganized central ministries recruited staffs of experts. In the provinces, new agents were appointed who were largely free of local interests, though some concession did have to be made to the regional traditions of the Habsburg realm. The core domains (excluding Hungary and the Italian possessions) were reorganized into ten provinces, each subdivided into

Martin van Meytens
MARIA THERESA AND HER FAMILY, **1750**
Although the setting is just as splendid, the portrayal of Maria Theresa with her husband and thirteen of her sixteen children suggests a domesticity that is absent from Louis XIV's family portrait of half a century before (see painting, p. 490).
Galleria Palatina, Palazzo Pitti, Florence, Italy. Scala/Art Resource, NY

districts directed by royal officials. With the help of these officials, the central government could wrest new taxes from the local diets. Meanwhile, Maria Theresa

brought important nobles from all her domains to Vienna to participate in its social and administrative life. She also reformed the military, improving the training of troops and establishing academies to produce a more professional officer corps. Thus did international needs help shape domestic political reforms.

Habsburgs and Bourbons at Madrid

In Spain the Habsburgs had little success in state building either at home or abroad. The king who followed Philip IV, Charles II (r. 1665–1700), was a sickly man, incapable of having children; and the War of the Spanish Succession seriously reduced the inheritance he left. Both the southern Netherlands and most of Italy passed to the Austrian Habsburgs, and Spain's overseas possessions often paid little notice to the homeland.

The Spanish nobility was even more successful than the Austrian in turning absolutism to its advantage. In 1650 the crown had been able to recapture Catalonia's loyalty only by granting the province's aristocracy virtual autonomy, and this pattern recurred throughout Spain's territories. Parasitic, unproductive nobles controlled the regime, often for personal gain. The country fell into economic and cultural stagnation, subservient to a group of powerful families, with its former glory visible mainly in its strong navy.

Bourbon Spain Yet Spain and its vast overseas possessions remained a force in eighteenth-century affairs. When the Bourbons gained the crown, following the War of Spanish Succession, they ended the traditional independence of Aragon, Catalonia, and Valencia and integrated these provinces into the kind of united Spain Olivares had sought eighty years earlier. They imported the position of *intendant* from France to administer the provinces, and although the nobles remained far more independent, the Bourbons did begin to impose uniform procedures on the country. In midcentury the ideas of enlightened absolutism that were visible elsewhere in Europe had their effect, largely because of a liberal reformer, Count Pedro de Campomanes. The most remarkable change concerned the religious order that had been identified with Spain since the days of its founder, Loyola: the Jesuits. They had become too powerful and too opposed to reform, and so they were expelled from Spanish territory in 1767.

In a sense, though, the Jesuits were to have their revenge. Spain's colonies in America were flourishing in the eighteenth century: Their trade with Europe was booming; they were attracting new settlers; and by 1800 they had over 14 million inhabitants. But they were still subject to the same absolutist control as the homeland. It was largely under the inspiration of disgruntled Jesuits that the idea of breaking free from Spain took hold in the empire, an idea that led to the independence movements of the 1800s.

Peter the Great at St. Petersburg

One of the reasons the new absolutist regimes of the late seventeenth and eighteenth centuries seemed so different from their predecessors was that many of them consciously created new settings for themselves. Versailles, Schönbrunn, and Berlin were all either new or totally transformed sites for royal courts. But only one of the autocrats of the period went so far as to build an entirely new capital: Tsar Peter I (the Great) of Russia (1682–1725), who named the new city St. Petersburg after his patron saint.

Peter's Fierce Absolutism None of the state-building rulers of the period had Peter's terrifying energy or ruthless determination to exercise absolute control. He was only nine when he was chosen tsar, and in his early years, when his sister and his mother were the effective rulers, he witnessed ghastly massacres of members of his family and their associates by soldiers in Moscow. Like little Louis XIV, endangered by Paris mobs during the Fronde, Peter determined to leave his capital city. Soon after he assumed full powers in 1696, therefore, he shifted his court to St. Petersburg, despite thousands of deaths among the peasants who were forced to build the city in a cold and inhospitable swamp. Well over six feet tall—a giant by the standards of the time—Peter terrorized those around him, especially during his many drunken rages. His only son, Alexis, a weak and retiring figure, became the focus of opposition to the tsar, and Peter had him put in prison, where Alexis mysteriously died. Peter refused even to attend his funeral.

Western Models Early in his reign, Peter suffered a humiliating military defeat at the hands of the Swedes. This merely confirmed his view that, in order to compete with Europe's powers, he had to bring to Russia some of the advances the Western nations had recently made. To observe these achievements firsthand, Peter traveled incognito through France, England, and the Netherlands in 1697 and 1698, paying special attention to economic, administrative, and military practices (such as the functioning of a Dutch shipyard). Many of his initiatives were to derive from this journey, including his importation of Western court rituals, his founding of an Academy of Sciences in 1725, and his encouragement of the first Russian newspaper.

Italian artists were brought to Russia, along with Scandinavian army officers, German engineers, and Dutch shipbuilders, not only to apply their skills but also to teach them to the Russians. St. Petersburg, the finest eighteenth-century city built in Classical style, is mainly the work of Italians. But gradually Russians

PETER THE GREAT AT ST. PETERSBURG
In the eighteenth century Peter the Great of Russia outstripped the grandeur of other monarchs of the period by erecting an entirely new city for his capital. St. Petersburg was built by forced labor of the peasants under Peter's orders; they are shown here laying the foundations for the city.
Tass/Sovfoto

took over their own institutions—military academies produced native officers, for example—and by the end of Peter's reign they had little need of foreign experts.

Bureaucratization In ruling Russia, Peter virtually ignored the Duma, the traditional advisory council, and concentrated instead on his bureaucracy. He carried out countless changes until he had created an administrative apparatus much larger than the one he had inherited. Here again he copied Western models—notably Prussia, where nobles ran the bureaucracy and the army, and Sweden, where a complex system of government departments had been created. Peter organized his administration into similar departments: Each had either a specialized function, such as finance, or responsibility for a geographic area, such as Siberia. The result was an elaborate but unified hierarchy of authority, rising from local agents of the government through provincial officials up to the staffs and governors of eleven large administrative units and finally to the leaders of the regime in the capital. Peter began the saturating bureaucratization that characterized Russia from that time on.

The Imposition of Social Order The tsar's policies laid the foundations for a two-class society that persisted until the twentieth century. Previously, a number of ranks had existed within both the nobility and the peasantry, and a group in the middle was seen sometimes as the lowest nobles and sometimes as the highest peasants. Under Peter such mingling disappeared. All peasants were reduced to one level, subject to a new poll tax, military conscription, and forced

public work, such as the building of St. Petersburg. Below them were serfs, whose numbers were increased by legislation restricting their movement. Peasants had a few advantages over serfs, such as the freedom to move, but their living conditions were often equally dreadful. Serfdom itself spread throughout all areas of Peter's dominions and became essential to his state building because, on royal lands as well as the estates of the nobles, serfs worked and ran the agricultural enterprise that was Russia's economic base.

At the same time, Peter created a single class of nobles by substituting status within the bureaucracy for status within the traditional hierarchy of titles. In 1722 he issued a table of bureaucratic ranks that gave everyone a place according to the office he held. Differentiations still existed, but they were no longer unbridgeable, as they had been when family was the decisive determinant of status. The result was a more controlled social order and greater uniformity than in France or Brandenburg-Prussia. The Russian aristocracy was the bureaucracy, and the bureaucracy the aristocracy.

The Subjugation of the Nobility This was not a voluntary alliance between nobles and government, such as existed in the West; in return for his support and his total subjection of the peasantry, Peter required the nobles to provide officials for his bureaucracy and officers for his army. When he began the construction of St. Petersburg, he also demanded that the leading families build splendid mansions in his new capital. In effect, the tsar offered privilege and wealth in exchange for conscription into public service. Thus, there was hardly any sense of partnership between nobility and throne: The tsar often had to use coercion to ensure that his wishes were followed. On the other hand, Peter helped build up the nobles' fortunes and their control of the countryside. It has been estimated that by 1710 he had put under the supervision of great landowners more than forty thousand peasant and serf households that had formerly been under the crown. And he was liberal in conferring new titles—some of them, such as count and baron, copies of German examples.

Control of the Church   Peter's determination to stamp his authority on Russia was also apparent in his destruction of ecclesiastical independence. He accomplished this with one blow: He simply did not replace the patriarch of the Russian Church who died in 1700. Peter took over the monasteries and their vast income for his own purposes and appointed a procurator (at first an army officer) to supervise religious affairs. The Church was, in effect, made a branch of government.

Military Expansion   The purpose of all these radical changes was to assert the tsar's power both at home and abroad. Peter established a huge standing army, more than three hundred thousand strong by the 1720s, and imported the latest military techniques from the West. One of Peter's most cherished projects, the creation of a navy, had limited success, but there could be no doubt that he transformed Russia's capacity for war and its position among European states. He extended Russia's frontier to the south and west, and, at the battle of Poltava in 1709, reversed his early defeat by the Swedes. This victory began the dismantling of Sweden's empire, for it was followed by more than a decade of Russian advance into Estonia, Livonia, and Poland. The very vastness of his realm justified Peter's drive for absolute control, and by the time of his death he had made Russia the dominant power in the Baltic and a major influence in European affairs.

ALTERNATIVES TO ABSOLUTISM

The absolutist regimes offered one model of political and social organization, but an alternative model—equally committed to uniformity, order, and state building—was also created in the late seventeenth century: governments dominated by aristocrats or merchants. The contrast between the two was noted by contemporary political theorists, especially opponents of absolutism, who preferred **constitutionalism.** And yet the differences were often less sharp than the theorists suggested, mainly because the position of the aristocracy was similar throughout Europe.

Aristocracy in the United Provinces, Sweden, and Poland

In the Dutch republic, the succession of William III to the office of Stadholder in 1672 seemed to be a move toward absolutism. As he led the successful resistance to Louis XIV in war (1672–1678), he increasingly concentrated government in his own hands. Soon, however, the power of merchants and provincial leaders in the Estates General reasserted itself. William did not want to sign a peace treaty with Louis when the French invasion failed. He wanted instead to take the war into France and reinforce his own authority by keeping the position of commander in chief. But the Estates General, led by the province of Holland, ended the war.

A decade later William sought the English crown, but he did so only with the approval of the Estates General, and he had to leave separate the representative assemblies that governed the two countries. When William died without an heir, his policies were continued by his close friend Antonius Heinsius, who held the same position of grand pensionary of Holland that Jan de Witt had once occupied; but the government was in effect controlled by the Estates General. This representative assembly now had to preside over the decline of a great power. In finance and trade, the Dutch were gradually overtaken by the English, while in the war against Louis XIV, they had to support the crippling burden of maintaining a land force, only to hand over command to England.

Dutch Society   The aristocrats of the United Provinces differed from the usual European pattern. Instead of ancient families and bureaucratic dynasties, they boasted merchants and mayors. The prominent citizens of the leading cities were the backbone of the Dutch upper classes. Moreover, social distinctions were less prominent than in any other country of Europe. The elite was composed of hard-working financiers and traders, richer and more powerful but not essentially more privileged or leisured than those farther down the social ladder. The inequality described in much eighteenth-century political writing—the special place nobles had, often including some immunity from the law—was far less noticeable in the United Provinces. There was no glittering court, and although here as elsewhere a small group controlled the country, it did so for largely economic ends and in different style.

Sweden   The Swedes created yet another nonabsolutist model of state building. After a long struggle with the king, the nobles emerged as the country's dominant political force. During the reign of Charles XI (1660–1697), the monarchy was able to force the great lords to return to the state the huge tracts of land they

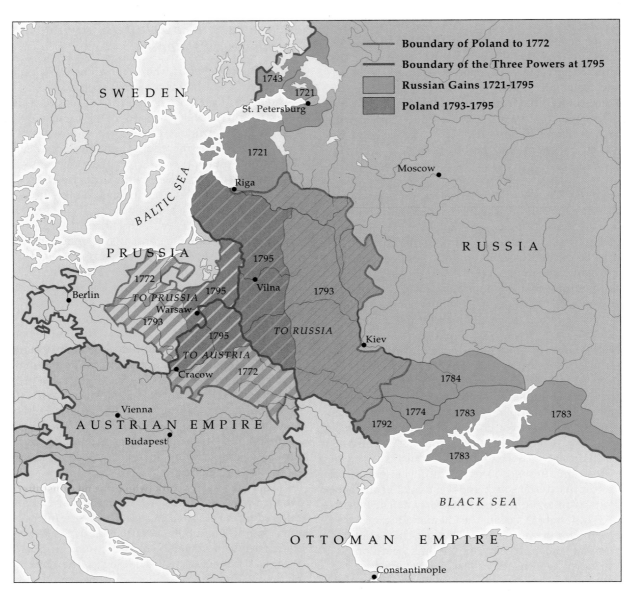

MAP 17.4 THE EXPANSION OF RUSSIA AND THE PARTITION OF POLAND
All three of the powers in Eastern Europe—Prussia, Russia, and Austria—gained territory from the dismemberment of Poland. Which country was the chief beneficiary of the partition? In addition to the territory it gained from Poland, where else was Russia expanding in the period 1721–1795?
◆ For an online version, go to www.mhhe.com/chambers9 > chapter 17 > book maps

had received as rewards for loyalty earlier in the century. Since Charles stayed out of Europe's wars, he was able to conserve his resources and avoid relying on the nobility as he strengthened the smoothly running bureaucracy he had inherited from Gustavus Adolphus.

His successor, Charles XII (r. 1697–1718), however, revived Sweden's tradition of military conquest. He won land from Peter the Great, but then made the fatal decision to invade Russia. Defeated at the battle of Poltava in 1709, Charles had to retreat and watch helplessly as the Swedish Empire was dismembered. By the

time he was killed in battle nine years later, his neighbors had begun to overrun his lands, and, in treaties signed from 1719 to 1721, Sweden reverted to roughly the territory it had had a century before.

Naturally, the nobles took advantage of Charles XII's frequent absences to reassert their authority. They ran Sweden's highly efficient government while he was campaigning and forced his successor, Queen Ulrika, to accept a constitution that gave the Riksdag effective control over the country. The new structure, modeled on England's political system, gave the nobility the role of the English gentry—leaders of society and the shapers of its politics. A splendid court arose, and Stockholm became one of the more elegant and cultured aristocratic centers in Europe.

Poland   Warsaw fared less well. In fact, the strongest contrast to the French political and social model in the late seventeenth century was Poland. The sheer chaos and disunity that plagued Poland until it ceased to exist as a state in the late eighteenth century were the direct result of continued dominance by the old landed aristocracy, which blocked all attempts to centralize the government. There were highly capable kings in this period—notably John III, who achieved Europe-wide fame by relieving Vienna from the Turkish siege in 1683. These monarchs could quite easily gather an army to fight, and fight well, against Poland's many foes: Germans, Swedes, Russians, and Turks. But once a battle was over, the ruler could exercise no more than nominal leadership. Each king was elected by the assembly of nobles and had to agree not to interfere with the independence of the great lords, who were growing rich from serf labor on fertile lands. The crown had neither revenue nor bureaucracy to speak of, and so the country continued to resemble a feudal kingdom, where power remained in the localities.

The Triumph of the Gentry in England

The model for a nonabsolutist regime was England, even though King Charles II (r. 1660–1685) seemed to have powers similar to those of his ill-fated father, Charles I. He still summoned and dissolved Parliament, made all appointments in the bureaucracy, and signed every law. But he no longer had prerogative courts like Star Chamber, he could not arrest a member of Parliament, and he could not create a new seat in the Commons. Even two ancient prerogatives, the king's right to dispense with an act of Parliament for a specific individual or group and his right to suspend an act completely, proved empty when Charles II tried to exercise them. Nor could he raise money without Parliament; instead, he was given a fixed annual income, financed by a tax on beer.

The Gentry and Parliament   The real control of the country's affairs had by this time passed to the group of substantial landowners known as the gentry. In a country of some 5 million people, perhaps fifteen to twenty thousand families were considered gentry—local leaders throughout England, despite having neither titles of nobility nor special privileges. Amounting to 2 percent of the population, they probably represented about the same proportion as the titled nobles in other states. Yet the gentry differed from these other nobles in that they

ENGRAVING FROM *THE WESTMINSTER MAGAZINE,* 1774
Political cartoons were standard fare in eighteenth-century newspapers and magazines. This one shows a weeping king of Poland and an angry Turk (who made no gains) after Poland was carved up in 1772 by Frederick the Great, the Austrian emperor, and the Russian empress. Louis XV sits by without helping his ally Poland, and all are urged on by the devil under the table.

had won the right to determine national policy through Parliament. Whereas nobles elsewhere depended on monarchs for power, the English revolution had made the gentry an independent force. Their authority was now hallowed by custom, upheld by law, and maintained by the House of Commons.

Not all the gentry took a continuing interest in affairs of state, and only a few of their number sat in the roughly five-hundred-member House of Commons. Even the Commons did not exercise a constant influence over the government; nevertheless, the ministers of the king had to be prominent representatives of the gentry, and they had to be able to win the support of a majority of the members of the Commons. Policy was still set by the king and his ministers, but the Commons had to be persuaded that the policies were correct; without parliamentary approval, a minister could not long survive.

The Succession   Despite occasional conflicts, this structure worked relatively smoothly throughout Charles II's reign. But the gentry feared that Charles's brother, James, next in line for the succession and an open Catholic, might try to restore Catholicism in England. To prevent this, they attempted in 1680 to force Charles to exclude James from the throne. But in the end the traditional respect for legitimacy, combined with some shrewd maneuvering by Charles, ensured that there would be no tampering with the succession.

Soon, however, the reign of James II (r. 1685–1688) turned into a disaster. Elated by his acceptance as king, James rashly offered Catholics the very encouragement the gentry feared. This was a direct challenge to the gentry's newly won power, and in 1688 seven of their leaders, including members of England's most prominent families, invited the Protestant ruler of the United Provinces, William III, to invade and take over the throne. Though William landed with an army half the size of the king's, James, uncertain of his support, decided not to risk battle and fled to exile in France. Because the transfer of the monarchy was bloodless and confirmed the supremacy of Parliament, it came to be called the Glorious Revolution.

William and Mary   The new king gained what little title he had to the crown through his wife, Mary (see the genealogical table below), and Parliament proclaimed the couple joint monarchs early in 1689. The Dutch ruler took the throne primarily to bring England into his relentless struggles against Louis XIV, and he willingly accepted a settlement that confirmed the essential role of Parliament in the government. A **Bill of Rights** determined the succession to the throne, defined Parliament's powers, and established basic civil rights. An Act of Toleration put an end to all religious persecution, though members of the official Church of England were still the only people allowed to vote, sit in Parliament, hold a government office, or attend a university. In 1694 a statute declared that Parliament had to meet and new elections had to be held at least once every three years.

Despite the restrictions on his authority, William exercised strong leadership. He guided England into an aggressive foreign policy, picked ministers favorable to his aims, and never let Parliament sit when he was out of the country to pursue the war or to oversee Dutch affairs. In his reign, too, the central government grew considerably, gaining new powers and positions, and

THE ENGLISH SUCCESSION FROM THE STUARTS TO THE HANOVERIANS

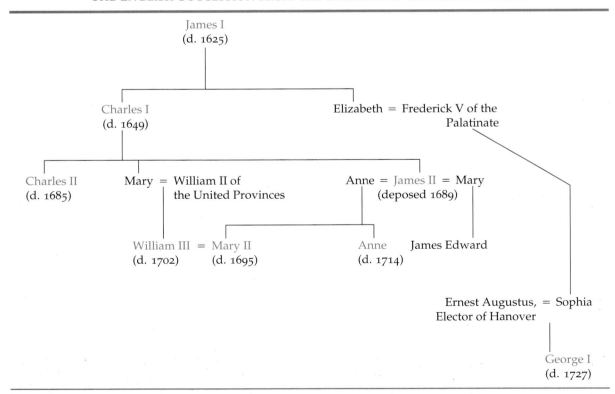

Note: Names in blue = monarchs of England.

thus new opportunities for political patronage. But unlike James, William recognized his limits. He tried to have the Bill of Rights reversed and a standing army established, but he gave up when these efforts provoked major opposition. By and large, therefore, the gentry were content to let the king rule as he saw fit, for they had shown by their intervention in 1688 that ultimately they controlled the country.

Politics and Prosperity

The political system in England now reflected the social system: A small elite controlled both the country's policy and its institutions. This group was far from united, however, as was apparent when a party system began to appear in Parliament during Charles II's reign. On one side was the **Whig** party, that opposed royal prerogatives and Catholicism and was largely responsible for the attempt to exclude James II from the throne. The rival **Tory** party stood for the independence and authority of the crown and favored a ceremonial and traditional Anglicanism.

Party Conflict   Because the Whigs had been the main advocates of the removal of James II, they controlled the government for most of William III's reign. They supported his war against Louis XIV (1689–1697), because France harbored both James and his followers (the romantic but ill-fated Jacobites, who kept trying to restore James's line to the throne). This was a fairly nonpartisan issue, but the Tories and Whigs still competed fiercely for voters. Because the qualification for voting—owning land worth forty shillings a year in rent—had become less restrictive as a result of inflation (which made forty shillings a fairly modest sum) and was not to be raised to a higher minimum until the late 1700s, England now had what would be its largest electorate before the 1860s. Almost 5 percent of the population (more than 15 percent of adult males) could vote, and although results were usually determined by powerful local magnates, fierce politicking was common. And in the election of 1700 there was a major upset: The Tories won by opposing renewal of war with Louis XIV, who had seemed restrained since the end of the previous war in 1697.

Within two years, however, and despite William's death in 1702, England was again at war with France, this time over the Spanish succession; and soon the Whigs were again in control of the government. The identification of the parties with their attitude toward war continued until 1710, when weariness over the fighting brought the Tories back into power. They persuaded Queen Anne, William's successor, to make peace with France at Utrecht in 1713; and they lost power only because they made the mistake of negotiating with the rebel Jacobites after Anne died in 1714 without an heir. Anne's successor was a German prince, the elector of Hanover, who founded the new Hanoverian Dynasty as George I (1714–1727). Since they firmly supported his succession, the Whigs regained control of the government when George came to the throne. They then entrenched themselves for almost a century.

The Sea and the Economy   At the same time, England was winning for itself unprecedented prosperity and laying the foundations of its world power. The English navy was the premier force on the sea, the decisive victor over France during the worldwide struggle of the early eighteenth century. Overseas, England founded new colonies and steadily expanded the empire. When England and Scotland joined into one kingdom in 1707, the union created a Great Britain ready to exercise a worldwide influence.

The economic advances were equally remarkable. A notable achievement was the establishment of the Bank of England in 1694. The bank gained permission to raise money from the public and then lend it to the government at a favorable 8 percent interest. Within 12 days its founders raised more than a million pounds, demonstrating not only the financial stability of England's government but also the commitment of the elite to the country's political structure. London was becoming the financial capital of the world, with her merchants gaining control of maritime trade from east Asia to North America. And the benefits of the boom also helped the lower levels of society.

English Society   With the possible exception of the Dutch, ordinary English people were better off than their equivalents elsewhere in Europe. Compared with the sixteenth century, there was little starvation. The system of poor relief may often have been inhumane in forcing the unfortunate to work in horrifying workhouses, but it did provide them with the shelter and food they had long lacked. It is true that thousands still found themselves unable to make a living in their home villages each year and were forced by poverty to take to the roads. And the many who ended up in London hardly improved their situation. The stream of immigrants was driving the capital's population toward half a million, and the city contained frightful slums and miserable crime-ridden sections. Even a terrible fire in London in 1666 did little to improve the appallingly crowded living conditions, because the city was rebuilt much as before, the only notable additions being a series of splendid churches. But the grimness should not be overdrawn.

After more than a century of inflation, the laborer could once again make a decent living, and artisans

William Hogarth
THE POLLING, 1754
Despite the high reputation of the polling day as the central moment in the system of representative government, Hogarth's depiction of it in this scene suggests how corrupt and disheveled the process of voting was. The sick and the foolish are among the mob of voters; the central figure looks bewildered as he is told what to do; on the right a bloated official cannot decide whether a voter should be allowed to take his oath on the Bible with a wooden hand; and all ignore the distress of Britannia, the symbol of Britain, in her coach on the left.
By courtesy of the Trustees of Sir John Soane's Museum, London

were enjoying a growing demand for their work. Higher in the social scale, more men had a say in the political process than before, and more found opportunities for advancement in the rising economy—in trade overseas, in the bureaucracy, or in the expanding market for luxury goods. It has been estimated that in 1730 there were about sixty thousand adult males in what we would call the professions. England also had better roads than any other European country and a more impartial judicial system. Yet none of these gains could compare with those that the gentry made. In fact, many of the improvements, such as fair administration of justice, were indirect results of what the upper classes had won for themselves. The fruits of progress clearly belonged primarily to the gentry.

The Growth of Stability

Like the absolutist regimes, the British government in the 1700s was able to advance state building—to expand its authority and its international power. This was the work not so much of a monarch as of the "political nation": the landowners and leading townsmen who elected almost all the members of Parliament. Their control of the nation was visible in the distribution of the 558 seats in the House of Commons, which bore little relation to the size of constituencies. In 1793, for example, fifty-one English and Welsh boroughs, with fewer than fifteen hundred voters, elected one hundred members of Parliament, nearly a fifth of the Commons. Many districts were safely in the pocket

NEW GALLOWS AT THE OLD BAILEY, ENGRAVING
It was an indication of the severity of English criminal justice that the gallows erected near the chief court in London, the Old Bailey, in the mid-eighteenth century was specially constructed so that ten condemned criminals, both men and women, could be executed at once.
© British Museum

of a prominent local family; and elsewhere elections were often determined by bribery, influence, and intimidation. On the national level, loose party alignments pitted Whigs, who wanted a strong Parliament and usually preferred commercial to agricultural interests, against Tories, who tended to support the king and policies that favored large landholders. But the realities of politics were shaped by small factions within these larger groups, and alliances revolved around the control of patronage and office.

War and Taxes   As the financial and military needs and capabilities of the government expanded, Parliament now created a thoroughly bureaucratized state. Britain had always prided itself on having a smaller government and lower taxes than its neighbors, largely because, as an island, it had avoided the need for a standing army. All that now came to an end. Starting with the struggle against Louis XIV, wars required constant increases in resources, troops, and administrators. A steadily expanding navy had to be supported, as did an army that reached almost two hundred thousand men by the 1770s. Before the 1690s, public expenditures rarely amounted to 2 million a year; by the 1770s, they were almost 30 million, and most of that was

spent on the military. In this period, as a result, Britain's fiscal bureaucracy more than tripled in size. The recruiting officer became a regular sight, and so too did the treasury men who were imposing increasingly heavy tax burdens.

Unlike their counterparts on the Continent, however, the wealthier classes in Britain paid considerable taxes to support this state building, and they maintained more fluid relations with other classes. The landed gentry and the commercial class, in particular, were often linked by marriage and by financial or political associations. Even great aristocrats sometimes had close ties with the business leaders of London. The lower levels of society, however, found the barriers as high as they had ever been. For all of Britain's prosperity, the lower third of society remained poor and often desperate. As a result, despite a severe system of justice and frequent capital punishment, crime was endemic in both country and town. The eighteenth century was the heyday of that romantic but violent figure, the highwayman.

The Age of Walpole   The first two rulers of the Hanoverian Dynasty, George I (r. 1714–1727) and George II (r. 1727–1760), could not speak English fluently. The

Samuel Scott
THE BUILDING OF WESTMINSTER BRIDGE, CA. 1742
The elegance, but not the squalor, of city life in the eighteenth century is suggested by this view of Westminster.
The Metropolitan Museum of Art, Purchase, Charles B. Curtis Fund and Joseph Pulitzer Bequest, 1944. (44.56) Photograph © 1993 The Metropolitan Museum of Art

language barrier and their concern for their German territory of Hanover left them often uninterested in British politics, and this helped Parliament grow in authority. Its dominant figure for over twenty years was Sir Robert Walpole, who rose to prominence because of his skillful handling of fiscal policy during the panic following the collapse of an overseas trading company in 1720. This crash, known as the South Sea Bubble, resembled the failure of John Law's similar scheme in France, but it had less effect on government finances. Thereafter, Walpole controlled British politics until 1742, mainly by dispensing patronage liberally and staying at peace.

Many historians have called Walpole the first prime minister, though the title was not official. He insisted that all ministers inform and consult with the House of Commons as well as with the king, and he continued to sit in Parliament in order to recruit support for his decisions. Not until the next century was it accepted that the Commons could force a minister to resign. But Walpole took a first step toward ministerial responsibility, and to the notion that the ministers as a body or "cabinet" had a common task, and he thus shaped the future structure of British government.

Commercial Interests In Great Britain as in France, the economic expansion of the eighteenth century increased the wealth and the social and political weight of the commercial and financial middle class. Although Londoners remained around 11 percent of the population, the proportion of the English who lived in other sizable towns doubled in the 1700s; and by 1800 some 30 percent of the country's inhabitants were urbanized. Walpole's policy of peace pleased the large landlords but angered this growing body of merchants and businesspeople, who feared the growth of French commerce and colonial settlements. They found their champion

in William Pitt, later earl of Chatham, the grandson of a man who had made a fortune in India. Eloquent, self-confident, and infused with a vision of Britain's imperial destiny, Pitt began his parliamentary career in 1738 by attacking the government's timid policies and demanding that France be driven from the seas. Though Walpole's policies continued even after his resignation in 1742, Pitt's moment finally came in 1758, when Britain became involved in a European war that was to confirm its importance in continental affairs (see pp. 523–524).

Contrasts in Political Thought

The intensive development of both absolutist and antiabsolutist forms in the seventeenth century stimulated an outpouring of ideas about the nature and purposes of government. Two Englishmen, in particular, developed theories about the basis of political authority that have been influential ever since.

Hobbes Thomas Hobbes, a brilliant scholar from a poor family who earned his livelihood as the tutor to aristocrats' sons, determined to use the strictly logical methods of the scientist to analyze political behavior. As a young man Hobbes was secretary to Francis Bacon, who doubtless gave him a taste for science. And the almost scientific reasoning is the essence of his masterpiece, *Leviathan* (1651), which began with a few premises about human nature from which Hobbes deduced major conclusions about political forms.

Leviathan Hobbes's premises, drawn from his observation of the strife-ridden Europe of the 1640s and 1650s, were stark and uncompromising. People, he asserted, are selfish and ambitious; consequently, unless

PORTRAIT OF THOMAS HOBBES
This depiction of the famous philosopher shows him with a twinkle in the eye and a smile that might seem surprising, given the pessimism about human nature in his *Leviathan*.
Art Resource, NY

restrained, they fight a perpetual war with their fellows. The weak are more cunning and the strong more stupid. Given these unsavory characteristics, the **state of nature**—which precedes the existence of society—is a state of war, in which life is "solitary, poor, nasty, brutish, and short." Hobbes concluded that the only way to restrain this instinctive aggressiveness is to erect an absolute and sovereign power that will maintain peace. Everyone should submit to the sovereign because the alternative is the anarchy of the state of nature. The moment of submission is the moment of the birth of orderly society.

In a startling innovation, Hobbes suggested that the transition from nature to society is accomplished by a contract that is implicitly accepted by all who wish to end the chaos. The unprecedented feature of the contract is that it is not between ruler and ruled; it is binding only on the ruled. They agree among themselves to submit to the sovereign; the sovereign is thus not a party to the contract and is not limited in any way. A government that is totally free to do whatever it wishes is best equipped to keep the peace, and peace is always better than the previous turmoil. The power of Hobbes's logic, and the endorsement he seemed to give to absolutism, made his views enormously influential. But his approach also aroused hostility. Although later political theorists were deeply affected by his ideas, many of Hobbes's successors denounced him as godless, immoral, cynical, and unfeeling. It was dislike of his message, not weaknesses in his analysis, that made many people unwilling to accept his views.

Locke   John Locke, a quiet Oxford professor who admired Hobbes but sought to soften his conclusions, based his political analysis on a general theory of knowledge. Locke believed that at birth a person's mind is a *tabula rasa*, a clean slate; nothing, he said, is inborn or preordained. As human beings grow, they observe and experience the world. Once they have gathered enough data through their senses, their minds begin to work on the data. Then, with the help of reason, they perceive patterns, discovering the order and harmony that permeate the universe. Locke was convinced that this underlying order exists and that every person, regardless of individual experiences, must reach the same conclusions about its nature and structure.

When Locke turned his attention to political thought, he put into systematic form the views of the English gentry and other antiabsolutists throughout Europe. The *Second Treatise of Civil Government*, published in 1690, was deeply influenced by Hobbes. From his great predecessor, Locke took the notions that a state of nature is a state of war and that only a contract among the people can end the anarchy that precedes the establishment of civil society. But his conclusions were decidedly different.

Of Civil Government   Using the principles of his theory of knowledge, Locke asserted that, applying reason to politics, one can prove the inalienability of three rights of an individual: life, liberty, and property. Like Hobbes, he believed that there must be a sovereign power, but he argued that it has no power over these three natural rights of its subjects without their consent. And this consent—for taxes, for example—must come from a representative assembly of men of property, such as Parliament. The affirmation of property as one of the three natural rights (it became "the pursuit of happiness" in the more egalitarian American Declaration of Independence) is significant. Here Locke revealed himself as the voice of the gentry. Only those with a tangible stake in their country have a right to control its destiny, and that stake must be protected as surely as their life and liberty. The concept of liberty remained vague, but it was taken to imply the sorts of

LOCKE ON THE ORIGINS OF GOVERNMENT

The heart of John Locke's Second Treatise of Civil Government, *written in the mid-1680s before England's Glorious Revolution but published in 1690, is its optimism about human nature—as opposed to Hobbes's pessimism. In this passage Locke explains why, in his view, people create political systems.*

"If man in the state of nature be so free, if he be absolute lord of his own person and possessions, equal to the greatest, and subject to nobody, why will he part with his freedom, and subject himself to the dominion and control of any other power? To which it is obvious to answer, that though in the state of nature he hath such a right, yet the enjoyment of it is very uncertain, and constantly exposed to the invasions of others. This makes him willing to quit this condition, which, however free, is full of fears and continual dangers; and it is not without reason that he seeks out and is willing to join in society with others, who have a mind to unite, for the mutual preservation of their lives, liberties, and estates, which I call by the general name, property. The great and chief end, therefore, of men's putting themselves under government, is the preservation of their property.

"But though men when they enter into society give up the equality, liberty, and power they had in the state of nature into the hands of society; yet it being only with an intention in every one the better to preserve himself, his liberty, and property, the power of the society can never be supposed to extend further than the common good. And all this to be directed to no other end but the peace, safety, and public good of the people."

From John Locke, *The Second Treatise of Civil Government,* Thomas P. Peardon (ed.), Indianapolis: Bobbs-Merrill, 1952, chapter 9, pp. 70–73.

freedom, such as freedom from arbitrary arrest, that appeared in the English Bill of Rights. Hobbes allowed a person to protect only his or her life. Locke permitted the overthrow of the sovereign power if it infringed on the subjects' rights—a course the English followed with James II and the Americans with George III.

Locke's prime concern was to defend the individual against the state, a concern that has remained essential to liberal thought ever since (see "Locke on the Origins of Government," above). But it is important to realize that his emphasis on property served the elite better than the mass of society. With Locke to reassure them, the upper classes put their stamp on eighteenth-century European civilization.

THE INTERNATIONAL SYSTEM

While rulers built up their states by enlarging bureaucracies, strengthening governmental institutions, and expanding resources, they also had to consider how best to deal with their neighbors. In an age that emphasized reasoned and practical solutions to problems, there was hope that an orderly system could be devised for international relations. If the reality fell short of the ideal, there were nevertheless many who thought they were creating a more systematic and organized structure for diplomacy and warfare.

Diplomacy and Warfare

One obstacle to the creation of impersonal international relations was the continuing influence of traditional dynastic interests. Princes and their ministers tried to preserve a family's succession, and they arranged marriages to gain new titles or alliances. Part of the reason that those perennial rivals, Britain and France, remained at peace for nearly thirty years until 1740 was that the rulers in both countries felt insecure on their thrones and thus had personal motives for not wanting to risk aggressive foreign policies.

Gradually, however, dynastic interests gave way to policies based on a more impersonal conception of the state. Leaders like Frederick II of Prussia and William Pitt of Britain tried to shape their diplomacy to what they considered the needs of their states. "Reasons of state" centered on security, which could be guaranteed only by force. Thus, the search for defensible borders and the weakening of rivals became obvious goals. Eighteenth-century leaders believed that the end (security and prosperity) justified the means (the use of power). Chasing the impossible goal of complete invulnerability, leaders felt justified in using the crudest tactics in dealing with their neighbors.

"Balance of Power" and the Diplomatic System   If there was any broad, commonly accepted principle at work, it was that hegemony, or domination by one

Louis Nicolas Blarenberghe
THE BATTLE OF FONTENOY, **1745**
This panorama shows the English and Dutch assaulting the French position in a battle in present-day Belgium. The French lines form a huge semicircle from the distant town to the wood on the left. The main attacking force in the center, surrounded by gunfire, eventually retreated, and news of the victory was brought to Louis XV, in red on the right, by a horseman in blue who is doffing his hat.
Photo: Gérard Blot. Château de Versailles et de Trianon, Versailles, France. Réunion des Musées Nationaux/Art Resource, NY. Giraudon/Art Resource, NY

state, had to be resisted because it threatened international security. The concern aroused by Louis XIV's ambitions showed the principle at work, when those whom he sought to dominate joined together to frustrate his designs. The aim was to establish equilibrium in Europe by a balance of power, with no single state achieving hegemony.

The diplomats, guided by reasons of state and the balance of power, knew there were times when they had to spy and deceive. Yet diplomacy also could stabilize: In the eighteenth century it grew as a serious profession, paralleling the rationalization of the state itself. Foreign ministries were staffed with experts and clerks, who kept extensive archives, while the heads of the diplomatic machine, the ambassadors, were stationed in permanent embassies abroad. This routinized management of foreign relations helped foster a sense of collective identity among Europe's states despite their endless struggles. French was now the common language of diplomacy; by 1774 even a treaty between Turks and Russians was drafted in that language. And socially the diplomats were cosmopolitan aristocrats

who saw themselves as members of the same fraternity, even if the great powers dominated international agreements, usually at the expense of the smaller states. Resolving disputes by negotiation could be as amoral as war.

Armies and Navies

Despite the settlement of some conflicts by diplomacy, others led to war. Whereas Britain emphasized its navy, on the Continent the focus of bureaucratic innovation and monetary expenditure was the standing army, whose growth was striking. France set the pace. After 1680 the size of its forces never fell below 200,000. In Prussia the army increased in size from 39,000 to 200,000 men between 1713 and 1786. But the cost, technology, and tactics of armies and navies served to limit the devastation of eighteenth-century warfare. The expenses led rulers to conserve men, equipment, and ships carefully. Princes were quick to declare war but slow to commit armies or navies to battle. Casualties also became less numerous as discipline improved

Engraving of a Military Academy, from H. F. von Fleming, *Volkommene Teutsche Soldat*, 1726
This scene, of young men studying fortifications and tactics in a German academy, would have been familiar to the sons of nobles throughout Europe who trained for a military career in the eighteenth century.

and the ferocity that had been caused by religious passions died away.

Tactics and Discipline   On land, the building and besieging of fortresses continued to preoccupy military planners, even though the impregnable defenses built by the French engineer Sebastian Vauban to protect France's northeastern border were simply bypassed by the English general Marlborough when he pursued the French army in the War of the Spanish Succession. The decisive encounter was still the battle between armies, where the majority of the troops—the infantry—used their training to maneuver and fire in carefully controlled line formations. The aim of strategy was not to annihilate but to nudge an opposing army into abandoning a position in the face of superior maneuvers. Improved organization also reduced brutality. Better supplied by a system of magazines and more tightly disciplined by constant drilling, troops were less likely to desert or plunder than they had been during the Thirty Years' War. At sea, the British achieved superiority by maneuvering carefully controlled lines of ships and seeking to outnumber or outflank the enemy.

As these practices took hold, some encounters were fought as if they were taking place on a parade ground or in a naval strategy room. Pitched battles were increasingly avoided, for even important victories might be nullified if a winning army or navy returned to its home bases for the winter. And no victor ever demanded unconditional surrender; in almost all cases, a commander would hesitate to pursue a defeated company or squadron.

Officers   The officer corps were generally the preserve of Europe's nobility, though they also served as channels of upward social mobility for wealthy sons of middle-class families who purchased commissions. In either case, the officer ranks tended to be filled by men who lacked the professional training for effective leadership. The branches of service that showed the most progress were the artillery and the engineers, in which competent middle-class officers played an unusually large role.

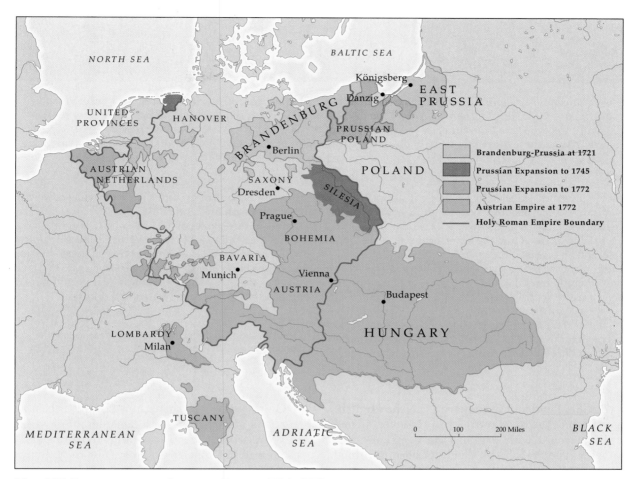

MAP 17.5 PRUSSIA AND THE AUSTRIAN EMPIRE, 1721–1772
The steady territorial advances of Prussia had created a major power in northern and eastern Europe, alongside the Austrian Empire, by the time of the first partition of Poland in 1772. Which was the most extensive of Prussia's gains between 1721 and 1772?
◆ For an online version, go to www.mhhe.com/chambers9 > chapter 17 > book maps

Weak Alliances A final limit on the scale of war in the eighteenth century was the inherent weakness of coalitions, which formed whenever a general war erupted. On paper these alliances looked formidable. On battlefields, however, they were hampered by primitive communications and lack of mobility even at the peak of cooperation. Moreover, the partnerships rarely lasted very long. The competitiveness of the state system bred distrust among allies as well as enemies.

The Seven Years' War

The pressures created by the competition of states and dynasties finally exploded in a major war, the Seven Years' War (1756–1763). Its roots lay in a realignment of diplomatic alliances prompted by Austria. Previously, the Bourbon-Habsburg rivalry had been the cornerstone of European diplomacy. But by the 1750s two other antago-

nisms had taken over: French competition with the British in the New World and Austria's vendetta against Prussia over Silesia. For Austria, the rivalry with Bourbon France was no longer important. Its position in the Holy Roman Empire depended now on humbling Prussia. French hostility toward Austria had also lessened, and thus Austria was free to lead a turnabout in alliances—a diplomatic revolution—so as to forge an anti-Prussian coalition with France and Russia. Russia was crucial. The pious Empress Elizabeth of Russia loathed Frederick II and saw him as an obstacle to Russian ambitions in Eastern Europe. Geographical vulnerability also made Prussia an inviting target, and so the stage was set for war.

Prussia tried to compensate for its vulnerability. But its countermoves only alienated the other powers. Frederick sought to stay out of the Anglo-French rivalry by coming to terms with both these states. He had been France's ally in the past, but he now sought a

MARIA THERESA IN A VEHEMENT MOOD

The animosities and ambitions that shaped international relations in the eighteenth century were exemplified by the Empress Maria Theresa. Her furious reaction to the event that destroyed Europe's old diplomatic system—England's signing of the Convention of Westminster with Maria Theresa's archenemy, Frederick the Great—suggests how deep were the feelings that brought about the midcentury conflagration. After learning the news and deciding (in response) to ally herself with France, she told the British ambassador on May 13, 1756, exactly where she stood.

"I have not abandoned the old system, but Great Britain has abandoned me and the system, by concluding the Prussian treaty, the first intelligence of which struck me like a fit of apoplexy. I and the king of Prussia are incompatible; and no consideration on earth will ever induce me to enter into any engagement to which he is a party. Why should you be surprised if, following your example in concluding a treaty with Prussia, I should now enter into an engagement with France?

"I am far from being French in my disposition, and do not deny that the court of Versailles has been my bitterest enemy; but I have little to fear from France, and I have no other recourse than to form such arrangements as will secure what remains to me. My principal aim is to secure my hereditary possessions. I have truly but two enemies whom I really dread, the king of Prussia and the Turks; and while I and Russia continue on the same good terms as now exist between us, we shall, I trust, be able to convince Europe, that we are in a condition to defend ourselves against those adversaries, however formidable."

From William Coxe, *History of the House of Austria*, Vol. 3, London: Bohn, 1847, pp. 363–364.

treaty with England, and in January 1756 the English, hoping to protect the royal territory of Hanover, signed a neutrality accord with Prussia, the Convention of Westminster. The French, who had not been informed of the negotiations in advance, saw the Convention as an insult, if not a betrayal: the act of an untrustworthy ally. France overreacted, turned against Prussia, and thus fell into Austria's design (see "Maria Theresa in a Vehement Mood," above). Russia too considered the Convention of Westminster a betrayal by its supposed ally England. English bribes and diplomacy were unable to keep Russia from actively joining Austria to plan Prussia's dismemberment.

The Course of War   Fearing encirclement, Frederick gambled on a preventive war through Saxony in 1756. Although he conquered the duchy, his plan backfired, for it activated the coalition that he dreaded. Russia and France met their commitments to Austria, and the three began a combined offensive against Prussia. For a time Frederick's genius as a general brought him success. Skillful tactics and daring surprise movements brought some victories, but strategically the Prussian position was shaky. Frederick had to dash in all directions across his provinces to repel invading armies whose combined strength far exceeded his own. Disaster was avoided mainly because the Russian army returned east for winter quarters regardless of its gains, but even so, the Russians occupied Berlin.

On the verge of exhaustion, Prussia at best seemed to face a stalemate with a considerable loss of territory; at worst, the war would continue and bring about a total Prussian collapse. But the other powers were also war-weary, and Frederick's enemies were becoming increasingly distrustful of one another. In the end, Prussia was saved by one of those sudden changes of reign that could cause dramatic reversals of policy in Europe. In January 1762 Empress Elizabeth died and was replaced temporarily by Tsar Peter III, a passionate admirer of Frederick. He quickly pulled Russia out of the war and returned Frederick's conquered eastern domains of Prussia and Pomerania. In Britain, meanwhile, William Pitt was replaced by the more pacific earl of Bute, who brought about a reconciliation with France; both countries then ended their insistence on punishing Prussia. Austria's coalition collapsed.

Peace   The terms of the Peace of Hubertusburg (1763), settling the continental phase of the Seven Years' War, were therefore surprisingly favorable to Prussia. Prussia returned Saxony to Austria but paid no compensation for the devastation of the duchy, and the Austrians recognized Silesia as Prussian. In short, the status quo was restored. Frederick could return to Berlin, his dominion preserved partly by his army but mainly by luck and the continuing fragility of international alliances.

Summary

If, amidst the state building of the eighteenth century, Europe's regimes were ready to sustain a major war even if it brought about few territorial changes, that was not simply because of the expansion of government and the disciplining of armies. It was also the result of remarkable economic advances and the availability of new resources that were flowing into Europe from the development of overseas empires. In politics, this was primarily an age of consolidation; in economics, it was a time of profound transformation.

QUESTIONS FOR FURTHER THOUGHT

1. Although Americans naturally prefer regimes that provide for representation and citizen participation in government, are there times when it is advantageous for a state to have an authoritarian or absolutist regime?

2. How important is the development of a capital city or a center of government in the process of state building?

RECOMMENDED READING

Sources

*Hobbes, Thomas. *Leviathan.* 1651. Any modern edition.

*Locke, John. *Second Treatise of Civil Government.* 1690. Any modern edition.

Luvvas, J. (ed.). *Frederick the Great on the Art of War.* 1966.

Studies

*Behrens, C. B. A. *Society, Government, and the Enlightenment: The Experience of Eighteenth-Century France and Prussia.* 1985.

Brewer, John. *The Sinews of Power: War, Money, and the English State, 1688–1783.* 1989. The work that demonstrated the importance of the military and the growth of bureaucracy in eighteenth-century England.

*Hatton, R. N. *Europe in the Age of Louis XIV.* 1969. A beautifully illustrated and vividly interpretive history of the period that Louis dominated.

*Holmes, Geoffrey. *The Making of a Great Power: Late Stuart and Early Georgian Britain, 1660–1722;* and *The Age of Oligarchy: Pre-industrial Britain, 1722–1783.* 1993. The best detailed survey.

Hughes, Lindsey. *Peter the Great: A Biography.* 2002.

Lossky, Andrew. *Louis XIV and the French Monarchy.* 1994.

Mettam, Roger. *Power and Faction in Louis XIV's France.* 1988. An analysis of government and power under absolutist rule.

Oresko, Robert, G. C. Gibbs, and H. M. Scott (eds.). *Royal and Republican Sovereignty in Early Modern Europe.* 1997.

*Plumb, J. H. *The Growth of Political Stability in England, 1675–1725.* 1969. A brief, lucid survey of the development of parliamentary democracy.

Raeff, Marc. *The Well-Ordered Police State: Social and Institutional Change through Law in the Germanies and Russia, 1600–1800.* 1983.

*Tuck, Richard. *Hobbes.* 1989. A clear introduction to Hobbes's thought.

Weigley, R. F. *The Age of Battles: The Quest for Decisive Warfare from Breitenfeld to Waterloo.* 1991. The best military history of the age.

*Available in paperback.

Glossary

absolutism Political doctrine that the monarch is the source of all authority and government in a kingdom.

Academy Quarter of Athens in which Plato established a school.

Aeneid Epic poem by Roman poet Virgil about the founding of Rome.

agora Central market of a polis.

Allah Islamic term for God that derives from the Arabic word *al ilah,* meaning "The God."

Amon-Re "Hidden"; an unseen, universal god of Egypt.

Anabaptists Individuals who, pointing out that the Bible nowhere mentions infant baptism, argued that the sacrament was effective only if the believer understood what was happening and that therefore adults ought to be rebaptized. Opponents argued that infant baptism was necessary so that a baby would not be denied salvation if it died young.

anarchists Radical activists who called for the abolition of the state, sometimes by violent means.

anti-Semitism Anti-Jewish sentiment used to reinforce conservative, antiliberal and nationalist politics.

appeasement The policy by antiwar governments in Britain and France to placate Nazi Germany. Culminated in the Munich conference giving Germany control of Czechoslovakia in 1938; encouraged further German aggression.

apprenticeship Method by which young candidates, or apprentices, studied a particular trade under a master of that skill before admittance into the guild.

Areopagus Rock in central Athens that gave its name to a powerful governing council.

Arianism Heresy based on the teaching of Arius, an Alexandrian priest, which denied that Jesus was coequal with God the Father.

assignats Paper money issued by the French revolutionary governments, whose value was backed by nationalized church lands.

aton Disk of the sun, worshiped by Akhnaton, an Egyptian pharaoh.

Augustus "Most honored"; name conferred on the first emperor of Rome.

balance of power The belief that no one state should be permitted a dominant role in international affairs, and that alliances among their neighbors ought to restrain ambitious rulers.

Baroque Ornate style of art, music, literature, and architecture that emerged in the seventeenth century, characterized by an emphasis on grandeur, power, drama, and rich color.

Bastille A fortress prison seized on July 14, 1789, by Parisians looking for munitions to repulse the royal army; the event symbolized the Revolution's popular support.

Beguines Pious laywomen who lived in communities outside of convents.

Beowulf Anglo-Saxon epic that illustrates the weakness of tribal kingship.

Bill of Rights Document (usually only in a constitutional system) listing the protections from government oppression enjoyed by individual citizens.

billeting Providing board and lodging for troops by making ordinary citizens house and feed soldiers in their homes.

biometry The application of statistical methods to the analysis of biology and medicine.

Bismarck, Otto von The chief minister of Prussia's king, he masterminded the unification of Germany through military aggression and nationalist appeals.

Black Death Great plague of the fourteenth century that spread throughout Europe and resulted in huge loss of human life.

blitzkrieg "Lightning war"; German military tactic in which enemies were overrun with lightning speed using tanks and air power; led to the quick defeat of Poland in 1939 and France in 1940.

Bolsheviks "Majority faction"; the Leninist wing of the Russian Marxist party; after 1917, the Communist party.

broadsides Brief pamphlets or leaflets, often satiric, making sharp comments about a major issue of the day.

Brumaire The coup d'état in 1799 that overthrew the Directory and led to the dictatorship of Napoleon Bonaparte.

cahiers Grievance petitions written by local electoral assemblies, to be presented to the king by the deputies attending the Estates General in France.

Caliph In the Middle Ages, he was the religious and civil ruler of the Muslim empires, as in the Abbasid Caliphate.

Carolingian minuscule New form of formal, literary writing that used capital letters for the beginning of sentences and lowercase letters for the text.

cartel An informal association of manufacturers or suppliers who maintain prices at a high level and set production limits to control market demand.

Central Powers Name given to the coalition including Germany, Austria-Hungary, Turkey (the Ottoman Empire), and Bulgaria in World War I.

Chartism A mass working-class movement in Britain between 1837 and 1848 that derived its name from the People's Charter, a document calling for universal male suffrage, frequent elections by secret ballot, and other democratic reforms.

chivalry A new code of behavior that refined the manners of knights and nobles and adapted them to life in a noble household.

Cistercians Monastic order founded in 1098; they emphasized the emotional devotion to Christ's and Mary's humility.

Civil Code (Napoleonic Code) A grand codification of French law under Napoleon, which preserved certain gains of the Revolution such as legal equality and the abolition of seigneurial property, while clarifying contract and family law.

Civil Constitution of the Clergy The French Revolution's 1790 reform of the Catholic Church under which priests and bishops were elected by the laity, and parishes and dioceses were redrawn; created opposition to the Revolution and a schism within French Catholicism.

Classicism A movement in the arts that seeks to recapture the style and the subjects associated with ancient Greece and Rome.

Colonial Mandate Designation for the former colonial possessions of Germany and the Ottoman Empire, which the League of Nations placed under the control of the various Allied nations after World War I.

colonus In the Roman Empire, a free man who was settled as a worker on the land of another.

comitatus A Germanic warrior band organized under the leadership of an established chief.

Committee of Public Safety A committee of deputies to the National Convention that set political and military strategy and formed the hub of the revolutionary dictatorship of 1793–1794.

common law Laws that applied to the entire kingdom and were thus distinct from local customs, especially associated with England.

commune In medieval and Renaissance Europe, a self-governing association created by townsmen and headed by elected officials.

Concert of Europe A loose agreement by the major European powers to act together to maintain the conservative order in Europe and repress liberal and nationalistic uprisings after 1815.

Conciliar Movement Advocates of the authority of General Councils, rather than the papacy, in the Roman Church, especially active in the 1400s.

Concordat (of 1801) The religious settlement with Pope Pius VII that made Catholicism the "preferred" religion in France but protected religious freedom for non-Catholics.

confraternity A voluntary association of people; in earlier times, usually associations of laymen who wanted to intensify their religious piety.

Congress of Vienna An international congress that met from 1814 to 1815 to set peace terms for continental Europe after the Napoleonic Wars; notable for its creation of a European balance of power and the restoration of old dynasties.

conquistador A Spanish minor nobleman who led his country's expeditions of conquest into Central and South America in the sixteenth century.

conscription Policy of requiring all males of a certain age to sign up for a nation's army.

Constitutionalism The political doctrine that authority in a state depends on consent by the governed, or at least by the leaders of the society.

consuls Supreme magistrates in the Roman Republic, always holding office in pairs.

Continental System Economic sanctions established by Napoleon under which all ships carrying British goods or trading with Britain, even those from neutral countries, were banned from European ports and subject to seizure.

Corn Laws British grain tariffs seen as benefiting the landed gentry at the expense of higher bread prices for urban consumers; an opposition movement by middle-class reformers led to the repeal of nearly all duties in 1846.

Cortes The legislatures of the Spanish kingdoms—Aragon, Castile, and Navarre—which were made up of representatives of the Church, the aristocracy, and towns.

Counter-Reformation Refers to those who see the Catholic revival of the sixteenth century as a response to the Reformation. Those who consider it a natural development within the Church refer to the revival as the Catholic Reformation.

courtly love The polite relations between men and women.

crusades In the eleventh through thirteenth centuries, a series of armed expeditions of Christians to the East to overturn Islamic rule of the Holy Land.

Cubism Art form pioneered by Pablo Picasso and Georges Braque in the early twentieth century that rejected the artistic conventions of three-dimensional perspective and naturalistic representation for a flat, two-dimensional perspective and an abstract style.

Cuneiform System of writing by pressing wedge (Lat. *cuneus*) into clay.

curia regis An assembly of men who advised the king and acted as his principal court.

curiales Councilors in the Roman Empire.

curia Town council in the Roman Empire; later means royal court and central directing body of the Roman Catholic Church.

Cyrillic alphabet Developed by Cyril, a Slavonic script based on Greek letters.

danse macabre "Dance of death"; popular artist motif that depicted people from all different walks of life dancing with a skeleton as a foretaste of their deaths.

decolonization The gradual postwar withdrawal of European nations from colonial empires and the rise of national self-determination in former colonies; initiated a new era of global politics that intersected with the Cold War.

deism Belief in the existence of a supreme being but arising from reason rather than revelation.

Delian League Alliance of Greek states headed by Athens; became the Athenian Empire.

demesne land Land, worked by serfs, that the lord held for his own crops and profit.

demographic transition A pattern of declining birth rate accompanied by a more rapidly falling mortality rate that is characteristic of modern societies.

dialectic The art of analyzing logical relationships among propositions in a dialogue or discourse. Later, a philosophical term for Hegel, who applies the term simultaneously to both world history and ideas. It describes the development from one stage of consciousness to a superior one through a dynamic process of the fusion of contradictions into a higher truth.

dictator In the Roman Republic, a supreme officer whose term was limited to six months; this limit was broken by Sulla and Julius Caesar.

Diet The legislature of the Holy Roman Empire and many German states, bringing together representatives of princes, cities, and the Church.

Directory The centrist republican regime in France between 1795 and 1799; characterized by a weak executive, political polarization, and instability.

Divine Comedy Written by Dante, a medieval poem of personal spiritual exploration.

divine right of kings The belief that a monarch's powers derived directly from God, and thus that treason was a kind of blasphemy.

Doctrine of Petrine Succession The traditional Catholic (and medieval) view that Jesus himself endowed the apostle Peter with supreme responsibility for his church.

doctrine of survivals A term first employed by the anthropologist Edward Tyler (1832–1917) to refer to vertigial cultural phenomena from the past that continue to survive even though they have lost their utility.

Dorian Greeks Last wave of Greeks to immigrate, speaking the Doric dialect.

dynasty A family, usually of rulers, that maintains its authority from generation to generation.

East India Co. (British) A corporation that initially traded with native groups in India but eventually exercised an oppressive colonial dominance over Indian affairs.

enclosure The act of consolidating and fencing in land used in open-field agriculture or village common land.

Entente Powers Name of the members of the Triple Entente of 1907—Britain, France, and Russia—which expanded during World War I to include Belgium, Serbia, Greece, Italy, Romania, the Soviet Union, and the United States.

entrepreneur A person who organizes and assumes risk in a business venture in hopes of making a profit.

Epicureans Followers of the philosopher Epicurus who taught that everything is made of atoms (*a-toma* in Greek) and recommended a quiet life free of powerful emotional attachments.

epicycles In traditional astronomy, small circular orbits, revolving around the main circular orbit, that planets follow as they move through the sky.

epistemology Theory of how one obtains and verifies knowledge or truth.

equestrians Originally the Roman cavalry; became the business class of Rome.

Estates In a number of countries in Europe, representative assemblies that were composed of three houses of representatives: the clergy, the nobility, and townsmen.

Estates General An assembly convened by Louis XVI in 1789 that represented the clergy, the nobility, and the Third Estate; once used to win support for royal policy, it had not met since 1614.

ethnic cleansing A coordinated assault to drive members of a specific ethnicity out of a particular region.

Eucharist Also known as communion; Christian sacrament offered during a religious service in which consecrated bread and wine are consumed in celebration of the Lord's Last Supper.

eugenics The study of the improvement of the human race through selective breeding to eradicate less desirable traits in society. An extrapolation from the work of Charles Darwin, it was popularized by his cousin Francis Galton (1821–1911), in the nineteenth century.

Eurocommunism An alternative program for Western Europeans who disagreed with Soviet policies (particularly the invasion of Czechoslovakia) in Eastern Europe.

evolution The process by which species develop through the natural selection of traits best adapted to the environment.

existentialism A twentieth-century philosophy asserting that individuals are responsible for their own values and meanings in an indifferent universe.

famine Period of severe food scarcity due to too much or too little rainfall.

fascism A philosophy or system of government that advocates a dictatorship of the extreme right together with an ideology of belligerent nationalism.

fealty An oath, often accompanying the oath of homage, in which the vassal swears to uphold his homage.

feudalism An economic, political, and social organization of medieval Europe. Land was held by vassals from more powerful overlords in exchange for military and other services.

fief Land given to a vassal from his lord in exchange for specified terms of service; sometimes called benefice.

"Final Solution" Based on Nazi theories of racial inferiority, the systematic extermination of Jews in German-occupied Europe in massacres and death camps like Auschwitz from 1941 to 1945. Also known as the Holocaust or the Shoah.

Five-Year Plans Plans for the rapid, massive industrialization of the nation under the direction of the state initiated by the Soviet Union in the late 1920s.

forms In the thought of Plato, perfect models of all things; any object we see in life is only an imperfect imitation of the object's form (in Greek, *idea*, meaning something that can be seen).

Franco-Prussian War The conflict from 1870 to 1871 that led to the unification of Germany and (indirectly) to the creation of the French Third Republic; signaled the rise of Germany as a military power.

Frankfurt Parliament The assembly elected in 1848 to unify the various states of Germany under a new liberal constitution and a single monarch; it was dissolved in 1849 when Prussia spurned its projects.

Freikorps German postwar paramilitary groups, consisting mainly of war veterans, employed by both the new republican government and especially by far-right political movements such as the Nazis; literally "volunteer troops."

"general will" Rousseau's idealized concept of popular consensus, under which individual interests are subordinated to the public good.

gentry Owners of significant country estates in England, forming a distinct social group immediately below the nobility.

glasnost A Soviet policy under Mikhail Gorbachev permitting a more open discussion of political and social issues and freer dissemination of news and information.

Golden Horde The capital of a division of the Mongol Empire at Sarai, on the lower Volga River.

Gothic Style of Western European architecture and art that developed in the twelfth century; the style is characterized by vaulting and pointed arches.

Great Schism Major split of the Church in the period of 1378–1417, in which two, and later three, popes fought over the rule of the Church.

Greek Orthodox Church Modern term for the Eastern Orthodox Church, whose main departure from Catholicism is their belief that, in the Holy Trinity, the Holy Spirit proceeds only from the father.

guerillas In Spain during the Napoleonic occupation, groups of irregular fighters who harassed French troops, restricted access to supplies, and punished collaborators; a pioneering model for modern guerrilla warfare.

guilds Associations formed by merchants and master artisans to defend and promote their interests and to regulate the quality of the goods they produced and sold.

Hanseatic League Association of northern European trading cities that by the fourteenth century had imposed a monopoly over cities trading in the Baltic and North Seas.

heavy-wheeled plow A heavy, powerful plow that cut more deeply into the ground, forming furrows that drained excess water. It permitted cultivation of heavier river valley soils.

Hellenistic Age In Greek history, the period 323–330 B.C.

helots Publicly owned slaves in Sparta.

heresy Any belief contrary to church dogma; from Greek *hairesis*, "choice."

hieroglyphs "Sacred carvings"; Egyptian style of writing using pictures.

hijra Muhammad's migration from Mecca to Medina in 622; it marks the beginning of the Islamic calendar.

homage An oath of allegiance sworn by a vassal to his lord.

home front In the new time of total war during World War I, civilians—mostly women and men ineligible for military duty—remaining at home assumed a primary role in the national economy; their continued efforts were held up as indispensable to the war being fought on the military front.

Homo erectus "Erect human being"; predecessor of the modern human species *Homo sapiens.*

Humanism An intellectual movement of the Renaissance that emphasized the importance of having the ability to read, understand, and appreciate the writings of the ancient world.

Hundred Years' War War between France and England fought in the fourteenth and fifteenth centuries. Allegedly sparked by a dispute over French royal succession.

Hussites Followers of Hus, the Bohemian priest whose practices attempted to reduce the distinction between priest and worshippers.

iconoclasm In the Byzantine Empire, a rejection of religious icons or pictures of Jesus, Mary, and the saints that led to the destruction of a number of these religious images.

imperium Power of command held by Roman officers.

Impressionists A group of artists who conveyed subjective experiences by capturing the effects of light and color on canvas.

induction Starting with observation, the logical process by which one moves to general principles.

indulgences Grants to sinners by the Roman Catholic Church that reduce time for their souls in purgatory before they can ascend to heaven.

Inquisition A special papal court instituted by Pope Gregory IX for the purpose of rooting out heresy.

intendants French officials who ruled the country's provinces as direct representatives of the king.

Investiture Controversy Conflict between the German emperor and the pope over who had the authority to appoint bishops and "invest" them with their spiritual symbols of office, the ring and the staff.

Islam Strong monotheistic religion founded by Muhammad.

itinerant justices English justices who traveled and heard both criminal and civil pleas. In both cases, they relied on the testimony of a jury.

iurisprudentes or iurisconsulti Jurists or advisers in the Roman legal system whose opinions shaped laws.

ius civile "Civil law," or law relating to Roman citizens.

ius gentium "Law of the nations"; Roman law as applied to noncitizens or to all cultures.

Jacobin Club An influential political club whose leaders propelled the French Revolution toward a democratic republic and supported the use of severe repression against the Revolution's enemies.

Jacquerie French peasant revolt in 1358.

jingoism Attitude of extreme and belligerent patriotism often used to gain popular support for war and other political causes.

Julio-Claudians Dynasty of related rulers from 27 B.C. to A.D. 68 in Rome.

July Monarchy The liberal constitutional monarchy established in France from 1830 to 1848, in which the House of Orléans replaced the Bourbons; its modest reforms benefited most the wealthy middle class.

June Days An uprising in Paris in 1848 by radicals and workers that was brutally suppressed by government forces of France's new republic; the event symbolized the conflict between liberal democracy and working-class militancy.

Junkers Prussian aristocrats whose large estates and tradition of military and bureaucratic service ensured their dominance within the Prussian state.

justification by faith A central tenet of Luther's theology: belief that one is saved through the grace of God rather than good deeds.

Justinian's Code Known as the *Corpus Iuris Civilis,* this was the codification of Roman law undertaken by the Byzantine Emperor Justinian in 528.

Keynesian economics Economic theories and programs ascribed to John M. Keynes and his followers. Keynes argued against a totally laissez-faire economy, urging governments to minimize the effects of boom-and-bust economic cycles by manipulating interest rates and employment (through public works projects).

Koran The Muslim holy book that contains the prophecies Allah revealed to Muhammad; it was written between 651 and 652.

kyrios Greek, roughly "master"—for example, head of a family; used for Christian God.

laissez-faire The theory in which individual self-interest and free markets, rather than state regulation or guild protection, stimulate economic progress.

"last decree" *Senatus consultum ultimum,* "final resolution of the Senate"; an instruction to a consul to "see that the state suffers no harm"; a declaration of martial law, first used in 121 B.C. in Rome.

latifundia Large plantations in the Roman world, worked mainly by slaves.

League of Nations International organization created in the wake of the end of World War I and located in Geneva; the forerunner to the modern-day United Nations.

legion Main unit of the Roman army, in principle 6,000 men.

levée en masse A military draft by the French National Convention in August 1793 of unmarried men between the ages of eighteen and twenty-five that recruited about 300,000 new soldiers.

Linear B Script used on Crete, as well as in Greece, to write the early form of Greek.

Lollards Followers of Wycliffe, a vocal dissenter of the church's leadership. This group became an underground rural movement.

Lyceum School established by Aristotle, meeting in and taking its name from a grove in Athens.

Maastricht Treaty Changed the name of the European Community (EC) to the European Union (EU) in 1992. It also enlarged the powers of its parliament and called for a coordinated foreign policy and a common European currency by 1999.

maat Egyptian concept of right order.

Magna Carta "The Great Charter"; English royal charter of liberties granted by King John in 1215. Intended to settle disputes over the rights and privileges of England's nobility.

Magyars The Hungarian-speaking population of the Hapsburg Empire who began to push for Hungary's independence in the 1840s.

Mannerism Art style that emerged in the sixteenth century in response to the serenity and idealization of the High Renaissance. Mannerism is characterized by distorted, esoteric imagery and a sense of artificiality.

manor An estate held by the lord that included land, the people on the land, and a village, usually with a mill. A fief might contain a number of manors or sometimes just part of one.

manorialism An agricultural, legal, and social organization of land, including a nucleated village, large fields for agriculture, and serfs to work the land.

Marxism The political philosophy of Karl Marx, based on the premise that economic conditions determine the nature of society. Marxists advocate the overthrow of capitalism, which they believe will lead to the establishment of a classless society.

memsahib A term of respect used by Indians to address female social superiors. Used in the nineteenth century to refer to British women in colonial India, the term came to connote the blatant ethnocentrism and spoiled behavior associated with these women.

mendicant Orders of religious men, followers of Sts. Dominic and Francis of Assisi, who preached among the poor townsmen and lived a life of begging.

mercantilism The belief that the amount of wealth in the world was fixed, and that a nation should try to gain as much as it could at the expense of other nations, either by accumulating more gold or, in a more sophisticated version, by improving its balance of trade—that is, by exporting more than it imported. This doctrine led to some governmental regulation of commerce in a number of countries in the seventeenth and eighteenth centuries.

Mesopotamia "Land between the [Tigris and Euphrates] rivers," home of early civilizations.

Messiah In Hebrew, *mashiah:* one anointed by God to rule; title given by Christians to Jesus.

metropole Term used to describe European countries in the context of the dominant economic and cultural relationships they had with their colonies.

Middle Passage The harsh voyage of slaving ships from Africa to the Americas during which an average of 10 percent of the slaves perished.

Minoan Name for civilization on Crete, derived from legendary King Minos.

monasticism Practice of withdrawing from daily life to devote oneself to prayer in isolated communities.

Muslims Those who submit to the will of Allah. In Western Europe, often referred to as Saracens.

nationalism A social and political outlook insisting that the state should embody a national community united by some or all of the following: history, ethnicity, religion, common culture, and language.

nationalization State takeover of privately owned businesses; used in fascist Italy and the Soviet Union, but also in postwar Britain and France, to promote greater economic efficiency and social justice.

natural history The science of the earth's development accomplished through the study of geology, zoology, and botany.

natural rights Liberties that should be common to all people by virtue of their nature as human beings; one basis for the French Declaration of the Rights of Man and Citizen of 1789.

natural selection A central feature of Charles Darwin's (1809–1882) theory of evolution that suggests that only organisms best adapted to their environment survive and transmit their genes to succeeding generations, whereas those less adapted are eliminated.

Nazism The body of political and economic doctrines put into effect by the National Socialist German Workers' party in the Third German Reich. A fascist form of government based on state control of all industry, predominance of groups assumed to be racially superior, and supremacy of the Führer.

Neoclassicism A style of art and poetry inspired by themes from antiquity and its conceptions of form and beauty.

Neolithic Age New Stone Age; date of beginning of agriculture, about 11,000 B.C.

Neoplatonism Influential school of thought during the Renaissance, based on Plato's belief that truth lay in essential but hidden forms.

Neostoicism A sixteenth- and seventeenth-century school of philosophy dedicated to the revival of moral values, such as calmness, self-discipline, and steadfastness, first advanced by the Stoics in ancient Greece and Rome.

New Economic Policy (NEP) Lenin's compromise on economic and social policy for the USSR during the 1920s.

New World Name given to the Americas by sixteenth-century explorers and settlers.

Nicene Creed Declaration made at Nicaea in 325 that Jesus was coeternal with God.

Nominalists Individuals who subscribed to a school of thought in medieval Europe that rejected abstractions as the subject matter of philosophy and focused instead on one's experience of individual, distinct beings and objects.

North Atlantic Treaty Organization (NATO) Created in 1949 to coordinate military forces from the United States, Canada, and ten Western European nations in response to perceived Soviet threats in Europe.

notables Locally prominent and wealthy individuals whose support for Napoleon and subsequent French governments was encouraged by state recognition and honors.

novus homo A "new man"; in Roman politics, a man elected consul with no ancestor who had held this office.

October Manifesto Declaration by the tsar of Russia in 1905 that provided Russia with a written constitution and guaranteed freedom of speech and assembly.

oligarchy The rule of a state by a small number, often the Wealthy citizens.

open-field system The division of agricultural land on a manor into three large fields. The lord held land for his direct profit in these, and his serfs also had strips of land in all three fields. The land farmed by each individual was therefore mixed in with, and open to, neighboring plots. The medieval system lasted long after serfdom ended in England and France.

oral tradition Tales, songs, and adages passed on orally that were the core of traditional popular culture.

Osiris Egyptian god of fertility.

ostracism Procedure in ancient Athens by which men could be banished from the city; voting was done by scratching names on *ostraka* (potsherds).

Ottoman Empire Powerful and much feared empire of the Ottoman Turks, whose holdings stretched across the Middle East and Europe; began as a small state in the fourteenth century but soon took over Asia Minor and surrounded Byzantine territory, resulting in the fall of Constantinople in 1453.

Paleolithic Age Old Stone Age; age of stone tools, ending about 11,000 B.C.

papal bulls Papal letters, closed with a lead seal, or *bulla*.

papal *curia* The central bureaucracy of the pope; it served as the central financial and judicial administration and selected the new pope.

parlements The chief law courts in the regions of France; the members, who owned their offices, claimed the right to approve royal legislation for their regions, and sometimes clashed with the king.

Parliament English legislature, consisting of a House of Lords whose members were nobles and bishops, and a House of Commons whose members were elected gentry and townsmen.

patricians Upper class, a small minority, in Rome; the status was heredity.

perestroika A policy of economic and governmental reform instituted by Mikhail Gorbachev in the Soviet Union during the mid-1980s.

pharaoh Title of Egyptian kings from the New Kingdom onward.

Pharisees Jewish sect that believed in resurrection and accepted non-Jewish converts.

Philippics Orations by the Athenian politician, Demosthenes, attacking King Philip II of Macedonia; used also to refer to speeches of Cicero against Mark Antony.

philosophes A group of French intellectuals who used rational inquiry to advocate intellectual and religious freedom and a variety of practical reforms.

plebeians The great mass of Roman citizens; they were not blocked from holding office.

polis Especially in classical Greece, a city that was also an independent state, not sharing citizenship with any other state.

Politburo The principal policy-making and executive committee of the Russian Communist party.

postmodernism A later twentieth-century approach to the arts stressing relativism and multiple interpretations.

predestination The belief that God has preordained whether a person will be saved or damned, and nothing can be done to reverse this fate.

prefect The chief administrator in each French department appointed by the central government; a hallmark of centralization established by Napoleon but lasting into the twentieth century.

Principate The Roman Empire from Augustus down to Diocletian, so named from the republican term *princeps*, roughly "first citizen."

protoindustrialization Heavy concentrations of pre-factory manufacturing, in which urban merchants employed rural households to produce goods, especially textiles.

psychoanalysis A method of analyzing psychic phenomena and treating emotional disorders that involves treatment sessions during which the patient is encouraged to talk freely about personal experiences and especially about early childhood and dreams.

public sphere Forums outside the royal court, such as newspapers, salons, and academies, in which the educated public could participate in debate on the issues of the day.

Puritans Devout Protestants who believed in a stern moral code and rejected all hints of Catholic ritual or organization.

raj British rule in India, which had spread through most of the subcontinent by the mid-nineteenth century.

realism The depiction of ordinary, everyday subjects in art and literature as part of a broader social commentary; a reaction against the themes and styles typical of Romanticism or of academic painting.

reasons of state Often known by its French name, *raison d'état,* the doctrine that, especially in foreign affairs, a state is bound by no restraint when pursuing its interests.

Reformation The period of major change and variance in the fundamental beliefs of Christianity. The demands of the faithful varied and intensified throughout Western Europe, making it difficult for the Roman Catholic Church alone to accommodate all of them.

relativity Einstein's theory that all aspects of the physical universe must be defined in relative terms.

Renaissance Rebirth of classical culture that occurred in Italy after 1350.

Restorations Attempts by the powers in Europe to restore the dynasties and monarchical institutions (including the Bourbons in France) disrupted by the revolutionary and Napoleonic upheavals.

risorgimento A term meaning "resurgence," used to describe the liberal nationalist movement that led to the unification of Italy by 1870.

Roman Catholic "Universal" church; Christian church headed by a pope.

Romanesque Style of Western European architecture and art developed after 1000; the style is characterized by rounded arches, massive walls, and relatively simple ornamentation.

Romanticism An artistic movement that rejected classical aesthetic forms and norms, and which emphasized personal experience, emotion, or spirituality.

sacrament Means by which God distributes grace. Luther retained only baptism and the Eucharist.

Sadducees Conservative Jewish sect that did not believe in angels or resurrection because such teachings were not found in the five books of the Old Testament, known as the Pentateuch.

sagas Adventure stories told in prose that cover the Viking period to about 1000, when Iceland converted to Christianity.

Saint-Simonians A nineteenth-century movement that called for the reorganization of society by scientists and industrialists to achieve planned progress and prosperity.

salons Social gatherings, usually organized by elite women, that sought to promote discussion of Enlightenment ideas.

sans-culottes Parisian militants, mainly artisans and shopkeepers, who called for repression of counter-revolutionaries, price controls, and direct democracy; helped bring the Jacobins to power in 1793.

satyr play Comic, often vulgar, play performed after an ancient Greek tragedy.

Schlieffen Plan In World War I, the German military plan specifying how the army would fight a two-front war: Germany would invade Belgium and the Netherlands on its way to France, score a quick defeat in the west, and then concentrate its forces against Russia in the east.

Scholasticism A form of argument, or dialectic, developed in the Middle Ages, particularly with Abelard and Thomas Aquinas.

Scientific Revolution The succession of discoveries and the transformation of the investigation of nature that was brought about in the fields of astronomy, physics, and anatomy during the sixteenth and seventeenth centuries.

Second Empire The reign of Napoleon III in France from 1852 to 1870; while authoritarian in nature, the regime fostered popular support through social programs and nationalist sentiment.

second front In World War II, the establishment of an Allied front in Western Europe to match the Russians battling the Nazis in the East; after several delays, the Allies launched the second front with the Normandy invasion in June 1944.

seigneurialism A system prevalent in Western Europe by which peasants owed various fees and dues to the local lord even if the peasants owned their land.

serf or villein Peasant who was personally free, but bound to the lord of a manor and worked the land on the manor.

serfdom A feudal system of agricultural exploitation in which peasants were bound to their lord's estate and owed him forced labor.

sexagesimal System of mathematics based on the number 60.

sexual selection The theory that the traits that increase an organism's (typically male's) success in mating and transmitting its genes are selected and perpetuated. Differs from natural selection, which focuses only on traits that influence survival.

shell shock New psychological diagnosis applied to those soldiers exhibiting signs of psychic distress during the First World War, thought to be caused by the near-constant shelling experienced in the trenches.

sister republics States and territories that fell under French control during the Directory and were reconstituted as republics in collaboration with native revolutionaries.

Skepticism Philosophy that questions whether human beings can ever achieve certain knowledge.

Slavophiles Russian intellectuals who opposed Westernization and saw Russia's unique institutions and culture as superior; some supported autocracy but also favored emancipation of the serfs.

social Darwinism The application of Darwin's scientific theory of evolution to society, often in the service of reactionary and even racist ideas.

social welfare State-run programs for social security, education, medical care, and family benefits.

Sophists Teachers of rhetoric in classical Greece, especially in Athens.

Stalingrad The place where Russians fought ferociously, street by street, to halt the German advance in 1942; marked the turning point of the war on the Eastern front.

state of nature Description in political theory of the condition of humanity before the creation of governments.

steam engine A machine patented in 1782 that converted steam into mechanical energy; provided a cheap and flexible source of power critical for early industrialization.

Stoics Followers, in Greece and Rome, of thought of Zeno, who taught that the wise man leads a life of moderation, unmoved by joy or grief, and stands by his duty according to natural law.

strategic bombing A military doctrine of aerial bombardment of populated and industrial areas; intended to destroy morale and the industrial capacity to fight. Initiated by the Germans on Britain, but most fully used by the British and U.S. air forces.

Sturm und Drang A literary and artistic movement in Germany that emphasized strong artistic emotion; a precursor of the Romantic movement.

subinfeudation The grant of a fief by a vassal to a subordinate who becomes his vassal.

Sunni-Shiite schism Division within the Islamic religion over who should rule after Mohammad's death.

syndicalism A movement in which worker's organizations attempted to destroy bourgeois capitalism and gain control of industry by general strikes.

Talmud General body of Jewish tradition.

tariff A duty or custom fee imposed on imports, often to protect local agriculture or industry from competition.

Tetrarchy Rule of four co-emperors of Rome under Diocletian.

Thermidorian reaction The period between the fall of Robespierre and the establishment of the Directory during which the Convention dismantled the Terror and attacked egalitarian politics.

thermodynamics The study of the relationships between heat and other forms of energy; becomes one of the bases of nineteenth-century physics.

three-field system Agricultural system in which two-thirds of the land was cultivated on a rotating basis; it replaced the two-field system and resulted in increased productivity.

Tory English political party committed to a strong monarch and a strong Anglican Church.

total war Unprecedented type of warfare in which all segments of society, civilians and soldiers, men and women, were mobilized in the hope of ensuring victory.

totalitarianism A twentieth-century form of authoritarian government using force, technology, and bureaucracy to effect rule by a single party and controlling most aspects of the lives of the population.

tragedy The supreme dramatic form in ancient Greece, usually treating a mythological theme and leading to catastrophe for some of the characters.

transubstantiation Belief that bread and wine are transformed into the body and blood of Christ during the Eucharist.

Treaty of Paris (1763) Peace treaty ending the British and French war for empire in which France surrendered Canada to the British and lost its foothold in India.

Treaty of Tordesillas Signed in 1494, the treaty confirmed the pope's division of the world between the Portuguese and Spanish for exploration and conquest. Under its terms, a line was drawn some 1,200 miles west of the Cape Verde Islands, with Portugal granted all lands to the west and Spain granted all lands to the east.

trench warfare Static, defensive type of combat seen mostly on the Western front of World War I, where a war of attrition was fought in a complex system of underground trenches and supply lines.

triangular trade A complex pattern of colonial commerce between the home country (Britain or France) and its colonies in which refined or manufactured goods were exchanged for raw materials or slaves from West Africa.

tribunes Ten Roman plebeians, elected to protect the common people; some of them became powerful political activists.

triremes Greek warship, powered by three banks of oars.

triumvirate "Body of three men," a term applied to two such cabals in the Roman Republic.

trivium and quadrivium School curriculum that became the standard program of study in universities. The trivium comprised the verbal arts (grammar, rhetoric, and logic), while the quadrivium comprised the mathematical arts (arithmetic, astronomy, geometry, and music).

troubadour A writer of vernacular romantic lyrics or tales who enjoyed the patronage of nobles around Europe in the twelfth through fifteenth centuries.

tsar Title adopted by the Russian king; the term was the Slavic equivalent of the Latin term *caesar*.

tyrant In ancient Greek states, a powerful man who ruled in a polis without legal sanction, not necessarily a cruel despot.

ultraroyalists French reactionaries who not only supported divine-right monarchy but called for the return of lands taken from the émigrés during the Revolution.

usury Interest of profit on a loan; it was prohibited by the Church.

Utilitarianism British reform movement that believed that society should be based on "the greatest happiness for the greatest number," and that sound governments could make such calculations.

utopian Having to do with an ideal society, as presented in Sir Thomas More's book *Utopia*, which means "nowhere" in Greek.

vassal A free warrior who places himself under a lord, accepting the terms of loyal service, fighting in times of war, and counseling in times of peace.

Vatican II Vatican council called by Pope John XXIII in 1962. Vatican II made the leadership of the Church more international, directed attention to the concerns of developing nations, and ordered that Masses be conducted in the vernacular instead of Latin.

Vulgate The Latin translation of the Bible in the fourth century, identified with St. Jerome, which became the medieval Church's standard text and was deemed holy in the sixteenth century.

war guilt clause Article 231 of the Treaty of Versailles, specifying that Germany alone was responsible for causing the First World War.

Warsaw Pact The Russian response to NATO; an international military organization established in 1955 that included the Soviet Union and Eastern European communist states.

Weimar Republic Left-liberal German government established after the war, named for the city where German politicians formed the republic; instituted universal suffrage, and wrote a new democratic constitution.

Wergeld Literally, "man-payment"; in Germanic tribes, as a means to prevent feuds, payments given in compensation for crimes committed; the amount of compensation depended on the social rank of the individual.

Whig English political party committed to a strong Parliament and religious toleration.

Yalta Conference In February 1945, the meeting between Roosevelt, Churchill, and Stalin to set the postwar order in Europe. The conference agreed on the creation of the United Nations but was unable to counter future Soviet dominance in Eastern Europe.

Zeus Sky god; the chief god in Greek myth.

ziggurat Terraced tower built of baked brick in Mesopotamia.

Zollverein A customs union established by Prussia among most states in the German Confederation that allowed for free movement of goods; promoted the economic unification of Germany.

Text Credits

Chapter 1

Page 11 From Robert F. Harper (tr.), *The Code of Hammurabi*, Gordon Press, 1904, 1991, (language modified). Reprinted by permission. **Page 22** From Exodus 15. Revised Standard Version of the Bible, copyright 1952 [2nd edition, 1971] by the Division of Christian Education of the National Council of the Churches of Christ in the United States of America. Used by permission. All rights reserved. **Page 23** From Jeremiah 11. Revised Standard Version of the Bible, copyright 1952 [2nd edition, 1971] by the Division of Christian Education of the National Council of the Churches of Christ in the United States of America. Used by permission. All rights reserved.

Chapter 2

Page 43 From Mary R. Lefkowitz and Guy M. Rogers, *Black Athena Revisited*. Copyright © 1996 by the University of North Carolina Press. Used by permission of the publisher.
Page 43 From Guy MacLean Rogers, *Black Athena Revised*, University of North Carolina Press, 1996, pp. 449–452, abridged.
Page 48 By Sappho, translated by Guy Davenport, from *7 Greeks*, copyright © 1995 by Guy Davenport. Reprinted by permission of New Directions Publishing Corp. **Page 58** From *Herodotus*, book VII, M. H. Chambers (tr.).

Chapter 3

Page 70 From Hugh Tredennick (tr.), Plato, *The Last Days of Socrates*, Penguin Classics, 1954, 1972, 1980, p. 76.
Page 72 From E. F. Watling (tr.), Sophocles, *The Three Theban Plays*, Penguin Classics, 1971, pp. 60–61. **Page 74** From Rex Warner (tr.), Thucydides, *The Peloponnesian War*, Penguin Classics, 1954, 1980, pp. 403–404, abridged. **Page 76** From E. C. Marchant, (tr.), *Xenophon*, Vol. 4, Harvard University Press, 1979, pp. 7, 35–42 abridged.

Chapter 4

Page 112 Plutarch, *The Life of Caesar*, ch. 66, M. H. Chambers (tr.).

Chapter 5

Page 121 From Tacitus, *Annals*, Book 1, ch. 2, M. H. Chambers (tr.).

Chapter 6

Page 163 From H. Mattingly (tr.) *The Germania*, Penguin Classics, 1970, pp. 11–12. **Page 175** From Timothy Fry (ed.), *The Rule of St. Benedict in Latin and English with Notes*, Liturgical Press, 1980, pp. 261–265. Reprinted by permission.

Chapter 7

Page 185 From *The Koran*, N.J. Dawood (tr.), Penguin Books, 1968, condensed.

Chapter 8

Page 229 From William Fitz Stephen, *Norman London*, Italica Press, pp. 52, 54. Reprinted by permission of Italica Press in cooperation with the Historical Association, London.
Page 233 From C. Warren Hollister, et al., *Medieval Europe: A Short Sourcebook*, 1992. Reprinted by permission of The McGraw-Hill Companies, Inc. **Page 238** From Norman Downs, *Basic Documents in Medieval History*, Melbourne, FL: Kreiger, 1959, pp. 64–65. Reprinted by permission.

Chapter 9

Page 254 From *The Letters of Abelard and Heloise* by Peter Abelard & Heloise, translated by C. K. Scott Moncrieff, copyright 1926 and renewed 1954 by Alfred A. Knopf, Inc. Used by permission of Alfred A. Knopf, a division of Random House, Inc. **Page 254** From *The Letters of Abelard and Heloise* by Peter Abelard & Heloise, translated by C. K. Scott Moncrieff, copyright 1926 and renewed 1954 by Alfred A. Knopf, Inc. Used by permission of Alfred A. Knopf, a division of Random House, Inc.

Chapter 10

Page 284 From Emilie Amt, *Women's Lives in Medieval Europe: a Sourcebook*, Routledge, 1993, pp. 195–196. Reprinted by permission. **Page 296** From C. Warren Hollister, et al., *Medieval Europe: A Short Sourcebook*, 1992. Reprinted by permission of The McGraw-Hill Companies, Inc. **Page 297** From Emilie Amt, *Women's Lives in Medieval Europe: a Sourcebook*, Routledge, 1993, pp. 264–265. Reprinted by permission.

Chapter 11

Page 309 From C. Warren Hollister, et al., *Medieval Europe: A Short Sourcebook*, 1992. Reprinted by permission of The McGraw-Hill Companies, Inc. **Page 317** From "Did Women Have a Renaissance?" by Joan Kelly from Renate Bridenthal, Claudia Koonz, and Susan Stuard, *Becoming Visible: Women in European History*, 2nd ed. Copyright © 1987 by Houghton Mifflin Company. Adapted with permission. **Page 325** From G.G. Coulton and Eileen Power (eds.), *The Trial of Jeanne d' Arc*, W. P. Barrett (trans.), Routledge, 1931. Reprinted by permission of Taylor & Francis Books. **Page 332** From Richard Knolles in John J. Saunders (ed.), *The Muslim World on the Eve of Europe's Expansion*, Prentice-Hall, 1966, adapted by Theodore K. Rabb.

Chapter 12

Page 340 Petrarch, *Epistolae Familiares*, 24.8. Passages selected and translated by Theodore K. Rabb. **Page 350** From D. S. Chambers (ed.), *Patrons and Artists in the Italian Renaissance*, London: Macmillan, 1970, pp. 128–130 and 147–148. Reprinted by permission. **Page 362** From Matthew Spinka (ed.), *The Letters of John Hus*, Manchester: University Press, 1972, pp. 195–197.

Chapter 13

Page 371 Adapted from Lucien Febvre and Henri-Jean Martin, *The Coming of the Book: The Impact of Printing 1450–1800*, David Gerald (tr.), London, NLB, 1976, pp. 178–179, 184–185. Reprinted by permission. **Page 375** Translation from the Latin by Theodore K. Rabb of Luther's preface to the 1545 edition of his writings, in Otto Scheel (ed.), *Dokumente zu Luthers Entwicklung*, Tübingen: Mohr, 1929, pp. 191–192. **Page 389** From E. Allison Peers, *The Life of Teresa of Jesus*, London: Sheed & Ward, 1944; New York: Doubleday, 1960, pp. 258–260, 273–274. Reprinted by permission.

Chapter 14

Page 397 Adapted from J. H. Elliott, *Imperial Spain, 1469–1716*, New York, 1964, p. 175. **Page 404** From S. E. Morison, *Admiral of the Ocean Sea: A Life of Christopher Columbus*, Boston: Little, Brown, 1942, pp. 670–671. **Page 404** From Kirkpatrick Sale, *The Conquest of Paradise: Christopher Columbus and the Columbian Legacy*, New York: Knopf, 1990, pp. 209–210, 362.

Chapter 15

Page 450 From Louis André (ed.), *Testament politique* (Editions Robert Laffont, 1947), pp. 347–348 and 352; translated by Theodore K. Rabb. **Page 453** Adapted from J. H. Elliott, *Imperial Spain, 1469–1716*, Edward Arnold, The Hodder Neadling PLC Group, 1964, p. 175.

Chapter 16

Page 465 From Giorgio de Santillana, "Galileo and Kepler on Copernicus", from *The Crime of Galileo*, Chicago: University of Chicago Press, 1955, pp. 11 and 14–15. Reprinted by permission of the University of Chicago Press. **Page 480** From Jan de Vries, *The Economy of Europe in an Age of Crisis, 1600–1750*, Cambridge University Press, 1976, p. 5. Reprinted by permission.

Chapter 17

Page 495 From J. M. Thompson, *Lectures on Foreign History, 1494–1789*, Oxford: Blackwell, 1956, pp. 172–174. **Page 498** From Albert Sorel, *L'Europe et la révolution française*, 3rd ed., vol. 1, Paris, 1893, p. 199, as translated in William F. Church, *The Greatness of Loius XIV: Myth or Reality?* Copyright © 1959 by D.C. Heath and Company. Used with permission. **Page 500** From John C. Rule, "Louis XIV, Roi-Bureaucrate," in Rule (ed.), *Louis XIV and the Craft of Kingship*, Columbus: Ohio State University Press, 1969, pp. 91–92. Reprinted by permission. **Page 520** From John Locke, *The Second Treatise of Civil Government*, Thomas P. Peardon (ed.), Indianapolis: Bobbs-Merrill, 1952, chapter 9, pp. 70–73.

Volume I Index